OUTSIDE THE GATES OF EDEN

OUTSIDE THE GATES OF EDEN

THE DREAM OF AMERICA
FROM HIROSHIMA TO NOW

PETER BACON HALES

University of Chicago Press
Chicago and London

PETER BACON HALES is professor emeritus of the history of art and architecture and director emeritus of the American Studies Institute at the University of Illinois at Chicago and the author of several books, including, most recently, *Atomic Spaces: Living on the Manhattan Project*. He lives and writes in New York's Hudson Valley.

The University of Chicago Press, Chicago 60637
The University of Chicago Press, Ltd., London
© 2014 by Peter Bacon Hales
All rights reserved. Published 2014.

Printed in the United States of America

23 22 21 20 19 18 17 16 15 14   1 2 3 4 5

ISBN-13: 978-0-226-31315-3 (cloth)
ISBN-13: 978-0-226-12861-0 (e-book)
DOI: 10.7208/chicago/9780226128610.001.0001

Library of Congress Cataloging-in-Publication Data

Hales, Peter B. (Peter Bacon), author.
  Outside the gates of Eden : the dream of America from Hiroshima to now / Peter Bacon Hales.
      pages ; cm
  Includes bibliographical references and index.
  ISBN 978-0-226-31315-3 (cloth : alk. paper) — ISBN 978-0-226-12861-0 (e-book) 1. United States—Civilization—20th century. 2. Popular culture—United States—History—1945–
I. Title.
  E169.12.H339 2014
  973.91—dc23

                          2013036230

Publication of this book has been aided by a grant from the Neil Harris Endowment Fund, which honors the innovative scholarship of Neil Harris, the Preston and Sterling Morton Professor Emeritus of History at the University of Chicago. The Fund is supported by contributions from the students, colleagues, and friends of Neil Harris.

♾ This paper meets the requirements of ANSI/NISO Z39.48-1992 (Permanence of Paper).

For Maureen Pskowski, who makes all things possible

Contents

An Introduction

Two charged images dominate American life from the end of World War II to this moment. One invokes pain and terror: the great cloud rises above the American city, unleashing a firestorm whose aftermath blows sickness, deformity, and death out into the landscape, enveloping the tidy suburbs and sowing poison on the farms, ranches, and wilderness spaces that ennoble the nation.

The other seems its opposite: an expansive community takes form and matures, united in optimism and prosperity, as young families in new homes cluster at just the right distance to encourage the continuing reinvention of democratic community while honoring the American ideal of individualism.

These are more than American nightmare and American dream—they are the settings for the central drama that the United States has acted out since the first reports of the atomic inferno that destroyed Hiroshima in 1945. In 1947 they filled the pages of the great picture magazines. Today they form the basis for pop fiction and movies and wildly successful video games. Playing *Call of Duty: Modern Warfare*, tens of millions have been caught in the blast wave as a city is flattened by atomic holocaust, and then, for long minutes, struggled to recover, then just to survive, and then, finally, resigned themselves to death amidst the wreckage. Or, in the *Fallout* and *S.T.A.L.K.E.R.* series, they have wandered and foraged, exiles in the postholocaust landscapes of the American West or the Soviet empire.

Or they have become gods of the suburban landscape, creating virtual creatures in their own image, "sims," and done the small detail work of feeding and clothing, motivating, socializing, and entertaining their simulacra,

1

shopping and teaching and exercising and inspiring them to live lives of gently ironic desperation.

Across the reach of America's preeminence and its embrace of empire, these narratives emerge and recede: fear and hope, catastrophe and celebration. In the midst of the virtual world, as in the concrete spheres of our nation and the nations we seek to influence and save, we reenact the myths and menaces of our histories. We yearn for something.

*　*　*

This is a book about the transformations of the American cultural landscape between the end of World War II and the first decade of the twenty-first century. During that period, more than sixty years in length, a nation that prided itself on continual reinvention and renewal faced threats to its very existence, alone and as part of a globe facing universal destruction by human technology.

The title is borrowed from a line by Bob Dylan, written during his most prolific period of prophecy, 1964–1967. During those years, his songs, by turns moody and aphoristic or headlong and hilarious, limned an America riven by doubt about itself and its place in the world, an America exiled from its sense of innocence, promise and entitlement, thrust *outside the gates of Eden* into a realm of danger, unwanted responsibility, and imminent nuclear apocalypse, yearning for a return to safety. But, as Dylan warned, there was *darkness at the break of noon*, a foreboding that *eclipses both the sun and moon*; we were, as one of his paler imitators declared directly, standing on *the eve of destruction*. Impelled by this sense of urgency, our culture produced a wild array of democratic art—movies, magazines, houses and subdivisions, TV shows, pop songs and the pocket radios to hear them on, countercultures small and large, and then, as one age merged into another, computer programs and video games that were built on the codes of mutually assured destruction from that earlier fear and made possible a strange new interpenetration of the real and the imaginative, the physical and the virtual—that strange, ambiguous country in which we now live.

Our cultural landscape is more than a simple collection of places. It contains the spaces we make, yes, but also the ways we find meaning in our surroundings, declaring them ours and then imbuing them with myths and memories that link our presence to the past and the future. It is found in houses and cities, but also in novels and songs, advertisements and movies and television shows. In all these spaces and places, real and imagined, postwar America teemed with anxiety.

For America, what our landscape means has always been critical to our identity, a place to wrestle for control of our sense of self, as individuals and as a nation and a culture. Our narratives, reaching back to the earliest European settlers and forward to the pontifications of teachers and politicians, declare our divinely ordained mission to occupy and expand, to exploit and transform, the ground beneath our feet.

Yet for all its bravado, America has always squatted uneasily on the land beneath it, unsure whether it was loaned, bequeathed, or stolen. If America is an Eden granted by divine decree, are we not always on the verge of expulsion? During the first half of the twentieth century, that unease seemed to dissipate as Americans found themselves growing increasingly comfortable with the longevity of their experiment and the success of their settlement. They built monuments, physical and imaginative, that explored the implications of a national civilization settled on a binding contract with nature. Even the Dust Bowl and the Depression failed to slow this process—the New Deal agricultural programs, the Hoover, Bonneville and Grand Coulee dams, the Tennessee Valley Authority, all attest to the momentum behind it.

But the events of August 1945 that ended World War II seemed to cancel the divine contract in ways warned of in older American narratives— Puritan, Indian, slave. A new, atomically unstable nature, unleashed on the world by this very nation, brought the threat of global eradication and the responsibility for global survival to national consciousness, beginning an era of deeply conflicted cultural signs, meanings, and interpretations and an often-wild gyration of debates about national self-image and action. Well into the twenty-first century, that cultural instability shows no sign of abating. Outside the gates of Eden, as Bob Dylan prophetically wrote in 1964, we continue to assess and repent our failures, adjust to our new environment of doubt and responsibility, and perhaps find some way to end our exile and return to grace.

Four generations of Americans have traced this trajectory. Even as the new era wrought by atomic weaponry threatened fundamental American beliefs about itself and its place in the world, the very forms of the debates were also rapidly changing. Through what medium was America to reconstruct its identity? Popular magazines, newsreels, movies, television, popular music, and then the technologies of the virtual: each of these media came into prominence, receded, and sometimes returned as sites for a complex set of debates about the meaning and mission of America.

In this book, *all* those media find their moments at center stage. As importantly, they each interacted (and continue to interact) with the changing material landscape of the nation—a landscape itself weighted with significance, serving as a medium for enunciating cultural crises and our responses to them. Not just "television," but television *sets*; not just pop music but the printed 45-rpm sleeves and the 33 1/3 album covers in which the technology was encased; not just Levittown the self-declared symbol of a new America but Levittown the suburban town; not just postapocalyptic video games but the machines on which they are played. Unearthing those things, examining their significance, teasing out their meanings: that is the purpose of this book.

The stories told here—from Bikini Atoll and *I Love Lucy* to a post-9/11 virtual world of tweets and *Sims* and the *Shadow of Chernobyl*—propose an America caught in an ongoing cultural crisis concerning its place on the global stage as a model civilization granted natural wealth and unique national privilege. This crisis, catalyzed by the atomic age and its responsibilities, brought veering responses—between isolationism and global engagement, between triumphalism and self-loathing, between utopianism and dread. Never once, however, did America waver in its conviction that it must take itself seriously, choose its mission properly, follow its path responsibly. Not just intellectuals, patriarchs, or politicians believed this: it was the American myth, gift, and peril that *all* Americans shared, even those most marginalized and disenfranchised.

To speak of these matters, then, not just in accessible languages and terms but in forms sufficiently subtle to do justice to the complexity and weight of America's moral conscience became the dominant obsession of the country in the decades after Hiroshima. 9/11, for all its looming rhetoric and its immense human and political consequences, pales before the cultural explosion that extends from Hiroshima and all it stands for. Indeed, as I will propose, 9/11 is perhaps best understood as a reawakening of the anxieties of the atomic age, most notably the fear that America's geographical invulnerability could be violently breached by what Harry Truman, speaking of Hiroshima, called "a rain of ruin from the air."

The terrors and responsibilities of the atomic age were (and are) rarely faced head on. They were too immense to grasp in full, and so the contest for meaning played out obliquely. One of the defining characteristics of the atomic age has been its double path: on one side, the high-toned oratory of politicians and pundits with their speeches and editorials, manifestoes and position statements; on the other, the sidelong, disguised expressions that permeate the common culture of picture captions, sitcoms, songs, and the other everyday artifacts of the era.

I speak of a single identity—*America*—throughout this book. By this I do not mean some forced commonality or a melting pot of cheerful consensus. Instead, I try to suggest the ways dominant and powerful institutions sought to create and control the meaning of America, while those at the margins fought to identify new media and means of expression, and use them to challenge the dominant voices.

Still, my attention is directed toward the most broadly popular cultural artifacts, forms, and media of this protean time. This is, after all, the era when democratic culture became fully a *popular* culture, with success defined by numbers—viewers captured, records sold, houses built, hours online. So a central theme of the book concerns the ways seemingly monolithic cultural institutions could be infiltrated by other voices, the ways themes and traditions, condensed to maximize the universality of their appeal, could be then reinflected by their audiences, redirected and rendered denser and more porous.

Each chapter examines a charged particle of American culture: charged by its influence at the time and since, but also by its connection to one or more interwoven themes that dominated American cultural life in a changing global environment.

First among these—most powerful, most terrifying, and most prone to surface, sink, and then reappear in a different guise with ever greater power and terror—is the possibility of nuclear warfare and human annihilation. World War II was the first American war in which the notion of eradication of whole "races," cultures, and nations was at the heart of the conflict. It ended with the deployment, from a distance, of an extraordinary new weapon of mass destruction. This changed America forever, thrusting it fully into its self-conceived role as global leader, as moral example, and as *civilization*, responsible for its own character and destiny, and responsible to the world as prime agent for its survival as a place of human habitation.

Invisible death rays that killed from a great distance; rogue unseen particles that brought mutation, sterility, pain, disease, and death to innocent and guilty alike; blossoms of sublime beauty that filled the skies, blinded witnesses, and then disintegrated everything below for hundreds, perhaps thousands of miles: these were shocking new realities for generations of Americans who sought some meaning, some narrative, to enfold and make sense of this terror, and some means to direct it to redemption rather than apocalypse.

In the face of such horrors Americans sought alternative dramas, huddling places, palliatives, and promises, from movies about perfect Christmases in shiny houses to virtual simulations of those houses featured in electronic games. Such diversions promised escape and denial but just as often served as conduits for recurrent paranoia and panic.

Today we have lost much of the sense of horror, fear, and powerlessness that accompanied the opening of the atomic age, though the cultural responses to 9/11 suggest how quickly it can reappear in new forms and with new shadow-enemies to threaten us. It is my responsibility as a historian to return a sense of that earlier moment and to reveal the process by which moment became moments, and moments became stages in a narrative of American power and responsibility countered by rages of powerlessness and loss of faith.

I speak of *stages* in two ways throughout this book. In the first instance, I am thinking of the dynamic of history, of the ways discontinuous objects, spaces, and events are recast into narratives, and of the contests among institutions, agencies, groups, and individuals to make, control, and transform those narratives. To control a cultural narrative is to make myths and, in our time, to make myths is to define experience and its significance.

In a second way I speak of stages as the sites where the national narrative, the American drama, was and is written, enacted, observed, and then reengaged in a continually mutating dynamic. It is a feature of the American experience right after World War II that we saw ourselves to be the principal actors on the world stage, and on the stage of history, both because of our newly created power of global destruction and because of our long-standing identity as "city upon a hill," a civilization divinely chosen and declared to be the model for a human utopia. You didn't have to be white, Protestant, and a descendent of the Puritans to believe this—it was a powerful theme hammered home in literature popular and elite, in politics high-flown and scrappy, in social debates and in economic contests from the first days of European settlement until at least the end of the twentieth century. When Martin Luther King Jr. stood before millions of Americans gathered on the Washington Mall or watching on television, his call for a national transformation was couched in that expansive, millenarian language. When George W. Bush declared a war on terror, casting American virtue against exotic "evildoers," he too was reiterating this sense that America was required to enact its narratives on the stages of the globe and of history.

This sense of *enactment* and self-dramatization wasn't limited to the high plains of visionaries. It was a fundamental feature of everyday life in the new American landscapes of the postwar years, landscapes of dramatic domesticity in which each woman and man, each family, was exhorted to act as a model for others in America and across the globe. To explore this theme, I have chosen the most iconic of postwar American communities—Levittown, Long Island, New York. Levittown isn't important simply because of its nature as a mass-produced, mass-market, middle-class instant community. There were many others, from Lakeside, California, to multiracial

Ronek Park, also on Long Island, that rose from the housing crisis following the war. But it was Levittown that became shorthand for a new type of American utopia. Even before it had physical form, Levittown held a central place in the mythos of postwar America. As an innovative answer to the housing shortage and as the staging ground for a new form of American communitarianism, it was announced with fanfare and analyzed with hyperbolic zeal by a burgeoning national popular press—not only weekly tabloid magazines but newsreels, social-uplift journals, and the movies.

It may seem strange to come upon Levittown in a Christmas movie, but there it—or a variant thereof—is, in the hands of a child asking Santa for a new life with a new family in a new sort of American landscape, in *Miracle on 34th Street*. This sort of conjunction between physical spaces and their representation in popular media isn't rare or unlikely in the decades after World War II. On the contrary, it was a feature of the new postwar America, and it is a central subject of this book. But themes, meanings, symbols, and myths change over time, or change emphasis, and so do the media that are central to a moment or message. I have organized the book around significant moments in postwar American history, and as each stage shifts, so too do the media that most dominated that stage and presented its particular concerns to a changing American audience. I begin with newsreels and mass-market magazines; continue with movies; turn on the television, as both a medium and a domestic object; then explore the novel technologies of the space age, from transistors to Telstar.

In the midst of this first part of the narrative, I have sought to tease out two important tensions between a dominant culture and a subjugated minority. The first is, of course, between white and black America. At first, I pose this as something closer to an absence than to an active resistance. This is a different analysis than the one commonly found in American history books of the last few decades. That's because I'm not looking at political movements or conflicts where the battles were granular and local, but at how the most influential forms of media and cultural representation chose to frame the national struggle for identity and meaning. Only later, when a new generation finds common cause with an older but marginalized black tradition, and new forms of popular media turn their attention to the rituals of racial injustice, will the conflict more fully emerge.

The second significant tension is between a culture run by and for men, and the women whose positions were largely determined for them, not simply by the traditional forms of family and legal structure but more surreptitiously and systematically by the forces of imagery and marketplace mythology. A chapter on the wildly popular *I Love Lucy* serves to anchor this theme and highlight the ways a sole woman, Lucille Ball, in concert with a writing team of women and men, sought to frame that conflict without violating the unspoken regulations of the television industry or the larger culture.

This is a story that has deep personal significance for me, for it is, in disguised form, the story of my own family—of a mother struggling to accommodate herself within the restrictions of an idealized but forced domestic life, raging against its limitations, yet for more than a decade prisoner in its often-gracious spaces. My experience with *Lucy* is, in fact, profoundly tied up with the days when, sick at home, I watched reruns of the show with my mother until she reached her limit, exploded from the chair, and disappeared to some obdurate domestic chore. Only in the 1960s, when her cause became common with that of her daughters, who had grown up believing they had a right and a responsibility to redefine the national mission and its utopian possibilities, did she reemerge as a figure of power and political savvy.

The postwar '40s and '50s presented one form of spatial duality—between the safe yet claustrophobic structures of the home and the living room, with its glowing television, and the conflicts of the wider world, battleground of American men in commerce, media, or war. In Levittown, the community became an extension of the nuclear family, its uniform houses and curving, protective streets buffers against danger. It was a place where women could control not simply their small havens of home but a larger and more communitarian environment devoted to raising a new, happier, and hopefully less fearful generation of Americans. The dangers of nuclear holocaust now clung to a new ideology of women's responsibility—to construct and watch over a safe haven and to protect and prepare the children of the atomic age.

With the opening of the 1960s, a new kind of duality emerged between the fixed domesticity of the living room and the fluidity of the streets and highways—a duality that came to represent different media for different generations: the television for grownups, the portable radio for the kids. The transistor radio and the popular music it allowed you to carry around with you became the dominant media of the generation born during and right after World War II. This tightly linked combination of artistic medium and communication medium enabled a new form of resistance to the steadily more powerful institutions of the dominant culture.

For this generation, the relationship to atomic fear and atomic holocaust was fundamentally different than it had been for their parents, who more or less embraced the paradox of responsibility and powerlessness over this extraordinary new technology of destruction, and the many products and projects that spun around or scattered off that nucleus. The children, how-ever, had never known a world *without* these conditions.

The children of the atomic age made their music a place for declaring their right to happiness and even utopia. Some transformed the lessons taught in their history classes and scout troops and youth fellowships and sought to make real—not imaginative—utopias, laying claim to the streets of the city and the great sweeps of the American wilderness. These were bold, even revolutionary acts of appropriation, laying claim to the mythic spaces that had defined American identity and American exceptionalism from the very first years of the colonial experiment. When Bob Dylan claimed the right to explore America's "gates of Eden," he did so from the most hal-lowed of American symbolic places—from Carnegie Hall in New York, from a stage at Newport, Rhode Island, from the steps of the Lincoln Memorial. In 1967, when the Diggers appropriated San Francisco's parks, they were occupying Frederick Law Olmsted's ideal urban pastorales, designed to si-phon off class warfare and redeem the regimented worker from drudgery and neurosis. When the Yippies tested their own *Intervention* (as the Dig-gers named their street actions), they did it on the floor of the New York Stock Exchange. When the commune builders fanned out from the cities and suburbs, they settled in sites that reclaimed the Puritans' "errand into the wilderness," located in sight of the "purple mountains majesty above the fruited plains."

Music, street actions, ritual exodus and return, were chronicled by the older media of *Life* and *Time* but also by the new medium of FM radio: these conjunctions of cultural drama and mass media confirmed the sense that Americans were actors on a stage, inventing a new narrative or adapting the older ones. The arrival of the virtual exploded this continuity, promising each of us our own personal utopia in which the inconveniences of time and space might be eradicated in an endless sphere of play.

I think of space and spaces as essential to understanding my subject, not least because the popular and mass media I work with so resolutely argue the case by their own attentiveness to spaces, places and their meanings.

In the virtual world, the promise of a culture without place seemed to af-ford a new sort of American utopia. Yet from the first, dominant forces and institutions already in place, though frayed by the counterculture, sought to control this new type of cultural creation and community. To explore this, I once again turn to the objects and inventions most celebrated, popular, or controversial. From the earliest successful arcade video game, *Pong*, to the return of suburban utopia and atomic holocaust as nostalgia and fantasy in *The Sims*, *Fallout*, and others, I tease out the tensions between the dominant institutions of American economic and cultural life and the surreptitiously revolutionary counteractions of everyday citizens.

We end this traversal of American cultural life at something approaching the present—a present instantly receding into history as this book is published. Its description of things cannot keep up with the changes in the physical and imaginative spaces in which it is archived and read. To fight that trend, I have proposed to continue the book in the virtual world itself, in the spaces of the blogosphere, where new artifacts, new essays, new narratives, and myths can be given their due. These appear, and will appear, at peterbhales.com.

Today it is tempting to see the events, themes, and artifacts of the Cold War era as dead matter, sealed in a vault of the museum of history, with the lights off to preserve it, the door locked to protect it from pillage. But just as the Cold War reconstituted the myths of other eras and centuries, from Puritan John Winthrop's "city upon a hill" to John L. O'Sullivan's "Manifest Destiny" and Frederick Jackson Turner's frontier thesis, so too is the virtual present a protean mash-up of Cold War dramas and a dynamic repository for the very symbols and myths that only seemed useful until the Cold War ended. Every Christmas, *Miracle on 34th Street* shows on TV in near-continuous rotation. There's not a time or place in any season where some cable station isn't broadcasting *Lucy* reruns. Yesterday, Dylan's *Like A Rolling Stone* was filling the elevator at a Dominick's supermarket in Chicago.

Twenty-five years ago, the Soviet Union was still a powerful adversary, demanding that America present its case with the fullest conviction, even as Ronald Reagan was threatening the world, if only jokingly and off-mike, with atomic holocaust. Even that nightmare has faded and then returned—in the warnings of pundits and in the games played on the iPhone of the person seated next to you on the subway. So too has the urgency of American self-invention and the fragility of our identity. This urgency and fragility are the subjects of the narratives we will trace; I see no sign that our obsession with reinvention will settle down anytime soon.

CHAPTER 1

The Atomic Sublime

The central image of the atomic age is the mushroom cloud: an icon once universal, powerful, and affecting but today almost forgotten, as the circumstances from which it arose and the world to which it spoke have faded into something else. It is an icon fundamentally American, steeped in the Protestant tradition, in which the most significant symbols are also the most sparse, austere, and, in consequence, most freighted.

In pictures, we see the mushroom cloud rising above the lush tropical isles of the South Pacific, bringing with it the rush of uplifted waters, greater than any waterspout or typhoon but somehow of that ilk, a product of nature, yet, paradoxically, the creation of men and a nation.

Or we see it rising from the desert landscapes in the great American West, blooming as light and then blinding, blotting out the harsh desert sunlight.*

Judging from the early photographs, it's odd that the mushroom was chosen to describe this new thing. The reference is to something too humble, too small in scale, too much an organism of dark, closed spaces, when the atomic cloud is born of open, unbounded landscapes and inconceivable light.

Indeed, it seems a strange sort of denial. To look at the film footage of bomb after bomb (as one can do these days, thanks to YouTube) is to see that the mushroom is only a single briefly held form among many taken by an

---

* These images are now readily available on a variety of websites, including *The Gallery of U.S. Nuclear Tests* (http://nuclearweaponarchive.org/Usa/Tests/) and *The Nuclear Test Image Gallery* (http://www.cddc.vt.edu/host/atomic/testpix/index.html).

1.1. Operation Ivy: "Mike," Enewetak Atoll. (Courtesy of the National Archives and Records Administration.)

atomic explosion. If anything it is uncharacteristic of the process in which a column rises, spreads at the top, and then leans, extrudes, and—finally—dissipates.

The cloud is gone from sight and it has nearly disappeared from memory despite its return as a novelty in the digital library of the Internet. Last of all to fade is its power to draw together and represent anxiety, fear, doubt, and sorrow, as well as grandiosity, heroism, sober realpolitik. But that too is going; the commentaries on YouTube treat these once-monumental events as curiosities of the past, presented in the same light as fiberglass dining-room sets and ads for Spam.

It is a fitting fate for the atomic age. The epoch that seemed at one time to be eternal has disappeared in much the same way it came into being. Like the culture it invoked, spoke for, and spoke to, this icon began from unformed energy, emerged into a nameless but imperative visual identity, radiated its messages, accepted our responses (terror, fear, awe, pleasure, a certain guilty regret) and then slowly, almost imperceptibly, faded into the atmosphere surrounding it.

*   *   *

In August of 1945, when the first representations of atomic explosion appeared in public, Americans had nothing before them but an as-yet insignificant image, a grainy, ill-defined reproduction of a photograph (itself made under difficult circumstances) within whose edges could be discerned a fuzzy plume rising above a cloudscape, seen from a great distance and at eye level or a bit above. They were looking, captions explained, at the explosion that destroyed Hiroshima from the first atomic weapon used in war. Within weeks they would be told repeatedly that they had seen both the end of things and the beginning—end of the war, but beginning of a new epoch in human power.

That image was simultaneously familiar and new; it invoked older icons from the war but connected them to an event without precedent. Americans

1.2. Operation Teapot: "Wasp Prime," March 29, 1955. (Photo courtesy of the National Nuclear Security Administration / Nevada Site Office.)

1.3. Atomic cloud over Hiroshima. (Courtesy of the National Archives and Records Administration.)

had already seen pillars of smoke rising from the destruction of wartime sites: munitions factories, military installations, urban centers on both sides of the divide between ally and enemy. The picture magazines had regularly shown them similar photographs of natural phenomena—cyclones racing up Tornado Alley, through Texas, Oklahoma, Kansas; waterspouts in the Caribbean and the South Pacific; hurricanes photographed by U.S. weather planes and captive-air balloons. Americans had developed a penchant for the photography of natural disaster, and the skinny vertical cloud, widening at its top, listing to one side, was a staple of the press: nature gone amok, striking at the innocent, reminding us of its power when unpropitiated.

From the first, then, this new image connected to nature, to the icons of nature personified—"nature's fury" or "nature's rage" or simply "raging elements" or "raging winds." But the earliest *written* descriptions of the bomb's blast were far more complex, more dynamic, reflective of the stakes. These first reports emanated, with little acknowledgment of the fact, from a single source. Whether rewriting military releases or looking to journalistic witnesses, editors and copywriters depended on the reporting of one witness: William L. Laurence, science writer for the *New York Times* and, secretly, a minion of the army's Manhattan Project, handpicked by its military overseer, General Leslie R. Groves. Laurence had been chosen as the supersecret program prepared to unleash its product and decisively enter the public stage.[1] He was brought in months before Hiroshima, learned the science, observed the technology, witnessed the teamwork of the scientific community at Los Alamos, and grasped the immense scale of the production enterprise, from its smallest labs in places like Ames, Iowa, to its monumental structures, monoliths of windowless concrete, rising out of the desert floor in Hanford, Washington.

Laurence demonstrated his fealty and earned the right to accompany the bombing flight over Nagasaki and then furnish the scripts that lifted the veil of secrecy that had hidden the Manhattan Engineer District from view for the life of the war. When General Groves spoke to the press, he spoke Laurence's words; when Truman made his announcement on August 7, 1945, warning of "a rain of ruin from the air the likes of which has never been seen on this earth," the president was reading the speech Laurence had prepared for him.[2]

Laurence's words derived from, and simultaneously established, the official language of the atomic age. His own report on the Nagasaki bombing was widely published, most fully in *Life* on September 24, 1945. It began with a string of metaphors: "A giant flash . . . a bluish-green light that illuminated the entire sky . . . a giant ball of fire . . . belching enormous white smoke rings . . . a pillar of purple fire."

> Awestruck, we watched it shoot upward like a meteor, becoming ever more alive as it climbed skyward through the white clouds. It was no longer smoke, or dust, or even a cloud of fire. It was a living thing, a new species of being. . . . At one stage, the entity assumed the form of a giant square totem pole, with its base about three miles long, tapering off to about a mile at the top. Its bottom was brown, its center was amber, its top white . . . it was as though the decapitated monster was growing a new head. As the first mushroom floated off into the blue, it changed its shape into a flowerlike form, its giant petal curving downward, creamy-white outside, rose-colored inside. It still retained that shape when we last gazed at it from a distance of about 200 miles."[3]

Lawrence originated what would rapidly become the standard description of nuclear detonation: he split the occurrence in two, with infinite power, sublimity, and triumph above, high in the skies, and horror, death, and destruction below.

What lay below, indeed, was the very reality American military figures and their propagandists wished to dispel. Lawrence's eyewitness report on Nagasaki carried the reader away from the darkness and into the light. Look up and see this glorious creation, "a living thing, a new species of being." His description of that new species might be seen as an unconscious sequence: first sun, then meteor, then mushroom, then decapitated monster, and finally a beautiful, delicate, roseate flower. By the time Laurence was through, the atomic cloud belonged to God and nature, and its powers for horror and destruction had been transmuted into redemption and resurrection.

*　*　*

Lawrence's narrative was compelling. It yoked the specific cruelties of a new weapon of war to the foundations of human experience, and thereby absorbed complex questions of culpability and the specific individuals and nations involved into a drama of types and universal messages. To look at the flood of images in the popular magazines and journals was to see, over the next months and then years, the imbedding of a narrative that declared a brooding drama and a glowing triumph. Heroes emerged, not just military heroes like Paul Tibbets, who piloted the Hiroshima bomber, or General Groves, but scientists at Los Alamos and Chicago, who appeared in the media as stereotypes—brilliant, thoughtful, yet activist intellectuals, men and women of the new elite, deserving of our trust. Depicted in the illustrated newspapers and picture magazines, these scientists worked intently at some unexplained experiment, or they stood before blackboards full of arcane symbols and formulae. And they gazed, with awe and triumph, at the mushroom cloud, artifact of their genius.

It was appropriate that the dominant medium for the presentation of a new atomic age was photography, for it froze the unthinkable, the infinite, and the terrifying into something incontrovertible, measurable, capable of capture and then release into familiar surroundings. The editors of the principal popular journals wrung everything they could from Hiroshima and Nagasaki, and when the military released pictures and scripted reports of the earliest test at Alamogordo, New Mexico, from that story as well.

By the end of September 1945, each site had adopted a particular symbolic function. Alamogordo represented the triumph of American knowhow, courage, and dedication. Hiroshima became the vengeance for Pearl Harbor, the necessary escalation required to save American lives and decisively end the war. The refusal of the Japanese to surrender, requiring the bombing of Nagasaki, proved that the enemy was as weird, as irrational, and as intrepid as the propagandists had proposed—a kamikaze nation. *Japs*: "savages, ruthless, merciless and fanatic," in Truman's words.

Over the fall and winter of 1945 and into the spring of 1946, journalism, propaganda, denial, and desire combined to form a stable fiction about a weapon terrifying in both principle and actuality. It became a fitting end to the war and a portentous test of humankind's capacity to seek good and resist evil. A campaign of this magnitude, this sharply focused, seems appropriate to the steady swell of frustration, fear, and doubt about the future that made this war's end unlike others. And so, like the ripples from a pebble dropped in a still pond, the atomic sublime expanded into its surroundings. Whether on purpose or by happenstance, the atomic cloud became the symbol of an atomic age—an isolated singularity became a universal inevitability.

It seems paradoxical that this emblem of the infinite, of absolute power and responsibility rendering "words and statistics, and even pictures inadequate,"[4] should become the trademark of the age in the form of a photograph mass-reproduced in popular illustrated journals on coffee tables, in dentists' and doctors' waiting rooms, and in the browsing area of the public library. But that was the magic of this icon—the way it could simultaneously domesticate the unimaginable while charging the mundane surroundings of our everyday lives with a weight and sense of importance unmatched in modern times.

*   *   *

Two American landscapes served as theatrical stage sets for the redemption of the American atomic empire in the decades of nuclear testing after the end of the war: the tropical paradises of the Pacific islands and the harsh sublime landscape of the American West. Both came with powerful associations. Both had been memorialized in books, movies, photographs, paintings, and music. Both would serve the staging of new myths.

The challenge was this: to test the bomb required an empty landscape— empty of people, and also of associations, myths, and symbols. This is impossible, at least as it concerns the American empire, because emptiness itself is a central element in America's origination myth: empty landscape in America signifies promise, a vacuum drawing new and renewed people and institutions. Preparing these landscapes for testing involved complex adaptations of mythology, symbolism, and association. Official propagandists began the process. Enthusiastic journalists expanded and promulgated the atomic narrative. Everyday citizens consumed, adapted, and passed it on. Landscapes of national promise and possibility became monuments of national sacrifice.

But what of those who lived there? The land had to be emptied, of course. It would be best of its people chose to make the sacrifice, offering redemptive absolution for the rest of us. Or its population might be deemed not human, or less than human; in that way, the moral cost of evacuation might be lessened. Both strategies came to be applied in the decades of nuclear testing.

The first postwar tests took place on Bikini Atoll in the Marshall Islands of Micronesia in 1946. Bikini was a logical choice because it was already a protectorate of the United States; it had been "liberated" from the Japanese (having been occupied by exactly 6 soldiers); it was small, with an exploitable deepwater port where obsolete naval vessels could be anchored, the better to see the effect of atomic weapons on the navy. Bikini was home to 167 natives, still (largely) unaffected by the modern. They could be evacuated, and, according to the reports of naval assessors, they were docile, grateful, susceptible to persuasion that took advantage of their devout Christian religiosity, and politically inept. With a minimum of fuss, a military representative was dispatched to present the case to the natives, a "replacement" atoll, Rongerik, was prepared, and the natives were evacuated, along with their outriggers and, in a concession to their Christianity, their chapel. (The saga of their outrageous mistreatment, their conversion from self-sufficient tribe to desperate, starving reservation dependents, their return to an inadequately decontaminated Bikini, and their subsequent reevacuation, is told eloquently elsewhere.[5])

The entire event was a matter of propaganda far more than one of science. The purpose of the test was political far more than scientific or military. Conflicts between naval and air forces over the future of the American armed services formed one subplot; the need to make atomic warfare imaginable as a military strategy formed another; the desire to send a strong signal to the new enemy in Moscow, a third.

This first postwar atomic test was conceived from the first as a theatrical event. Thousands of radio stations ran remote feeds; 175 reporters and numerous senators, congressmen, UN observers, and a cabinet member were among the 42,000 or more witnesses to converge on Bikini Atoll. By the time the bomb finally went off, less than a year after Nagasaki, somber moral reflection had successfully dissipated into something closer to a festival atmosphere. We might oversimplify by contrasting the titles of two articles, less than six months apart: "What Ended the War," in *Life*'s September 17, 1945, issue, and *Newsweek*'s "Atomic Bomb, Greatest Show on Earth," of February 4, 1946. Not just the titles, but the substance of each article reflected the shift. *Newsweek*'s Washington editor and bureau chief, Ernest K. Lindley, announced the advent of atomic tourism: "Many who have had these firsthand experiences have felt words and statistics, and even pictures inadequate to convey their impressions to others. They doubt that anyone who has not been an eyewitness can sense finally the power of the atomic bomb."[6]

The Bikini test wasn't just spectacle; it was a spectacle of nature, with the American as its caretaker. And at its core lay one of the founding myths of American civilization: the noble savage, primitive, technologically innocent, but wise to the universal laws that linked the divine, the natural and the human into one. Transplanted from the North American wilderness to the South Sea Islands, this prophetic type served the old functions in a new Eden: not the frontier but the globe. Here too, though, his role was the same: to symbolize the passing of one order and the ascendance of the new, to bless this transition even as he and his people were pressed aside, relocated, and then abandoned.

The South Seas, and Bikini by extension, were part of a long theme of native stereotyping. The Bikini elders and their families emerged as stereotypes drawn not just from American Indian precedents, but from European paintings (Gauguin especially), American novels of the Pacific (from Hermann Melville to James Michener), and newly popularized anthropology texts (notably Margaret Mead's studies of adolescence, sexuality, and society in Samoa, New Guinea and Bali). The resulting picture was a paradox of sorts. The native peoples were simultaneously "primitive" (even Mead used the word in her subtitles), and representative of the ideal American character: they were both Indians and settlers, "noble savages" and Enlightenment *philosophes*, occupying an Eden whose sacrifice would redeem the postwar world.

It was a resonant and effective myth, forged in the war itself, though with roots reaching back to the birth of American imperial endeavors with the conquest of the Philippines. If the native peoples were innocent, childlike, in need of help and protection, their protection justified and explained in some measure the immense death toll of the Pacific Theater, as American marines, sailors, and airmen died by the thousands to capture small outcroppings in the midst of an infinite ocean. If they reincarnated the American democratic experience on a new frontier of ocean islands, then they became Americans too in some associative sense. To save them, then, was to reenact the defense of freedom, liberty, democracy—American values made universal.

This, at least, was the thinking of editor-turned-author James Michener, drafted into the Pacific fleet, trapped in a desk job on Espirito Santo in the New Hebrides, and then reassigned as a naval supply officer in the Solomon Islands. In mid-1944, at age 37, he began his first serious writing, a series of short stories, thinly veiled observations and memoirs of his experience of the war in the Pacific. Using enlisted men and officers as his editors, he sought to produce a work that recorded the complex experience of life in these islands, and—more surreptitiously—to explain and justify American sacrifices in this long, long campaign. Sometime in the spring of 1945, he sent it back to New York to see if it was publishable.

Michener's manuscript took the complex mythos of the South Sea Islands and made it a deeply American story. In his tales, civilized men discovered the hollowness of their civility, had their characters tested without benefit of New England heritage or New York money, and, too often, failed the test. Against this critique of East Coast cultivated traditions, Michener proposed other forms of heroism and character: wisecracking idealists with convictions so powerful they must keep them hidden until finally they might sacrifice their lives or their honor to defend those convictions; native women who embodied the virtues of the natural man but were not so easily dismissed or pressed aside. What had started as a collection of amusing anecdotes meant to explain the tedium and terror of the Pacific Theater came into print with a deeper, darker vision of human frailty and resilience.

Michener finished *Tales of the South Pacific* as America and the globe debated, loudly and publicly, the significance of the new atomic age. His complex, ironic description of a common humanism (informed by his Quaker upbringing) seems utterly in tune with these debates. Yet never in *Tales of the South Pacific*, never in his memoirs, does Michener mention the atomic holocausts that ended the war, and that absence was a powerful presence in the novel. Moreover, between the time he started the novel and the release of the finished product, his island paradise had become a sacrificial zone, permanently contaminated by atomic radiation.

Michener's tale of native nobility and sacrifice and imperial imperiousness and responsibility appeared in print just six months after the first test explosion at Bikini. His noble savages were frail, unattractive, inbred islanders clinging to a once-glorious history. They were, to quote Michener's mouthpiece, the lieutenant Tony Fry, "like the little Jew ... some sawed-off runt of a Jew in Dachau prison. Plotting his escape. Plotting to kill the guards. Working against the Nazis.... You probably wouldn't invite him to your house for dinner."[7] For Michener, the moral quandary of imperialist responsibilities lay in recognizing the underlying values beneath the homely, malodorous surface of humankind.

Not so the noble savage of Bikini. This was propaganda for a broader audience, and no one took the risk of putting a toothless ugly oddity in front of the cameras. Bikini's noble savage was a man named Juda. He was, variously, "King Juda, their leader," sometimes "their local chieftain," and, once, "Bikini's tall, tawny Paramount Chief Juda, manor lord of 160 Christian islanders."[8] His actual relationship to his tribe and to the larger governance structure of the islands was complex, ambiguous, and even dangerous. (The decision as to which island should be their new home was determined in large part by concerns about tribal and clan conflicts with other islanders, matters the U.S. government never fully understood.) But Juda was essential to the story told of the evacuation of Bikini.

Two versions of this evacuation story run parallel, both reported by Naval Commander Ben H. Wyatt, military governor of the Marshall Islands and the principal U.S. liaison with the Bikinians. Both versions start the same way: the naval commander went to Bikini after military and scientific experts had determined that this was the best island, the most appropriate military target, and the one least disruptive to the peoples of Micronesia. He made the trip on Sunday, February 26, 1946, to ask permission of the Bikini islanders to sacrifice their home to the goal of global peace, the end of warfare. There, immediately after their Sunday Christian worship service, Wyatt took his case to the assembled islanders, and they willingly agreed to give up their home.

Thus far, Wyatt's two versions, one released near the event as the official report, the other a recollection for posterity written in 1952 after the atomic testing program had become an established part of American and global life, correspond. From here, the single clean historical narrative begins to diverge. Interests intervene, reports become stories, and point of view becomes increasingly crucial. Wyatt's first, official report has Juda respond immediately to America's request, as if he knew the minds of his native followers intuitively—and that's consistent with the more general figure of a noble savage.

In the face of it, though, that story strains credibility. It complies too perfectly with the needs of the navy and the testing program: instant permission, and beyond even that, an affirmation that this ambiguous event was, in the eyes of the wise innocent, a "wonderful undertaking" (Wyatt's paraphrase of Juda).[9] By 1952, the story had been further cleaned up and dramatized. In this later version, Wyatt added a discreet pause during which he left the natives to debate the question privately; he walked on the beach in silent contemplation until Juda came to him (leader to leader) to report the decision: they would sacrifice their island for the cause of humanity.

Neither story exactly corresponds to the newsreel that Americans saw in 1946. There, Wyatt can be seen delivering his speech to a group of natives who sit cross-legged on the sand in the shade of the coconut palms, with the clear water and the broken horizon, sunstruck, behind them. He speaks in English, and though there is an interpreter, we don't hear him; indeed, it is as if the natives understand the message intuitively. King Juda rises, walks forward, announces to the naval man the decision of the people, and it is over: the narrator's voice rises up and the scene shifts. This isn't the finish of the play. It's rewritten in the newspapers and magazines over and over. Juda becomes a figure closer to godlike. From one iteration to the next, Wyatt becomes gentler, more humane, "soft-spoken," and "sensitive." The atomic test becomes, according to Juda, "the will of Heaven." Wyatt's words become more forthright and the process far clearer: "The U.S. wants to turn this great destructive power into something good for mankind,'" *Time* reported him as saying. "The Bomb would be dropped on Bikini. For their protection, and for progress, would the islanders help by leaving their home, perhaps forever? Juda took counsel.... At length he gave his decision: 'If the U.S. Government needs to use our houses for the goodness of mankind, then by the kindness of God we are willing to go.'" As the accounts multiplied, the natives grew steadily more exotic: the *New York Times* had them festooned in frangipani: "primitive they are, but they love one another and the American visitors who took their home," the subtitle read. The *National Geographic*, legendary for its depictions of bare-breasted native women and loin-clothed men, called them "brown people" who "had progressed to using kerosene lanterns and a few imported steel hand tools . . . [whom] modern civilization suddenly overtook." *Life* went further: these innocents had agreed because the U.S. had promised that the evacuation was necessary "for the good of mankind."[10]

Life ended its article with a photograph of Bikini, and in the caption, the atoll itself became alive, conscious, a willing participant in its immolation: "Pacific Island of Bikini Calmly Awaits the Atom Blast," explained the caption. And in the magazines, especially, the island mutated into something more; that mythic island paradise imagined, desired, owned by all. "In a Blue Lagoon," *Time* titled its first piece. "Something to remember . . . a long crescent of gleaming sand, well grown with palms and other vegetation and framing one side of a lagoon of incredibly blue and green water," said the *National Geographic*. "A small outrigger canoe dashed past toward the beach, where sailing outriggers were drawn up and boys played in the water. . . . The setting was idyllic."[11]

Setting, characters, drama. "Atomic Age: The Goodness of Man":

Under Bikini's palm and pandanus trees, bright in the South Sea Sun and dark in the shadow of the Bomb, primitive man and progressive man held palaver. The U.S. Navy's soft-spoken, sensitive Commodore Ben Wyatt might well have wondered why progress had to sacrifice this lovely coral atoll, instead of an empty wasteland, a dismal slum or a plaguesome Buchenwald.

Bikini's tall, tawny Paramount Chief Juda, manor lord of 160 Christian islanders, took comfort in the will of Heaven.[12]

The Bikini story developed over months into this seamless, "idyllic" narrative of peaceable innocents in an animate paradise, willingly offering themselves and their home as sacrifice "for the good of mankind," with "the kindness of God," to a soft-spoken, diffident representative of a nation reluctantly pressed into service as the protector of humankind.

We can see this evolution, as did most Americans, by looking at the newsreels that ran before feature films in movie houses throughout the country. With their portentously voiced narrators, dramatic silhouette shots, close-ups of sternly determined faces and images of masses of men (and sometimes women) racing to some common task, these newsreels became a staple of the wartime years. What most viewers didn't notice was the source of the imagery: military propaganda cadres who provided the raw footage from which companies like Universal and Paramount edited and pasted, overlaying bold graphics and text, narrative voices, and sound effects. By the end of the war, the newsreel industry had a two-decade-long place in the lives of most moviegoing Americans, who might have felt cheated without the voice of Ed Herlihy or one of the other narrators to reassure and rearrange the events of the week into some orderly coherence.

The events of 1945, 1946, and beyond provided a transition between World War II and the Cold War, and the consistency of visual propaganda from one to the next suggested a seamless coherence of two forms of war. At the center of this transition are the stories of those first atomic tests at Bikini. Each week Paramount and Universal, the two principal newsreel producers, devoted significant attention to the events at Bikini, weaving a narrative that took the everyday events of America in its first postwar year— stock car races, hotel fires, bathing beauty contests, demobilization and housing crises, vacations, and celebrities—and framed the whole in terms of global power and responsibility, personal awe and fear.

Universal's series began on January 25, 1946, with an announcement, almost in passing, that the U.S. government had decided to test more nuclear weapons. It wasn't until mid-March that Universal presented the first full-scale narrative on the subject, and it was here that the promise inherent in a visual medium presented to a rapt audience in a darkened theater, annexed itself to the atomic story. Universal had the entire wartime experience of its audience upon which to capitalize; all the habits of propaganda shifted easily over to the new tale. Indeed, one can almost feel the palpable sense of relief as the company's narrators, editors, and writers found themselves smoothly redeployed into a new arena that comfortably resembled the past.[13]

"First Pictures—Pacific Isle Waits Atom Bomb!" shouted the headline on the poster at the local movie house. Universal's poster style was to present tiny snippets in the form of mock newspaper articles; the mimicry improved the credibility of the presentation, even as the purple prose and hyperactive punctuation aped the breathless style of the narrator in the newsreel.

BIKINI ATOLL, MARSHALL ISLANDS—the scene for "Operation Cross-roads"—the tiny crescent-shaped island where the special atom-bomb tests will soon be held—shows natives leaving for new homes and advance crews readying site for historic blast.[14]

The newsreel itself was a masterpiece of the genre: from the opening Air Force footage, nearly identical to so many wartime reels of airborne bombers high above the clouds, to the arrival at Bikini, seen from a bomber's-eye-view, and thence down onto the waters of the atoll, with the narrator's voice fusing the rough edit where Air Force footage stopped and Navy footage began. Narrator Ed Herlihy's praise of the new technology of radiation-sensing remote-control drone aircraft reminded viewers that scientific progress made a new form of casualty-free warfare possible, ensuring no American lives would be endangered "when they fly into the radioactive cloud over the atomic test grounds, palm-studded Bikini Atoll in the Marshall Islands, where Universal cameraman Floyd Trahan took these first pictures." Universal's copywriter yoked together the new atomic nature with the old Edenic one; mentioning the cameraman's name was meant to assure viewers the footage was authentic, that the journalist was independent of the military, that the news producers were courageous and intrepid, and the newsreel medium was up-to-date and authoritative.

In that context, the tale of Chief Juda and the natives assumed a central role, and it was smoothed and distilled as each week's newsreels appeared. In this early Universal newsreel, the evacuation was presented almost brusquely: a desultory shot of the supposed native assembly, overlaid by Herlihy's portentous voice: "American officials discuss plans with the Bikini natives for the evacuation of the atoll." Sometime before, it's implied, the larger questions of rights and compensation for exile from their home were settled. Besides, assures the narrator, "the islanders are a nomadic group, and are well pleased that the Yanks are going to add a little *variety* to their lives." What could the omniscient narrator have meant with that subtle emphasis? That evacuation was a more pleasant version of their normal rootless ways? That the bombing itself would serve as entertainment for a jaded tribe of lotus-eaters? (In fact, as the newsreels returned, week after week, both these implications resurfaced, as the narrator recast Rongerik Atoll into an ever-more perfect paradise, "where there is more rain and better coconuts," and as a grinning Juda was brought back to watch the first test, and other natives were imported to admire the second.)[15]

When the film caressed a bevy of giggling girls, when the narrator reminded viewers that "the inhabitants are missionary-educated," devout Christians despite their bare skin and skimpy garb, when the men of the tribe waved happily from the PBY vessel and industriously offloaded the timbers of their primitive church to rebuild it on Rongerik: this was preparation for the culminating assurance that even "the natives will be safe from the atom-bombing tests at Bikini—these tests, which are so highly important to the world, tests that will help chart the future for us all." Here the significance of the natives became clearest—not merely to ratify the validity of the tests, nor simply to reaffirm the new role of the bluff, honest Yank as policeman and guardian of the globe, but to assure American citizens, everyday viewers of movies, families on a Saturday or couples on a date, that they too were safe, could rest easy, abandon their skepticism and become, like the natives, happy emigrants to the shores of a new world.[16]

* * *

On June 6, 1946, right in the midst of the newsreel sequence devoted to the Operation Crossroads testing, Universal released "Damage Foreshadows A-Bomb Tests." It was the first detailed motion-picture footage of Hiroshima and Nagasaki's aftermath. The film received full treatment:

> From the shattered cities of Hiroshima and Nagasaki in Japan comes visual evidence of the staggering power contained in the blasts of atomic fury now undergoing tests in the South Pacific . . . the most terrible weapon known to science.

"That ghostly shading on the bridge walk is the only remaining evidence of what was once a man," intoned the narrator, as the camera played over a vague darkening in the pavement. "The bomb blast consumed his body entirely but cast his imprint on the stones where he stood to meet his fate. . . . Steel window frames were forced outward by the terrific concussion. School chairs are streaked with its dazzling light. Science still seeks to uncover the complete secret of the atom's mighty power."[17]

This was the other narrative of the atomic age: dire warnings of vulnerability, devastation, the erasure of past stabilities, memories, promises. School chairs streaked with dazzling light, the schoolchildren vaporized, their innocence betrayed; everything strong and invulnerable rendered weak, useless. But shaping the atomic story was an incomplete process, not a duality but a dialectic: science still seeks to uncover the complete secret of the atom's mighty power, and so we must place our faith in science, in the scientists and in the military and social institutions that support and make possible their search for knowledge.

As Juda and his tribal council, guests of the American military, waited eagerly to watch the atomic extravaganza, they foreshadowed the countenance Americans were being encouraged to assume, giving our faith to God and America, simultaneously weighed down by the burden of such terror and power and relieved of its weight by the solicitous institutions of the new atomic culture. What were we to be? What but eager witnesses to "the gripping story of the bomb explosion and subsequent damage scenes," as Universal promised in its press release, awestruck and overwhelmed by "the mighty atomic bomb," "the smashing blow of the deadly plutonium weapon," "a stab of light as brilliant as lightning," caressing with our eyes "the appalling damage wrought" while we remained, protected evacuees, wards of the state. We watched, but from the darkness of the theater, looking upward at the black-and-white images, listening to the narrator, witnesses not to the experience but to its recreation—as "the film highlight of all time!" When, in August, Universal presaged its footage of the second Crossroads test ("history in the making, a scene that excites even the most experienced newsman!") it ran confiscated Japanese footage of the carnage at Hiroshima and Nagasaki. By this time, though, the question of identification had grown confused. Were we the victims? Or was this too a part of the "greatest show on earth," "the motion picture spectacle of all time," subject for our awe and our delectation, as we, like King Juda, got "a front row seat at the bomb blast"?[18]

*　*　*

Exactly what happened at Bikini is hard to piece together from the various official versions. How did a significant native population find itself shuttled off to a vastly different atoll where they could not sustain themselves or their culture, where they would become beggar-clients of the United States, receiving rations in a manner closest to the dehumanizing doling out in the most desperate Indian reservations of the nineteenth century? Exactly how was a naval officer with a Bible and a translator able to make that forced exile seem desirable? Thus far we have three distinct, but interrelated, narratives of the events at Bikini in 1946. The first two, by Ben Wyatt, are consistent in their themes if differing in their chronologies: the U.S. military asked permission of a primitive but innately generous tribe and, through its leader, were granted the right to sacrifice their habitat for the good of mankind, and in return the military helped the tribe migrate to another, better, island paradise.

The newsreels built on this base to produce the most consistent and far-reaching version. In the darkened movie houses, rapt audiences watched as the natives, joining with the rest of the world, witnessed a great spectacle of scientific-military triumph that also declared American supremacy and served to warn those who might oppose it.

And so it comes as a shock, even today, to reach behind the scripts of those newsreels and find the messy primary material of history, to discover how fully the rough splintered edges of historical fact put the lie to every part of the composite script of American Cold War exceptionalism that found its way into common knowledge.

In the air force film reels held at the National Archives is the raw footage of the evacuation of Juda and his 166 fellow natives from Bikini Atoll. It is here that one can piece together the actual circumstances of the Bikini test and see the ways the historical events were revised, reshot, and edited until the unsettling, morally fraught reality became a perfect, and more necessary, myth.

If you know the actual chronology of Operation Crossroads, it's unsettling to watch the Navy-shot reels of raw footage in their proper sequence, from the reconnaissance of the atoll to its immolation.

President Truman gave his imprimatur to the bombing of Bikini on January 10, 1946, and blasting of the harbor began immediately. Naval Commander Wyatt didn't arrive to ask the permission of the Bikinians until exactly a month later, on Sunday, February 10, 1946, by which time the atoll was already a casualty of American plans.

In the context of the historical record, this is unsettling on the extreme, for by the time Wyatt met with the natives, they had been subjected to a month of blasting, dredging, and construction. How did they maneuver their outriggers past the navy vessels in order to fish? What explanation had they been given as they were herded onto a smaller and smaller part of their island home?

Wyatt's account, and the narrative presented in the finished newsreels, suggests that he was the advance man, that the response of the natives actually mattered. According to his accounts, Wyatt flew in and went up to the native church, where services had been shattered by the tumult of his arrival. Taking up a Bible, he reported, he preached to the natives; he "compared the Bikinians to the children of Israel whom the Lord saved from their enemy and led into the Promised Land," and he asked, "Would Juda and his people be willing to sacrifice their island for the welfare of all men? . . . After all plans had been explained to them and all personal questions answered their local chieftain, referred to as King Juda, arose and stated that the natives of Bikini were very proud to be part of this wonderful undertaking, and if it was the desire of the United States Government for them to live elsewhere they would be very happy to do so."[19]

But there's something wrong here, some further falsehood is at work. As the raw footage flickers on the screen, the stable narrative of the emerging atomic age agitates and then disintegrates. The film of Wyatt's meeting, it turns out, was made not on Sunday, February 10, but nearly a month later, on Sunday, March 3, the last Sunday before the evacuation. This is not a documentary of the action unfolding as it occurs. It is a dramatic reenactment or else a complete fabrication.

In either case, the cameramen filmed that March 3 outdoor scene at least twice, to correct errors in the camera angle, bad sound, and the recurrent failure or refusal of the natives to recite their lines correctly. Next the cameras moved to the final church service, and then to the native graveyard, where Juda and his people were instructed to say farewell to the bones and spirits of their ancestors buried there. And this too is a dramatic set-piece containing a moral contradiction. If these are nomadic peoples happy to hitchhike on a navy PBY to their next island, why do they have such a graveyard, and why do they mourn the loss so poignantly?

In the real time—in the awkward present of the raw footage, with its accidental inclusions and arresting details destined to be edited out, corrected, resected—the entire event grows more shameful, more difficult to watch. The cameramen are impatient. They insist on retake after retake. "We were very confused," reported Bikinian Kilon Bauno some years later. "I couldn't understand why they had to do everything so many times." As the retakes grind on and on, Juda himself grows visibly angry, tired, and impatient. Finally Juda walks directly up to the cameraman; staring directly into the lens, he says, "All right; is that all?" and walks off. Soon it's clear the light is dying and they'll have to continue on Monday; the military record later shows that Wyatt decided to postpone the evacuation by another day in order to assure that the movies could be complete and satisfactory.[20]

From the reels of raw footage, then, a new narrative emerges. Having already doomed Bikini, having already determined that its natives would have to be removed to the island reservation of Rongerik, having already begun the systematic destruction of the atoll and its complex natural and human ecosystem, the U.S. military recognized the necessity of forging a triumphalist narrative that could awaken, modernize, and apply older American myths of expansion and dominion. Military public relations specialists scripted this new narrative and recruited a native populace into playing the roles apportioned to them.

The jumble of unhappy incidents found in the raw footage is not what appears in the smooth finished narrative of the atomic sublime. Instead, we watch and listen in the darkened theater as "the evacuated ruler of Bikini, King Juda, gets a front row seat at the bomb blast [he's wearing military clothes—not a uniform, but khakis], as he arrives aboard the *Mount McKinley*, and is greeted by Admiral Blandy, Joint Task Force 1 Commander." In the final newsreels, we see publicity shots of the two of them together: Blandy gracious, Juda excited and grateful.

This finished newsreel ends, as it should, with the atomic sublime, the mushroom cloud, emblem and icon, trademark of the American atomic empire, lifting "a million tons of water, alive with deadly rays," as the narrator intones, "awe-inspiring in its significance for man, who learned how to control the atom, but must now learn how to control himself."

This seems the perfect close: a caution directed back to America (when America alone held the secret of atomic warfare), yet also deflected from a call for American political and military restraint to a more amorphous and less charged call for human restraint.

Over the next fifteen years, the discourse would evolve in stages, from a debate about the moral stain on the nation and a new and highly charged form of exceptionalism, with all its incumbent doubts, to a sense of increasing vulnerability, as the first Soviet test in 1953 broke the American atomic monopoly, followed by the first well-publicized air-drop test in 1951, the first hydrogen bomb test in 1953, and finally the successful testing of a Soviet intercontinental missile capable of carrying atomic holocaust to every American city and household.

Terror invoked and then released. Guilt awakened, transformed to responsibility, transferred to the institutions of power and authority. What is left but the pleasure of witnessing this event, again and again—of experiencing, if only in the mediated, controlled, and artfully composed forms central to postwar American culture, the rush as "awestruck, we watched,"[21] while the "atom bomb, greatest show on earth" affirmed the power of the new American empire, an empire demanding of its citizens fealty to those heroic individuals, vigilant groups, and necessarily powerful institutions that had taken the weight of responsibility and the relentlessness of atomic anxiety on themselves, leaving us spectators to the grand sweep of history.

But that's not what ends the vintage newsreel footage in the gleamingly clean National Archives repository in College Park, Maryland. Over time, the original film stock has worn, been broken, and been repaired. Parts of it have disappeared. Some of the reels are silent, and we see the visual narrative without the instructive directions of the voiceover. Some flicker and fade to white. This one is a casualty. We hear the narrator describe the sight, saying the words that will close the final version, the one released to movie houses in 1946: "Awe-inspiring in its significance for man, who learned how to control the atom, but must now learn how to control himself."

That's the end in those seamless, edited versions. But there's something tacked on to this outtake, something unsettling that undoes the careful work that rendered the atomic sublime a seamless apologia for the American atomic empire. The narrator continues. "There is but one defense against the atomic bomb, and that is distance. . . . But distance will mean nothing without world": and here the sound abruptly dies.

World peace, we imagine. *World cooperation. World government.* All of these fit the discourse of the atomic empire; but so do *world dominion, world supervision, world rule by the wise forces of democracy and order.*

Of course it's just an artifact of age, of the decay of the film. We should resist the temptation to see it as a metaphor for other losses—of memory, of certainty, of objective truth—that accompany our steady recession from the events of another era, more terrifying than our own, when total annihilation was experienced as an everyday possibility.

But today, the film's frailty, its ephemerality, its hesitations of meaning, suggest a different feel to the postwar American empire, more tentative, more deeply marked by doubt, but also more fluid, more adaptable, less absolute. Comparing the raw footage with the finished narrative, we see a culture in the process of being constructed, and the flaws in its foundation and its finish are clearer to us.

This will be a recurrent theme in the production and reproduction of postwar American culture, as old myths are adapted, reinvoked and imbedded in new forms, old symbols recast, and old narratives reborn across the American landscape, now set uneasily in a wider, global geography of power and doubt.

CHAPTER 2

Bombing the West, 1951

In the pictures that memorialized the atomic bombing of Bikini Atoll—in the newspapers, the picture magazines, and the newsreels—the great cloud rises in the midst of the atoll's sheltered waters, with massive naval vessels lifted in its coursing upward tower. In the foreground, however, a different picture shows: palm trees wave gently, and two grass-roofed huts sit on stakes, open to the tropical breezes. If you look closely, you will see that scruffy amphibious carriers and other pieces of junked or cast-off military equipment strew the beach; there are four trash barrels, one knocked on its side; a picnic table sits forlornly, at some remove from the native structures. But it would take a magnifying glass and a high-resolution reproduction to draw a 1948 viewer's attention to these disruptive details, and that wasn't how Americans saw the picture. Most of them saw it first as it came off the wires, grainy and hard to read, the massive ships mere dashes of black against the towering column of the atomic explosion. Even in a double-page spread in *Life*, the focus was on the cloud, and the foreground's discernible elements were the grass huts and the palm trees, and even the most attentive viewer might be forgiven for failing to notice the telltale stripes painted on the palms, stripes meant to measure the height of the tsunami that would come, soon enough.

The picture confirmed that conjunction of paradise and atom bomb and located Bikini in the imaginative, the fantastical, rather than the real. Even before that first test on July 1, 1946, two French designers had begun marketing a tiny two-piece bathing suit for women, named after the atoll. In late November, a party to celebrate the completion of the Operation Crossroads test sequence featured a cake made by St. Louis bakers, with a mushroom

2.1. Operation Crossroads. (Courtesy of the Department of Defense.)

cloud formed of angel food puffs, cut by Vice Admiral "Spike" Blandy and his wife, who was wearing a mushroom-cloud hat,* and watched over by a smiling Rear Admiral F. J. Lowry. The event, widely reported in the press, came off as a light entertainment, part of a developing string of relocations of the bomb from fury to fun.[1]

In 1948, the United States shifted testing to Enewetak Atoll at the westward edge of the Marshall Islands, thereby moving the atomic age down the road toward normalization, setting it in a landscape of military and industrial efficiency. For while Bikini had been relatively unscathed by wartime, Enewetak had been the site of a bloody battle and was then converted wholesale from atoll to military base. Once again the newsreels were full of images of Enewetak's bulldozers and Quonset huts, airstrips, and monitoring stations. With its history as a Jap defense site, and then as a Yank forward station, Enewetak lay outside the discourse of paradise and innocence. It was the place of pragmatic, Cold War realpolitik, a bustling military base tied to the older, cleaner, clearer war of just a few years back.

Above, reconnaissance aircraft recorded an increasingly spectacular panorama of atomic fireballs. Enewetak was planned as the principal testing

---

* There is some dispute as to whether Mrs. Blandy's choice of hat was deliberate or coincidental.

site for the atomic age, and the Sandstone series of 1948 began the process. That spring, three test weapons were exploded at approximate two-week intervals.

The official photographs released to an eager press recorded an escalating sequence of sublimity. The first test, X-Ray, illuminated the atoll and its waters with its fiery head. The second, Operation Yoke, was a painterly splash across the dark surface of the Pacific.

Enewetak would continue to serve this dual role—industrial normalcy below and up close, natural sublimity above and from a distance—throughout the Cold War's intensive atomic testing era. Test series were conducted on the atoll in 1951, in '52 with Operation Ivy, the first thermonuclear H-bomb test, and then in '54, '56, and '58. The images themselves poured out as U.S. government agencies caught on to their seductiveness, lavishing increasingly elaborate photographic apparatuses, and releasing steadily more—and more

2.2. Admiral Blandy and his wife posing with an atomic cake and atomic hat. (Stock Montage / Archive Photos / Getty Images.)

2.3. Operation Ivy: "Mike," Enewetak Atoll, November 1, 1952. (Courtesy of the National Nuclear Security Administration / Nevada Site Office.)

sensational—pictures to grace the covers of *Life* and double-page spreads in *Look, National Geographic,* and many other magazines.

But by 1950, the Korean War and increasing tensions between the United States and the Soviet Union, amplified by public knowledge that America was no longer the sole atomic power, pressed military authorities to find a test site in the continental United States, at a safe distance from potential sites of warfare and with few of the logistical or transportation complexities entailed in the South Sea. Early in 1951, President Truman approved a site in Nevada, in the desert seventy-five miles northeast of Las Vegas.

The first test series, named Ranger, took place just weeks after Truman's signoff. But it was hardly visible: military officials hastily assembled the teams and equipment, and everyone was wary of the effect on civilian sentiment of testing in the United States proper, especially with a complicated war being fought at some distance and with a threat of nuclear escalation. Few pictures of the tests were released; fanfare was kept to a minimum.

The second series, however, was a different story. Buster-Jangle, a joint operation of the Department of Defense and the Los Alamos scientific-military team, entailed the first active field operations in concert with atomic testing, sending some 6,500 American soldiers into mock-atomic conflict, complete with newsreel, photographic, and journalist teams working under the careful eye of the Atomic Energy Commission and the military. Operation Ranger was the rehearsal, Buster-Jangle the opening gala.[2]

Buster-Jangle introduced Americans to atomic spectacle set in the larger mythos of the American West. The site, its subsectors nicknamed "Frenchman Flat," "Jackass Flats, "Yucca Flat," and "Pahute Mesa," had all the qualities of a setting in a B Western—low mountains in the background, cacti strewn at intervals across a vast, sandy, hostile desert swept by burning sun and blinding sandstorms. The military propaganda newsreel for Exercise Desert Rock, the mock-atomic battle conducted under Buster-Jangle: Dog, described the site in appropriately forbidding but also familiar terms: "this remote desert area" where "wind, sweeping across the desert, provokes violent

2.4. Corporal McCaughey, "Exercise Desert Rock. Troops of the Battalion Combat Team, U.S. Army 11th Airborne Division, watch a plume of radioactive smoke rise after a D-day blast at Yucca Flats as the much-prepared Exercise Desert Rock reaches its peak," November 1, 1951. (National Archives and Records Administration, Records of the Office of the Chief Signal Officer.)

dust storms," soon became part of the deeper American myth of Manifest Destiny—"in a land where lizards and sand flies are the only living things, a tent city, Camp Desert Rock, now stands."[3]

Here was one of the first clear signs that American mythos and Cold War atomic strategy were being more or less consciously interwoven by military writers, filmmakers, and propagandists. Up to this point, that linkage occurred without rhetorical exploitation—it just seemed a coincidental conjunction of an appropriately empty, otherwise useless landscape and a new purpose. The powerful new visual form and symbol simply appeared, as if natural, in the images and narratives accompanying the atomic testing regimen.

But *this* was not mere conjunction. Under new pressures to normalize the idea of atomic testing and even atomic warfare to a restive American population riven with Cold War anxieties and faced with a legacy of portent surrounding the effects of atomic warfare, American military propagandists and their "civilian" Atomic Energy Commission counterparts began to craft their narrative, draw its symbols into play with each other, and set them in an order that reclaimed and reawakened an older cluster of American myths, of divine exceptionalism and Manifest Destiny, played out in the now-completed drama of a sweeping continental campaign to acquire, exploit, tame, and civilize a wilderness empty but for savages, hostile, and unforgiving until the hand of the American could turn it to rich pastoral harvest.

Tied to this mythos was another, as old as the doctrine of Manifest Destiny itself: the notion of divine utility to the lands given to the Americans. On one extreme of this cluster of ideas and images lay the doctrine that "the Americans bring the rains with them,"[4] that "rain follows the plow"[5]—that the simple presence of the divinely ordained Americans would turn desert into pastorale. At the other end was a proposal, also made at the first moments of serious American westering, that each part of the West followed a "type," and each type was appropriate to some purpose: valleys watered by rivers or creeks were to be farmlands; grasslands would serve as cattle and sheep range; mountains were filled with rich mineral deposits and covered with necessary timber. The deserts, however, were meant to be left alone— their function was aesthetic, philosophical, spiritual in tone. They were to serve as reminders of the wastelands of Old and New Testament *hegiras* and the testing grounds of Judeo-Christian exceptionalism. Their hostility, vastness, and extremes were there to evoke the sublime.[6]

This structured narrative of the American West provided a description of the American landscape as a place of purpose and meaning, and it made the Great American Desert suitable for atomic testing. Moreover, it set that testing, with its shocks of light, sound and energy, its cataclysmic transformations of botany and wildlife (mesquite and chaparral spontaneously combusting, cacti set aflame, corpses of jackrabbits and coyotes strewn across the blast zone) as continuations of a larger natural process of geological and biological change wrought by the presence of man—not destructive, but transformative.

A more elaborate film for Troop Test Smoky, accompanying Operation Plumbbob in 1957, showed just how well military propagandists came to apply and extend the linkage between the American narrative of a desert land conquered and put to use and a new era of incursion and exploitation. *Troop Test Smoky* was produced with a wider audience and a broader purpose in mind than many of the earlier and more ham-fisted films, whose public lives seemed to come in snippets edited into the weekly Universal Newsreels. This was an official newsreel, complete in and of itself, its length, visual format, and tone closely matched to the commercial productions, meant to be inserted into the sequence of shorts that appeared before the feature at every American movie house. The narrative voice had the appropriately stentorian tone, and when it receded, it was replaced by skillfully edited cuts of "live" action.

The film began with a carefully scripted prologue stolen from Depression-era documentaries and newsreels familiar to Americans who'd lived through it: thirteen field soldiers, white and black, all-American, like us, naming their home towns. Elmhurst, Illinois; Dorchester, Massachusetts; Cheyenne, Wyoming; Columbus, Georgia; Portland, Oregon; New York City; Louisville, Kentucky; Liberal, Kansas: these were the first eight, after which the pace picked up, and the places blurred into the American geographical tapestry: Missouri, Minnesota, Arizona, New Jersey. These soldiers were American lawmen, bringing order to the vast terrains of the West against the unspoken backdrop of a globe in turmoil, a wide-open international society whose governance had failed it, in need of a sheriff and a posse. That this film appeared in 1957 placed it firmly within a broader American vogue for Westerns—not the B Westerns of the '40s and early '50s, but the TV Westerns that had begun to sweep the airwaves in the later '50s.[7]

Troop Test Smoky was the official version of a much wider process by which the atomic sublime and the Great American West conjoined to create a new, global narrative of American exceptionalism and Manifest Destiny. In newsreels and widely distributed publicity and public-interest pictures,

2.5. "Sands Copa Girl, Linda Lawson, is crowned "Miss-Cue" by military personnel participating in Operation Cue at the Nevada Test Site, May 1, 1955." (*Las Vegas Sun* Archives, University of Nevada, Las Vegas Special Collections.)

this atomic landscape became populated—by happy-go-lucky American
soldiers, awestruck civilian witnesses, and beauty-queen American god-
desses dressed in atomic *dishabille*.

The conjunction of sexuality, fertility, and atomic transformation dated
back to that rather arbitrary naming of an "itsy bitsy, teenie weenie" two-
piece bathing suit after the atomic test at Bikini Atoll. By the late '50s, the
novelty of the bikini had given way to more elaborate, Americanized, versions: the mushroom-cloud hat worn by "Miss Cue," Queen of Operation
Cue (1955), and the atomic costume worn by Copa Room dancer Lee Merlin,
winner of the Miss Atomic Bomb contest, in 1957.[8]

These pictures inscribed the atomic explosion as a thought balloon above the head of an otherwise vapid Vegas ornament (at least, as the *Las Vegas Sun* portrayed her), or as a benign, fluffy ornament to the body. What radiation these pictures implied was of the benevolent sort: "personality," or "sexiness" or "verve;" "radiating loveliness instead of deadly atomic particles," as an earlier Miss Atom caption read.[9]

Lee Merlin would be the last Miss Atomic Bomb. Shortly after she was crowned, Plumbbob's operation went wrong, dumping fallout across the great sweeps of desert landscape, borne by those winds described in that first military newsreel, the "violent dust storms" crackling with deadly flakes of irradiated desert material—sand, cacti, sand flies, and lizards—sucked up into the vortex of the atomic sublime.

The cloud bore down on the soldiers of Operation Desert Rock VI;

2.6. Operation Plumbbob: "Smoky." (Photo courtesy of National Nuclear Security Administration / Nevada Site Office.)

afterward, the newsreel blithely reported that Geiger counter tests revealed no danger and showed soldiers being briskly swept down with a household broom. As it turned out, the radiation counters the men had been given could not record amounts of radiation exposure greater than the military-determined maximum-safe dosage of 500_r. More than three thousand men would later be found to have taken dangerous levels of exposure.

As of 1980, however, only ten of the soldiers had contracted leukemia; by the military code, this was a light casualty rate for soldiers engaged in a wartime action. What could not be counted in the military's moral or tactical calculus was the swath of civilian deaths, injuries, and diseases in the wide oval of fallout precipitation brought by the prevailing winds off the Nevada Test Site throughout the '50s. These were ranchers, sheepherders, and farmers, rural folk and Western hamlet residents and townspeople; by rights, they were the innocent settlers whom the lawmen had come to protect. "Downwinders," they would come to be called.[10]

This narrative, in which the innocent were injured by the heedless pragmatism of atomic testers, was not the one that played out in newspaper and magazine articles or in Saturday matinee newsreel shorts. It could have: it was part of a larger American narrative rarely described and even more rarely celebrated, a legacy of waste and decimation. Indian tribes force-walked from reservation to reservation; piles of buffalo and bison heaped up and rotted by the railroad line; whole species wiped out of sky or land; settlers uprooted or killed off by ranchers and corporate farming interests.[11]

The eerily gorgeous color photographs of dawn atomic tests from the middle and later '50s provided a thrilling Technicolor alternative to this harsher picture of the West. Those photographs and the stories that accompanied them in newspapers and magazines like *Life* and *National Geographic* fit the new atomic West neatly within the movie Western traditions of the recent past. But an earlier photograph, one of the first to be released showing action at the Nevada Test Site in November of 1951, better records the darker and less romantic ways in which the atomic explosion might insert itself into the larger mythos of the Wild West. Made by photographer Donald E. English for the Las Vegas News Bureau, it was widely distributed on the wires and used as a stock photo. It showed the puff of the atomic cloud, not quite a mushroom, more like an isolated thunderhead, in between the armatures for neon casino logos (including, prominently, Vegas Vic) and the older, more forlorn signs attached to the liquor stores and hotels of Glitter Gulch, the gambling core of Las Vegas that stretched out from the railroad station.[12]

2.7. Donald E. English, Atomic test, Nevada Test and Training Range, November 1, 1951. (Las Vegas News Bureau Archives, University of Nevada, Las Vegas Special Collections, 1951.)

It wasn't the picture alone that spoke to the new conditions of an atomic age brought home to the American continent, though that conjunction of the abjectly human and the blankly natural was part of it. It was, rather, the caption some inspired copywriter for *Life* gave the picture: "Wherever You Look, There's Danger in Las Vegas."[13] This was something closer to the historical actuality of the frontier West, a place of random threats, wild gambles, rare triumphs, irregular failures, rarely with a Hollywood-style forewarning. It spoke to the randomness and incomprehensibility of events that happened when you ventured into the wilds and deserts without an appropriate sense of humility or adaptability.

Vegas, and Nevada, existed in postwar American mass culture as legendary sites full of larger-than-life narratives in a still-renewing myth of westering, and in that imaginative landscape, the Technicolor explosions and radioactive-rattlesnake dangers of atomic testing fit with ease. In newspaper supplements, picture magazine covers, and weekly newsreels, they moved across the vectors of culture to join the other postwar epicenters—

the dream cities of New York and Hollywood, where the reiterations and reinventions of the American Dream were being constructed; and the new suburban environs outside of those cities—Lakewood, California and Levittown, Long Island—where new communities, self-described frontiers of very different sorts, were coming into being to counteract or deny the anxieties now located in the brilliantly lit deserts of the West.

CHAPTER 3

Tracking Shot

MIRACLE ON 34TH STREET AND THE BIRTH
OF AN ATOMIC AMERICA

Miracle on 34th Street begins clumsily. Partly that's because it's meant to. The camera tracks down a New York street, behind a man. But the credits obscure the man and the street, blaring forward into the center of the screen in a busy, near-chaotic stream of names and titles, most of them too small and too rapidly replaced to be read or savored. The music is overbearing, a harsh fanfare of horns playing up and down a major scale. As the credits fade we see the street more clearly and the man, who seemed up to that point simply anonymous.

The man has a beard and a prosperous overcoat and an overblown British accent, and he's arguing with a shopkeeper about the appropriate order of reindeer in a storefront decoration. Right there, we realize the premise of the movie: here is a sweet but delusional man who believes he's Santa Claus. The rest of the movie will no doubt play this out to a saccharine conclusion of one sort or another.

Then the scene abruptly shifts. There's a shot of the newspaper ad— "Macy's Annual Thanksgiving Parade To Welcome Santa Claus"—and then the movie explodes into a disorderly rapture of noise, narrative confusions, and symbols. In the center of a crowd at the staging ground on 77th Street stands a woman we will come to know first as Mrs. Walker and then, after her transformation, as Doris. Mrs. Walker is bossing people around. They are characters who will go on floats, but no one tells us this. They press awkwardly forward for their assignments. The scene is gracelessly shot, with figures difficult to discern and the order and meaning of the discussion baf-flingly obscure. An officious little man with a moustache, Mr. Shellhammer, pushes up to announce a catastrophe: "That rub-a-dub-dub three men in a tub float just isn't big enough. We can get the butcher and the baker in, but the candlestick maker . . ." Mrs. Walker interrupts: "I'm awfully sorry Mr. Shellhammer, but I've got enough to do to take care of the people."[1]

This is the first in a long series of allegorical statements that will sur-face through the rest of the movie. Who is she that she must take care of the people? This is, after all, a Christmas story; in fact, it's a recasting of *the* Christmas story into a new environment, part fairy tale and part shopping excursion.

Mr. Shellhammer rushes off, but the impression is clear: this is a world of overloaded senses and overloaded symbols. There's too much, too many, and not enough room for everything. When our bearded, delusional street stroller comes up to tell Mrs. Walker that her hired Santa is drunk, his own stability and assurance begin to show themselves. He and Mrs. Walker in-spect the culprit and observe his vaudeville-act drunkenness. Behind them, we are seeing the Puritan feast of Thanksgiving turned into an ugly little ad campaign, with the Pilgrim, a hot-air balloon, sharing space with the trick-sters and the clowns. As did the audiences in 1947, we are seeing the illusions of the movies torn aside by drab sets, mechanistic camerawork, bad acting, bad directing, and the illusions of our national culture blown up or ripped to shreds by greed and self-absorption, both corporate and individual.

In the middle of this, Mrs. Walker looks at Kris Kringle and sees a re-deemer. She asks him if he will take the role. He demurs, but then a thought strikes him—no, more accurately, given the way he cocks his head at that moment, a voice speaks to him. "The *children* mustn't be disappointed," he muses. It is not simply a statement: more than a message in a message-movie, it is an imperative spoken by a divine representative brought to earth for a purpose, brought here to preach certain gospels.

At the moment Kris Kringle accepts his earthly incarnation as Santa Claus, as *Mr. Macy's Santa*, everything in the movie changes. The next scene presents us with the parade, festive, joyous, working its way down 5th Ave-nue. Suddenly the street looks good; the light has turned from muddy indis-tinctness to a lovely clarity. And we see Kris Kringle atop his sleigh presid-ing over all, giving order, benevolence, and grace to the scene below. From our angle of view, 5th Avenue has returned to its place as the site of ticker-tape celebrations; for the audience of 1947, scenes and sites like this clari-fied the difference between war and peace, signaling the newly normalized world in which fantasy and fun were once again permitted.

3.1. Kris rides in the Macy's Thanksgiving Day Parade, film still from *Miracle on 34th Street* (1947)

Still, the street retains its august heritage. At this instant it has become a Roman triumphal entryway, and Santa Claus is the hero. The camera work disappears, and in its place is a sense that we are once again spectator-participants in a narrative, in the unfolding of a myth. The movie has started. Over the next ninety minutes, the audience will see the American future unfold: the hardhearted businesswoman will become a softly yielding housewife-to-be; a naive lawyer will grow up, shoulder his responsibilities, and take on the role of husband, father, and breadwinner; a child will lose her jaded nihilism and become an innocent again; a new family will move from Manhattan to Long Island; the city, no longer needed as a place to live, will become instead the site of a new form of consumer capitalism; the new shrine will be Macy's and the new demigod Mr. Macy himself. Morality will be reinserted into the corporate headquarters of downtown and the family rooms of the suburbs.

*   *   *

Miracle on 34th Street is one of the crucial documents of American culture after World War II. It is a narrative that begins with the broken pieces, fragments, and fragile connections of America at war's end and proposes a way that they might be reassembled, fitting into a coherent whole that could be, simultaneously, a narrative of national life, a landscape, and a set of instructions to a worried citizenry. Central to all of this was the shift in national focus from the old duality of city and country, to a new one, of city and suburb.

What should surprise us here isn't the arrival of the suburb. It's the lateness of that arrival, to the movies, at least. Throughout the twentieth century,

American life had increasingly included the suburbs. From Los Angeles and Chicago to Wilmington and Boston, Americans had been moving from the cosmopolitan apartment to the suburban tract house in significant numbers since the 1880s. But the cultural mythology of American life hadn't kept up with this shift in demographics and geography. The popular literature, the movies, the magazine stories and their illustrations still focused on the old duality. Norman Rockwell's covers for the *Saturday Evening Post*, for example, set their sentimental vision of America within the older tension between city and country. From the savage satire of *Babbitt* to the lyrical sentimentalism of *Our Town*, literature, theater, and film followed Rockwell's lead.

Meanwhile, Americans themselves were remembering those '30s documentaries on the bleak hopelessness of American rural life and writing the countryside out of their futures. When *Fortune* hired the Roper team to do a national survey of living preferences in 1946, only 3.5 percent wanted to live in "a small town distant from a city," and the 26 percent who voted to live "out in the country" were almost entirely farm families voting to stay where they were, on their lands. Where people wanted to live in 1946—53 percent of them, according to the *Fortune* survey—was the suburbs.[2]

If America's cultural geography was to catch up with shifting national conditions, a new genre would have to appear, one that recast the imaginative map to include, even feature the suburban landscape, one that could redefine rural life so that its cultural messages, its heritage of values and beliefs, could carry forward into postwar life; one in which the city might be reimagined as well. *Miracle* was the first; it defined a generation of suburban idylls in movies and television from plot and characters to settings and camera angles and the most mundane of props.

Let's replay a scene from *Miracle on 34th Street* that resonates even today. Little Susie, Doris Walker's fatherless daughter, friend of lawyer-neighbor Fred Gailey, lifelong cliff dweller at 5th Avenue on Central Park, reaches into her dresser to draw out a folded and wrinkled page from a Sunday supplement. The handsome bearded old man, Kris Kringle, is sitting by her bed as she unfolds that paper and hands it to him. If we are vigilant, we see that it is a page from a real estate section, and one of the two pictures on *our* side shows what looks to be one of the first publicity shots of Levittown, Bill Levitt's much-celebrated mass-production suburban Long Island housing development.

What Kris Kringle sees, however, is a different picture, and we see it too, in a matter of moments. It too is a suburban house: two-story, pitched-roof, custom-built, with windows fronting the two brick-and-clapboard facades, small-paned "colonial" windows, and all the little details of status and heri-

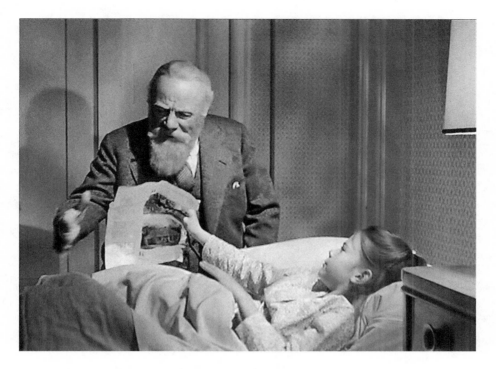

3.2. Kris, Susie, and the secret Christmas wish, film still from *Miracle on 34th Street*

tage, details of the sort exactly lacking in Levitt's bargain-basement Cape Cod of that year.

This is Susie's dream house and, more important than that, it is the secret Christmas present she desires and that she has finally come to trust Kris—Santa—enough to show him. This seems a pivotal moment, since the plot of this movie—one of them, anyway (it's a plot-crowded movie)—revolves around Susie's cynical rationalism, drummed into her by her mother, an embittered divorcée, and the erosion of this skepticism in the face of Kris Kringle's steady benevolence, empathy, and faith. And the director, George Seaton, has chosen to do his very best by the entire scene, letting it climax with the ring of simple directness that so touches us at *this* moment, as Susie carefully unfolds that newsprint page and shows Santa and us the new American dream.

We look for quite some time at this picture, once in this scene and then, to reinforce the image, again, for an even longer time, at the opening of the next. The shot sits there, with the picture filling the frame, for close to four seconds, long enough for us to get a really good look at it, but not so long as to belabor the point. Susie wants this Christmas present, and the central imaginative event on which this entire narrative hinges is this: Kris Kringle,

3.3. Susie's dream house, film still from *Miracle on 34th Street*

Santa Claus, takes her absurd, grandiose, impossible desire seriously. That's why the discussion between the child and the old man is so important. It marks the shift from one economic system to another, from industrial capitalism to consumer capitalism, from working to wanting as the central impulse of the economic system. This particular scene is startlingly undramatic, and yet starkly affecting, and we know why. This is the scene that sets the largest plot in motion, by linking all the others into one. Susie wants to leave the city and move to the suburbs.

"That's a tall order," exclaims Kris Kringle, and he echoes the larger forces behind him. For this to happen, working mother Mrs. Walker must abandon her professionalism and her pride of place in the workplace—prizes hard-won by the exigencies of the Depression and the demands of wartime home front life. She must become not the competent, intelligent, experienced Mrs. Walker but the softer, more indolent Doris, casting aside her formal identity for her informal, intimate first name, domestic and homely, not brisk and energetic. For this to happen, the lost father must be forgotten, and a new father found, a father capable of sentiment, faithful and true, but committed as well to the workplace values that will put bread on the table. Not only that, but the audience of 1947 will have to be convinced that the picture her daughter shows us on that newspaper page isn't a fraud, a trick, a bait-and-switch.

This is an especially tall order if you look at the supply-and-demand curves for housing in the immediate postwar years. Americans may have wanted to live in the suburbs, but the suburban dwellings available to them, the ones they could afford within a feasible commute from their work, were pretty thin and pretty picked over. Even before the war ended, the new drama was the waiting list. All over America, GIs and their families were trudging out to sales offices clutching real estate sections just like the one Susie had collected, and finding not a lovely landscaped lot with a cottage nestled therein, but a muddy postage stamp with a half-built box in its center. One of the miracles in *Miracle* would be its persuasion of millions of Americans that a box could, and would, become a home.

Miracle doesn't shy from the poker table; it ups the ante. To a moviegoing audience in 1947 it must have seemed strange that Susie didn't like what she had, and the movie's makers emphasized this incongruity. Susie lived in a spacious, lightstruck apartment right on Central Park, with a bedroom to herself, and a piano, and a steady, soft-spoken black servant, Cleo, to take care of her. To the vast majority of Americans of 1947, this was an extravagant dream. Postwar housing shortages were a dire fact of life; in 1946, 64.6 percent of Americans reported experiencing the housing crunch, close to 20 percent were "doubling up" in housing, and nearly half believed the housing situation wouldn't be eased in the foreseeable future.[3]

Media coverage of the situation only increased the sense of crisis. "No Vacancies: This is Year's Saddest Phrase" was the headline for the feature in *Life*'s tenth-anniversary issue in June of 1946, and its variations hammered at American readers from newspapers, magazines and newsreels throughout that year, and into 1947. Returning GIs who lived with their families in outbuildings, garages, even cars, were always good for a headline or a human-interest picture. A double-page picture spread in a 1946 issue of *Life* counterpoised an aerial shot of half-built houses in a California instant suburb, with a photo of a family huddled improbably under an umbrella on a park bench, evicted, *Life* reported, when the landlord needed his house back.

Americans flocking to the movie theaters in the summer of 1947 were in many cases fleeing the overcrowded apartments where they doubled or tripled up with parents or in-laws, sharing a room with their infants and young children, cooking and eating in shifts, fighting over bathroom privileges, dreaming of a day when they might have a place of their own. In their eyes, Susie must have seemed an ingrate, a spoiled whiner who had no inkling of how good she had it.

And even today it seems a bit odd. In 1947, children asked Santa for a football or a doll. Susie wanted a new America.

Susie asks for this Christmas present, with all its corollary changes in the social, cultural, economic, and geographical landscape, and Kris Kringle, Santa Claus, takes her seriously. But it's not preposterous—neither the desire nor, in 1947, the satisfaction of that desire. "It's awfully big for a little girl like you," Kris told her in the bedroom scene, but for Susie it's not big at all; it's just the right size for expanding hopes and ambitions, spreading fantasies, a topology of play, "a backyard with a great big tree to play swing on," a hearth with a working fireplace, a sunstruck house upon a hill. This is what American families dreamed of in 1946. *Life* pictured it for its readers in a series titled "1946 Dreams," "based on the hard statistics of consumer demand and manufacturers' unfilled orders."[4] *Life* went beyond the simple text-and-picture layout for this one: its editors commissioned photographer Bernard Hoffman for one of its special assemblages, in this case helicoptering in to one suburban plot all the ingredients of the postwar American Dream, down to the television and the new car.

Life assembled all those American desires into one double-page spread; *Miracle on 34th Street* showed Americans *how* it was going to happen, in a series of narrative moments set, one after the other, in the most important locales of postwar American life.

We've watched the earliest scenes set in the urban street, unappetizing, trashy, gray, and unpopulated as a place of utility and of living, but available as a place of ceremony, as a sacred space for cultural rituals like the Thanksgiving Day Parade to take place. We've gone into two urbane apartments, places that draw together the elegant living of upper class metropolises and the comfortable conditions of a squeaky-clean and orderly middle-class life. Mr. Gailey—Fred—has a place as equally well kept. He's young enough to stand in for all the returning veterans, mature enough to have sacrificed, for the sake of his country and the moral salvation of the world, a professional life already in motion. This can explain why he's a bachelor to an audience of married ex-GIs and their families.

Susie's mother, Mrs. Walker, can be understood and forgiven (remember, we are attempting to reclaim the mental and emotional habits of 1947, not project our own values backward to that moment) and allowed to transform, if we observe her spaces and the ways she lives in them. At the beginning of this movie, we knew her as a remarkable professional woman, the middle-class substitute for Rosie the Riveter and all the other women who stayed home and took over the means of production. And like them, she was discomfiting to a postwar America concerned about jobs for returning GI and the possibility of a postwar recession or even a return to the Depression. Manufacturing production was still undergoing painful dislocations in the shift back from war production to peacetime consumer goods; shortages in almost everything were the norm; the government faced a huge national debt about to be "called in" by the millions of citizens who'd obeyed the admonitions and bought the war bonds, savings bonds, savings stamps, and defense issues; and the public and private sectors confronted an aged, Depression-damaged infrastructure (the National Housing Agency reported that, of forty-one million housing units, fully ten million were in such a shambles they needed to be demolished, and everything from railroads to sewer lines was in equivalently sorry shape). Women had moved into the workforce in significant numbers during the Depression as men lost the better jobs and women sought to provide family income in any way possible. The wartime years saw the consolidation of those gains as these women and many others took over everything from industrial jobs to the sort of professional tasks Mrs. Walker performed. After D-day, and more dramatically after VE-day, the potential labor war between working women and returning veterans began to shape up as a crisis. The Selective Service Act had promised soldiers that their jobs would be waiting for them when they came home; working women had been told, loudly and repeatedly, that they were necessary, valuable, talented, and successful.[5]

The promise of work for returning veterans, the shrinkage of defense jobs, the lag in demand, all ensured that the economic system alone could not solve this problem. As a result, government, business, and the media found themselves in the position of creating what they had assumed to be inevitable—a tidal wave of women *voluntarily* leaving the work force and heading home. They would change the minds and the desires of American women in an all-out assault of advertising, propaganda and persuasion.

In this campaign, preparations for the moment of demobilization began much earlier than the war's end. The overall themes were relatively consistent: to shift the domestic propaganda campaign orchestrated by the national advertising agencies, the Office of War Information, and the advertising and editorial departments of the mass media from a policy designed to encourage women to enter the workforce and lauding their contributions to one that focused increasingly on a postwar life in which women would no longer need to work and could return to even more crucial and rewarding tasks located in the home. "Amazons in the Arsenal," read the headline in *Nation's Business* for July 1943; "Aprons and Overalls in War," was the title in

FAMILY UTOPIA

The posed scene above is an honest representation of the dream of most U.S. families. Fanciful as it looks, it is based on the hard statistics of consumer demand and manufacturers' unfilled orders. Beginning with the trim

Colonial house and its generous plot which affords an op portunity for gardening, what Americans want in 194 are (*from left background, working to foreground*) conver ible station wagon, $2,890; blankets and towels (*being c*

3.4. Bernard Hoffman, "1946 Dreams," *Life*, November 1946. (Bernard Hoffman / Time & Life Pictures / Getty Images. LIFE is a registered trademark of Time Inc. Photo by Bernard

d), $50; aluminum ladder, $22; set of stainless-steel tchen pans, $33; automatic washing machine, $241; levision-phonograph-radio, $1,795; vacuum cleaner d gadgets, $107, being unloaded from truck with plastic hose, $15; electric stove, $266, with (to right) dishwashing unit, $299. Behind the bemused couple is a freezing unit, $200. On aluminum porch furniture, $115, sit percolator, $17, toaster, $19, and iron, $10. Behind is a lawn sweeper, $37. Farther to right is power mower, $200; aluminum slide, $37; doll carriage, $35, and a portable radio, $60. Hovering over them all, the dream's supreme moment just before waking, is helicopter, $48,500.

CONTINUED ON NEXT PAGE 59

the *Annals of the American Academy of Political and Social Science* for September of that year. But as war's end neared, the crucial question rose: "Can the Girls Hold Their Jobs in Peacetime?"[6]

The question of women's freedom to choose their futures was a complex one, and it evolved in often confusing ways over the years surrounding the end of the war. When *Life* ran its controversial "American Women" editorial in January 1945, the editors proposed that women would have to claim their place, resisting their own impulses to shop, consume idly, and live lazily, aided by "the oversolicitous American male." The essay aroused a firestorm of responses, nearly all angrily accusing the magazine of condescension and bias. A year later, for *Life*'s sister publication *Fortune*, anthropologist and women's pundit Margaret Mead recast the argument in subtler terms. Both women and men, she proposed, "are becoming increasingly conscious that something is wrong with women's place in the modern world," even when "it is possible for society to do almost anything with the relationships between men and women." When she made her final point, however, it wasn't in terms of the workplace, but the home. "Elimination of the semivoluntary slavery to housekeeping that we now impose on married women in the U.S.," she wrote, "should open the way for an equally significant set of inventions in that key spot of our civilization, the home, where not "things" but human beings are produced and developed."[7]

Margaret Mead's essay should be seen as a response on the part of the Luce publishing empire not just to its gaffe more than a year before, but more directly to the disturbing results of its survey on American women, published in August of 1946. *Fortune*'s survey revealed that men were more likely to marry a working woman than one who had never held a job, but they shied away from women with highly successful careers, didn't think women were more appropriate than men for any of the jobs *Fortune* listed and agreed that, once married, women should quit work—not just while they had young children in their care, but throughout the marriage. The vote wasn't overwhelming in this last case, but it was sufficiently strong to lend credence to a campaign, already in full swing, to move women out of the workplace and into the home.[8]

One group that did seem to have a clear grasp of the import of this confusing stew of spaces, places, people, occupations, and the larger social and economic future of the nation was the advertising profession. During the last years of the war, a swell of ad campaigns in the major popular magazines targeted women. While the articles and editorials might have extolled a new deal for women, the ads presented a different message. In an unhappy present, women appeared alone or with a child, overwhelmed by the demands on them—as in the Rinso ad campaign of 1945, or the Tender Leaf Tea campaign with "doing it all yourself these days?" the recurrent caption. In the postwar future, though, these ads promised an idyll in which American women rediscovered romance with the return of their men, and eagerly slipped from work clothes to wedding dress and then housedress. In some cases the products themselves invited such tactics. Oneida/Community Silver spent the war without the raw materials essential to its products. After D-day, the company ran an immensely popular campaign featuring melting, movie-star embraces and the theme song "Back Home for Keeps." "Today, at Community, we speed away at our war work," read one full-page ad, full color inside the cover of *Life*'s May 7, 1945 issue—one of the most expensive ad spots in the national media. "But when the war is won . . . then go to your jeweler's . . . Together! Choose your very own Community. Its loveliness will be yours to treasure when your man's *back home for keeps*."[9]

The campaign was aimed squarely at reintroducing women to the idea of a new role for themselves, a role within which the purchase of domestic luxuries became an essential part. As with each of these ads, the punch line was the future in which leisure and romantic attachment were inextricably linked with consumption. Oneida/Community's campaign was a huge success—so huge, in fact, that *Life* reported Oneida had, within the first weeks, mailed out close to a million copies of the ads in poster form where, Oneida boasted, it appeared "on the walls of girls' colleges . . . in high schools, even in the barracks."[10] But its double message was only the most sentimental version of a terrifically successful national advertising trend that emphasized a future in which women wouldn't have to go it alone—would, in fact, be free to return to the safety, leisure, and protection of a perfect home. "It's Spring Again—It's Two Again" was the headline for a Chesterfield's cigarette ad that ran in the spring of 1945. "Just the way it used to be," burbled the copy; "two to grab for the morning papers. Two places to set at the table . . . and Two Chesterfields over Two cups of Coffee" The illustration, though, showed him in a business suit, her in a silk dressing gown. He was off to work; she wasn't.[11]

Mrs. Walker, then, begins as an ambiguous cultural icon inserted into a tense moment in American life. She represents—she stands in for—the highly successful, professional working woman able to balance work and home, able to raise her child on her own and to keep the American way of life productive and efficient at the same time. She begins, in other words, as an appropriate icon for a movie released in, say, 1944 (though in that case, her husband would have been killed in the war, not divorced as a cad). But this is not 1944, it's 1947, and the details of her life increasingly undercut her

3.5. *Life*'s inside front cover, May 7, 1945

role as model American woman. In the first scene, after all, we're reassured that her work is in fact maternal and nurturing; she can't help Mr. Shellhammer with the Three Men In a Tub float because it's her job "to take care of the people." She's competent but harried in her professional role, and she softens considerably the moment she pushes her way through the parade-watchers at the doorstep to her apartment building and softens more when she's in contact with her daughter, Susie.

That Mrs. Walker is a mother was meant to be a surprise to audiences of 1947, for no part of the movie had given indication that she's anything but a working woman, of the sort common enough during the war. *Miracle* would help to define a new trajectory for American women, and so Mrs. Walker had to be in some ways an unstable character—unstable in the sense that she fails to conform to old stereotypes but assembles her identity from pieces of the familiar. Her entry into her own home after the parade is meant to evoke tension. She calls for Susie, but she's simultaneously looking at the mail on the telephone table just inside the living room, and that stereotypically male

3.6. *Life*'s inside back cover, May 7, 1945

gesture carries the tension of her roles directly into the home, leaving it not a haven (as she implied when she promised Mr. Shellhammer that she was going home to fall into a hot bath) but a place of contest and irresolution.

A few short scenes that reinforce Mrs. Walker's uncomfortable place in the home, introduce Susie as a child alternately instructed and chastised, and show us Fred Gailey's bachelor life: that's the last we'll see of the domestic sphere for a while. But the sequence helps to provide the transition between an incomplete home and family, and an equally uncompleted workplace—Macy's, serving here as the stand-in for all of consumer capitalism. Not yet, though.

* * *

Though few today might recognize it, much of *Miracle on 34th Street* was shot on location in Macy's Department Store, on Herald Square in New York City. Even in 1947, the filmmakers presented an unconventional picture of that shrine of downtown shopping. There's little of glamour in the depiction. Again, the movie works against the stereotype. It's supposed to be winter and the Christmas shopping season. Moviegoers at that time had watched for two decades as film stars, dressed in furs or prosperous overcoats, leaned over the display counters, attractive shop assistants at their beck and call, picking out the perfect gift for their beloved: Fred Astaire for Ginger Rogers, Bing Crosby for his sweetheart-of-the-reel. The stores gleamed, their high ceilings ascending to heaven like cathedral spaces.

Here, though, the filmmakers had already provided two very odd precursor shots of Macy's. One showed Mr. Shellhammer's office; it was cast in opposition to Mrs. Walker's apartment as they talked on the phone about that fabulous new Santa while Susie practiced the piano. The worlds of home and work were simultaneously sundered and united; the home was the woman's, the office was the man's. And it seems a perfectly unremarkable office, with a window overlooking the street, a desk, and desk lamp and not much else.

If you weren't observant, you might not have noticed the model caboose on the desk or the toy sailboat on the radiator. In both spheres, woman's and man's, the home and the consumer workplace, children's play is central but almost ignored by the camera.

The next scene is more striking. It's a high-angle shot of the crowd in a city square, and a man in a uniform is addressing the cheering, packed-in, roiling crowd. It's not Hitler, though, nor Mussolini, although the shooting is lifted wholesale from the newsreel and propaganda footage Americans saw time and again during the war, of the enemy. This time it's Santa Claus in Herald Square, announcing that all sorts of toys and gifts are available at

3.7. Mr. Shellhammer's office, film still from *Miracle on 34th Street*

Macy's. Kris's mouth moves out of synch with the words. It's clearly a dub job; the filmmakers aren't even careful, because they want us to see the artificiality, and to make the connection.

And then we're inside Macy's, but not in the glamorous store. We're in the employees' locker room, and there's Alfred, a fat, swarthy teenager with a Brooklyn accent, sweeping up as Kris puts on his outfit. The boy signals the future of all those apartments that are going to be abandoned—they'll go to the melting-pot immigrants whose good hearts and cheerful work-ethic will provide us with the production capacity we'll need.

Over the next hour, we'll see a frenzy of shopping, in the foreground, the background, around the corner from the action, and often central to the plot's narrative. But this will be shopping set within a new proposal for postwar American capitalism, and the movie gives us a critique, a proposition, and an endorsement in a few tightly structured little scenes. First, Alfred tells us what's wrong with the old model: "There's a lot of bad 'isms' floatin' around, but one of the worst is commercialism. Make a buck! Make a buck! . . . Just make a buck!" Then Kris proposes a consumer-satisfaction model to replace it—don't "push" products people don't want (Mr. Shellhammer's solution): send people wherever the best product at the best price can be found. But how can any store survive? Compete on service, the customers tell Mr. Shellhammer, and Mr. Macy, and "you'll be seeing plenty of my business from now on."

Alfred's critique of capitalism is pretty extreme: commercialism is up there with the other "bad 'isms'"—Fascism, Nazism, and of course the newly threatening one, Communism. Alfred's the working-class boy. We'd better fix our economy quick or we'll find our work force looking around for another. But the movie's proposal turns everything upside down. Bad capitalism operates brutally, because it assumes a marketplace of scarcities—scarce goods and scarce demand. The new, consumer capitalism Kris proposes assumes abundance of products and of shoppers. The problem, Kris tells us, isn't with immoral greed. It's a fault in the inefficient supply-and-demand chain. Kris proposes a postwar economy in which all that planning skill and experience left over from the New Deal and the wartime years is remobilized, sent out into the free world, to ensure that everything runs smoothly. From an economist's standpoint, it's a rather innovative proposal: a cornucopia model of consumerism in which there's so much supply that everyone's wishes can be granted, yet demand rises steadily in concert with supply, preventing a precipitous, overstock-sale of a price crash.

In fact, what turns Kris's fanciful dream into the pragmatic reality of postwar America is the increasingly powerful voice of advertising and publicity, which can fine-tune the realms of supply and demand, production and desire. When Mr. Macy likes Kris's idea, he sets his ad men on the job of maximizing the benefits. Mr. Macy's got it pretty right: "we'll be known as the helpful store, the friendly store, the store with a heart" he tells the ad men, "the store that places public service ahead of profits . . . and consequently, we'll make more profits than ever before." Pretty soon we see Mr. Macy and Mr. Gimbel fighting over the chance to contribute to an x-ray machine to an old-folks' home; both of them want the rewards of publicized corporate sponsorship. Every store is competing on service; every shopper is happy, purse strings are permanently untied, charity, and goodness overflow, and American business sees the best Christmas ever.

All this takes place in the actual space of American consumerism, Macy's Department Store. It's not spectacular, but it's festive, crowded with shoppers, a *community*. This may have been the most important visual feat of the movie—the way it articulated in understated visual form the idea that American consumerism could be a community-building function. All those shoppers! Some of them are working class, like little Peter's mother, the first to experience Kris's plan. Some are middle class, like the girl who's going to get figure skates and *her* mother. Some of them represent the most cultivated and elite American classes, like the foster mother of the little refugee girl to whom Santa magically speaks Dutch. This is a melting pot of classes and origins.

The movie disentangles the unity of Macy's into its parts, each defined in its peculiar locales. We're taken behind the scenes to learn just how American business works, or will work. In the front, where the customers are, it's not a fairy-tale place of escape, but it's brisk and well scrubbed. Mr. Macy's own office doesn't seem like much; sure, there are drapes on the windows and the walls are fully wainscoted, but the desk is homely and the chairs are anything but lavish.

The appearance of Mr. Sawyer, the sham psychoanalyst who eventually tries to have Kris committed to a mental hospital provides the movie's fourth important theme. Mr. Sawyer's form of business, and of psychology, satirizes and undercuts the dour picture of America found in the so-called social problem movies of just that time, films like *The Best Years of Our Lives*, a 1946 Oscar-winner that followed three returning WWII vets as they seek, with little success, to readjust to postwar American life. Mr. Sawyer's psychological misdiagnoses reflect the sham psychology of neuroses, anxieties, and phobias, not the cheerful psychology of warm material gratification *Miracle* proposes. With the right psychology we can move forward, forging new communities; with the wrong one we are trapped in fear of a dangerous, unknown, possibly catastrophic future in which we have little personal agency and no collective power.

Yet the reality of wartime and immediate postwar life conformed much more closely to the picture presented in *The Best Years of Our Lives*, and in fact *Miracle* does contain and confront these conditions, though in oblique and even disguised in form. Mrs. Walker is not a widow, and her husband is not away at the war. She divorced him. Fred's bachelorhood is a suspicious one. He's not the Hollywood man. He works for a large law firm but gets himself fired because he's too dreamy. In his own way, he's as much a failure as an American man as Mrs. Walker is a failing American woman.

All three, in fact—Susie included—are lost souls, out of right relation with their proper sexual, gender, generational, family, work, and social roles. In the "social problem movie" genre, the dissatisfaction, depression, and maladjustment of the characters are found to be within, the result of trauma and injury experienced in battles with an outside world that is, at best, indifferent and random, at worst actively malevolent. Characters struggle to come to terms with the conflict between their internal sense of justice and morality, and the alienness of their surroundings. And this narrative didn't just appear in social problem movies—it was prevalent in popular media immediately after the war. The solution urged by *Ladies' Home Journal*, *Harper's*, *Coronet*, or the newspaper's advice column, was to turn to a kindly professional—often medical, sometimes psychiatric, sometimes psychoanalytic, who would help with "adjustment."

Miracle on 34th Street presents a dramatically different path to happiness. Consumerism, not depth or social psychology, is the cure. The maladaptations and neuroses of the principal characters in the movie are the result not of internal strife but of environmental circumstances. What's needed is a way to retune the externalities of American life so that social harmony can return on the grand level of postwar economic life and on the intimate level of the American family. It's all about place, about reconnecting the American narrative with its proper traditions of exceptionalism, expansionism, communitarianism, and prosperity.

That's what Kris must then do: he must move Doris, Susie, and Fred into a new house in a newly privileged American landscape. There Doris will find the perfect match for her instincts to help and nurture and her desire to make a difference. There Fred will be freed of the ghosts of war and return to a firm sense of sacrifice at work and reward at home. There Susie will have her swing and her tree, her backyard, and a real school—not the "progressive" one she's going to in the city (probably Ethical Culture or Montessori!).

The move to the suburbs envisioned by Fred, by Susie, by Kris, and finally by Mrs. Walker isn't artificially yoked to the old themes of frontier yeomanry and of picturesque rural cottage life. A forceful tradition in the history of the American cultural landscape—perhaps *the* dominant tradition in that history—sets American privilege in an evolving vision of virtue and redemption found there in that house on cultivated soil. What's unusual, almost alien to the dominant American culture of the time, is that strain of cosmopolitanism, professionalism, skepticism, rationality, and social fluidity that is the province of the American city. *Miracle* simplified and clarified Manhattan's urbane geography and, by extension, America's. But it also shifted the meanings of the urban spaces and places, reinflected and transformed them to suggest what the city will become once everyone has moved to the suburbs to live. First and most important, it will become a place of professional work, of white-collar work in attractive surroundings. We see Fred's law office, and it has a marvelous view of the skyscraper sublime that was Manhattan as a business and professional center. We see the judge's chambers, plush, sober, spacious. We see Bellevue, and the courthouse, and we see the post office. It's the only place where working-class labor is shown, and it's not manufacturing—nothing's *made* here, except connections.

In fact, manufacturing *was* moving out of the cities, though not as dramatically as *Miracle on 34th Street* would have it. We think of Levittown, Long Island, as a place where the women drove the men to the station, and the men, in their suits and ties, went into the city to work. Actually, many—most—of the Levittown workers didn't go back to the city, and they didn't necessarily wear white shirts or polished cordovans. They went in the opposite direction, further out along the Island's highway corridors, working in the aviation and high-tech industries that had sprung up out there. Moving to Levittown *shortened* their commute rather than lengthened it. This was also the case with Lakeside and the other suburban developments outside Los Angeles, so too with Daly City in South San Francisco and Skokie in Illinois.

That's why the post office scene is important to the movie. It's the place where industrial techniques are shown to have transformed the service sector, and where working-class Americans now direct their muscle power and their assembly-line rote skills to new forms of urban labor. Once again, the moviemakers had shot this scene on location, in the mail sorting facilities, and the camera lingers on its high-speed assembly line efficiency for sixteen long seconds before Susie's letter to Kris shows up on the screen. Then the plot's linchpin scene plays out in that sorting room: the assembly line worker calls over his supervisor, and they have a friendly, cooperative, conspiratorial confab that results in all those bags of mail addressed to Santa going over to the courthouse, freeing Kris and proving his legitimacy.

It's another one of the little miracles that make up *Miracle*: the scene lasts over a minute, during which time we get a chance to see the new postwar capitalism working. Labor and management aren't just at peace; they're friends and collaborators, working together to make for ever-greater efficiency. As the two conspirators talk out their plan, we get a chance to look around at the smooth workings of this new manufacturing zone, and it looks pretty good. It's skilled work, and the workers look satisfied and proud. Black men and white men work side by side. The place is clean and well-lit. It doesn't look like the post office we might know from our excursions to

3.8. Postal workers examining the letters to Santa, film still from *Miracle on 34th Street*

get the Christmas package two days before the holiday. Again, the miracle of postwar American prosperity turns out to be found not just on 34th Street, not just in the retail sector, but pervasively, as a complete system applying the innovation and efficiencies of wartime defense production to a new consumer economy. By the time the movie shows us Kris's liberation from Belleview, and we are granted a moment of lingering tourist pleasure looking at the twinkling lights of the now-pristine winter streets while Fred and Doris kiss and make up, we've seen nearly all aspects of the American city recast as sites of a new prosperity.

This isn't actually the way things will turn out in America. The shift from one economic system to another and one American geography to another will be painful, difficult, and marked by strikes and labor strife, racial discord, recessions, and scandals. Cities will age and begin to crumble. And the new suburbs won't look like Susie's dream. That's part of the reason we may like the movie so well, these days. It doesn't show us what things are like; it feeds our nostalgia and our fantasy of an American past that is idyllic and uncomplicated. We remember Susie's dream house perhaps better than our own. That's the role of cultural mythology: to redraw the past in ways that deny its contingency and pain; to present the future in ways glowing enough to drive us toward it; to propose the present as a place only we find uncomfortable, terrifying, or chaotic; and to promise us this pain is temporary, this chaos illusory.

*   *   *

It seems a little strange, doesn't it? That a movie so relentlessly devoted to tracing the migration from city to suburb should spend so little time on the goal, on the house itself, but, even more importantly, on the community and the social life that exist there. All but a tiny portion of the movie's running time takes place in Manhattan, and it looks better and better as the movie goes along. The plot, the settings, even the most mundane details of individual scenes put the movie in contrast to the dominant belief of the postwar era, that to move from city to suburb was to move from social anomie, isolation, anonymity, to a tight-knit social community of like-minded people. Work is rewarding, the commute is interesting and full of vistas of urbanity and nature alike, and nearly all the interior spaces we see are encouraging, bright and friendly, or at least bright and efficient. We don't get a look at the more chaotic side of city life after that first set of establishing shots.

Part of the trouble lies in the subject. It might be easy enough to depict a darker Manhattan, but it was hard in 1946 to portray a vibrant or thrilling or even warmly sociable suburban landscape. Partly that's because there weren't many, yet—any affordable postwar ones, that is. There were older, much more expensive, attractive suburbs, and there were the raw new ones just going up outside of Los Angeles (Lakeside) and on Long Island (Levittown). What was there to show? Think for a moment of the images of Levittown that would appear in *Newsweek, Time, Life* and the other magazines in 1947 and 1948.

Raw yards with spindly saplings and struggling shrubs, rooms too small for the photographer to get a good picture without a superwide angle lens. Young mothers with babies and small children, struggling to adjust to the new world of low density and what it meant: driving its circuitous routes and avoiding the cul-de-sacs, finding the grocery store and the dry cleaners, seeking other families like their own, children their children will like, babysitters, and boiler repairmen. These aren't minor transitions when you've lived in a dense urban neighborhood like Manhattan, or a place like Queens or the Bronx, where everything's close in. The city is richer in diversity and opportunity, more efficient than the suburbs, at least until you've learned your way around. But soon! Utopia! This was the lesson extolled in article after article about Levittown, for example, but also for the other new suburbs that Levittown so often stood in for. The mass market magazines talked about babysitting collectives, about laundry pools, about school bus meetings and playgroups. They provided surreptitious instruction manuals for a social life that participants in the new suburban experience were having to invent for themselves with little training or experience.

Miracle doesn't take this difficult theme for itself. Media and other voices had sung the praises of the suburban future. That left the makers of this movie free to work with economy and thereby to pack the few images of suburban life with density and resonance, to make them not settings but emblematic symbols.

That's certainly the case with Susie's picture of her dream house. She takes it out of the drawer and unfolds it, and we can see that it's been folded and unfolded countless times. This is her security blanket.

Knowing how important it was to the child, how repeatedly and obsessively Susie parsed that illustration, movie audiences naturally looked it over pretty carefully—and the movie's producers gave them time to do it, just as they made sure that the picture would contain triggers to the wider net of associations that made suburban living so deeply, even unconsciously, desirable in 1947. The big chimney in the picture bespeaks a hearth and fireplace; the low windows of the first floor, sheltered by eaves, give it some of the quality of a cottage and imply a view from within of the idyllic natural setting that is itself domestic. Big trees surround it, that's the most impossible detail, but also one of the most important. New suburbs didn't have big trees, because cost-containment by the contractor—the whole mass-production miracle that Levittown introduced—required the use of cheap, unwooded farmland and the wholesale leveling of the site. But just as the saplings in front of Levittown houses invoked the promise of future pictur-esque idylls, so here Susie's illustration represents a fantasy—but a fantasy that you, we, all of us, can work to make real.

When we drive to the *real* fantasy, to the house itself, we are in the com-pany of the tentatively complete nuclear family. Fred is at the wheel. The street is wide enough for two parking lanes *and* two driving lanes. There aren't any sidewalks. There are trees, leafless but tall, next to the colonial revival houses. Then suddenly we're on the hood of the car looking back at the occupants. The three of them are in the front seat. Then we switch again: we're in the car, watching Susie. Behind her, through the rear window, the houses and their lawns and yards and trees: Susie cries to Uncle Fred to stop.

And he does. This matters, too. Children speak and we obey their instruc-tions. She leaps from the car, and rushes up the walk toward the entrance. As her mother chases after her, we see the sign: SALE, on the front lawn. We also see that this is, in fact, the house Susie showed Kris, and us, many scenes ago.

3.9. On their quest for Susie's Christmas present, film still from *Miracle on 34th Street*

3.10. Susie's dream home, Manhasset, Long Island, New York, film still from *Miracle on 34th Street*

It is up on a rise, and for a moment we will look down from it to the valley below, full of lovely houses on curved streets and cul-de-sacs.

As Doris and Fred run up in chase of Susie, the camera moves from panoramic shot to near-close up. The house is two storeys, flagstone below, clapboard siding above. There are shutters on the small-paned windows in front. Inside, though, the house is full of light. The front door opens into a foyer right off the living room, with a coat closet behind the door, and an open stairway on the right leading to the second floor.

The living room into which Susie rushes is huge; off it is a dining room, with a hidden kitchen implied. It's important to notice that this house bears little resemblance inside to the house we saw outside. The fireplace is in the wrong location—it's been moved from the side to the rear—and a large bay window has been added next to it. But that's the point.[12] This entire scene is shot in a fantasy house that stands in for a fantasy house, and that one stands in for another fantasy house, each one simultaneously ancient and modern. The house links past American values with new ones, hearth and home, rural farmhouse and ancient oak, transported into a recently completed suburban subdivision. For Susie's redemption, and their own, Fred and Doris will buy the house. They will marry, live here, and all will be well.

* * *

Miracle on 34th Street is a religious movie. That's why the word "miracle" appears in the title. But what is the miracle, and what theology does it articulate? These questions and their answers clarify central aspects of postwar American culture. They also bring into sharp relief the ways popular art forms like the movies reflected, reinforced and transformed their surrounding culture.

Start with the obvious: *Miracle on 34th Street* is a Christian movie: Christian in themes, in characters, but also in its mythology and in the traditions from which it draws and on which it depends. A man comes from outside, claiming to be a divinity or, more appropriately, an agent of the divine. He preaches a new gospel of kindness and seeks to overturn the tables of the greedy. He develops a small discipleship and then a steadily increasing following of believers and enthusiasts. He is declared an enemy of the powers that be, is persecuted at the hands of a cynically opportunistic semiofficial religion, is lost and then, miraculously, resurrected. He gives his last and greatest gift and leaves this world, but his preachings live on.

Miracle on 34th Street recasts the Passion of Christ. That's how its makers conveyed their messages without an interpreter, a manual, or a codex. Playing this mythology beneath the overt narrative, disguising the characters, writing the movie as a sentimental comedy-drama: all these served to slip the cultural significance of the movie past the vigilant censors of a cultural elite who had good reason to oppose most of its dogma.

"The whole of New York awaits the opening of the Christmas shopping season, crowds line the street, a great illusion can be built or shattered."[13] This was the *New Republic*'s enthusiastic review of the movie. But the magazine's reviewer replicated the moviemakers' strategy, perhaps unconsciously, by leaving unspecified just what this "great illusion" was. A child's belief in Santa Claus, yes: but an adult's faith in Christianity or capitalism could as easily have been the referent. The Christmases of 1946 and 1947 were, in fact, the make-or-break moments for the postwar American economy. Had shortages been too severe, or shoppers too penurious, the nation could have tipped into hyperinflation or into recession or worse. The shoppers who crowded Macy's in this movie were emblematic to almost any newspaper-reading American—their presence, and the solution to shortages proposed by Kris Kringle, could be read as fantasy or as reassurance with equal logic, to the majority of Americans nervous about a postwar spiral of inflation or the return of the Great Depression. The future of the American economy in June of 1947 lay with the willingness of American workers and consumers to have faith that times would be good, better tomorrow than today. With that faith, Americans would shop, charge, work to pay the charge, and in working make the goods they and others would desire, purchase, and charge again. A great illusion can be built or shattered—the illusion at the heart of consumer capitalism.

"The most real things in the world are things that neither children nor men can see,"[14] reminded the *Saturday Review*; that too could have applied as well to the direction of the American economy. For what built the postwar suburbs wasn't the economy of save-and-spend but of borrow-and-spend. The prosperity that made large-scale home purchases possible was also dependent on demand that forced production, production forcing hiring, labor, overtime, and the paychecks that resulted fueling future purchases.

Miracle wasn't alone in preparing Americans for a revolving-charge card, and then a credit card, economy. Indeed, *It's A Wonderful Life* was more direct: our hero George Bailey tells Mr. Potter, the tightfisted evil capitalist, that American citizenship, built on home ownership, required mortgages, required borrowing if it was going to remain successful. Otherwise, all we'd have would be a disaffected immigrant working class without a stake.

As *Miracle on 34th Street* ends, we are left without any doubt as to what will happen. Fred and Doris will buy Susie her house, with an FHA-VA mortgage, paying it off over thirty years at less than they currently pay in rent. But the premise of the movie's ending is more clever, for it proposes that Kris Kringle has *given* Susie, and Fred and Doris, that house. There too "a great illusion can be built or shattered," the illusion that the new American suburb is a place of rewards without payments, losses, dangers. Susie looks out the large plate-glass door at the back yard. "There is! There is!" she cries: her dreamed-of tree with its swing is there after all. That's nature in the suburbs—grass soft as silk, trees that bend to take the child in their arms. Everything is tamed, everything's a gift. Fred's new work will be so rewarding it won't seem like drudgery to take the car to the train to the subway, and the pay packet that disappears into the mortgage and the heat bill and the electric bill and the property taxes will be gift and not pay at all. The light pours into that final scene as if there were four suns, one at each of the compass points. Doris's life within these walls won't seem like prison here. She will bask in the light of this miraculous suburb on a hill, far from 34th Street.

The movie worked its miracles back in the anxious days of 1947. Though *Miracle* shies away from saying much about the war, the hints it gives us are powerful. When Kris tells Susie that boys dream of B-29s, most Americans would remember that the B-29 was the plane responsible for long-range bombings of Japan and then, on two days in the summer of 1945, of Hiroshima and Nagasaki, ushering in the atomic age as an age of urban destruction.

If the city's so great in this movie, why do people want to leave it? The image of Hiroshima flattened by the atomic bomb provided a powerful incentive to Americans to get away. It was a fantasy, of course, that moving to

Manhasset (or Morton Grove, Daly City, or Lakewood) would keep one safe. But it was a powerful, necessary fantasy, one repeated throughout the next two decades with greater and greater hysteria and less and less grounding in reality. When Eisenhower authorized the wholesale construction of super-highways, the bill was named the National Interstate and Defense Highways Act of 1956; it promised exits for citizens from target cities, and the means to get military and medical relief into the bombed-out centers. Today we know the freeways well enough to recognize this as a folly of gridlock. But this too would be the miracle antidote to the depredations of the atomic age.

The other recollection of the war just past, remember, is the Dutch refugee girl whom Kris befriends and whose hope he renews. This is the orphan that Susie won't have to be, because her mother has chosen a new role, a new profession, as mother, wife, householder, director of consumption and engine of capitalist transformation and renewal; because Fred has chosen domestic love and the thralldom to labor at a distance in order to make it possible; because the entire cast of characters, audience included, have by the end of the movie come to accept, to celebrate, and to realize, the miracles of postwar America.

Miracle on 34th Street lies situated between eras and serves as only one of many icons of culture, in mass and popular media, that bridged the canyon between a moment of doubt and terror, and a sigh of relief, between the flash of the atomic bomb and the moving truck pulling in front of the Levittown house. It is surprising that what is basically an ingratiating B movie, made on the fly, written and produced from a pitch, could sustain the weight of so much analysis, could prove to be so rich, could seem so indispensable to American life. But for its moment it was a necessary perfection: a movie at a moment when movies and their rituals of community-in-the-dark were still central to the glue holding the nation and the culture together; a story that could collect around it so many American traditions, be invigorated by them and reinvigorate them, could adapt the iconography of Christianity, democracy, and capitalism and cram all those symbols, sometimes layering them one on another, and still have the story work. But that is the way that America's culture held itself together: moving forward, looking backward.

Miracle and its medium would soon be supplanted by other media and other cultural artifacts: mass-market illustrated magazines, television, popular music, and then the novelties-turned-necessities of the virtual world, such as the Internet, mp3 players, video games, smart phones, GPS, and Google maps. At each moment, technologies of cultural communication would adjust to crises of culture; systems of cultural production would emerge, often adapted, even cobbled together, from older media and older traditions and systems of meaning; new objects of culture would emerge from those systems, nestling ingratiatingly into the everyday and thereby becoming the vessels of controversy, connection, and transformation.

Not all would find their core in the central mythos of American space, the opportunities it afforded, the responsibilities it required, the unique coherence it seemed to bring into being, to reinvent and reenergize, crisis after crisis, time after time. But it is hard to find a moment in American life from the bombing of Hiroshima to the virtual worlds of the present, when that enduring American myth of exceptionalism played out in the gift of space would not inflect the myths and the symbols that cohered America, and made it a culture.

CHAPTER 4

Looking at Levittown

In the spring of 1951, a brief letter appeared in *Newsday*, Long Island's first and only daily newspaper. Headlined, and doubtless "improved" by an editor at the daily, the resulting block of text looked a bit like a news story or an editorial:

LEAVE LEVITTOWN ALONE WEEK

Levittown—How about *Newsday* or any other organization promoting a long overdue "Leave Us Alone in Levittown" week? Just one single week is all we want. One week where nobody bangs on our front door selling yo-yos for "the kiddies," or broomstick handles for "mothers." And should the plan go through, we will have one full weekend where people with absolutely nothing at all to do cannot ride through our town trying to peek through windows, stopping in the middle of the road to see what has been done to this house and that. It would be a glorious week for us residents. We're only humans—not freaks. We just want to live a normal life without being the object of salesmen who must assume they are dealing with weak-minded, newly married couples. And in that one week, perhaps some of the Levittown political groups would even stop hammering down our front doors at 10 o'clock in the evening and come around at a more decent hour if they must come at all. Please, leave us alone for one week.—P. G.[1]

P. G.'s letter seemed to encapsulate a larger mood infecting not just the legendary mass-production, middle-class suburb and its community but the larger American moment. P. G.'s woes, and those of her fellow Levittowners, reflected the celebrity of her community. Something was happening there, and across the spectrum of American society—news, politics, culture, economics—representatives had come to study, to bear witness, to exploit.

Salesmen headed the list, and they marked the new culture of consumption that was sweeping in to replace the abstemious wartime years and the more desperate years of the Depression before it. They came to Levittown because they knew they could find families with disposable income and the need for things; there weren't grandparents or kin around the corner ready to lend toys or broomstick handles or carpentry tools—these were young families who'd moved away from their roots to live in this new place, and they hadn't brought much with them, because they were young but also because there hadn't been much in the way of closet space or storage in their basement-less, garage-less houses when they first moved in. And they had a little money in their pockets. It was a matter of pride for builder Levitt's organization that renters had no costs beyond their deposit; purchasers, too—no closing costs, no down payment, no "ups" or "overs," and no surprises. There weren't revolving credit cards or bank credit cards in their wallets or purses; debt was hard to come by if you rented or bought from Bill Levitt.[2]

By 1951, when the Levittown pioneers read P. G.'s letter, thousands had been at home for three or four years. They'd put flooring down in the attic; maybe they'd already turned that raw space up the stairs into a bedroom for the child and a clutter room for everything they needed and had started to acquire or knew they'd need again soon. The purchasers of the newer-model California ranches had carports, and many of them had already converted them into fully enclosed garages to house the car, but also the lawn mower, the rakes and pruners, the boxes of Christmas ornaments, the crib that waited for the next child.

Levittown was good salesman territory. It was easier work than the city; there were women at home during the day, and to get to the face-to-face part of salesmanship you didn't have to confront a building superintendent or ring twenty doorbells and then climb the endless stairs looking for the apartment number of the person who'd buzzed you in. P. G. might complain, but she was probably also buying—cleaning supplies from the Fuller Brush man, vacuums from the Hoover guy, encyclopedias a volume at a time, from Encyclopedia Americana or Encyclopedia Britannica or the World Book, so that the set would be complete when the kids (the first of whom by this time were on average five years old and heading for kindergarten) had to do the new Cold War homework, mastering atomic tables and chemical bonds that their parents had never needed to study, learning a geography that had changed with the war and was changing after the war, requiring that they memorize the location of small islands like Enewetak and new nations like Indonesia and whole areas of the world that had previously been *terra incognita* for anyone not majoring in history or geography in college.[3]

P. G. was also upset—or so she pretended—that the life of Levittown had become America's life, a daily or weekly soap opera or, more accurately, a wallboard opera. Writers for the *New York Times* and *Newsday* were competing with photographers and journalists for *Life* and *Look* and *Time* and even *Coronet* and *Architectural Forum*. Some of these people were setting up big cameras on tripods in the middle of the street, knocking on doors to ask permission to trample the lawn or come in and photograph the living room decor.

P. G. wasn't exactly kidding about the fishbowl effect, either. People did come to Levittown, on the weekends especially, to rubberneck. The truth was that many Levittowners themselves had first seen the site on a weekend excursion; like their later counterparts, they'd read about this novel feature of the postwar American landscape that was springing up just about an hour's drive from Manhattan, a half-hour from the Bronx. These rubberneckers went home and talked it over and, the following weekend, headed out with the lawn chair and the blanket and pillow to camp out in the lines that had formed around Levitt's sales center. Back then, in 1947, '48, '49, they'd been the gawkers, and they'd wanted in to this place. They'd arrived and, over the year or two or three it had truly become a place, their place. Now they were more than a little put off by having their rituals of communitarianism looked at as if they were—P. G. said it—freakish.[4]

But no one could read this letter, then or now, without also recognizing the tone of pride, the desire to use the wider public forum of *Newsday* (not the *Levittown Eagle*, after all) to make a declaration: Levittowners *weren't* "only humans." They were special. They were the models for the new America, and theirs was the city upon a hill, under construction. P. G.'s complaint was deceptively simple: we are inventing postwar capitalist culture; stop interrupting us.

Looking at postwar America, it's tempting to caricature that landscape the way those visitors peeping in the windows did. It's easy to forget that Levittown's lifestyle came into being after two full decades of social, political, and economic chaos, chaos that broke apart long traditions of family, work, love, and community.[5] The Great Depression had removed much of the freedom to define oneself that was a hallmark of the American dream. The war had replaced one set of anxieties with another. The postwar era promised a third: politicians, capitalists, and social theorists all feared painful lurches in the economy, insecurities in the job market, breakdown of families as men returned from war and women from work, a culture-wide malaise.

Levittown was a celebrity community because it offered the promise that American citizens, resilient, optimistic, and energetic, were going to put the pieces back together again—hooking up with capitalists to buy and labor, with politicians to vote and legislate, with social theorists to engender a renewed, appropriately adapted democratic society. Media giants from the most elite to the most populist put Levittown at the center of national and international attention precisely by making the promise that there, in its houses and on its streets, a new template for human progress was being worked out.

Remember too that P. G. assumed she could speak for others, that her experience and her annoyance were shared, that Levittown was anything but the soulless collection of look-alikes proposed by various pundits, that it was instead a community of people who were capable of communal emotion. And she knew what it had taken to forge this community: not homogeneity of origin, ideology or class—for Levittown wasn't at all homogeneous, seen up close—but rather the combination of shared experiences and accepted differences that had brought residents to that state of consciousness that P. G. embedded in the tone and the content of her letter, a peculiar sense of acting in a drama, on a stage, without the lines quite set or the audience fully visible. What P. G. wouldn't have admitted was the ways that community had gained its cohesion not only through tolerance and inclusion, but also through intolerance and exclusion.

P. G. might have wished, in her letter, for a return to unselfconscious community life, but she wasn't going to get it, and I'm not sure she really wanted it, anyway. Levittown had come to stand in for a much larger revolution, "a revolution in epitome," as one writer termed it;[6] it had become a sort of shorthand for the much larger sweeps of postwar American life. People would keep on driving past her house, some with interest, some with disdain, some with envy. (*Time*'s July 3, 1950, issue reported that "one elderly dowager regularly takes her friends through Levittown in her chauffeur-driven limousine to show 'what Levitt has done for the poor people.'"[7]) Not long after P. G.'s letter appeared, Yale University graduate student John Liell would show up with a small army of student assistants, handing out questionnaires and asking for interviews; he and his crowd would bring a new cry from the community: *will all the sociologists please leave us alone!*[8]

*   *   *

P. G.'s letter appeared in *Newsday* just six months before a corollary announcement. On November 20, 1951, William Levitt declared that the last phase of construction on Levittown, Long Island, had begun; once it was done, there would be no further expansion—Levittown would be complete.

Levitt's proclamation probably surprised most readers. Over the past four years, his development had extended through six or more "phases," beginning as a veterans-only rental project of some seven hundred houses, until it was, in 1951, the single largest detached-housing development in the world, encompassing some four thousand acres on which the firm had built more than seventeen thousand houses. Now the ceaseless annexation, with its rumble of supply trucks and inconvenient rail sidings crossing the busy roadways, its army of workers and the noise, dust, and mud that existed at the frontier line where neat curvilinear streets met the treeless expanses of potato fields was all to be stilled. As Levitt leveraged parcel after parcel of adjacent farmland into acreage for his houses, other builders, other developments encroached from other directions. The suburban frontier was closed; there was no more free land available for the expansive world of the ideal postwar suburb.

The end of expansion meant more than just the silencing of hammers and the settling of dust. Levitt built his empire by exploiting the ambiguities—political, social, economic, and cultural—of the landscape he had transformed. By sprawling across multiple municipalities and school districts, he avoided close scrutiny; by building common facilities—from swimming pools to schools and shopping centers—he gave the illusion he was creating a benevolent communitarianism in his name while leaving himself the option of "donating" these facilities to the municipalities and taxing bodies and pushing the responsibility for their upkeep off the Levitt organization and onto the citizenry.

Levitt's abdication announcement proposed a different picture of Levittown than P. G. implied in her letter. Soon there would be cracks in those pools, liability insurance bills for the playgrounds, heating bills for the community centers, property tax fights and school bonds to pay off. The oligarch of Levittown had brought civilization to the potato fields, and now he was heading out of town.

His leaving forced the next stage in the transformation of the suburb. Levittown had been a paternalistic community—somewhere between a very large family and a company town. Those who came to Levittown in those early years may have presented themselves as pioneers, but they weren't as independent of spirit or as devoid of resources as the term implied. They'd had much of their lives handled for them; streets and taxes, sewers and recreation facilities, zoning regulations and economic incentives for businesses were managed by the Levitt organization or by the surrounding municipalities into which Levittown had been dropped. Even the racial composition of the community—only members of "the Caucasian Race," as Levitt's long-enduring racial covenant put it—could be conveniently placed at the door of the developer.

Levittown was by nature a community in which self-sufficiency was not a goal, and in this too the self-styled image Levittowners presented of themselves as latter-day inheritors of the westward settlers, out on the frontier, their belongings in moving vans rather than Conestoga wagons, but pioneers nonetheless, was a comforting fiction, linking present to past.

Part of what lay under P. G.'s letter was this very American confusion of self-styled individualism, self-invented communitarianism, and uneasy paternalism. P. G. communicated, a bit unwillingly, the concession that Levittown was a contemporary, still-incomplete version of the newly popular historic restoration tourist sites, like Old Sturbridge Village in Massachusetts or Colonial Williamsburg in Virginia. But whereas the life characters at Old Sturbridge or Colonial Williamsburg were trained actors in costume, doing rote activities and giving prepared speeches, Levittowners were dressed in their regular clothes—and they were suddenly costumes—and they were doing their everyday tasks—and now they were significant activities—and they were talking to each other—and their conversations were turning into speeches.[9]

P. G.'s double message—her yearning for privacy and her bemused, chagrined acceptance of publicity—corresponded to the two revolutionary spaces composing Levittown: womblike interiors serving as huddling places, and fluid communitarian backyards and public spaces, both of them counters to the vast and terrifying alien spaces of the atomic test sites appearing at the same time in other American frontiers, contained and transmitted into American homes in glowing color picture essays and bleak black-and-white sequences detailing, alternately, the triumph and terror of the atomic age.

While Levittown's spaces were new, surprising, and significant, they were also evolutionary, and they reached back to the past, to older American land patterns and deeply imbedded American myths about land and landscape. In this too I think we can see the dialectical connection to the terrors of a new and awful Sublime. Faced with an unhappy novelty, Americans were glad to see, walk on, and live within a landscape of secure traditions.

Levittown began as mere topography; on it was imposed a pattern or set of patterns that organized that topography in new ways and gave it new significance, simultaneously local and national. The pattern comprised objects and artifacts—roads, power lines, streets, curbs, sidewalks, community buildings, private houses, front and backyards, trees, and shrubs. Between and among these, residents and visitors enacted rituals—repeated, significant actions—individually and as a community. Out of all these, drawn together in a shifting transforming whole, came an image of American utopia for the postwar years.

*   *   *

Levittown was and was not most of the forms we ascribe to it: land, landscape, landmark. Land in America has the connotation of emptiness, expansiveness; it's wilderness, or desert, or open prairie; if it's used, it's ranchland or farmland, with the houses few and far between, the roads straight and empty, leading out to the horizon.

Levittown wasn't land in that sense. Land was what was under the place, and before it. And it wasn't a landscape in any of the conventional terms by which Americans understood the concept. Landscape was what people came out from the city to find on Long Island—the vast manicured estates of the North Shore, those Gatsby-esque visions, or the seashore sublime that Robert Moses had rendered accessible, sand dunes and vast expanses of beach available to the masses. Those who stumbled on Levittown in those first months of 1947 had come out through the flat agricultural middle of the island, discovering in the midst of an endless-seeming flat grid of mass-production farms this strange phenomenon of a couple of little houses and a modernistic glass-and-steel "sales center" with a patient line of people waiting in the mud.

Even after it was fully built, spreading across many square miles, Levittown wasn't a physical landmark discernible from a distance, the visible icon around which one organized one's sense of place. *Life*, the *American Magazine*, *Time*, and even the *New York Times Magazine* sought without success to make a single photograph that conveyed the iconic status of the place, and they all conceded failure, settling on arresting aerial views that conveyed the vastness of scale and the repetitiveness of form with admirable clarity.

But these were like x-rays—they didn't convey the experience a real person might have with the site from a distance or right up in it. Still, then and now, residents, journalists, politicians, pundits, and visitors approached Levittown as if it *were* a legible topographic feature, towering above the flatlands, a beacon visible from as far away as Manhattan. By treating it this way, they made Levittown a landmark on an imaginative geography, a mythic geography of America, one that included the history of the nation as it was written in textbooks and then taught in public schools, and as it was assembled

4.1. Tony Linck, "Aerial View of Levittown, Long Island," *Life*, June 1, 1948. (Tony Linck / Time & Life Pictures / Getty Images.)

from the popular visual icons of the past century and a half. Almost before it was invented, Levittown was part of that pantheon of privileged places reaching back from the frontier town to the New England village.[10]

The GIs and their wives who were first in line to sign the leases and rent the first Levittown houses lined up and camped out for the chance, and the newspapers and magazines—local, like Long Island's *Newsday*, regional, like the *New York Times*, national and global, like *Time* and *Life*—memorialized the event, making it simultaneously a mark of the housing crisis, and a camp-out, an adventure in roughing it in the countryside of Long Island.[11]

Recalling those preconstruction days, the young couples and just-families who would sign those leases spoke of driving out to "the country" or taking a weekend drive into "the countryside" to look at houses, to escape the heat, to be alone, away from relatives and parents with whom they were "doubled up," in the parlance of the day. And these couples *were* young, in years (on average, in their early to mid-twenties) but also in attitude and experience, in self-identity. They had perhaps lost a year or two or three, waiting out in the South Pacific with Michener for the next big strike, or stateside, in secret facilities, supply dumps, or factories making everything from uniform buttons to the enriched plutonium for the bomb that irradiated and eradicated Nagasaki. They were back, alive, and they had a strange sense of themselves, strange, that is, to those of us who weren't there: still boys and girls, teenagers who'd picked up where things left off, and communitarians who'd been bound together by shared time in the barracks or the factory. There was a festive air to the cold nights out on Long Island, and the families huddled under blankets waited for morning and the chance to put down their deposits on houses they'd not seen in neighborhoods still unimaginable, sharing a sense of something important about to happen.

They were camped out in front of the model house and the sales center; behind that, there wasn't anything to see. In the early 1990s, Bill Levitt recalled that there were exactly 3 trees in the entire expanse of the first parcel of optioned land, some 1,200 acres. The roads were mostly dirt roads and there wasn't electricity except the temporary lines Levitt had set up to run the spotlights on the model houses and illuminate the inside of the sales center. It was cold enough for jackets and hats and blankets while you slept—had it been high summer, the fireflies would have provided light, the locusts and cicadas and crickets the sounds that made this campout an adventure in the American landscape.

(The model houses did give an artificial air of promissory transformation: they were fully *landscaped*, with shrubs and grass and trees. The illustrations accompanying the ads in newspapers were more explicit and more fantastical: they showed huge bowers looming over the cottage-like Cape Cods. Residents in that first wave were about evenly divided. Many were shocked at the spindly saplings, raw earth, and scraggly shrubs that awaited them when they pulled up with the moving van—they'd expected something close to the ad or the model. The rest tended to be pleased with what they got—the saplings were fruit trees, along with a maple in front and an evergreen at the rear; the bushes were Japanese shrub and mountain laurel.)

Landmarks are usually the monumental residues of historical significance, natural history in the case, say, of Yellowstone National Park, or human: the U.S. Capitol; Los Alamos, New Mexico. Sometimes they are monuments to past events or heroes. Levittown wasn't any of those. It wasn't even Levittown yet, at least not before December 31, 1947. It was a landmark to a history that hadn't happened yet.

And this was a characteristic understood by everyone involved from the very first, if you are to believe the accounts. This quality of self-awareness, the sense of being lucky enough to make history as ordinary citizens—to make a history *of* ordinary citizens, a democratic, everyman history—drew the residents-to-be, and the journalists, architectural critics, sociologists, salesmen, teachers, shopkeepers, and all the rest who chose to make this their home.

Though most critics and historians of the Levittown transformation have focused on the houses or—more recently—the communities, Levitt himself always declared that the real work was done on the much larger scale of the landscape itself. That work began before he even entered the navy in 1943 to build barracks as a Seabee, when he exercised an option on the first 200 of the 1,200 acres of potato fields he'd contracted for and then strong-armed his brother and father into continuing to exercise the option by purchasing the next 200 acres, and then the next, one parcel a year.

By the time Bill Levitt left the military the firm had close to 2 full sections of land on which to build. Most of the geography of the United States depends on the Jeffersonian model of a vast rectilinear grid imposed on the land in 640-acre "sections" (1 square mile) that were meant to house between 1 and 4 typical farms, and Levitt's land resembled the typical flat rectangles of agricultural land that stretched westward along the agricultural frontiers of the nineteenth century. Upon this, Levitt chose not to build in the most cost-effective and efficient way. Rather than following the grid, he imposed a complex combination of parallel streets, cul-de-sacs, curved sets of 2 and 3 corner-cutting streets, and dead ends. The 750-square-foot houses sat on lots of approximately 70 × 120 feet—1/7 acre—small enough for easy maintenance, large enough to provide the sense of land ownership that Levitt considered a fundamental of American values. ("No man who owns his own house and lot can be a communist," he once declared. "He has too much to do."[12]) While most lots faced each other across parallel streets or backyards, when you look at the home movies or the snapshots people made of the kids playing, what you see is anything but a receding grid. The social scale is intimate; every few houses, there's a dead end or a curve that interrupts the headlong tricycle race or the runaway kickball.

To drive through these was similarly intimate. The town was built around a series of through-ways, wide routes between the new parkways; you turned off the Wantagh State Parkway onto the old Hempstead Turnpike or off the Hempstead onto Wantagh Avenue and then onto the residential streets of your neighborhood. You couldn't drive too fast, and the process of sweeping and stopping, turning, looking, all made for a sense of *being within* rather than *passing through*.

Levitt's plan imposed a hierarchy of scales onto the landscape. At the most panoramic, there was the entire settlement, steadily expanding and bounded by potato fields before 1951, closed in by other towns and neighborhoods by the time Levitt left his creation behind. Tighten the angle, though, and you saw a cluster of perhaps a thousand houses loosely organized around the Levitt-built community buildings: recreational structures with large swimming pools and shopping centers with supermarkets and smaller stores, usually in two buildings arrayed across a parking lot. Closer still, and you saw the neighborhood. Some were large, approaching three hundred houses. Some were quite small, eighty or fewer. But off the main thoroughfares, street widths didn't differ, and so the notion of a neighborhood was fluid and boundaries were unclear.

Most early residents agree that it was the presence of young children and the desire for more that took them out of their apartments and neighborhoods to stand in line or sign the sales contract.[13] Levittown immigrants helped to clarify the postwar reconception of childhood and its needs. First was space—open space, outdoors, where children could play safely and more or less under the eye of a parent or parents. (Remember Susie's headlong rush to the back door in *Miracle*, looking to see if there was, indeed, a protected childhood sphere.)

In a gridded street plan, almost any street is a potential shortcut; streets in Manhattan, Brooklyn, and the Bronx, from which most Levittowners were emigrating, were dangerous playgrounds. Levitt resolved that problem with plans that weren't simply replicas of other, older suburban models. The very scale of Levittown, even of its various building stages (Levitt loved to call them "neighborhoods"), was too large to partake of the traditional older suburb's deliberate isolation from traffic systems—most traditionally built as a separate set of streets connected to the main thoroughfares at only one or sometimes two points. Instead, Levitt used the irregularities of the outer-access roadways, the vagaries of land parcels he'd optioned, and the public spaces of recreation and shopping to disrupt the rectilinearity—often just a little bit—and confuse the rationality afforded by the urban grid. The result was to filter car traffic, to slow it down, and to make drivers attentive.

But the very arrangement of access points from outside to inside meant that most of the cars on the street belonged to people of the neighborhood. Regular openings from the major thoroughfares into the dense housing core encouraged commuters to turn into their cluster; difficulties moving from one cluster to another—not least the confusion afforded by the regularity of the houses themselves—further impeded the sort of shortcutting that characterizes city driving. Once you were in your cluster, you didn't drive fast because you knew there were neighbors, people who knew you, watching from their lawns or through their windows. The children on the street might well be your children; almost certainly they were children you knew.

This is not to say that the constant play of children in, around, and across the streets wasn't a matter of serious concern for those who did use the streets in older, more conventional urban or interurban or even rural fashions. A truck driver's letter to the editors of the *Levittown Eagle* in the early summer of 1951 suggested the tension between old and new landscapes and their users: "Too many children from three to six years of age playing in the roads, uncared for . . . unseen by an approaching driver to be crushed beneath the wheels.[14]

His warning echoed a *Levittown Tribune's* 1949 editorial about the three failures of "manners and morals" in the new community. Not just children in streets made its list; so too did women with baby carriages using the streets instead of sidewalks. "For gosh sakes, women, get your baby carriages on the sidewalks where they belong," wrote a resident in 1949 to the *Tribune*; "You only walk in the road to be contrary or to yakaty yak with your friend."[15]

As would the trucker a couple of years later, this resident misunderstood the action of his neighbors. This was a declaration of independence, a staking of turf. The streets belonged not to through traffic nor to truckers or delivery vans servicing the stores at the edges—they belonged to women and children. Drive slowly, carefully, as we do, they were saying. *You* are the unwelcome presence in a new landscape in which streets might be playgrounds and the sites of sisterly communion and gossip.

Slow, attentive traffic; houses that, in a classic Levitt innovation, had the kitchen windows aimed out at the street; long stretches of daytime when few if any cars even traveled on the streets: all these encouraged the children to take those streets as their communal turf, and the mothers to develop a fluid (sometimes dangerously fluid) process of communal childrearing.

In the home movies and photographs of Levittown from that era, you can, once again, see the streets in the way that first generation understood them to be. Tricycle races and roving bike gangs, kickball and baseball and capture the flag and ringolevio all played out across the seven-striped flags of the streetscape: front lawns, sidewalks, grass-and-curb transitions, then the street, then on the other side curb, sidewalk, and opposite front lawn. Cars parked in front of the houses only made the games more interesting, breaking up the space in unpredictable ways, day-by-day and hour-by-hour.[16]

But while the informal patterns of play meant that children defined the cultural terrain of adults, adults still kept pretty tight control over the behavior of children. While the kids played in the backyards or the streets, mothers took turns watching out the windows and passed responsibility off via telephone networks. On weekends, fathers congregated in the yards, working on cars, working in the yard, cooperating in one attic expansion remodeling job after another in what some residents likened to a suburban barn raising tradition; while they did, they too kept watch over the kids. (One resident told sociology student John Liell that "many, but not necessarily all, of the social activities of immediate neighbors are caused by the fact that baby sitters are now always available—and immediate house-to-house visiting can be safely done with parents checking the children at frequent intervals."[17])

Then there were the backyards. Levitt forbade fences and hedgerows used to demarcate property lines; he understood that buyers looking out the back would never guess the cramped dimensions of each lot, especially after 1949, when the "glass window wall" along the rear-facing living room made the back into a panoramic vista. With houses backed up to one another, the depth of the rear lots doubled; because of the irregularity of the streets, these open spaces swelled and breathed, seeming even more irregular and organic than they were.

Into this space the children charged, out the back doors, down the gentle slopes or up them, heedless of the invisible lines between one property and another, unaware of the significance of a lawn of pure bluegrass and one mixed in with cheap Sears seed, except insofar as an unmowed lawn was better to hide in and a close-cropped one made for better football. The common green of the New England village never had the fluid commonality of Levittown's backyards.

For some, this new freedom, this socialism of children and dogs, was too much. A resident wrote on a questionnaire handed out by John Liell in 1951: "No fences—this is the one thing that causes more trouble, open fights and vicious silent battles than anything else. Why? Because it is a city of children (I have four of them), and children need fences for themselves. . . . That is the only thing wrong and a serious problem."[18]

But the majority of Levittowners, children and their parents, disagreed. Take the Tekulas' house on Gleaner Lane.[19] Charles Tekula moved his family into one of the ranch models with the big picture window in the back. Joanne and Charles Jr. went from diapers to First Communion in that house. Gleaner Lane cut across between Barrister Road and Stonecutter Road. But Stonecutter was actually U shaped, so Gleaner, Hunter, Stonecutter, and one or two others created a complex set of spaces with rear areas that looked every which way. Charlie was in diapers when he first confronted "the hill." Looking today at photographs his mother, father, and aunt took of their life there, one can't quite tell where anything is. There's a picture of Charlie "on the huge hill we had behind our house, looking north at the backs of

4.2. Charles Tekula's sister playing "horsey" with her mother in the front yard of the Tekula house in Levittown, Long Island, c. 1950. (Courtesy of Charles Tekula, Jr. and the Tekula family.)

homes on Stonecutter Road;" Charlie is probably two years old, and behind him, the older houses on Stonecutter have trees that rise above the roofs of the houses; in another, we look at Joanne in diapers playing horsie on her mother's back, in a view "looking south to houses on Bloomingdale Rd. You know how big those trees are now," writes Charles; in the picture, the spindly sapling is perhaps three feet high.

The freedom of the streetscape and the backyard prairies of Levittown had their contrasts in the formal organizations meant to supervise, train, and inculcate those same children. Brownies and Girl Scouts and Cub Scouts and Boy Scouts were extremely popular; so also were league-based child and youth sports. All these were tightly structured activities with parents hovering nearby and adults setting the rules and enforcing order. They were excellent training grounds for the destinies of these children: small, local dens or troops beneath regional chapters with a national organization at the top. They replicated the corporate structures that were, at that very moment, moving into a dominating position within the American and the global economy. Achievement to be rewarded was uniformly determined: Eagle Scouts nationwide had all learned the same knots, mastered the same woodcraft, done the same group tasks.

Rusty Arnesen's experience was in many ways typical. He grew up in

Levittown in the '50s and early '60s; his stories reflect the next stage in community—building after the earliest frontier days of the '40s and early '50s, described so well by the Tekula family's images and memories.[20]

In Arnesen's pictures, the houses show some wear and, outside, trees have grown to full size and grass has had time not only to set down roots but to develop that particular combination of hardiness and bare patches that makes a true suburban lawn. So too with the institutions, informal and formal, that cemented Levittown's place as a baby-boom community devoted to the nuclear family and the raising of children.

Arnesen's is a story of Cub Scouts and block parties, of all-day neighborhood barbeques and Halloween pageants, and then, in the early '60s, of teen dances and teen "nightclubs" designed to extend the combination of childhood freedom and adult supervision into the turbulent years of adolescence. Arnesen's family lived at 14 Swallow Lane; his father Carl was a disabled veteran of World War II, confined to bed and wheelchair. This didn't limit Carl's involvement in the community; on the contrary, it seems to have fostered an extended network of clubs and activities that reached from the neighborhood outward to the larger Levittown community. Carl was involved in veterans' organizations that provided him with companionship and his family with advocates and friends. He was also an organizer and adult supervisor of children's activities, from overseeing daily play to serving as commissioner of a Cub Scout pack with his wife as a den mother.

4.3. Rusty Arnesen in the family kitchen, early 1950s. (Courtesy of the Arnesen family.)

Arnesen senior and fellow disabled veteran John Cochrane founded the Northside Five Baseball League, where, in 1954, 120 children played in the open common areas behind the Arnesen home; by 1958, it had become the Levittown Athletic Club, with boys' and girls' leagues, membership cards, and uniform patches.

For Rusty, the result was a world of safe adventure, an idyllic suburban childhood in a child-centered community. "Levittown was a very children—and youth—friendly environment when I grew up there in the fifties and sixties," reported Rusty Arnesen. "There were always kids on my own street to play pick-up games and sports with. Stick ball and touch football in the street and baseball or basketball in the school yard were sports where you could find enough kids from your street or, if need be, the next, to form teams. We also played 'kick the can,' tag, 'rang a leario' [sic] 'capture the flag,' hide and go seek, and 'Johnny on the pony.'" At the most local and informal level was Rusty's neighborhood gang—children from the surrounding homes. While the parents knit their social web, the children did the same. "There were many activities centered around our 'block' or immediate neighborhood in Levittown," noted Arnesen. "We played in the street, around our houses and through the neighbors' backyards, with little complaint from the neighbors. In the summer we played past dark or until our parents made us come in."[21] The clusters of houses provided the basis for children's playgroups, and these often served as templates for the parents' own informal associations. Writing in *Harper's* in 1953, Harry Henderson reported that "the main way of getting to know people . . . was 'through the children.'" From these introductions came the glue of association—informal babysitting arrangements, PTA meetings, baseball coaching, or just the informal arrangement of families eating or drinking or watching TV together while their kids played. "Block parties were common," recalled Arnesen. "All of the neighbors on a street would get together and set up tables and chairs, often blocking off part of the street. The parties were pot luck and often lasted most of a day and into the night."[22]

Between the casual but tight knitting of these groups and the more formal institutions the lines were blurred and fluid. The freedom of baby-boom childhood in suburbs like Levittown seemed also a danger as those children became teenagers and adolescent individuation, rebellion, and social insecurities replaced the easier terrain of elementary school. Because Levittown was something close to an instant suburb, and because its residents moved into the community shortly after the end of World War II, there were few of the institutions and folkways that made those transitions from childhood to adulthood less wrenching for parents and children alike. Levittown's worries about juvenile delinquency were amplified versions of a national obsession with the moral fabric of baby-boom children.[23]

Levittowners responded with an array of organizations and activities for teenagers meant to channel, harness, and render harmless the dangers of adolescence. "In addition to the community pools, parks, village greens, bowling alleys, skating rink, ice cream parlors, and movies," Arnesen recollected:

> We had many other activities available to us. We had dances at all of the schools, both high schools and grammar schools, public dances at the Levittown Community Church and Levittown Hall. In the summer, there were square dance lessons and dances held in the Levittown Shopping Center parking lot and a large fireworks display every fourth [sic] of July. There was a carnival held every summer, with cakewalks, games and other contests held in the parking lot of Northside School. The recreation director of Northside kept the Gym open during the summer for a number of activities and games for kids. The classrooms were also open, with adults teaching crafts and art.

Residents of many other booming suburbs in Cold War America—from Branford, Connecticut, to Lincolnwood, Illinois, to Daly City, California—will recollect similar rituals of restrained passage. What was perhaps different in Levittown was the intensity, borne in part out of the critical mass of suddenly maturing adolescents, and in part out of the lack of longer-lived, multigenerational traditions that Levittowners like the Tekulas and the Arnesens had left behind when they moved from the older communities in Queens and the Bronx and even the farm towns of Long Island and New Jersey.

Rusty Arnesen still has the membership card to the Teen Age Nite Club that was a peculiar feature of Levittown's adolescence. "In addition to dances, movies and more standard activities for teenagers," Arnesen reports, "'teenage nightclubs were popular for a while in the sixties. I sang in a couple of bands that played at these, in the mid-sixties. They charged a membership fee and, I think, an additional admission charge. They also served pizza, other snacks, and soft drinks, and the club was fairly popular for a while."

Arnesen's club was The Swaray, a clever respelling of the more formal French—and debutante—term *soiree*. Hip spelling ("nite club") and the promise of exclusivity ("Private Member" reads the heading on Arnesen's card) made the club a status symbol, and a mirror of adult recreation, too.

But this was not an unrestrained world of the sort promised in the rock-and-roll songs of the time. The rules on the back of The Swaray membership card made sure of that. Members were reminded:

1. Absolutely no alcoholic beverages
2. Girls must wear skirts or dresses
3. Gentlemen must wear jackets & ties
4. Ages—15 to 19 exclusively

Arnesen's membership card presents a strange combination of new suburban values and old New York City urban neighborhood traditions—adaptations of the old ethnic and neighborhood "social clubs" to the demands of teenage life. There too Levittowners sought both to invent a new developmental map from childhood to responsible adult citizenship and to fit the new experiences of raising children in the expanding spaces of the postwar cultural landscape into something more familiar.

They weren't fully successful; as Levittown's children entered adolescence their differences sharpened, and the broad swath of childhood broke up into tense strokes of subgroup and gang. In Levittown, the juvenile delinquents—JDs and juvies—were most commonly called "rocks" for the music they listened to and the idols they mimicked in hairstyle and costume and gesture, but also for their posture—they were *hard guys*. In the high school they were known as bullies; in at least one case, a turf war outside a local Levittown pizza parlor resulted in a knifing.[24]

But the final transitions through which teenagers move seemed to turn Levittown into a miniature place; the houses got smaller and smaller as the children got larger and larger, and the fluid floor plans gave little escape for adults or teens. Kids drive too fast; the streets shrank and the shriek and squeal of tires going around the corners or racing to the cul-de-sacs woke up parents and young children; the headlights shone in the corner houses and the loud radios tuned to 77 WABC and 55 WINS playing Chuck Berry and the Shirelles and then the Four Tops and the Beatles pushed the houses closer to each other and constricted the streets. Everything contracted.

This was the opposite of the panoramic impulse that dominated not just media presentations of the community (the aerial views and the statistics of scale) but residents' own attempts to comprehend their experience. Perhaps the most striking of Rusty Arnesen's treasures is a photograph of Cub Scout Pack 323 at the Long Island Cub Scout Jamboree. Under the watchful eye of Cubmaster Carl Arnesen, the boys built a scale-model replica of their neighborhood. "My father planned our entry for the exposition so that it

4.4. Cub Scout Pack 325 with model of the Levittown neighborhood, c. 1955. (Courtesy of the Arnesen family.)

was easy for each scout to construct his individual part of it," Arnesen wrote in a letter. "He obtained the blueprints for Northside School and made a scale model, in sections, so that we could fit the sections together. He also laid out the plans for each model of Levitt home on two flat pieces of cardboard, one for the walls and one for the roof. Each scout was able to pick out his own model of home, fold both parts of the house along the dotted lines and paste the roof to the bottom part. The scout then had a scale model of his own home." Together, the scouts colored in their houses, added "trees and bushes of green sponge and twigs, and mounted each on green cardboard to simulate grass. After the exposition, each scout could keep the scale model of his own home."[25]

Just like the photographers for *Life* and *The Architectural Forum* and the rest, Mr. Arnesen had a good deal of trouble figuring out how to make his commemorative picture so that the houses could be visible and the sweep of the neighborhood simultaneously revealed and encompassed. His work was in some ways even more difficult, for he had to include the boys. The resulting photograph includes the sawhorses that supported the plywood base, and the posterboard with the Cub Scouts' den number prominently displayed. The sign of community; the materials of construction, the architect-builders, the residents: all are contained within the frame.[26]

*   *   *

Cubmaster Carl Arnesen's system for producing scale models of the Levittown houses replicated many of the celebrated features of the Levittown construction process: readily available mass-market materials were used and a uniform template was developed for the houses, so that variations from one house to another could be added on rather than built into the houses, making construction easy, something a relatively inexperienced worker could do rather than a highly trained—and expensive—custom craftsman.

In some ways, the resulting product had a similar quality of miniaturization and orderliness. Intriguingly enough, these scouts didn't have much interest in recording the inside of the houses. Perhaps they knew them too well. Perhaps the houses were just too small to accommodate childhood energies and so the primary focus of their lives was outside, where they could gain some measure of control and exercise their inventiveness without the constrictions of the small rooms and thin walls. Or perhaps it was simply that the larger panorama was easier to make than the detailed modelwork of the insides of houses, where their parents and the adults who might have owned the houses before them had already sought so vigorously to put their own personal stamp on the regular sameness of the interior plans.[27]

Most architectural historians speak with some surprise of the reputation for novelty appended to Levittown and the Levittown house. The mass-production strategies the Levitts applied weren't new at all. No cellars; slab foundations with radiant heat pipes already built in; units (from walls and ceilings to entire bathrooms) designed in four-by-eight-foot increments to match the stock sizes of wallboard and lumber; everything possible, from windows to doors to stairways, assembled before transportation so that on-site construction was fast, regular and essentially skill-less: all these were strategies proposed, detailed, worried over, and obsessively repeated during the long construction-free years of the Depression and the war, long before Levittown came into being. If you read an architectural magazine, a builder's magazine, or even *Popular Mechanics* or *Fortune* or *Life*, you already knew what it would take to build a house cheaply and efficiently.

The transformation of the land was the primary obstacle and the great opportunity exploited by Bill Levitt and the his organization. If you accepted the proposition that suburban housing for the democratic masses should be a scaled-down version of the American ideal, from Andrew Jackson Downing

4.5. Tony Linck, *Building Materials and Workers Needed for a Single Levittown House, Life,* June 1, 1948. (Tony Linck / Time & Life Pictures / Getty Images.)

to Lewis Mumford, you weren't going to build cheap houses. So Little Susie's house in Manhasset from *Miracle on 34th Street* may have been just down the street from Levittown in the imaginary world of the movies, but in the real world it was an economic class away. Its houses were prohibitively expensive because you couldn't grade the property—you just about had to chisel it out of the rock. For Susie's subdivision, putting in streets, sewer lines, electrical power, water lines, curbs and sidewalks—all the responsibility of the suburban developer—required the sort of craftsmanship and engineering appropriate to the medieval guilds. All that guaranteed a painstaking hand-crafted result and a price tag of, say, $22,500, about three times the cost of the first Levitt houses. Just how Uncle Fred and Doris afforded the house isn't a secret. They were upper-middle-class professionals, double-income, with

lots of defense bonds to cash. The neighborhood they drove through following Chris's instructions closely resembled not Levittown but Strathmore,
the Levitt organization's prewar project in Manhasset, complete with Tudor
half-timbering and turreted towers, or substantial brick Jeffersonian models
with garages nestled into the tall trees the Levitts were canny enough *not* to
uproot.[28]

Levittowners knew they couldn't afford those sorts of places, even if
they'd been available—which, given the housing shortage, they weren't.
About the highest compliment any Levittowner paid to the Cape Cod model
was that "it was adorable." Most remembered thinking it was "kinda cute."
And it was. Given the extraordinary cost constraints, Levitt still managed to
supply little neocolonial decorations, picket fences, fruit trees, appliances
that were up to date and name brand. Brother Alfred, the architect for the
firm, managed to take the base Cape Cod model and produce no fewer than
five different versions, some with picture windows, some without, some
with ornamental fenestration or split roofs—different in color, look, and
feel on the outside.

Inside was a different story. For the first couple of years, if you entered
the empty Levittown house—as homeowner, as relative, as guest, as a kid
like Susie racing into the new home—you faced an internal plan that was
utterly uniform—from the cutouts on the stairwell to the color of the walls
and floor to the types of appliances and cabinets and the toilet.

To look at the house plan for the Cape Cod today is to engage in a necessary delusion, because the plan doesn't show anything but outlines, and it
doesn't include the dimensions. The house's total square footage (described
variously as 720, 730, and 750 square feet) was divided among five rooms,

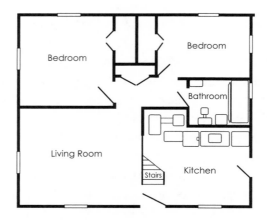

4.6. Plan for the model Cape Cod house, Levittown, 1948

4.7. Sandy Adams's kitchen at 83 Horn Lane, c. 1954. Only part of most Levittown rooms could be shown in an amateur's picture, because the rooms were too small to get a full vantage point. (Courtesy of Sandy Adams.)

including the single cramped bathroom. Still, those outlines are telling. You walked into a tiny entryway; directly in front of you was what residents and visitors often called "the stairway to nowhere." Though he was hardly more than a toddler when he used to visit his Uncle Paul's Cape Cod, Brian Mc-Cabe reported remembering "very clearly that the stairway to the second floor seemed to just end at the ceiling. I can remember Uncle Paul magically opening up the ceiling and taking me up into the 'secret' room."[29] This sense of an unfinished place contrasted with the shinily painted walls and floors of the living room to the left and the kitchen to the right.

The basic orientation of the house was a combination of historical precedent, social engineering, and sheer financial pragmatism. The result, however, was to engender a more open, informal social life within the family, with decreased privacy and increased contact in the most intimate of moments.

The bedrooms were in the back in these first-issue homes. They were small, buffered by the double closets that, once filled with clothes and shoes, boxes and toys, would absorb noise and provide some sense of privacy. Even when the house was empty, its rooms should have felt cramped, even claustrophobic. But few Levittowners ever experienced the house this way. For each new resident, that empty place was a *tabula rasa*, a blank slate on which each family could inscribe the identity of its members. Paint the walls, ceiling, floors. Fill the cabinets with cans and boxes, the closets with clothes, the walls with decorations, the space with furniture—your furniture.

The Levitt organization understood early on just how important was this process of individual initiative, of making the place home. The *Levittown Eagle*, Levitt's house organ, ran articles full of decorating tips and kudos to the individualism new residents applied to their houses. In 1951, Levitt even sponsored a home-decorating contest for residents who'd recently bought into the new-model $9,000 ranch house.[30]

Levitt's contest was an odd mixture. Meant to encourage the transformation of uniform spaces into individual ones, it set individuality and "courage" within the narrow confines of accepted interior-decorating orthodoxy. Levitt hired four New York City decorators to determine the winners; "the fact which chiefly impressed the judges," according to *Life*, "was that most homeowners did not know how to furnish small rooms to make them look more spacious and uncluttered. . . . This is a knack which the average housewife should learn."[31]

This contest occurred late in Levittown's growth period. By then, Levitt himself had worked hard to vary the interior details as well as the exterior ones. *Life* understood that this was a different sort of proposition than one might find in a custom builder. There, home buyers expected to pay for a quality of distinguishability, an appearance of uniqueness within a general style—Tudor, modern, colonial, French provincial—giving both acceptability and panache. When *Life* wanted to describe Levitt's experiment in diversity, the magazine found a family that was "'trading up'—Levittowners could now buy a new house each year, as they would a new car," reported the magazine, and posed the Bernard Levey family in front of their original 1948 home, their current 1949 model, and the 1950 model they had ordered. "When the '51s come along" *Life* reported, "they may buy again."[32]

Levitt wasn't offering uniqueness from house to house, but from *model to model*. Each successive year offered "improvements" over the previous version. And the principal changes weren't trivial. They were, in fact, redolent of meaning; Levitt wasn't adding features—he was adding symbols. The 1949 model had three powerful innovations. The first was the name: it was the "ranch," a house model with only minor changes in its outside design— minor functional changes. The shifts in window type and roof line and in the exterior cladding all were meant to shift the house from New England to California, home of the ranch house, symbol and fashion of the moment for a new, leisured, prosperous, Edenic American future. With high, thin,

SAME ROOMS, VARIED DECOR

CLEVER INTERIORS WIN PRIZES IN IDENTICAL LEVITT HOUSES

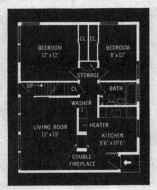

The big housing developments, which over the past few years solved the shelter problems for hundreds of thousands of Americans, have also created some difficult decorating problems for the new homemakers. Faced with furnishing a house that, inside as well as out, was identical with hundreds of houses all around, they found it troublesome to give their homes individuality, usually in small space and on small budgets. A few months ago William Levitt, the biggest U.S. development builder, recognizing the problem he helped create, held an amateur home-decorating contest at Levittown, Long Island among the first 500 buyers of his newly built $9,000 homes. He offered prizes of $1,000, $500 and $250 for the best-decorated homes plus five $50 runner-up prizes. As judges he got New York decorators Melanie Kahane, Ted Muller, Edith Hernandez and Beatrice West. Their decision has just been announced and on these pages LIFE shows various views of the prize-winning interiors.

The houses, whose ground floor plan is shown at left (carport omitted), are all identical to the last bit of brick and piece of pine paneling. The average income of Levittown homeowners is $80 to $100 a week; carrying charge for houses is $61 to $68 a month. The fact which chiefly impressed the judges was that most homeowners did not know how to furnish small rooms to make them look more spacious and uncluttered. Since the average home has shrunk 200 square feet in the past 10 years and most homes built today are small, this is a knack which the average housewife should learn. The prizewinners showed a feeling for scale and used ingenuity in making the most of every inch of space. The views of the living rooms of the three prize houses (below and opposite) look toward the

stairs leading to the second floor where one room is finished. (Other views are on following page.) First prize went to the home of Mr. and Mrs. Mel Gervey (she is seated, below), whose furniture is all in proper scale for the house. The sectional chairs against the stair wall are in perfect proportion to the height and size of the living room. Shades of two colors used as the decorative scheme enlarge the room. Textures —brick, glass, cotton on the floor, nubby fabrics, copper—add sparkle to the muted color scheme. The bamboo screen at the right of the lounge chairs, which is used to conceal an extra entrance to the kitchen and bedrooms, makes the room seem less a passageway.

Second prize went to Mr. and Mrs. Charles Field (top, opposite page), who showed excellent taste in using traditional furnishings and suitable accessories. Choice of dark green for the walls makes the small living room look friendly, warm, large. Only one printed fabric is used, a good rule for small rooms.

Mr. and Mrs. Thomas Hagan's home (below, right) won third prize because of its courageous blend of colors and complete individuality. The owners created a smart, big-city interior right in the center of a development. The judges liked the olive walls—even the brick and pine paneling were painted—and the dramatic gold-and-silver tea paper on the wall behind the stairs. They also commended the lavish use of white (masks on wall, triple lamp, ash trays) and the strategic touches of black (magazine rack, table) which keep the bright colors from overpowering the room.

Among all the houses judged, 35% of the interiors were modern, 20% traditional and 45% were an eclectic mixture which in many cases turned out to be an unsuccessful hodgepodge.

FIRST PRIZE

4.8. "Same Rooms, Varied Decor," home decorating contest winners Mr. And Mrs. Mel Gervey, *Life*, January 14, 1952. (© The Picture Collection Inc. Photograph © The Estate of Leslie Gill, courtesy of the Robert Mann Gallery.)

LEVITT ADDS 1950 MODEL TO HIS LINE

New house has carport, tile bath and a television set—for $7,990

Last month Levitt and Sons, the country's biggest housebuilders, unveiled their 1950 model house in an atmosphere suggesting an auto show combined with a Christmas preview. The effect on early audiences was almost as heady, even though New York house shoppers have come to expect wonderful surprises (automatic washers, built-in barbecues) inside anything Levitt builds. In addition to the radiant heating, fruit trees and other extras included in previous Levitt packages, they found his 1950 version, for the same $7,990, had a television set (p. 147), a carport (which to the carless can be a porch), tiling in the bathroom and abrasion-resistant walls. During the first showing weekend the throngs that inspected two four-room-plus-attic models and the various exhibits bought 252 houses from the corps of uniformed salesmen behind a sales counter. This total Builder William Levitt regarded as somewhat disappointing—the weekend was partly rainy—although he could comfort himself with the fact that even before the showing 1,000 persons had bought 1950 models without having seen them. At last week's end 2,400 of the 4,000 houses to be built this year were sold, a third of them to people already occupying Levitt houses.

This carried out the auto-show parallel and introduced a peripatetic element in the traditional American pattern of "settling down in the suburbs." Instead of settling down, Levittowners (residents of the 6-square-mile, 10,000 Levitt home area which is actually part of Hempstead and Oyster Bay townships but is recognized as a separate entity on maps) could now buy a new house each year, as they would a new car. While Levitt does not accept older models in trade, Levittowners have no trouble in finding buyers. The Leveys, shown at right posing before their sequence of Levitt homes, rented one of the Cape Cod homes Levitt built in 1948 (*top picture*) to see if they liked it. They did, so they bought the 1949 model and now have ordered a '50, selling the '49 for only $256 less than they had paid in on it. When the '51s come along, they may buy again.

This convenient practice, however, may come to a stop. When his 1950 building program is done, Mass Builder Levitt will have room in Levittown for only 2,000 1951 homes. Still, having sold $200 million worth of houses in the past 21 years (LIFE, Aug. 23, 1948), it is rather unlikely that Levitt will merely retire and settle down in the suburbs.

BERNARD LEVEY, his wife and children stand before their three Levitt homes. He is a truck supervisor.

1948

1949

1950

CONTINUED ON NEXT PAGE

4.9. Bernard Hoffman's three photographs of the Bernard Levey family in front of their successive Levittown houses, *Life*, May 22, 1950. (LIFE is a registered trademark of Time Inc. Photo by Bernard Hoffman. © The Picture Collection Inc. Reprinted with permission. Article: © 1950. The Picture Collection Inc. Reprinted with permission. All rights reserved.)

horizontal windows replacing the old, shuttered double-hungs, and the entrance moved from center to side and the roofline flattened and shifted to accommodate angled decorative supports in the front, Levitt's architectural detailing made the same basic box look longer, lower, implying an open plan within. This was a design meant to correspond to the promise of Western and Californian lifestyles of freedom, leisure, and ease.

Within, the '49 house had a rather remarkable two-way fireplace, between kitchen and living room. This innovation renewed the focus on home and hearth that had been implicit in the Cape Cod models of 1947 and 1948, and it used the hearth as a means to link the space of house labor with the space of community and family. *Life* would later point to similar virtues in a discussion of other house designs, particularly those penned by American women, that removed the wall between kitchen and dining room, even consolidated the three into one evolving space.[33] Levitt couldn't go that far—he needed those walls between kitchen and living room—but the two-way fireplace offered the same promise that women could participate in the warmth of family and still watch over the dinner and the wash.

The fireplace was a signifier of cultural conservatism meant to counter the modernity and freedom from history implied by the California ranch moniker. The final innovation moved this side of the equation further: it was the shift of living room from *front*, where visitors entering the house were immediately welcomed, to the *back*, where a long, wall-sized picture window and a doorway out to the back patio opened the living room to outdoors and, more importantly, to the intimate, informal, neighborly, communitarian space of the open backyards, the common area, rather than the sidewalk and street, the formal and efficient areas where the car was parked to take you to work and where the school bus came. Now rather than watching the kids from the kitchen, you watched them from the living room—from the space of leisure rather than labor.

Critics of Levittown and the larger suburbanization phenomenon it represented have tended to miss the view from the picture window. In the early Levittown Cape Cods, "picture windows" looking out onto the street were an option; one could buy a house with small front windows more readily. But in either case, one didn't look directly into another resident's house; instead, the view showed front yard, sidewalk, street, and sidewalk before the neighbor's property became the object of sight. You looked out your windows at the transition between the private space and the public. And when the picture window did appear as the major innovation of the 1949 model ranch, it was a very different event than most critics have suggested. The window was huge; it covered the entire rear wall of the living room, and it went from floor to ceiling. Broken out into twelve horizontal rectangles, at least some of which could be cranked or slid open, the window-wall (as it was often called) was simultaneously transparent and transitional. Recent cultural critics have pounced on the "fishbowl effect" of this window, warning that it violated privacy more than it brought nature indoors. But they're wrong; they've not looked at the snapshots of residents nor listened to the reminiscences. They've also not noticed just how extensive was the vista of the double backyards, nor the effect even minor curves and stretches of the grid pattern made on the way you looked out your windows to the back or what you saw.

In fact, the picture window was only part of the transitional space Levitt offered in the 1949 ranch. A snapshot from the Tekulas' collection showed the back door opening to a makeshift patio, which accommodated the kids in their inflatable pool and three metal lawn chairs.

In Sandy Adams's backyard at 83 Horn Lane, the area immediately behind the picture window became an early home improvement project. A concrete slab turned it into a patio, soon filled with lawn furniture (including the miniature sling chair for young Sandy!) and even a picnic table. The Adamses didn't just stop there; they added a homemade border out of lumberyard scraps and planted flowers along the space between that border and the concrete patio. In both cases, it's worth noticing the ways the outdoor furnishings were arrayed. They're aimed out at the vista, not back at the house. Given the choice, Levittowners turned out toward the common areas, rather than turning their back on them and looking back at their private property.

4.10. The Tekula children in their backyard inflatable pool. (Courtesy of Charles Tekula, Jr. and the Tekula family.)

4.11. Sandy Adams's improved backyard patio at 83 Horn Lane, summer 1952. (Courtesy of Sandy Adams.)

The picture windows served complex and multiple functions. They brought air, light, and noise from outside in, expanding the space of the living room and giving it a quality of celebratory community. With the upper windows open, on a spring or fall afternoon after school let out, you could hear your kids, smell the new-cut grass, look at your growing things, catch the call of other women to their children or each other, hear the snap of laundry in the wind and the periodic muffled sound of cars driving by on the streets. If you had little ones—and in the early '50s most Levittowners did—you could put the playpen out there, as did the Tekulas, or you could improvise more expansively, as did Brian McCabe's Uncle Paul. He went to the garden supply store and bought the stakes and netting usually used to protect tomato plants and backyard garden plots from marauding animals. Then he made an enclosure for his daughter Florence, big enough to allow her to run, crawl, and play, but small enough to ensure her safety. Then if the parent needed to retreat from living room to kitchen for a little while, there was no need to worry; the open windows gave you the aural monitoring you needed while you shifted the laundry or put the roast in the oven or answered the phone.

The picture window didn't exaggerate the crowded homogeneity of these suburban communities. Instead, it celebrated their expansion of scale:

4.12. Brian McCabe's Uncle Paul and cousin, early to mid 1950s. (Courtesy of Brian McCabe.)

backyards that flowed with picturesque indeterminacy from what you owned, what was yours, to what was common.

If we return to the snapshot Brian McCabe has of his Uncle Paul's backyard, we can see something of the effect. Uncle Paul's house was close to a corner, and so he looks across an expanse of open grassy landscape, a common green, at the backs of houses that are slightly more than ninety degrees to his. Notice also that he and his neighbors have honored the covenant forbidding fences, and so the line that separates properties isn't clear. Remember: the land looks common, but it's really not—it's just the assemblage of privately owned backyards. Originally, Levitt forbade fences to accentuate this sense of spaciousness, but even after he had left the picture, most first-generation Levittowners kept the spaces unbounded.

This wasn't a decision without inconvenience and complication. Dogs roamed free, often in packs, children too, tracking mud and trampling gardens. Neighbors were often faced with confrontation and compromise at the edge between *my* space and *yours*. These formed major impediments to the utopian fantasies Bill Levitt proposed when he advertised that "here in Levittown all of our 37,000 men, women and children have a common purpose: to be happy, friendly, neighborly."[34]

Yet Levittowners didn't give up on the promise of those open quasi-public spaces they saw beyond their lawn chairs, patios, kiddie pools, and clotheslines. Nor did they shy away from the complex fluid transitions between public and private, between seeing and being seen, to judge by the photographs—they kept their shades up during the day and the windows open when the weather was good; they let everything in, including the eyes of their neighbors.

A house that served as a ranch headquarters; children and dogs out on the range; the unfenced public lands; walls that enabled you to expand or contract your house, your space, and your view at your own desire; a hearth at the center of the inside space, serving to reiterate the gravitational pull of family and friendship while simultaneously serving to open up the distinction between "living" and "working" spaces: Levittowners loved these innovations. The Leveys weren't the only ones to sell their older models to move up to this new lifestyle. And when the 1950 model arrived, it too had as its principal innovations, two features that seemed adventurous then and, now, seem happily inevitable: a carport and a built-in television.

Levittown's new models changed the meaning of these first, seminal postwar living spaces. The 1947 and '48 houses were tightly enclosing, womblike, miniature spaces, pushing the family into close proximity when inside. The interior spaces were relatively dark once you put up curtains on the windows to afford a modicum of privacy from the houses so near to you on either side. The entire effect promised a huddling place, shelter. That's part of the reason the kids spent all their time outside, no matter the weather. The house seemed built, surreptitiously, around adult fears and adult responses.

This was the paradox of the Levittown house, and the larger lifestyle of the suburban family who bought into the dream. On one side, these first houses were deeply private; they were too small, really, for parties, for houseguests, for committee meetings or any of the other communitarian functions that extended the individual beyond the family. On the other, this very quality forced residents out of their homes, out of the privacy and insularity of the middle-class house, out onto the street, the backyards, the common spaces and places and functions. Children and grownups alike exploded from the houses into the fluid space of community.

So we might be granted the indulgence to speculate, to ask: why were the first spaces inward-facing, drawing their symbolism from similarly inward-dwelling American colonial pasts; and why, over time, did the Levitts modify their designs to make them more fluid, open, continuous with the public spaces and integrated into the outside? Levitt himself was frank: he did it because it enabled him to sell more houses more quickly; people wanted these innovations, and they wanted the new symbols more than the older ones he'd started with. But we're then left to ask why buyers came to prefer the new designs over the originals. We might be tempted to simply say that Levitt was finally getting things right. The first generation of houses sold fast because the demand was high and indiscriminate. The second and third generations had to satisfy other desires in a competitive housing market.

But that begs the question: why *did* buyers and residents come to be drawn to the new, more open, fluid, and less protective environments of the later houses? It's a question that might be answered in some part by looking back at the atomic sublime, at the fading of fear and the normalizing of fear that occurred between 1947 and 1951. The first years after the end of the war were among the most disturbing for Americans confronting the atomic age. This was that early moment, when the horror of Hiroshima seared the imagination and the question of American responsibility was uppermost.

Then there was a dip of sorts: the pattern, as it turned out, that characterized the years from 1945 through the mid-1960s, of aroused anxieties, cultural response, and then diminution of fear and a return to normalcy. As Levitt began to sell the 1949 houses, Americans were coming to accept— temporarily—the notion that we were in the midst of an atomic age, had survived its first stage, and must now learn to live with its consequences. In 1948, the first extraordinarily seductive images of atomic testing surfaced, with the sequence of above-ground tests held in the South Pacific at Enewetak Atoll. Then, in the summer of 1949, the Soviet Union detonated its first atomic bomb. In 1950, Klaus Fuchs confessed to selling atomic secrets to the Russians, and Americans found themselves embroiled in the Korean War. Huddling under the protective eaves of the home seemed increasingly futile and absurd. At the same time, the promises of an American future of prosperity, shared wealth and leisure, common pleasures and common responsibilities, came increasingly to dominate the pages of magazines, the editorials of newspapers, the speeches of politicians.

Indeed, this was the paradox of an era, reflected in the paradox of the Levittown house—a small, dark, claustrophobic private space that residents treated as, simultaneously, a toy, a hobby or craft project, the excuse for communitarianism, and the staging ground out of which one launched—as kid, as mother and housewife, as young husband and father, as American man or woman—into the open spaces where community might be found or, more appropriately, constructed, through a combination of spontaneity, of structure, commonalities discovered, shared, and also made. Historian and visionary Frederick Jackson Turner had it right. Speaking before the World's Columbian Exposition in the summer of 1893 in Chicago, he declared that the American frontier encouraged the continual reinvention of American democracy, the rejuvenation and reconstitution of American institutions. That's what happened in Levittown.

Or at least, that's the way Levittowners saw it—then, when it was still a process, and later, when it was the object of nostalgia and memory. It's not entirely clear, reading the letters, essays, editorials, diaries, and commentaries, looking at the snapshot photographs, interviewing the veterans, whether Levittown pioneers made that image themselves, giving it to the national press and the national culture as a sort of postwar gift. Perhaps the news reports, the importuning of photographers, the musing of editorial writers and the pontificating of the publicity hound Mr. Levitt himself, all combined to provide Levittowners—confused over their new environment, a bit lost now that they were out of their city, their neighborhood, their kinship group—a readymade identity, and one which offered them celebrity, importance, a place at center stage in the evolving drama of postwar America.

Doubtless Levittown came into being as a cultural landscape and landmark out of the push and pull of both processes. Just a few months after P. G. wrote her "Leave Levittown Alone Week" letter and two months before Bill Levitt pulled out of Levittown for greener pastures, *Collier's* sent photographer Leo Choplin to celebrate the community's four-year birthday. To make his birthday portrait, Choplin didn't just rent a plane and shoot the obligatory aerial view. Nor did he haunt the streets looking for the perfect street scene, the emblematic family, the most memorable house, yard or neighborhood. Instead, he inveigled the sponsorship of Sylvania Electric Products, Inc., the Levittown civil defense director, and thousands of Levittowners. Over a period of days, he orchestrated a view of the town lit by 1,500 Sylvania flash bulbs, one per yard of the visible panorama encompassed by his camera, mounted on the water tower at the west end of town. *A Town Takes Its Own Picture* is the title for the spread.[35]

The *Collier's* writer, one Sey Chassler, made the exchange condescendingly one-sided—as if the magazine was responding to the importunings of tens of thousands of residents: "Welcoming every chance to make news with the enthusiasm of a starlet," he wrote, "the town got a whopping new opportunity"[36]

The picture's a novelty item—a night-shot color photograph bled across two pages, with its stripes of car lights in front and dots of light at the rear, as the distance leaves the houses increasingly dark. In the center of the space, though, each house is lit like a stage set. There are silhouettes in front of the house, but they aren't the residents—they're the engineers from Sylvania, a team of twenty who passed from block to block and house to house to illuminate each of the seventy-five successive exposures. The houses stand in

A Town Takes Its Own Picture

THE houses of Levittown, Long Island, New York, mass-produced by superenergetic Levitt & Sons, Inc., contain 16,746 families nourished on national publicity. Welcoming every chance to make news with the enthusiasm of a starlet, the town got a whopping new opportunity some weeks ago, when photographer Leo Choplin asked it to help him take the biggest flash photograph ever attempted.

For his stunt, Choplin consulted with Sylvania Electric Products, Inc., and they let him have 1,500 of their largest flash bulbs, lighting engineers and a brace of walkie-talkies. Thus prepared, he climbed a 200-foot water tower near the west side of town and got set.

The suburbanites pitched in. Levittown's director of civil defense, Robert E. Lackey, a veteran blinded on Saipan, assigned a group of his auxiliary police to alert the town to the huge flashes, block off the affected streets and handle the flash bulbs under the direction of Sylvania's engineers. Keeping in touch with Choplin via walkie-talkie, a 20-man crew set off the bulbs in batches of 20, some 70-odd times. As the bulbs flashed in area after area, Choplin simultaneously opened and closed shutters of three different cameras.

After four hours of blinding flashes, astounded couples and kids went to bed; Bob Lackey had proved that his civil defense team could give and take complicated orders, and Leo Choplin had the amazing color photograph on these pages. One question remained: What was the big idea? Well, next month is Levittown's birthday, and if this isn't the biggest, brightest, most ambitious birthday card ever presented to a four-year-old, what is?   SEY CHASSLER

Engineer Dick Martensen instructs town civil defense boss Bob Lackey

Photographer worked three cameras at same time, got but one good shot

Photographer's aid counts 1,500 flash bulbs used for Levittown's snapshot

Biggest flash picture ever made celeb

4.13. "A Town Takes Its Own Picture," double-page spread, *Collier's*, September 22, 1951. (Photographs by Leo Choplin.)

town's fourth birthday. It took four hours, covered 600,000 sq. ft., used light output equal to 3,688,580 standard 60-watt bulbs

for their occupants, who have chosen or allowed themselves to be defined by their celebrity spaces: street, house, carport, backyard.

The picture itself continues to confuse and to tantalize us. The houses in Choplin's photograph look simultaneously toylike and endearingly inviting. The stripe of lit houses, with darkness before and behind it, seems more like an oasis than a dehumanized Pavlovian experiment in social uniformitarianism. The engineers, arms above their heads to focus and direct the flashes, seem to be saluting each house in succession. Yet the houses look abandoned too, evacuated. The glare of the flash lights resembles the harsh light the Atomic Energy Commission used to illuminate its experimental "Doom Town" in the Nevada desert two years later, in the first live-televised exhibition of the effects of atomic weapons on American suburban houses. Looking at Choplin's photograph, we might wonder if these are houses whose interiors shelter happy families tucked into their beds or clustered around the new built-in television; or if these are simply facades, artifices in the stage show of American life.

One of the telling side comments tossed off in Sey Chassler's brief commentary is this: to make the picture, Choplin had to consult with the town's civil defense director, "Robert E. Lackey, a veteran blinded on Saipan," who "assigned a group of his auxiliary police to alert the town to the huge flashes." Suddenly the experience from the ground looks quite different. First, Lackey's brigade fanned out, dressed in the Civil Defense Auxiliary uniform of white jumpsuit, black holster belt, black shoes, and white helmet emblazoned with the CD logo; this was an opportunity to reassert the legitimacy of the auxiliary, to remind Levittowners of the imminence of atomic threat, to hand out civil defense pamphlets and brochures. Then a crew of twenty Sylvania men in their own corporate jumpsuits marching resolutely from street to street over four hours, carrying strange machines that they aimed in unison at a row of houses, from which there emitted a sudden blare of light and a small din of hot explosive pings, while the residents hid within, a few peering out from behind the half-drawn curtains or around the edge of the picture window.[37]

Choplin's picture implied a suburb denuded by atomic holocaust, its residents wiped away or huddled in fallout shelters. And Levittowners bought their share of shelters; their children learned their share of civil defense survival strategies. But that was only a part of the story. On the morning after Choplin's men and machines packed up and left, Levittowners opened the doors and the children ran out into the street to play; they stood in the kitchen, watching the children in the street, and used the wall phone to call neighbors, friends, members of the community to talk about the latest brush with the momentary, blinding, disconcerting and flattering blaze of public scrutiny.

Levittown was, then, a paradigmatic Cold War cultural landscape, simultaneously huddling place and open community, with neither extreme particularly far from the other. The houses were private, but the lives within them were for the most part public—shared around via gossip but also by the commonality of the experience. Levittowners shared far more than they didn't. Because they were almost entirely FHA/VA mortgage recipients, they were veterans of the war—soldiers if male, or war workers if female. And they were almost uniformly young. They might be afraid for their children's futures, anxious about their proximity to New York, a prime target for atomic attack, and without much seniority in their new jobs. But they were also optimistic. Things were going to work out. They were model citizens in a new, model America, and they were acting the part rather well.

* * *

Levittowners were a remarkably stable lot. Though their incomes rose (or, in a few cases, fell), though they took on the increased responsibility of full adulthood and then maturity, though their children grew up and shrank the houses and then left and didn't come back, a surprising percentage of Levittown pioneers remained in their houses.

This wasn't what anyone really expected. When Harry Henderson wrote about the place for *Harper's Monthly* in 1953, he agglomerated it with Park Forest, Illinois, and Lakeside, California, two other legendary postwar developments. Again and again in his two essays, Henderson spoke of the inevitable transience of the populace; he quoted residents joking about "the first wife, the first house" as an emblem of the postwar generation's optimism about its prospects.

But Henderson was wrong about Levittown, and so were those residents he quoted. The census data records a process of inflow but little outflow. Ralph Martin, onetime resident and longtime literary champion of the place, writing in 1956, was more attentive to this; he noticed that Levittowners rising in the economic ladder, bulging out of the small bedrooms as they had more (and more) children, facing needs or wants they hadn't had when they were twenty-two or twenty-six and this place seemed like heaven, built out rather than moving out.[38]

Why did they stay? Why did they expand and refit and invest, dormering first one side and then the other, winterizing the carports, then enclosing the breezeways, pushing out to the edges of the lots and jackhammering out the slab floors to put in cellars? The answer wasn't in the mechanics of financing or the stagnation of incomes or the unavailability of upscale housing into which to upgrade. They made their changes *in order to stay*, because their commitment was to the particular American communitarian democracy they believed they had made and were continuing to make. They were actors on a stage and the play wasn't over.

You can hear it in the analogies they used. "When we first came out here, it was like one big barn raising," Martin records Dr. Bernard Winter as telling him. Winter looked at Levittown and, in one phrase, linked it to nineteenth-century pioneer expansionism, to *Oklahoma!* and to Martha Graham's *Appalachian Spring*. Dr. Winter wasn't proposing a community of rugged individualists (that was Martin's take); he saw home remodeling as a community exercise, knitting individuals and families into a larger whole. In the final episode of his 1953 two-part essay, Harry Henderson chose to see Levittown as a place of "rugged American collectivism," and he liked his proposal so well he made it the title of the article.[39]

But there was more to Levittowners' settledness than the ties of community. To have left would have meant betrayal of their own identities as well; for they had come to imagine themselves as the embodiment of that community and thereby as pioneers and paragons of the new America. The dogma proposed by critics of the postwar suburban landscape was one they accepted, accepted and celebrated: they were the products of their environment. But of course they imagined that environment in a very different way than did, say John Keats, in his brutally mean-spirited and wickedly funny satirical excoriation-of-a-novel, *The Crack in the Picture Window*.

In the early '90s, Hofstra University, a Long Island institution with Levittown's most assiduous historian, Barbara Kelly, on its faculty, embarked on a television documentary about Levittown. The timing was fortuitous: Bill Levitt was still alive, though not for long (shortly after declaring himself ready to build his empire again—"I just need another six months," he told the camera—he died). Many of the others who had come to live and stayed were also eager to be filmed, reminiscing in their Levittown living rooms, with the paneled stairway behind them, the stairway leading to the old expansion attic Levitt had included in order to make the square footage of his little house sufficient to satisfy the regulated minimums in Nassau County.

These residents confirmed and amplified much of what we've seen, and it's worth viewing the documentary, if only to hear the stories told in the broad New York and Long Island accents, and to see these young men and women grown old. But many of them ended with a narrative of loss; they reported that the Levittown they lived in at the end of the twentieth century was different than it had been, a community that had lapsed from its youthful energy and its promise. But even as they mourned its decline they did it with a certain dramatic flair, a sense that this too was part of the drama they had made, and were making still. They had improvised the production of a new American utopia and they weren't about to give up the stage. Like Bill Levitt, struggling for every breath, telling his story from the sterile confines of a convalescent hospital, they declared they were still in play, still in the play.

CHAPTER 5

Levittown's Palimpsest

COLORED SKIN

To open the 1960 census to the pages where Levittown's statistics are laid out in neat rows is to see a revolution caught in a moment's broken gesture. Even historians who routinely consult the census for everything from family median income to number of appliances per household might not notice at first the evidence of that revolution. But it's there.

It's there most notably in a fundamental change in the questions census takers asked about race. For the first time, the old bifurcation between "White" and "Non-White" broke into smaller shards of identity by race: "Negro," "Japanese," "Chinese," even "Filipino." White, however, remained a monolith.

On one level, the breakout of racial categories might be seen to presage the identity politics that would emerge a decade later. I think something more complicated is at work: the census change reflected the roiling shifts in national discussions about race over the previous decade; the census by its very questions activated new sensitivities to racial difference; and the results provided important evidence of conditions that would soon engulf the nation in a great wave of civil rights protest and change.

For its first years, Levittown wasn't just overwhelmingly white: it was entirely white. The Levitt organization's people didn't rent homes to *Negroes* or *colored people*, and after they began to sell, they didn't sell to them either. In addition, those who rented were forbidden to sublet to nonwhites, and those who owned were also enjoined by restrictions in the bill of sale from selling to anyone not white or, more precisely, not "Caucasian," to quote from the Levitt rental contract and the later sales agreement.[1]

No one at the time should have been surprised by this. In the newspapers, new subdivisions aimed at integrationists and people of color had to advertise the fact in the real estate ads: "No restrictions! No discrimination!" read one. Ronek Park, also on Long Island, opened in 1950, with a declaration by its builder, Thomas Romano: ""Dedicated to the Proposition that All Men Are Created Equal . . . and no UnAmerican, Undemocratic restrictions as to race, color or creed!"[2] His manifesto was comforting, but it wasn't creed that mattered on Long Island. Jews and Catholics were surreptitiously banned from many places but rarely from housing developments. It was race that separated Ronek Park from Levittown. Ronek Park and its fellow nonracial subdivisions ended up being overwhelmingly or entirely black—there just weren't enough white Americans willing to overcome their fears to make Romano's utopian experiment work.[3]

Veterans—black veterans, anyway—may have been outraged by Levittown's racial covenants, but only a naive or heroically stubborn few could have expected otherwise. Throughout the war, housing in military barracks and defense plants had segregated soldiers and workers by race as well as gender. Conditions for blacks were pointedly worse than for whites, and their labor was persistently undervalued. This had been the pattern, and there wasn't much evidence that things would rapidly change when war was over.

Even after Harry Truman integrated the armed services in the summer of 1948, the reality differed from the edict. Racial segregation in the military wasn't officially ended until 1954, and even then, forms of de facto segregation were endemic. Outside the military, racial integration continued to be a rarity, and the legal restrictions on integration were extensive and common in housing, union membership (and hence in trade and occupation), and schools and universities. Not just private citizens, not just businesses and corporations, but federal agencies urged the continuation of racial segregation, especially in housing. Black veterans had left segregated neighborhoods to go to war, they lived in segregated circumstances throughout the war, and they returned to separate housing, separate communities, after the war. There were exceptions but no one pretended they were otherwise than exceptional.

To break the pattern required a revolution of thought, attitude, and political will, and a shift in legal precedent as well. It didn't happen at Levittown. When a particularly stubborn black vet named Eugene Burnett tried to get a purchase contact from a salesman back in 1949 or 1950, the salesman apologized; it wasn't him, he said, it was just that the developer hadn't yet decided whether to rent to colored people.[4] He was being gentle; in fact, Levitt's rental contract from the first clearly required the tenant "NOT TO PERMIT THE PREMISES TO BE USED OR OCCUPIED BY ANY PERSON OTHER THAN MEMBERS OF THE CAUCASIAN RACE," and put the clause in capital letters for emphasis. Had Levitt decided differently, no doubt he would have offered a separate section of the development to nonwhites and those who might want to rent or buy in that area. But he didn't need to: Ronek Park served that function. And by leaving it to others, Levitt saved himself the conflicts that would inevitably have occurred.

Levitt's salesman bumped responsibility up to the developers. The decision by Jewish American builders like the Levitts to continue the policy of segregation seemed to many a hypocrisy in the face of German genocide and racialism. But Levitt saw himself as a salesman, a businessman, and in his eyes, moral courage was bad business. In the later '70s, Levitt defended his stance; he told reporters that he had faced impossible pressure from outside, from renters and buyers nervous about their property values, to start with. He later told historian Stuart Bird that the market *required* him to segregate: "originally we would not sell to a black person because it was an old story that if we sold to blacks, whites would not buy."[5]

Levitt also bumped the responsibility upward to the banks, which routinely refused to make big-block loans to developers of integrated housing. The banks further shunted the blame to the government, whose loan guarantee programs specifically enjoined lenders from offering integrated housing. The Federal Housing Administration on which Levitt and the other master builders of the postwar era depended for their financing, was quite clear: no "inharmonious racial or nationality groups." "If a neighborhood is to retain stability," FHA regulators explained, "it is necessary that properties shall continue to be occupied by the same social and racial classes." Levitt's covenant was nearly word-for-word the template proposed by the FHA as an example of "suitable restrictive covenants."[6]

This policy of "redlining," in which the government drew boundaries separating "safe" (read: "white") investment areas from those considered too risky, also pushed the blame elsewhere. This time it was the citizenry who were at fault; the spokesmen for government loan programs announced that their agencies were not in the business of altering social policy but of lending money for housing in a way that ensured the economic success of the developments and not their racial profile. Americans (meaning *white* Americans) wanted the freedom to choose white-only communities, and it was not the FHA's right to limit American freedoms.

There was evidence to support the FHA/VA proposition that forcing social integration of suburban housing would ensure not just racial conflict but something closer to chaos, at least as banks and government banking agencies might define that. One of the first black residents of Levittown reported he'd been offered his house by a friend—white—who was moving. When word got out, the seller received a visit from neighbors, who offered to pay a premium to ensure that the sale fell through. And given the opportunity for integration, the new home-buyers of the postwar years weren't interested in joining what at best they considered a risky social experiment. Bernice Burnett, one of the first to buy in Ronek Park, reported that of the first few hundred houses, only perhaps one or two families were white. How Romano managed to get financing for his community remains a mystery.[7]

There's no need to point out the paradoxes inherent in this story of failed policy. White residents throughout the era claimed that their attitudes weren't set by hatred or fear of people but by a genuine concern that their hard-won investment in home ownership would be taken from them as property values plummeted after integration. The banks wouldn't lose, they said—they'd still have to pay their mortgages—but they'd end up with more paid out than they could recoup if they sold. Had Levittown been a typical working- and lower-middle-class community, this phenomenon of Americans whose houses contained their entire savings (including all they hoped to use to supplant Social Security for their retirement) would probably have followed patterns elsewhere: "white flight" into self-segregated communities further out in the widening rings of suburban development.

In the United States, integration finally became a governmentally sanctioned and even advocated policy in 1954. That was the year of *Brown v. Board of Education,* the year the Supreme Court announced what to any but the most naive Americans was a self-evident fact: to sequester facilities by race was to guarantee better facilities for the majority race, the race with economic, political, and social power. Nineteen fifty-four was also the year the FHA/VA regulators abandoned redlining and even warned client banks against the policy. And it was the year the Department of Defense made an active policy of desegregating the bases and the immediately surrounding areas.

That was also the year the Levittown covenants fell.

This brings us back, then, to the 1960 census and its flurry of surprises. The first is the ratio of black and white residents six years after the collapse of legally sanctioned institutional racism. In 1960, the U.S. population was just under 11 percent "Negro." New York City, the nearest metropolitan feeder for Levittown, was a bit over 7 percent "Negro." Levittown's percentage of black residents was .0008705, less than 1/10 of 1 percent.

To map these numbers across the physical and social spaces of Levittown we return to the census. There were about fifteen thousand houses in Levittown in 1960. There were fifteen occupied by black families, about one per thousand houses. If you were a white kid going to school, what would that mean? That you never saw a black kid, except, perhaps, at a distance, a dark face far down the hallway.

The next statistic further confounds. The total of black Levittowners, fifty-seven, fits logically within those fifteen houses—about four people per house, which was the approximate average in the rest of Levittown. But the mix is wrong: forty-eight women and girls, nine men and boys. This is no culture of poverty at work; Levittown was a stable, middle-class community, and in that demographic, black families were as stable as white. Why, then, this disproportionate absence of men?

We can find a revealing answer by panning out from Levittown to the larger picture the census shows us, of race and geography in the United States at the end of the '50s. Look at the numbers on the other cities and towns of New York State; for that matter, look only at the ones on the two-page spread of the census on which Levittown appears. What you find are cities and towns with solid black populations—industrial towns, like Newburgh, New York, on the Hudson River, 39.6 percent black; Niagara Falls, close to 7 percent. In these, and in most of the other cities and towns with substantial black communities, men and women are equally represented.

But there are others where the Levittown pattern appears. Locust Grove: fifty-six black women, one black man; Massapequa, just south of Levittown, forty-six and four. In Massapequa Park a little further to the east, twenty-eight black females were listed in the census column; there were no men at all. Merrick had a hundred and forty-eight black women and girls and nineteen black men and boys. (Actually, the numbers are even more skewed, as most of the male blacks, there and elsewhere, were children.)

To know something of these communities is often to have the quandary resolved. Take Massapequa. It was a resort town on Jones Beach, with resort hotels that needed maids and cooks; this form of domestic labor brought with it, often, a place to stay. Black maids and domestics were counted in the census. In other communities, summer homes for the rich or landed estates required domestics, too.

Up and down these columns of numbers, the pattern clarifies. In communities needing servants, black women and their children make up the small enclave of black workers counted in the census. Once it had been different; when photographer James Van Der Zee was growing up in the Berkshires in Massachusetts, his family was part of a small community that included carpenters and tradesmen as well as male domestics—butlers and menservants. By the later '50s, that pattern had shifted, as fashions among the wealthy changed, but also as male servants found better-paying jobs in the factories, while women and children still eked out their livings in the kitchens and laundry rooms.

The list of towns and cities on that double page of the census embeds Levittown in a larger history of racial separation and racial space in America. From towns without a single black resident to towns with substantial black populations, one can trace the history of the region: towns and cities that needed workers—to break the strikes, to fill the vacancies in the factories during the wars, to clean the rooms and houses and serve the estates—found those workers and kept them, and the integrationist laws of the '50s did not bring about a revolution. For the rest of the area, for the rest of the nation, white communities stayed white, or they turned black. They didn't, with very rare exceptions, become truly multiracial communities.

Levittown never became substantially integrated. As late as the 1970 census, only 0.1 percent was demarcated as "Negro"—at a time when the population of the nation was just over 11 percent black. As of the 2010 census, the census tract for Levittown had a population of 46,137, of whom 470 were African American, just over 1/10 of 1 percent.

Most American blacks stayed away from Levittown. Though it was inexpensive even in the later '50s, it didn't become a place of starter homes for the black middle class of New York or the rapidly increasing numbers of well-paid black union workers in the defense industries. The unwelcoming reputation of the place preceded it. As *Brown v. Board of Education* began to be implemented two or three years after the landmark 1954 decision, the Levitt firm's Pennsylvania version, housing mainly working-class ethnic families whose men worked the steel mills, was the scene of ugly conflicts over integration, and that reputation redounded on the earlier Levittown, as well, particularly in the black community.[8]

As had Levittown in so many cultural arenas, in this one too it became a place of legend and myth—the place where, after the war, the line of American identity was redrawn to include Jews, Catholics, Irish, but not blacks. In black America, Bill Levitt's explanations seemed more than weak; thanks to the black press and the rich underground communication system, most African Americans knew (as most white Americans didn't) that Levitt had continued to include Caucasian-only covenants in his new developments, had sued the state of New Jersey to allow him to write such contracts, and had testified before Congress defending white-only housing development. Black veteran Eugene Burnett had tried to buy back in 1950, and he reported forty years later: "I will never, ever in my life forget the experience and the feeling that I had when I rode back to Harlem that night." For blacks, the myth of Levittown was a photographic negative of the picture that had arisen throughout the rest of the nation and the globe.[9]

To white Levittowners, though, the question of race was more complicated than they knew it seemed to their black counterparts. There was the fear of financial ruin if the community "went black." But there was also something else—a distinction based on race as an indelible mark of *difference*. To longtime Levittowners, particularly to the first generation who stayed in their original houses and were proud to be counted as pioneers in the 1960 census, the few black settlers were first of all *not their kind*—not the pioneers, not the still-childlike veterans and young veteran's wives, not the ones who'd invented Levittown and been invented by it. These blacks were not actors in the Levittown drama. Theirs was another drama, one seen on television after 1954, a drama set in places like Kansas City and Selma, Alabama. In *that* history play, the Levittowners weren't heroic pioneers but weak-minded escapists from the difficulties of the American utopia, settling for hypocrisy. Not a pleasant self-image—Levittown as huddling place—it was a picture that further ensured Levittown's isolation.

And the decisions of Levittowners to draw the line at the color line is particularly ugly and particularly significant on the national stage, not only because Levittown was such a visible actor on that stage, but because while religion and ethnic background and even class were distinctions Levittowners proudly integrated into their self-declared polyglot democracy, blackness of skin was ineradicable and could never be celebrated within the drama of the new American life. In its long history of racial exclusion, then, Levittown was again a model, a drama, a passion play of Cold War American utopianism and its failures. What was transparent in the census data for Levittown was perhaps hidden, disguised or implicit across the American cultural landscape, but it was there.

CHAPTER 6

Mr. Levitt's Television

Levitt's house designs weren't set in stone; they changed from year to year, sometimes dramatically. The model-year marketing system, complete with annual rollouts and ad campaigns extolling the contemporaneity, the now-ness of the new, reflected the Levitts' wholehearted adaptation of the Detroit production system to the needs of American housing. "Progress in housing," as one press release put it, was a tenet of the Levitt organization. The goal was market share and profit for the company, and achieving it meant accurately reading the market.

In the 1950 California ranch, and in all the 1950 houses, one of the more novel incentives to moving up or moving in was a built-in television included in the price of the house. Set into the paneled wall made by the staircase to the expansion attic was an Admiral with a thirteen-inch screen and two oversized knobs, and it beamed its picture into the living area at right angles to the double-sided fireplace that was another feature of that year's model.

Television was still a novelty in 1950, but everyone saw its arrival as something between a trend and a cultural tidal wave. Threatening long-established media of communication and cultural cohesion, from movies to radio to picture magazine to newspaper, television promised to be a new feature in the American cultural landscape, even as it changed the existing landscapes of everyday life—living rooms, houses, neighborhoods, communities, nation, and globe. Simultaneously an object and an apparatus, it changed the ebb and flow of American domestic life, and its glow promised a new way of seeing the world—simultaneously a window, a panorama and maker of dreams, and a new way of fostering unity and shared purpose in the family, the community, and the nation.

TELEVISION SET is built into living-room wall, has a 12½-inch screen.

6.1. Levittown's very first built-in television, featured in "Levitt Adds 1950 Model to His Line," *Life*, May 22, 1950. (LIFE is a registered trademark of Time Inc. © The Picture Collection Inc. Reprinted with permission. Article: © 1950. The Picture Collection Inc. Reprinted with permission. All rights reserved.)

In the Levittown house, the Admiral competed with the newly added fireplace as a giver of warmth and light and as a gravitational center for family life. Architect Alfred Levitt (Bill's brother) was toying with ideas about the hearth, about the center of family attention, and about the symbolic connection between older ideals of hearth and home. Levitt's house that year was a California ranch, not a colonial. Levitt had decided that the demand for nostalgia and reconnection with the national past, so powerful during the first years after the war, was played out; he had sensed the great shift that would take the national culture toward fear and anticipation of the future. California was it—the new America—and the California ranch was its architectural symbol. Open plan horizontality, interpenetration of indoors and outdoors, casual living, and casual socializing: that was to be the new wave, and the Levitts were already in the midst of this. That it meant expanding the original house from 750 to 800 square feet was only part of this shift from the notion of house as shelter to house as social environment. Alfred Levitt had been watching the Levittowners and he recognized the trend and capitalized on it.

Theirs was an architecture embracing symbolism rather than form or function, and the very fact that it revitalized home sales and motivated a number of Levittowners to "trade up" indicates how potent that symbolism was.

Levitt's 1950 ranch extended the previous year's innovation—the shift of living room from front to rear and the addition of that picture window wall at the back. And the TV competed with that panoramic vista, even if only metaphorically, its small screen promising to open out onto a national and global vista.

The picture window was a hit; so too were the patio and the carport that came in the 1950 ranch. The fireplace, which opened onto the kitchen as well as the living room, was a brilliant stroke of compression—in the kitchen, it referred to the American colonial mythology of the fireplace as a pioneer's cooking source (and Levitt advertised that his families cooked stews and even barbequed in that fireplace), while on the other side, it offered its traditional face as a source of warmth, light, and visual delight. Drafty and impractical, it didn't get much use after the first winter.

But that didn't matter. Levittowners weren't staring in reverie into the embers; they were clustered around the other hearth, the "electronic hearth," as it has often been called, radiating a colder, bluer light, equally hypnotic.

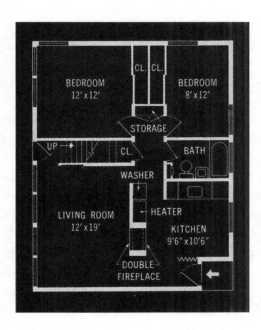

6.2. Floor plan for Levitt ranch, 1950, *Life*. (LIFE is a registered trademark of Time Inc. © The Picture Collection Inc. Reprinted with permission. Article: © 1950. The Picture Collection Inc. Reprinted with permission. All rights reserved.)

Levitt's offer of the television as a built-in feature made sense for all concerned. That paneled wall running up the stairs was a perpetual decorating nuisance. Levitt's decision to supply a television as a built-in saved an immense amount of space and kept the natural flow of traffic from front to back from awkward interruption by obstacles. In 1950, televisions came in one dominant form: heavy, obtrusive pieces of furniture, big, hot vacuum tubes and large transformers in a cabinet whose massive and (usually) dark wood presence demodernized the tube and put it within a tradition of older entertainment forms—pianos, especially, and then gramophones and, more recently, older cabinet radios. Most television makers conceived of their wares as monumental inheritors of that centuries-long tradition, with the heavy wood and blocky assertiveness of the cabinet testifying to the substance and significance of what's within: aristocrats' privileges made available to all.

Levitt's placement of the television into the wall removed it from the realm of furniture, stripping it of its fireside chat-radio nostalgic anachronism and presenting it as it imagined itself to be, an invisible conduit between the home and the world. Getting the television's long, massive, delicate picture tube, circuitry, sound amplifier, and speaker out of the box and laying the picture-plane flush with the wall changed everything. Putting it off-center accentuated the change, removing it from the context of decoration, of pictures-on-a-wall. This was a new and particularly American medium, a medium of directed democracy and consumer capitalism, and the Levitt TV accentuated that claim.

Levitt's decision to add the television was another in the series of prescient events that characterized the builder's strategies. In April of 1950, 5,343,000 televisions graced American homes—9 percent of American households. By the end of that same year, more than 8,000,000 sets were in place. By 1954, more than half of all American households had television.[1]

This sudden increase occurred despite a relative dearth of television stations. In 1948, the FCC froze the issuing of licenses for new stations at 107 nationwide. Some cities had no stations at all, and once outside the urban core, television reception dropped off dramatically. Only a few cities had more than one station. But Levittowners weren't impoverished in this regard; indeed, suburban developments in the Los Angeles and New York areas were the richest TV sites in the country, with seven stations in each, competing to gain market share in relatively cutthroat fashion.[2]

Levitt offered his 1950 house hunters an innovation, not a novelty. Building the TV into the wall declared it was a permanent feature of the new postwar American life. You didn't *buy* the television. It came with the house, and you paid for it in the mortgage. This was a clever bit of subterfuge on Levitt's part; the televisions he supplied were relatively cheap by the standards of the time, and putting them in the monthly payment meant the cost was amortized over thirty years, dramatically increasing its final price, as you paid interest on the loan. Long after your first television had broken and been replaced, and replaced again, and again, you were still paying for that first model.

And that original TV didn't last long. You can see it in the photographs Levittowners took of their living rooms. Levitt bought ten thousand identical televisions in 1950; by 1952 or '53, the first ones had already been replaced, as you can see in the prizewinning living rooms of Levitt's 1952 decorating contest, celebrated in *Life* in garish color.

Over the next few years, the pictures made by the Tekulas, the Armstrongs, the Arnesens, and many others show a bewildering array of different models inserted into those walls—and rarely were they notably larger or fancier, either.

It's significant that when these TVs did break, the owners put others right in the same place. They too participated in the imbedding of the television set into the physical form of the postwar house, and they too expressed the oddly doubled quality of the television, simultaneously an appliance to be hidden and a marvelous new feature of everyday life.

But there was more to that television's location in the wall. It also reflected the indeterminate, transitional role of the TV in the early 1950s, part visual object in itself, part a frame for visual displays, part a window into the virtual conduit that led from the suburbs to the city, and through the city to the world. The Levitt house television wasn't just a picture tube inserted into the paneling; it had a frame, a plastic-gilt frame. The knobs too had gold-paint edges (over time, they wore off). Turn on the TV and the first thing that happened was that you heard a buzz and a solid, annunciatory *whump*. Then there was a wait as the vacuum tubes and the big picture tube "warmed up." Then the picture began to resolve across a blue-gray plane.

Turned off, the slight bulge of the screen made a diminished, fish-eye panorama of the house it reflected. Oddly enough, this accentuated the flatness of the gray surface, its ambiguous quality of two-dimensionality gave the hint that something lay behind it. As the picture appeared, that flatness resolved into a moving space, deepening into a proscenium stage or, more evocatively, into a cone that drew you toward it. In 1950 or thereabouts, television watchers weren't pressed back in their seats by the spectacle of television. They leaned into it—more and more, over the space of the show. That's what the photographs show us. Even women, watching the television while

6.3. Second- and third-prize winners of the Levitt Home Decorating Contest, featured in "Same Rooms, Varied Decor," *Life*, January 14, 1952. (©The Picture Collection. Reprinted with permission. Photograph by Leslie Gill © The Estate of Leslie Gill, courtesy of the Robert Mann Gallery.)

6.4. Charles Tekula as a toddler in front of family's second built-in television, c. 1952. (Courtesy of the Tekula family.)

they iron or fold laundry, are still bending a bit awkwardly toward the image. They want simultaneously to see it better than they can and to be drawn into its illusion.

This wasn't just a matter of the small image, though. In some part it was a response to the makers of televisions, whose ads in the early years of the '50s had a recurrent visual motif: a young family brought together, often dressing up for the occasion, actively engaged with the screen and what was behind it—as in the 1950 DuMont ad, in which even the youngest child appeared to be in a suit that matched his father's.[3]

The thirteen-inch, black-and-white television that was the common form of the '50s had a peculiar quality: it was a window you looked *into* and *out through* simultaneously. Originally, the phosphor-coated front plane of the picture tube was named a "screen" by engineers who were thinking of it as a destination for electron beams—they saw it from within. But most television watchers understood that word to refer to something else, to something more mysterious. Screens hide, or at least obscure, what's behind them; in home decorator parlance, they separate one space into two. Levittown houses were small, and so were the houses in Lakewood Park, California, and the other new suburbs. The television screen suggested that there was something behind the wall, something more than the picture tube; it expanded the domain of home. It turned the home into an embarkation point for the wider world and a destination for new information. In this,

6.5. Joanne Tekula in front of the family entertainment center, Easter 1959. (Courtesy of the Tekula family.)

6.6. Dumont TV ad, 1950

the screen masked not just the cone behind it but the funnel leading out from it to the new world. To lean into the screen, then, meant not only that you were trying to see more, and more clearly, but that you were, perhaps unconsciously, striving to pass through the glass surface and into the realm of light, celebrity, consequence.

Of course there is that other precedent for understanding the television as a screen: the movie screen. In 1951, New York-area movie houses saw a precipitous 40 percent decline in viewership, while in non-television locations, moviegoing actually increased. Harry Henderson reported that the suburbanites he'd polled in 1952 and 1953 saw television as an economizing tool; an evening out, with the movie, food, the bar bill, the transportation costs, became an evening in.

The new screen that replaced the old transformed American space in fundamental ways. The vast, elaborately decorated movie palaces were once filled with a breathing, laughing crowd of people in the dark, and those people leaned back in their seats, looking upward, overwhelmed by the monumentality of the faces, bodies, spaces above them. You might not interact with your fellow audience members, but you knew they were there, you knew they shared your responses, not least because you could hear them laugh, fidget, squirm in their seats, or reach for a handkerchief. There in the dark, you were part of a community of participants.

Against that, compare the living room into which the television projected its images. The television made living rooms into public spaces different than the public spaces of the movie theaters. For one thing, most living rooms stayed lit by more than just the TV light; as a consequence, there was a different sort of sociable, interactive dimension among those in the room rather than an agreement to form an audience of anonymous viewers, as happened with the movies and their dark, dark environs. In living rooms with the TV on, new social groupings came into being; older ones expanded or contracted or changed in character or significance. And a new imaginative relationship between the individual, the family, and the larger world began to form, a relationship that would eventually come to be called not imaginative, but *virtual*.

*   *   *

When television came to Levittown it was more than a novelty. It was a major intrusion in the developing social mores and family patterns of middle-class American suburbanization. And television in *Levittown* was more than a shift in behavior in a relatively small community. Because Levittown had already come to symbolize the new cultural landscape of prosperity, leisure, family, and community, sociologists, writers, pundits, and their readers treated this new phenomenon as a harbinger. Harry Henderson studied Levittown in 1953 along with other instant suburban communities, and he reported in *Harper's Magazine* that "these are the first towns in America where the impact of TV is so concentrated that it literally affects everyone's life. Organizations dare not hold meetings at hours when popular shows are on. In addition, it tends to bind people together, giving the whole community a common experience."[4]

By the time Henderson got to the mass-produced suburbs, television was big, and the patterns were relatively fixed. In the earlier years, when television was a rarity, the TV had served as a social lubricant. In 1948, *McCall's* moved Levittowner Helen Eckhoff into the celebrity seat when its editors chose her to represent Levittown for an installment in its "How I Keep House" series. Like the other featured housewives in the series, Eckhoff had been chosen as a model of the new feminist virtues of scientific housekeeping; she reported with pride the various ways she applied her scientific management skills to keep housekeeping to its most productive. She'd reorganized her kitchen into an assembly line, with separate areas devoted to different aspects of motherhood and homemaking: baby, food prep, cleaning.[5]

Eckhoff and her husband were true pioneers: they'd bought a television even before Levitt offered the built-in, and she reported on her success at using the TV as a feature of a sociable life. By saving time in the kitchen and structuring childrearing right, she declared, "Bob and I have just about as much social life as we ever did. Naturally I don't gad about, but there's always time to have people over. On Saturday night we usually have a television party. Refreshments are simple and we don't use many dishes, so it's just as relaxing for me as the guests."[6]

Eckhoff's "television parties" were gussied-up versions of a common occurrence in the everyday life of TV in the postwar years. Writing in a survey of viewing habits a year before the Levitt built-in appeared, William J. Baxter of the Baxter International Economic Research Bureau reported that "every television set owner soon discovers that he is doing a lot more entertaining than formerly and that his bills for food and beverages are up sharply." Baxter also alerted readers to "cases where the 'gang' would all flock to the home of the first person in the group who has a seven-inch set, and then desert him for someone with a ten-inch set. If a person wants to make friends and climb socially, he should get as big a set as possible and tell all his acquaintances about it." One reporter commented that Levittown's pioneer television families complained they had to sleep in shifts to accommodate the constant stream of guests.[7]

In the late '40s and early '50s, most Levittowners reported looser social events than Eckhoff's: people assembled in the houses with TV, often without formal invitation, to watch their favorite shows, sometimes to the consternation of the homeowners, and families organized potlucks around sports and theatrical "specials." The new forms broke with older models of upward mobility, with the notion that each upward step could be marked by specific social forms, costumes, and rituals and amplified the new fluidity of class in America—a fluidity celebrated in *Life* magazine's April 11, 1949, rewriting of Russell Lyne's "tastemakers" article in *Harper's*, in which *Life* recast the original to suggest that Americans could now put on and take off the trappings of caste and class—and provided a marvelous visual guide showing how to do so.

Baxter's description of a "gang" that traveled from house to house reflected some of that informality of relationships that we've seen in the connection of Levittowners through children and backyards. These new communities were marked by their youth, and they were extensions of the wartime habits of informal clustering. Men and women in the services made their friendships and broke them quickly and easily. Women too still had the habit of friendly interconnection that came with wartime dislocations and unpredictable futures, shared kitchens, and sacrifices. Harry Henderson put it well, when he wrote his second essay on the new suburban social world for *Harper's*: "Gone also are most rituals and ceremonies. If you want to know someone, you introduce yourself. There is no waiting for the 'right people.' You 'drop in' without phoning."[8] TV parties were extensions of the weekends spent working on the expansion attic or teaching each other how to overhaul the carburetor on a second-hand Chevy.

Television parties weren't for the most part raucous occasions. They were marked by their own decorum. When you watched TV, you *watched* it, in those early years. You didn't stare into its embers or keep it on all day just to keep you company—not yet, anyway. Televisions were expensive and they wore out fast if they were used that much. That doesn't mean the television was rarely on—to the contrary: by the mid-1950s, Americans had their televisions on more than five hours a day, and, as one Levittown pioneer recalled, there was always "at least one person engrossed in a situation comedy, children's show, or variety show."[9] From a ceremony to a ritual to an integral part of daily life, television imbedded itself in the American cultural landscape—living room, house, region, and nation.

As this process evolved, the institutions and authorities seeking to regulate, direct, and exploit the postwar American family and the larger national culture looked with a measure of alarm at the new medium. This was in part a matter of competition—newspapers, glossy picture magazines, newsreels: all these sites where American life was fed back to its citizens, ordered, amplified, packaged with remonstration and praise, were also in direct competition with and threatened by the commercial and cultural success of television. There, a chorus of critics, pundits, and even home decorators weighed in with their warnings about the dangerous intrusiveness of TV and the importance of disguising, conventionalizing, or controlling its seductive presence.[10]

But few Americans wasted their time actually *doing* what the social pundits urged. The entire picture presented in these alarmist responses conflicted

6.7. The Tekula family in front of their entertainment center, Easter 1959. (Courtesy of the Tekula family.)

with the evidence presented in Levittown. Bill Levitt didn't hide the TV and neither did his buyers. The TV was instead a fixture, the way a light was or a window seat. If Levittown was as emblematic as everyone thought it was, why weren't its residents taking the advice of the magazines? Why, years later, were they inserting new televisions in the same spot or cutting an even larger chunk out of the wall to accommodate their newer, larger set or make it part of a more elaborate "entertainment center" with the addition of a hi-fi setup, as did the Tekula family, when they hinged the paneling, added a small service door above the set, and put the record player and amplifier below the new, larger TV set?

The surge in warnings about television's intrusiveness and the necessity of maintaining control over its presence, I suspect, reflected not the disquietude of television owners and users but of the media threatened by this new form—magazines, newspapers, books. Writers on television in the late '40s and '50s often spoke of it as a window—sometimes as a physical window, sometimes as a metaphorical one. They were noticing the ways that the television screen seemed to exist as a visual portal between two types of space: physical and virtual. Often these writers seemed intent on confusing the matter further, suggesting that this portal was more literal—that actors and personalities were somehow using the TV channel to dematerialize and to reappear in the living room itself. They were worried that the television had somehow violated Americans' sanctuary. Behind their words lay the recurrent atomic-age myth of the house as huddling place, as fallout shelter. But in this case the rays and waves weren't atomic in origin—they were cultural, mass cultural. Critics, editorialists, even comedians like Harry Hershfeld bemoaned the television as a portal through which intrusive new characters were invading the home.[11]

These remonstrating voices of authority and propriety warned that television was the cause of an unhappy siege on personal and family identity, and not what most people saw it to be—a part of the larger shift toward informality and fluidity in social, spatial, and cultural categories. They missed the sense in which they were right, however. For television was supplanting a very particular form of sociability: the mixing of strangers in dynamic settings. Movie houses were one thing; what TV increasingly edged out, for those outside of the teen years, were nightclubs, supper clubs, restaurants, bowling alleys, and dancehalls, all of them places where you engaged with fellow Americans who might be very different than you—richer or poorer, of some exotic background, older or younger, with whom you shared, however, a commonality of interest: in the foxtrot, in mastering a split, in roller skate balletics, in big-band jazz. As we'll see, *I Love Lucy*, the single biggest hit show of its time, mirrored this with perfect irony—you stayed home from the Cuban, tropical-themed nightclub in order to watch Lucy commit every misdemeanor in the book to get to that very club.

The pundits, however, warned not of a breakdown of informal social interaction among disparate parts of a democratic polity; they were worried about a breakdown of civility and propriety, of formal nicety and proper manners on one hand and a collapse of the walls and boundaries protecting the sanctified home from a vulgar mongrelism of ethnicity and class on the other.

Something else was happening to the TV-having home. It was becoming a unit in a cybernetic apparatus and, over time, the producers and marketers of television—along with government bureaucracies and corporate advertisers—would realize this, and exploit it. There was a *screen* which connected to a *channel*, one that enabled viewers to pass through to the virtual spaces of television. And the cultural geography of the nation—and the globe—was changing as a result.

*　*　*

Pundits, writers, humorists, and critics took on television, and they did so in a peculiar way—as a part of the landscape, a geographical feature, and not just a new form of entertainment. Most of the writing on the subject ignored that screen/channel connection in favor of other analogies: a window between a proscenium stage and the family's private box seat, or a magic carpet enabling escape from the narrow confines of the everyday to exotic new places in the globe. In both cases, television served as a means to render the landscape, whether outside or in, fluid, malleable, stretched or shrunk (most often shrunk) by the channeling of television.

Television programmers saw the matter similarly, at least in the first years. They made shows that aped high theater, Broadway, and vaudeville—all of them providing novel variants on the old proscenium. Meanwhile, travelogue-style segments or shows came to symbolize that other, outer reach. Network marketers touted the range of the TV camera and promised it was revealing the globe and offering a better view than any wealthy aristocrat or capitalist had ever been afforded—and producers, cameramen, writers all sought to live up to the claims.

The difficulty with all this lay with the physical realities under which television actually appeared. Close your eyes and listen to a '30s radio show and you're afforded a remarkable illusion of sonic transportation. Footsteps in the hallway sound like footsteps in the hallway. Pretty soon, you're able to make a visual leap and see the spaces in which Johnny Dollar or Matt Dillon is hidden, waiting for the bad guy. You're invited to a process of imaginative creation that's strikingly similar to the way most people read fiction—dime-store novels or Edith Wharton.

There's little to suggest that this willing suspension of disbelief took place with early television, or that an illusionary world welled up from within. No one watching an early thirteen-inch Admiral mounted in a wall or a sixteen-inch Motorola in a bulky piece of furniture thought for a moment that Milton Berle was actually going to step into the living room. He was trapped in the tiny, fuzzy, black-and-white set with its tinny, worse-than-radio sound and its interruptions of narrative to allow for commercials, which increasingly moved abruptly out of the performance and into some other space and sound environment, and then another (as multiple ads were piggybacked on a "station break"), before returning you, disruptively, to the space and sound of the show itself.

Television wasn't an illusionistic medium, to be blunt, and its visual style didn't try particularly hard to overcome those limits. Inside its often-elaborate furniture housing, the actual set was small; you controlled it, more or less, with your hands on the knobs—and, etiquette evidence tells us, people loved to play with the knobs, to remain in physical contact with the object. Besides the problems of people who dropped in uninvited to watch *their* show on *your* TV, and people who overstayed their welcome, the most common TV-related complaint written in to advice columnists involved guests who insisted on taking over the set's adjustments and switching its channels. The common explanation for this eagerness to manipulate the set's features—contrast, focus, tonal range, volume of sound—is that the picture was too lousy and the sets too unreliable. There's truth to this. Television watchers became resigned to the realities of the television reception; they understood that it wouldn't in fact take them on a magic carpet ride or offer them the opportunities of verisimilitude on the one hand or imaginative excursion on the other. It was just what it was. Touching the buttons, playing with the reception, viewers reconfirmed the physicality of the television set, and the clumsy ephemerality of the visual and sonic information it was projecting.

Remember too that television watchers, unlike radio listeners, had a precedent against which they could compare the experience of television: the movies. And don't think that movie producers, faced with precipitous declines in viewership and revenue, didn't try to exploit their advantage. Widescreen, Widelux, better and better color, louder and more elaborate sound systems, even abortive attempts at 3-D and vibrating seats: all these expensive innovations sought to enlarge the difference between the seductive mirages of the movies and the tinny box in the living room.

None of these strategies worked. Television continued to eat into the movies despite its technical roughness and its inability to provide a convincing out-of-body experience. In fact, the better the movies got at giving an illusionistic experience, the more people stayed at home and watched TV. Clearly, people were finding a different kind of experience in that act, an experience that marketers, critics, and even producers tended to miss. That image of television watchers arguing among themselves as to who could, should, or should not touch the knobs, bang the set, adjust the antenna, serves as a reminder that the power of television lay precisely in the fact that it didn't have power over its viewers—that they had power over it instead. They could turn it on or off, get up and leave or wander in, ignore the commercials, talk over the show, fall asleep in front of it, eat, drink, make love, all without any obligation to the set, to its moral power or its messages. (Harry Henderson quoted one Levittowner who told him: "Until we got that TV set, I thought my husband had forgotten how to neck."[12]) Everything that was wrong with the set as an illusion-machine was *right* with it when it came to the role Americans found for it within their lives.

There's a great deal of talk in the histories of TV about something called the "golden age of television"—a time when talented, even brilliant, writers, directors, and actors were collaborating with network executives to produce "teleplays" ranging from adaptations of Shakespeare to Paddy Chayefsky's celebrated *Marty*, a drama generally conceded to represent the high point of golden age television.

But the ratings don't support the contention that these golden age tele-dramas were what people wanted to see. Certainly they *saw* them—the same way they went to school board meetings or science fairs at the junior high school—dutifully. *Marty* appeared on May 24, 1953, on the *Philco TV Play-house*, the most celebrated of these teledrama anthology series. It was there, for example, that viewers of the show's first season in 1948 had seen *Cyrano de Bergerac* adapted to that fuzzy, black-and-white, thirteen-inch Admiral, Zenith or DuMont, a live production complete with José Ferrer and a cast of hundreds milling about on seven completely different stage sets, at least one of them designed to reproduce the seventeenth-century Parisian streets. The production, like all of what was done on *Playhouse* in the first year was a product of Actor's Equity, which was seeking rather desperately to deter-mine a way to make television into another outlet for Broadway stage plays, and thereby keep its union members employed and happy.[13]

The *Philco TV Playhouse* ratings show a clear trend. Nineteen fifty was the first year of published ratings, and the show was third. Over the next three years it dropped steadily in popularity—twelfth in 1951-1952, seventeenth in 1952-1953, when *Marty* aired, and nineteenth in 1953-1954. By 1955, it had dropped off the top twenty-five and was cancelled.

The Texaco Star Theater told a different story. It was hot when it appeared in 1948 and it stayed that way; it debuted on the Nielsens at number one two years later, and remained in the top five through 1954. But it was a show made for the very qualities that marked television's failure as a medium of verisimilitude. If the screen was blurry and the sound tinny, *Texaco* host

Milton Berle in an outrageous costume, yelling, prancing, and domineering the proscenium made a perfect counterpart; he accepted the denigration of the theatrical stage and made a new sort of vaudeville variety show to match the new medium—brash and hilarious, but never much more than trivial. It was TV.

So was *Arthur Godfrey* in its two incarnations—*Arthur Godfrey and His Friends* and *Arthur Godfrey's Talent Scouts*. There again viewers had the chance to watch "stars" who weren't stars, as regulars and as "discoveries." And Godfrey himself was a disarming presence, a living-room nonintrusion, though in a far different way than the clownish Berle. The *New York Daily News* television critic set down the source of his popularity: "It is his friendliness, his good cheer, his small-boy mischievousness and his kindly philosophy . . . or maybe it's his magnetism, his personal attractiveness."[14] This was a presence appropriate to the miniature set—there wasn't anything frustrating or dutiful to the act of watching—or half-watching—Arthur Godfrey.

The first decade of television seems marked by two opposing streams of creative production. One sought to adapt older patterns of formal, live, direct entertainment—Broadway, vaudeville, the serious theater, opera, classical music, jazz—to the new medium. This wasn't particularly successful, and so writers, directors, and programmers moved in another direction— toward finding forms that *were* appropriate to the peculiar qualities of the new medium. Employing this kitchen sink experimentation, programmers had spectacular hits and misses. Those that worked—the Berle formula, the Godfrey formula—provided interim strategies while programmers tried to determine just what it was that people wanted from their televisions.[15]

By the mid-1950s, the TV offerings had coalesced, and so had the patterns of TV watching. The result was a synergy between audience and producer, a feedback loop that was rendered almost instantly more efficient and immediate with the introduction of the Nielsen ratings to television in 1950.

Looking at the list of top-rated shows as the system settled down, we can see the trends: in the earliest, pre-Nielsen years, it was marked by an amalgam of adaptations, from theater, from radio, from vaudeville, from Hollywood, from the sporting arenas (boxing matches were among the most popular of early TV offerings, not least because viewers at home saw the fights with greater immediacy than if they'd been there, thanks to cameras that could capture the ring from above, or show close-ups of the clinches and the KO). Within a season or two, this fluidity gave way, and a look at the newspaper schedules shows true television genres appearing—shows people will watch by *type*, so that a loss of interest in *Hopalong Cassidy* brings *The Lone Ranger* or *Martin Kane, Private Eye* combines with *Man Against Crime* to become *Treasury Men in Action*, and then later spins out to *Dragnet* and *Perry Mason*.

By the mid-1950s, the Nielsen ratings had grown significantly more sophisticated, and so had the advertisers and producers who pored over its details. The opportunity to parse the top twenty-five or, more astutely, to look at the raw numbers, breaking them out by the gender of the viewer, the age, the financial status, the purchasing habits, made the Nielsens indispensable, the keys to what shows lived and died, but also what shows were stolen, copied, adapted or refined.

Television critics and historians today have the names for the resulting genres. Comedy-variety: by 1955, *The Ed Sullivan Show* was at the top. Family variety: *Disneyland* appeared at number six in 1954–1955. Crime and punishment: *Dragnet*, number four in 1952, top ten through 1956, when a new genre, the Western, subsumed its function in a new and mythically more resonant guise. Domestic sitcom: *I Love Lucy* arrived in 1951–1952 at number three and stayed at one or two through 1957. Crooner shows. Quiz shows. Drama-variety. By early 1951, television's producers had come to understand how to make the new medium work.

In the Levittown houses, and in all the houses that Levittown stood for, then and now, televisions glowed—in more and more houses, for longer and longer periods, and then in more and more rooms, as second televisions became a feature of suburban life. By the mid-1950s, television watching had changed, had stabilized, marked not by scarcity and novelty but by plenitude and normalcy. In fact, television had become a symbol of the promise of the new American landscape—in which normalcy *was* plenitude.

But this process changed the rhetoric of television. The other media continued to trumpet the threat of TV—its capacity to monopolize, to hypnotize, to colonize—their protests better understood as attempts to protect themselves and simultaneously to generalize a very real threat to their own power and influence. But most Americans showed by their behavior that they didn't take the threat seriously—they were comfortable with the freedom to ignore the television.

Television parties disappeared. So did the problem of the unwelcome guest-as-television-watcher. But so also did the fantasy, so often eulogized, of family television or, more accurately, of television as a means of uniting families in a common social space and a shared experience. It's not to say that family watching wasn't important—Nielsen ratings demonstrate that family shows at the right times did indeed garner whole-family audiences— but this phenomenon was far less influential than pundits and producers had predicted. TV didn't unite the nuclear family, knitting parents, teens, and children into one happy homogenous, consuming entity. Instead, the television became a more complex part of the cultural geography of American life, as teenagers got *their* shows, and housewives theirs, children, too.

Significant cultural productions simultaneously *reflect, protect,* and *inflect.* They respond to their audiences by mirroring their languages, myths, fears, and desires, or they wouldn't survive; but simultaneously, they alter those attitudes, those emotions and beliefs, and they recast the forms in which they're imbedded, remaking myths, reinvigorating and transforming symbols. In so doing, they serve to insulate the culture and its people. They offer both familiarity and orderliness—a map of the terrain, a reminder that we've traversed something similar, and the assurance that there are others here with us.

TV started by aping older cultural media—theater and the movies. And it periodically returned to those older modes. But the action wasn't in these proscenium performances or the inept attempts to compete with Panavision. It was in the rest of television—in the programs that embraced, appropriated, and rejuvenated the central myths of American culture, bringing the anxiety and guilt that came with the new, into the fabric of continuity and tradition.

These shows weren't short skits nor were they lengthy dramas. They had the truncated, schematic structure of fairy tales and fireside stories, children's books and schoolroom history texts. They fit within thirty-minute time slots (rarely, they extended to an hour) and, because they were interrupted once or even twice by commercial breaks, necessarily they had discrete segments. In the first part, we were reintroduced to the characters—stock characters well known to viewers, with fixed, schematic qualities representative of American traits—and then to the particular problem that would be the core of the show, along with a series of hints and cues to the larger meaning of the issue. The middle segment explored the problem more fully, amplifying it to a crisis; and then the finale reasserted the power of traditions, institutions, social bonds.

But this was only part of the story. Just as children listened to fairy tales with a strange obsessive fascination that involved more than the plot or characters alone, so with television, viewers were freed by the stock features of character, plot, and structure to pay a sort of oblique attention to the rest of it—to the setting, the pace, the costumes, and references, and from all these to build a larger narrative. If you weren't paying attention, you hardly noticed the way it was redefining American life in the Cold War environment. Its steady, almost unwavering rhetorical persistence rendered it nearly invisible while organizing a great deal of cultural information.

That's what's so interesting about television's early years, and so important: the way it brought into being a new form of public discourse that was simultaneously ingratiating and entertaining, while admitting, even in its most grandiose moments, to its own triviality. Yet this triviality was a sort of Trojan horse; Levittowners bought the second television for the kids or the bedroom and they kept the sets on for longer and longer periods, murmuring in the backgrounds, lighting up a room through which one might pass, or in which one might sit, watching and listening, as its rejuvenated versions of American myths and memories played themselves out.

Yet that very promise of reassurance bound up in the recurrence of the trivial—the show, the commercial, the half-hour slot, the weekly schedule, the arrival of a new season increasingly recasting its predecessors—was set against other, and more complex, reversions of fear and the promise of comfort. Late-night television watchers with their sets on at 1:30 in the morning on Thursday, September 16, 1953, saw the screen go blank and an announcement replace their programming: the first CONELRAD emergency broadcasting system test. Three years later, at 3:10 in the afternoon on Friday, July 20, 1956, viewers and listeners to television and radio heard a 1-1/4 minute announcement of a second test. At approximately the same time, the Atomic Energy Commission was detonating a particularly dirty H-bomb (technically, a "thermonuclear device") named, perhaps with irony, "Redwing Tewa." Second-to-last in a long series of thermonuclear tests at both Bikini and Enewetak atolls named after American Indian tribes, "Tewa" blew a substantial hole in Bikini.[16]

Television watchers didn't see "Redwing Tewa"; they had witnessed two earlier tests in the Redwing series: "Lacrosse" on May 4 and "Cherokee" on May 20—or at least, television reporters on the deck of the USS *Mt. McKinley* had observed the shots. What viewers saw, instead, on that CONELRAD screen, was a gray blank, on which CONELRAD ALERT was inscribed, as the announcer (an Air Force voiceover specialist from the Lone Mountain film division, source of most of the official atomic test footage during the era, recorded onto a vinyl record sent to all U.S. radio and television stations) described the test, with a coda crediting the United States Air Force Orchestra and the United States Air Force Band for the music that would occupy the rest of the test's time.

The voice, stentorian and officious; the music, stirring and patriotic; the words, bold; the typeface, simple, efficient, without ornament: CONELRAD's announcement epitomized one conception of television's potential—as a superb tool for ensuring uniform, obedient responses by a properly attentive American population. But television watchers rarely complied with this

Cold War bureaucratic dream—that first night, most were asleep, a few restless, bored, insomniac, watched their screens go blank, probably with more irritation than panic; and that afternoon three years later, a summer's Friday afternoon, few would have minded the interruption of CBS game show *The Big Payoff*, or NBC's *Matinee Theatre*. The test would be over by the time *Queen for a Day*, that sob-story housewife giveaway, came on at 4.

CHAPTER 7

The Incredible Exploding House, Yucca Flat, Nevada, March, 1953

Houses, actually. Two of them, identical, built in the atomic testing range at Yucca Flat, Nevada, close to Frenchman Flat, costing $18,000 each: boxlike, two-storey suburban colonials with outdoor chimneys and full basements.

In their rooms on the first and second floors, mannequins arrayed in tableaux. In the basement, a young woman, incongruously dressed in *décolletage*, in a small makeshift lean-to shelter the Civil Defense had been pressing every citizen to build, without much success. Together, the two houses constituted the entire built environment and the population of a community known as Doom Town. In the predawn hours, one light on in each house—nightlights for the family.[1]

These ersatz citizens in their American dream homes waited to be destroyed and then remade: as time-lapse photographs, as television images, as the basis for one of the first carefully scripted prime-time television docudramas, when film teams for the national networks would troop into the ruins to photograph the destruction, interview the experts, view the (plastic) bodies and see the sheltered ones huddled, protected, unscathed, in their Civil Defense–approved havens. But the program disintegrated.

* * *

7.1. Fabricated suburban colonial house, Nevada Test Site, 1953. (Courtesy of the National Archives and Records Administration.)

Upshot-Knothole* was the name of the test series scheduled for that spring of 1953. It wasn't the first set of above-ground atomic tests to take place on American soil, nor was it the first within the spectacular desert outreaches of Nevada. And it wasn't the first to have civilian spectators. For the 1952 tests, the Atomic Energy Commission had provided bleacher seating for a relatively small number of journalists, politicians, and officials, at a slight uplift known as "News Nob."[2]

But Upshot was the first attempt to fully script the performance of an

---

* The naming of tests at this early stage was largely the provenance of the scientists, whose names were deliberate obfuscations, often ironic or joking, or private messages—some concerning the purpose of the test ("Upshot"), some the actual technologies or theories being tested ("Knothole") and then the location in the test sequence ("Annie"), which conformed roughly to an alphabetical sequence, though often scrubbed or postponed tests would confuse the series.

atomic test, with an elaborate cast of characters, a carefully constructed set, and a plan to beam the orchestrated results into a national audience of TV watchers via live network television.

From the bleachers, and now from in front of the TV, the test site took on a decidedly theatrical quality. Stage left and some miles away was the tower where the bomb would be detonated, and from which the mushroom cloud would rise. Stage center and much closer were those two suburban houses, one of them 3,500 feet from ground zero, the other a half-mile closer to News Nob. Stage left: troops, about a thousand, in bunkers and trenches they'd dug into the desert floor. Stage right was a Greek chorus of journalists, onlookers, and privileged visitors. Over the course of the test and the dramatic events it caused, they would comment, first to each other, then to the audience of citizens watching at a distance, huddled around the small ovoid screens of their televisions.[3]

As *Newsweek* later explained it, "Civil-defense workers from every state, headed by the new chief of the Federal Civil Defense Administration, Val Peterson, had been brought to Nevada to get a firsthand story for the folks at home."[4] *Life* put it more bluntly: "The Federal Civil Defense Administration wanted to exploit the test to inject an overdue sense of urgency into its campaign to organize a sensible defense of American cities."[5]

There was a reason for this conversion of military test into public spectacle. Over the years following Hiroshima and Nagasaki, atomic fears had waxed and waned. When the Russians announced their first successful test, American apprehension had grown, as the possibility of atomic warfare grew ever more likely. But the steadily more spectacular pictures of atomic tests, at Bikini and Enewetak in the Pacific, and at Frenchman and Yucca Flat in the Nevada desert, had reassuringly pushed the symbol of the atomic age back into the realm of wonder and beauty. "New Looks at the A-Bomb," in *Life*'s May 26, 1952, issue, revealed the payoff of treating the tests as hyperactive spectacles, replete with a direct, unabashed embrace of atom bomb fashion. Photographers, journalists, and "some 200 distinguished guests" watched from News Nob as "the mushroom cloud, pink, luminous and beautiful, swirled up into the sky. The first public performance of the bomb seemed safe and almost easy," declared *Life*, "but out at ground zero all life was scorched."[6]

Nineteen fifty-two's test series—Tumbler-Snapper, it was named—took place in the midst of the Korean War, when the use of tactical atomic weapons was a matter of active debate. Soldiers there might have to march into atom-bombed battlefields, and the notion was deeply unsettling. The military had been deploying infantry into the Nevada test sites since 1951 to

7.2. "The atomic cloud formed by the detonation seems close enough to touch, and tension gone, Poth and Wilson do a little clowning for the camera." U.S. Marine Corps publicity photograph dated May 1, 1952. (Still Picture Records Section, Special Media Archives Services Division [NWCS-S], National Archives at College Park.)

gather information on troop behavior, and official pictures and press releases appeared to reassure Americans that atomic warfare was safe (for the aggressor American) and even entertaining. A picture widely distributed from 1952 exemplified this. Its caption, authored by one of the AEC's public information officers, spoke volumes: "The atomic cloud formed by the detonation seems close enough to touch, and tension gone, Poth and Wilson do a little clowning for the camera."[7] The mushroom cloud, no longer a menace, had become an optical sleight of hand.

But there was another catalyst for the full-tilt move of Atomic Energy Commission officials into public-relations spectacle in 1953. After the end of the previous test season, *Life* and other media outlets had acquired, and released, a series of horrifying nightmare pictures of the aftermath of Hiroshima and Nagasaki. *Life*'s initial scoop was titled "When Atom Bomb Struck: Uncensored;" the subhead was "First Pictures—Atom Blasts Through Eyes of Victims."

TEN MINUTES AFTER THE BLAST YOSHITO MATSUSHIGE SNAPPED HIROSHIMA'S "WALKING DEAD," LATER WASHED THIS DEVELOPED FILM IN CREEK NEAR CITY

LIFE
Vol. 33, No. 13   September 29, 1952

WHEN ATOM BOMB STRUCK—UNCENSORED

A collection of scratched and dusty photographs, retrieved from half-forgotten files, has just struck Japan with the impact of a delayed fuse bomb. For the first time Japan has seen—and been shocked by—visual evidence of what happened to the people of atom-bombed Hiroshima and Nagasaki. And the collection, published here for the first time in the U.S., has the immediacy of today's news pictures for any people who live in the not illogical fear of being caught themselves in an atomic blast or in the terrible work of tending those who are.

Like the rest of the world the Japanese knew only the physical facts of atomic destruction, the statistics of death, the stories of what happened under the mushroom cloud. But, with one or two exceptions, pictures taken by five Japanese photographers in the first hours of terror after the blasts had been suppressed by jittery U.S. military censors through seven years of the Occupation. In that time many negatives were damaged or lost. Some, processed in inferior wartime chemicals, deteriorated beyond use. Nonetheless, early this year,

HIROSHIMA'S VIEW OF CLOUD

even before the Occupation formally ended, enterprising Japanese publishers began rounding up those photographs still left. Last month, with U.S. censorship abolished by the peace treaty, the publishers rushed into print with three books and a 26-page newspaper supplement. They sold out almost overnight and publishers ordered fresh editions.

In Japan it had been feared the stark record would touch off new waves of anti-Americanism. But the lesson of the pictures went much deeper than that on the people who had started the war which led to Hiroshima and Nagasaki. Almost with one voice those who saw the long-suppressed photographs renewed a heartfelt cry—nearly forgotten since the Korean war and the threat of Russian aggression—for pacifism, neutrality and peace at any price. In Nagasaki, at a memorial to those who died there, a teen-aged survivor voiced the common fear: "With all my might, as I once cried out for water out of thirst while crawling among the charred bodies on that fateful day, I should now like to cry 'peace, peace.'"

19

7.3. Opening spread, "When Atom Bomb Struck—Uncensored," *Life*, September 29, 1952. (LIFE is a registered trademark of Time Inc. © The Picture Collection Inc. Reprinted with permission. Article: © 1952. The Picture Collection Inc. Reprinted with permission. All rights reserved.)

This was exactly the theme AEC officials sought to bury with the new "open" tests of that spring. Of course there was the brutal shock of the pictures themselves: peeling emulsion standing in for peeling skin, peeling skin standing in for deeper and more hidden wounds. But there was also the implication that censorship by the military and the AEC wasn't meant to shield enemy eyes from military data but to keep Americans from seeing atomic warfare from the victim's angle. Despite its lip service to American atomic policy, *Life* had allowed its writers to end the revelations with the warning that "the long-suppressed photographs, terrible as they are, still fall far short of depicting the horror which only those who lived under the blast can know."[8]

Life's release of the Hiroshima and Nagasaki pictures was in some ways the culmination of a longer and more untidy trend in the representation of atomic warfare, and atomic energy more generally, in popular media. Historian Ferenc Morton Szasz collected and studied atomic-themed comic books for decades, and in them he saw a narrative emerging that was far from the one American military strategists wished to see. In comic after comic, atomic weapons fell into the hands of rogue individuals and groups; atomic power went awry; radiation and poisons threatened the nation and the globe; atomic energy itself broke free of scientific and bureaucratic restraints to become a personified evil. In the comics, superheroes from Superman to Captain Marvel came to the rescue, but the comics almost invariably ended with a warning about the dangers of atomic power run amok. And of course few Americans reading these comics had illusions that some superhuman force for good was in fact waiting in the wings to stop a threat that was anything but fictitious; as if to bring this home, the four-part comic book series titled *Atomic War*, released in 1952, depicted in graphic detail the destruction of New York, Detroit, and Chicago, followed by protracted and escalating global warfare. A better case against the arguments for a winnable atomic war and a defensible American continent could probably not have been made.[9]

Life's revelatory picture essay appeared in late September of that same year, providing wrenching photographic close-ups of what the comic books had painted in bold washes of color and form. That left AEC, the Federal Civil Defense Administration and army officials the long winter season to contemplate the untidy effects of this wave of media on the campaign to normalize atomic warfare, and devise a public relations strategy that could put them back on track.

Upshot-Knothole-Annie was the first test of the new season. Civil Defense and AEC officials designed this showdown to the music—cool jazz piped through the PA system at News Nob. As if to compete with the epic hyperbole of the big Hollywood films of the day, military planners brought in that cast of onlookers, numbering close to a thousand, to do the crowd scenes. Each had been vetted for their photogenic and picturesque potential— "local politicians, bus drivers, the press agents of the Las Vegas casinos and even several of the more influential gambling house proprietors ... civil defense representatives, including governors of many states, police and fire chiefs, even public-spirited housewives," according to *Life*'s correspondent. This was the first test, *Life* noted, to feature its own "portable lunch counter dispensing hot dogs, sandwiches, coffee and Coca Cola." And it was the first in which network television cameras had been placed to enable live early-morning national coverage of the blast, with a complex logistical scenario to allow the network evening news teams onto the site to present the aftermath of destruction on prime-time television and radio news that very evening.[10]

Annie's pageant started auspiciously. The weather held fine, the bomb exploded. The live coverage went off without a hitch. *Life* reported that "millions of Americans, just finishing breakfast or still drowsy from sleep, watched it on TV." But the Civil Defense officials had planned a second TV pseudo-event to coincide with prime-time news in the populous East Coast market—an excursion into those "model American homes," as the AEC press release called them, to graphically demonstrate the virtues of home atom-blast shelters.*

It didn't fare well. A shift in the wind patterns pushed the "hot cloud" over both houses, and fallout was sufficiently severe that only a single AEC official made it in—clad in protective clothing and dropped at house 2 by helicopter. He stayed only a few minutes and was then airlifted out. (One of the visiting locals, Klien Rollo of Cedar City, Utah, reported to the *Iron County Record* that the head of Civil Defense, Val Peterson, "was flabbergasted by the amount of dust and debris present even at two miles distant from ground zero"—dust and debris, it seems, that the witnesses, as well as the locals, found swirling around them.[11]

The evening television news coverage was heavily curtailed. No TV cameras entered the houses, and the alarm of the officials never made it out on the network feeds. Instead, Civil Defense representatives hastily assembled

---

* Because the AEC and Civil Defense did not yet publicly acknowledge the pervasiveness or danger of fallout, these shelters were meant only to protect against the blast shock and the wind burst immediately following an atomic blast.

a puppet show, using "a model of the model house" to point to the safe havens where (if you didn't factor in fallout, and they didn't) their mannequins had successfully survived an atomic attack.[12]

By the end of the evening, what had been planned as a tightly controlled television docudrama had been transformed by the realities of atomic holocaust into an absurdist teleplay that ran counter to the script. To watch government experts playing dollhouse with models while the announcer explained that the real site was awash in death rays and atomic contamination was to hammer home the very truths this test had been designed to dispel: atomic warfare was unpredictable; the effects were much more violent and dangerous than acknowledged by experts or imagined by witnesses; and Civil Defense planners were ill-prepared for the result. This test had been meant to establish the knowledgeable authority of civil and military defense officials. Instead, it presented them as incompetent, even buffoonish, driving President Eisenhower to order "a complete reexamination of the realities of atomic warfare" on the grounds that the public had witnessed the "inadequate progress of civil defense."[13]

The event turned out to be a public relations disaster, thanks in part to the complex ambitions of government and military propagandists. It also came from the confusion between test and theater. The event overlaid two stories, both of them meant simultaneously to alarm and reassure American viewers. One was military, the other civilian. Eight hundred and fifty soldiers had been brought in and dug into trenches close up to the blast. The bomb went off nearly over their heads; after a suitable delay, they then left the trenches and advanced toward ground zero. They weren't there to test military strategy or troop readiness—that had already been established in the Desert Rock maneuvers of 1951 and 1952. Their primary role was to demonstrate to reporters stationed with them that the weapon wasn't scary enough to deflect them from their duties. This part of the docudrama went off without a hitch. Journalists huddled in the foxholes, recording soldierly reactions to this new form of trench warfare. The GI's comments seemed blasé; they complained the show wasn't good enough. *Newsweek* quoted a major—"I didn't think it was worth coming out here for"—and an artillery officer—"Charge Six of a one-five-five would hurt your ears more." This was exactly the sort of comment desired: it shaded atomic warfare into conventional warfare.[14]

The trenches, soldiers, jeeps, and armored personnel carriers arrayed across the desert provided ingredients for scripted news pictures of a prepared military well-equipped to handle the rigors of this new form of warfare. Everything about the military side of the test countered the unspoken anxiety that America was unprepared for a nuclear war, that its soldiers were ill-equipped, physically and mentally, for the new warfare.

The other side of the American dance between triumphalism and terror was situated in the arena of Civil Defense, where every scripted detail contributed to an allegory about everyday people and their everyday lives interrupted by the sudden flash and blast of an atomic attack. Those suburban houses out in Yucca Flat, with their carefully dressed mannequins arranged in deliberately sociable poses making up the cast of characters, were center stage in the spectacle. Civil Defense stagers set mannequin families at the dinner table, clustered in the living room, peacefully abed. A team of official photographers and filmmakers from the AEC's Lookout Mountain Studio shot footage of these scenes of domestic bliss before the blast, the anticipated foil to a before-and-after contrast that would graphically prove the case for Civil Defense.

(What wasn't publicized was the substantial modification of those two houses to minimize the horrific effects that would have occurred to a normal suburban house. Special paint, asbestos shingling, and the addition of closed metal venetian blinds all ensured that total devastation of the two houses by fire would not occur, and only the so-called blast effects would be recorded.[15])

Everything was organized so television viewers would walk away with a reassuring picture of what it was supposed to take to survive an atomic bomb—above all, faith in the appropriate bureaucracies of government. Americans' do-it-yourself skills would solve a simple problem ("build-it-yourself fallout shelter"), and wary readiness would be the new American condition, replacing the deeply fatalistic scenario imagined by most Americans: that atomic destruction was so severe and death so horrific that there was no point in preparing.[16]

As Civil Defense had planned things, the mannequins in house 1's shelters should have survived the horrific destruction to pick their way out of the rubble of their flattened house, while those in house 2, further away, should have emerged into a relatively untouched domestic landscape. House 1's occupants should have walked from the flattened zone about a mile or so, where they would encounter the occupants of house 2, sweeping up some broken glass, rearranging the furniture, and ready to welcome their refugee fellow citizens. By compelling contrast, those in house 1 who'd ignored the call to take shelter, reluctant to leave the supper table or the TV show, should have been shown to have suffered a horrific death.

U.S. News and World Report, the Cold War's loudest American cheerleader, gave its readers that party line, complete with hastily acquired photographs from Lone Mountain Studios, released by the AEC to United Press International, the newspaper photo outlet. The report seems to have been developed almost entirely from the press releases:

> Destruction is fairly complete within about a mile of the center of an atomic target. That rule of thumb still holds. But most families, even in industrial cities, live outside of such a 10-block radius from probable targets. American-style houses and cars, outside of this lethal distance from 'Ground Zero,' can become fairly good bomb shelters. That's shown now for the first time.[17]

U.S. News and World Report ended the article by reiterating some good old America-first rhetoric: "Even families living close to target areas may have a good chance of survival merely by living in an American-type house or driving an American car, and taking very simple precautions." The words parroted the message planners had hoped journalists and witnesses would report: atomic war is survivable, even winnable; atomic attack can be neutralized with a little planning; American know-how, American manufacturing, American cars and houses could win the "hot" war just as, five years later, in the fabled "Kitchen Debate" with Khrushchev at the American National Exhibit in Moscow, Vice President Nixon would declare that American consumer goods had already won the Cold War.

If you'd read "When An Atomic Bomb Hits Your House or Auto"—for that was the title of *U.S. News and World Report*'s article—you'd have thought the test demonstration had been seamless in execution and in message. In truth, nearly everything had gone wrong.[18]

Planners had set out to destroy house 1 while leaving its basement shelter untouched. Lesson: build or buy a shelter—and support the Civil Defense initiatives—if you don't want to be vaporized. The dramatic stop-action photographs *Life* later published came from AEC cameras trained on that home, and they were horrific indeed.[19]

The sequential images of the shock wave devastating house 1 were assuredly not what Americans had grown used to seeing when atomic holocaust was represented in popular culture. No: they expected the spectacular sublimity of the mushroom cloud, seen at panoramic scale, preferably with witnesses pointing and staring, agog at the scene.

To shock and terrorize without awakening a state of fatalism was the Civil Defense Administration's brief. What emerged instead was a split-screen drama. From the safe distance of News Nob, where the observers sat in their makeshift theater seats, the entire event was disappointing, even a bit boring.

7.4. Eggleston time-lapse photographs of the destruction of the test house, Nevada Test Site, 1953. (Courtesy of the National Archives and Records Administration.)

As *Life* reported, "hardly had the mushroom cloud gained its full height before it became apparent that the audience was disappointed. A middle-aged woman in a lumberman's shirt remarked to a colleague, 'I really didn't mind it at all. I rather expected something much more violent.'" Onlookers used to seeing full-page Technicolor shots of mushroom clouds rising from the desert or emerging from the blue of the Pacific were unmoved by the distant pygmy cloud hardly visible in the predawn sky. Those who watched it on TV had even less to remark on—a white flare rendered in grainy gray on the small TV screen.[20]

On the other side, the pictures of the destroyed house and the battered, even dismembered, unsheltered mannequins, combined with the ongoing unofficial reports of fallout and its depredations, contradicted the can-do, can-survive message that had been scripted into the show. Now the photogenic everydayness of the mannequin families worked against the planned effect; mannequin babies torn and crushed, limbs missing, looked too much like real children or treasured dolls ripped apart by a sadist or a madman.

That wasn't the worst of it, though. The dénouement came in the third act of the journalistic play, two months later, when *Science Digest* ran an unusually long feature by Chicago-based writer Michael Amrine.[21] Amrine had pored over the abortive television and journalist tours of the houses. He had probably also polled some of his neighbors and friends and read the dailies. His article stressed what was already becoming the dominant theme of atomic literature and reportage: true, the blast effects and the fire are bad, but they're consistent with conventional, expected parts of warfare, though ratcheted up an order of magnitude. What was unfathomable was the fallout, with its unpredictable intensity, unpredictable path, and unpredictable consequences. Fallout was coming to represent the truly terrifying new horror of the atomic age, and the studied avoidance of the issue by Civil Defense officials was not going to erase it from American consciousness.

Much of Amrine's report was devoted to dismantling the reassurances offered by officials. Of the common explanation that the radiation from fallout was no more than one might expect in a radium-illuminated watch dial, he quoted a scientist's retort: "I'm used to radiation from radium, and from watches, but if I looked out and saw Michigan Avenue *paved with radium-dial wristwatches*, personally I'd call it remarkable."[22] Amrine went on to open wide the full Pandora's Box of the never-to-be-expressed: genetic damage resulting from fallout exposure and the unwillingness of scientists to attest to its harmlessness; cataracts on the eyes of Hiroshima citizens; even Nobel Prize–winning atomic geneticist H. J. Muller's prediction that "there would be as many 'genetic deaths' in Japan as there were outright casualties from the two atomic bombs." Amrine's language was dramatic: he described clouds "full of sizzling radiation dust," "radioactive rain," and "radioactive hailstones," enveloping victims and creating "a chain of hereditary weakness in the progeny of survivors for countless generations to come."[23]

Science Digest was a popular magazine directed to a general audience. Usually its articles were similar in theme and tone to those of its sister publication, *Reader's Digest*; "How Far Away Is a Rainbow?" "The Dumbest Cluck on the Farm," and "Your Jiggling Heart" were typical titles of stories from the same issue in which "Atomic Clouds" appeared. The goal of this article was unabashed, as Amrine put it in his last sentence, "in raising questions about radioactivity it shocked thoughtful people out of the habit of swallowing the bromide that 'the A-bomb is just like other bombs, only bigger.'"

Amrine confirmed the steady deadening of the sense of atomic reality as Americans came increasingly to depend on television as a substitute for personal experience. In cases like Yucca Flat, the effect of unreality was doubled by its conjunction with the tourist experience, in which certain sites became icons, shrines, pilgrimage destinations, but to approach them was to have their magic removed, to find them shrunken, dull, everyday. Even in 1953, that lumberjack-shirted woman in the crowd of witnesses was disappointed that atomic destruction wasn't "something much more violent," even as the house in front of her lay flattened, the intervening landscape stripped of all vegetation, the flash blinding, the blast earthquake-like in its intensity. The atomic holocaust had shaded imperceptibly into a tourist attraction, with its qualities of scenic excess, emotional thrill, and inevitable letdown.

Science Digest sought to reclaim the horror of atomic holocaust; *National Geographic*, by contrast, celebrated an atomic American landscape. The *Geographic* titled its June 1953 essay "Nevada Learns to Live with the Atom," neatly inserting atomic tests into the world of American tourist attractions, between the ebullient excesses of Las Vegas and pioneer sites of the frontier West. Amidst the wastelands of the Great American Desert, interspersed with the human wreckage of abandoned mines and ghost towns, the atomic sublime seemed right at home. Set against a backdrop of this scale—at least as *National Geographic* writer Samuel Matthews told the tale—tests like this one weren't really destructive; they altered the landscape, sure, but the way earthquakes and volcanoes did. "Animals Take Blasts in Stride" ran one subhead. "Town Scared Only Once" ran another. You might be "Jolted Almost Out of Bed," but "who wants to get up at 5 a.m. just for that?" For "the Sheahan family and their nine employees," living 30 miles from the shot tower at the Flats, the tests amounted to a personal festival, a chance to experience the "tremendous fireworks . . . atomic science produces inside this country."[24]

"To Nevadans, the atomic tests are only one more superlative in a State endowed with already spectacular history and scenery." This became Matthews's message. He started by recounting his own thrilling experience of the test, in the trenches next to a sergeant whose face "lifted in startled wonder" as, "within the massive cloud, paint was spilled in pastel shades. The spreading mushroom became bright pink. Purple shaded to lavender, orange turned pursy rose, and the hues flooded and overlapped in great rolls and waves of cloud. Higher and higher the cloud boiled against the bright blue-green of dawn. On the very summit ice crystals formed, cascading over the rim like pure-white surf in the sky."[25]

If you believed Matthews, men and women, waitresses, gamblers, and ranchers all over Nevada and the Great West followed the testing schedule and then, on test day, waited for the observation planes to cue them to head outside for the fireworks. "'That's how we know when to go outside to watch the flash,' Eva Vaden, Flathead Indian waitress of the near-by Oasis Café, told me." Matthews's choice of Vaden was felicitous: the magazine had treated the natives of the Marshall Islands as noble savages when it celebrated the evacuation of Bikini Atoll in 1946, and now the Indian served to place the atomic sublime firmly within the fabulous features of the American West.

There was still the problem of fallout, radiation sickness, genetic monsters, human and otherwise, walking the salt-sowed earth: all the iconography of atomic terror *Science Digest* had so convincingly invoked that same month. Matthews dealt with it by presenting a brief, authoritative statement by the Atomic Energy Commission "reassuring the Nation" that "'no person has been exposed to a harmful amount of radiation from fall-out. No person has been injured by blast waves. Successive tests have not resulted in the accumulation of a hazardous amount of radioactivity in the soil.'"[26]

Most of the dailies and the weeklies illustrated their stories with the official sequence of the exploding house. *National Geographic* by contrast used only three of those pictures among a full twelve photographs in a layout that re-presented the test as little more than an anecdote in a larger set of stories about the triumph of scientific endeavor over the dangers of the atom; about the straightforward, unterrified responses of everyday citizens to the spectacle of the mushroom cloud; about the sheer beauty of the explosion itself; and, perhaps most importantly, about the integral relationship between the spectacles of atomic explosions and the spectacles of a sublime American landscape. Americans had prevailed over the hostilities of this desert; in turn they gained sustenance from its awesome beauties. Congruently,

840   National Geographic Photographer Volkmar Wentzel

Observers Listen to an Army Briefing on the "St. Pat" Atomic Blast

7.5. Army briefing with Monopoly's Rich "Uncle" Pennybags, 1953. (Volkmar Wentzel / *National Geographic* Stock. Used with permission.)

Americans had prevailed over the terrifying possibilities of atomic explosion and in turn have come to embrace and find renewal in its beauties.

The first photograph in *National Geographic*'s sequence was mundane, a picture of everyday men in workman's caps and shirts seated in a makeshift outdoor theater while a man at a podium gesticulated toward a primitive schematic drawing of the explosion, the GI trenches, the "display area," and News Nob. Behind him, pinned to the backdrop, was a picture of the Monopoly's Rich "Uncle" Pennybags, recognizable from endless pieces of good news at "Community Chest" or bad news at "Chance."

The first full-page photo spread lay opposite. It could not have been more different.

Taken by *Las Vegas Review-Journal* photojournalist Alan Jarlson and widely circulated in national newsweeklies and pictorials, the spectacular photograph found its most sympathetic home here. Jarlson had scouted the picture well beforehand—or, more likely, AEC public relations officials had done the prep work for him, as they had for others, and the Sheahans, and their Groom Mine, had been offered up to journalists, photographers, and newsreel cameramen, to whom they provided homely visual details and homespun wisdom. But it was only Jarlson who chose to shoot the blast from the Sheahans' perspective.

Jarlson's bet paid off. It was an ideal spot from which to witness a spectacular event, as Jarlson framed the photograph—a desert wilderness with a

841   Alan Jarlson

Atomic Dawn, Many Times Noon's Brightness, Greets a Nevada Family 20 Miles Away

Nobody lives closer to the Yucca Flat test site than the Sheahans, who have watched a number of nuclear tests from their lonely Groom Mine property. Cleo the cat (left) let out a shrill meow and scurried for shelter after this blast. One Nevada atomic flash was seen as far away as Kalispell, Montana, 780 miles north.

7.6. Atomic dawn with the Sheahan family, 1953. (Photo by Alan Jarlson for *National Geographic*. Used with permission.)

mountainside for emphasis: Jarlson's picture fit neatly within a long tradition of nature images celebrating America's natural wonders appreciated by quintessential Americans, reaching back to Emanuel Leutze's *Westward the Course of Empire Takes Its Way* of 1860 and Frederick Edwin Church's *Our Banner In the Sky* of 1863. It was a full-on clothing of atomic holocaust in the garb of the romantic sublime.

Jarlson's photograph emphasized a sort of respectful awe in the face of grandeur. And he took the picture from an angle that placed his viewers as witnesses of witnessing: readers in 1953 looked at this family and, past them, at the desert landscape and then, beyond that, the great white circle of light that is the extraordinary new feature of the American landscape. The halo of the atomic explosion illuminated the clouds with a holy light and there, below, revealed an open valley, expansive and inviting.

Jarlson let the light bathe his nuclear family as well. Silhouetted against the darkened foreground, their faces and bodies were lit with a halo by the brilliance of the atomic explosion. And to make his picture complete (and to compensate for the lack of house or cabin, any other sign of domestic settlement), Jarlson included the family cat in the lower left corner of the picture; it too watched the blast.

Jarlson's picture implanted the atomic explosion firmly within the bosom of grand Western scenery, of sublime nature there to be witnessed by resident and tourist alike. So too he rendered the test a comfortable, and comforting, part of the American family, a technological innovation to be watched and wondered over, like television, but brighter, bolder, more entrancing. Beyond these, however, Jarlson managed to set the blast within a context of religious imagery—it was a holy thing, a manifestation of God in the American landscape, a modernized, Americanized version of the burning bush. In this, the picture only amplified and updated a long tradition of American attachment to its landscape, understood as a place of religious sanctity.

(Later that same year, the Sheahans would become alarmed by the increasingly "dirty" detonations of the rest of the Upshot-Knothole series. One such shot, Harry, dropped pieces of the tower from which the bomb was suspended on their land; individual shards picked up by a magnet buried the needle on the Sheahans' recently acquired Geiger counter. Shortly thereafter, Sheahan would seek to sell his property to the AEC, but his hardship claim, after some delay, was rejected. His wife would then sue after contracting cancer; her claim too was turned away. By the end of the series, more than 35,000 kilocuries of radioiodide had been released as fallout, concentrating in milk and bringing some 28,000 cases of thyroid cancer and at least 1,400 deaths, as near as the Sheahan ranch and as far away as New Hampshire.[27])

Jarlson's photograph was a triumphant visualization of the atomic sublime, in which terror is translated to beauty and danger is always held at arm's length. So too was the *National Geographic*'s smashing double-page spread, one page devoted to the explosion ("The Atomic Mushroom Leaps in Fiery Fury from Yucca Flat"), the other to soldiers advancing toward ground zero ("Ready for Combat, Troops 'Attack' in Dust and Smoke").*

To insert the atom bomb into the fabric of American landscape mythology was the unfulfilled dream of the publicists and propagandists in charge of the scripting of Upshot-Knothole-Annie. That was the reason for their wholesale importation of picturesque American democratic "types." That was the reason for the elaborate planning of side trips to the right locales, by journalists and photographers and, abortively, by television camera crews. Indeed, that was the reason the Civil Defense Administration chose to build those houses in such perfect reproduction of the dream suburban home of 1953. And, perhaps unconsciously, there was reassurance in locating that destructiveness in the great desert of the West, where it competed with earthquakes and brush fires, landslides, dust storms, hot springs and geysers, wildly exaggerated rock formations, and tall, forbidding mountain peaks. The cruel hubris of man entered the sublime power of divine landscape: it became the property, and the responsibility, of God, not man.

This wasn't a new theme, by the way. It was present in the earliest rationalizations by witnesses to the first explosion at Alamogordo, New Mexico, during the war. It was evident in the words of Harry Truman, addressed to the Japanese belligerents and the American home front after the first devastations of atomic war had scorched the earth at Hiroshima. To give the responsibility of atomic holocaust back to God, while retaining, conveniently, the political and global power it could wield, was an ideal circumstance. Time and again, Americans embraced the tactic.

What *is* remarkable about this 1953 version is the way that government failed in its attempts to promote the cause, while the mass media—newsreels, photography, journalism—stepped in to salvage what they could of the propaganda catastrophe. This was a skill learned by journalists, photographers and other representatives of the public arts during the New Deal, honed during the wartime years, and now applied without the direct instructions of government or military figures. It signaled the centrality of these media to the making, reinforcing, and redirecting of national mythology.

---

* "Dust and smoke" was the official phrase whenever the fallout cloud was described.

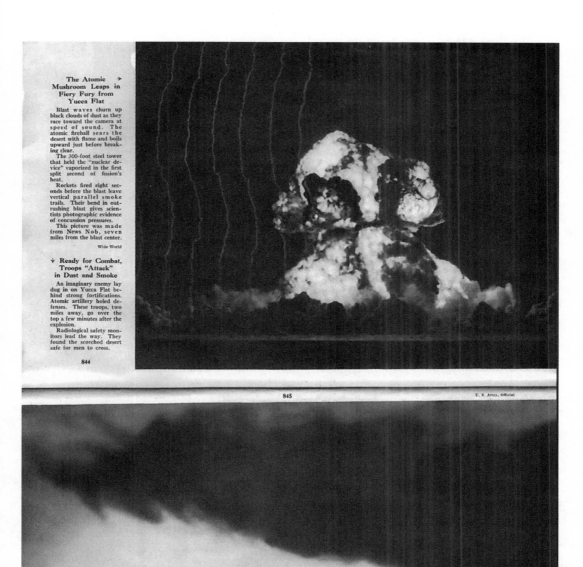

**The Atomic →
Mushroom Leaps in
Fiery Fury from
Yucca Flat**

Blast waves churn up
black clouds of dust as they
race toward the camera at
speed of sound. The
atomic fireball sears the
desert with flame and boils
upward just before break-
ing clear.

The 300-foot steel tower
that held the "nuclear device" vaporized in the first
split second of fission's
heat.

Rockets fired eight sec-
onds before the blast leave
vertical parallel smoke
trails. Their bend in out-
rushing blast gives scientists photographic evidence
of concussion pressures.

This picture was made
from News Nob, seven
miles from the blast center.

Wide World

**÷ Ready for Combat,
Troops "Attack"
in Dust and Smoke**

An imaginary enemy lay
dug in on Yucca Flat be-
hind strong fortifications.
Atomic artillery holed de-
fenses. These troops, two
miles away, go over the
top a few minutes after the
explosion.

Radiological safety mon-
itors lead the way. They
found the scorched desert
safe for men to cross.

844

845

U. S. Army, Official

7.7. Double-page spread from "Nevada Learns to Live With the Atom, *National Geographic*,
1953. Photographs by Volkmar Wentzel. (*National Geographic* Stock. Used with permission.)

Yet this was a role already being removed from the purview of those older and more experienced media and redirected to new media and new forms within those media. When military and Civil Defense officials planned out their Upshot-Knothole program, the preponderance of attention went not to press photographers and print journalists, but to television crews. In 1953, though, that redirection turned out to be premature—the TV couldn't hold the image to its proper form, couldn't record its gorgeous colors, and couldn't present its scale: it could only diminish and trivialize.

By contrast, the technical photographs of Harold Edgerton's EG&G team won the day. Those high-speed stop-motion "photographs" of the houses being destroyed easily overshadowed the puny, diminished visual puff of the live television broadcast.[28]

But Edgerton's pictures couldn't be returned to a narrative; they were snapshots seen through eyes blinking from unbearably brilliant light; they were trace memories of trauma. Smashingly powerful, they became the most reproduced and most seen of all the Civil Defense Administration's productions.

In the end, they were too successful. Rather than encouraging obedience to the instructions of Civil Defense, they became goads to fatalism. Government officials, newspaper and magazine editors, writers and layout people all had to work overtime to contain their terrifying force, and set the diminished result within a larger context of remonstrance and reassurance.

Television failed. But the future lay with television. Even at this early moment, the very diminishment and incapacity of that medium had served the planners, even if inadvertently—for millions of viewers got their first reckoning through that small gray screen, well before they encountered the terrifying realism of Edgerton's photographs. And we must remember why it was that officials paid such attention to television: it was already a ubiquitous part of American family and home life, especially among the most influential, vocal, powerful, and rich portion of the citizenry—the middle class. Television had the potential to present the same image from the same camera in millions of American living rooms. It was the medium of the future, but not yet, at least when it came to making bold, histrionic statements of national purpose.

The immediate failure, and incipient triumph, of television and its new form of cultural rhetoric may have been one important lesson of the incredible exploding house fiasco of Yucca Flat, Nevada, in March 1953. But the less evident event may have been more significant: the uniting of atomic holocaust, American nature, and the suburban home into one complex and highly charged myth.

It was a fool's errand, this campaign to present atomic holocaust as a survivable natural event. Four months earlier, on November 1, 1952, Operation Ivy had vaporized Elugelab Atoll in the first successful test of a hydrogen bomb. Even as Civil Defense and AEC officials were preparing their 1953 campaign, its message had been rendered moot; no house could survive, no makeshift shelter protect against the vastly more destructive new weapon.

Lookout Mountain Studios had filmed Operation Ivy, and by the time the scripted events of Upshot-Knothole Annie were playing out, the studio had a black-and-white rough cut of the thermonuclear event. By December of 1953, when a more elaborate color version had begun to circulate in official circles, AEC's "Classification and Information Services" bureaucracy was engaged in a furious debate about the wisdom or necessity of releasing the film to the public. It was not until April 1954 that the film went public, and it ran repeatedly for weeks on network television. It was a terrifying testament to the conjunction of the power of nuclear holocaust and the power of television that President Eisenhower was obliged to speak directly of the matter. "The greater any of these apprehensions, the greater is the need that we look at them clearly, face to face, without fear, like honest, straightforward Americans," he told the nation, in a televised address.[29]

But such a clear, honest, and straightforward look at the newly amplified nuclear age was not to be. Within the year, the Civil Defense Administration would try again, rebuilding the nuclear neighborhood, setting up bomb shelters and populating them with mannequins for the test sequence given the homely name of Teapot (suggesting atomic warfare was "a tempest in a teapot" and evoking the nursery rhyme, "short and stout," further diminishing the event). This time, *Life* returned to show a house far less damaged and mannequins still relatively unscathed, in postures more comical than frightful.

It was in 1957 that Lookout Mountain Studios produced its finest, and most duplicitous, collation of films and photographs, depicting the disastrous Plumbbob series, with its seething clouds of fallout and its irradiation of the nation's milk supply as a luscious lollipop of a confection, America's soldiers as prepared for anything, and America's cars, trucks, buses, houses, and towns readily adapted to protect us from the inconveniences that came with such a thrilling spectacle. But it was too late. The very thing that Civil Defense and the U.S. military had feared—an organized anti-nuclear-warfare movement, capable of repeatedly declaring the futility and the horror of atomic war—had come into being. Nineteen fifty-seven was the year America's pediatrician, Dr. Benjamin Spock, joined a consortium of highly respectable American public figures to found the Committee for a Sane

Nuclear Policy. It was also the year Nevil Shute's acclaimed nuclear apocalypse novel, *On The Beach*, hit the bestseller list; two years later, it would be released as a major Hollywood movie, directed by the hugely successful Hollywood producer Stanley Kramer, with a stellar cast that featured Gregory Peck and Ava Gardner. Striving to control, to redirect, the imagery of atomic holocaust, official bureaucracies and military propagandists would never quite manage to stay ahead of the narrative.

CHAPTER 8

Lucy!

At approximately the moment that two perfect suburban mannequin families waited to be blown asunder in the atomic desert of Nevada for the sake of a planned primetime TV event later canceled by radiation and fallout, nearly three-quarters of American TV watchers were engrossed in another explosion of a far different, atomically unstable, family. It was Monday evening, January 19, 1952, and Lucy Ricardo was about to give birth to Little Ricky on *I Love Lucy*, while in Hollywood, California, actress Lucille Ball was, in real life, giving birth to Desi Arnaz, Jr.*

Of all the shows to appear on the built-in screens of Levittown's televisions, and all the other televisions that glowed across America, none had the resonance or longevity of *I Love Lucy*. Its effects are with us still, as a point of comparison with each new iteration of the American family, from celebrity marriages in the supermarket tabloids to the travails of gay marrieds dealing with an obstreperous toddler on prime-time TV.

The show debuted with the story of two young marrieds in New York City, he a somewhat unsuitable Cuban bandleader of a husband, she a vaudeville veteran trapped in domestic bliss and struggling to escape. It ended with a family in the suburbs—kids, house, lawn and all—some six years later. It took the trajectory of *Miracle on 34th Street* and gave it an antic energy, a claustrophobic sense of urgency, an emotional honesty far more recognizable than the posturing sincerity of Doris, Fred, and Mr. Kringle. Most

---

* Though the televised and actual births took place on the same day, the fictional birth was recorded some months before; just exactly what time of day Desi Arnaz, Jr., was born is not publicly recorded.

importantly, it described in disguised form the uneasy place of the ideal of American womanhood in Cold War America.

Even the supporting actors had an acidulous bite. *Lucy*'s Fred wasn't a professional man with a gently idealistic turn of character, ready to believe in Santa and take a serious-faced child as his own. He was a cigar-chomping, bald, hoarse-voiced, misanthropic landlord whose true pleasure lay in watching other people duke it out—in the ring, or upstairs from his own apartment at the Ricardo's, where he'd egg Ricky into confrontations with Lucy, displacing his own frustration and hatred of his wife, Ethel. Everyone knew that Fred drank hard whiskey when he wasn't on screen: drank, swore, and pushed Ethel around just as much as he dared and no further. He didn't work and he didn't want work. Ethel wasn't much better. She had a voice that could etch her initials on her husband's whiskey tumbler and a distaff version of Fred's petty meddling viciousness. These were survivors; you knew they'd live through the atomic attack on Manhattan, shielding their own bodies with those of Ricky and Lucy. In the great fallout-shelter debate of the mid-50s— should you take a gun inside to ward off your neighbors when they came begging for the provisions and the protection that was barely enough for your own family?—everyone watching *I Love Lucy* knew where Fred and Ethel stood.

And they were just the supporting cast. Americans nationwide tuned in to CBS at 9 p.m. on Mondays to watch a prison drama of sorts in which four loudly inflated, joyously self-pitying cellmates schemed to escape their circumstances and slowly, undramatically, those circumstances changed without enlarging the scope of the characters or granting them serenity, wisdom, or contentment. It took the American Dream and turned it inside out.

Moreover, week after week, *I Love Lucy* directly addressed one of the central tensions in postwar American life—the role of women (and of men!)— and it did so in ways that profoundly undermined the picture of suburban-homemaker bliss so heavily touted by America's most powerful institutions.

If you perused the ads, read the magazines, and watched the rest of the TV lineup during the *Lucy* years, you'd have seen two broadly drawn caricatures of the new American woman: the happy, well-adjusted homebound director of consumption, making happy workers and happy well-adjusted children; and the anxious, bitter, maladjusted neurotic whose frustrations found their source within—in liver imbalance or constipation, or unspoken "female trouble" or a mild mental illness—and needed only a pill, a better cigarette, a new couch, a vacuum cleaner, to be righted. What you didn't see were professional women, working women, women in part-time jobs to provide the extra income necessary to satisfy the demands of a new consumption lifestyle: women, in other words, who populated the postwar world in significant numbers and provided a context and a contrast to the idealized American housewife.

Lucy filled a gigantic gulf between the idealized and the actual experiences of women in the Cold War years. Not until Betty Friedan's declaration, "Women are *People* Too!" in the September 1960 issue of *Good Housekeeping*, was there a voice, a personality, a persona, that could speak to what Friedan would call "a strange stirring, a dissatisfied groping, a yearning, a search that is going on in the minds of women."[1] Nowhere, that is, except *Lucy*.

Lucy hit the 1951 fall season with a roar.[2] It premiered on CBS in a plum spot. *The Hollywood Reporter* announced that *Lucy* "fulfills, in its own particular niche, every promise of the often harassed new medium." *Variety* declared it "one of the slickest TV entertainment shows to date . . . Monday's preem was a resounding click." By February, *Lucy* was getting major play in the big-circulation weeklies. By the end of that first season, it had pushed Milton Berle out of the number-one slot and muscled that long-running and hugely popular variety hour into the corner. By April, Lucille Ball was on the cover of *Time*, upstaging the great battle over Communism in America, *Chambers v. Hiss*.[3]

Producer, writer, and behind-the-scenes genius Jess Oppenheimer put the case for *Lucy*'s significance directly. "To me," he wrote, "a situation comedy series is much like visiting a friend's family. You don't know what they are going to say, but you know how each person is going to react in a situation and how each of them talks. The more consistency there is, the more comfortable you are, and the more you can enjoy everything that happens."[4]

That was part of the function television began to take unto itself—to offer structure to the social opportunities and the anxieties of the new American life—and *I Love Lucy* represented the front line, in this as in so much of the evolving medium. *Lucy* was a remarkable blend of novelty and normalcy, of innovation and repetition, of topicality and safety.

People watched *Lucy* every week, on the same day and at the same time, for the entire first life of the show, from the fall of 1951 to May 1957. By the end of that first season, more than eleven million of the fifteen million American families with TVs were tuned to *Lucy*—one-fifth of the American population, but a significant fifth, the trenders. And year after year, the numbers went up. By its final season, *I Love Lucy* had 43.7 percent of TV-watching households, and by then, nearly 80 percent of American families had TVs.[5] There were few other mass culture events so firmly anchoring American life, from the commonality of ritual to the commonly shared narrative, to the common topic of conversation the next day among citizens otherwise separated by deep crevasses of difference.

Families clustered around the electronic hearth, intently watching allegories about proper life, proper behavior, acted out in studios, beamed simultaneously to an entire nation. That was the ideal of early Cold War television. *Lucy* fulfilled and yet exploded that idyll. The idealized suburban families of *Leave it to Beaver* or *Father Knows Best* or *The Donna Reed Show* never came close to the sweeping popularity of *Lucy*, where viewers gathered to see a desperate, thwarted woman and a slippery, fast-talking *Cubano* uneasily yoked by marriage, ambition, and necessity struggling to stay afloat in a cutthroat city.

* * *

Lucy and *Lucy* were both hybrids, ideally suited to populate the postwar American cultural landscape. Lucille Ball was simultaneously movie-star gorgeous, vaudeville blowsy, and rubber-face, rubber-body clownish.* Film studio executives hadn't known what to do with her, and television executives weren't much more visionary.

From the first moment of her appearance on *I Love Lucy*'s pilot, what set Lucille apart from other actors or comedians and Lucy apart from other comic television characters was the sense that she shared a core experience with everyone around her, and the sense of those around her—the writers, the live audience members, those at home in Levittown and Lansdowne, city, suburb and farm—that they were all in on something, something that could be disruptive and threatening, or could be slyly, even uproariously, tipsily, transformed.

From the beginning, *Lucy* grounded itself in the opposite of the prevailing suburban Cold War idyll. It was relentlessly urban in setting. Its family wasn't even a family until that child-bearing episode two years into the show; Lucy and Ricky weren't calm, selfless, or wise enough to raise a child. And the show thrived on tension—not tension resolved, but tension impossible to resolve or escape, modulating in rises and falls, in repeated patterns of loud and soft, direct and oblique, female and male. And at the core of *Lucy* was that broader conflict, better left unspoken, better acted out than admitted or acted on: the continual struggle, and continual failure, of the characters to carve out an alternative to the prevailing archetype of the ideal

---

* The first seasons often showed her as plump and dowdy; in real life she was twice pregnant during the filming of the first two years of the show, including the pilot.

Cold War life, and in mirror image the continuing struggle, and continuing failure, of viewers to live out, and live up to, the newly delineated roles of proper Cold War citizenry.

The pilot episode set the tenor of the show. In synopsis, it would appear to have a simple enough plot and an obvious enough theme. Bandleader Ricky is about to audition for his own television show. Lucy wants in. She deep-sixes Ricky's guest star in order to take his place. She's wildly successful—so successful that the network chooses Lucy and not Ricky for the series. She turns it down in order to save her marriage and her man.

It's in the details that both plot and theme upend expectations. Lucy auditions as a male, a clown. Ricky sees through her scheme, but he lets her play it out, lets her upstage him and win the contest between man and woman. When he comes home, defeated, she's neither repentant nor exultant. She's both, and Lucille Ball used every bit of her talent to play these two conflicting emotions simultaneously. When she asks him what *he* wants her to do, he reiterates his sardonic caricature of the newly ascendant ideal of the Cold War suburban housewife: "A wife who is just a wife. . . . [to] clean the house for me, hand me my pipe when I come home at night, cook for me, and be the mama for my children." It's a miserable slavery he envisions for Lucy, and up until now she has fought him all the way—fought and won. Now, it seems, she relents. She hands Ricky his pipe, and then she tells him she has a surprise.

For her capitulation to be complete, that surprise must be the announcement that she's pregnant, with the child who will complete this family, take center stage in her life, resolve her frustrations, and provide her with the new and appropriate role. And Ricky is thunderstruck, overjoyed. But Lucy's surprise is *not* the kid that Lucille Ball was at that moment bearing in real life.* It's a pie that she's baked, and given all the slapstick that has come before, we know what to expect. We wait for the pie-in-the-face ending that will defuse all this tension. And it doesn't come. Instead, we're left with the asymmetrical frontal shot of two failures, a man bested by his wife and failed in his ambitions, standing, disgruntled; a woman tousled, double-chinned, in an apron, holding an obviously inadequate offering to the kitchen god.

That's the final shot, but it's still not the final word on male–female relations in the pilot. For audiences had already seen, and loved, the audition scene at the nightclub. We know that because the pilot was shot in front of

---

* Lucille Ball was pregnant, not with "little Ricky," who was to provide such drama the next season, but her daughter, Lucie Arnaz, who would never appear as a real or fictional character on *I Love Lucy*.

8.1 Last image of the pilot for *I Love Lucy*

a live audience, and no laugh track was added. We also know that because of the way the cast—not just Lucy and Ricky, but the extras playing patrons of the nightclub, and the band members in the background—are so palpably reacting to the improvisatory craziness that Lucy, Ricky, and the writers have brought to the scene. Ricky knows it's Lucy playing the clown-mime, and he eggs her on. He thrives on her increasing wildness. She starts to act outside the script (we know this from Oppenheimer's memoir); he steps up to the challenge. The actors playing band members and nightclub patrons start to crack up. The audience response swells in the soundtrack, and there are pauses in the action to settle things down enough so that the dialogue can be heard. At one point Lucy cracks Ricky up and actor Desi just gives up the attempt at self-control. This is great stuff.

So Ricky's failure and Lucy's triumph create a genuine comic and dramatic dilemma. By rights, Lucy *should* win. But when Ricky comes home, he slumps disconsolately in his chair, his husband-throne. Suddenly this slapstick comedy has turned very serious. For a moment, the postwar American woman really *is* going to take the job away from her man—and the fact that he's Cuban and an entertainer and a bit of a buffoon isn't enough to dull the knife-edge of this postwar anxiety.

Then she lets him dictate their future, and there's a palpable relief of tension. But that also threatens to puncture the entire comic premise, to evacuate all that antic energy that made the nightclub scene so spectacularly successful. How, then, to construct a resolution that adheres to the necessities of that cultural moment, while maintaining the tension that drives the comedy?

The writers, and Lucy and Ricky too, maneuver their way out of the dilemma by leaving it hanging. Somewhere in that final scene, it becomes clear the conflict's not located *between* man and woman, but *within* each of them. Ricky says he just wants Lucy to be a docile, obedient servant to his wishes. But we've already seen him thrive on the energy of her rebelliousness—it saves him. Lucy promises Ricky she's going to be a good wife, but we don't believe it for a minute. Both Lucy and Ricky want the two antithetical outcomes—the nuclear family and the egalitarian alternative. This little half-hour pilot presented American viewers with a mirror of their own ambivalence, their own irresolution. No wonder CBS bought the show; no wonder it ran for years; no wonder it drew the largest audiences of any show of its time.

*   *   *

I Love Lucy discovered, renewed, even invented crucial features of the American cultural landscape that other shows, other media, and other cultural icons couldn't give their due. It recognized, reflected, and played with the new space-time continuum of the Cold War.

One can think of *Lucy* as having multiple time-identities: the half-hour; the week that intervened, into which, I've proposed, viewers could themselves speculate, imagine, interject, and argue over just *what was going on at Lucy's* while we weren't watching; the stretch of the season; the retrospective of summer reruns; and the long sweep of the show's six years. This sort of game had been played in radio, from which Lucille Ball and the show originated, but it was novel in television

So too with space. Up until *Lucy*, television had pretty ham-handedly tried to reproduce the spatial richness of the movies, or it severely restricted the space within which a show played out. Radio, by contrast, had always succeeded by employing suggestive hints from which the audience constructed an expansive world. *Lucy* too conjured its geography by suggestion, and it wasn't the geography pundits and propagandists for the new American lifestyle urged on us.

We think of American life in the Cold War era as centered in the suburban subdivisions that sprang up during the first years after the war and continued to grow throughout the next two decades and beyond. Certainly this was the story that the principal news media took up and developed into a repeating soap opera. Magazines like *Life* and *Newsweek*, even the tonier ones like *Harper's*, spotted the demographic trend and saw the opportunity to make an American narrative out of it—a family epic. That's what *Miracle on 34th Street* presaged; it's the passion play Levittowners lined up to audition for. It was the establishment myth of the era.

Lucy provided an important alternative to the suburban world, both for the urban dwellers still in the big cities and for those who'd already moved out. It romanticized city life, but it also shrank it, derided it, made it into a place which you'd be glad to leave behind. The romantic city was always outside the apartment window or the camera's gaze, in spaces to which Lucy sought to escape. The claustrophobic, dystopian city was what the camera lingered on: the crowded apartment, the dingy fire escape, the outmoded kitchen.

Lucy gave the glamorous city to Ricky. It was the place to which he rushed, excited, in the morning; it was the place of monumental challenges and heroic conquests, implied but rarely revealed, from which he returned at night. Its allure was rendered all the more palpable by Lucy's yearning. The city of desire was right outside the picture window in the living room of the apartment, a panorama of light, scale, and drama in front of which Lucy fumed and schemed to break out of the domestic sphere that was her fate.

The apartment was Ricky's staging ground, a place to rest, relax, and regroup. It was Lucy's prison. Anyone who has lived in a New York City apartment knows that its universal common characteristic is its size: *too small*—too small for the scale of living appropriate to its occupants. Even a rudimentary blueprint plan of the Ricardo apartment shows the three rooms—bedroom, living room, and kitchen—to be crammed with furniture, so crowded, in fact, that it's difficult to imagine how four people could sit together in the living room without kicking each other, impossible to imagine how two people could have undressed, slept, awoken, dressed and exited without killing each other. *Lucy* revealed the urban life that suburbanites had rejected and pointed up the comparative spaciousness of even the smallest suburban house. But the claustrophobia of city domesticity didn't apply to Ricky, who could leave at any time, day or night, and did. It was instead the legacy of crushing inequity against which Lucy fought so valiantly, so hilariously.[6]

The living room belonged to both sexes. Because it was Ricky's too, it took on a certain inviting quality. Pendent to the living room was the kitchen, a stage for the playing out of conflict and comedy, highlighting the narratives and themes of thwarted womanhood by presenting the woman's sphere as essentially impoverished.

The kitchen was, first of all, dingy. It was painted a muted color that came out as middle-register gray in the black-and-white set, as did the appliances and the countertop. The refrigerator door was even dirty around the handle, a mark of its age but also of Lucy's refusal to make do.

8.2. Lucy's first kitchen

It was utilitarian, drably so. In an age of novel kitchen appliances, of stylish sinks, and recognizably new refrigerators and stoves—an age, that is, in which the model year planned obsolescence of the automobile and the Levittown house extended fully into the kitchen, including such novelties as Formica countertops and all-steel minimal-modern cabinetry, diffuse overhead fluorescent lighting, and the like—what marked out Lucy's kitchen was its lack of any indications of respect or interest.

Observations tumble over one another here: compare *Ozzie and Harriet*'s kitchen (1952–1953) or the kitchen in *Father Knows Best* and you see the difference immediately. Partly that was a matter of suburbanization, but it was also a result of the odd relegation of Lucy's domestic life to a class well below hers—to the drab surroundings of *The Honeymooners*, the skit-series in the comedy-variety *Jackie Gleason Show* (in weekend prime time from 1952 to 1959) that sketched the cramped lives of bus driver Ralph Kramden and

8.3. Ad for Hotpoint featuring Ozzie and Harriet's kitchen, 1953

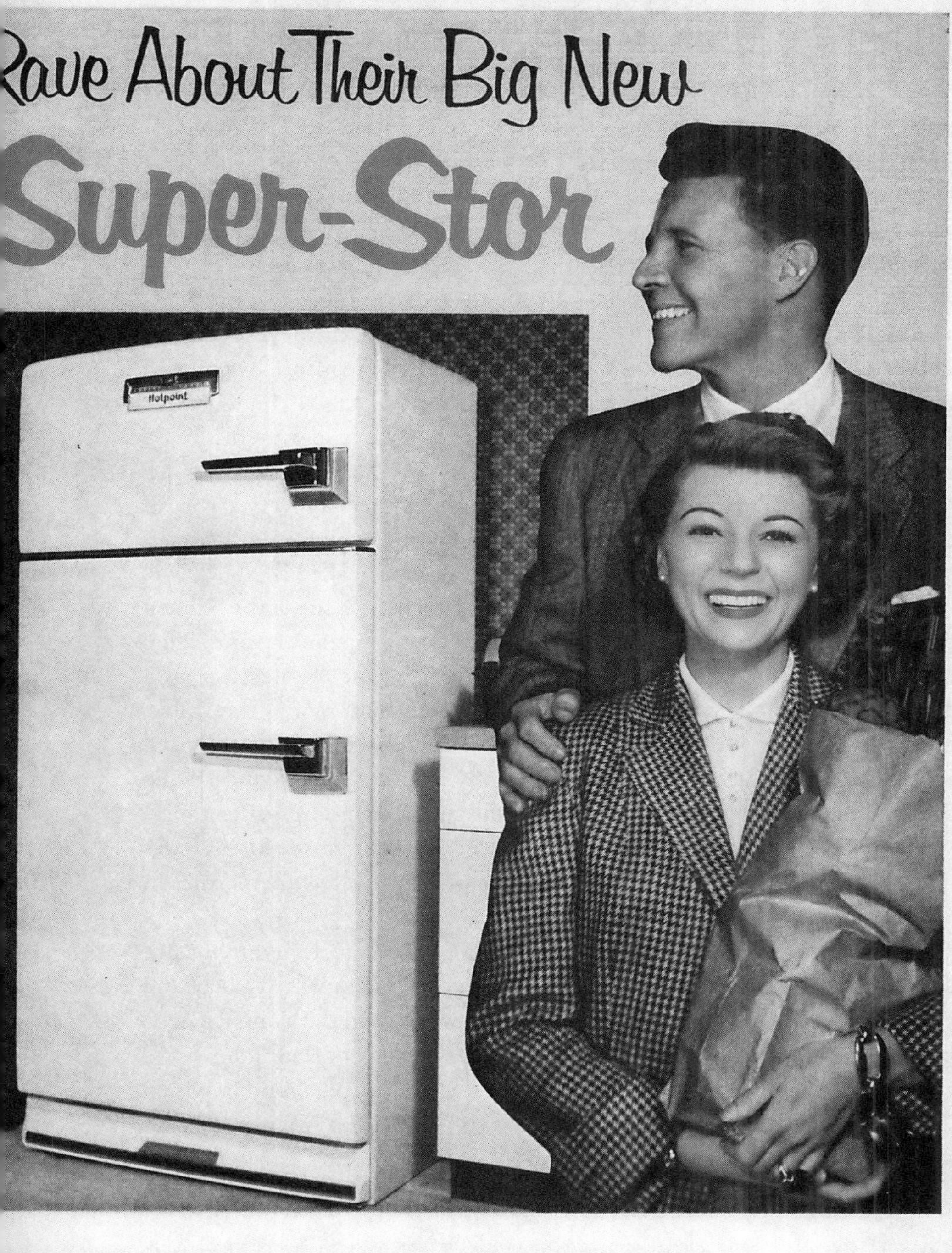
Rave About Their Big New
Super-Stor
Hotpoint

his wife Alice, trapped in a working-class tenement life from which they'd never rise or even escape.*

On top of it, the social life in that kitchen was deeply impoverished; whereas Lucy and Ricky "laughed, loved, and lived" in the living room, the recurrent theme played out in the kitchen was Ricky's absent presence as he ate his breakfast behind his newspaper, unappreciative of the meal, unappreciative of Lucy's appearance, her conversation, her very presence. The kitchen was a space not of informality and give-and-take between two separate but equal spheres of agency (as it was in the suburban domestics of the '50s and '60s) but of the master-servant relationship of the sexes.

Giving Lucy the drably old-fashioned, unappetizing room wasn't just a slap in the face to her, nor even a simple declaration of misogyny. Lucy redecorated the living room, she conspired to get new furniture or paint or better light in there. She chose not to do the same for the kitchen. It was a prison in part because Lucy *saw* it as such, as a place below attention. It's important to stress here that a woman, Madelyn Pugh, was writing this show along with two men, and that she was evidently integral to every aspect of the script, from the gags to the final draft. In addition, Lucille Ball herself read the scripts with a drill sergeant's eye and a tyrannical will.

The result was evident in the subtlety with which the issue of the kitchen played out. In an era that saw Margaret Mead praising the multiprofessional capabilities of the American housewife, dignifying the "profession" as a form of high-skill labor repaid in currency greater than money (gratitude, status, love, creative flexibility, status, even power, both within the family and in the larger economy—that is, *buying* power)—Madelyn Pugh and Lucille Ball and their male collaborators spat on the suburban premise, the housewife promise, with every gesture in that kitchen.[7] For them, the kitchen was a stage to explore, rather than to resolve, the conflict over women's roles in Cold War America.

There's an episode we have to introduce in order to fully emphasize the revolutionary treatment of *Lucy*'s kitchen, the one in which Ricky and Fred bet the girls that they can be better housewives than the women can be breadwinners. It's the "Candy Factory" episode (formally titled "Job Switching") that opened the second season, most famous for the scene in which Lucy and Ethel are subjected to an assembly line speed-up and resort to eating the chocolates rather than be found wanting and fired.

---

* In some senses, *Lucy* had a good deal in common with *The Jackie Gleason Show*: both of them pitted celebrity and entertainment success—"How sweet it is!"—against the drab backdrop of urban apartment life. But Jackie celebrated his escape; Lucy fought and lost.

8.4. The assembly line scene from the "Switching Places" episode during *I Love Lucy*'s first season

That scene is extraordinary: it draws from Charlie Chaplin's *Modern Times* and carries in an attenuated form the same class struggle themes. Work is demeaning; bosses are mean spirited, inhumane slave drivers; the environment is dreadful and the physical demands of mass production are taxing even as the specific tasks are mind-numbingly repetitive and unrewarding despite the skill they require.

(But that's the *old* work. The new work, the work that Ricky does, and the work that Lucy wants, is of a different order.)

The scene is brilliant, no question about it.

So we tend to forget the counter-scene, though to read the script is to see how essentially identical a critique of woman's work that one is, as well. It takes place in the kitchen: Ricky is making *arroz con pollo*, Cuban chicken with rice, and we see both the fabulous-exploding-pressure-cooker-chicken-hits-the-ceiling gag *and* the endlessly-swelling-malevolent-amoeba-of-cooked-rice gag.

It's a scene that could be (*will be*, in other shows and other media) granted its full place as a sight of desperation and hopelessness. And its thematic punch was in a way greater than the toned-down radicalism of the candy factory scene; the haplessness of these men, and the comeuppance for their own hubris (Ricky was so proud of his little housekeeping "innovations" until this came along) has to be set against the developing sense that it's not Lucy's and Ethel's shortcomings that overwhelm them in the workplace or at home—it's the nastiness of the system itself. The episode ends with Ricky

8.5. Catastrophic kitchen scene from "Job Switching"

and Fred proffering chocolates as their peace offering, twisting the knife one final time: the men have had their just deserts and yet will go forth tomorrow to their light-struck freedom of street and club, bar and park; while Lucy and Ethel have lost their taste for one of the few rewards a woman is given, on her birthday, on Easter, on Valentine's Day. They have come through this misadventure not enlarged and extended, but distended, deadened, even poisoned.

That the next week's episode is utterly different seems to reflect the disjointed logic of television. But television wasn't exactly disjointed, even then. Rather, it was developing a new sort of logic, knitting itself together across the week-by-week of episodes on the same show, and even across the channel-by-channel of different shows that might follow each other over the course of an evening. *I Love Lucy* was one of the most important sites for the sort of experimentation and innovation that brought that new logic into being.

In this case, the sequel to "Job Switching" was "The Saxophone," another classic episode in which Lucy sought to join Ricky's band as saxophonist, knowing only one, dreadfully lame, approximation of one song, "Glow Worm." The episode serves multiple purposes. It returns the fatal hubris to Lucy (reasserting the dominant misanthropic theme that Lucy is, always, not just wishing to escape but believing with "typical" self-deception that she has the wherewithal to do so) and the sphere of breezy competence and even artistry to Ricky.

It reintroduces the essential dyad between the apartment's confinement and the brilliantly lit stage of the Tropicana. Most of all, though, it returns us to the largest narrative of *I Love Lucy*: the story of upward mobility as an interpenetration of space and time. "Job Switching" described the fatalistic proletarian world made infamous by the "Honeymooners" episodes of the *Jackie Gleason Show*. "The Saxophone" took apart the dreams of success, celebrity, stardom, and escape and placed it in a new landscape of limitless possibility. For that was what Lucy dreamed of, and what she could never attain.

We need to pause for a moment and confront what seems a series of fundamental contradictions and to point up the ways the show encouraged the contradictions even as it seemed to resolve them. *Lucy* presented the glamorous, celebrity city to an audience predominantly located in unglamorous suburbs. It treated the home, and family life more generally, as claustrophobic. It presented a woman trapped, desperate to escape, destined never to succeed, to an audience at least half of whom were women who were in similarly constricted circumstances, granted similarly constricted roles and opportunities. And it pretty much ignored the central function of the Cold War nuclear family: childrearing.

8.6. Lucy as a hipster, from "The Saxophone" episode during *I Love Lucy*'s second season.

But what *I Love Lucy* did with these themes was fully bound up with the pact between the cast of characters and the audience. In each case, the very qualities evoked—anxiety, frustration, conflict—could be recognized by the suburban viewer, and simultaneously recognized as located in spaces, places and circumstances emphatically *not mine*. Women could empathize with Lucy's frustration, binding their own to hers, without having to face squarely the fact that their frustration was equally as systemic, equally as permanent and inescapable, because *Lucy is different! Lucy is crazy!* She ignored her child! She connived against her husband! She sought a stardom and significance far beyond her bad, "Glow Worm" talents!

Men, too. Ricky was, after all, a sort of exaggerated stereotype of postwar American maleness: his identity was bound up in his workplace success; he palled around with his male buddies; he loved the fights. But holding Ricky up to comedic ridicule, showing his absurd vanity, his preening, the gap between his vision of himself as a *real man* and his own demeanor and behavior—all this could awaken male viewers' fears (Am I like that? Are people laughing at me behind my back? Am I inches from failure?), and in so doing dramatically ratchet up the energy and tension men might bring to watching the show. But they, like their wives, could take comfort in the differentness of their circumstances. Ricky didn't live in Levittown. Ricky was a foreigner. He was a "spic." He was an entertainer. He wasn't even a musician— he waved that wand around, he banged those little drums, but mostly he just preened and postured for the amusement of his audience—*people like us*.

Finally, though, it's important to see that *I Love Lucy* also embedded all its cultural conflicts in an envelope of comforting consensus. It was, in the end, not that different than all the other domestic sitcoms in which a conflict arises, the wise parental heads step in, and all is resolved. But with *Lucy*, the audience took on the parental role; *you* saw the solution, and when Lucy and Ricky resolved their conflicts, you were comforted. If they didn't, you saw that your solutions, your circumstances, in fact, *would* have resolved them, and you were comforted. If she'd only pay attention to the child, she'd see how rewarding her life could be—as mine is, when I look beyond the momentary frustrations of everyday life. If he'd only get a *real* job, he wouldn't have to turn himself into a caricature every night at the club. If they'd only move to Connecticut, have another child, develop community connections and relationships, they'd be relieved of the tensions and frustrations of city life.

Lucy did finally take that last piece of advice. But doing so took the fundamental creative tension out of the show and broke the complex connection between cast and audience, between *them* and *us* as *them* and *not-us*. Sensing the emptiness ahead, Lucille Ball, and *Lucy,* exited gracefully and, thanks to the miracle of reruns, returned as nostalgia.

* * *

The first two seasons of *Lucy* set the foundation. They were seasons about stability: Ricky had the same job in the same nightclub; he and Lucy had the same apartment within which the fundamentals of their romantic and social life are stable; Lucy's disappointments and frustrations were recast week after week. Ricky redecorated the club; Lucy got new furniture. Outside the show, in the larger dyad of performance and audience, this stability provided reassurance both in countering the fears and instabilities of the Cold War years, and in mirroring or providing enlightening contrast to the work and leisure, public and family life experienced by those who watched the show. As I've said, *Lucy* operated in something close to real time, and thereby it salved the impatience of Americans caught up in the dream of upward mobility and economic progress and the reality of an increasingly repetitive and regimented life. To watch *Lucy* every Monday at the same time was to redeem repetition as security.

Naturally, one very big transformation occurred in those first two seasons: Ricky and Lucy had a baby. But this in some ways simply confirmed the pace of change in postwar life, reaffirmed the centrality of the inward-focused family, providing comfort at a moment when even the most bland and mundane of cultural outlets were peddling fear and even panic.

Just a few weeks before the first Lucy pilot aired, *Popular Mechanics* ran (at the urging of the government, and almost certainly with government editorial help) a series of articles titled "If the A-Bombs Burst—Here Is What to Expect, What You Can Do Today to Prepare Yourself, What You Can Do Then to Survive."

The first installment began with a New York City secretary declaring, "There's nothing you can do to save yourself " and "a nervous executive" in Chicago reacting to a lightning flash: "he can't help wondering whether the bomb would demolish his home and kill his family in a suburb 14 miles away. . . . Now, 4-1/2 years after the atom bomb dropped toward its first target, the threat of a nuclear fireball hangs over every major American city . . . the crushing reality that an atom bomb destined for his neighborhood might even now be winging its way across the curve of the world."[8] Articles like these weren't simply meant to present the facts; they were often grippingly specific and horrifically suggestive. Here's one passage from the second installment of the *Popular Mechanics* series: "White coughed until he

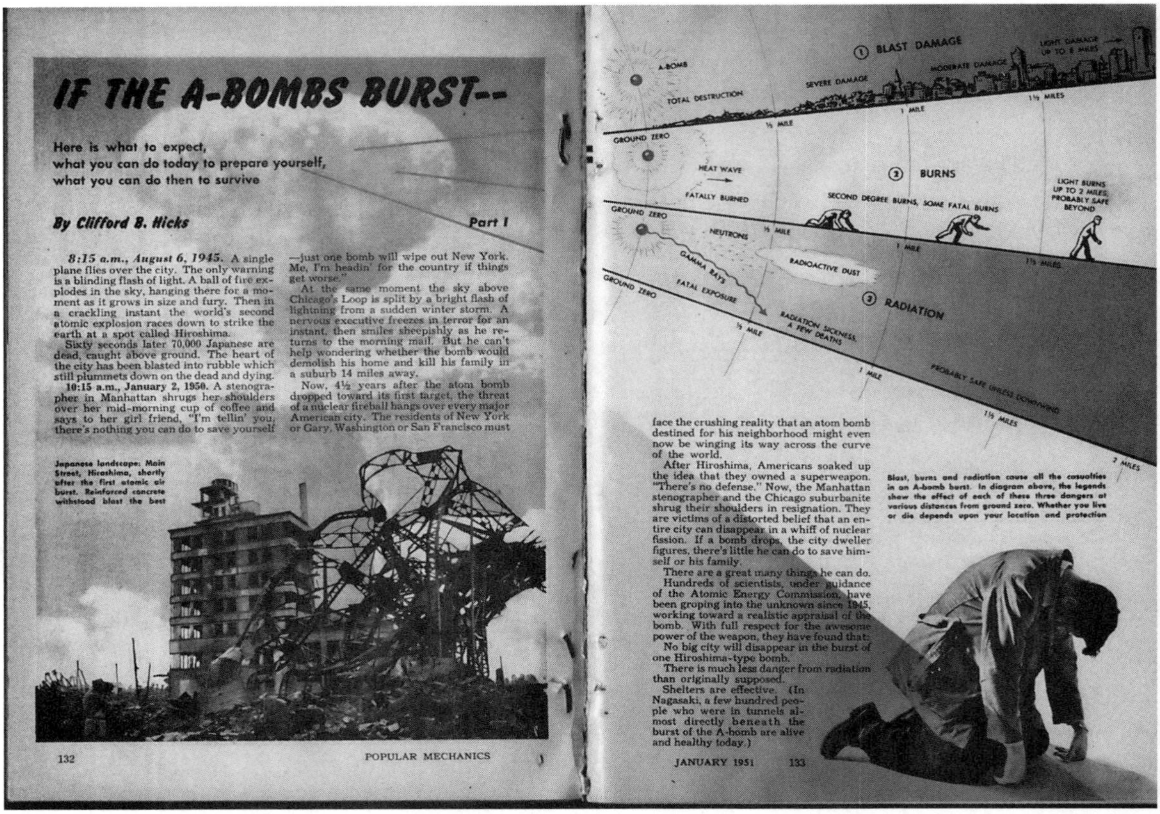

IF THE A-BOMBS BURST--

Here is what to expect, what you can do today to prepare yourself, what you can do then to survive

By Clifford B. Hicks

Part I

8:15 a.m., August 6, 1945. A single plane flies over the city. The only warning is a blinding flash of light. A ball of fire explodes in the sky, hanging there for a moment as it grows in size and fury. Then in a crackling instant the world's second atomic explosion races down to strike the earth at a spot called Hiroshima.

Sixty seconds later 70,000 Japanese are dead, caught above ground. The heart of the city has been blasted into rubble which still plummets down on the dead and dying.

10:15 a.m., January 2, 1950. A stenographer in Manhattan shrugs her shoulders over her mid-morning cup of coffee and says to her girl friend, "I'm tellin' you, there's nothing you can do to save yourself—just one bomb will wipe out New York. Me, I'm headin' for the country if things get worse."

At the same moment the sky above Chicago's Loop is split by a bright flash of lightning from a sudden winter storm. A nervous executive freezes in terror for an instant, then smiles sheepishly as he returns to the morning mail. But he can't help wondering whether the bomb would demolish his home and kill his family in a suburb 14 miles away.

Now, 4½ years after the atom bomb dropped toward its first target, the threat of a nuclear fireball hangs over every major American city. The residents of New York or Gary, Washington or San Francisco must face the crushing reality that an atom bomb destined for his neighborhood might even now be winging its way across the curve of the world.

After Hiroshima, Americans soaked up the idea that they owned a superweapon. "There's no defense." Now, the Manhattan stenographer and the Chicago suburbanite shrug their shoulders in resignation. They are victims of a distorted belief that an entire city can disappear in a whiff of nuclear fission. If a bomb drops, the city dweller figures, there's little he can do to save himself or his family.

There are a great many things he can do.

Hundreds of scientists, under guidance of the Atomic Energy Commission, have been groping into the unknown since 1945, working toward a realistic appraisal of the bomb. With full respect for the awesome power of the weapon, they have found that:

No big city will disappear in the burst of one Hiroshima-type bomb.

There is much less danger from radiation than originally supposed.

Shelters are effective. (In Nagasaki, a few hundred people who were in tunnels almost directly beneath the burst of the A-bomb are alive and healthy today.)

Japanese landscape: Main Street, Hiroshima, shortly after the first atomic air burst. Reinforced concrete withstood blast the best

Blast, burns and radiation cause all the casualties in an A-bomb burst. In diagram above, the legends show the effect of each of these three dangers at various distances from ground zero. Whether you live or die depends upon your location and protection

A-BOMB
TOTAL DESTRUCTION
SEVERE DAMAGE
① BLAST DAMAGE
MODERATE DAMAGE
LIGHT DAMAGE UP TO 8 MILES
GROUND ZERO
½ MILE
1 MILE
1½ MILES
HEAT WAVE
FATALLY BURNED
② BURNS
SECOND DEGREE BURNS, SOME FATAL BURNS
LIGHT BURNS UP TO 2 MILES, PROBABLY SAFE BEYOND
NEUTRONS
GAMMA RAYS
RADIOACTIVE DUST
FATAL EXPOSURE
③ RADIATION
RADIATION SICKNESS, A FEW DEATHS
PROBABLY SAFE UNLESS DOWNWIND
2 MILES

132 POPULAR MECHANICS

JANUARY 1951 133

8.7. Double-page spread, "If the A-Bombs Burst," *Popular Mechanics*, January 1951

vomited, steadied himself, and then clawed his way to the top of a mound of brick and steel beams. From here he surveyed what remained of his block. Somewhere beneath his feet he heard the muffled scream of a woman."[9]

Bombarded with such images in magazines that normally offered celebrity gossip, or fashion and cooking tips, or domestic improvement schemes,* it's not a wonder that many Americans reported doubts about bringing children into the Cold War world. *Lucy* showed something different, a scenario that resolutely denied the images of eradication and horror, a narrative in which audiences could see their mirror images living the trivial and the personal in rapt self-importance, as they conceived, gestated, and then gave birth in real time and nearly on camera. That Lucille Ball was herself pregnant and gave birth at nearly the very same moment as did Lucy only em-

* That same issue of *Popular Mechanics* included "New Trees From Old," "What's New for Your Home," and "Beautiful Finishes With Plastic Veneer, Part I."

phasized more emphatically the messages of reassurance and reaffirmation. Not just Lucy and Ricky, but Lucille and Desi too rejected the calculus of horror.

The first two seasons formed the foundation from which the show and its people grew increasingly fast paced and frantic. The writers and producers sent the Ricardos and the Mertzes out on dream vacations: out along Route 66 in a car trip to Hollywood, off to Europe to capture some culture. Of course nothing ever worked out the way Lucy wanted it to, and the show stressed the reach of yearning, the impossibility of fulfillment, the abjectness of failure, the return to start again.

In each excursion, Lucy and Ricky desired, and they failed to achieve their desire. Because the message was that it wasn't *getting* that mattered—it was *wanting*. This may help us account for the strange phenomenon of eight million women watching themselves thwarted each week and returning to watch their own humiliation again, again, and again. This wasn't just repetition compulsion at work. It was the affirmation that the energy of desire, so central to Lucy's own identity, was neither a pathology nor a prison, but rather a value.

This isn't to say that *I Love Lucy* didn't follow a trajectory of upward mobility. It did, though in tellingly incomplete ways. Lucy and Ricky, after all, found the money and the opportunity to tour Europe—and in so doing, they mirrored a peculiarly mass culture–infused set of desires, traveling only through the most stereotypic tourist destinations. And they did manage a move from the cramped apartment to the spacious suburban greensward of Westport, Connecticut, a similarly reductive caricature of the American suburb. But every achievement was marked by a pointed attentiveness to what was lost as well as gained. The move to "the country" was particularly plangent; it occurred in the very last season of the show, in the spring of 1957, and lasted just thirteen episodes, of which most were fraught with regret over the move and, uncharacteristically, a palpable self-consciousness of loss on Lucy's own part. Just as Lucy achieved an idyllic ideal of American Dream success, the show itself folded. Desire achieved wasn't the point of the show, and Lucille Ball and Desi Arnaz announced to their writers, staff, and fellow actors that the show would end.

To viewers of television who grew up not on *Lucy* but on more recent fare, the final installment seems peculiar in the extreme. There's no climax; in fact, the last two episodes explicitly recycle plots and themes that have been used multiple times through the life of the show. There's no summing up, no culmination to 180 half-hour glimpses of this American story, so avidly watched by so many.

But that too is of a piece with the show as a whole. Every episode of *Lucy* began with an intimation of liberation, transformation, transcendence; every episode ended with a return to the conditions of the past—every episode, that is, except the birth of little Ricky. In that one, something monumental *did* happen, and it took multiple episodes to undo that sense of momentousness and restore the essential narrative. Little Ricky faded away, returning here and there as a stage prop or a plot device. Even the switch from one apartment to another turned out to be no change at all, for the new place was simply a mirror of the old one, with an added, almost unvisited additional room, necessary in order to maintain the unchanged quality of the rooms viewers *did* see—keeping the child and his crib, his toys and his noise, out of the familiar spaces of living room and kitchen.

And so, even with a birth, with the creation of a new life on television for the very first time, *Lucy*'s function remained essentially conservative. In the face of the American promise of rapid change—upward mobility, prosperity, the transformed life of the suburbs—or sudden catastrophe—the neighborhood turned to rubble, "the muffled scream" of a woman buried under the ruins of her house or yours (*Popular Mechanics*' description—remember?—of the effect of nuclear attack on America)—*Lucy* gave a measured pace to the imaginative, and the real, lives of Americans who watched the show. Just as the television itself became a physical anchor for the domestic spaces of Americans, so this single most popular show of all time provided a cultural anchor for the drifting identities of postwar Americans.

Lucy sharpened the sense of cultural time, but it blurred the sense of place in American life. When Lucy, Ricky, Fred, and Ethel embarked on their road trip from New York to Hollywood, it was *almost* a Route 66 tour, at *almost* the moment when such road trips were shifting from exotic events to common family vacations. But it sent the two couples not to real locations but to fantasy ones (like Bent Fork, Tennessee, invented home of television's Tennessee Ernie Ford), accentuating how television was reinventing American geography: hillbilly South, cactus-strewn desert, sunny California. The Ricardo's European travels took them to travel-poster destinations, and in so doing confirmed the ways Americans were already colonizing the globe, not just by occupying it, but by insisting that it conform to their preconceptions and expectations.

And when "Lucy Wants to Move to the Country" became not an episode but a complete shift in the show's locale, Lucy and Ricky moved not to a sharp-focus satire of the new American sprawl, but rather to a blurry, idealized suburb. How did Ricky make it home at 3 a.m. from the club? What trains ran? Did Lucy pick him up at the station in the predawn hours? Or did he drive himself?

Even as it drew away from the local and place became an abstraction, *Lucy* remained precise in its timing. While Lucy and Ricky were settling in to their Connecticut home, the new arteries of the National Interstate and Defense Highways Act—the freeways and superhighways of the future, the catalysts of a second wave of postwar suburbanization—were cutting through city neighborhoods and older, inner-ring suburbs, slicing through farmland and recalculating the relationship between American space and American time: the first expanding, the second shrinking to a steadily more rushed and inadequate pace. A couple of miles from Ricky and Lucy's new home, the Connecticut Turnpike was about to be completed. A year after the show ended (in October 1958), that tollway opened, cutting travel time from two hours to less than one, and Westport became a newly middle-class suburban destination.

The timing of *Lucy*'s suburban move was also reactive, retrospective. Lucy and Ricky pulled their child from urban schooling at just the moment when millions of other white families were doing the same, reacting to *Brown v. Board of Education*, the Supreme Court's landmark decision in favor of school desegregation. That ruling, in 1954, was followed by a more conservative call in 1955 for change with "all deliberate speed," assuring that transformation in the racial fabric of the nation "would be a progression of action," as Chief Justice Warren later wrote. Lucy and Ricky, like a majority of their white, middle-class viewers whose children in 1954 were educated in racially isolated schools, extricated themselves from the traumas of racial integration. In the process, *Lucy* declared the full ethnic assimilation of that crazy *Cubano*, Ricky Ricardo, who asserted his own integration by defending the right of segregation.

Of course no TV series overtly told the story of white flight, of the Levittown, Pennsylvania, race riots (white residents threw the rocks, not the other way around), and working-class urban blockbusting. *I Love Lucy* never mentioned Negroes or the Supreme Court or even education. Television attracted by its power of denial, by the way it could recast the everyday in a form that conveniently missed the most difficult and painful of cultural struggles. Like the screams of a burned and buried neighbor during an atomic holocaust or the realities of marital strife, infidelity, and divorce in the postwar nuclear family (realities experienced in spades by the Ball-Arnaz family but assiduously hidden from public view), *Brown v. Board of Education*, and the racial strife it addressed and catalyzed, became a presence by its absence.

By the time *Lucy* moved to "the country," the palpability of the show had dissipated into ideality. Where the apartment had drawn energy from the physical density of the set—its replication of real construction on a Hollywood soundstage giving it a reassuringly realistic look, sound, and feel—the Westport house exemplified television's emerging role as a creator of *prospective* myth: it was exact down to the colonial furniture (fake) and the late-model Ford (real, because you could buy it on time). Viewers of the show in 1953 might look at where they'd once been or where they were soon to leave; by 1958, they were looking at the place they hoped to go to but would never realistically attain. The Westport house completed the chain of upward mobility. It was closer to the Beverly Palms Hotel suite where the family lived during that ill-fated Hollywood sojourn than it was to a tiny home in Levittown—a description of fantasy not a goal toward which to work.

But it differed from the Hollywood hotel in an important way. Out in California, the Ricardos faced disappointment when Ricky failed to make it in the movies, and that tension saved the show's episodes. Time after time, what energized the plots came from below, from a dark repressed awareness of failure and out-of-placeness that one or both of them felt. In Connecticut, the family succeeded, and the show died. The house, symbol of American Dream achievement, was too perfect. Even the kitchen—*especially* the kitchen—lost its crackling presence as a symbol and an enactment of domestic imprisonment and claustrophobia. In the old kitchen, eating was crowded chockablock with the stove and the sink; in the new house, there was a dining nook for breakfast, but a separate dining area in the vast living room had a china buffet, and out on the patio was a picnic table and, eventually, a barbeque. When Ricky had tried to cook in the apartment, his failure brought home the lessons of gender-specific work. Out here in the idyll of the suburbs, men and women had separate domains for cooking, and domesticity participated in the larger promise of seamless leisure. Facing a future of bliss punctuated by minor mishaps, Lucy and Ricky, Jess Oppenheimer, Madelyn Pugh, and Bob Carroll, Jr. closed down the production.

By a stroke of telling irony, though, the end of *I Love Lucy* had its rationale, both public and private, in the public and private lives of the couple who populated it. Lucille Ball had started the show to rescue their rocky marriage, bringing them together on the set. She'd risked everything to guarantee that it be filmed not in New York but in California, ensuring stability off-screen as she and Desi made mayhem and instability a staple of the screen. As early as 1952, the couple were exploiting this mirror-image of lives, giving interviews that played up the story of an American marriage saved by hard work, stability, and togetherness. And the journalists took the bait, not least because it made such good journalism: "By giving up movies and nightclubs for their TV show, *I Love Lucy* (Monday, 9 p.m., CBS), Lucille and Desi now have all their weekends free, and work only four days a week—together," reported *Time* in February, after the show topped the ratings. "In brightening up their own lives, they have done quite a lot to make a cheerful half hour once a week for millions of televiewers. . . . Says Lucille, 'We try to be an average married couple getting into unaverage situations.'"[10]

Three months later, the magazine was back for a retrospective of the first year, and the themes were identical. Lucille Ball had gained a stable role in television to replace the unstable one granted her by movies, said *Time*, but that wasn't all; "the show also allows her time with her ten-month-old daughter Lucie Desirée [*sic*], and for the first time in eleven years of trouping, gives her a home life with husband Desi. Says she: 'I look like everybody's idea of an actress, but I feel like a housewife. I think that's what my trouble was in movies.' Actress Ball was a long time arriving at the calm waters of motherhood and housewifery."[11]

The show began on the premise of an unstable fictional life making possible a stable "reality." It ended with an unstable reality—a marriage collapsing under the weight of infidelities, conflicts over autonomy, and money—pressing against a torpidly stable imaginative and mythic televisual life. But this was part of the power of the show, part of what it promised: a new form of reality in which the distinction between the box of the living room and the living room's box blurred, and the two experiences commingled.

There's an early *Lucy* episode, aired in May of the first season, that remains perhaps the single most popular of all. Originally titled "Lucy Does a TV Commercial," it's known in the vernacular as the "Vitameatavegamin" episode. Ricky finally has his own TV show, and he's responsible for making the commercials. Since his show is marginal, the sponsors are, too—not auto manufacturers or tobacco companies, but quack patent medicine purveyors. Lucy wants to use this chance to vault herself into a television career, but she plays the part too well. Viewers of the reruns, from the '60s on, remember it as one of the most spot-on depictions of slow, steady drunkenness and as a drop-dead Lucille Ball triumph.

But there's an earlier, smaller, but perhaps more significant skit in the same episode, in which Lucy, hoping to convince Ricky to let her act in a commercial for his televised show, disembowels the couple's television and places herself inside it, pretending she's a televised phantom and not a real woman.

8.8. The Ricardos' television, *I Love Lucy*, season one

It's not just that the Ricardos have a television that's arresting. Oddly sequestered in a corner, it faces a desk at an unwatcheable angle, and Fred has to drag it out into the room to get Ricky to sit down in front of it to watch a boxing match.

And it's not the way that Lucy's presence *inside* the set reflects the larger conflation of televised experience and lived experience—or even the way that Lucy's quest finally mirrors that conflation: she wants to quit being a real actress playing a thwarted actress trying to become a real actress, and become a real actress playing a fictional actress. It isn't even the way that Fred and Ricky sit to watch the television—on the edge of the furniture, as if it were something worth paying attention to, something even worth putting on one's living room manners for.

It's the dismembered television itself that we should be looking at. For the scene ends when Lucy discovers that the inner workings of a television can be removed whole, taken from the furniture case that disguises its technology. In the reality of Ricky and Fred, and the reality of the designers of living room televisions in the early '50s, the cladding disguised the new and disturbing personality, disguised it and also simultaneously made it possible to move the thing to a corner (as it is at the beginning of the episode) and rendered it unwieldy when the necessity came for bringing it out into company.

But Lucy didn't get that. She didn't realize that the television was a full-blown entity dressed up in a proper costume; she thought it was an intricate architecture of tubes and transformers, rheostats, and switches. She took the thing apart, piece by piece, piled the parts up, and hid them in the closet. When she brings them out, the scene ends with a signature *Lucy* combination of abjectness, surrealism, and clowning.

The pile of parts is, like Lucy, abject; it's also hilariously unlikely. And it marks a wonderfully complicated twist in the tale of television's steady incursion into American life. By taking the TV apart, Lucy has triumphed over her rival for Ricky's attention. She has declared the importance of the real over the artifice—she's *acted* on all those warnings in the non-television media that TV is going to ruin American family and community life. But

8.9. Inside the Ricardos' television

8.10. The impossible pile of parts

she's also broken the TV. Now there's no means for Ricky to see her performance when she finally makes it onto the commercial, the first leg up in her
dream career as a television celebrity.

That pile of parts looks like so many other piles of parts depicted between
August of 1945 and the dismembered culture known vernacularly as "the
'60s": the taken-apart atomic bomb that appeared in *Life*, and its hydrogen-
bomb update circa 1952; the *Popular Science* exploded-view of the pieces
that made up antiballistic radar; numerous diagrams showing the inner
workings of Sputnik, the Soviet winner in the contest for outer space satellites, launched in 1957. *Popular Mechanics* was hugely popular during that
era; using its schematics and its step-by-step instructions, fathers and sons
built model airplanes and miniature battleships, repaired the toaster ovens,
souped up the carburetors, and constructed winning science fair exhibits
on every aspect of Cold War technology. *Popular Mechanics* was also the magazine that ran the government's terrifying ghostwritten jeremiads about
"survivable" atomic warfare and the necessity for Civil Defense cadres and

fallout shelters. Fathers and sons pored over the plans for those shelters, and some of them dug up the back yard or cinderblocked a corner of the cellar to build one.[12]

For the men and boys reading *Popular Mechanics*, that pile of parts might have represented a warning about thinking too hard, taking too much apart; more likely, though, at the more conscious registers of the mind, it represented a challenge, a metaphor for the larger demands of democratic life in Cold War America. Time to get out the soldering iron, the government-printed electronics handbook, the instruction manual, the back issues of the magazine, and get to work.

*　*　*

By the time *I Love Lucy* reached its real-time culmination of the postwar American Dream, depositing the family in the suburban Eden and granting them the material trappings of upper-middle-class stability, it had lost its force or, more accurately, its role in the culture had changed. From a celebration of the creative ferment and the endless possibilities of Americans with soldering irons and pressure cookers and schemes upon schemes for escape and elevation, from a recognition of the prisons of social and cultural behavior, tradition, mores and models, it became instead a force to conserve the broad outlines of the American ideology. Upward mobility; geographical mobility; global hegemony; male freedom and female domesticity; celebrity over meritocracy; material prosperity tied to social propriety: these became the recurrent themes, the core concepts of the show as it wound to its end. But almost any show could encompass these reassurances. By the later '50s, they were built into the medium itself.

Yet *Lucy* never left. Production ended, and the following year, *I Love Lucy* reappeared as reruns, and there it has remained, in syndication into the twenty-first century. The show ran in primetime through 1958 and 1959, while new, hour-long "specials" reintroduced the Ricardos and Mertzes in real time.

The result was an odd dissociation of time and space; one could see the older, somewhat wearier, certainly more successful foursome the same week that their young, anarchic ancestors blew up chickens and took apart televisions. Over time, however, the nostalgic and retrospective came to dominate, and finally to vanquish, the more complex, irresolvable, and rebellious counterpart. More precisely, over time this older-younger version of Cold War Americans fighting for their liberties and their opportunities came to occupy the sites and sights of history—the past, daddy's time and mommy's, back when television was black and white and there was only one in the house, and people, middle-class *white* people, actually lived in apartments in the city.

By the summer of 1958, when *I Love Lucy* finally cycled out of prime time, American televisions were typically color and not black and white. They were to be found less exclusively in the living rooms and more commonly in the family rooms, the bedrooms, even the kitchens of middle-class houses. There they competed with media of cultural connection and entertainment that television had thought to have vanquished long before: phonographs and radios, where the simplified plots and broad cultural themes of the half-hour television show could be easily distilled to three minute songs. *Lucy* became the place one came home to, the retrospective and comforting murmur of the repeated episode, the memorized line, the imitable gesture. Other forms had begun to emerge, in other media, to take on the role of rebellious, anarchic individualism, optimism, and energetic cultural appropriation that *Lucy* had exemplified.

CHAPTER 9

Technologies of Space and Place, 1962

Throughout the '50s and early '60s, while televisions expanded, radios shrank. Television's incursion into the domestic, cultural, and public spheres mimicked the expanding screen and its accompanying cabinet. Nine-inch, then thirteen-, seventeen-, twenty-one-, and twenty-three-inch screens were the planned obsolescence temptations of 1948, '50, '55, '59, and '62, respectively; each promised a larger vista behind and beyond the surface in the virtual space drawn into the living room by the electrical impulses exciting phosphors that painted themselves along the inside of the glass, in the vacuum. Purchasers turned on the sets to discover that the images didn't get particularly sharper or more detailed, because the limits of the signal itself precluded this. But there wasn't a wave of returns or complaints to manufacturers; viewers *felt* they were more completely immersed in an experience of visual immediacy, despite the evidence to the contrary.

To some extent, the very pervasiveness of advertising for the new and larger sets ensured their reception. In magazine and newspaper ads, manufacturers repeatedly linked the size of the television not just to the vividness of the escape it offered but also to the sociability that would enter any living room with such a set.

In ad after ad, neighbors and friends assembled, often in dress and demeanor that implied a certain status attached to the event; or families came together, happily communing: children, teenagers and parents smilingly immersed in a benign, parallel sociability. In both sorts of ad, the television

9.1. Motorola ad, 1951

served as a sort of relay, connecting people without necessarily demanding much in return.

Larger sets changed the nature of the viewing experience, shifting its promise from verisimilitude to atmosphere, from picture plane to glowing space. (Unlike the movies, where the inherent resolution of the 35-mm print and the high quality of lenses both in cameras and projectors meant that the picture could remain sharp even when steadily enlarged, TV had a built-in limit to its visual acuity.) The expanding screen declared dominion over a greater area around it in the living room. It had to. If you continued to watch from the location where you'd sat before the bigger set was delivered by the appliance store, you felt a sense of disappointment in your purchase; instead of a glowing and seductive picture, the images on the screen seemed washed-out and indistinct—you were too close, and the illusion fell apart. So you backed your chair up and contrast improved, as did the sense of illusion. The triangular territory known as the "viewing area" widened and deepened with each new and larger set until, in many cases, the television console ended up dominating not a wall but a corner, while its cone of influence paralleled the walls on either side and colonized the entire room. More

9.2. Magnavox ad, 1958

people could watch at the same time; all the family could be comfortably placed, seeing equally well, and guests could be accommodated with ease. But if the TV was on, the living room was under its sway, and any activities were bound to be distracted by its visual and aural presence.

To suit this widened arena, the volume went up, and the television's blare came increasingly to leak beyond the single room and into the rest of the house. (GE's 1960 flagship color set had *two* 21×9-inch low-frequency woofers and a corresponding pair of electrostatic high-frequency tweeters.)[1] New patterns of home design and remodeling during the later '50s and early '60s exaggerated the effect. Dining rooms disappeared, becoming "nooks" in the kitchen or transition areas between living room and kitchen, and the walls separating the kitchen from living areas came down, replaced by "snack bars" and pass-throughs, open counters and even stoves and sinks, so that the housewife could do her work while sharing the television with the rest of the family.

New homes were the most likely to have these innovations, and the families moving into the rapidly expanding suburban real estate landscapes spreading outward from the freeway interchanges that radiated from the major cities were exactly the ideal citizens presented as the new Americans in the mass media, particularly the print media. Their taste in the new open-plan home and its social rearrangements became the raw material for numerous features. Just as *Life*, *Look*, and the other mass-circulation weeklies had touted Levittown a decade earlier, now they, and their successors and niche-dwelling counterparts, found the opportunity to celebrate the new suburbanites and their homes. One result was a craze for remodeling pressed by home builders, building-supply companies, furniture makers, department stores, and even specialty domains like the window industry and, naturally, the appliance makers.

These companies sought ready vehicles for their ads, and as a result, home improvement and home beautification magazines like *Better Homes and Gardens* and *House Beautiful* thrived. These outlets pushed new home designs and proposed ways to make older houses new again, or at least novel. And they spread their influence far beyond the magazine racks; home design, new-home models, and remodeling projects were common fare in the free calendars that lumber yards and building supply houses distributed. Banks too got in on the trend, promoting their own mortgage and home-improvement loan-inducing calendars. When *House Beautiful* marketed its calendars to banks and savings and loans, its editors adapted the best of their annual projects, plans and home-improvement hints, putting color set-pieces on the front and projects and proposals illustrated in black-and-white on the back. The 1959 calendar, for example, pushed the idea of an open window between kitchen and living-dining room; "with surface cooking units set into pass-through counter," October's editor advised, "hostess is able to keep food at proper temperature until ready for serving. Pass-through can be closed off by sliding doors." Ideally, food, conversation, and parental monitoring flowed back and forth; in point of fact, as many of the etiquette books and advice columns revealed, it was the television's presence that held sway, to the discomfiture of many, and with the result that new forms of television etiquette had to be devised.[2]

Locating the television, both physically and experientially, became part of a larger discussion about social activity—and solitary activity, as well. Television offered itself—in ads, in magazines like *TV Guide*, in strange little snippets of TV that simultaneously mimicked and idealized TV watching—as a flexible companion. For women trapped in the home doing chores that were simultaneously boring and demeaning, daytime TV offered a means of drawing off resentment and replacing it with fantasy from the love lives on the soap operas to the winnings on game shows like *Queen For A Day*, which migrated from radio to television in 1956 and ran until 1964. For those after-school kids, there were kiddie shows and Westerns and, of course, *American Bandstand*. Evening television was meant to be sociable, but in fact it was far less so than it had been in the early years.

The early '60s thus saw a contradictory place for the television, both as a cultural presence and as a physical one. Once introduced as a novel and important form of cultural glue, a means of knitting family, community, and the nation together, informing and uplifting, the TV had become something of an invisible force, attracting, deflecting, and inflecting those within its aura. It succeeded in ingratiating itself; it expanded its influence by reducing its physical authority.

The permeability of television's messages, in sound and light, accentuated by the simultaneous move to open-plan family and public spaces, left little place for the radio as part of the ceremonial public life of the American family. In home-improvement magazines and ideal-home calendars, radios disappeared from the decorating schemes; one would have thought that the medium had simply vanished.

But this was a chimera. Radios continued to sell; the percentage of households with radios crept upward from its 94 percent mark in 1950 to peak at 96.4 percent in the early '60s, while revenues and income roared upward after a brief, recession-induced pause in 1960. Listenership increased and time listened increased, as well. The data propose not a medium in retreat but one continuing to thrive in a new form.[3]

Radios had shifted their domains. No longer domestic features, they now served as escapes from domesticity. And escape routes were much in demand by the early '6os. While the formal and communal areas of the ideal American house opened up to the television's influence, the unstable electronic nucleus of the nuclear family seemed to fling occupants and occupations in a centrifugal expulsion to outer rooms, where doors could be closed, the insistent sight and sound of the TV shut out, and individual activity could hold sway. And that was where the radio reasserted itself, in a seeming exile that was in reality more like a novel form of intimacy.[4]

Where were those family members who weren't clustered in the living room around the TV? If at home, they were in the individuated spaces of the house, in kitchens, workrooms and laundry rooms, studies and dens, and in bedrooms, gluing Green Stamps into booklets, sewing Simplicity kilted skirts, building model rockets or kits of "Big Daddy Roth" kustom kars, B-52 bomb-delivery jet aircraft, the Invisible Man and the Invisible Woman.[5] With this new market in mind—those working at hobbies or home labor that kept parents and children in the house but left them with a good deal of attention to spare—radio set manufacturers engaged in a frenzied battle to produce radios that could get as far from the living room corner, and as far into the everyday lives of citizens, especially teenagers, as possible. Radios transmuted, becoming more like friendly companions than formal presences. Smaller, increasingly zany in design, they inveigled themselves into their users' lives. They stopped looking like furniture—or like anything but themselves: boxes with two knobs and a dial, or a knob that *was* a dial. You reached to turn them on the way you reached for a pack of cigarettes—half-consciously, reflexively, for comfort.

I've been talking of radios as if they were animate, symbiotic, squeezing themselves into the lives of Americans of the early '6os. While this might seem odd, even misleading, it's a reflection of the ways manufacturers sought to sell the radio while its position in the household was under siege by the new technology of television. No longer marketable as a piece of imposing living-room furniture, the radio could be rebranded as a sort of pet. And Americans responded. As early as 1955, *Time* ran an article on "the new average radio listener": the editors reported that "he treats his radio like a constant companion who is pleasant to have around but can be comfortably ignored."[6]

The statistics on radio purchases clarify the outlines of that phenomenon. In 1950, the U.S. census began to track the popularity of a new form of radio, the "portable/clock" radio. That year, large radios were outselling these smaller versions five to one. Five years later, smaller radios were close

ACTUAL SIZE

KING-SIZE SOUND

Radio Receiver Department, Utica, New York

In spades! General Electric engineers fashioned seven transistors and many other precisely made components into a tiny, yet *powerful*, radio receiver.

Understandably proud of their achievement, they insisted that a handsome case be designed to house it. It was, as you can see.

This pocket portable (model P-8523) makes a splendid gift. It comes in a jewelry box, with earphone, battery and carrying case. See it, *hear* it at your General Electric dealer's. Costs about $40.

It's there now, along with many other portables, table models and clock-radios, both FM and AM, by General Electric, America's number ONE manufacturer—and seller—of radios.

Progress Is Our Most Important Product

GENERAL ⓖⓔ ELECTRIC

MODEL P-865

FM/AM portable with AFC—General Electric's finest. 11 powerful transistors pull in distant stations. Heavy-magnet speaker delivers console-quality sound. About $125.

MODEL P-9051

Seven transistors power this sleek new portable. Fits neatly in your shirt or skirt pocket. Comes complete with battery, earphone and carry strap. Just $29.95* takes it all.

MODEL P-860

The Sportmate. Eight transistors and a heavy-magnet speaker give big sound everywhere. Rugged construction; exceptional pull-in power for a set its size. Only $39.95.*

*MANUFACTURER'S SUGGESTED RETAIL PRICE OPTIONAL WITH RETAILERS.

9.3. GE radio ad, 1962

to twice as popular, and by 1959, the ratio was well over two-to-one. Americans were buying radios to place by their bedsides and their children's; they were buying radios for the workshop, for the kitchen shelf or counter, for the corner of the living room or family room, where the small box didn't interfere with the big box but could be used when what it offered was clearly superior.

Smaller radios inserted into increasingly diverse environments played to increasingly diverse audiences, as well. Televisions were expensive, even in 1963, especially in comparison with radios. A "portable" television with a thirteen-inch screen and a handle for carrying it from room to room (and still requiring an AC outlet to power it) cost around $139.99—about one-tenth of the cost of a compact car (and down from $179.95 in 1959)[7]—while a battery-powered pocket radio sold for less than a tenth as much. This was Christmas-present cash and after-school job cash, and that was ideal, for as we've seen the new market for radio was increasingly youthful: the children of the baby boom, now in mid-adolescence.

So while television seemed to win the *scheduled* entertainment battle, radio managed to retain and even enhance its quality of intimate connection, almost below consciousness. To actually *watch* television required one's attention. The peculiar visual quality of the image demanded a particular adjustment of eye and mind, and to look away was to destroy the illusion. Similarly with the vocal and aural on TV: jokes flew, plot lines demanded a particular sort of rapt attention, and social distractions like conversation or movement broke the narrative flow and aroused the anger of fellow watchers. Radio could be listened to with full concentration while doing everything from ironing to soldering a plumbing repair or assembling a model airplane—activities that were solitary but demanding.

Equally importantly, the smaller radios could be moved from place to place, for they worked on batteries rather than AC. As transistors replaced miniature tubes in the last years of the '50s, battery life increased dramatically, as did reception quality and even volume, while the radios themselves shrank steadily. Between 1959 and 1965, Japanese-made (though often American-branded) miniature portables swept the market. As a consequence of this shift in listening, radio developed a new sort of sonic ambience, and a new sort of rhetoric. This wasn't literally tonal—Bob and Ray, probably the most successful radio voices of the Cold War years, were relaxed almost to blandness (that was the basis of much of their humor), yet if you moved up the radio dial a bit, you might hear someone like deejay Harry Harrison on 77 WABC in New York, one of a host of radio personalities with a hopped-up, even strident delivery. What was shared was the goal of a new form of intimacy.

Just *how* that intimacy was achieved, and with what style, depended on the audience. And the radio audience increasingly bifurcated as the '50s ended and the '60s began. Older and younger listeners who had tended to share musical and listening taste now found themselves in very different streams; adults listened to the radio for sports, news, and information (and despite television's successful incursion into the news business, radio still could offer information on a 'round-the-clock basis rather than twice a day, and radios were on more than televisions before noon); adolescents and young adults listened to pop music radio. And this latter audience was the expanding one, the one whose allegiance could be retained even as the rest of the airways battled it out with television.

In those years, radio had a potent new combination of technology, audience, and programming. This alchemy—miniature radios, teenagers, and AM pop music—moved out of the enclaves of bedroom and work room and into the public spaces of streets and parks, beaches, and community centers, the quasi-public spaces of malt shops and soda fountains, and the surreptitious assembly points where a newly mobile generation could combine, disperse and recombine in fluid patterns that defied older forms of social control. The result was a contest over regulation of identity—individual, social, and cultural—that pitted parents and their social controls against the desires for freedom and autonomy on the part of an educated, self-assured and increasingly cohering generation.

The baby boom children of the later '40s had entered adolescence, and they sought privacy and a place of their own. With luck and family prosperity, they found it in the bedroom, where they could do their homework without eternal supervision, in physical, emotional, and intellectual circumstances that might not satisfy their parents: lying on the bed or the floor, sprawled on a chair, with a telephone, perhaps one of the new small Princess phones with the night-light dial, readily available to call friends or classmates for diverting gossip or homework help, and with a radio by their side to provide them with their own envelope of social belonging.

But this was an isolation not entirely desirable to the gregariousness and sociability of that stage of development. In addition, it was the privilege of only a few, even in the middle class. For the crowded children in Levittowns and all the older, smaller houses that still formed the bulk of dwellings during those years, a transistor radio with its earphone speaker plugged in offered escape from the claustrophobia of daily life. Through its electronic node, a teenager could secretly connect with a larger, louder, more resonant social gathering.

Pop music radio drew that youth audience out of individual bedrooms and into some larger, transcendent social landscape. Between 1962 and 1963, television and radio managed to work out a sort of truce, carving up both the physical spaces of the American home, and the wider spaces of cultural imagination. In the fall of 1962, TV sent out its latest call for Americans to stay home, indoors, in their safe, private places, to watch the new season of shows that were old and familiar. Meanwhile, teenagers were being importuned to party with vampires, zombies and "coffin-bangers": "you can Monster Mash!" sang Bobby (Boris) Pickett. Venus had come down from the heavens wearing blue jeans ("with a pony tail!," sang Jimmy Clanton), and Chubby Checker was raving about dancing with his "pussycat."

Downstairs, the living room glowed with the light of the television, while parents watched the hits of that season: *Dick Van Dyke*, *Candid Camera*, *Bonanza*, *The Beverly Hillbillies*, *Andy Griffith*, *The Lucy Show*. Upstairs, or out on the street, at the park or the parking lot, teenagers were dancing with monsters, misfits, surfers and Bahamian limbo-virtuosi. Two cultures were emerging, linked to different technologies of information and entertainment, located in different places—in the home, and within the imaginative geographies that were increasingly determining the flow of cultural information, practice, ritual, and the sense of community identity.

CHAPTER 10

Two Satellites, 1962

The November 3, 1962, *Billboard* "Hot 100" had an unusual number of featured fast-risers: the Four Seasons' Philly-Italian falsetto hit "Big Girls Don't Cry" had leapt from 66 to 17 and was now at 4, on its way to number 1 in a couple of weeks; Philly-sound Chubby Checker was pushing the "Limbo Rock" just two down; Elvis had "Return to Sender" at 10 (it had hopscotched 68, 20, 10, but Elvis was Elvis). Black shouter Little Eva was shouldering in; lounge lizard Mel Tormé was next up; then folk-revival pleasantry with Burl Ives. Marvin Gaye was higher up, and so were the Tijuana Brass and the Everly Brothers. It was a listing typical of the new pop music scene: black and white, rockabilly and urban doo-wop, performer-composed and Brill Building industry–manufactured. Down toward the bottom with its own bullet was a strange little shrieker of an instrumental named "Telstar."[1]

Some of these songs would keep jumping, and some would stay hot for a while. A few would do both, rise rapidly and then hold on at the top for weeks. Little Eva had a run—the teenage babysitter for Brill Building songwriting team Carole King and Jerry Goffin had her follow-up to the fabulous "Locomotion," "Keep Your Hands Off My Baby," start at 90, and then leap to 62, 42, 29, then 19, slowing to 16, 13, and finally stall at 12 before plunging. Elvis's hit had legs—it just went on and on—but it never made number 1. "Telstar" was the shocker. A sound-effects instrumental by an unknown British band that was penned, recorded, and "enhanced" by a producer destined for ignominy and suicide, it borrowed slavishly from the sound of surf instrumentalist Dick Dale, whose first album had made it to England not long before. Arriving in the Hot 100 at 85 with a bullet,* it floated into the "top 40" two weeks later then rose steadily, week by week: 18, 13, 7, 5, and then number 1.

If you haven't heard the song, it's worth logging on to a music site and sampling it. You'll immediately recognize the unlikeliness of the tune to any claim of cultural significance. With its odd little organ sound and its too-soft tremolo guitar, it seemed anything but the sort of hit destined to push past Chubby Checker, Elvis, Mel Tormé and the Four Seasons to hit number 1 on Christmas week, holding holiday songs at bay, staying on top into January, and hanging on in the top 40 into mid-February. But there it was.

"Telstar" wasn't just a top 40 novelty tune like its 1962 colleagues, "Monster Mash" and "The Chipmunk Song." It was the product of a confluence of cultural conflicts, reflective of the dynamics and complications of the new democratic culture at a moment of high tension and unexpressed possibilities. It sat at the cusp between two phases of American culture as it stretched from the end of World War II to the end of the millennium, and it expressed its place with sufficient verve that Americans paid attention. A product of the Cold War, it was a harbinger of counterculture utopias that would press at the dominant center—at old men and politicians and television and living rooms, credit cards and mortgages—picking pockets, stealing children, and redistributing the booty via new forms of communication and expression aimed directly at a new audience of Americans.

Before it was the title of a song, Telstar was a communications satellite, a product of Cold War defense industrial technologies and organizations linked to the dominant corporate economy and promising a new era of global cultural homogeneity.

Lightweight and solar-powered, it was a leading-edge application for the transistor technologies invented and perfected by Bell Labs, the R&D arm of AT&T. AT&T in turn was among the largest and richest American corporations, a government-sanctioned communications monopoly that was also a major defense and aerospace contractor. Telstar expressed its forebears; while the satellite was developed by the "independent" Bell Labs, and owned by AT&T, it was propelled into orbit by NASA rocket shot from Cape Canaveral in the first privately sponsored space launch. In addition, its role as a relay of telephone, television, and data stream transmissions was shared out among an international consortium of quasi-public communications

---

* The phrase "with a bullet" has been a part of pop music parlance at least since the '50s; in fact, *Billboard* rated its fast risers with a solid star. I've stayed with the vernacular.

10.1. Telstar assembly at Bell Labs, publicity photograph. (Courtesy of the NASA Glenn Research Center.)

10.2. NASA Telstar takeoff. (Courtesy of the NASA Glenn Research Center.)

entities, including the British General Post Office (the national telephone monopoly) and its French counterpart.[2]

Telstar was part experiment, part prototype, part public relations stunt. Because of its low and rapid orbit, it could only transmit in durations of twenty minutes or less—not enough for a full television show, but enough for specially tailored political and corporate events, from presidential press conferences to scripted "conversations" between officials on different continents. From the first, it exemplified a space-age version of what historian Daniel Boorstin called the "pseudo-event": carefully controlled artifices of immediacy from which all risk and chance had been removed, but which, skillfully done, could still draw on an illusion of grittiness and realism. The first transmission, made on the afternoon of July 10, was particularly harrowing for the Bell Labs scientists, for they were required to conform to international television schedules; the first image showed the American flag waving in front of the giant reception telescope, leaving Bell Labs developer Eugene O'Neill with "a vivid recollection of a young fellow lying on his back holding the staff, the breeze provided by a large fan, with the PR program manager shouting, 'Hold it steady, dammit, hold it steady!' (The "Star-Spangled Banner" was added later as more appropriate audio.)" The opening shot was followed by short speeches from the chairman of AT&T and Vice President Lyndon Johnson.[3]

This was just the first of a series of manufactured events, many of them run by, sponsored by, or monitored by the USIA, America's Cold War information agency.[4] The first full-length (twenty-minute) transmission, on July 23, was a mock news program with feeds from El Paso (longhorn cattle, "home, home on the range"), Huntley-Brinkley television news from Washington, an excerpt from a press conference with President Kennedy, and video views of Niagara Falls, Cape Canaveral, a Cubs game at Wrigley Field in Chicago, the Golden Gate Bridge, the Statue of Liberty, Mount Rushmore, and the Mormon Tabernacle Choir singing "A Mighty Fortress Is Our God." One shot, of three hundred buffalo at the Custer State Park in South Dakota ("a home where the buffalo roam"), caused the producer to declare that he'd paid for the shot and damned if he wasn't going to use it: "At air time, we'll get them to run onscreen on cue," he promised a reporter.[5]

Telstar could move not just propaganda but data streams, and in that regard it showed the way for a dramatically shrunken globe in which space-age technologies offered forms of virtual instantaneity, both spatially and temporally. This combination of hyperbole, orchestrated utopianism, and technological whizbangery was what inspired British music producer and composer Joe Meek. He witnessed the early promotional events on television in London and conceived a pop music celebration of this new era in global telecommunications. Meek's vision of Telstar differed dramatically from that of, say Lyndon Johnson or AT&T's chairman, Fred Kappel. Meek was a pop music impresario, recording engineer, and producer, and he'd been responsible for significant hits by some of Britain's most prominent pop musicians. He'd also sponsored and recorded American music legends like Big Bill Broonzy, introducing them to the British Isles; and he'd made much of his career producing British musicians who rehearsed major American musical trends, from jazz to Texas swing to bluegrass.[6]

What Meek couldn't do was move the stream in the other direction. Musically, the UK was a distant colony, maker of derivative music, longing to enter into dynamic reciprocity. British music shared a vibrant youth scene, albeit far more class-defined than the American version, and a pool of very high-talent musicians, composers, and lyricists. Meek saw Telstar as a symbol of a new era, in which a globalizing, reciprocal, dynamic alternative culture would come into its own, taking over the means not only of production, but of transmission and reception.[7]

Meek wrote "Telstar" with his co-composer Geoff Goddard while watching one of the first transmissions over the satellite, possibly that image of an American flag that O'Neill had helped to bring into being.[8] Meek's initial draft was a blend of his signature "special effects" (for which he'd made a name already), Goddard's snappy little skiffle melody over a standard pop progression in A, and an adaptation of what Dick Dale had been doing in California, making his first "surf music" instrumental album, *Surfer's Choice*.[9]

Looking for a Dale-like sound, Meek called in a backing band he'd put together the year before to record and tour with his principal stable of singers. The Tornados were a practiced studio and club-date band, capable of quickly picking up a mood and more-than-competently laying down a track. They combined a reedy electric organ, a tremolo-drenched guitar, and a competent rhythm section and followed Meek's antic bidding. Their song was in the can in a single quick session.

There really wasn't much there, actually: little musical ambition, anyway, and no lyrics to salvage it. To get the song up to radio length (three-plus minutes), Meek had the band repeat the entire thing, modulated up a fourth, while someone hummed along in the background. It was still just over two minutes. So, after the Tornados left, Meek began to muck about. Within the song, he added the watery sound of an early synthesizer called the clavioline. Then he tacked special effects to the beginning and end, in an attempt to link it directly to its eponymous source, giving it the timely hook that might pull it into the charts.[10]

"Telstar" worked, and that's the mystery. Compare it to Dick Dale's "Surf Beat" or "Let's Go Trippin,'" from around the same time, and you can see just how musically lame the piece was. But listening to Meek's previous outings is revelatory: he must have *wanted* this sound, for the others aren't at all like this—they're more technically assured, lively, and they push the beat in true rock-and-roll fashion. This song hangs off the back of the rhythm by its fingernails. The Vox Continental organ dominates, with the clavioline pouring over the top of the background, through which you can hear drums, bass, and guitar as if you're under water. The special effects that linked the song most directly to the satellite—a collage of noises at the beginning and the end (variously reported as recordings of rocket launches and of Meeks's toilet flushing, but probably neither)—were rudimentary, cheesy even for those days.

Yet you could easily read a narrative into its wordless unfolding, and that narrative could expand to global proportions or shrink to fit the accepted form of the pop-song-in-three-minutes: intro, theme, chorus, modulation, hook, repeat, coda. Meeks had composed the song to the pop pattern—that's part of what made it hit-worthy. But he also built the musical plot as a version of the televised mock-up of Telstar in space—probably the one he and millions saw on TV as they waited for the first broadcast—which showed the satellite approaching, present, receiving and beaming, and then receding, from a vantage point in outer space. It was a matter of point of view transliterated from the televisual to the audiophonic: for the duration of the song, you listened, weightless, out past the Van Allen belt.

The song was a near-instant British hit, charting in August and staying there for more than four months. It was a perfect summer tune; what was a little strange was the way it stuck around through the fall, reaching number 1 in the UK and holding there for five full weeks while Elvis assaulted listeners with "Return to Sender," Ray Charles released "I Can't Stop Loving You," and numerous British hitmakers sought to win the day. Then, just as it should have saturated the market, soured the ear and disappeared from the top 40 radar, something changed: "Telstar" began to rise on the *American* charts.

* * *

On the other side of the Atlantic, "Telstar" entered a dramatically different cultural context. Here in the States, the satellite Telstar stood for the consortium of institutional, political, economic, and cultural forces that had come to dominate Cold War America: a vast monopolistic corporation, a high-tech lab devoted simultaneously to consumer goods and defense tools, governmental agencies from the USIA and the CIA to the FCC—and, of course, television, notably the Big Three networks. Here's President Kennedy's script for the dedication ceremony: Telstar was "another indication of the extraordinary world in which we live. This satellite must be high enough to carry messages from both sides of the world, which is of course a very essential requirement for peace, and I think this understanding which will inevitably come from the speedier communications is bound to increase the well-being and security of all people, here, and those across the oceans. So we are glad to participate in this operation developed by private industry, launched by government, in admirable cooperation."[11]

Heady stuff, and certainly the success of Telstar was a relief and a cause for celebration, after the debacle of the Russian Sputnik satellite triumph in 1957 and subsequently the regular sight of American rockets blowing up—on the launch pad, just after takeoff, or high in the atmosphere—as high-tech components (some of them designed by Bell Labs) shorted, behaved erratically, or fizzled out. Kennedy's rhetoric also echoed his renewed version of America's Manifest Destiny, the "new frontier" he'd proposed when he accepted the nomination a year earlier: American expansionism extended to "the uncharted areas of science and space."[12]

By September, Kennedy himself seemed emboldened by Telstar's success. At a speech in Houston on September 12, he invoked Pilgrim leader William Bradford, called on America to "set sail on this new sea" of space travel, exploration, and national expansion, and declared that "the vows of this Nation can only be fulfilled if we in this Nation are first."[13] Though he proposed a moment later that "there is no strife, no prejudice, no national conflict in outer space as yet," he'd been thinking since shortly after taking office that the high ground in the Cold War now lay with the *image* of power and superiority transmitted to the globe, and he saw the conquest of "outer space" as a compelling rhetorical weapon in this war of myths and images—both the global image of the United States and the American self-image, so damaged by technological failures, by the prospect of a renewed nuclear arms race, by relentless diplomatic and imperial probings by the USSR. In April of 1961, he'd sent a memo to the chairman of the Space Council, asking plaintively, "Do we have a chance of beating the Soviets by putting a laboratory in space, or by a trip around the moon, or by a rocket to land on the moon . . . ? Is there any other space program which promises dramatic results in which we could win?"[14]

"Dramatic results" were exactly what Telstar offered: a picture of American technology triumphant, but also benevolent, egalitarian, generous to the world. Kennedy's celebration of the satellite "high enough to carry messages from both sides of the world" was nearly identical to Joe Meek's. It was in the matter of *what* messages would be sent, and by whom, that they differed so profoundly.

Kennedy's call for Manifest Destiny in space needed some pacific imagery attached to it. Though he'd suggested that outer space was a frontier of scientific discovery, a conflict-free zone, his confidence was in part made possible by a very different incursion into space, completed just a day before Telstar's launch. On July 9, 1962, after a string of costly, humiliating, and technologically sobering failures of launch rockets, guidance systems, triggers, and the like, the Atomic Energy Commission succeeded in its most

10.3. Official NASA publicity photograph of Telstar, produced by photo compositing. (Courtesy of the NASA Glenn Research Center.)

ambitious of nuclear tests: Starfish Prime, in the Operation Dominic test series, launched from Johnson Island a few hundred miles to the west of Hawaii, 248 miles up, deep into outer space, where its hydrogen bomb blew a 1.45-megaton hole in the Van Allen radiation belt, unleashing a spectacular light show and interrupting power in Oahu with an electromagnetic field strong enough to set off burglar alarms and blow out the fuses for the street lights.[15]

The resulting darkness was probably welcome for the thousands of tourists who'd assembled to witness the test. Hotels on Oahu and the main island "offered roof-top bomb watching parties," recalled atomic veteran Cecil Coale, who was in the South Seas as part of a team from the Electro-Mechanics Company under contract to use their magnetometers to measure the flux in the earth's magnetic field brought on by outer space nuclear explosions. Coale described the view: "a brilliant white flash" that "erased the darkness like a photoflash. Then the entire sky turned light green for about a second. In several more seconds, a deep red aurora . . . formed where

10.4. "Starfish Prime." (Courtesy of Los Alamos National Laboratory.)

the blast had been. A white plasma jet came slowly out of the top of the red aurora ... and painted a white stripe across the sky.... The visual display lasted for perhaps ten minutes before slowly fading."[16]

Coale expressed the relief and exhilaration of the military-scientific community as they watched the spectacular specular fireworks they'd set off in outer space. It was about time. Dominic had been a test series fraught with conflict. After three years of an informal test ban, the USSR had abruptly changed course and restarted the arms race. Meeting with Soviet nuclear scientists on July 10, 1961, Khrushchev had called for a new series of atomic tests designed "to show the imperialists what we could do." In August he announced the resumption of tests, and testing had begun immediately thereafter. On October 30, 1961, the Soviets set off the largest nuclear explosion in history, a 50–58-megaton bomb,* more than three times the power of the

---

* There is lively and still unresolved debate as to the yield; Sakharov and others on the Soviet side reported it as fifty-eight megatons, and so have a number of American researchers, but others have argued the tonnage was lower. In either case, the yield was by far the largest in the history of atomic testing.

largest American bomb. The weapon was actually a cut-down version of a 100-megaton design—a device so huge that it could never have been delivered or used militarily. Had it been deployed as a public relations weapon, however, it would have so increased atmospheric fallout that millions of premature deaths in the Soviet Union alone would have resulted.[17]

The Tsar Bomba test dramatically raised the stakes in the rhetoric of the Cold War. Kennedy's response coincided with the desires of a number of hawkish nuclear scientists eager to test weaponry, strategy, and delivery systems heretofore left on the drawing board, and one confluence of these concerned outer-space warfare. Could the United States deploy a nuclear weapon that could wipe out or disable incoming Soviet missiles and bombs? What effect would such an explosion have on atmospheric radiation, electromagnetic fields, and other still-speculative elements of atomic warfare?

Over a period of months, a string of tests, both in Nevada and the South Seas, resulted in an equally spectacular string of failures—and further amplified American anxieties. Then came Starfish Prime, a smashing success, both scientifically and rhetorically. By that point, the atomic bureaucracy was desperate for a dramatic counter to the successes of the Russians and the string of American losses, and they had risked a flood of pretest publicity. On Hawaii's resort islands, a number of hotels held rooftop viewing parties; publicity releases had gone out not just for this test but for each of the nine postponements and the previous launch blowups. (*Life* counted not one but two such failures; perhaps it was confusing Bluegill's June 3 destruct as part of the sequence). Despite the long odds, though, tourists once again lined the shorelines and *Life*'s bureau sent high-level editorial representatives,* and scattered photographers through the South Seas to get the full panorama, including prize *Life* staffer Carl Mydans, whose picture from Samoa was the final in the series of double-page spreads of the dazzling visual effects. The result was a front-cover, eight-page spread, including not only color and black-and-white panoramas but a pair of views of awestruck spectators, some with their jaws literally agape at the spectacle. "Space Bomb in Color: Eerie Spectacle in Pacific Sky," *Life* titled the issue.[18]

"It Was as if Someone Had Poured Blood on the Sky," read the headline for Starfish Prime, followed by "A Scientific Revelation Above Samoa," on the final spread of Mydans's pictures. These were typical of the portentous pronouncements *Life*'s copywriters considered necessary to the journal's

---

* Notably Dick Stolley, who would later acquire the Kennedy assassination film from Zapruder, run the Washington bureau of the magazine, and found *People*, and Tommy Thompson, another celebrated *Life* writer and editor.

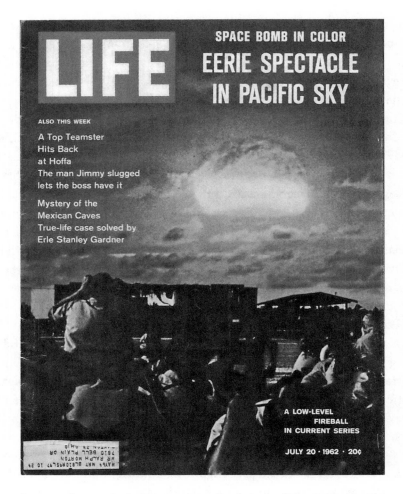

10.5. *Life* cover, July 20, 1962. (LIFE is a registered trademark of Time Inc. © The Picture Collection Inc. Reprinted with permission. Article: © 1962. The Picture Collection Inc. Reprinted with permission. All rights reserved.)

role as an interpreter of world events to an often-frightened and as-often-numbed American public.

Invoking biblical apocalypse was scary enough to require an antidote, and the magazine found it in the story of Telstar, the little satellite that could, and a homely septuagenarian whom *Life* flew to the launch for a picture opportunity. Just a page after the H-bomb: "Another Wonder Sears the Sky." So read the headline, but the story itself focused on "Mrs. Louise Bucker of Milwaukee, AT&T shareholder ... [who] went to Cape Canaveral to watch her 1/14,760,000 interest in the real Telstar streak skyward in the dark dawn." Across the two-page spread showing Mrs. Bucker in time-lapse as the Telstar-bearing Thor rocket arced across the opposite page, *Life*'s editors declared that "man pursues his fiery destiny." Sublimity, terror, apocalypse, domesticity, capitalism, heroics, and space-age destinarianism: all in one issue.[19]

Americans reading *Life* that July weren't privy to the complex scientific-military implications of the Dominic series. For them, the visual spectacles presented on the pages of *Life* represented a return to the old dialectic of beauty and terror, triumphalism and fatalism, that had been interrupted by the test ban. *Life* was right on target to set Mrs. Bucker and Telstar in contrast, and then to cite John Glenn immediately thereafter, for in so doing the journal recast the narrative of the atomic age, not disruptively but cumulatively. Defense was one necessity in the battle for technological progress and eventual triumph; world communication and world understanding were others. Glenn's space travel, Telstar's stock-shares-into-space: these were tangible signs of "man's adventure" seen benevolently.

Life quoted Shakespeare ("Man, proud man") while it warned that Telstar "forebodes intercontinental Ed Sullivan," trivializing grand achievements and contributing to the general corruption of American purpose. Over the fall of that year, though, most Americans would have been more than content to see the heavens applied in so mundane a fashion. Instead, the months after Telstar's launch and Kennedy's bold pronouncements were punctuated by increasingly terrifying signs of the impending apocalypse, of blood poured on the sky and the horsemen riding the flaring auroras of revelation above Samoa. In September, exposés of the dangers of test-explosion radiation to Soviet and American astronauts sullied the picture of heroic space destinies as the Soviets called on the United States to reschedule tests to protect cosmonauts, and NASA officials revealed that they were monitoring astronaut Wally Schirra, his spacecraft, and his spacesuit for radiation overdoses.

Then atomic brinksmanship and its accompanying terror reached an epochal climax. On October 22, President Kennedy announced that the Soviets had set up nuclear missile sites in Cuba, and missiles and warheads were on the way. Two days before, nuclear test Checkmate had detonated almost a hundred miles into space, signaling a continuation of resolve to test the limits of atomic brinksmanship and saber rattling. Two days after his speech, Kennedy quarantined the island nation, proposed to intercept and inspect ships on the high seas, and reinforced Guantanamo base with an infusion of troops. On the 26th, Bluegill Triple Prime exploded, producing a fireball visible in Hawaii. That same day, the Soviets launched two successful airborne nuclear tests.[20]

In the intervening years between then and now, the resolution of the crisis has developed a reassuring triumphalist quality: Kennedy stood up to

10.6. Double-page spread, *Life*, July 20, 1962. (LIFE is a registered trademark of Time Inc. Photos by Yale Joel. © The Picture Collection Inc. Reprinted with permission. Article: © 1962. The Picture Collection Inc. Reprinted with permission. All rights reserved.)

... 'IT WAS AS IF SOMEONE HAD
POURED BLOOD ON THE SKY'

r time before the memory of man, the
ight sky rose unreachable above him.
remote dark dome reflected only the pin-
k of stars, the moon's changing face, the
ora's subtle glow, the jagged webs of light-
g. But now man was no longer a mere ob-
er of his sky. He had tumultuous light-
gs of his own. Last week he loosed them,
loding a giant hydrogen bomb hundreds
miles in space over the Pacific. As the in-
lible flash spread over millions of square
es of ocean man looked up in awe and
nder at what he had done.

n the Hawaiian Islands rain dripped from
rattling palms on the day the shot was
posed to go off. The clouds were thick.
waiians, recalling nine postponements and
failures in earlier attempts to send up
bomb, saw the gray sky and concluded
t nothing would happen this time, either.
the earlier low-level shots, such as that
wn on the cover, they had seen nothing
ll.

ut at noon short-wave radio sets began
pick up monotonous voices broadcasting
e checks from Johnston Island 800 miles
he west, launching site for the Thor rocket
ich would thrust the H-bomb aloft. Gradu-
word spread that another countdown had
eed begun. Later in the afternoon, weather
scientific and observation planes began to
off from Hawaiian airfields, headed west,
l by night the crowds started gathering
doors. LIFE regional editor Dick Stolley
tched them. "There were coeds in muu-
us, college boys in swimsuits, tourists in
wly purchased resort wear, sleepy kids.
ne carried transistor radios to keep track
the countdown." On Waikiki Beach, boys
ught their dates. In Pearl Harbor, sailors
ught up in an orderly row on the dock along-
e their submarine. A show girl from the
yal Hawaiian Hotel slipped outdoors in her
eaf skirt, hoping to see the shot between
s. Other spectators, seemingly undisturbed
the symbolism, watched from a cemetery.
e weather grew worse and veteran observ-
began to expect another postponement.
t at 10:45 the word came that the Thor
cket was off its pad and rising. Honolulu
io stations cut their programs and broad-
t the continuing countdown for the explo-
n as the rocket climbed for 15 minutes. Stol-
heard the remote counting voice from
nston Island "grow higher, almost girl-
." It read off the final five seconds. Then
was precisely 11 o'clock.

LIFE Correspondent Thomas Thompson
s watching from a hotel courtyard. "The
e-black tropical night suddenly turned into
ot lime green (see pp. 26, 27). It was bright-
than noon. The green changed into a lemon-

E SHOCK, THE SHOCKED. Eight hundred
es away, the space bomb lights the sky and
cloud banks near the Hawaiian island of Maui
ft). Buildings in foreground are a secret instal-
ion built to study the blast. Meanwhile on Wai-
ki (right) spectators gape in the searing light,

ade pink and finally, terribly, blood red. It
was as if someone had poured a bucket of
blood on the sky." Stolley, on Waikiki Beach,
saw the blast as "white and hot, like the flash
of a breaking electrical circuit. It turned almost instantly to bright bilious green, a color
so unexpected that watchers on the beach
gasped. Great green fingers of light poked
out and through the clouds. From the center
of the blast, a red glow began expanding upward. It was not the familiar orange of the
tropical sunset but a deep, solid red, and the
people afterwards groped for words to describe it. The glow bubbled aloft and boiled
in the sky. A quarter-moon—some people
thought it was the fireball—showed through
occasionally as the clouds broke (see pp. 28,
29) and its face glowed not pale but a rich,
strange yellow."

S ome 2,000 miles southwest from Hawaii,
LIFE Photographer Carl Mydans watched
from the island of Samoa. There were no
crowds. Mydans and another newsman stood
alone in a deserted mountain pass, and saw
what Mydans called "the greatest rainbow in
history. . . . First two bright lines came up off
the northern horizon, curving away from each
other, looking like feathers in a glass. The
white lines of the earth's magnetic field curved
round from north to south and in between
them there were colored lights dancing. After
six to eight minutes the rainbow faded but it
left something behind I'd never felt with rain-
bows: elation, awe, and an unearthly fright."

In Hawaii there was the same fear. One family had kept its children up late to watch from
the beach. The parents saw their kids staring
wide-eyed at the tormented sky and they
shuddered. Another elderly couple on the
beach covered their eyes. Most of the watching crowd was silent. "There was none of the
go-team-go atmosphere of a missile launch,"
Stolley reported. "The crowd stood strangely
still, as if braced for a thunderous wave of
noise. There was no noise, of course, and we
constantly had to remind ourselves that what
we gaped at was taking place 800 miles away.
We stood there, with only the gentle sounds
of sea and civilization murmuring around us."

As tests go, the man-made inferno was su-
premely successful. It was a crucial part of
our effort to deter a nuclear war by keeping
our nuclear superiority. The Pacific blast may
lead to better weapons for us—and perhaps
even a defense against enemy missiles. It came
at a time when we seemed to be triumphing
wholesale in tests of strength and skill with
nature: digging canyons in the earth with other nuclear blasts in Nevada; orbiting an intricate star which brought pictures from one side
of the Atlantic to the other with the speed of
light. But the scientific and technical importance of the events seemed to pale in the bright
fury of the blast which climaxed them. There
were prayers all across the Pacific last week
—prayers across the world—that man's headlong mastery of his universe would always
stay as wondrous, and as safely remote, as on
the awesome night when we set the sky on fire.

CONTINUED

ANOTHER WONDER SEARS THE SKY

MAINE

FRANCE

THE PICTURE

Another Thor rocket put another remarkable object into space last week—a satellite called the Telstar which sent a crisp TV picture across the Atlantic. Telstar picked up signals from a domed station in Maine (*top, left*) and relayed them to another in France (*center*) where sets received a bandbox-bright image (*bottom*). Telstar had been launched by the government for the American Telephone and Telegraph Company, whose shareholders got a nice piece of sky in their pie.

SHAREHOLDER IN A SATELLITE. Mrs. Louise Bucker of Milwaukee (*above*), A.T. & T. stockholder, examined a Telstar model last fall (LIFE, Sept. 29). Last week she went to Cape Canaveral to watch her 1/14,760,000 interest in the real Telstar streak skyward in the dark dawn (*right*).

10.7. Double-page spread, *Life*, July 20, 1962. (LIFE is a registered trademark of Time Inc. © The Picture Collection Inc. Reprinted with permission. Article: © 1962. The Picture Collection Inc. Reprinted with permission. All rights reserved.)

MAN PURSUES HIS
FIERY DESTINY

The spectral light over the Pacific and the glimmer of millions of TV tubes last week illuminated an understanding with fate that man made long ago. When he first discovered that fire was not an undiluted benefit—and promptly burned his thumb—man did not put out all fires everywhere and forever. He chose, in his moment of anguish, to keep the fire—and all its benefits—and to take the risks and the consequences that attended it. Since then it has been his nature to go on burning his fingers—to tinker, to meddle, to *try* things, occasionally to be hurt, even to the death. The beauties and bounties of the ages have been his rewards: the other side of the understanding.

The past months, weeks and days have been triumphant for man—U.S. man, in particular—exploiting his side of the understanding. Telstar —though it forebodes intercontinental Ed Sullivan—has also the promise of untold reward. So too has the fantastic blast in the Pacific sky. But it is foolhardy to predict what these things may one day mean. Though the explosion was undertaken in the name of defense, and the Telstar launched in the most peaceful of interest, both remain part of man's ancient, two-sided understanding. Here he stands today, blowing on his fingers, making plans still more vast.

Man tinkers, man meddles—and some say fearfully that he should not. But thereby is revealed a misunderstanding of what man is. He is far more than what Shakespeare, in one of his dourest moods, said he was—"Man, proud man . . . like an angry ape, plays such fantastic tricks before high heaven as make the angels weep."

John Glenn is a man, and very much a part of man's adventure. After his orbital flight Glenn explained one tiny fraction of what remains to be done. He said that if his reach represented the diameter of the earth, he had been but two scant fingers' width above its surface. But 50 years ago, man had journeyed upward only the breadth of a hair. In rising so far so fast, man has pursued his roving destiny, accepting both the risks and the rewards. The fire that once could only warm his food and illuminate the walls of his cave now propels him, as he knew intuitively it one day must, toward the stars.

the Russkies, Khrushchev stood down, the missile-laden ships slunk back to harbor in the Soviet Union.[21] To world citizens at the time, however, the end was anything but clear-cut, for military and diplomatic professionals and ordinary citizens alike. After nearly two decades of anti-Soviet propaganda portraying Russian leaders as dangerous, volatile, aggressive, primitive, and duplicitous, American suspicions ran high, and to turn on the morning news was to sit by the radio or television with breathing shallow and prayers close to the lips.

In that last week of ambiguous resolution and unspoken anxiety before the Cuban missile crisis resolved, the novelty Halloween tune "Monster Mash" fell out of the top spot on the hit parade, replaced by "He's A Rebel," the Crystals' second hit, and their first on Wall of Sound producer Phil Spector's Philles label. The *Billboard* Hot 100 of November 3 seemed to reinforce the contention that pop music's relations to the broader streams of its culture were tenuous. Love dominated, love and isolation, self-involvement, fad (Chubby Checker's "Limbo Rock" had risen from 33 to 23 to 18 and then had broken into the top 10 at number 8) and predictability. Such a lineup might suggest the isolation of youth culture from looming adult responsibilities and fears, or it might propose the music as a place of safe retreat, a predictable, rigorously structured form that could serve as a haven from what lay on the horizon, for the world, the nation, and the individual.

It might be worth glancing farther afield before concluding one way or the other. We might, for example, return to the opening scene of *Miracle on 34th Street*, that tracking shot of a man walking down a New York City street. But let's move the time forward to 1962, and put a man in place of a deity.

Photographer Garry Winogrand is considered one of the masters of the mordant strain of modernist visual arts that emerged in the '60s from the celebratory heroicism of '50s American expressionism. His was a visual universe of broken connections, dazzling visual slapstick at the edge of despair, a social landscape of demonic children, sad imprisoned animals, desperate lockstep businessmen, primordially sexual women, all trudging an urban landscape slipping into entropic chaos but not quite there yet. There was no Santa on the sidewalks of Winogrand's New York, though there were midgets, legless cripples on makeshift wheelie-carts, astronaut look-alikes trying to pick up ice cream cone–balancing women, pantheists worshipping the fire-god in a smoldering garbage can.

Early in 1963, just weeks after the missile crisis, Winogrand formulated the text to his application for a Guggenheim Fellowship, perhaps the most prestigious and most competitive of artists' grants offered in the United

States, then or now. Winogrand would become only the third photographer to receive such an honor.

> I look at the pictures I have done up to now, and they make me feel that who we are and how we feel and what is to become of us just doesn't matter. Our aspirations and successes have been cheap and petty. I read the newspapers, the columnists, some books, I look at some magazines (our press). They all deal in illusions and fantasies. I can only conclude that we have lost ourselves, and that the bomb may finish the job permanently, and it just doesn't matter, we have not loved life. I cannot accept my conclusions, and so I must continue this photographic investigation further and deeper. This is my project.[22]

Winogrand despised self-analysis or pontification. But he sometimes spoke of his experiences as the Cuban missile crisis unfolded. He told of walking the streets, stopping at an appliance store window where a wall of televisions showed the crisis unfolding. To his friend John Szarkowski, he spoke of "despair out of fear for the life of his family and himself and his city, and . . . his own impotence to affect the outcome. Finally it came to him that he was nothing—powerless, insignificant, helpless, and that knowledge, he said, liberated him. He was nothing, so he was free to lead his own life."[23]

Winogrand's response was imbedded simultaneously in the high culture of his day (to which he aspired) and its popular culture (of which he was a part, seeking to extricate himself). His career had begun in advertising. He'd entered the Museum of Modern Art not through the serious photography for which it was known but as part of the vast, bathetic, mass-culture paean to world peace and unity, Eduard Steichen's 1955 group show, *The Family of Man*. By the early '60s, he was a successful commercial photographer, mixing advertising with editorial work while simultaneously making a start at the practice that would set him in the pantheon of modernist artists. He felt his kinship to the expatriate and denationalized artists of the modern era—Goya and Picasso, Hemingway and Stein. Yet he was perhaps more a typical American than he might have seemed: an immigrant son swimming the seas of postwar cultural life. Beneath the tortured surface of his Guggenheim essay lay the deep sense of alienation and dread that he shared with so many Americans of his time. Asked once what it was like to watch the Cuban crisis unfold on multiple televisions in a shop window, he replied that it was strangely social; he was one of a crowd of people pressed up against the glass, three or four deep, when the evening news came on, and he watched televisions "flying out the door" as those with the cash to spend and no TV at home bought their first sets in order to follow the course of events, perhaps the last American narrative. Strangely social and yet utterly lonely, he went on. No one spoke, there was some shuffling and a little push-and-shove to get a view, but it was as if one were in a city already populated by "ghosts and zombies."[24]

Winogrand's response to the Cuban missile crisis represented one alternative an American might choose: to find liberation and escape simultaneously in the realization of individual powerlessness. Adults like Winogrand discovered in that moment a culmination of nearly two decades of fear, of manipulation—and awareness of that manipulation, even if that knowledge didn't free them from the anxiety, the doubt, and the instinctive reactions it was meant to provoke. If the long-term rhetoric of the Cold War had developed to persuade the American polity to put its trust in the largest institutions, the most powerful political forces, the best-armed among the military, the missile crisis threatened to snap the elastic connecting the individual to the state and its policies.

Of course, the alternative was denial, perhaps the absolute denial that showed itself in one of the most raucous New Year's Eves in New York City history, or the relative denial that came with retreating to the house, the hearth, home and family, to spend the holidays huddled together as if in a fallout shelter, waiting for memory to fade.

Looking at the top 40 suggests there was a third way, a way taken primarily by teenagers and young adults for whom powerlessness wasn't a revelation but a condition: teenagers, young adults, black men, women of all colors, artists, Jews, men with the wrong desires (Joe Meek was one; his relationship with his business, creative, and romantic partner Geoff Goddard was on the rocks or already finished by the time "Telstar" hit the *Billboard* Hot 100). Powerlessness was a condition. Opting out, leaving the expected narrative, as Winogrand did, was a response that wrested power from powerlessness. Over the next year or two or five, the pop music world would be rife with songs that proposed this option: the Drifters, singing King and Goffen's "Up on the Roof"; Petula Clark singing, *I know a place where the music is fine and the lights are always low*; Bob Dylan calling, *take me on a trip*. Timothy Leary would soon urge Americans to "turn on, tune in, drop out." By the end of the decade, this utopian refusal would have lost its force. Joni Mitchell would turn Woodstock into a dirge aria. Crosby, Stills, Nash & Young singing *we're finally on our own*, having *found her dead on the ground* at Kent State, would ask, *How can you run when you know?*[25]

During the week in 1962 that saw the Cuban missile crisis come to a head, the week that "He's a Rebel" beat out "Only Love Can Break A Heart" for number 1, Meek and the Tornados broke into the American market. "Telstar" entered on November 3 at 85. At that moment it might have been evidence of *Life*'s warning that the culture fostered by the satellite might offer nothing more than "intercontinental Ed Sullivan." Only love, not politics, not global apocalypse, might break a heart, the top songs told their believers.

And yet. For those in radioland, transistors, outer space, Thor missiles and unlikely asteroidal rumblings could be the property not just of McGeorge Bundy but of anyone with a transistor radio, a 45-rpm record player, and 99¢. Cheerful, stupid, repetitive, recorded in an apartment, featuring keyboard sounds that might have come from a child's toy and a vocal part hummed with the pitch-imprecision of shower operas in your own bathroom, "Telstar" was simultaneously liberating, cynical, and optimistic. On the week that the United States unleashed its final atmospheric nuclear test (Tightrope, on a Nike Hercules missile, yield "low," height approximately fourteen miles), "Telstar" was number 71 with a bullet.

Week after week, it rose like a rocket: 85, 71, 39, 18, 13. On December 8, 1962, it broke into the top 10. That was the week that the newspapers and magazines announced the breakdown of the actual satellite. "Telstar Is Silenced by Circuit Problems," reported *Aviation Week* on December 3. In fact, it was Starfish Prime that did in Telstar; having irradiated the Van Allen belt on the day before Telstar was launched, the outer space nuclear test produced an unrelenting burst of electrons at every rotation. Checkmate, Bluegill Triple Prime, and Kingfish added to the radioactivity, knocking out transistors in Telstar's command decoders and silencing its relays.[26]

As news of the satellite's failure spread, two chain reactions diverged. In official circles, Telstar's loss was kept very quiet; *Life* didn't report it, nor did the newsweeklies. On December 24, Queen Elizabeth constructed her broadcast Christmas greeting around the satellite: "Mankind continues to achieve wonders in technical and space research but in the Western world perhaps the launching of Telstar has captured the imagination most vividly," she declared; "this tiny satellite has become the invisible focus of a million eyes." Nowhere did she mention its silence.

On December 24, Americans probably didn't listen to the queen, but they did listen to "Telstar"; it hit number 1 that week, guaranteeing appearance in the airplay rotation at least once an hour. While Frankie Valli and the Four Seasons were falsetto doo-wopping "Santa Claus is Coming to Town" (number 34) and Bing Crosby's "White Christmas" was in a virtual dead heat with The Chipmunks' "Chipmunk Song (Please Christmas Don't Be Late)" at 46 and 47, "Telstar" was the song you heard in the car on the way to work or

Christmas shopping; it was the song to relieve the rush of the season, and it mediated between the promise of the Christian holiday and the conditions of a world on the brink. Compared with the top albums of that season—ranging from the slightly swank sounds of the Norman Luboff Choir to the sweater-clad crooner compilations getting steady airplay during the weeks immediately before Christmas—"Telstar" was an unlikely holiday hit. It had everything those didn't: it was primitive, cheesy, cheerful, and ominous at the same time, with a chipper rhythm that kept you shopping, cooking, wrapping, driving that season. It made its own beat: *apocalypso*.

Over the next weeks, scientists at Bell Labs worked frantically to find a workaround for their star satellite. Sometime after the first of the new year, one in their ranks proposed turning the circuitry off, waiting for the excess radiation to dissipate, and then turning the satellite on again. By this time, its elliptical orbit had placed it out of the Van Allen belt, and the repair was a success. This was news the dominant institutions—government, military, and corporate—could tout, and this time the triumph made the magazines. Even *Business Week* ran a piece—"Repair Job in Space: Telstar's Troubles."[27] That same week, "Telstar" fell out of its number 1 spot, though it held on at number 2 for a couple of weeks thereafter. By early February, when the satellite emerged from darkness and, bombarded by renewed radiation, failed permanently, "Telstar" was down to 36. February 16, and the song and satellite were both gone.

Atomic radiation had foiled the transistor revolution Telstar seemed to promise—seemed, that is, to the likes of President Kennedy and Queen Elizabeth, to AT&T's chairman, Fred Kappel, and perhaps to Mrs. Louise Bucker, stockholder. Theirs was a techno-utopia bringing world understanding in terms that could guarantee progress and profit, packaged in a gift wrap of institutional propriety. But down on earth "Telstar" was celebrating another transistor revolution, and the transistor radio was making that celebration nearly universal.

Diamonds and furs were heavily advertised presents that Christmas, but the holiday season's real hit was the portable transistor radio. First appearing in quantity in the later 1950s, these radios had achieved near-universal market penetration by 1962; now they were called, simply, transistors. Miniaturized to shirt-pocket size and featuring six, seven, or more transistors to increase sensitivity and acoustic quality, sold with earplugs that compensated for the tinniness of the small speaker, these were prime items on the lists of teenagers and young adults alike. And the flood of these radios from the cheap-import market in 1960, '61, and '62 pushed the price down relentlessly.

That season saw prices drop to $14.99 and then lower still as retailers competed for the post-crisis Christmas dollar, making them appropriate purchases, especially during a season when families nested in retreat from a year of terrifying news and in anticipation of one that might be even more harrowing. As radio historian Michael Brian Schiffer has pointed out, "Small transistor portables, equipped with ear plugs, elegantly solved the rock-and-roll problem. By bestowing these radios as gifts, parents could wall off the offending music."[28] Transistors offered a compromise between propriety and permissiveness; perhaps parents understood that the bonds of authority, weakened between them and their nation's principal institutions, could also be weakening between the generations within the household.

On May 7, 1963, NASA, Bell Labs, and AT&T launched Telstar 2. Nearly identical to the first except for added radiation shielding for the command decoder transistors, this one was set for a higher orbit—high enough to avoid much of the Van Allen belt and, perhaps even more importantly, high enough to bring its transmission capability over a half-hour, making it a viable tool for network TV. Down on the ground, though, it was spring, and teenagers were listening to Little Peggy March singing "I Will Follow Him" and Peter Paul & Mary doing "Puff, The Magic Dragon." The trio had already made a name for themselves singing the songs of a young folk composer named Bob Dylan, whose second album, *The Freewheelin' Bob Dylan*, was released that month, rising to 22 on the album charts. "The Times They Are A-Changin'" wasn't on that album. But they *were* changing.

Both Telstars transformed the cultural geography of Cold War America. Both rose and fell; both were relays of complex messages presented more or less clearly, more or less garbled, more or less faint. Both presaged utopian futures. That these would clash was inevitable, though the play-out of this cultural warfare would take most of a decade to escalate, and the decade would come to stand for that war—though, like most conflicts imbedded in contradictory premises uneasily coexisting under one identity, as one nation, this civil war would also be confused, sporadic, marked by torn allegiances and broken families.

CHAPTER 11

Portable Communities

RADIO, 1963

> Well, I remember seein' some ad
> So I turned on my Conelrad
> But I didn't pay my Con Ed bill
> So the radio didn't work so well
> Turned on my record player—
> It was Rock-a-day Johnny singin,' "Tell Your Ma, Tell Your Pa
> Our Love's A-gonna Grow Ooh-wah, Ooh-wah"[1]
> BOB DYLAN, "Talkin' World War III Blues," 1963

By 1963, radio and television had diverged sharply in their programming, in the domestic geography they staked out, in the demographics of their audiences, and in the cultural spaces they both claimed and brought into being. Television sought consensus in product and audience. Radio responded to the loss of its function as a national unifier by celebrating diversity.

Radio was poised for a revolutionary shift. All the elements were in place: the audience had decentralized throughout the house and out to the motel room, the vacation cabin, the beach, the hangout, and the car (where radios were the second most-chosen option, right behind heaters). In urban apartments, where space was at a premium, in poor homes where television was a distant dream, in rural areas where there wasn't any TV signal, the radio remained the dominant technology of mass communication. Black or

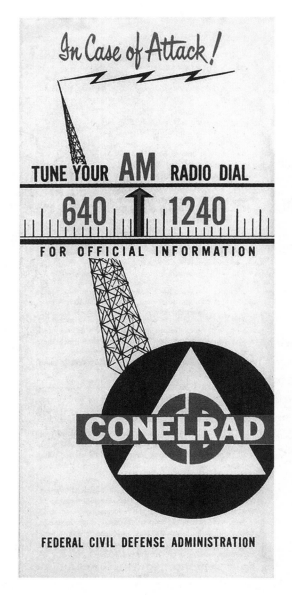

11.1. The official CONELRAD pamphlet, 1953

"race" music, "hillbilly," "bluegrass," "country," and "western" music could be heard on almost any radio anywhere in the United States at any given moment. Bob Dylan, still Bobby Zimmerman in 1956 and living in Hibbing, Minnesota, helped his father sell televisions in the family furniture and appliance store. At night, he transported himself across the country and across its musical and ethnic history, leaning into the radio in his bedroom as the distant signals, amplified by darkness and cloud cover, magically appeared on the dial, between CONELRAD* markings and network shows with broader appeal.

Small, fiercely independent radio stations offered content that was anything but bland or official. "Clear-channel" radio stations broadcasting from the Mexican border with huge transmitter wattages pushed everything from right-wing politics to quack nostrums, but they also sold musical forms that stood for, and spoke to, a culturally complex American populace. Gospel stations, union stations, "race radio" broadcasters, Mexican and Polish stations, Texas swing shows, and political tirades all competed in the ether. Where the signal originated didn't matter. Mexico, North Dakota, California, Ohio: this was *everywhere* music, to paraphrase cultural historian Daniel Boorstin.[2]

Radio attached itself most of all to the children of the postwar baby boom, many of them teenagers. With increasing amounts of disposable income and with a yen for independence and the time to indulge it, American teenagers as a class became radio owners and listeners. In the process, they inherited the wildly diverse airwaves, even as their presence, their heft in the ratings, served to shift that programming.

The radio they demanded, and the radio to which they listened, was vastly different than that of their parents. While the clock radio awoke husband and wife to news or to news and music radio, most commonly the network radio broadcasts, teenagers awoke to deejay music on their own stations and with their own playlists.

These rock-and-roll teenagers formed a different generation even than the ones who had made that musical form popular in the '50s. It's striking to consider the different circumstances of teenagers turning 16 in 1954, in 1958, and in 1963. The first would have been born in the depths of the Great Depression, and then, during the war, may well have spent the years from age 6 to 10 without a father in the household and often with an absent working mother, being raised in day care, by neighbors, or by grandparents or other members of an extended family. If the reunited (or reconstituted) family moved to the suburbs in the early '50s, this child was already entering adolescence—was 13 in, say, 1951. This was almost exactly the tale that underlay *Miracle on 34th Street*, and that somber, overly adult, emotionally suppressed child, Susie, with her yearning for the stabilities of home and the financial and emotional security it promised.

The second child in that family would have been conceived in 1942 in

* CONtrol of ELectromagnetic RADiation: the Cold War national defense emergency radio broadcasting system.

the rush of war-bride marriages as men went off to battle, experienced the earliest childhood years in the straitened circumstances and decidedly un-nuclear family constellations of the war, and then had a father reappear, with all the upheaval and tumult that such an event might be expected to catalyze. Moving to the suburbs in '51 at age 9, she or he would have shifted schools in second or third grade.

These two clusters of rock-and-roll children were offspring of conflict and instability, material straits turning to comparative prosperity, upend-ings of family and wrenching shifts of place. The first group gave rise to the wave of "juvenile delinquency" or at least the fad of fear about it (*Rebel Without a Cause*, released in 1955, was both a consequence and a cause of a burst of discussion about the dangers of America's rootless, rebellious youth), but the majority of its members had strong experiential ties to their younger brothers and sisters of the second group—rebellious, perhaps, but also de-sirous of a social community and wary of cutting the ties of family. (Indeed, the plot of *Rebel Without a Cause* didn't concern teenage rejection of family, but rather the deep, unrequited need of those teens for stable and loving families to compensate for the instabilities of their childhoods.)

The teenagers who bunched around age 16 in 1963 differed markedly from this profile of early austerity and later comfort. They were conceived in the years after their fathers returned from war, born into the upwardly mobile, increasingly affluent American dreams of the Cold War years. Im-portantly, there were so many of them that from childhood they had a sense of themselves *as* a generation. If their families moved to suburbs like Levit-town in the early '50s, they were still young enough to experience a conti-nuity of playmates and classmates, and a stable physical, social, and cultural geography. Their insecurities were Cold War insecurities: like their parents, they were inundated with images of atomic weaponry, warnings of atomic warfare, and routines of atomic defense, from "duck and cover" exercises in the classroom to fallout shelter rehearsals at home; but unlike their parents, they didn't have the contexts of Depression life or of conventional warfare in which to set these images and manipulations. The lessons they learned early in life (the *Duck and Cover* filmstrips were released in the early '50s), were reinforced in the middle of childhood (the *Gaither Report* on the rela-tive civil defense capabilities of the United States and Russia was leaked in 1957 and brought a flurry of new fears), and reappeared as they entered ado-lescence, with the Berlin crisis of 1961 and the Cuban missile crisis of '63.

Their fears, in the main, didn't concern loss of love or lack of food, shel-ter, or clothing. Theirs were less immediate but more pervasive, more global, anxieties: the fear of annihilation, not just of themselves and their families, but all of civilization, all life on the planet. Their responses were communal and sociable; they sought a certain safety in their own numbers, and the movies they watched and starred in reflected that. The string of popular teen-utopia "beach blanket" movies of the early and mid-1960s often interwove family unity with the discovery or creation of a family within their teen peers. In fact, we can compare the dysfunctional yet yearning teen "family" from *Rebel Without a Cause* to the sheltering families that surrounded Gidget in her sequel, *Gidget Goes Hawaiian* (1961), in which the teen's nuclear family flies to the ideal isle and Gidget boomerangs between their reassuring presence and the freedom of a teen society of surfers and "beach bums."

Teens crowded the beaches in the summer of 1963, and they brought their radios. Some carried the larger and higher-fidelity portables like the Zenith Royal 790 or the Silvertone 800/Sears 4223, both of which debuted in 1963. These had amplifiers and speakers powerful enough to project beyond one beach towel—they could make a party. Others brought the trendier shirt-pocket transistors—the Zenith Royal 40 (1963) or the already legendary Sony models. These didn't offer much in the way of sound projection, but then, fidelity and nuance weren't the goals on a public beach—the point was to be seen with the radio and to be heard listening to the right music and the right songs on the right stations. Out there, in the world, the radio's function was social. It was a means of using sound and music to declare your identity to others and to draw others of similar identity to you. While you waited, alone, for friends to arrive, the radio provided a cocoon.

Radio manufacturers were more than aware of this phenomenon. They designed and advertised for this market and its particular demands. As early as 1959 and 1960, Motorola and Zenith were selling direct to teenagers with ads that pitched the radio as an icebreaker and a maker of communal experience.

Take a look at the ad. What did Motorola think these kids would be listening to? The radio's dial isn't clearly delineated, but it doesn't look like the arrow was pointing to 640 or 1240, CONELRAD's atomic-attack instruction stations. Judging from the clothes, it looks like fall, at the beginning of the school year, when social insecurities were high and when social relations were fluid, and when teens still had summer-job money in their passbooks. Probably it wasn't the first week or two of school, though—when "My Boyfriend's Back" promised that a summer of vicious rumors of a girl gone wild were about to be put to rest (*He's gonna save my reputation, hey la, hey la, my boyfriend's back!*). Perhaps the radio was playing Bobby Vinton's "Blue Velvet," a hot number with a sentimental twist that had boys and girls both sighing as they slow danced. Or "Sally Go 'Round the Roses," by the Jaynettes, a girl

Pocketful of power

Portable Model 8X26 has 3-position carrying handle-stand, earphone jack for private listening. Colors: Maple Sugar, Charcoal.

Like carrying a full <u>10-tube radio</u> in your pocket! This pint-size power-plant packs 8 transistors and 2 germanium diodes. Extra amplifier transistor in RF Stage produces 5 times more power to get more stations. 3-section gang Tuning Condenser has 9 times more power to select desired stations, reject unwanted stations. Audio transformer delivers 30% more audible volume without distortion. Plays hundreds of hours at peak performance on penlite batteries you buy for pennies.

More to enjoy **MOTOROLA**

Specifications subject to change without notice.

11.2. Ad for a Motorola transistor radio, 1959

group whose hit took a classic childhood skip-rope song and made it about as dreamy and sad as it could get. Trini Lopez's cover of Peter Paul & Mary's version of Pete Seeger's civil rights protest song, "If I Had a Hammer," a danceable version that eviscerated the song, threw away the protest guts, and left a very hip skin, was hanging on in the top 10; "Surfer Girl" by the Beach Boys was making its slow slide after having been introduced a little too late in the summer season to make number 1.[3] Sam Cooke's smokin' version of "Frankie and Johnny" was in the top 20. If you really, really wanted to dance, though, you put on "Heat Wave" by Martha & the Vandellas, even if your parents might forbid it for its description of orgasmic-swooning crush— the very sort you just might have had by the end of the first month back in high school.[4]

The transistor radio afforded two freedoms for American teenagers of the early '60s, and both of them suggested the beginnings of an alternative to the dominant, middle-class, middle-age culture, an *isoculture* that preceded the counterculture, located not on college campuses but in high school parking lots and the spontaneous community places and events that these adolescents were making and using. One was a freedom to move, and to move with their communities intact—to migrate on a daily basis within the relatively constricted geographies their adult tenders had granted them, without losing their sense of who they were, as individuals and as a community, a generation. The other was a freedom to move beyond those restricted places, to enter an imaginative geography of far wider area and far more fluid boundaries—and to do so without the control of adult supervisors and censors. Yes, radio stations were owned and operated by adult, capitalist conglomerates and corporations. And yes, the deejays were primarily adults themselves, beholden to their employers and to the rules of top 40 radio. But the very nature of that radio format, like so much of the supposedly conformist and authoritarian mass-communications world, was still a function of capitalist supply and demand. By 1963, teenagers had enough market heft and enough self-confidence to *make* the music, both as musicians and as audiences. In the process, they were expressing, describing, mapping, and settling the cultural landscapes of their moment and those of their futures, imagined and real. Lesley Gore's declaration, "You Don't Own Me," which hit the Hot 100 at the end of 1963, simply confirmed what the rest of that year's Hot 100 had been saying all along.

* * *

Portable communities *on the air*—that was what radio offered teenagers. By 1963, a cluster of elements had aligned: the teen audience, rock-and-roll music (broadly defined), radio stations whose programming strategies had evolved into sophisticated market-driven wedges of consumers and advertisers, and deejays.

Deejays were the catalysts in this mixture. From the early years of Alan Freed's "Moondog," who howled, punned, panted, rhymed, ridiculed, and revered the driving forces behind rock and roll and its blacker, darker, sexier R&B source, deejays introduced audiences to artists, artists to audiences, and audiences to each other. By the early '60s, though, the market for pop music radio had stabilized in most of the larger markets. As Ben Fong-Torres documents in his study of disk-jockey culture, Todd Storz and others standardized the musical offerings, introducing a format known as "top 40," by which program or station managers determined the most popular hits using statistics drawn from record sales, and then set those forty songs as the repeated fare of the week. As the top 40 model spread from the mid-size, middle-American venues like Omaha (from which Storz emerged), standardization spread as well, until by the early '60s more and more major-market deejays operated by a "clock" that was set by station managers—news, ads, promotions, contest, weather, patter, music, all locked into certain moments in the hour. Standardization to the point of near-automation now threatened to supplant the more fluid, personalized forms of the previous decade.[5]

This might seem a stifling system, but it was significantly more porous than its name implied. First, only a few stations in any radio listening area could thrive on a rigid top 40, clock-based format—perhaps two or three in major metropolitan areas where there were enough listeners willing to jump from station to station just to hear their particular favorite song in the top 40 mix. Even these stations couldn't sustain the same forty songs indefinitely; listeners and buyers tired of songs, and to keep their loyalty required that new songs enter the mix at regular intervals, and record companies, eager to replace lagging sales for one tune with runs on another, pressed the stations to air new songs.

Out of this came the payola scandal of the late '50s and early '60s as record labels, particularly the smaller ones with more at stake, bribed and rewarded station managers, program managers and disk jockeys for introducing new sides. The investigation of payola resulted in the demise of some of those labels and some of the more prominent disk jockeys as well (Freed was the most famous to go down). It also tightened playlists at many of the larger and more prominent stations, but the need to rotate and innovate remained. Deejays from different markets talked on the phone to each other, and some even traveled into regions near and far to cull trends and steal routines. When a San Francisco deejay named Bill Gavin began to send around mimeographed newsletters and then moved to a radio syndicate as a programming consultant, he built a network of deejays and programmers throughout the rest of the country (he saved the West Coast for himself) through which the *Bill Gavin Record Report* could identify songs and trends, locate regional hits, and make predictions.[6]

The result was, paradoxically, to introduce novelty into individual markets while encouraging a more homogeneous sonic palette nationally. Even the station managers and syndicate executives recognized that no audience would stay with utter repetition, and they sought ways both to distinguish themselves from other stations and to distinguish their offerings on a weekly, daily, even hourly basis. Here again, deejays were critically important. From the earliest rock-and-roll disk jockeys, a tradition had developed of "personality" broadcasting: Alan Freed's "Moondog" was only one among many who used the tricks of voice, impersonation, alliterative speech, puns, double entendres, sing-alongs, and personal "contests" encouraging listeners to call in, all to foster a loyal audience and engender a sense of community. Within markets, deejays fought tenaciously to gain and hold their people, and they routinely competed across regions as well, stealing each others' routines, or meeting, informally or formally, to share ideas and strategies. The result was a combination of intimacy and showmanship that emphasized radio's promise as an aural theater of the mind.[7]

If you listened, you heard a deejay address you directly: *your* deejay spoke *your* language; you called in to make requests; your station had contests, so if you had a car you put a bumper sticker on it and the "roving WAVZ mobile" might radio in your license plate giving you just a few minutes to call back and win, or they called your house and if you remembered the secret of the day, hour, or minute, you won; your high school got named, and maybe you, too. You might get tickets to a concert, even backstage passes and chances for autographs of the musicians. If your school was big enough or voluble enough in its fan base for the station or deejay, you might have a deejay party or even a dance with a live band.[8]

In the process, the line between the imaginative social landscape you floated into and out of on radio waves and the physical spaces you occupied daily and nightly began to blur. You belonged to a group of amorphous dimensions and indeterminate locations. What you knew, and what mattered, was that you shared your tastes, your experiences, your ways of dress and talk, and most importantly your music with others, others who might be on your street or around the corner or far from you.

The music was more than chords, rhythms, and notes; more than voices and accents and harmonies; more than lyrical clichés or stories; more than moods that soothed or energized you—though it was all those things. It was a code you shared with those like you, and it was the stream of messages those songs conveyed, directly and surreptitiously. The music was fluid, adapting to the changes of season and circumstance. It reflected your circumstances, but it also defined for you the theater within which your circumstances took on a larger form. It made a stage, and you strode on it, in imagination at least; your costume was chosen for you, but it was yours, after all—it fit you. If it didn't, you were free to switch stations.

To say that American teenagers of the Cold War generation lived by the rhythms of pop radio isn't an exaggeration—it's an understatement. As a consequence, they became arguably the dominating force in the medium between the end of the '50s and the arrival of FM as a major force in the late '60s. They were the largest audience, and they, and their just-older cohort, were the principal producers of content, imagery, mythology.

Radio offered two powerful incentives to its teen and young adult audiences: freedom and community. And while both of these can be understood through the lens of space, place, and movement, the site of pop radio's gifts lay in the realm not only of space but of time as well. Television promised escape to fantasy places, but it required its viewers to define their lives around its schedules and to stay at home to watch.* Pop radio liberated young listeners from a sense of their physical constraints and their adult-controlled time schedules, and into a more fluid imaginative space-time continuum.

The top 40 format's very repetitiveness made the prison sentence of school less onerous. You didn't miss anything while you were in school. You got out in the parking lot or onto the sidewalk or the school bus and you were back with your kin. There were differences *within* the hour—what high school Cousin Brucie featured; what time the "pick hit" of the week came on, and in what order those forty songs were played—but if you wanted to hear the Exciters singing "Tell Him" (number 1 on WABC and WMCA for the first week of 1963, edging out "Telstar"), you knew you'd hear it within the hour. And your imaginative geography ranged far beyond that which television offered your parents.[9]

The song spoke directly to you. *I know something about love,*† the Exciters

---

* Bars with televisions in them, mainly for watching sports, represented the principal exception to the rule, and they weren't yet ubiquitous; you might go next door to watch a show, but you were just shifting living rooms. So-called portable televisions were heavy, bulky, and tiny-screened.

† Throughout the discussions of popular music lyrics, I have chosen to italicize lyric fragments and passages to emphasize their spoken and listened-to nature, rather than quotation marks, which treat them as documentary shards.

told you, and then they gave you some useful advice. Simultaneously, the music linked you to the community with whom you shared experience—the broadcast. If you were listening and the music affected you, you could be sure that millions of others nationwide shared your emotion. Every week that the song rose in the charts, you felt your community enlarging, your experiences held in common by a larger and larger body of Americans. You belonged.

Radio's top 40 played against the backdrop of the news, of history small and large. Other radio, *old* radio, emphasized long newscasts, interviews, panels, specials. When the Cuban missile crisis of October 1962 brought the world to the brink of nuclear conflict and forced America to face the possibility of mushroom clouds rising from the heart of Miami, Washington, New York, and Boston, grown-up radio devoted itself to minute-by-minute of the terror. Top 40 radio, by contrast, gave a brief, rapid-fire string of headlines, lasting perhaps three minutes, including commercials.

This didn't mean that the circumstances of the day, the region, the nation and the world disappeared from a top 40 listener's consciousness. If anything, a news spot that emphasized an airline crash, failed international test-ban treaty negotiations, tax reform, traffic pileups, and the economic outlook, all in two minutes and thirty seconds, was *more* disconcerting rather than less. Top 40 news emphasized the distance of young listeners from any power over the news, reinforcing with its telegraphic style the sense of observing at a distance, as in a dream, unable to move. (*I'd like to help you son, but you're too young to vote*—Eddie Cochran, "Summertime Blues")

After the news, the rest of the hour offered solace, as it promised to speak directly about *your* crises, the ones that affected you and that you might affect: love, sociability, insecurity, hope, set within an intimate space. Or it opened outward into spaces of freedom and celebration: streets full of dancers, rooftops unfolding under the stars, on beaches and oceans, streets and highways. It set the drama of your life to music.

*　*　*

Radio music mapped two principal utopias for teenagers and young adults. Both were spaces of freedom and independence. Both were created *by* young people themselves, and that identification between audience and artist was what transformed the process from simple commerce to complex cultural creation. The creators made dream worlds out of real worlds, and the listeners affirmed the reality and the dream.

From one coast came an urban geography of streets and dance halls, apartments, and rooftops. This was the music that emerged from the Brill

Building and its neighbors on Broadway in New York City: music composed mostly by young white couples and performed mostly by black ensembles just as young and if anything more urban in origin and outlook.

Al Nevins and Don Kirshner founded Aldon Music in the belief that sound and music could provide qualities of authenticity that would draw the expansive teen audience. Starting the company in 1958, when *American Bandstand* was hot and the lush, string-and-horn "Philly Sound" dominated, 21-year-old Don Kirshner seemed to be bucking trends—but actually he was anticipating them. Working with Al Nevins, a longtime producer and successful musician in his 40s, turned out to be a brilliant act of synergy.[10]

Kirshner and Nevins had a surefire system for making hits. They replicated teenage experience by hiring teenagers to write, collaborate, and perform. Kirshner was a songwriter, committed to reaching *his* generation, and he rapidly assembled a string of like-minded and similarly youthful writers. Carole King and Gerry Goffin were both 19 when they joined up, and so was Neil Sedaka (his writing partner, Howard Greenfield, was 21). They worked in tiny spaces with tinny spinets, day and night. The Aldon factory at Broadway and 49th in New York City was so successful that the more established companies across the street in the Brill Building proper soon adopted this youth-commune model as well.

By 1962 and '63, the machinery was well oiled and the results extraordinary. Songwriters worked in pairs, often romantic pairs—Mann-Weil, King-Goffin—to keep boy and girl perspectives. "It was insane," reported Barry Mann of the Mann-Weil team. "Cynthia and I would be in this tiny cubicle. . . . In the next room, Carole and Gerry would be doing the same thing, and in the next room Neil [Sedaka] or someone else. . . . The competition, and the pressure, I suppose brought out the best in us."[11] The wash of music provided not just competition but ideas, chord progressions, rhythms, lyric notions. Mann recalled, "Sometimes when we all got to banging on our pianos you couldn't tell who was playing what."[12] With an early draft done, the writers commonly auditioned it to their colleagues. Often the result was to rewrite the lyrics, melody, or both (and to talk about which performers such a song should go to for recording and performance).

Once written, the songs still weren't ready to leave Aldon. The teams routinely recorded demos, mixing their own talents with a stable of on-demand musicians, that could be shopped to producers. The demos often involved arrangements sufficiently sophisticated that they could be rapidly adapted by the singers when the contract was signed and the label's musicians entered the studio. Even then, however, the Aldon collective was often deeply immersed in producing the final record. Sometimes the writers themselves served as pop stars—Neil Sedaka was the most prolific and famous of these, but Carole King had begun her career as a performer, and others appeared, pseudonymously, on record. Ellie Greenwich and Jeff Barry, who signed on with Aldon competitors Lieber and Stoller, had hits in 1963 as the Raindrops.

The musicians who performed on the demos, too, often ended up featured on the final releases. And these musicians, young, often black or Latino, contributed to the milieu from which the composers might construct a song. The music that resulted had an immediacy and authenticity that swept aside the surface clutter of clichés and stereotypes, and set narratives. In fact, one could consider those seeming failures of literary and musical merit as something quite different—as disguises for the underlying messages of subcultural unity, and as mediators between the raw experiences that gave rise to the songs, and the young listeners. Sometimes these functions combined, to slide a song's content past the censors—parents, station managers, or FCC monitors—while leaving the content accessible to the knowing teen.

Two songs—one a success, one a failure—serve as examples. Both were composed by Carole King and Gerry Goffin, and both involved their babysitter, Eva Boyd. Boyd was 17, working on and off as a substitute singer for the black girl group the Cookies. The Cookies were long-standing members of the demo-musician community, and they were established as performing and recording artists as well. Eva Boyd was just a few years younger than King and Goffin when the couple wrote a song called "The Loco-Motion," based on a dance Boyd had brought to the house. The beat—pushed, syncopated, even broken—came right out of the black music of Eva Boyd's childhood in South Carolina: gospel, R&B, and blues. Goffin and King had been immersed in its urban forms—they'd written for the Cookies before. That Little Eva would end up recording the song, with Carole King singing backup, also spoke for a different form of racial interplay than had characterized the conversion of race records into white hits in an earlier era.

"The Loco-Motion" was one of many songs that Aldon produced through which teenage listeners responded to their own sense of community, and of isolation from those outside their generation. *Everybody's doing a brand new dance, yeah*, Little Eva sang, and Carole responded, *Come on, baby, do the Loco-Motion*. Everyone was doing the dance—everyone, that is, except all the grownups, the squares, the censors, and *you*. You'd better start now: you were a baby, maybe Carole's baby sister, or maybe Little Eva's, or maybe just a baby not yet initiated into the community of teenagers. Listen to the song, on the radio, listen to Eva and Carole, and they'd teach you how—after all, *my little baby sister can do it with me, it's easier than learning your ABCs!* Learn the dance, and you'd join the joyous community of dancers, singers, revelers. Of course if you didn't pay attention to the lyrics (they were dumb, they were doggerel, they were repetitive), if you didn't bounce to the beat (it was so commonplace, so unsophisticated, so primitive), you wouldn't even know you'd missed the opportunity.

Little Eva's song was a huge hit in 1962. It made number 1 in August, not long after Eva arrived at the Goffin-King house badly beaten by her boyfriend. Goffin and King's response was to write one of the most controversial songs of pop history: "He Hit Me (And It Felt Like A Kiss)":

> He hit me and it felt like a kiss.
> He hit me but it didn't hurt me.
> . . . .
>
> If he didn't care for me
> I could have never made him mad
> But he hit me and I was glad.
>
> Yes, he hit me and it felt like a kiss.
> He hit me and I knew I loved him.

King and Goffin produced a song that was nearly documentary in its transcription of a domestic violence victim's rationalizations, chilling in its depiction of the mutual bonds of sadomasochism in the relationship that hovered in the background, telling in its description of a woman so bereft of power that violence inflicted on her could be at least an affirmation of identity—an identity as slave: *he made me his.* It described a narrator who accepted the pact; it was a confessional, and if you listened to it, you shared that confession. You weren't being invited to join this woman; you were simply required to listen. She could tell you this shameful story because you and she were part of the same family; you listened because you had to. She had taught you the "Loco-Motion." She had shared her joy. You owed her something in return.

But the song was, finally, too direct and naked. Without the disguises, it attracted the censors' attention and was banned from radio airplay. Still, "He Hit Me" was at the edge of a larger strain of music to come out of the Brill Building environs in 1962 and '63, one that hinted at social realism and social protest. In '62, Mann and Weil wrote "Uptown," and the Crystals recorded it:

> He gets up each morning and he goes downtown
> Where everyone's his boss and he's lost in an angry land
> He's a little man
> . . . .
> But then he comes uptown where he can hold his head up high
> Uptown he knows that I am standing by
> And when I take his hand, there's no man who could put him down
> The world is sweet, it's at his feet, when he's uptown

It surfaced in March and made it to the 13 spot in the Hot 100 while only hitting 18 on the R&B charts, an indication that black music was losing its racial isolation. Perhaps more significantly, the chart story of "Uptown" suggested that serious lyrics expressing cultural disaffection, and linking that disaffection to a crossracial utopian isoculture, could emerge from the fecund, complex world of teen music.

Like "He Hit Me," "Uptown" was striking for its naturalism, to use the literary term. "Uptown" encapsulated a very local black experience—*uptown* was Harlem, after all, and the experience of racial degradation and compulsory obeisance to white power was palpable. Mann and Weil had been listening to the black musicians with whom they worked, listening with respect and directness, and "Uptown" was the result. Yes, it was sentimental; yes, it used clichés in abundance, but these were the sentiments of the speakers, the clichés familiar to black and white teens alike.

There was little of the protest movement's fervor in these songs. In this world of teen life, the small things, properly attended to, could expand sufficiently to make "a little man . . . tall"—love, respect, friendship, the exuberance of a body reveling in youthful physicality, doing the Loco-Motion.

What's remarkable isn't that "He Hit Me" was censored but that so much else was allowed—so much freedom within the chains of adolescence, so much freedom of expression within the constraints of mass culture. Of course there were limits to the liberty of that pop music. "He Hit Me" went to Phil Spector, a brilliant young producer then working for (tellingly) Liberty Records. When the song died, Spector got the point. His next tune was "He's a Rebel," which combined the theme of the outsider teen with a more traditional girl group romance lyric, and he left Liberty to form his own label. By the middle of 1963, he'd perfected his famous "Wall of Sound" production techniques and produced his masterwork, a Greenwich-Barry tune, done by the Crystals: "Da Doo Ron Ron."

"Da Doo Ron Ron" represented a different sort of teen culture song: it contained not a shred of social commentary. Instead, it celebrated teenage life, a world of parties, of sexual attraction, of flirtation and romantic possibility, of faith in one's own private future despite doubts about the future of the human species or the planet:

> I met him on a Monday and my heart stood still
> Da doo ron-ron-ron, da do ron-ron
> Somebody told me that his name was Bill
> Da doo ron-ron-ron, da do ron-ron
>
> Yeah, my heart stood still
> Yes, his name was Bill
> And when he walked me home
> Da doo ron-ron-ron, da do ron-ron

"Da Doo Ron Ron" also spoke in tongues; the signature repeated line was a return to the older doo-wop nonsense lyrics of the late '50s, and its seemingly mindless repetitiveness kept the minds of censorious parents and radio program managers from noticing just exactly what happened right after the song ended—what happened "when he walked me home." So it also *was* a sort of pig Latin: many listeners thought it to be *They do run, run, run, They do run, run*, an expression of the rapidity of memory, hope, fantasy, friendship and love. The telescoped geography of the song conveyed the limits of teen life—school, hangout, sidewalk—but suggested the intensity of emotional life that could live there. It portrayed teen life as a sort of ghetto experience. In this regard it reflected the Jewish writers and the black singers who had made it. It was a great song, but its greatness was held in a small form. It was a dramatic retreat from the expansive social commentary of "Uptown," the euphoric celebration of "The Loco-Motion," the claustrophobic naturalism of "He Hit Me." It never quite made it to the top of the hit parade; at its height, at number 3, it was bested by the Japanese-language novelty song "Sukiyaki" at number 2 and, at number 1, Lesley Gore's "It's My Party," one more saccharine, the other more declarative. It was close, but it was just a little too compromised.

Below it on the Hit Parade, Nat King Cole sang "Those Lazy, Hazy, Crazy Days of Summer," and Sam Cooke did "Another Saturday Night (And I Ain't Got Nobody)," Little Peggy March declared "I Will Follow Him" at number

17, while directly beneath, at 18, the Shirelles declared her a "Foolish Little Girl" (*Foolish little girl, fickle little girl*). Indeed, it wasn't a happy time to be a girl or young woman: the airwaves were loaded with exhortations to properly diminutive conduct, from 1963's first number-one hit, "Go Away Little Girl," past "Butterfly Baby" (Bobby Rydell) and Steve Lawrence's "Poor Little Rich Girl," to Lesley Gore's early-December hit, "She's a Fool." Yet even in this swamp of misogyny and masochism, there lay another undercurrent in which the combination of young white female songwriters and young black female singers and girl groups declared by the power of their voices the right to speak, and in speaking, expressed some of the complexities of female identity at a turning point. It culminated in Gore's "You Don't Own Me."

*　*　*

The pop music emerging from New York and its surroundings around 1963 pitted the spontaneous expressions of postwar teens speaking to one another, against a dominating and highly structured institutional system which sought to reach into new markets by exploiting creators and musicians.

To describe this as a guerilla war wouldn't be fanciful. At every turn, one side or the other sought advantage, made sorties and incursions into the other's turf. The lives of the singers, writers, and producers—their dramas and narratives—represented more than ephemeral statements to the girls (especially) and boys who listened to the music and followed its fairy tales in the teen pop magazines. In their songs and in their lives, King and Goffin, Greenwich and Barry, Mann and Weil, all confirmed to their fans that a life of spontaneity, authenticity, and youth could carry over into adult life. Similarly with the girl groups themselves. Most were black; most were shown in photographs—on dust sleeves for 45s and covers for LPs, and on posters and promo materials in stores—in clothes that were neither outlandish nor identifiably racial or class-based. In fact, these girls and women often took on the fashions of suburban women's club denizens: white gloves, puffy dresses, hose and high heels. As King and Goffin redefined marriage, these girl groups took on and redefined female and feminine fashion. Their poses too were emblematic: communal, proud, even defiant, they stared right back when you looked at the picture. When a white group like the Shangri-Las shared the visual podium with a group like the Crystals, there was more commonality than difference.

Yet there were also major campaigns from the other side. Corporatized, television-style culture institutions didn't simply accept a new and more passive role as distributors and facilitators of this new indigenous youth culture. They sought to modify it, to adjust its parameters and redefine its themes, to return women to pussycats and men to sweater-wearing soon-to-be-inheritors of the white-collar job. And when they could, they sought to buy outright not just the cultural productions, but the very apparatus itself, and even to own and control its creative producers. Much has been written, on one side and the other, concerning the financial shenanigans of the pop industry. Certainly few of the musicians were well paid or recompensed in proportion to their creative work, and especially not the black musicians. Neither were many of the composers and lyricists. Teams like King-Goffin and Mann-Weil had to produce hit after hit to maintain anything like a middle-class lifestyle. That financial insecurity bonded them to the musicians with whom they worked, and kept them connected to their listeners as well, but it reflected a larger question of creative ownership hidden beneath the entire apparatus of popular music at the time.

When Columbia Pictures–Screen Gems Productions bought Aldon from Kirchner and Nevins in April of 1963, the shock within the cubicles was palpable. The transfer took some time to work out, and for a little longer the communal atmosphere remained. But Columbia/Screen Gems was a movie-and-television factory seeking simultaneously to acquire the backlist of the Aldon creators, and to put the firm on a "proper" footing, pressing it into an institutional model in which spontaneity and individuality were abhorred, in which formula and cliché and repetition, always necessary elements of the popular music Aldon produced, became not just dominant but all-consuming. By the end of 1963, the commune was disbanded, the teams were dispersed, and Kirchner himself was at the helm of a larger but far more sanitized company, whose black voice was the still-lush-pop Nina Simone rather than Little Eva, and whose typical hits came from grown-up musicians like the Sonny Lester Orchestra, performing songs like "Dreamy Islands of Hawaii," perfect for a suburban backyard luau-themed barbeque.

In the face of it, Columbia/Screen Gems had succeeded in eliminating a powerful voice of independence and rebellion, even as it had brought teen culture back to the grownup-controlled, television-dominated entertainment center. For the institutional and corporate forces of culture, the less there was dancing in the streets and the more there was watching in the living room, the better.

What's striking, though, was how unsuccessful was the takeover in quelling the street revolution that the Brill Building rebels—white and black, composers and performers—brought to the radio and, through it, to a national audience. One consequence was the development of a new geographical locale for energetic pop that complicated racial dichotomies: Detroit.

"Uptown," a hit in 1962, formed one bookend to the urban streetscape of this prelude to youth revolution; the other was Martha & the Vandellas, singing in the late summer and fall of 1964 a song written in Detroit by Marvin Gaye, Ivy Joe Hunter, and William Stevenson, all mainstays of the emerging soul label, Motown:

> Calling out around the world, are you ready for a brand new beat?
> Summer's here and the time is right for dancin' in the street!
> Dancin' in Chicago (dancin' in the street)
> Down in New Orleans (dancin' in the street)
> In New York City
>
> All we need is music, sweet music
> There'll be music everywhere
> There'll be swingin,' swayin,' and records playin'
> Dancin' in the street
>
> Oh it doesn't matter what you wear, just as long as you are there
> So come on! Every guy grab a girl,
> Everywhere, around the world
> . . . .
>
> This is an invitation across the nation
> A chance for folks to meet
> There'll be laughin,' singin,' and music swingin'
> Dancin' in the street

A national takeover of the streets by the young, the dispossessed—*an invitation across the nation, a chance for folks to meet ... all we need is music*—this song countered the inward-turning tenement romance of "Uptown" and invoked 1963's civil rights movement street actions, culminating in the March on Washington. More meditative was the Drifters' 1963 hit, written by Goffin and King: "Up on the Roof." There, above the demands of the streets and the claustrophobia of the domestic was a landscape opening to the skies, the stars, the infinite. In none of these—nor in "Da Doo Ron Ron" or even "You Don't Own Me"—did the new life enact itself in the home. A new cultural geography was taking shape, mapped in music and even, perhaps, created by it. As importantly, it was an imaginative landscape you *danced through*—a landscape not of constraint but of freedom; even when the lyrics circumscribed that freedom, the beat, the push, the anthemic peal of other teen voices, the *music*, was a symphony of possibility.

* * *

Brill Building pop or Motown soul: these were urban forms celebrating urban freedoms and populated by a polyglot mix of white, black, Hispanic, and ethnic kids—kids whose distinctive regional, racial, and ethnic accents were smoothed and rendered common by the rigors of rhyme and meter and the shared language of melody and harmony.

Within this musical culture there were distinct tugs, one toward a happy ending that eased rebellious, energetic teens into responsible, obeisant adulthood, and the other toward some less-defined new world, in which the constraints imposed by adult mores and institutional imperatives and regulations were finally thrown off. This was the strain celebrated with "Dancing in the Streets."

The more conservative track was exemplified in the work of Ellie Greenwich and her husband/partner, Jeff Barry. This was natural enough: Greenwich had grown up in Levittown, gotten a college degree from Hofstra, and taught school before switching full-time to songwriting and joining the Brill Building team of Lieber and Stoller. The songs she wrote with Barry were mostly sunny; their protagonists longed to get out of the confines of their suburban houses, out *the front door* to *a movie show* and, somewhere out there, to get *some lovin' and some kissin' and a-huggin*,* but the trajectories of their largely female narrators and listeners were often conventional. "Not Too Young to Get Married" (1963, performed by Darlene Love) headed to "The Chapel of Love" (written with Phil Spector in 1963, charted by the Chiffons, 1964), declaring *I won't be happy till I make him happy and the wedding day is set* ("The Kind of Boy You Can't Forget," by Greenwich and Barry themselves, as the Raindrops, 1963) and thence, one assumed, to a recapitulation of their parents' lives and their own.

The exception was their most famous and long-lasting hit, "Leader of the Pack." On the surface, it followed a darker trajectory. The narrator's boyfriend was from *the wrong side of town*, but he had managed to found an alternative society (the pack) celebrating heroic daring. She loved him, for she knew that he wasn't a criminal—he was "maladjusted," to use the term of the time or, as she said, *I knew that he was sad.* Together they would make a relationship that transcended the narrow constrictions of class and propriety.

* These are all quotes from "Wait Til My Bobby Gets Home," Darlene Love's 1963 hit.

But that wasn't what happened, and while the tragic ending with its revving-engines soundtrack and broken-glass effects was sure to tug at the sentimental side of teen listeners, the underlying theme was more like the warning Greenwich might have gotten from her Levittown parents: stray outside the bounds and you'll be punished. The entire *mise-en-scène* seemed to invite tragedy: an informal meeting at a teens-only hangout rather than a properly supervised introduction and courtship; the illicit thrill of a motorcycle; the untoward assumption of gang leadership; the ring (code for sexual favors granted or at least promised)—not legitimate marriage, not the chapel of love, but coupling outside the bounds of the social.

"Leader of the Pack" was a perfect compromise: it celebrated rebelliousness and freedom, then it punished those who embraced it. It was a smash for the Shangri-Las, hitting number 1 on Thanksgiving 1964, and charting along with Motown's "Dancing in the Streets." But it made its rise sandwiched between two examples of a very different teen geography, anchored not in the urban, polyglot world celebrated by the Brill Building teen writers, but in a lily-white, prosperous, athletic teen society located in Southern California and dedicated to the beach-and-surf life. Above on the charts was Jan and Dean's "Ride the Wild Surf." Below, an odder and more elegiac dispatch from the same world: "When I Grow Up to Be a Man," by another high-school pop band, the Beach Boys.

California surf music was a phenomenon. It emerged in 1962, swept popular music in 1963, then mutated rapidly into self-parody or psychedelic experimentation. In its brief heyday, though, it recast the celebratory freedoms of the American West, revitalizing them with teenage swagger. While the parents stayed indoors, watching the domesticated Westerns *Petticoat Junction* and *Bonanza*, their heroes lumbering along the rutted trails of the past in *Wagon Train*, the children were outside, in the freedom afforded by year-round good weather and a social landscape defined by postwar affluence—public parks and public beaches, a vast semi-urban landscape organized by wide streets and boulevards, enabling rapid travel from suburbs like Hawthorne (where the Beach Boys lived, in something approaching a West Coast Levittown) to the Rendezvous Ballroom in Balboa (where Dick Dale and the Deltones, originators of "surf-guitar" instrumental music, played every Friday, Saturday, and Sunday night), and from there to Santa Monica Beach or Muscle Beach in Venice.

Cars were mobile property—the teen equivalent of the mortgaged house of their parents and their futures. Yet their role wasn't to locate or anchor social and cultural life in geographical place. Instead they were the catalysts to a form of expansionism, a conquest of territory at the western edge of the continent, furthest point of America's long dance with Manifest Destiny. Now, it seemed, the young adventurers were thrusting further westward out into the ocean itself; or bouncing back, redirecting their energies and their messages eastward as they invited others to join them here; or sending themselves upward and outward from the physical geography of nation, continent, and globe to the ethereal, the space above where Telstar reigned and the radiowaves, where their fellow-citizens met.

Like their Brill Building counterparts, they sent postcards from an imaginary land of promise. But they were in many ways the coastal opposites of the Brill Building teens with their multiracial urban flair. White, apparently (if not actually) comfortably middle class, raised in houses in the postwar Los Angeles suburbs, the Wilson boys, cousin Mike Love, bassist Alan Jardine, and their fellow travelers (including Jan and Dean, for whom they wrote, accompanied, and harmonized) defined the California dream as teenagers understood it. They'd recaptured their world from the giddy girl-meets-boy beach movies and presented instead a complete, coherent, and compelling isoculture, with a geography that linked the beaches, the wildly, dangerously weaving streets up the hills, the flat straight roads of the Valley, the postwar shopping centers, the leisure-industry offshoots like "malt shops" and movie theaters, into a coherent social matrix—coherent, that is, to those who could understand its languages, master its folkways, prove themselves in its places of contest, display themselves with the appropriate bodily, sartorial, and mobile finery.

You could be there, if you were lucky. Or you could listen, carefully, enthusiastically, to the radio, from the middle of 1962 through the end of 1964. If you did that, you could see that world in your mind's eye. If you bought the records—the singles and especially the albums—you could anchor your imagination in photographs of surfboards, two-piece bathing suits, blond athletic male bodies, wildly modified cars with huge engines and extravagant decorations.

(The album art of the Beach Boys' first few albums made California living into fantasy centerfolds. *Surfin' Safari* showed the band hanging onto a surfboard in and atop a modified '30s pickup on a Southern California beach marked by white sand and a border of protective cliffs; *Surfin' USA* showed a lone surfer in perfect form on an awesome wave. *Surfer Girl* showed them all dressed identically in surfer-prep outfits, carrying a single board at water's edge.)

Along and within the geography of the surfing life, the Beach Boys defined a particular teen lifestyle that was built around classic American

11.3. Album cover for The Beach Boys, *Surfin' Safari*, 1962

values like hard work, know-how and creativity, and physical prowess, but peeled away from the corporate and the capitalist spheres of their parents. In this imaginative utopia, young men were surfing from dawn to dusk, rebuilding, customizing and then racing their cars, celebrating the local patriotism of the high school ("Be True to Your School," 1963) while turning their backs on the larger patriotism of nation. The Beach Boys and their fictional personae simultaneously chafed at the restrictions of middle class adult life and yearned for its rewards.

A string of solid hits marked out the teen landscape of Southern California, the freedom it offered, and the machinery required to fully take advantage of its possibilities: new, fast American production cars to shrink the distance between home, beach, hangout and high school ("409," a paean to a Detroit production engine); jet airplanes to take you from Redondo Beach to Australian and South African surfspots ("Surfin' Safari").

11.4. Album cover for The Beach Boys, *Surfer Girl*, 1963.

"Go West, Young Man, and grow up with the Country," John B. L. Soule had declared in 1851; Horace Greeley had repeated the cry in 1865, seeking to redirect the dangerously rootless Civil War veterans from urban revolution to wilderness expansionism, and now the Beach Boys were trumpeting the same call, a call that would be echoed, though in complex, evolved form, and with a different geographical nexus, when in 1967 John Phillips of the Mamas and the Papas would write a song-ad for the Monterey Pop Festival:

> If you're going to San Francisco
> be sure to wear some flowers in your hair
> . . . .
> Summertime will be a love-in there

The Beach Boys may or may not have understood the tangled, dangerous balance between revolution and geographical expansionism that Greeley had sought to tilt toward order and away from anarchy. Nor did they yet grasp the anarcho-syndicalist utopia John Phillips would draw from the Haight-Ashbury lifestyle and write into code. *Their* revolutionary utopia was a direct extension of the wealth and leisure—promised leisure, anyway, and promised wealth—that postwar America had generated. They swaggered over the entire California landscape, taking over its beaches, its boulevards, and its freeways in a paean to mobility without direction or purpose. Yet they also seemed to want the sweaters, the fraternity pins, the girls, the secure path of upward mobility and eventual maturity in a new American landscape of eternal prosperity.[13]

Theirs was a curiously aimless mobility, in part because every part of the landscape through which they moved with such swagger was, in their lyrics, paradise. But this was more than a simple matter of climate and scenery. The California of the Beach Boys was formed out of the prosperity of a vast humming defense industry: Northrop's sprawling aerospace complex was less than a mile from the Wilson's house. Their fathers had worked in that great machine, and the pastel late-model cars that granted the Boys their mobility, the drum sets and tape recorders and guitars that enabled them to make their music, were gifts from those fathers—fathers who could also be cruel, violent, desperate, anxious, and depressed, fathers who could climb the economic ladder and fall from it. Liberated by their music from the necessity of entering that hardscrabble white-collar world, the Boys also had no avenue from youth to adulthood.[14]

> Get around round round I get around
> From town to town
> Get around round round I get around
> I'm a real cool head
> Get around round round I get around
> I'm makin' real good bread
> Get around round round I get around
> I get around

These were the lyrics of their very first number-one hit single. Yet the 45's dust jacket showed not rock-star surfer dragsters, but college BMOCs complete with sweaters and loafers, climbing the steps of what looks to be one of UCLA or USC's signature California Collegiate buildings. The contradiction between the two, song and picture, reflected a complex ambivalence between adulthood as life sentence to be avoided, as patrimony to be inherited, or as territory to be staked out, claimed, fought for, and then transformed and made one's own.

This was the question that drove "When I Grow Up to Be A Man," released in August of 1964, as "I Get Around" was dropping slowly down the charts. "When I Grow Up" was a disappointment, rising only to 9, while co-surf/muscle-car musicians Jan and Dean were selling "Ride the Wild Surf" and the Shangri-Las were warning of the dangers of falling in love with the leader of the pack. Yet it was, finally, among the most courageous of the self-examinations and self-declarations, and self-inventions of the postwar generation.

> When I grow up to be a man
> Will I dig the same things that turn me on as a kid?
> Will I look back and say that I wish I hadn't done what I did?
> Will I joke around and still dig those sounds
> When I grow up to be a man?

As the song moves through its plangent questions, the background vocals whisper each succeeding year:

> Will my kids be proud or think their old man is really a square?
> (eighteen, nineteen)
> When they're out having fun, yeah, will I still wanna have my share?
> (twenty, twenty-one)

The final verse smashes together two contrasting moments: the youthful present, but understood fully only as it is fading into its opposite—an adulthood tinged with loss and regret:

> What will I be when I grow up to be a man?
> (twenty-two, twenty-three)
> Won't last forever
> (twenty-four, twenty-five)
> It's kind of sad
> (twenty-six, twenty-seven)
> Won't last forever
> (twenty-eight, twenty-nine)

It's kind of sad
(thirty, thirty-one)
Won't last forever
(thirty-two)

Striking, isn't it? The terrifying beat of the heart that is demarcated in years—14, 15, 16, 17, 18, 19, 20, 21—but not stopping there: *it's kind of sad (26, 27) . . . it's kind of sad (30, 31) won't last forever (32)*. The boys of eternal summer had conquered the last American frontier; they could surf its ragged edge, race its freeways and dance in its parking lots, but they could find no way to conquer time.

"When I Grow Up to Be a Man" signaled a split in sensibility for the Beach Boys, signified by the two very different worldviews of composer-singer Brian Wilson and lead singer Mike Love. Wilson left the band's live show, moving into more and more complex and hermetic studio production using sidemen and multitracking and producing increasingly introverted and ambiguous songs, helped along by collaboration with the ambitious and sophisticated lyricist and producer Van Dyke Parks. By contrast, Love lived for the touring, continued to push the celebration of teen leisure and freedom, and complained bitterly about the experimental and abstruse trend, telling Wilson at one point: "don't fuck with the formula."[15]

Over the next few years, the Beach Boys released songs in both modes. The brash muscle-car and surfer-king celebrations of California life, however, lost freshness and verve, seeming increasingly like repetitions rather than reiterations. By contrast, Wilson's work pushed toward a new trend, marked by the allusive work of the San Francisco sound, and culminating in the 1966 number-one hit, "Good Vibrations." On the West Coast, the youth culture was mutating radically.

And back East, from the wreckage of Brill Building pop came a song written for a young female singer whose voice, interpretation, declaration, would lay down the gauntlet for the male-dominated surf sound:

You don't own me
I'm not just one of your many toys

* * *

Teen sensation Lesley Gore's smash-hit popularity almost exactly spanned 1963, sprawling slightly on either side. She'd arrived as a girl group sob-sister: first it was "It's My Party (And I'll Cry If I Want To)," then the teen-girl revenge follow-up, "Judy's Turn to Cry." This was a shallow freshet from the stream that had nurtured so many solo-woman songs, most recently the smash of 1963, "I Will Follow Him" (*follow him wherever he may go … there isn't an ocean too deep, a mountain so high it can keep, keep me away*) by Little Peggy March. But there was a certain tone in Gore's songs—the sound, perhaps of assertiveness, a certain reveling in revenge and a celebration of manipulativeness—that hadn't been present before in the girl-puppet masochism that dominated the feminine pop genre.

Then came "You Don't Own Me," a slow 6/8 declamation with a Phil Spector Wall of Sound style to it. "You Don't Own Me" appeared in the Hot 100 after Christmas; no doubt Gore's record producers and promoters were satisfied to watch it surface, in the last week of December, 1963, at 72; and then, in the next weeks, charge upward: 49, 37, 18, 13, and then hit the wall of the Beatles, holding right below them at 2 for three weeks before the Beatles' second hit pushed it down. Even then, it survived the British Invasion for weeks before dropping out of the Hot 100.

Gore's anthem to freedom was just the sort of song censors and network execs would have loved to see disappear, but of course they couldn't make it happen because it was too hot to handle. Gore's song, written not by her but by two Brill Building songwriters, John Madara and David White, was a dramatic step forward in tone. *You don't own me … you don't own me … you don't own me … you don't own me*, Gore intoned; the line returned at every moment when courage might fail or the listener, *that boy*, try to push back.

One of the emphatic messages of the West Coast sound was its brazen declaration that this was a landscape, and a lifestyle, for boys and men. Girls and women might be objects of interest and attention, but it was boys who did the surfing, while the girls looked on, boys who built and raced the cars while the girls stood admiringly by, preening and waiting to be noticed.

That women might not *want* to be "on display" might have been news to the Beach Boys; it was probably also news to the hipsters and playboys who read Hefner and kept his magazine in their desk drawers as they worked at the United Broadcasting Corporation. But it would have been a part of the common parlance of the most recent iteration of American feminism, exemplified by Betty Friedan's *The Feminine Mystique*, also released in 1963.

Gore's was more than a girl group independence lament; it was on the verge of declaring war on the entire continent of images of happy-but-neurotic American housewifery that underlay so much of the economic system of postwar capitalism in the States. *I'm not just one of your many toys*, said the narrative voice, and the implication turned identity and personal value away from consumerism and toward something that awaited clarification.

The declaration of woman's independence was only one part of the song's significance. The overt femininity of the voice in the first verse wasn't there in the chorus; it was a teen lament. *Don't put me on display*, cried the teen to parents, but also to coaches, teachers, and even Cold War American authorities who were using the American teenager as a symbol of freedom and spontaneous conformity.

> I'm young and I love to be young
> I'm free and I love to be free
> To live my life the way I want
> To say and do whatever I please.

This was the missing lyric to the Beach Boys' Bill of Rights; it was the core sentiment extracted from a host of earlier songs written by Brill Building prisoners and sung by black women waiting in a full-ashtray, overheated demo room: a declaration of independence by the nation of youth. To be young no longer meant imprisonment—suddenly there *was* a cure for the *summertime blues* Eddie Cochran had sung about in his rock-and-roll prison chant just a few years before. But freedom didn't mean access to a car *to go ridin' next Sunday*, as Cochran had imagined. After all, the Beach Boys had declared: *I'm gettin' bugged driving up and down the same old strip*. It meant *to live my life the way I want, to say and do whatever I please*. Freedom *to* move, into new spaces real and imaginative, had become a freedom *movement*, linking the teenager's declaration of empowerment, autonomy and liberty, with other and perhaps more profound movements—most notably the civil rights movement and the ban the bomb movement.

Thank God the Beatles were there to propose innocence and fun again—a retreat to teenage life whose greatest lament might be, not "You Don't Own Me" but "I Want to Hold Your Hand."

Lesley Gore, the Beach Boys, and the Beatles fought it out on the charts in 1964, not 1963, and that conflict, its resolution, and the splits in cultural formation and consumption that resulted are part of the mature phase of the counterculture and its contests with the dominant consumer-consensus culture. The Beatles may have started with innocence but they didn't last long in that realm; their very popularity—and the extraordinary lyrical and musical ability of the quartet, enabling them to not to parrot but to compose, not to reflect and mediate but to express, champion and transform—made them leaders and communicants of the wider trend that Gore herself had declared: *to say and do whatever I please*. Within months after they'd first appeared on the Hot 100, the Beatles were accepting a joint from Bob Dylan at a party in London, and soon thereafter they were declaring a landscape they shared with him, one that interwove imagination and action: "Within You Without You." By 1966, Paul McCartney was playing that track for Brian Wilson, declaring it was inspired by his experimental music.[16] Meanwhile, Dylan was poised to change everything, bringing protest music to a transcendentalist high and hitting the top 10 in the fall of 1965 with a bullet, hovering at 2 with a song, twice as long as the longest acceptable single (at six minutes) and with a rough anguish that turned aimless mobility into angry alienation: "Like A Rolling Stone."

CHAPTER 12

Dylan's America

He arrived in New York in January of 1961; that week, the *Billboard* top 10 included Elvis Presley singing "Are You Lonesome Tonight," the theme from the movie *Exodus,* by grand-piano duo Ferrante and Teicher, "Corinna Corinna," a remake of the 1958 R&B hit by Big Joe Turner performed by sweater-crooner Ray 'Tell Laura I Love Her" Peterson, and the Shirelles singing "Will You Still Love Me Tomorrow," the first number-one hit penned by Carole King and Gerry Goffin. Already Dylan had defined himself by his transience. He left Hibbing, Minnesota, traveled to the University of Minnesota student slum of Dinkytown, and hitched to Chicago in the winter of 1960, then to Madison, Wisconsin, and finally to New York City. Sometime out there he had changed his name from Robert Zimmerman to Bob Dillon and then to Bob Dylan. He had begun his musical life as a rocker, playing piano; he had listened to the high-watt nighttime radio growing up and absorbed western swing, country music, blues and race, and pop; he would later shock interviewers by praising singers like Rick Nelson (whose version of the old folk-blues tune, "Milk Cow Blues" hovered at number 80 that week of January 16, 1961). He'd been performing a sort of bland revivalist pop folk in Dinkytown until he discovered Woody Guthrie; a bad case of bronchitis turned his voice from a pleasant, smooth anticipation of the baritone on *Nashville Skyline* to the roughened, whining, tenor that would become his trademark.[1]

In the coffeehouses and folk clubs of Manhattan, he told and retold his identity: he'd been a carnival worker; he'd herded cattle; he'd come in from New Mexico, from Colorado, from California, from the unnamed West; he derived from American Indian stock; he had no parents; he was estranged from his family. He claimed all of America as his genetic map and his cultural history.

As he had in Minnesota, he continued to absorb musical influences with extraordinary rapidity and depth; he stored ancient melodies and chord structures from every form of American music and, behind it, the music of Africa, Ireland, Russia, of the Jews, the Muslims, Gospel, and shape note.

His first album was a rapidly recorded pass through a piece of this gigantic repertoire. Remarkable about it was the way that one type of song became another: the geography of genre, of heritage, of musical form was transient, too. Black gospel turned to hillbilly whine; St. Louis blues turned to Delta. The slave spiritual "In My Time of Dyin,'" ended up as a combine of multiple, differently named versions by Josh White, Blind Willie Johnson, and a number of Dinkytown and Greenwich Village folkies. By the time Dylan was done with that song, it had sunk back decades, his guitar strings so dead that his repeated thumb hammering on the E string and a thin metal lipstick holder in place of a proper slide seemed to be disintegrating an instrument found in a trash can in the rain. His version of a Roy Acuff/Hank Williams "Freight Train Blues" was played so fast that the articulation of the words seems impossible and the long, long, long enunciation of the *oooooo* in the chorus is as hauntingly stretched as a train whistle crossing North Dakota.

Bob Dylan came out in 1962; it demarcated a new American cultural geography, not of the present or future but of the past. Few collections of music so ambitiously trod America's mythic geographical heritage, nor so irreligiously melded such antithetical places. In Dylan's book, however, this combine was the America he had come to claim—and to claim to be *from*: "the wild West" ("leavin' the towns I love the best," a Texas swing lyric[2]); but perhaps more significantly, along the length of the continent's spine, down the river from Minneapolis to the gulf, and then back along Highway 51. One of the freedom roads, and a route in the Great Migration, Highway 51 stretched from New Orleans (where it split from its dark twin, Highway 61), up through Mississippi to Elvis Presley's home in Memphis, and on to Cairo, Illinois (where Huck Finn and Jim had hoped to land, making Jim a free man), crossing the waters on a narrow bridge, passing west of Chicago, and ending in northern Wisconsin less than two hundred miles from Hibbing.

In this first album, the voice and accompanying guitar and harmonica belonged not to one person but to an actor assuming with absolute assurance and conviction personae that were almost impossibly distant from the young, white, Midwestern Jewish boy on the album's cover—not just a dead black man come back from the grave to request dignity, or a wild cowboy, or even an American hillbilly singing a song about a British Redcoat forbear, but a dying female prostitute in a Storyville whorehouse.[3] *Bob Dylan*, the album and the artist's persona, resuscitated a long tradition of American self-expression: the hard-bitten vernacular individual, veteran, and inheritor of the nation's troubles, traveling its spaces, finding the places, the citizens, the moments when her authentic soul pierced the surface of platitudes, desires, proprieties. This justified the odd, even off-putting harshness of the voice; this explained the weary rubato of the rhythms or the fast, driven intensity of revelation. Dylan solved the problem of authenticity by defining it not as a matter of certifiable experience but of dramatic passion and consummate conviction.

Yet for all its ferocity, the album's antiquarianism seemed strange. Across the pop music scene, the focus was on the present and future—on the rooftop and at the candy store and on the suburban sidewalk for the slow walk home, and on the life that love would bring. That music too was an escape from the present, from the news barked quickly on the hour and the longer, more lugubrious performance at 6 or 7 p.m. on the TV. Dylan's was part of a different sort of retreat; the entire early folk scene seemed drenched in other times and other places—Elizabethan courts, rural Irish landscapes, Virginia settlements. But Dylan brought something entirely different to this enervated antiquarianism, embodied most of all in the piercing faux sincerity of his soon-to-be-girlfriend, Joan Baez. Dylan's songs took the trappings of other places and times, and invested them with the intensity, the fear, the murderous recklessness in the face of oblivion, that would mark his map of the American present.

Atomic anxiety pervaded the early albums. As Dylan mapped it in the composite of his songs, America was a nation drenched in fear and impotence, populated by drifters who had no reason to stay where they were and no better place to go, no place free of the specter of instant annihilation or slow, awful death. Dylan's shifting persona, however, drew these voiceless, hopeless nomads into a single American oversoul, embittered, dangerous if awakened into awareness of its collective power. "A Hard Rain's A-Gonna Fall," on his second album, 1963's *The Freewheelin' Bob Dylan*, was a song set in a dreamscape: the prodigal son traveled *10,000 miles in the mouth of a graveyard*,* passing mountains, highways, forests, and oceans. Dylan was reprising the travels of his hero and mentor, Woody Guthrie, who sang of an America of oceans, mountains, highways, and forests in "This Land Is Your

---

* Again, as in the previous chapter, where the lyrics are meant to be heard as sung or spoken, I have dispensed with quotation marks and placed the lines in italics, to indicate their oral, and aural, emphasis.

Land," his most celebrated, misquoted, and misunderstood work. Dylan had heard the *real* song, with all its Wobbly leftist populism, back in Minnesota. Its celebration of the country was also a call to radical occupation, rejuvenation, and redemption. Now Dylan envisioned the consequences of failure: an America in which the forest dripped blood, in which the wealth of the "highway of diamonds" was laid waste, in which the innocent child, America, now lay surrounded by wild wolves, an America whose rights and freedoms had been abrogated: its poets and its people wandering, wounded, across the devastated landscape.

"A Hard Rain" described an America stripped of purpose, promise, and hope, and as a result the claims and consequences of American exceptionalism were also stripped:

> Where the people are many and their hands are all empty
> Where the pellets of poison are flooding their waters
> Where the home in the valley meets the damp dirty prison
> Where the executioner's face is always well hidden
> Where hunger is ugly, where souls are forgotten
> Where black is the color, where none is the number.

Dylan's tone, his language, for all its seeming hyperbole today, rang in harmony with its sources, high and low. Dylan took America's folk and popular heritage away from its claimants, the Harvard students with Appalachia-made dulcimers, nostalgic for an authenticity they knew nothing about, but also from corporate entertainment conglomerates quick to exploit and to bowdlerize the music of protest and refusal, turning union organizing anthems into hootenanny tunes to be sung by sweater-clad counterfeits like the Brothers Four. He also took the drive and verve of popular music and roughed it up again. The result was music that never quite reached the hit-machine world, work of an ambition and scope no popular American musician has approached before or since, work that demanded commitment of its listeners and formed the revolutionary anthems of the counterculture. Dylan's music didn't just reflect the American moment; Dylan *revealed* that moment in the music, in the constantly transforming dynamic of language, tone, texture, melody, and music combined in ways always meant to challenge.

Dylan's American voice combined not just regions and generations but historical moments, bringing them into a revolutionary present. The righteous upstanding gentleman founding fathers mixed with the ebullient oratorical voices of the expansionist nineteenth-century Americans like Andrew Jackson and Horace Greeley, declaring Manifest Destiny to explore, extend, transform, and redeem the great wilderness, and they in turn melded with the populist reformers and revolutionaries who believed their songs and speeches might rouse the polity to reclaim the nation. Dylan's lost boy, his Tom Joad, would go back out to minister to those he'd seen, sick, hungry, desperate, voiceless. But he would do it with song.

*　*　*

Dylan's first albums were rife with transience. With Dylan, or more accurately, with his narrator, listeners traveled from a great West now stripped of promise, a place fit only for leaving, then passing through a South marked by vicious racism and segregationist violence, arriving in a New York in ruins, victim of an atomic attack,* only to leave again in search of some haven never found.

There was an alternative to rootlessness, itinerancy, and wandering exile: to bring about and then settle in a new American utopia. *Come gather 'round people wherever you roam*: these words began Dylan's 1964 album, conceived in the heady days of 1963. That roaming might end with mass assembly, and mass assembly lead to fundamental change, was a tenet of those days, and the songs Dylan wrote carried that imperative: Dylan ordering Americans to gather round him, to listen, and then to act.

There were good reasons for Dylan to think that he and his songs could change a nation. National press coverage of his concerts, his music, and even his everyday life focused on his role as seer, as prophet, for a new generation of idealized activists remaking America; his anthem to transformation, "The Times They Are A-Changin,'" covered by the passionate but mellifluous Peter Paul & Mary, had reached number 2 on the charts by the summer of '63; he had appeared before something close to two hundred thousand Americans at the March on Washington that August; he had conquered Carnegie Hall. Heady times, indeed, and Dylan might be forgiven for taking on with such alacrity the role he'd treated with doubt and even refusal just months before.

The songs he wrote that spring, summer, and fall of 1963 and released as *The Times They Are A-Changin'* in January of 1964 might be seen as primers for social action, or perhaps more accurately sermons, alternately evangelical, visionary, funerary, and jeremiadic in tone. Much about this album surprised Dylan's topical song fans nonetheless. Places intruded with visceral

* This is the trajectory of the first half of side two of *The Freewheelin' Bob Dylan*: "Bob Dylan's Dream" to "Oxford Town" to "Talkin' World War III Blues" to "Corinna, Corinna."

and tactile clarity: the broken-down South Dakota cabin of Hollis Brown where the rats destroyed the flour; the blasted industrial landscape of Hibbing, Minnesota, where *the mining gates locked and the red iron rotted*; a Baltimore hotel where Hattie Carroll *carried the dishes and took out the garbage*.

These songs declared a moral and spiritual drought afflicting the landscapes of America, from the settled cities of the East, bastions of law, precedent, tradition, to the farms and mines of the frontier West. Against these, new landscapes or transformed ones emerged: within the songs and in an America across which Dylan and his music marched.

Newport, Rhode Island, where Dylan took the Folk Festival by storm in July 1963, had been an iconic site of American privilege—the privilege of the elect, Puritans of the earliest New England villages, and then of the merchant classes, from slave-trading days to the present. Just a few weeks before, Dylan had taken activist-singer Pete Seeger up on a call to go down to Greenwood, Mississippi, to play for a voting-rights rally. If he was out of his element there, he didn't show it: in a typically challenging move, he performed "Only a Pawn in Their Game," a richly complicated analysis of the forces behind the murder of civil rights worker Medgar Evers, to an audience of about three hundred, nearly all of whom were black.

On the pastoral greenswards of the Folk Festival, Dylan assumed his place in the ranks of the ancient ones honored in his world: Delta bluesman Mississippi John Hurt, Ramblin' Jack Elliott (Guthrie's comrade and heir apparent), Mother Maybelle Carter, the Reverend Gary Davis. There he introduced his masterful critique of the ideology of American exceptionalism, "With God On Our Side." With Joan Baez singing harmony in her piercing voice, the song seemed sure to filter into the wide porches and verandas of the mansions and summer homes surrounding the festival site.

Then a month later, Dylan stood on the stage beside the Washington Monument and looked out across the most celebrated of American commemoration sites, the National Mall, as an ocean of Americans, mostly black, claimed the site for their own.

Dylan helped to open that August celebration of redemptive transformation; Martin Luther King, Jr., would close it with his most famous speech. The day's events began with the performances of a delegation of Greenwich Village folk singers: Joan Baez first, then Odetta, Josh White, Peter Paul & Mary, and then Dylan. None of the singers aroused much interest, but at least Baez and Peter Paul & Mary sang with clarity and passion. Dylan's appearance was a letdown in what was a minor sideline to the main events of the day. He opened with his biblical-righteous anthemic "When the Ship Comes In." Joan Baez joined him; she didn't know the words and couldn't

12.1. Bob Dylan singing "When the Ship Comes In" with Joan Baez, March on Washington, August 1963.

read the cheat sheet on the podium, so for most of the song she sang an inept wordless harmony. He exited the stage and was reintroduced as "a singer from New York," to mixed applause. He then sang "Only A Pawn In Their Game"; his nasal whining voice and the vagaries of the sound system made the words nearly incomprehensible, and he quickly lost his largest audience—some two hundred thousand crowded all the way back from the stage at the Lincoln Memorial, past the Reflecting Pool, to the Washington Monument.[4]

Dylan and Baez may have made little impression on the vast black audience on the Mall, but they did serve a very different purpose. Seeking to defuse the racial charge of the march, which Soviet propagandists had already propagated globally as a evidence of American hypocrisy and injustice, the U.S. Information Agency hastily purchased a dual portrait of Dylan and Baez rehearsing offstage and disseminated it to USIA outlets worldwide, showing a softer, younger, whiter, and more romantic picture of the event.

It was a long day. It's doubtful Dylan remained on the site,[5] but it's nearly certain he heard King's speech at the end—as most Americans did, via the uninterrupted coverage of CBS television and the now-arrived cameras

12.2. Spinning the March on Washington, a United States Information Agency publicity picture. (Courtesy of the National Archives and Records Administration.)

of ABC and NBC. The presence of more than thirty-five network cameras and more than five hundred technicians, interviewers, and commentators marked the full transition to a different media economy. While the Universal Newsreel of the event took weeks from March to movie house, enabling writers, editors, and narrators to craft an interpretation of the event, the networks were faced with responding immediately, cutting in and out of regular programming,* frantically writing copy for the news narrators to read, editing film to bring viewers up to the live action when coverage returned. In a prelude to what the Vietnam War would do to the corporate control of media, the event itself overwhelmed the mechanisms of correction, shading, and interpretation from above. Instead, the networks, desperate for drama, took the narrative given them and simply amplified it.[6]

Nowhere was this more evident than in the coverage of King's speech. King's magisterial formality and the slow pace of his words combined with the static form of the man-at-the-podium shot, required the directors to jump cut to the panoramas, the audience response close-ups, and the Lincoln Memorial behind King, with its array of white and black authorities,

---

* CBS ran continuously after 1:30; the other two networks wove in and out of coverage.

somber, marked by gravitas, to maintain some visual drama. The resulting montage, with King's words overlaying it, ended up controlled not by the corporate media but by the organizers' rhetoric and the picture they had planned so carefully to show the nation and the world.

King's speech began with rhetorical authority. He had learned, as had Dylan, that drawing from deep popular memories and long-known sources was not theft or plagiarism but a means of tapping a spring of cultural memory in listeners. King started with reference to the Gettysburg Address, a document American schoolchildren, white and black, had been memorizing for a decade or more. When King moved forward from that, however, his speech grew heavier and more difficult, both in rhetoric and in message. King advanced the Negro cause with militancy. Passages often dripped with irony and contempt, as he addressed at moments the American black citizenry, racist white America, American integrationist liberals, and the nation as a whole.

The memorable ending of King's "I Have A Dream" speech was improvised, a variation on a speech King's coactivist, Archibald Carey, Jr., had given a decade earlier. It is a consummate example of a long tradition of African American sermonizing, a tradition King had mastered over many years of study and practice. It was not the brief of particulars found in the earlier section, not the set of demands or the call to justice, and yet it is the part everyone remembers.[7]

In the videos of the moment, we see King pause, look up from his script, simultaneously outward at the sublime landscape of a quarter-million people occupying the stateliest of American sites, and inward—not quite in prayer, not quite groping for words or images, but rather waiting as the inner and outer worlds come into harmony.

Then he begins. Looking out, he acknowledges Americans who "have come fresh from narrow cells . . . battered by the storms of persecution and staggered by the winds of police brutality . . . the veterans of creative suffering." This complexly ambiguous phrase is recast, with an equal but different ambiguity: he urges them to "continue to work with the faith that unearned suffering is redemptive." His black listeners understand what he means, though. They respond from the audience, and from the stage where, among others, Mahalia Jackson speaks back to King, urging him on. With this shift in focus clear, King speaks again directly to his militant black audience, leaving the others—the racists, the well-meaning white integrationists, the sheltered, mildly inquisitive television audience—to observe a discussion from which they are excluded because they have *not* experienced a life of undeserved suffering. (Later, King will return to this assurance of a reward earned for injustices withstood, when he recasts the old slavery promise of heaven into something more tangible, immediate, echoing and extending Dylan's earlier conflation of the eternal with the immediate.) "Go back to Mississippi," he tells them, "go back to Alabama, go back to South Carolina, go back to Georgia, go back to Louisiana, go back to the slums and ghettos of our northern cities, knowing that *somehow* this situation can and will be changed."

He pauses for a moment. The doubled imagery of a prison cell of suffering at the arbitrary hands of others, matched by that list of Southern states, conveys to him a further biblical passage, a metaphoric landscape, "the valley of the shadow of death" from Psalm 23. Countering that landscape of doubt, fear, and suffering comes the prophetic landscape of reward that underlay so much of slavery's music and metaphors for the centuries of that American iniquity. But here, again, King pauses. He stops because he senses a trap, perhaps, or because he wants to emphasize the next and most significant moment in his argument: this time, not Heaven, but here. In America. This linkage between the private suffering and the public good is matched by the introduction of the dream sequence, a personal dream matching and transforming, even replacing, a dream-myth: the American dream. "I have a dream," he confesses, looking, close up, more vulnerable than he has before. "It is deeply rooted in the American Dream." This seems odd: the American dream imbedded in popular discourse in 1963 is one of economic mobility and prosperity. But King insists on reaching behind that narrowing interpretive stream to the wider river of American possibility and promise, in which *freedom* can, and must, mean something more than an unfettered marketplace on which individual desire will be able to play itself out.

King raises the debate, raises the stakes, and also raises the rhetorical gaze of speaker and listener from the valley of despair. He does this by invoking the Declaration of Independence, a strategy derived from other, earlier sermonizers on race in America: "I have a dream that one day this nation will rise up and live out the true meaning of its creed: 'We hold these truths to be self-evident, that all men are created equal.'"[8]

Then he returns to the visual imagery of landscape. He stands on the steps of the Lincoln Memorial. That vantage point, the designers' created illusion, a sweep so vast that it appears the curvature of the earth has begun to obscure the base of the Capitol building, works on King, and he works on it in return. His bird's-eye view descends to a specific scene of "the sons of former slaves and the sons of former slave owners" sitting down at a table "on the red hills of Georgia." The metaphor seems a little mixed—it reflects King's brilliant epiphany to sweep the collective vision across the landscape of America, as so many other memorable icons of American culture have done, uniting its disparate parts in one harmonious whole. King isn't ready yet. He keeps his listeners in a rhetorical and visual swing between the specific, the cruel locality of events, and the sweeping panorama of a possible future. The speech dips and retreats, cutting in to show first a "sweltering" hell then an oasis, first a drooling Governor Wallace, then King's own children, then a handheld circle of black and white children dancing together "as sisters and brothers."

With this, King sweeps out and back, returning to the valley of death, but this time drawing from Isaiah's millenarianism: an American Eden regained by redemptive suffering and a deepened and renewed exceptionalism as a result. Turning from the valley, he moves to the mountaintop, and to Deuteronomy—the mountain of prophesy, Mount Pisgah, whence God had shown Moses a promised land, promised but deferred until a new righteousness redeemed the nation of Abraham. For King, however, conquering this "mountain of despair" leads him to a declaration of ownership over the redeemed land, over America. King moves on to intone America's informal national anthem, "My Country 'Tis of Thee,"[9] in which liberty has bound itself to the mountainside: in a vast and fast-moving panorama, King transports his listeners from New Hampshire to California, and then back to the South, to "Stone Mountain of Georgia . . . Lookout Mountain of Tennessee . . . every hill and every molehill of Mississippi."

Landscape and music bound together; King returns to the final line of that song—"let freedom ring"—and then uses the music of bells, with its associations, to shift rapidly from vista to locality and then to society—to a millennial America singing, hands joined, "the old Negro spiritual": "*free at last.*" With this, he is done; the next event is the benediction, and the march is over.

Though King's speech utterly overshadowed Dylan's earlier performance, both men shared a similar vision, with its strengths, its inspiration, its inconsistencies, and its consequences. As had Dylan, King reached back through—indeed *spoke through*—the long traditions of American sermonizing and African American calls for justice. He too took on voices and made them part of a renewed vision in a reinvigorated heritage. Just as Dylan had reached to the triumphalist literature of black culture as well as white, King went to the icons of white America, from whence he reclaimed the rhetoric of American optimism, from the resolute statements of the Declaration to the national anthem and its fellow songs. Rejuvenating and expanding these anthems, King knit the country back together; his speech reunited the ideals of the past with the promise of the future. But in the exhilarated improvisation at the end of his speech, King spoke as if this change *must* come. King's own education and heritage, steeped in the language and the rhetoric of the black church but also in the roots of American Puritanism, with its distinction between the elect and the damned, and its avowal of a predestined promise to that elect: all this fostered his heady vision of inevitability.

Like King, Dylan succumbed to the confident inescapability implicit in this Puritan doctrine. Like King, he reclaimed America's mythology from the privileged, the powerful, and the possessors, granting it to red-iron miners and hardscrabble farmers and domestic laborers, to Hollis Brown and to Hattie Carroll. To them, Dylan promised in the last lines of that first song sung at the Washington Monument:

> And the ship's wise men
> Will remind you once again
> That the whole wide world is watchin'
>
> The foes will rise
> With the sleep still in their eyes
> And they'll jerk from their beds and think they're dreamin'
> But they'll pinch themselves and squeal
> And know that it's for real
> The hour when the ship comes in
>
> Then they'll raise their hands
> Saying we'll meet all your demands,
> But we'll shout from the bow your days are numbered.
> And like Pharaoh's tribe
> They'll be drowned in the tide
> And like Goliath, they'll be conquered.

There was something of irony here, particularly to older, more seasoned, or more directly threatened members of the movement. At the March on Washington, black activist Dick Gregory turned in disgust from that early event block of self-serving, earnest, white do-gooders daring to lecture the assembled masses: "Stand behind us," he declared. Don't stand in front of us."[10] For black radicals like Gregory, for poor sharecroppers to whom Dylan had sung earlier that year, for the desperate and forgotten, Dylan's triumphalist crowing appeared unseemly, out of place.

Yet here Dylan's role as a stand-in for a widely sweeping population of young Americans, white, middle class (or at least prosperous), comes into play. Mass movements promise not to elevate or aggrandize the individual but to absorb individual angst, alienation or suffering into a millenarian wave; for a moment, a white boy from Hibbing might be able to imagine some kinship, some commonality, with the others. Dylan's theft of slavery spirituals and their redemptive promises, his gleeful smashing together of eschatology and social revolution, survived the sobering challenge implicit in King's more sustained, and more consummate, conjoining vision of a new America.

Dylan brought his combination of protest songs and calls to action to Carnegie Hall that fall, on Halloween night, for a concert that cemented his place at the forefront of his generation. Between the March on Washington and the October 31 concert, President Kennedy had committed, however reluctantly, to the cause of integrating America, federalizing the Alabama National Guard and allowing the integration of the public schools of Birmingham. Governor Wallace had responded by declaring his candidacy for the Democratic ticket for the presidency. On the TV, the national evening news was full of images of rage, violence, and hatred. Then came the Sunday school bombing. A white Klansman, part of an offshoot group calling themselves the Cahaba Boys, placed a bomb under the steps of a black church that had been used by integration protest groups in the past, timing the blast to occur as Sunday school was letting out. At the funeral of three of the four murdered girls, King declared: "At times, life is hard: as hard as crucible steel." It was a line so brilliant, so apt that no writer could fail to take a lesson from it. After the funeral, the cortege swelled to eight thousand, including eight hundred interracial ministers from Birmingham alone. Kennedy's failure to step forward aggressively and King's public support of a halfhearted federal response to the bombing unleashed a torrent of internecine conflict within the movement—not just the immediate civil rights movement, but the larger sea change coming to America.[11]

Dylan was not yet ready to give up on the hope of a multiracial, triumphalist, utopian America. The Carnegie Hall concert was a performance with careful scripting behind it, as the set list makes clear. Beginning with "The Times They are A-Changin,'" passing through a string of intimate portrayals of humble desperate people and sharply drawn places—not just the farms and small towns, but the penitentiary at Red Wing, Minnesota, and the boxing ring where Davey Moore died—and ending with the story of Hattie Carroll and then that anthemic avowal of vengeance on the powerful but unrighteous, "When the Ship Comes In," Dylan's performance that night took back the American landscape and promised a renewed mission for national ideals in "the hour that the ship comes in." Once again, redemptive settlers would disembark in a promised land, abashing their enemies, blessed by their God. Sheltered from the near-chaos within the civil rights movement after the bombing, far from privy to the conflicts within the Student Nonviolent Coordinating Committee, unable as yet to grasp the sense of daily danger and invisible menace that had come to dominate African American experience in the South, in the movement and, increasingly, throughout America, Dylan reveled in his place as a rallier to the causes.

*　　*　　*

Newport, Washington, Carnegie Hall: three privileged American sites occupied, if only temporarily. The bleak reach of Elm Street in Dallas five months later fronted a different ceremonial space: the "grassy knoll" of Dealey Plaza, a vestige of a 1930s-era, WPA-landscaped parkway through which three of Dallas's main thoroughfares pinched together to pass underneath a wide swatch of railroad tracks before enabling an entrance to the Stemmons Freeway. Across that space of green interrupted by concrete gray and asphalt black, the Lincoln Continentals and Cadillacs of President Kennedy's motorcade sailed like ships coming in at midday on November 22, 1963.

The gathering of the new America that Dylan had envisioned in "The Times They Are A-Changin'" could not compete with the surreal horror of the months that followed Kennedy's assassination. Between November 1963 and May 1964, when the album was released, a different tableau dominated: a frenzied circus of images and an equal frenzied parade of those seeking to make those images, make, interpret, and exploit the pictures of one Kennedy slumped in a car, of another in short pants walking to the funeral, of a Givenchy-clad widow playing out the role as if it were the final act of the Camelot passion play.[12] Theories and schemes, conspiracies, films for sale, pictures for sale, assassins for sale: "For me," reported Dylan, "it was just insane."[13] Like so many of his generation, he couldn't integrate this event into his evangelical worldview without upending the picture once again. And this was what he did. Within hours of the assassination, he'd told his friend Bob Foss, "What it means is that they are trying to tell you: 'Don't even hope to change things.' If you try to put yourself up against the forces of death . . . forget about it, you're done for."[14]

By the time *Times* was released as an album in January 1964, Dylan had recast his song sequence. Where once his set list ended with "When the Ship Comes In," now Dylan ended the album with a direct slap in the face to his earlier self and his earnestly self-satisfied audience: "Restless Farewell." There his narrator declared directly that he would *bid farewell and be down the road . . . down the line . . . be gone . . . till we meet again . . . bid farewell and not give a damn.*

* * *

After January 1964, Dylan rapidly released—both musically and psychically—the wandering minstrel who had served him and his protest listeners so well. His next album was *Another Side of Bob Dylan*, a critical and audience disappointment, all but devoid of topical, political, or protest songs and marked by complex personal investigations of love and isolation. *Ain't no use to talk to me: it's just the same as talking to you*, he declared at one point. The album, with its long, Kerouac-esque, Beat-indebted liner notes, had been mostly written on the road, retracing some of the routes Jack Kerouac and Robert Frank had taken on celebrated Beat road trips in the mid-1950s in search of an America to counter the televised and suburbanized sanitation that dominated popular perception. During that time, Dylan also wrote early drafts of two songs that would appear on another, more significant, album: 1965's *Bringing It All Back Home*.

Another Side was a postcard from that trip, chronicling an uneasy transition. *Bringing It All Back Home*, released some eight months later, is the album in which Dylan fully recast the landscape of the American imagination. Gone is the nostalgic, retrospective, tone, defined in his earlier work by his "folk" invocations of crossroads and highways, of fictitious small towns and warm stove-lit cabins. The songs move from the past and future tenses that had dominated the previous albums, and into the present, a present located not in dying mine-towns or millennial utopias but in urban detritus and the absurdist, doomed attempts to make sense of it or—barring that—retreat once more.

The album is clearly divided: its two sides are as different lyrically and thematically as they are sonically. Side one is entropically urban, antic, absurdist, propelled by the clattering, mistake-laden immediacy of improvised rock and roll. It begins, with "Subterranean Homesick Blues," in a city, in a neighborhood overrun by spies, police, feds, all poised to crack down.

Hiding in the urban underworld, running to the countryside, Dylan and his collaborators discover only mirror-places of absurdity, hypocrisy, authoritarianism. The narrator follows his girl Maggie (who, in the subterranean homesick city, had rushed in to warn of police surveillance) out to the safety of the countryside, only to find a mirror of the System: forced labor, small wages, petty, vindictive bosses, a place where the promise of tolerance and personal freedom is unmasked as an equally stultifying forced conformity. Nature too is a mess, not a solace or a retreat. An urban hipster in dark sunglasses, you'll *stumble, and land in some muddy lagoon . . . when it's nine below zero, and three o'clock in the afternoon.*

This raucous album side ends with Dylan's long, hilarious recasting of high-school American history class, "Bob Dylan's 115th Dream." *Moby Dick's* interminable length and impossible antiquarianism of language and plot has left only the CliffsNotes précis, and that, as well, too hastily reviewed before the test to be trustworthy—Captain Ahab is now Ahab the Arab from the pop song of 1962. The *Mayflower* arrives on American shores, and a plan to fleece the natives (*Captain Arab he started writing up some deeds; he said, "Let's set up a fort and start buying the place with beads"*) is foiled by the savvy locals, New Yorkers all: cross-dressing waitresses, bunko-artists, protest marchers, cops who arrest the crew and ticket the ship for parking violations. As the narrator leaves, abandoning his friends, he encounters Columbus; time has turned fully backward, and the cycle of exceptionalist promise done in by human corruption will begin again.

Despite its description of a world of urban paranoia, failed utopian communalism, corrupted Nature and a near-inescapable conspiratorial authoritarianism watching over all, the first half of *Bringing It All Back Home* is anything but dark. Instead, it is vaudevillian, humorous, even joyous. This first side is both a description of the landscape of American corruption and a set of instructions for living within it, disguised, a guerrilla warrior in a land of promises broken, denied, or forgotten. But we're all in the same boat; by the end of the album's side, we're on that boat, together, leaving this place to Columbus: *good luck.*

The second side is dramatically different. The music is sparse, the acoustic guitar plays in an empty room, and somewhere outside, in the first and last songs of the side, a lonely electric guitar tentatively responds. In brief stabs, a harmonica speaks, coughing, after the narrator's voice has finished a verse.

Take me on a trip upon your magic swirling ship, cries the singer—to whom? In the logic of the album, the narrator has somehow landed on an exile island, having left America to Columbus. This island is internal, mental, imaginative. It is the obverse of that landscape of the damned found in "A Hard Rain" and returning in "Gates of Eden," the next song on this side. The trees don't bleed, though they are haunted and frightened; the singer passes beyond them:

. . . out to the windy beach,
Far from the twisted reach of crazy sorrow

Yes, to dance beneath the diamond sky with one hand waving free
Silhouetted by the sea, circled by the circus sands
With all memory and fate driven deep beneath the waves
Let me forget about today until tomorrow

Both "Mr. Tambourine Man" and "Gates of Eden" were written during or shortly after the frantic roadtrip of 1964. And both responded to a wave of disillusionment, even despair, that swept the generations of postwar Americans after the assassination of Kennedy. In April, Johnson and his Soviet counterpart Khrushchev announced a cutback in nuclear weapons material procurement, signaling a possible trend toward atomic stand-down, if nowhere nearly as dramatic a one as most peace activists had hoped in the aftermath of the 1963 Test Ban Treaty. By midsummer 1964, it appeared that war and conflict had just shifted from one global arena to another, as Congress passed the Tonkin Resolution, ensuring rapid escalation of the Vietnam War.

That spring, summer, and fall of 1964 were dominated by image wars, and wars over images. On October 24, two weeks after the Chinese exploded a nuclear device and Khrushchev was deposed, Dylan played Philharmonic Hall in New York. *Of war and peace the truth just twists*, he sang, beginning "Gates of Eden" halfway through the first set. Few in the audience failed to understand just what he meant.[15]

This was the concert at which Dylan introduced two of the bleakest songs of his career, "Gates of Eden," and "It's Alright, Ma (I'm Only Bleeding)," and removed from the set list the triumphalist chant of "When the Ship Comes In." In its place:

Darkness at the break of noon
Shadows even the silver spoon
The handmade blade, the child's balloon
Eclipses both the sun and moon
To understand you know too soon
There is no sense in trying

This was the beginning of "It's Alright, Ma," which would appear as the penultimate song of *Bringing It All Back Home* in a few months' time. In the Philharmonic concert the song was more than sobering—it was the keystone of the evening. For nine-and-a-half minutes, the words poured out of Dylan, and over the audience. Images fell like hard rain:

Disillusioned words like bullets bark
As human gods aim for their mark
Make everything from toy guns that spark
To flesh-colored Christs that glow in the dark
It's easy to see without looking too far
That nothing much is really sacred

The concert itself was a transition; the album completed the transformation. Not just the wild, anarchic repossession of rock and roll, R&B, race music and Brill Building pop, though that was an essential ingredient to the almost gleeful embrace of a newly improper America that dominated the first half of the record. The hushed, empty-room feel of the second side was also different than the counterpart in the Philharmonic concert. Partly this was a result of the sustained argument presented by four songs on this quiet half of the album, laid out in an inexorable and unrelieved sequence over twenty-three minutes.

Whereas those at the concert were drowned in the rapid flood of words, listeners to the album had the leisure to plumb the depths of individual songs and of the album as a whole, as a work in multiple movements. Few who bought this album bought just one copy. Many listeners wore out that second side, poring over the words, awash in the imagery pouring out from the voice in the room. These songs rewarded, as well. "It's Alright, Ma" was anything but a top-pop song. At just under eight minutes in length, this was an epic; Allen Ginsburg later described the Dylan of that time as "a column of air"[16] and in this song, the air rushed out, and in, and out again, like wind in dry grass.

Another song about eviction, "It's Alright, Ma" was also a letter home. It describes a sort of desperate, rapid-eyed search for retreat, safety, solace, with every glance recording a different cul-de-sac. Successively, promise after promise is revealed as platitude: consumer capitalism, religion, the nostrums of teachers and commencement speakers. In this maelstrom, *you lose yourself, you reappear . . . alone you stand with no one near*. From this come the two promises the song offers, and requires, for survival: private love and public refusal.

On the album, "It's Alright, Ma" was significantly shorter than its concert version. The words didn't change, though—only the rapidity and headlongness of the delivery. In concert, Dylan slowed the song enough that individual images could be snatched, if not contemplated. On the album, the promise of repeated listening enabled a more rapid-fire delivery, as if falling down stairs in a dream. In the album's version—that is, listened to over and over—the song divides into two parts. The first half records the increasingly desperate search for meaning and place in traditions, systems, and institutions. That portion ends with a declaration: *I got nothin,' Ma, to live up to.*

The second half of the song returns to those institutions, now seen not from desperation or desire, but from alienation and refusal: *strict party platform ties, social clubs in drag disguise.* The song ends with a declaration of the freak's code: rejection, active, defiant, absurd. *"Walk upside-down inside handcuffs, kick my legs to crash it off, say okay, I've had enough, what else can you show me?* Written in the present tense, it is a recounting of events that have already occurred. This is past. But it is also present, and future: *life, and life only.*

The final chorus, sung by the narrator to his mother, completes the manifesto: *If my thought-dreams could be seen, they'd probably put my head in a guillotine.* And this is both the tragedy and the liberation: not to let those thought-dreams be seen (even by that *trembling, distant voice, unclear* of the beloved); instead, to live within.

The consequence of this choice is eternal exile. And so the album culminated with the elegy of "It's All Over Now, Baby Blue." *You must leave now, take what you need, you think will last.* While others—seasick sailors, reindeer armies—return to their homes, we do not: *The highway is for gamblers, better use your sense. Take what you have gathered from coincidence.* We are called forth by a trickster, by a vagabond dressed in our clothes. Indeed, he *is* us—us as we are, or have been or will be. We must strike another match (*darkness at the break of noon*) and start anew.[17]

*　*　*

Much has been made of the bitterness, bile, and vindictiveness of "Like A Rolling Stone," Dylan's next manifesto, released as a single on July 20, 1965, six months after *Bringing It All Back Home.* But the chronology seems backward: the song hit the airwaves a week *before* the fabled and ill-fated Newport "electric Dylan" performance. The introspective and imagistically complex forms of the quiet exile songs had been received with respect, attentiveness and enthusiasm by audiences. Dylan had begun to experiment, with great enthusiasm, with a return to his old rock-and-roll self. He was in the beginnings of what would be his longest and probably deepest relationship, with Sara Lownds.

It might be more appropriate, then, to see that song as a near-seamless continuation of the narrative in the previous album, and of its musical, lyrical and thematic development. *Strike another match, go start anew, it's all over now, Baby Blue* shifts smoothly toward *nobody ever taught you how to live on the street, but now you're going to have to get used to it.*

What has changed between "Baby Blue" and "Rolling Stone" is, in part, the cast of characters or, more accurately, the ways these characters are arrayed across the grimy spectacle of late-modern life. If there is anger and bile, it is directed not at some shadowy cabal of the powerful and wicked, but at the pervasive, all-consuming seductiveness of contemporary consumer culture and its corresponding "society of the spectacle" with its capacity to transform money to sex to power to entertainment and even art, and back to money in a moment, in an ad, in a gesture made on the street or a sleek designer pet carried on one's shoulder, in the performances of *the jugglers and the clowns . . . when they all did tricks for you.* Dylan's song described a victim of this seduction, *a princess on a steeple*, a figure so caught up in the temptations of celebrity spectacle as to have become in consequence a seduction herself—*throw the bums a dime in your prime.* Witnessed at the moment of discard, the impossible moment now inevitable, witnessed by one who knew.

The scenario of the song is straightforward: pride falls. *Once upon a time* a girl who *dressed so fine* meets her fate; abandoned by her *diplomat, who carried on his shoulder a Siamese cat* as they rode together in the open car, *a chrome horse*, through the parade route—5th Avenue? Mardi Gras? Dealey Plaza, Dallas?—*Miss Lonely* now must go down to the street itself, where the narrator, *the mystery tramp*, awaits, a *Napoleon in rags* to guide her through the new world, the real world, she'll occupy now. (The song requires its sequels: the songs of *Highway 61 Revisited*, which take our lost innocent—take *us*—on that tour.)

Considered this way—that is, not as an example of vengeful *schadenfreude* but as the testimony of a battle-hardened witness documenting the inevitable alienation that accompanies modern life—"Like A Rolling Stone" extends Dylan's critique of American culture, setting it within the same landscape—cityscape, actually—but seen from a different angle, by different eyes.

> How does it feel
> How does it feel
> To be on your own
> With no direction home
> A complete unknown
> Like a rolling stone

The strategy of "Mr. Tambourine Man," in which the song was meant simultaneously to be listened to and *sung* by the audience, recurred even more potently here. On the liner notes to the album that opened with "Rolling Stone," Dylan punned on the homonym I/eye: "I cannot say the word eye any more. . . . when I speak this word eye, it is as if I am speaking of somebody's eye that I faintly remember. . . . there is no eye—there is only a series of mouths—long live the mouths . . ."[18]

All that summer, young Americans sang the chorus, some waiting for the radio play, some listening to the single again and again, some simply coming on its reiteration, thanks to pop radio's top 40 playlist regulations. When it reached the top 10 in August 1965, it was played approximately four times an hour on the big commercial pop stations. When it hit number 2, it was playing stations like WAVZ in New Haven, Connecticut, and WMCA in New York with sufficient frequency that its length—six minutes—was wreaking havoc with the very play formula that required its repetition. If you wanted to hear it, in any top-40 market with more than three stations (and that meant, almost any part of the well-populated zones of the East, Midwest, and West) you could push the buttons on the car radio or turn the dial of the pocket transistor and it would be out there somewhere, playing. Everyone hipped to pop music and living by the radio dial memorized it; everyone sang it: *How does it feel?* Exiled, stripped of ideals (or at least of certainties), we were feeling ourselves all over to find the wounds.

On the album, the song had a very different feel. *Highway 61 Revisited* was Dylan's culminating protest album, his final and most devastating critique of America, laid out as an alternative to the dominant culture's *roadmaps for the soul* sold by the *national bank at a profit*. The apocalyptic crack-of-doom snare hit that opened "Like A Rolling Stone" also served as the opening salvo for *Highway 61 Revisited*, but "Rolling Stone" was closer to a prologue to the album, whose framing device was, once more, that highway running from Minnesota to New Orleans, a river of a highway, running alongside the Mississippi River of Huck and Jim's salvation, incarceration, and eventual redemption.

Though the album and song title suggest we've been here before, the return is deceptive. In his first album, Dylan had taken us not along U.S. 61 but its more benign parallel on the other side of the Mississippi, Route 51. The road Dylan now drives us to is the Blues Highway written into so many of the precedential songs of migration and exile on which Dylan was building this album, with its stridently electric, Chicago blues–based sound (including on one take the drumming of Sam Lay, Howlin' Wolf's sideman). And with that crackle and howl of spontaneous, mistake-riddled set of songs, the album rendered an alternative roadmap for the alienated and unmoored.

Highway 61 Revisited bristles with references to American geography: the urban spectacle of New York in "Like A Rolling Stone," the corrupted Western frontier town of Tombstone; the arterial freight train's whistle in "It Takes a Lot To Laugh, It Takes a Train to Cry," the highway and the thruway seen out the window "From a Buick Six"; the urban den into which Mr. Jones wanders in "Ballad of a Thin Man," the mansions of the rich where "Queen Jane Approximately" is set, the border town of Juarez in "Just Like Tom Thumb's Blues," and, of course, that extraordinary word-picture, set on a dead-end street, part third-world corruption and stench, part Venetian decadence, part Parisian pretentiousness, part New York glib and London hotel: "Desolation Row."

Dylan didn't name the album "Like A Rolling Stone," though that song, released as a single well before the album itself was recorded, catapulted Dylan into pop and rock-and-roll stardom. Instead, he named it after a song that appears fully two thirds of the way into the album, buried in the middle of the second side. It is a hard-rocking tune, a three-chord takeover of a Bo Diddley/Chuck Berry form, reaching back to Muddy Waters and the Chicago bluesmen from whom guitarist Mike Bloomfield, playing stabbing slide here, had learned his chops.

A police whistle, an ambulance siren, punctuates the song and eventually ends it. It's a fadeout as the emergency vehicles race away from Yucca Flats, Nevada, where, for the benefit of the press, the U.S. military have just finished staging a rehearsal for Armageddon:

> Now the rovin' gambler he was very bored
> Tryin' to create a next world war
> He found a promoter who nearly fell off the floor
> He said I never engaged in this kind of thing before
> But yes I think it can be very easily done
> We'll just put some bleachers out in the sun
> And have it on Highway 61

Somewhere, Dylan must have seen that picture or series of pictures from *Life* in 1952, perhaps in the family living room in Hibbing; perhaps in a doctor's or dentist's office in Hibbing or Duluth: the journalists and witnesses, in their special dark sunglasses, seated in bleachers, staring at a mushroom cloud in the desert some miles away. Now, though, atomic holocaust was the

GUESTS ON NEWS NOB waiting for the blast surround AEC Chairman Gordon Dean (*front row,* *third from right*). At left halfway up hill is mirror in which Photographer Eyerman took picture at left.

AN ATOMIC OPEN HOUSE

AEC plays host to cameras, newsmen and TV at blast on Yucca Flat

12.3. Opening page of "An Atomic Open House," *Life*, May 5, 1952. (LIFE is a registered trademark of Time Inc. Photo by J. R. Eyerman. © The Picture Collection Inc. Reprinted with permission. Article: © 1952. The Picture Collection Inc. Reprinted with permission. All rights reserved.)

province of a *roving gambler* and *a promoter*. Or perhaps that was always the case: it just took Dylan to say it and the counterculture to hear it.

U.S. 61 never went anywhere near Nevada. Nor did it go to Mount Moriah in Jerusalem, where *God said to Abraham, "Kill me a son."* It did, however, go to Duluth, Minnesota, where Abraham Zimmerman's son Robert was born. Infanticide, divine decree, atomic holocaust: all took place *out there on Highway 61*. America the trash-heap of history, groaning under the weight of piles of army-surplus *red, white, and blue shoe strings*; no-longer-fashionable, defective princess phones; biblical prophecies; the promises of American exceptionalism and divine blessing; Manifest Destiny; old photographs of the Mount of the Holy Cross; tossed out paintings from the refurbished U.S. Capitol*—all were piled up out there.

And then "Highway 61" ends. The siren fades, *after the ambulances go,*† and the motorcade heads for Dallas.

"Desolation Row" is the world that's left for us after Dealey Plaza and the death of American innocence. It is America without enabling myths, without promises and American Dreams. Yet it is also America populated by mythic figures. Not the melting pot and no longer the prison yard, now it is America the staging ground. It is where we live, and its denizens are who we are. Asked in an interview what he'd do if he were president, Dylan said: "I would immediately rewrite 'The Star-Spangled Banner,'" and little school children, instead of memorizing 'America the Beautiful,' would have to memorize 'Desolation Row.'"[19]

At the moment Dylan *was* singing this song, and in the moments, days, weeks, months, and years after, the American counterculture was shaping itself into distinct camps: political radicals, new Old Left activists, hippies, freaks. All of them are found on "Highway 61," and on "Desolation Row." But Dylan's album defined with particular clarity what it meant to be a freak. It wasn't that Dylan threw his lot in with that group—with those who had passed beyond the aesthetic of cool to a formalism of alienation, in which the conditions that created loss, marginalization, impotence, exile, and disenfranchisement became the raw material for a new culture, stealing books, ideas, musical notes and phrases, comic-book moire dots and abstract expressionist brushstrokes, secreting them in lofts, factories, apartments, squats for the time when they might be recast or perhaps only seen in new combination, that being enough to make culture anew. No: Dylan

---

* Including Emmanuel Leutze's 1861 *Westward the Course of Empire Takes Its Way*, which crumbled in a closed-off stairway for years.
† "Desolation Row"

made them possible, by observing them, by describing them, by assembling them together, there on "Desolation Row." There, all of us were freaks. And there, a special beauty awaited.

*   *   *

As Dylan was writing, performing, recording, and releasing *Highway 61 Revisited*, his picture of a postmodern America stripped of progress and its utopian corollary promises was sweeping other media and artists. Within a year, Dylan would be visiting Andy Warhol's Factory, he and his friend Bob Neuwirth courting (or being courted by, depending on the account) Warhol's "superstar" Edie Sedgwick as pop held sway. Roy Lichtenstein's appropriations of comic book expressionism, Claes Oldenburg's monumental soft sculptures of consumer goods, from electric mixers to military tanks, Warhol's own announcement that "everyone will be world-famous for fifteen minutes": all these reflected and refracted Dylan's portrait of American alienation. Within another year, Warhol himself would appropriate Dylan, sponsoring the relentlessly urban, avant-garde art rock premiere of his "Factory band," the Velvet Underground, in 1967. With its grimy, gritty sound, its direct references to the Chelsea Hotel, *The Velvet Underground and Nico* was simultaneously an *homage* to Dylan (Dylan had written "I'll Keep It With Mine" for Nico, and it appeared on her 1967 album, *Chelsea Girl*) and an extrapolation from his work. This was an album that returned to the prison-yard of urban modernism, with its extended lines from the electric viola of John Cale and its dirge-like prison-march rhythms laid out by drummer Maureen Tucker and guitarist Sterling Morrison. Lyrically too the album retreated toward the romanticism of the Beats, with its celebrations of transvestitism and sadomasochism.

By that time, Dylan was long gone. He'd written a hilarious portrait of Edie Sedgwick, Warhol's "Girl of the Year" for 1965, describing the way her *brand new leopard-skin pill-box hat . . . balances on [her] head just like a mattress balances on a bottle of wine*, and the song made it onto *Blonde On Blonde*. So did "Visions of Johanna," another of his extended views of New York. Much was different about this treatment, though. Unlike the densely populated spaces of *Highway 61 Revisited*, this song was nearly empty. The song unfolded like a film, each verse a separate location. The camera moved from a loft where *the heat pipes just cough*, where *the country music station plays soft but there's nothing, really nothing to turn off*, panning to look down on an empty lot where the transvestites and prostitutes who would populate the songs of the Velvet Underground played head-games with the night watchman, and then cutting to a close-up of the female lead; then to a party and a pointless confrontation, followed by another pan, this time to the museum, where *infinity goes up on trial.* The song ends on the street outside the loft, in the early-morning hours. Once again, the *ragged clown,* the *Napoleon in rags,* the *mystery tramp,* returns: *the fiddler now steps to the road.* This is the end of things: *everything's been returned which was owed.* All debts are settled, all offences redressed. *The harmonicas play the skeleton keys on the rain* and Dylan's longtime persona, the trickster Tiresias, once again is gone.

This time for good. While the Velvet Underground took the stage for Warhol's *Exploding. Plastic. Inevitable.* multimedia performances, Dylan moved out of the Chelsea Hotel, disappearing into the Hudson Valley rural retreat of Woodstock, New York. On November 22, 1965, exactly two years after the assassination of John Kennedy, Dylan married Sara Lownds, and less than two months after that, their first child, Jesse, was born. Seven months later, a motorcycle accident provided him with a chance to retreat from touring and public appearance and he took it.

Over the next months, he returned to musical form, writing more than thirty new songs, many of them rehearsed and recorded in the basement of Big Pink, an unpretentious house in the woods of Saugerties, New York, rented by members of his touring band, the Hawks—soon to become the Band. Relieved from touring duties and with a newly negotiated recording contract granting him significant freedom, he returned to the vast archive of American musical forms he had heard and, with his extraordinary musical and lyrical memory, internally recorded. Week after week, he taught the Hawks the great American songbook, from Stephen Foster to Blind Willie McTell, from Clarence Ashley up to and including Bobbie Gentry.

While Dylan and his band worked up these tunes on languid summer afternoons, three hours south of them, Newark was awash in riots, declarations of revolutionary uprising, rebellions that accelerated as the forces of national order were called in to quell the disturbances. A ten-year-old boy, shot in Newark, graced a *Life* cover. Network news footage showed troops with shotguns being disbursed to each corner; as the camera panned from above, it turned the street into an impromptu billboard emblazoned with the words "Black Power." San Francisco's streets were dense with tens of thousands of young transients, many of them drawn there by John Phillips's song, written to advertise the Monterey Pop Festival down the peninsula, recorded by his friend and ex-bandmate Scott McKenzie in a smooth tenor that promised *gentle people* with *flowers in their hair* on the streets during a *love-in. All across the nation,* Phillips and McKenzie declared, *such a strange vibration. People in motion. There's a whole generation with a new explanation, people in motion, people in motion.*

Inside Big Pink, the motion seemed Brownian rather than revolutionary, utopian, or directed. Dylan's "Like A Rolling Stone" had emboldened those tens of thousands (and many more who didn't quite make it to San Francisco that summer) to imagine a life *on your own, with no direction home*. That summer in San Francisco, Black Panthers Bobby Seale, Huey Newton, and Eldridge Cleaver were listening obsessively to Dylan's "Ballad of a Thin Man"; Newton saw the song as a description of class and racial alienation and a call to revolutionary action.[20] Dylan had failed to show up at Monterey Pop; he'd remained silent on the collapse of the civil rights movement.

The songs Dylan wrote while in Woodstock were themselves anachronisms. They almost fit within the language and musical forms of the American songbook. But they didn't. They also seemed to emerge logically from their titular sources: the King James Bible, American folk tales of frontiersmen and women, of outlaws and lawmen, saints, drifters, gamblers, landlords, immigrants, hobos, jokers, thieves, lovers spied by the water, and messengers.

When Dylan was ready to record, he didn't take this band into the studio. Instead, he collected a small, tight set of songs, brought them to a Nashville studio, and recorded them with just a drummer and a bassist, both of whom had worked with him on *Blonde On Blonde*, and a late-addition Nashville pedal-steel player.

John Wesley Harding was a dramatic break with the noisy, mimetic cacophony that had characterized so much of Dylan's work from *Bringing it All Back Home* on. It wasn't rock, folk, or country, but rather some stubborn mutation. Similarly, it was neither strikingly original nor respectfully derivative, and it was certainly not fashionable in tone or in lyrical shape. It was as if Dylan had stopped in his tracks, gone back to pick up something he, his audience and his nation had dropped along the highway—a compass, say, or a roadmap—and then struck out on an entirely different track.

If he did, he didn't do it alone. *John Wesley Harding* assembled a cast of archetypal American characters, but the songs themselves disconnected these characters from the narratives they were meant to populate, relocating them in a sort of temporal, spatial, and cultural limbo. Frankie Lee Sims, a blues singer, Lightnin' Hopkins's cousin, lost his last name and became a gambler. John Wesley Hardin: Dylan misspelled the name of his outlaw-hero and stubbornly retained the misprision, running it as the album's title across a picture of Dylan in a rural landscape, dressed in what seems to be nineteenth-century outlaw garb—a tanned leather jacket and country hat—accompanied by apparent reincarnations of two American Indian guides and a mountain man or lumberjack.

Quiet, sparse, populated by mock allegories that often failed (or refused) to deliver their message with the depth and force of true allegory, the album might well be judged a failure, given its place and its maker. But it was Dylan's most commercially successful, certifying gold in three months. As importantly, it had "legs," even though Dylan refused to release a single from it, a standard tactic to draw new listeners and buyers to an artist with an established audience.* The album sat well on the turntable; it could be talked over, sung with, parsed, its images meditated on, its lines quoted. Dylan had told Allen Ginsberg "how he was writing shorter lines and that every line had to mean something. He wasn't just making up a line to go with a rhyme anymore. Each line had to advance the story, bring the song forward. . . . There was to be no wasted language, no wasted breath. All the imagery was to be functional rather than ornamental."[21] As a consequence, individual lines themselves seemed, at first, the best part of the album:

> to lend a helping hand . . .
> she meant to do me harm . . .
> Judas pointed down the road and said, Eternity! . . .
> Eternity, though you might call it Paradise . . .
> It's not a house, he said: it's not a house, it's a home
> please don't put a price on my soul . . .
> stay free from petty jealousies . . .
> live by no man's code . . .
> and hold your judgment for yourself . . .
> for his tongue it could not speak, but only flatter . . .
> if ye cannot bring good news, then don't bring any . . .
> nothing is revealed.†

Over time and repeated listenings, however, an atmospheric whole emerged, a hazy, perhaps deceptive, landscape: muddy, often cold, not inhumane but unbeholden to the humans who wandered its spaces from town to town, false-front tavern to one-room shack, looking for something and failing to find it. It was an album meant to defy the expectations and hopes of those who had come to Dylan for answers, for revelations, for instructions. Like its

---

* Most of Dylan's albums tended to sell very well for the first few weeks (for his fan base eagerly awaited each release) and then die.

† These individual lines come from, in order, "John Wesley Harding," "As I Went Out One Morning," "The Ballad of Frankie Lee and Judas Priest" [three lines], "Dear Landlord," "I Am a Lonesome Hobo" [three lines], "The Wicked Messenger" [two lines], and again, "The Ballad of Frankie Lee and Judas Priest."

characters—saints, syphilitics, bank robbers, lost lovers, immigrants—you too wandered, with no direction home.

* * *

Nothing is revealed.

The quality of anticipation, even dread, permeates this album, and renders it fundamentally different from the antic existentialism, the prison-yard sensibility of its immediate predecessors. Even the love songs that end this album's song sequence—"Down Along the Cove" and "I'll Be Your Baby Tonight"— suggest not that love itself is temporary, but rather that the stage on which love is set is only rented. The album's other songs, particularly their single lines and couplets, are full of omens: "The Wicked Messenger" declares, "*The soles of my feet, I swear they're burning!*" But neither he nor his audience can tell what this portent means. A *bolt of lightning* strikes the courthouse where the drifter is on trial—though for what, no one seems to know—and *as everybody knelt to pray, the Drifter did escape.* Has evil been returned to the world? Has a miscarriage of justice been averted? Not even the drifter himself knows.

These songs seemed to be pauses in the midst of narrative or even different renderings of the same pause in the same narrative. Their hushed quality wasn't so much for the purpose of encouraging listeners to pay closer attention to what was being said; they were hushed because both narrator and listener were listening for the sound of the rush, the roar, the wind after the calm in the midst of a hurricane, the race of sound and force when the atomic shock wave hit, the clash of heaven and earth on the opening of each of the seven seals of the Book of Revelation. Over the course of four albums, Dylan had been drawing back from the political, the social, and had reached the limit of his panoramic vision: he was watching the infinite and waiting to see what happened.

Yet this was not a retreat from advocacy to privacy; rather it was a shift of tone in a continuing vocation of prophesy. The achievements of *Bringing It All Back Home*, *Highway 61 Revisited*, and *Blonde On Blonde* lay in the means by which he assembled a vast array of disturbed pieces of American cultural experience, both contemporary experience—the quotidian moments of daily life and the melodramas of politics, crime, sex, celebrity, high art—and the roots, sources, and traditions that underlay the contemporary, fed it, gave it significance. A song like "Subterranean Homesick Blues" ripped out, in one sustained riff after another, antic pictures drawn from and drawn *as if* noir B-movies, working at such speed that the disparate elements crammed together to form the critical mass of the song. This was a method particularly apt to the moment in American cultural history, when radio and television had reached a screaming pitch of informational overload and the more traditional media were overcompensating in competition.

As Dylan was writing, performing, and recording those albums, Marshall McLuhan was touring in support of his book, *Understanding Media*, published in 1964, in which he argued that contemporary America was in the midst of a revolutionary information age, with new forms of media overwhelming those that demanded more complex and interactive responses. Dylan's achievement with those albums and with the infamous electric concerts of 1965 and 1966 was to accept and test McLuhan's propositions, and prove them wrong by making forms of music that were simultaneously "hot" (intense, attention-grabbing, even overwhelming) and "cool" (requiring engagement to complete the experience), overwhelming in their density and yet drainingly demanding precisely as a result.

Dylan's *assemblage* songs reproduced the struggle simultaneously to comprehend, to take in, and to fend off, the waves of images, sounds, ideas, imperatives, promises and threats found in "late-Capitalism." By contrast, *John Wesley Harding* was a report from a distant place, a place one went to wait as the world collapsed.

And so we come to "All Along the Watchtower." It appears toward the middle of the album, after an introductory triad of songs has set out the themes, the terms, the stakes: the problem of doing good, of taking a stand ("John Wesley Harding"); the existence of deceptive forms of evil and good and the unreliability of appearances ("As I Went Out One Morning"); the martyrdom of prophets, even when those prophets only prophesy the end of prophecy ("I Dreamed I Saw St. Augustine"). After "All Along the Watchtower," the songs seem to trail off, to retreat from prophecy to narrative, then anecdote, then cliché.

In case you've forgotten, here are the lyrics in their entirety:

"There must be some way out of here," said the joker to the thief
"There's too much confusion, I can't get no relief.
Businessmen, they drink my wine, plowmen dig my earth.
None of them along the line know what any of it is worth."

"No reason to get excited," the thief, he kindly spoke.
"There are many here among us who feel that life is but a joke
But you and I, we've been through that, and this is not our fate
So let us not talk falsely now, the hour is getting late"

12.4 Album cover for Bob Dylan, *John Wesley Harding*, 1967

All along the watchtower, princes kept the view,
While all the women came and went, barefoot servants, too.

Outside in the distance a wildcat did growl
Two riders were approaching;
The wind began to howl

It is the briefest of songs—or, more accurately, the densest and most condensed. It begins after it has ended: the two characters who speak in the
first two stanzas are the two riders who approach the watchtower in the final
verse. But that's to assume that we are reading the piece. We aren't. The song
is meant to be heard, and then replayed, in various forms, over some time:
it's demanding, in that it urges us to listen the way Dylan did—with a mu-

sically and lyrically photographic memory—and then replay, reordering, even, recasting in a different medium, what we've heard.[22]

So let's consider this as a cinematic piece, an extension of the formal strategies applied in "Visions of Johanna." The narrative begins in relative close up: two riders in the desert, passing the time in a debate about the richness of the earth and the ingratitude, the greed. Then, as Dylan says, "the scope opens up."[23] The pop existentialist's proposal, "that life is but a joke," is dismissed. We are called to account.

With that, the cinematic scope opens as well. These two are riding some vast plain, some wilderness, approaching a citadel. This is the Plain of Moab, above which rose Mount Pisgah, whence God brought Moses, showing him the land "promised of Abraham," promised—but denied—to Abraham, to Isaac, to Jacob, and now to Moses himself.[24]

Moses is buried there on that plain; perhaps the joker and the thief will pass by that grave, unmarked and undiscovered. Impotent rage, unheard prophecy, nihilism: *You and I, we've been through that, and that is not our fate. So let us not talk falsely now, the hour is getting late.* Now the camera pans back from these two, back across that plain, back to the watchtower at the foot of Mount Pisgah. As we watch the procession of worldliness—princes in their finery, the swaying procession of their women, along the high, open walkway, servants coming and going—a wildcat growls, the wind rises, and the screen goes black, the song ends.

John Wesley Harding deceived. It was quiet, ingratiating, with an unobtrusive country-roots feel that swelled at the end with the addition of pedal steel guitar whiz Pete Drake on the last two love songs. It invited you to put it on and listen, late at night. But if you did—if you listened—the disquieting conjunction of the moment and the Eternity behind it crept up. The pastoral plains and hillsides of America: that's what Dylan seemed to be offering as retreat, solace, alternative to the prison-yard of "Desolation Row," shrunk by its last verse to a single room in which you were trapped *just about the time the doorknob broke.* "John Wesley Harding" opened so quietly, so unassumingly, the guitar strum simple—anyone could play it—and the lyrics too an offering of moral simplicity. But it didn't work out that way. You looked too hard at the cover, and the figures around Dylan didn't offer a happy reunification of outlaws, Indians, and mountain men.

These were strangers, outsiders to America, and the landscape behind was chill and barren. Inside the album, the pastorale became the Plain of Moab. In the fields, down along the cove, in the frontier town and the county courthouse, the American archetypes began to assemble. All stood watch, waiting for the next thing. Something had to come. But it hadn't yet.

CHAPTER 13

Hendrix on Mount Pisgah

Besides, what could they see but a hideous and desolate wilderness, full of
wild beasts and wild men? . . . Neither could they go up to the top of Pisgah,
to view from this wilderness a more goodly country to feed their hopes.
WILLIAM BRADFORD, *Of Plimouth Plantation,* 1647

John Wesley Harding was released on December 27, 1967—quixotic timing,
two days after the end of the Christmas season. The production-to-release
schedule was unusually tight, though: Dylan had finished in the Nashville
studio on November 29.

Its profound debt to the language and literature of American religious
experience was easy to overlook in the secularized worlds of the later 1960s.
Dylan's plays on the imagery of Old and New Testaments seemed, to many,
simply strange, a part of his larger retreat from the America of his time.
Even those with some familiarity with American Protestant iconography
would have been baffled by the odd conjunctions and misprisions bedded
in the songs.

Dylan's application of this biblical imagery in the album was far from
declamatory or eloquent. It was, instead, sparse, even meager, and "All Along
the Watchtower" was the most restrained and recondite. Based, loosely, on a
passage from Isaiah predicting the fall of Babylon, it contained references
to the crucifixion, borrowed from the Book of Revelation and set its story
across a landscape compiled of many sites in the biblical world. Over the

whole, a sense of mood trumped clarity of narrative; one could feel the air more easily than track the events. Perhaps Dylan was seeking to write in a time-signature appropriate to revelation, recording a history that unfolded outside of time.

Listeners at the time could be forgiven for reading too much, or too little, into the song. For Dylan, however, the language of religious apocalypse was deeply familiar. He had listened to Gospel music and to the late-night preachers on the radio in Hibbing. With his *idiot savant* ability to imbibe and imitate, he had mastered a huge repertoire of African American blues and spiritual songs. Moreover, he had been studying the Bible, particularly the Old Testament and the Torah, even before the shock of his father's death in June of 1967, and his return to Hibbing for the funeral.[1]

Most followers of music, then and after, though, don't hear Dylan's version of "All Along the Watchtower" when the song plays in their head. Sometime in December, a prerelease demo tape of the song made its way to Jimi Hendrix through Dylan's publicist.[2] Within weeks of hearing it for the first time, Hendrix had recorded what is generally considered—even by Dylan himself—the definitive interpretation. Dylan had stolen from Gospel and the core of American black spirituality to produce an existential mood-piece. Hendrix took it back, and then some.

* * *

The Jimi Hendrix Experience was an unlikely group to cover the spare, brooding "Watchtower," with its stripped-down three-chord musical structure and its brief conversational narrative. By the time Hendrix began working on the song, he'd evolved his style from its earlier roots in blues and R&B, into a swirlingly psychedelic form unlike any other music being recorded. But Hendrix was deeply excited by the song from the start, and proud even of the earliest, four-track version the band produced in London in the first weeks of January 1968. Using Traffic's Dave Mason on acoustic twelve-string rhythm guitar, Hendrix worked obsessively on the recording, driving bassist Noel Redding out of the studio and taking over the bass part himself. Rerecording in New York a few weeks later, Hendrix picked apart and reassembled the London take, adding elements, multi-tracking guitar parts, redefining the sonic space and palette using the much more elaborate twelve-track facilities of the Record Plant studio.[3]

Completed, the result was stunning, and even more remarkably, it was recognized as such by record label executives, who released it as a single from *Electric Ladyland*, the double album on which it was the penultimate track. English and American audiences responded enthusiastically, pushing it into the top 5 in England, and the *Billboard* top 20 in the States—a major achievement at a time when the Hot 100 was still dominated by the Beatles' end-game singles "Hello, Goodbye" and "Hey Jude."

Hearing Hendrix's final version, especially on a good stereo, turned up loud, was bracing then, as it is now. The song opened with an off-off-beat rhythm part that anticipated Hendrix's swooping lead tone, itself more straightforwardly off-beat, so that, when the vocal line arrived, the song's musical and rhythmic logic dropped from the sky like a revelation. The guitar playing is among the very best Hendrix ever did; the pyrotechnics, including passages with glass-slide, wah-wah, fuzztone, delay, and other effects Hendrix was having made for him at the time, seem not gratuitous or overblown but apt, bringing a searing emotionality to a song that Dylan had sung as if he were observing from a great distance.

Over time, "All Along the Watchtower" became one of Hendrix's standards in live performance, and it remains one of the most heard of Hendrix's many memorable songs.

Yet Hendrix's interpretation is anything but straightforward. With its long pauses between sung lines, the song might have attracted a guitarist looking for a call-and-response opportunity to display guitar-solo prowess. Hendrix didn't approach the problem in that way. Instead, he ran his guitar parts around the vocal, allowing them to emerge and recede in ways not implicit in the Dylan version. Indeed, his vocals are deeply expressive, with accelerations and retards, stutters of syllables, rises and falls in volume and in melodic line.

Despite the combination of passion, intuition, virtuosity, and craft that Hendrix lavished on the song, there was one place where he was oddly lax. At telling moments in the song, he failed to get the lyrics right.

This is a particularly significant deviation. Hendrix revised the recording many times in two different studios, and yet he never took the opportunity to "punch in" corrections to the lyrics. Moreover, among the many recordings of live performances of the song, Hendrix consistently failed to fix his initial mistakes—if mistakes they were. At times, he mumbled; at times, he simply stopped singing midway through the first verse, where his most aberrant misreading takes place.[4]

It's especially odd given that the lyrics to this song are short and direct. Moreover, Hendrix was not particularly prone to slips of lyric. His own lyrics were linguistically complex, full of quick twists and turns, yet he never seems to have misspoken them. Even more interesting is to hear Hendrix performing, letter-perfect, the Beatles' "Sgt. Pepper's Lonely Hearts Club Band" without a lyric sheet, with Paul McCartney in the audience, around that same time. And when he worked in the studio, he routinely sang with lyric sheets in front of him.

It's worth considering, then, that this was not a mistake but a revision or, perhaps more accurately, a transgression. That Hendrix could *never* perform the lyrics correctly suggests a rupture of rationality, a reversion to the unconscious—to resistance, to transference, to displacement: the fundamentals of the psychoanalytic and psychohistorical method.

There's much to support the idea. Hendrix adored Dylan; his biographers agree that he transformed his look, both onstage and off, to make himself more Dylan-esque. His early lyrics, when they veer outside of their rootedness in R&B, soul, and blues, often seem like unfortunate imitations of Dylan's work. "And the Wind Cries Mary" contains many of the tropes Dylan used so masterfully; over time, Hendrix would develop facility with the loose metaphoric allusiveness that marked the mature Dylan, but at least at first, he was simply an adoring fan.

The idealization was mixed into a stew of ambivalence, however. Hendrix's girlfriend at the time reported that he was trying out a number of songs off Dylan's *John Wesley Harding* album, notably "I Dreamed I Saw St. Augustine," but turned away from that track as "too personal to Dylan for anyone else to be able to cover it. . . . Then he thought he would do 'All Along the Watchtower,' but he was terrified that Dylan would laugh at him and the critics lay into him."[5]

In some ways, presenting himself as a Dylan interpreter *was* a gesture fraught with temerity. There were many who had made the attempt and subjected themselves to ridicule, from Bobby Darin to the Golden Gate Strings. There were many more whose versions achieved pop success by flattening and simplifying Dylan's synergy of primitive music and highly sophisticated lyrics, winning them temporary celebrity and the eternal contempt of Dylan himself. What none of them along the way had done was rough-up Dylan: bring his work back to its origins in the dual rivers of American musical culture: African American blues and Anglo American traditional music.[6]

*　*　*

Jimi Hendrix spent most of his musical life as a sideman for a variety of soul and R&B acts. He observed the flamboyant performance stylings of his employers, ranging from B-list Motown singers like Buddy and Stacey[7] to the legendary Little Richard. He had also learned something of the ways that black performers had to work within long-held racial stereotypes when they crossed over into mainstream, mass-market musical media. Sexuality, wild extravagance, menace: the *bad nigger* played against the buffoonish, incompetent, pratfalling caricature—*dumb nigger*—most commonly seen in blackface Vaudeville and the movies. Hendrix had followed his mentor Little Richard into a variant on the first, in which exaggerated performance combined with sexual menace into a sort of mad, Dionysian composite—*wild nigger.*

But Hendrix was unsatisfied with the ways blackness played out—in his life, in popular music, in American culture more generally. Multiracial himself—part Cherokee, both of his parents were close to half-white—he had traveled through a wide variety of more or less uncomfortably multiracial environments, from his childhood Seattle and his racially integrated (if brief) high school career, through a briefer stint in the paratroopers, and then as sideman performing in a string of low-end music venues like Nashville's Del Morocco Club, where black performers played black and white music to black and white audiences, and eventually as guitarist for Little Richard, who played all-black "chitlin' circuit" venues, upper-echelon Harlem clubs, mixed-race rock-and-roll shows, and all-white concerts and dances.

Hendrix worked with Little Richard on and off until 1965, when he left the band and returned to New York. There he stayed in the uptown and Harlem circuits looking for gigs, even as Dylan's music was defining the city's downtown sound. Signing on with the all-black Isley Brothers (with whom he'd worked before), he played around the area, from New Jersey resorts to New England venues, on bills that included Booker T. & the MGs, an integrated band with a brilliant white guitarist, Steve Cropper. He began actively collecting records from the British Invasion, in particular a significant crop of English blues and blues fusion groups, like the Yardbirds, Them, and the Animals—young white men who were deeply in love with the black American blues and R&B traditions and were knocking out original reinterpretations of classics Hendrix had been playing on the black circuit, but with a far wider crossover audience and with a willingness to move beyond the narrow restrictions of the black musical and performance traditions within which Hendrix had been chafing for some time.

Throughout 1965 and much of 1966, Hendrix performed and toured with Curtis Knight & The Squires. The band was hot, playing a number of the Midtown and Greenwich Village go-go spots and dance clubs. For a time in 1966, they served as house band for the Cheetah, one of the most celebrated of New York City go-go clubs. Late in 1965, Hendrix signed on to tour with Joey Dee and the Starliters, a fully integrated group with a white, Jersey-Italian front man, a long-standing string of dance hits (most notably "Peppermint Twist"), and a stint in Europe, where their opening act was a new British quartet whose reputation was built on their interpretations of R&B standards: the Beatles. With these bands, and with others who hired him during these years, Hendrix found himself playing in front of all-white audiences, sometimes in places where social integration was unheard of— places like Revere, Massachusetts, an all-white waterfront town north of Boston, where he played with Dee late in '65.[8]

Mainly, however, Hendrix spent those New York months trying to find a place within the multiple scenes of that city. It wasn't easy. Those years were volatile ones within the geography of race in New York, as in the rest of the United States, and it spilled over into music. Hendrix tried crashing Harlem but was rebuffed as too primitive and showy. He made his living in Midtown, in the discos and go-go clubs, but the music and the scene left him unimpressed. He was listening to avant-garde jazz, experimental music, and post-Beat singer-songwriter stuff, and that was all downtown.

Greenwich Village was the locale for true ferment. Partly because of the heritage of avant-garde jazz performances at places like the Vanguard, the clustering of Beats, and the folk revival of the early '60s, the Village had developed a reputation as a cultural tourist site and, in consequence, one of the richest locales for performers and musicians. By the middle of 1965, Hendrix was frequenting the music and performance clubs looking for ways to break into the scene, and by '66 had formed a small band to back him: Jimmy James and the Blue Flame.*

The choice of a stage name, part soul-train alliteration and part Chicago bluesman in its sound, suggests Hendrix's evolving, unstable, musical, performative, and racial persona. Hendrix stood at the fringes of a variety of celebrity musical societies, many of them uneasy with each other—Harlem soul and R&B, midtown party disco with its high-society slummers and its fashionistas and art-school graduates, the Village with its often incompatible strains of radical politics, avant-garde literature, "out" jazz, good-time hootenannies, purist folk music, singer-songwriter expressionists and experimental pop-rock.

New York was the destination for ambitious avant-gardes in a wide variety of media, a place to transcend the limits of genre and style, to reinvent one's art and oneself—but not one's race. Even in the circles of the Village, Negroes were usually specimens, role models, exotics—a combina-

---

* The Blue Flame was no second-rate pickup band; Randy California (who later cofounded Spirit), and Jeff "Skunk" Baxter (later of Steely Dan and the Doobie Brothers) were both members.

tion of long-defined American racial stereotypes now admired rather than abhorred. Hendrix was in many ways already an ironic caricature of those stereotypes. He had observed the possibility of an identity that could play on race as he played the guitar—inventively, left-handed. He had begun to raise the gain on the guitar, the volume on the amp, and to use booster circuits to overload the preamp and power amp stages ("slamming the tubes"), to play with feedback, modulating, working at the edge where he might lose control, but didn't. He was beginning to do the same with the question of race. He was willing to transgress unspoken but long-held rules—to bring the black-to-black ironic performances of racial stereotype from the Negro circuits and the all-black shows of Harlem down to white audiences, and to do so while blending that irony with a genuine menace, to play with the stereotype of the ecstatic, emotive black, the hypersexualized, rapacious, vengeful Negro field hand going after the plantation owner and his women.

Yet there's evidence even this early that he was considering the ways that layering stereotypes, personae and identities one on the other might afford something even more radical. When he moved his base of operations from Harlem to the Village, he began to dress differently; there were elements of the cowboy, the soldier, and the gypsy in his evolving costumes. He was ranging up and down the chronological ladder as well, with anachronisms of nineteenth-century dandyism, English Edwardian and Regency dress, military medals and epaulettes from centuries earlier.

Some of this he was taking from his study of English pop music, which was also drawn to these flamboyant, even insulting references admixed in ebullient rebelliousness. Where the Mods, particularly, were attacking England's rigidly stratified class system, with its fastidious cues to class identity (accent, hairstyle, shoe- and boot toe, and working and leisure fashions), Hendrix's application drew a similar strategy into the American racial system.

Hendrix was also borrowing heavily from Dylan, whose chameleon-like shifts of identity had impressed him. Hendrix was learning his techniques from looking at the album jackets of British bands, and he was doing the same by observing Dylan's transformations from the Midwestern proletarian to the sexually ambiguous dandy to the less readable typologies he presented on the covers of *Highway 61 Revisited* and *Blonde On Blonde*. Hendrix was also looking over the publicity pictures that moved from press packet to pop music fan magazines and industry newspapers, and the underground broadsheets that were just beginning to burgeon. He understood what effect these had on young fans, the ways they offered promises of new lives, countercultural networks that transcended physical geography. Hendrix was working on something, but he hadn't yet worked it out.

Like so many other cultural reinventions, it required a sort of *hegira*, a voluntary exile, a sort of asylum-seeking, all crammed into a brief six months, to remake Hendrix into one of the most revolutionary visionaries of the counterculture. Discovered by Animals bassist Chas Chandler, who was seeking clients for a new career as a promoter, Hendrix left his half-forged New York self and headed to London, to form a new band and to complete his transformation.

* * *

The Jimi Hendrix Experience emerged from this exile-into-possibility. Chandler and Hendrix rapidly chose two British musicians to form the band: guitarist-turned-bassist Noel Redding and jazz-drummer-turned-rocker Mitch Mitchell. Embracing fluidity, Hendrix chose two remarkably adaptive musicians, both of whom brought new hybrid musical identities with them. The Experience was a trio and that was important: the form was unusual within the worlds of rock, blues, R&B. There were broad precedents in rockabilly and jazz: solo performers with rhythm section sidemen (Buddy Holly, for example), and combatively inventive jazz trios in which masters of their instruments played off each other's brilliance.

The Experience had an obvious counterpart on the London scene: Cream. Hendrix had jammed with them shortly after arriving in London, and his thinking about the nature of a musically inventive setting for his work jibed with theirs. Cream was a fiercely collaborative trio, more like an avant-garde jazz ensemble in the creative tensions built around a musical identity that had no acknowledged leader and in which the battle for leadership was constantly playing out.

Hendrix once recalled, "I was thinking of the smallest pieces possible with the hardest impact," but he and his managers also were playing with a more traditional leader-with-sidemen identity, evident in the choice of the Jimi Hendrix Experience as the name. Yet that suggestion belied the musical reality, for Mitchell and Redding were anything but quiet sidemen. (Listen to "If 6 Was 9" from the second album, *Axis: Bold as Love*.) Playing in a trio that aspires to more than gentle performances is extraordinarily difficult. There is no mercy: every note, right or wrong, can be heard by the audience, and by the other performers, and the struggle to simultaneously *listen* and *create* is exhausting and only rarely exhilarating.

The Jimi Hendrix Experience was, then, a paradox of musical and performative identities. At first, it wasn't even clear that Hendrix would be the lead singer; he took the role reluctantly and only slowly grew into it. But it's almost inconceivable to imagine what the Experience would have been had there been a white bass player singing lead and a left-handed black guitar virtuoso standing to one side. For what rapidly emerged as the visual and performative style of the Experience was a provocative racial irony, in which the traditional format of the white leader and diffident darkies supporting him (or her) became instead something dangerously different: a flamboyant upending.[9]

Photo shoots for the cover of their first album, *Are You Experienced?*, and the supporting photographs used for publicity and promotion, for inside shots, for the images on 45s, and for posters sold on tour emphasize this play on racial hierarchy. In the proof sheets of a shoot by Gered Mankowitz, for example, the series begins with a brooding individual portrait of Hendrix in a British army officer's ornamental jacket; over the following eleven pictures, we see Hendrix, the band, and the photographer, all collaborating on a series of variations portraying Hendrix as the wild, sultry, brooding, or thoughtful heroic center, while the two white boys, the diminutive one forward, the taller behind (to further distinguish Hendrix and his sidemen by scale), playing cocky, fey, anxious, coy. Their outfits too echo, in diminished form, Hendrix's own.

The cover for the English release of that first album made the relationship even more explicit: Hendrix is at center, seeming at first to be seated on the shoulders of his sidemen, who lean out from behind him on either side. In a composition borrowed from religious paintings, Hendrix has opened his cloak to surround and protect his two acolytes. Here is the black plantation owner with his white sharecroppers; the factory owner with his workers, the patriarch with his womenfolk. The photographer, Hendrix, Mitchell, and Redding, and probably Chas Chandler, have drawn on a secularized imagery long dispersed into the collective cultural unconscious, and the effect is neither novelty nor menace, but reassurance, an offer of benevolence and protection.

Yet the piece carries complex ironies beyond its initial surprises. As it comes to race, something has happened in this picture: in the lighting and the printing of the color image, Hendrix's blackness of complexion has been deemphasized, even as Redding and Mitchell's faces have been darkened, so that they are close to equivalent. Hendrix's "natural," a hippie variant on the Black Power afro, has lost some of its flamboyance, while Redding's own Dylan-esque hair is in something closer to Hendrix's natural than, say an unpomaded Italian pompadour or a French aristocrat's wig. (It would be a while before Mitchell would give in and perm his hair into the wildest of all three naturals.) The exotic clothing, drawn from Carnaby Street, but also from the black performers with whom Hendrix had worked in the years leading to the formation of the Experience (notably Little Richard), also brings the three together into a common, willfully chosen difference, a self-declared exile not only from conservative tastes but from the accepted stereotypes of racialized fashion.

The overall effect is to reconceive the idea of cultural marginality in America. To move to the margins is, for white men, an act of will, of solidarity with their black brothers. To flamboyantly layer racial marginality with gender and sexual identity, to admix sacred and profane, to compress centuries of fashion, to denigrate and appropriate signs of privilege: all this is to declare a counterculture of will.

Were this high art or culture, we might find many precedents. But this is pop music; it is resolutely pop music. Just as Jack Bruce and Ginger Baker were highly qualified jazz musicians who chose power-pop and blues-based forms with Cream, Mitch Mitchell turned away from the status of elite jazz

13.1. Gered Mankowitz, proof sheet of Jimi Hendrix and the Experience, 1967. (Photograph by Gered Mankowitz. © Bowstir Ltd. 2012/Mankowitz.com.)

13.2. Bruce Fleming, album cover photograph for British release of *Are You Experienced?* (Photograph © Bruce Fleming.)

to embrace Hendrix's extraordinary cohabitation of popular and folk musical forms. The idea wasn't to declare an avant-garde of artistic and cultural refuseniks; it was to inflame a generation of children and adults who had grown up in the promise of a mass-culture, middle-class utopia and then found it wanting. Hendrix was also situated at the edges of that musical isoculture I have located in the early '60s in pop radio. Hendrix was drawing on the earlier generation of cross-racial, countercultural radio music; he spoke to the same desires as had Martha & the Vandellas in 1964 with "Dancing in the Street," or Mitch Ryder and the Detroit Wheels doing "Devil with a Blue Dress On," both songs penned by William "Mickey" Stevenson while he was in the writers' stable at Motown. Hendrix had worked those soul-train gigs; he had listened to the trans-racial radio of the late '50s and early '60s, and he had early learned that the radio could redefine the racial implications of music, could send messages of liberation, promise, and rebellion to places far from their origins.

But look carefully at the British cover picture and one other feature, almost hidden, reintroduces racial and sexual menace. While Redding and Mitchell are entirely asexual, Hendrix sports a prominent bulge in the left side of his pants, almost hidden in the dark inking, artfully printed "down" to get it past the judging eyes of parents, record store managers, censors. Photographer Ron Rafaelli, one of the most celebrated of rock photographers at the time, did another series of the three musicians, along with two topless blonde groupies, shot in a field in Hawaii. The shoot resulted in another standard Hendrix poster, produced for the psychedelic publishers Visual Thing. Hendrix too was naked from the waist up, showing his taut, near-emaciated upper body, and again one could see, this time clearly discernible against the white of the trousers, Hendrix's penis (dressed to the left, again). In this picture, Mitchell and Redding stayed far in the background. There was no question that the women, blonde, gorgeous, Playmate-sexy, were Hendrix's.

This relatively straightforward appropriation of the black sexual predator-victor, declaring his mastery over the paler, more diminutive and deferential white "boys," was not a finished product, at least for Hendrix. While Hendrix and his merchandising crew sold that Raffaelli picture as a poster through many tours, Hendrix sought to nuance and complicate the sexualizing play of these first forays into visual identity-making. He was unsatisfied with the UK cover picture for *Experienced* and sought out a photographer whose reputation lay with the early psychedelic design forms—the swirling scripts, overwrought colors, and distorted forms that were meant to mimic something of the acid experience. He found his catch in Karl Ferris, a photographer in the rock industry around London who had recently received notoriety as the maker of the Hollies' *Evolution* album art.[10] Ferris took the exaggerated script and the high-key colors he'd applied to the Hollies' album, adding a fish-eye lens that resulted in a distorted circular photo image, and the result was a rough draft of what would become the U.S. album cover.

The new image of Hendrix and the Experience projected a transcendent acid-based psychedelicism that implied much of the hippie social and political sensibility. This was the primary message of the music and lyrics of that first album, as well. The lyrical themes of Hendrix's early songs emphasized transience, freedom, refusal to commit, rootlessness, travel, quest, rejection of a restrictive status quo—racial, social, sexual, spiritual. It had taken Dylan many albums to erase his political and social commentary, to turn his back on America's dreams and imperatives. Hendrix did it from the first.

Song after song extolled the rejection of dominant cultural mores and institutions, from marriage to capitalism to the work ethic. Images of disapproving bourgeois onlookers eying the resolute nonconformist appeared in "Stone Free," to be more fully fleshed out in the wonderful lines of "If 6 was 9" on the second album, completed just months after the first was released in the States:

> White collar conservatives flashin' down the street
> Pointin' their plastic fingers at me, ha !
> They're hopin' soon my kind will drop and die but Oh!
> I'm gonna wave my freak flag high, high!

Both these early albums featured lyrical efforts that proposed an astral, astrological, or transplanetary perspective, in which alternately the narrator spoke from outside the planet or traveled (or longed to travel) beyond the confines of a restrictive, soul-crushing earth. The yearning for escape, the fantasy of escape, the promise of escape seemed to dominate Hendrix's thinking.

Here we must again see Hendrix flaunting his blackness, using its caricatures to his own ends. Languidness, hedonism, an opt-out from the work ethic—none of these qualities true in the real Hendrix, who was known to have worked nonstop for weeks at a time to perfect his version of "All Along the Watchtower"—were the properties of the lazy Negro, the slave Jim in *Huck Finn*, the shiftless no-good in *Amos and Andy*. The themes of transience and escape recollected the runaway slave. The sexuality too played on the grotesque stereotypes of the Negro predator, raping white women, deserving of lynching. Hendrix took these stereotypes back from their white racist makers. What's wrong with sexual pleasure, he asked. Why should we live by the regulatory regimes of the bosses?

Sexual freedom, freedom from outmoded social and political institutions, and freedom to press the boundaries of convention and individual identity: all came laced with the language of psychedelics. It is difficult to overestimate the influence of psychedelics on Hendrix's evolving sensibility, or on the kinship proposed between artist and audience through the ritual sharing of the psychedelic sacrament. Now a new ritual evolved, in which the musician's experience of psychedelic liberation and transcendent enlightenment became channeled into musical and lyrical forms that sought to replicate the experience, so that the listener could find in the music a reenactment of the musician's experience, or could personally enter a melding of transcendent states.

(Lying on your back on the floor of a room, speakers on either side, tripping on Owsley, listening to Hendrix.)

Hendrix's lyrics sought to *describe* the acid landscapes, the out-of-body experiences, the synesthesial porous transfer of sight to sound to smell to touch, the transformation of time (stretched or abbreviated), the shifts of space and place, inside and outside. The music simultaneously sought to *replicate* these experiences and to *induce* them. Even as early as the first album, certain songs ("Purple Haze," "Manic Depression," "Love or Confusion") used extraordinary guitar effects, notably swirls of feedback and multiply layered guitar tracks. In some of these early songs, Hendrix moved dramatically away from the blues-based modalities of his past, and from the Appalachian modalities of the "hillbilly music" he'd avidly consumed on the radio as a child and young man, modifying complex jazz progressions to embrace the Indian and Eastern scales and hints of the raga forms that had very recently infiltrated English pop music through the Beatles and the Rolling Stones. These had come to stand metaphorically for the alternative, spiritual universe that Eastern mysticism offered to those Westerners whose liberation from their cultural norms afforded them the opportunity to embrace inner and outer peace and transcendental expansion of self and soul into something larger. The music of the Jimi Hendrix Experience was unlike anything being played by anyone, and it offered entry to sonic and spiritual vistas unimagined before.[*]

With the release of *Axis: Bold as Love*, a second, much more mature album out or about to be out at the end of 1967, Hendrix had a brief rest before the second North American tour, scheduled to begin in the first weeks of 1968. It was at that moment, near Christmas, that he returned to his obsession with Dylan and chose "All Along the Watchtower" as the object of that fierce, conflicted engagement with the principal mentor, rival, and opponent of all toward which he yearned.

*　*　*

Dylan was, face it, the antithesis of the grandiose, hippie, transcendentalist, postracial, post-conflict balloon on which Hendrix hoped to float to utopia. The brutal, acerbic wit; the cruel skill of caricature; the cynical, distant, ob-

---

[*] The chorus and instrumental segments of "If 6 Was 9" are remarkable—a descending string of 7sus chords replaces the V in the traditional blues box; the solo guitar is an indefinable synthesis of raga, jazz, and "out" playing.

serving superego of Dylan's best work; the very work Hendrix was seeking to emulate (while magically—impossibly—eradicating its cruelty, its nihilism): all of these represented a dagger poised above the inflated, hyperbolic identity Hendrix had become in just a year and more. No wonder Hendrix's girlfriend Kathy Etchingham reported that Hendrix was wary of approaching Dylan's most recent work.[11]

Hendrix didn't just cover the song. He didn't just reinterpret it. He snatched the song from Dylan. The result was more than simply a marvelous homage. It was a performance that defined both men's careers and identities. It returned Hendrix to a place where psychedelic transcendentalism and black culture could intermingle; it made Dylan black.

We can start with the voice. Dylan sang the song in a high, nasal, hillbilly voice, largely without inflection, and very much square to the beat, at least by comparison to his earlier styles. Hendrix's voice had a different kind of urgency. Dylan sounded like a dry deacon reading the Bible passage of the week. Hendrix sounded like a preacher, warming up to the full testimony of the sermon.

There's no coincidence here. Hendrix understood the biblical quality to the song, its references to an Old Testament tale; its simultaneous intimation of a world in which Christ had not come and all still waited for the Coming. Hendrix expressed the apocryphal references as well, the imaginative effort by Dylan to conceive the moment before the Coming, or perhaps the moment when it became clear that the desire, the yearning, would not ever be fulfilled—that no savior had come, and none was due in town, soon or ever.

Hendrix spoke-sang the song as if he were back in the Pentecostal church of his childhood, where he'd first come to hear, love, and learn music, in an environment where music was fraught with the need to express both the message and the emotion that accompanied that message.[12]

Next, the cadence. Hendrix had already mastered a sort of conversational rhythm to his singing, and the lyrics as he sang them stretched until they might give way and then rushed back, word toward word, syllable toward syllable. Hendrix understood that there was punctuation in the song, and he put in commas, dashes, semicolons, ellipses. At one point, his dramatization of the two characters reached a striking illusionism: *but . . . uh . . . but you and I we've been through that. . . .* As that second verse recovered from the stammer, the thief grew increasingly more assured, more passionate, as Hendrix acted him out. By the end of the last couplet, the force of conviction and the power of it raised the narrative to a vista. *So let us not talk falsely now: the hour is getting late! Late!!*

The last verse as Dylan sang it had that sense of quiet, of waiting. Not as Hendrix saw it: the drama was happening in the real time of the song's telling, and the rhythms of the music carried the event to its fade to black.

Reaching into the song, Hendrix rediscovered its roots in Christian evangelism, black and white, the place where, in tent meetings and revivals, in storefront churches like the ones he'd known as a child, *gospel* returned as a living force, a Holy Spirit, a great wind made up of the gusts of souls gone but not lost.

One can think of the deliberate shifts of grammar and syntax that Hendrix interjected into the song as a process of returning the song to its blackness, to its roots in the African American religious experience. Dylan says *some way out of here*, expressing in right-angle-syllable words the thought-maze the joker is experiencing. Hendrix says *some kinda way outta here!*, and the joker comes alive, desperate, shocked that he, the landowner, keeper of the company store, has been so disrespected. Dylan says "I can't get no relief," drawing from the black and rural roots of his music. Hendrix moves plurals to singulars ("Plowmen" to "Plowman") and verb forms into black vernacular—"*say* the joker to the thief," in Hendrix's opening lines; in the last line, "the wind *begin* to howl."

Again, it's important to look at Hendrix's own writing and his interpretations of other songs, including Dylan's, to see that this sort of shift isn't inadvertent. When he wanted to, Hendrix could write, speak, and sing with formal, even Anglican, correctness. By the time he'd started working on "Watchtower," he had developed a sort of easy, groovy vernacular that combined speech patterns of most casual American dialects: there were interjections that hinted at Irish, Appalachian, and other white ethnic and regional sources, as well as multiple regional black dialects. He had ingested an immense library of popular musical and speech forms, and melded them into his easy drawling stage voice. Taking Dylan's epic biblical landscape study, Hendrix applied this skill with language and its dramatic forms. Weaving in revivalist shouting, Delta and Chicago blues lines, soul singing, R&B exclamations,* and even the stern remonstrances of matriarchs and elders in the black church, Hendrix returned the song to its swirling heritage in the African American musical styles from which Dylan had first crafted it.

But it wasn't simply that Hendrix was "blacking up" or, more accurately, "reblacking" the song. In the assuredness of his performance, its absolute liberation from hesitation and self-doubt, Hendrix also made the dialectal

---

* Lines like *Bernadette!*, from the Four Tops or James Brown's sharp interjections are syncopated across the fabric of the music.

revisions and the shifts in style imply more than simply an older American musical heritage. He also reinterpreted the allegory itself, changing its meaning, its emotive sense, its menace.

The shift in the last line is important in just this way. When Dylan sang the song, it ended resolutely in the past—*the wind began to howl*. We watched from afar something that *had already transpired*. Some of this may refer back to the Puritan Protestant conceptions of predestination and prefiguration. What happened in the past, in the Old Testament, would happen again—in the End Times. Dylan was playing with the anagogical tradition of American Protestant religion. But this doctrine left the listener in a peculiar limbo between a God-dominated past and a God-dominating future. The present was a hollow space of regret, fear, and anticipation.

In Hendrix's reading, however, everything is right here and we are with it: Dylan's *Outside in the distance* becomes *Outside in! the* cold! *Distance!* The space between past and future, between history and foretelling, has imploded at that last line: *and the wind begin to howl*. Moreover, the wind has lost its singularity; it has become instead a host of individual gusts, rising and falling with Hendrix's voice and guitar, mounting to hurricane force, transforming into a band of malevolent, vengeful demons that *begin to howl*. As Hendrix shouted that last line, the hair on the back of your neck prickled. You fought the urge to look behind you, especially as the guitars washed around the sonic space surrounding you.

Hedrix's version didn't end with Dylan's lyrics. Under the swirling bursts of guitar, Hendrix's voice could be heard, declaring:

Oh
All along the watchtower
Gotta beware: gotta beware—I will
Yeah—yeah, baby
All along the watchtower

What will he do? Only what he has already done—liberate the song, repossess it, as a part of black culture, black *religious* culture. But to read this as a part of African American gospel and religious traditions requires as well that we see Hendrix allying his individual voice with a broader stream of righteousness. This is a spirituality far from the psychedelic, global, transcendent spirituality one finds in most of the rest of Hendrix.

Yet it is not exactly a cry of political outrage. It is far from the Panthers' menacing cry, "by any means necessary." In London, as he worked up "Watchtower," Hendrix found himself upbraided by one of his best friends, a black-liberation thinker (and actor-musician) named Ram John Holder, who charged Hendrix with failing to recognize his responsibility to the forces of black liberation, in the UK and the States.[13] Yet it is worth returning to the twin roots of that phrase, "by any means necessary," to understand the ways that Hendrix immersed himself in the larger movement to bring dignity to the African American strain of American culture. "By any means necessary" achieved its full play in a speech by Malcolm X in 1965, a speech that Hendrix surely had read and discussed with his black-power friends and acquaintances during that time:

> We declare our right on this earth to be a man, to be a human being, to be respected as a human being, to be given the rights of a human being in this society, on this earth, in this day, which we intend to bring into existence *by any means necessary*.[14]

For Hendrix, however, the very nature of his music was bound up with the progress of personal liberation, racial liberation, human liberation. And in this, he was closer to the later Malcolm and further from the political radicalism of the Panthers. In an earlier speech introducing the phrase, Malcolm X had been talking about black identity, black *male* identity, and claiming violence as a right in the face of racial genocide. In this later speech, however, Malcolm X was claiming a set of rights for *all*. The disenfranchisement and dehumanization of slavery was, by the end of Malcolm X's life, enfolded within a larger political and philosophical discourse that returned it to the Existentialist philosopher who had indeed first coined the phrase: Jean-Paul Sartre.

In this later and more universal declaration, Malcolm X also expanded the tools claimed for rehumanization. "By any means necessary" meant by the means at hand, the means that might work, the instruments one could reach, and wield, that might lever human society from one position to another. Hendrix's tools weren't simply a white Stratocaster, a Fuzz-Face, an Octavia, a stack of Marshalls, a wah-wah, a glass slide. They were also the powers to wield vocabularies of style and heritage on the guitar, vocabularies of spoken dialect, vocabularies of cultural exchange, and to mix those vocabularies to make a new language that liberated rather than limited human imagination, human desire.

Hendrix understood Dylan, but he also understood that Dylan could be the raw material for appropriations and transformations that might resonate in a complex moment. Dylan refused the countercultural, the communal, the transcendental; Hendrix sought to make of it something truly liberating.

Think, for example, of the way Hendrix used Dylan to turn a California jazz-pop festival into the first major volley in the counterculture. Playing Monterey Pop, and in the process introducing himself and his band to what would soon become *his* audience, Hendrix decided to play "Like a Rolling Stone"—not only play it, but rewrite it by providing a new contextual introduction, excising a critically important segment of the lyrics and, of course, using his virtuosic guitar as a metaphor for meditation. Hendrix began by dedicating the song to "everybody here: everybody with any kind of hearts and ears . . ." and in the process, proposed its mood to be communal, not adversarial. Then, coming out of the guitar solo, he removed the angriest, most bitter of the verses, interjecting, reassuringly: *Yes: I know I missed a verse . . . don't worry*. Compressed like that, the song became more intimate, more communal.

And yet it was also being sung by a black man to a predominantly white, middle-class audience who had grown up in the era of *Brown v. Board of Education*, who had seen, just a year before, the Watts riots and the slum conditions through which a black urban populace raged and responded. "To be on your own . . . with no direction home . . . like a complete unknown . . . like a rolling stone." Hendrix wasn't just declaring the internal experience of the black man in America; he was inviting his white listeners to join him or to discover that they had already joined him, at margins where, nevertheless, their ignorance, privilege and hypocrisy might give way to ironic self-awareness and to the beginnings of a moment when *we*—Hendrix, Mitchell and Redding, you and I—might "declare our right on this earth to be a man, to be a human being, to be respected as a human being, to be given the rights of a human being in this society, on this earth, in this day."

Just a month after Hendrix performed this song at Monterey Pop, Newark exploded in riots. The day after the band quit an ill-conceived tour with white pop legends the Monkees, Detroit erupted. A week later, Milwaukee. An American apocalypse seemed to loom. Hendrix, walking into Harlem's signature club, Small's Paradise, found himself taunted by black patrons and had to be spirited out of the place. Returning to London, Hendrix began obsessively listening to the prerelease reels of *John Wesley Harding*. Waiting in the studio to record the first versions of "All Along the Watchtower," he read Robert Christgau's lengthy attack on the counterculture at Monterey Pop, his own coming-out party; Christgau decried the false consciousness of the hippie movement, yearned for the authenticity of black R&B, and dismissed

Hendrix not once but twice. First, he called him "a transplanted American Negro." Then he devoted an entire paragraph to trashing Hendrix's self-made identity, his performance, his abilities as a musician, a guitarist, and a singer:

> Hendrix is just another Uncle Tom. Don't believe me, believe Sam Silver of *The East Village Other*: "Jimi did a beautiful Spade routine." Hendrix earned that capital S. Dressed in English fop mod, with a ruffled orange shirt and red pants that outlined his crotch to the thirtieth row, Jimi really, as Silver phrased it, "socked it to them." . . . I suppose Hendrix's act can be seen as a consistently vulgar parody of rock theatrics, but I don't feel I have to like it. Anyhow, he can't sing.[15]

Listening to Hendrix's reclaimed performances at Monterey,[16] it's a challenge to credit Christgau with having actually listened to what was in front of him. The Experience performed "The Wind Cries Mary" letter-perfect, and the guitar playing, with its references to R&B and soul rhythm and its post-blues solo work, had no counterpart at the festival. Hendrix's playing on "Killing Floor" brought forms of early, "primitive" blues from the Delta and the electric blues of Chicago's postwar scene into a fierce, feedback-driven present. The bizarre atonalities at the opening of "Purple Haze," are still, to my guitarist's ears, utterly inventive and strange, and his vocal lines were far closer to in-tune than those of almost any of the other performers struggling with that difficult sound stage in July of 1967, when monitor speakers were largely unheard of and one stood in front of the stack of amps, straining to tame them and to hear your fellow musicians. On top of it, any sophisticated critic should have heard Ravi Shankar (who also played Monterey) in the raga-influenced insertions that occur in the solo of that song. Hendrix reinvented feedback with "Foxy Lady," starting the song with a casual suggestion, "Dig this." While the solo he does isn't as compact and startling as the one that would appear on the U.S. version of *Are You Experienced*, some months later, it is still extraordinarily inventive, and his extreme bends of note (through which every guitarist winces to hear the bad-tremolo-springs-Stratocaster going wildly out of tune) rise and fall to and from the notes with an accuracy that belies the technical impossibilities of that moment.

Christgau's lacing critique attacked not only Hendrix but the very movement in whose embrace he had found himself. In Christgau's eyes, Hendrix's blackness was not just inauthentic—it was antithetical to black dignity and identity, undermining the work of a century of troubled African American freedom. Christgau's dour Puritanical jeremiad against the lazy optimism of audience and performers at Monterey could have been penned by Dylan himself at this most disillusioned moment.*

For Christgau, Hendrix exemplified the willful spilling of moral authority—the ultimate American moral authority, that of the righteous enslaved—on such unfertile human soil as the Monterey Festival represented. It is hard to imagine just how painful it must have been for Hendrix to have read that article, nor the urgency that the critique added to Hendrix's quest to deepen his musical and lyrical themes and to forge a substantial synthesis of global musical forms.

This, I suggest, is the undertext of his treatment of "All Along the Watchtower." Hendrix evicts Christgau's claims; he makes the critic's critique seem itself like the posturing of an arrogant, privileged white partisan of a now-discredited predecessor to the present. But that's incidental to the performance, to its urgency, its mastery, and its prophecy.

*   *   *

There remains that slip of the tongue, that failure of lyric at the end of the first verse. Hendrix produces a muffled muff: *None will level on the line; nobody of it is worth / nobody offered his word*. Why can't Hendrix declare, as does Dylan—that *None of them along the line know what any of it is worth*?[17]

What changes in the meaning of the song as Hendrix misspeaks it? In Dylan's allegory, the important message is one of language, speech and prophecy: *let us not talk falsely, now*. Undergirding this message, however, is the older heritage of Judaism, and its mutation toward Christianity, the Torah becoming the Old Testament. The joker speaks the role of a Judaic God, who has chosen a people, offered them wine and earth, only to find them turning away, squabbling, ungrateful, spoiled.

Hendrix takes the shift further: from Torah to Old Testament, to New Testament and finally to the Apocrypha and the Book of Revelation. Dylan's message: *they* are unworthy and *they* will be punished. Straightening Hendrix's tangled syntax, tangled to retain the rhyme (earth/worth), we get this: *nobody offered his word*. All are unworthy. This is a fundamental Protestant tenet: all sinners before an angry God. Hendrix has removed from this song its deep roots in Judaic narratives, in which a people chosen of God fail, again and again, to appreciate and ennoble their position, and he has replaced it with an American Christian notion of universal sin requiring universal redemption.

---

* Of course, Otis Redding was treated much like Hendrix under Christgau's pen, who also didn't seem to notice the presence of Booker T. and the MGs or proto-world music African artist Hugh Masakela.

But this is not a white evangelical in the burned-over districts of tent revivals and ecstatic mass redemption. It is a black man, enunciating these lyrics in the dialect of the black man.

This is, finally, a profoundly African American rewriting of the Gospels. As African slaves forced to worship a white Christian God, Hendrix's forebears had recast the story of the Chosen People. They had staked a claim to that position, by nature of their suffering, and the injustice of their circumstances, and in the process stripped from the narrative the image of a spoiled, ungrateful, slothful people confronted by a vindictive God, replacing it with a picture of martyrs who turned their faces to the heavens.

And so does Hendrix. His thief spoke with the roughened eloquent oratorical style of Martin Luther King, Jr., and the long line of African American preachers behind him, upbraiding those who had weakened in faith or turned to the false gods of fame and wealth and transient pleasure, returning their eyes to the heavens whence their salvation would come. As Hendrix recorded that song, America itself teetered on the edge of social, political and moral chaos. As he mixed it, at the Record Plant in New York, Bob Dylan was in full retreat, living the life of the comfortable exile in Woodstock. As he released it, on September 4, 1968, Martin Luther King, Jr., was six months dead, two months of near-continuous urban rioting had paused and then resumed, with the Glenville shootouts and the ensuing Cleveland riots, and the chaotic protests and ensuing police riot in Chicago as the Democratic National Convention made American political utopianism seem a foolish hope, indeed. There might be landscapes of redemption and promise, but for now there was this: a moment of instability, into which dread and hope might both be poured, and now . . . and now. . . .

> The hour is getting late! Late!
> Beware! Beware! I will!

> Neither could they, as it were, go up to the top of Pisgah, to view from this wilderness a more goodly country to feed their hopes; for which way so ever they turned their eyes, save upward to the heavens, they could have little solace or content. . . . Yea, let them which have been redeemed of the lord, show how he has delivered them from the hand of the oppressor. When they wandered in the wilderness, out of the way, and found no city to dwell in, both hungry, and thirsty, their soul was overwhelmed in them.
> WILLIAM BRADFORD, *Of Plimouth Plantation*, 1647

CHAPTER 14

Counter-Landscapes

We are stardust
We are golden
And we've got to get ourselves
Back to the garden
JONI MITCHELL, "Woodstock"

Back in the Sixties, sometimes it felt that the daily events we were living
were also happening on another, almost mythical, level. Still, reality is
messy and sprawling.
JOHN CURL, *Memories of Drop City*

Dylan's *John Wesley Harding* announced what fans already knew—that he
had moved his sensibility from the city's hard-edged streets to a pastoral retreat, with a corresponding change of voice, from sharply observed descriptions of the social streetscapes of America to suggestively drawn, imaginative, evocations of interior spaces in which settings seemed not decisive but
deceptive.

As Dylan was writing his meditation, Theodore Roszak was formulat-
ing a different manifesto, *The Making of a Counterculture*. Roszak coined the
term for the phenomenon that came when the youth cultures of the '50s
and early '60s merged with the political protest movements of the same
era—black and white, civil rights, and peace—and took on the questing lan-

guage of the Beats to form a critical mass, conscious of itself as a dynamic critique of the American experience.

Dylan had in many ways anticipated the general momentum of the counterculture. Years earlier he had chronicled the detritus of the consumption technocracy, describing the enemy as a "man with a Bic pen" who "wants eleven dollar bills—and you've only got ten": the model of consumer debt-slavery condensed to a single image.[1] His critiques of the political sphere had dissolved into a disillusioned recognition of the unlikeliness of political change and a search for alternatives. *John Wesley Harding* offered none of the rousing calls to action of the early Dylan, none of the biting social critique of the electric years, none of the dreamy hedonism of *Blonde On Blonde*; in their place was an allusive portrait of a drifting nation in a drifting time.

Meanwhile, his audience was gathering around a collective mission: to reclaim the American landscape, to "liberate" it, as the communards of 1966 and beyond called the process. As Dylan retreated, they moved forward; as his work grew oblique, even recondite, their language—vocal and bodily—became more direct and confrontational.

Though the roots of the counterculture took hold across the geographies of America—city, suburb, and rural—still, a majority of counterculture citizens were children of the postwar suburbs. They were born there or moved there or, if they didn't, they were steeped in the popular culture of suburban life—the very magazines, movies, TV shows, and music in which we have been immersed here. They played War, and Cowboys and Indians, and House, recapitulating the three resurgent, rejuvenated American myths.

Their education took place at a moment when American teachers, curriculum writers, textbook publishers, and parents were seeking to develop a new American curriculum to satisfy complex and often contradictory demands: global understanding, national patriotism, scientific and technocratic mastery, creativity and adventurousness, obedience to authority. Looking to American history or, more accurately, the myths of America's history, the Cold War's education technocracy built a powerful narrative set in a rhetoric of assurance, in tone alternately portentous and triumphant. It reflected the dominant narrative known by most Americans (white Americans, that is), and it was almost persuasive.

The Cold War generation was schooled in myths of American freedom, individual and collective, set within narratives of land and landscape. The heroes of early childhood, in stories, books and, rapidly, on television, were agents of Manifest Destiny: Daniel Boone, Davey Crockett, the Conestoga wagon emigrants of the Oregon and Santa Fe trails, the Indian fighters, the cowboys. In school, American history was told as a thrilling narrative of suc-

cessive excursions out into the wilderness that awaited habitation and transformation. The Pilgrims and Puritans appeared not as religious zealots and
radical isolationists, but as freedom lovers intent on conquering a new world
of wilderness and savagery for a future that included not just their descen-
dents, but hosts of Europeans (mainly northern and northwestern Europeans) yearning to breathe free. The Virginia landowners, founding fathers and
mothers all, weren't slaveholding defenders of an agrarian aristocratic past
but successful tamers of virgin lands, developing new crops and new forms of
agriculture appropriate to the new lands. By secondary school, when American history mixed with the modern discipline of "social studies," the doctrine of American exceptionalism united the narratives of Manifest Destiny
and westward movement with triumphalist discussions of American scientific innovation destined to make "the desert bloom" and lands of plenty feed
a grateful globe. In the textbooks, in the newsreels and copies of *Junior Scholastic* and *Senior Scholastic*, in the special reading lists of the college-bound,
the dogma of America's transformative landscape reinforced itself.

Just as the suburban landscape became increasingly restrictive, shrunken,
and regulatory and the suburban home increasingly claustrophobic, the
nostrums of high school textbooks came to many Cold War teenagers to
seem more like nagging recitals than uplifting inspirations. Those who
entered college or university in the early- and mid-1960s often found that
a different, more critical analysis of American lands awaited them, an intellectual and academic version of the Dylan songs—like "The Lonesome
Death of Hattie Carroll" and "With God On Our Side"—that railed against
the hypocrisies of America's self-declared exceptionalism. That era saw a
counter-literature of American landscape writing, writing that made its way
into college humanities and social science classes and, increasingly, into the
courses meant to satisfy general education requirements in the sciences.[2]

But it was the combining of these often disparate strains that formed
the synergy of the counterculture: works that linked the critique of a preda-
tory American expansionism to a quasi-spiritual nature movement. In the
intellectual history of the counterculture, though, these two strains acquired
third, fourth, fifth, and even sixth strands to form the strong weave of that
broader phenomenon: rediscovery and yearning to emulate Thoreau's
retreat into a life of enforced simplicity and self-sufficiency; arguments
against a technocratic urbanism and in favor of a humanistic city-design
sensibility, championed by Jane Jacobs in her seminal and popular *The
Death and Life of Great American Cities* (1961); works embracing Native American natural religions, like Paul Neihardt's *Black Elk Speaks*, first published
in 1932 but rediscovered on college campuses and in counterculture com-

munities, circulating hand to hand until the demand brought forth a best-selling paperback edition in 1971, and the wildly successful series of books on the mystical peyote rituals of purported *nagual* Don Juan by Carlos Castaneda; polemics of feminism from Simone de Beauvoir's *The Second Sex* (republished in paperback in 1961) to Betty Friedan's *The Feminine Mystique* (1963); and works of landscape design like Ian McHarg's *Design With Nature*, published in 1969 in part from lectures and presentations given at universities and in public presentations for some years before.

The counterculture's critique came out of this complex admixture of historical revisionism and romanticism, science and pseudoscience, philosophical and quasi-religious impulses. Binding these together became a project not of established American scholars and intellectuals, but of very young, often callow but passionate advocates, only sometimes coherent, who began to assemble this Babel of ideas into something new. It wasn't in philosophy seminars or serious journals that this movement found its calling. It was in action, action in what came to be called "the real world."

The counterculture was a patchwork of strategies—if strategies they could be called. Away from its grandiose manifestoes, in the small gestures of lives and actions, two value systems emerged and often clashed: one invested in taking and redeeming the local, the other in transcending it.

One might think of both imperatives—occupation and settlement, or transience and freedom—as representing different modes of reclaiming America, delineated along lines of sight and points of view. Those who sought to claim real land, to homestead the city neighborhoods, the urban parks, the rural New England lands, the arroyos and mesas of New Mexico and the spectacular California beaches and wild mountains of Bonny Doon and Santa Cruz and Marin imagined themselves close to the things of earth and nature. When they looked up, they looked to sun and sky. We will hear the voices of those who lived this most powerfully in the journals and letters coming from the communes, most especially those who lasted more than a few weeks. Theirs was the zoom lens and the microscopic focus: redemption in the small everyday rituals of planting and weeding, of building and cooking, eating and sleeping *close to the earth*, in the slogan of the time. By contrast, the transients sought to rise above, to soar and float, to encompass. Theirs was the panoramic view from an airplane or, more tellingly, from a satellite or an astronaut's window.[3]

In the most pragmatic sense, in the judgment of results set against claims and promises, the counterculture was a failure. No grand revolution, no mass emancipation or redemption resulted from the utopian calls from 1967 to 1972. Saying this, flat out, we can then move past the grandiose and utopian to the historical and pragmatic. We can, perhaps, return to our narrative, to houses, spaces, newsreels, movies, 45s, albums. We can see the counterculture with a little less anxiety, as one in a long line of American utopian, transformative movements, seeking to claim the most resonant of American myths and at the same time to recast those myths to new ideals and new ends.

These gestures of utopianism were strewn across North America, in cities and countryside and wilderness, though notably not in the suburbs that represented their parents' utopian site In the words of core counterculture figure Peter Coyote, this was a generation "that had taken as its collective task the rethinking and recreation of our national culture."[4] In the rural reaches of New England, in the high deserts surrounding the Puebloan tribes in New Mexico, but also in the streets of Chicago in '68 and the neighborhoods of the Haight in San Francisco, new communities, not virtual or imaginative but physical and local, caught the attention of the margins and the mainstream of the dominant American culture, until their humble, tentative, often doomed experiments resonated as symbols and their narratives resonated as origin myths.

People in Motion: Haight-Ashbury, San Francisco, 1965–1967

The epicenter of the counterculture was the Haight-Ashbury, specifically the intersection of Haight and Ashbury streets. The scene extended to include the surrounding neighborhood of older houses, small apartment buildings, and two- or three-storey commercial structures that abutted Golden Gate Park to the west-by-southwest, the panhandle of the park to the north-by-northwest, and the historically African American neighborhood of the Fillmore District to the east-by-northeast.[5] Behind it, Ashbury and its parallel streets rode the hills up to the Twin Peaks.

Haight-Ashbury's status as the anchor of the hippie movement was the culmination of a process linking media, message, and action in a feedback loop. As the defining events of the counterculture occurred at sites strewn along the coastline from Monterey northward past San Francisco into Marin County, reports drew acolytes and enthusiasts toward the West Coast. This migration reached reportable dimensions in 1965, and at the same time a number of events were devised to cater to this new audience-community, giving rise to further migration. By the end of 1966, the geography of the counterculture had found its axis in Haight-Ashbury, as a name, place, imagined ideal, staging ground.

To look at the chronology of events that spiraled centripetally into the Haight, and centrifugally from it, is to see the dialectical tension between placelessness, marked by nomadism, migration, and "flow," and an emerging sense of place staked, claimed, and held. Two forms of geographical liberation pervaded the narratives of the counterculture: liberation *from* place, where place was understood as a prison in a grid; and liberation *of* place, as the counterculture's populations swept into a location, taking it over, "freeing" land, neighborhood, or city, claiming the power to make or recast its identity.

Such duality often coexisted within a single site or moment in the counterculture's history. The Merry Pranksters, for example, were a loose confederation of freaks and hippies who clustered around the novelist and LSD prophet Ken Kesey. In 1964, they settled in La Honda Ranch, Kesey's compound in the Santa Cruz Mountains south of Palo Alto, and with Kesey's blessing transformed the site with hidden speakers, prayer bells, cameras, sculptural installations, structures useful and useless, theatrical stages, an entire array of improvised interventions in a sylvan setting. For some years (roughly 1964–1967), the group remained at the ranch in a parodistic reconstruction of an American fable: a western ranch with a patriarch and matriarch, a foreman, ranch hands, seasonal workers: *Bonanza* on acid.

But if it was a western family ranch, it was also a tribal gathering: it was both cowboy and Indian. La Honda was a home from which the Pranksters could embark and to which they could return. Perhaps the most celebrated of these excursions was the one they made in the summer of 1964, on board Furthur, a converted schoolbus, and memorialized in various forms as *Ken Kesey's Intrepid Traveler and His Merry Band of Pranksters Look for a Kool Place*. A peripatetic road trip, the Furthur excursion was simultaneously a tour of hostile country, a set of guerrilla skirmishes, momentary occupations and retreats, and an antic upending of the postwar family vacation.[6]

The Prankster's trip set one side of the counterculture's geography, of *no-placeness*, of fluid migration and mobility without set ends, directed outward as theater and pan-parade, and inward as the stimulus for internal transformation, both individually and within the tribal group. At the same time, the Pranksters' original goal was to reconnoiter, occupy, and perhaps (if only briefly) liberate that most recent site of American self-congratulation: the New York World's Fair. An invented, temporary celebration of material prosperity and progress, overseen by New York planning czar Robert Moses and Victor Gruen, the architect known as "the father of the shopping mall," the World's Fair was the locale for Ford's introduction of the Mustang and the site of Walt Disney's first successful public exhibition of Audio-Animatronics for

14.1. Lisa Law, *Furthur in the Great Bus Race with Ken Kesey on the Hood, Aspen Meadows, Tesuque Pueblo, Santa Fe, New Mexico, 1969.* (Photograph © Lisa Law.)

the Pepsi Pavilion's "It's a Small World." Kesey and the Pranksters arrived at the fair in their converted and laboriously handpainted 1939 International Harvester school bus. They spent their time erupting in spontaneous music and street theater, fueled by psychedelic drugs. Filming their antics against the backdrop of the fair, the Pranksters returned to La Honda to make their own alternative American epic, not a Western, but an Eastern.

La Honda and the Furthur bus were two extremes in the dialectic of place and placelessness that the counterculture occupied. The Pranksters were perhaps the most luminous legends of that movement, and also the most elusive, insiders who stayed outside, launching forays into the Haight and its surrounding environs, thereby increasing its reputation as the destination for the great migration of the Summer of Love.

The Haight embodied both place and placelessness. It was a specific location. It was a destination for transients. On a map of the counterculture, you would see Haight-Ashbury marked by a star: it was the capital. Surrounding it were other sites, and nearly all the seminal events before the Gathering of the Tribes/Human Be-In of January 1967 occurred beyond the Haight—at sites like the Calliope Warehouse (south of Market), the Fillmore (Geary Boulevard, near Japantown), and the Longshoreman's Hall, a cavernous venue just off Fisherman's Wharf that hosted the Prankster/Bill Graham multiday Trips Festival.

Nevertheless, it was the Haight that became the legendary epicenter of the counterculture. Haight-Ashbury had advantages as a nexus. Dense with cheap housing, the Haight had parkland on three sides (the Panhandle, Golden Gate Park, and Buena Vista Park), encouraging outdoor gatherings, and a ten-block stretch of low-rent storefronts, enabling establishments like Ron Thelin's Psychedelic Shop and the Free Clinic to find homes and maintain them despite the low-to-nonexistent profit margins of counterculture businesses and support organizations.

The temperate climate of San Francisco and the often chaotic and over-crowded "private" dwellings pressed the hippies out into the conjoining public spaces. In American history, the broader conception of public space had long been controversial, unstable, a legal, political, and social battle-ground. Laws and regulations to organize, orchestrate, control and limit activities on public streets tended to appear at about the same time as urban commercial, economic and social life became self-sustaining. Partly this occurred as density required regulation; partly as multiple interests sought to dominate the street and in the process to convert it to their purposes. Less a place of sociability, the street became increasingly a part of the economic system.[7] Parks too became locations of closely regulated and scripted leisure, meant to reward the rich with a vast play-and-display ground, and to provide the poor with just enough respite to defuse any revolutionary fervor while training them in proper behavior.[8]

Haight-Ashbury, then, lay at the intersection of two types of public space in the American city, each containing something of the longstanding American tension between benevolent visions of nature and human nature (with the concomitant celebration of spontaneity and freedom), and suspicion of darker and more destructive forces in human and environment that required regulation and law to suppress. The fragile truce between these two antithetical visions became a central place for the counterculture's intervention, and its most direct agents were the Diggers.

"Founded" as a radical offshoot of the San Francisco Mime Troupe, the Diggers sought to live as if the anarcho-syndicalist revolution had already come. Though their titular leader and central thinker was ex-mime writer-actor Emmett Grogan, the Diggers argued that there was no Emmett Grogan—that various Diggers took the name at whim.

14.2. Charles Cushman, *Haight Street Hippies*, view of Asbury from Haight, 1967, and *Haight Street at Masonic, March*, 1967. These pictures were made after Haight was returned to two-way status. (Photographs courtesy the Cushman Archive, Indiana University Library. Charles W. Cushman Collection: Indiana University Archives.)

A typical Digger broadside, printed up and placarded on walls, lamp-posts, street trees, and handed out on the street in the fall of 1966, excoriated the regulatory arenas of public space and proposed a new conception of the public sphere, simultaneously spontaneous, liberating (of participant and site alike) and provocatively confrontational:

> PUBLIC streets on riot with truckloads of arms protecting the
> private property of super-charging merchants. . . .
> PUBLIC streets where loneliness crowds silent, up-tight sidewalks . . .
> Where in the street can two fingers touch . . .
> Where in the street can you take off your shoes and sing and
> dance without disturbing the death called peace . . .[9]

Crosswalks, stop signs, and stop lights symbolized the minuscule, often unconscious ways that institutions and officials regulated and limited personal freedom and activity. In a page stolen from Jane Jacobs's *Death and Life of Great American Cities*, the Diggers and their community sought a return to the older urban street life of sauntering, greeting, conversing, and socializing. One of their most potent interventions involved an action called The Intersection Game, which simultaneously disrupted the flow of traffic, making drivers and riders aware of their investment in the regulations they unconsciously obeyed, and took the streets back as places of free play. Diggers, fellow travelers, and even passers-by tried to work out every possible way to cross an intersection, accompanied by giant puppets whose presence flummoxed the cops sent to restore a smooth flow of commuter traffic.

This Intersection Game was a huge success. Not just on the Haight, but on the parallel streets that formed the larger pattern of commuter traffic, gamers took over a string of intersections, causing near-complete disruption of "normal" traffic on Haight and surrounding streets, especially as drivers abandoned their cars to join the game—a triumph for the Diggers as enemy troops switched sides.[10]

Digger broadsides simultaneously catalyzed and reflected the tribal consciousness of those at the center of the broader movement in 1966 and through much of 1967,[11] as the steadily increasing community of counter-culture immigrants spilled onto the streets, where symbolic action could be quickly, almost spontaneously called up, and as quickly disappear before being fully quelled or dispersed. Or they sprawled out through Golden Gate Park all the way to Ocean Beach, accommodating a full range of activities, from the spontaneous and private wanderings of an acid trip or the final stages of various acid tests and music events that wound down around bonfires at the beach, to the complex combination of spontaneity and planning that resulted in the participation of between twenty thousand and thirty thousand at the Gathering of the Tribes/Human Be-In on January 14, 1967.

The Gathering of the Tribes was a seminal mass-event. "It was like awakening to find you'd been reborn and this was your new family . . . one of the grand mythic events of the Haight mystique . . . the notion of a meeting without any purpose other than to be," wrote participant (and later historian of the Haight) Charles Perry.[12] The reporting on it in magazines and newspapers as widely spread as the *New York Times*[13] and *Time*, turned an underground movement into a national and even global phenomenon.

The Be-In was a far greater success than its planners had envisioned. It wasn't just the scale of the crowd; it was also the way that scale transformed the event. Because the sound system was puny, designed for a much smaller

14.3. Lisa Law, *Allen Ginsberg and Gary Snyder Circumambulate Golden Gate Park, Human Be-In.* (Photograph © Lisa Law.)

venue, it failed to draw full attention to the stage and the musicians and speakers—political, artistic and spiritual—who paraded on and off, plagued by periodic power outages, microphone failures, and other frustrations. Instead, the audience *became* the event. Musicians set up throughout the crowd, forming spontaneous ensembles, often with unlikely combinations of instruments and styles. The poet Gary Snyder blew a conch shell as he and Allen Ginsberg circumambulated the park. An unknown figure parachuted into the Speedway Meadows field just to the east.[14]

The Human Be-In offered a model for the spontaneous liberation of a public space on a mass scale. It also set the parameters for the increasingly structured and scripted liberations and happenings of the movement over the seminal year of 1967. Perhaps most important, it awakened a group of promoters, mostly from the music industry centers in Los Angeles and New York, to the possibilities of marketing to this evidently large and relatively densely packed denizens, and the result was the Monterey Pop Festival, held on June 16–18 of that year.

Monterey Pop was in many ways the antithesis of the Human Be-In, a death knell for the core values of spontaneity, cooperation, and liberation that had characterized the Haight-Ashbury mystique. Whereas the Gathering of the Tribes had been largely leaderless and spontaneous, Monterey Pop featured a limited partnership that included record producers, musicians, publicists, and concert promoters. As Haight historian Barney Hoskyns put it, Monterey was "a trade fair for the rapidly expanding music business ... the birth of the rock industry as we know it today."[15]

Perhaps the most direct form of this commercial marketing innovation was the hit song "San Francisco," written as a promo for the festival. The song fed the notion of a summer trip to the West Coast, with Monterey Pop as one of the stops and the Haight as the other. The song's popularity fed the stream of young people whose summer vacation plans dramatically increased the number of ticketholders at Monterey Pop, but also upticked the reputations, and the record and concert sales, of bands that played there—many of them represented by the network of producers and marketers who stood behind the festival, notably Lou Adler, who represented among others the Mamas and the Papas and Scott McKenzie.

Monterey Pop's seductive anthem promised listeners around the country and the globe that the Haight-Ashbury Summer of 1967 "will be a love-in there." The result, however, was to overwhelm the complex and often-fragile social ecologies of the counterculture, swamp the limited spatial and geographical resources of the areas "liberated" over the previous year, violate the truces with the dominant culture and its institutions, and fragment the collectivity. Hordes of itinerants arrived, many of them underage runaways whose legal status pressed the police and social service agencies into an antagonistic relationship with the crash pads and with groups like the Diggers and institutions like the Free Clinic. Tourists, long drawn to San Francisco's picturesque environs, began to include a tour of the Haight along with the requisite trips to Chinatown, North Beach, Fisherman's Wharf, and the cable cars—until Haight residents started an active campaign to discourage them, spraying tour bus and tourist station wagon windows with paint—acts that further alienated the area from the larger community, and the police in particular. As San Francisco Mime Troupe and Digger veteran Peter Coyote noted, "A number of older hands realized that the area was poised to become unlivable." Soon thereafter, in an important symbolic move, Psychedelic Shop owner Ron Thelin closed his store, declaring his experiment a victim of "liberators," panhandlers, and the collapse of the counterculture's social and economic order.[16]

While the Digger programs of free food and goods, spontaneous celebrations, and liberation performances continued for months after this, the larger program centered on the Haight was effectively finished. The streets had lost their allure, both as staging grounds and as symbolic spaces for invention—musical, economic, social and political—in the Haight itself.

But the imaginative utopias that the Haight stood for, if only briefly, afforded possibilities for other circumstances in which the counterculture's search for liberation could be enacted. Soon the Diggers were pushing for a mass exodus from city to countryside and participating in the development of a string of communes and counterculture living environments where the experiments in utopian living could be more directly tested.

These weren't limited to back-to-the-land retreats. In New York on August 5, 1967, a group calling itself the New York Diggers adapted the Intersection Game. The New York Diggers' game, however, was more fully political, with a specific goal in mind (New York City's designation of a street block on the Lower East Side as a pedestrian mall), and with a much more organized plan, including a previously negotiated agreement with the police and the city allowing the protest to go forth.[17]

The New York Diggers' most famous intervention, the liberation of the New York Stock Exchange on August 24, 1967, showed something of the spontaneity of the San Francisco originators, perhaps in part because of the influence of Abbie Hoffman, who had traveled to San Francisco some months earlier to observe the Diggers and their work, and Jerry Rubin, a Berkeley political activist who had participated in the Human Be-In. Where this differed dramatically, however, was the site; moving to an icon of American capitalism, the Diggers threw money from the visitors' balcony, causing a near-riot on the exchange floor, a very satisfying demonstration of the intersection of individual and corporate greed. But the event didn't seek to actually take over or transform the site itself—it wasn't local in that sense, in the sense that the Diggers' Haight engagements had been. The ground was moving, both figuratively and literally. Within months, the center of counterculture activity would abruptly shift, first to New York, and then to Chicago, with the San Francisco Diggers retreating in a rural back-to-the-land campaign, and the New York Diggers reincarnated as a political force confronting national politics in the Chicago '68 "action."

Liberating the Grid: Chicago, August 18–30, 1968

The New York Stock Exchange liberation presaged the next important countercultural contest, Chicago '68. There the Yippies, an offshoot of the New York Diggers formed early in 1968, would mount a very different, perhaps even more momentous, culture-shaking campaign in which the separated goals of personal liberation and political liberation would be rewoven.

Chicago '68 has come to serve as a tagline for a complex assembly of distinctive strains of American cultural and political protest in Chicago during the days before, during and after the National Democratic Convention, held at the Chicago International Amphitheater on August 26-29, 1968. Because President Lyndon Johnson was expected to be nominated for re-election, the Vietnam War protest movement had targeted the convention as an opportunity to build on the dramatic success of the April 15, 1967, assembly in New York City, which had brought well over a hundred thousand protesters. That action had cemented the organization known colloquially as the "Mobilization" or "Mobe," shorthand for the National Mobilization Committee to End the War in Vietnam, which brought together numerous protest organizations, with agendas ranging from Old Left Socialism and pacifism to New Left cultural activism. The mobilization committee had proven itself capable of massive grassroots organizing on relatively short notice by gathering some fifty thousand demonstrators on October 21, 1967, at a protest rally at the Pentagon in Washington. With a strong organization and the momentum from a string of protests that spring, and with a clear symbolic opponent in Johnson and a highly-charged political event with guaranteed media coverage, Mobe moved aggressively to ensure a political protest action that would maximize pressure to end the war.[18]

Central to the discussions by the organizers were the issues of violence and order. The Mobilization's organization agreed that a successful group action would require that protesters remain orderly and nonviolent, if the goal of dramatically widening the constituency of the antiwar movement was to take place. By October of 1967, when planning for Chicago '68 began in Mobe, there had been sufficient publicity around the hippie movement and sufficiently clear evidence of a mass of young people ripe for "organizing" and "mobilizing" that Mobe leaders sought to reach out to what they understood as the leaders of the counterculture—and that led them to the self-advertised leaders of the Youth International Party, Yippie![19]

Seeking an alliance that could politicize and radicalize the hedonistic, utopian counterculture elements, Dellinger and the other leaders of Mobe reached out to the Yippie! constituency, seeking to interweave the Movement's antiwar protests with the Yippie! Festival of Life, a planned spontaneous action announced by the central figures of Yippie! in a manifesto released by the Liberation News Service on January 16, 1968. "We demand the policy of ecstasy," wrote collaborators Ed Sanders, Paul Krassner, Jerry Rubin, and Abbie Hoffman. "We are the delicate spoors of the new fierceness that will change America. We will create our own reality; we are Free America."[20]

Alongside this tone of militancy the founders of Yippie! posed a language drawn from the Haight. Historian Michael William Doyle has found a February 1968 letter from Rubin to Allen Cohen, then the editor of the *San Francisco Oracle*, in which Rubin described the Chicago action as a ramped-up combination of West Coast psychedelic and political utopianism: the Chicago Action would be "an international festival of youth music and theater . . . 500,000 of us dancing in the streets, throbbing with amplifiers and harmony. We are making love in the parks. We are reading, singing, laughing, printing newspapers, groping and making a mock convention and celebrating the birth of FREE AMERICA in our own time . . . New tribes will gather in Chicago. We will be completely open, everything will be free."[21]

Debating Old Left organizer and Socialist Worker Party presidential candidate Fred Halstead at the Labor Forum in New York in January of 1967, Rubin articulated the hard-edged, revolutionary ideology of Yippie!: "I support everything which puts people into motion, which creates disruption and controversy, which creates chaos and rebirth." Yet moments later, he described a very different vision of the Chicago "festival of youth, music and theater," one that seemed to take into account the hostility and the power of the opposition, and the inevitability of confrontation rather than liberation. Imagine, he said:

> Chicago is in panic. The American Youth Festival has brought 500,000 young people to Chicago to camp out, smoke pot, dance to wild music, burn draft cards and roar like wild bands through the streets, forcing the president to bring troops home from Viet Nam to keep order in the city while he is nominated under the protection of tear gas and bayonets. . . . Repression? Repression turns demonstration protests into wars. Actors into heroes. Masses of individuals into a community. Repression eliminates the bystander, the neutral observer, the theorist. . . . The street is the stage. *You are the star of the show.* And everything you were once taught is up for grabs.[22]

By February, Rubin was publishing his proposals for liberation in Chicago in alternative newspapers across the country. Interviewed, he spoke of "*confronting* them;" he envisioned festival-goers "blocking traffic, throwing blood, burning money . . . milling-in . . . and the Yippies being wanderers will be all over the city."[23]

Rubin's two diatribes turned the Diggers' spatial liberation campaign into a militant form of anarchism, simultaneously creative (dancing!) and destructive, placeless and fixed. No longer a flat social playing field, the street became a proscenium, raised up, on which one acted oneself into the consciousness of others by direct confrontation, and by the projection of confrontation via the media, notably television's network news. As Rubin, Hoffman, and others envisioned it, their takeover of Chicago would be part medieval morality play, part *I Love Lucy*, projected into every American living room in prime time. They weren't just taking over the literal streets of a literal Chicago. They were annexing the information pathways of Marshall McLuhan's new communication culture.

And so two different forms of protest action emerged. In Mobe's order-obsessed protest movement, it was all about place: about locating the rallies at the sites of the Convention. Mobe focused on the largely ceremonial, formal garden setting of the Grant Park area immediately across from the delegate-filled Hilton Hotel on Michigan Avenue, the monumental concrete-and-stone functionality of the Chicago Amphitheater at 43rd and Halsted and, to a lesser extent, the more than six miles of streets that lay between the two. Mobe fought for permits within a traditional orthodoxy of free speech, right of assembly, and the definition of *public* in the public spaces of street, park, and venue.

By contrast, the Yippies focused on a fluid, largely placeless, performative space, one that used the parks *and* the streets as conduits, information and performance pathways, escape routes, and backdrops for actions directed at an audience reading about, hearing or seeing dramas charged with symbolic significance. For the Yippies, Chicago's lakefront ribbon of parks north of the Chicago River formed a perfect staging area for actions that could flow into Old Town, or into staid North Michigan Avenue, over the bridges and down into Grant Park, the venue chosen by Mobe, only to redirect, retreat, and return.

But the planners in both movements were naive if they thought the Chicago political, legal, and police forces would be amenable to the strategies that had persuaded New York City to allow the Mobilization's parade and rally the previous autumn, or San Francisco authorities to grant the Be-In's organizers their permit for the polo fields in Golden Gate Park. Chicago bureaucrats were far too skilled in the arts of obfuscation, delay, ambiguity, and bland inaction, strategies that had served them well during the civil rights movement, desegregation, and before. Chicago's protest organizers found themselves outfoxed: permits for concerts, food distribution centers, and toilet facilities were held out as imminent, and then withdrawn until, by the time the throngs began to arrive, almost all the hedonistic, festival-based events were collapsing.

Yet the Chicago political establishment was also naive, thinking its temporizing strategies would force the movement to collapse. In fact it was movement they failed to take into account—the breadth of the counterculture's informal communication network and the momentum of countercul-ture transience. To the far-flung communes like Drop City, to the Haight, to the Lower East Side, to college and university campuses, the word went out, and the rideshare notes on Laundromat and transient hotel bulletin boards and student union notice-boards signaled a new site of migration.

By mid-August, when it became clear that the tribes were in motion, en route, while the locations for everything from toilets to musical stages had still not been confirmed, the stance of spontaneity became a practical necessity. Bands and performers backed out as permits were conclusively denied, and the mass migration of peace-loving counterculturists shrank. Those who did come and those locals who participated were committed to a more militant and confrontational process than the original Yippie! move-ment had envisioned.[24]

The Yippie! festival action proposed exactly the city bureaucracy most feared. They sought an America which could be joyously stripped of its des-tinarian traditions, living in an eternal utopian present, with "no place to go." To liberate the present into that atemporal paradise, they were willing to foment disruption and possible violence. *When you ain't got nothin' you ain't got nothin' to lose.*

But the center of the Yippie! actions lay in the promise of a televised drama in which, as Rubin had said, "you are the star of the show." And as that drama intensified—and as television's yearning for greater and greater intensity of visual and sonic impact edited chaotic footage into tightly wrought scenes to replay on network news—even the proper, rule-defined protests of Mobe became part of the larger screenplay. Over the course of the convention, propriety came to seem less and less a virtue; the festival's doctrine of spontaneity spread to the Mobilization's people, not least out of necessity, as police "rioters" beat up everyone from foul-mouthed freaks to white-collar grandfathers, forcing mass currents of migration into and out of the parks and the streets.

The police, of course, also found themselves swept up as actors in the drama, played out for a national and international audience, in newspaper and magazine articles, graphic photographs and, naturally, television. As they responded to the taunts and tossed objects of some of their adversaries, police came increasingly to look like truncheon-wielding loutish villains, perfect foils for a media machine hungry for a dramatic narrative and in-creasingly finding *itself* victim of police violence.

Moreover, the open spaces and ceremonial design of Grant Park made for an ideal public battleground, visible from the protected windows of Michigan Avenue's skyscrapers and leaving the political protesters of the

Mobilization particularly vulnerable to attack and violence, which then made for smashing TV. By contrast, Lincoln Park turned out to be a brilliant stage for the sort of actions the Yippie! leaders had envisioned from the first. With its irregular terrain and picturesque features, it was an excellent site for guerrilla action, with groups assembling and then dispersing, quick skirmishes and rapid retreats, under cover of darkness. A rock thrower one minute could be a sleeping hippie or one-half of a strolling couple the next.

These strategies were sufficiently frustrating to the cops, however, that they responded by widening their reactions until, during the worst of the police riots, they were attacking, beating, handcuffing, and imprisoning indiscriminately. In effect, the police escalations seemed tellingly to confirm one of Yippie!'s central tenets: that the Vietnam War's militarism, its authoritarian and tyrannical temptations, and its violence had infected the national culture as a whole—that Vietnam was being reenacted on American soil. As the counterculture's guerrillas replicated the strategies of the Viet Cong and the NVA, the police became the blundering intruders, caught in older conceptions of conflict, out of tune with their environment, brutal and brutish.[25]

The mental images of a different conflict, one perhaps never real but powerfully mythic, swept not just the police but the protesters as well. The Vietnam War failed at least in part because its participants in America clung to a set of images based not in the realities of the present but the popular mythology of the past, considering Vietnam as if it were Dunkirk or Iwo Jima. So also the domestic proxy war of protest and response was equivalently slave to a myth of moral war and American virtue in the fray.

Probably the most destructive aspect of this in the America of August '68 concerned protest actions held in Grant Park on the afternoon of Monday, August 26, and the battle to liberate, to retake, and to control a particular landmark: the John Alexander Logan Monument.

That statue was charged with significance for both sides. One of those conservative monuments to military heroism, the statue was set on an artificial hillock that formed the highest point in Grant Park. Moreover, sculptor Augustus Saint-Gaudens had replaced the traditional raised sword with an American flag.

The Logan statue action came on the heels of a particularly frustrating day after the arrest of leaders Tom Hayden and Wolfe Lowenthal, and an angry march to police headquarters that culminated in the arrest of the march's titular "leaders," a white woman riding on the shoulders of a black man. Returning to Grant Park, protesters passed cadres of police and National Guard troops, and a group broke off with a repeated call to "take the

14.4. Peter Bullock, *Demonstrators Crowded around General Logan Monument*, Grant Park, 1968. (Courtesy of the Chicago History Museum.)

hill!," rushing up the hillock to the General Logan statue.[26] Within minutes more than a thousand people had completely filled the hillock and spilled down at some distance, to the streets on the south and west, and the railroad viaduct to the east.

This was a telling event. For the protesters, Logan's statue symbolized the militaristic, jingoistic, flag-waving, mindless patriotism they so strongly opposed. Taking the hill was both a reenactment of childhood games of Capture the Flag, and a flaunting of the power of mass protest to counteract and even defeat the organized militia of the state.

For the police, it was a galling symbolic defeat. Both hero and flag were being denigrated, even defiled; after less than ten minutes, a group of heavily armed cops waded into the crowd to retake the statue and the hill. They swept up the hillside, beating protesters as they went, dragged the riders off the statue—with the exception of the final rider, a boy who took the event as his moment of celebrity at his peril, perching atop Logan's shoulders and

14.5. Proof sheet of the Grant Park Demonstrations, 1968. (Courtesy of the Chicago History Museum.)

chanting "Peace, Peace!" Police broke his arm and kicked him repeatedly in the groin before arresting him.

Though the incident once again points to the symmetry between military failures in Vietnam and the images and ideologies of protesters and authorities alike, its outcome suggests that the protesters had the upper hand. In the face of weaponry, they had irony, and with that tool were able to resist the intractable hardening of positions that would have led them to far greater peril and defeat. The melee ended with televised images of cops beating up kids and young women, and protesters massed peacefully at the edge of the park, across from the Hilton, where their speakers were recorded by news reporters, providing a vivid contrast with the images of police violence.

Chicago '68 didn't end with a revolutionary bang. Police and National Guard troops eventually and decisively routed the demonstrators. This outcome deeply disappointed the political organizations composing Mobilization. But for the Yippies, the entire drama confirmed their picture of a failed, militarized, ideologically empty, dominant culture wielding its authority against a vibrant, life-affirming, celebratory counterculture capable of living *as if*—as if the world were already different.

As importantly, for the festival adherents, the very fact that Chicago '68 became a drama confirmed their existential ideology. *They* had controlled the narrative—by predicting it, by participating in it, by turning it in directions they desired through their strategies and tactics, and by making that narrative public—by forging an oblique alliance with the dominant forces of journalism and television. The fact that theirs remains the dominant popular narrative of the events of late August in Chicago 1968 confirms their triumph. Few consider the other side: the most basic violations of civility and the escalating forms of cultural provocation aimed at the police and National Guard, from constant obscenities and insults that working-class Chicagoans considered calls to violence, to bottle- and rock- and shitbag-throwing incidents, incidents of spitting on the police, and recurrent refusal to respect even the most basic rules of urban life. Few consider the extraordinarily limited options Daley and his people had. What? To allow the Festival of Life in Lincoln Park, complete with forty rock bands and a hundred thousand counterculture denizens? To give over the parks for sleeping, but also for a host of illegal activities not tolerated in the everyday life of the city? To grant permits for marches through the city streets that would have halted urban life—economic, social, political, cultural? To turn against the party in power—a party that had made and sustained the Chicago Machine?

None of this adheres to the common picture of those days. Instead, a heroic narrative of spatial and cultural conquest emerges: for more than a week, the counterculture's most extreme ideological fringe liberated a city, its parks and streets, its history and its image in the nation and the world.

Looking Down on Sweet Valleys: Part-Time Pastorales at Woodstock and Altamont, 1969

Chicago's battles were played out on topographies both actual and symbolic. So also with that most legendary of countercultural events, Woodstock. Woodstock reiterated the duality between the local and the transcendental, between place and placelessness, transience and settledness.

There, at Yasgur's Farm in Bethel, New York, the magnet that drew the transient was that very image of place, and a very particular American place, simultaneously liberating and needing liberation. The American farm, set in bucolic rolling hills, interspersed meadows and pastures, woodlots, ponds, and small lakes: this was the site as it came to be memorialized, in pictures and words.

But Woodstock was and is a site of cultural remembrance even more than one of physical event. We think of Woodstock in terms profoundly colored by the inflated rhetoric surrounding it. Even more, we are affected by the way the filmed tribute recorded and transformed the place and the event. We hear Crosby, Stills, Nash & Young singing their counterculture anthem, "Long Time Gone"; we see the process of site preparation set against sweeping panoramas of the bucolic setting; we watch as photogenic innocents in stereotypic costume, their youth glowing from their faces and bodies, cross the wide screen. And then the music begins.[27]

That is to say, we see this event as a great pilgrimage and not a haphazard assembly of disjointed purposes and inharmonious subgroups, their expectations at every turn disrupted and frustrated; no one sure what the place will look like or even, precisely, where it will be; those with tickets unpleasantly surprised to find they've been conned or, at the least, outflanked by crashers and opportunists; those there to hear the music of their heroes exiled at great distances from the stage and the action, the sound from speakers muffled and lo-fi, worse than their car radios; those seeking a measure of pastoral escape seated in a vast sea of noisy, migrating, stumbling others, the skies above them, and the music, interrupted by the irritating high-volume din of helicopters coming and going (some bearing musicians otherwise marooned in the sea of abandoned cars, some bringing medical teams and evacuating the sick and injured, some carrying television crews, and some even there to help the promoters' film crews record, exaggerate and transform the refugee camp into "a song and a celebration," as Mitchell's lyric recorded it). All of that *before* the rains, the mud, the overflowing portapotties and miserable prison-camp food, inadequate water, bad drugs, lost companions, long delays between sets, dropped performers, bad performances, warnings from the stage, wandering psychotics, thieves and rapists and more general opportunists, lost cars and the long, miserable trek home.[28]

To trace the conversion of event into myth, we might begin by distinguishing the final site in Bethel Woods from the expected site at or outside Woodstock, New York. Yasgur's Farm was not the destination to which those hundreds of thousands imagined they were going. They knew nothing of this out-of-the-way rural place in the mid-west part of the state or of the

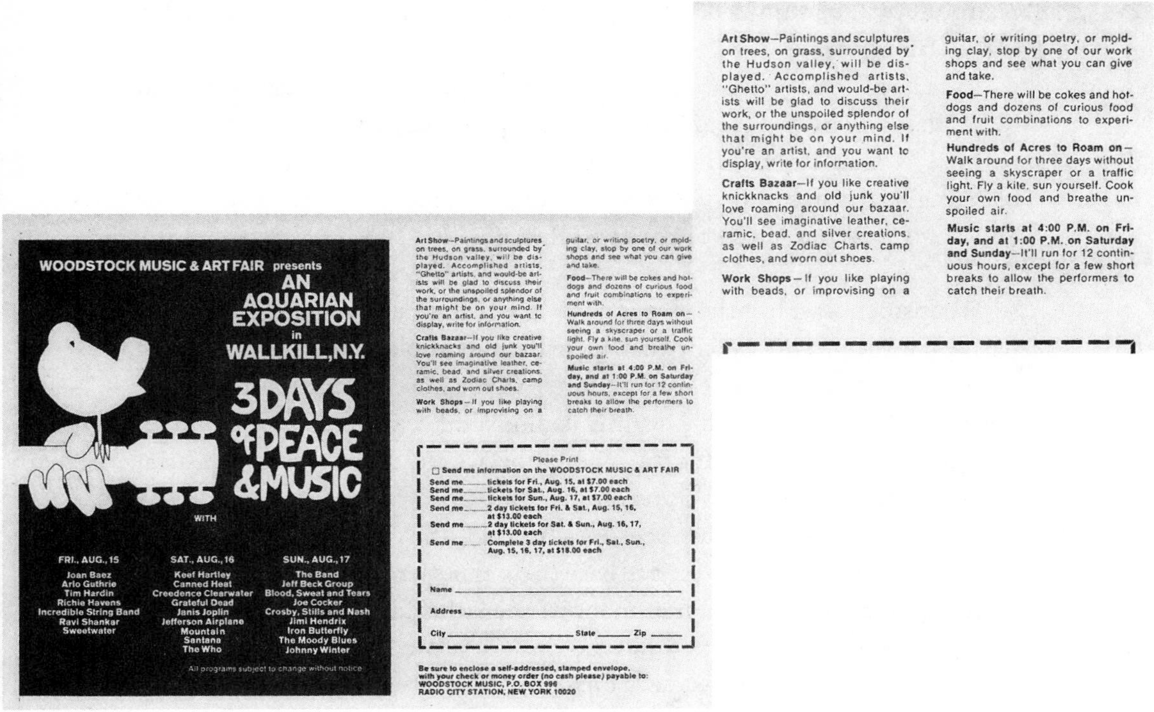
WOODSTOCK MUSIC & ART FAIR presents
AN
AQUARIAN
EXPOSITION
in
WALLKILL, N.Y.
3 DAYS of PEACE & MUSIC
WITH
FRI., AUG., 15
Joan Baez
Arlo Guthrie
Tim Hardin
Richie Havens
Incredible String Band
Ravi Shankar
Sweetwater
SAT., AUG., 16
Keef Hartley
Canned Heat
Creedence Clearwater
Grateful Dead
Janis Joplin
Jefferson Airplane
Mountain
Santana
The Who
SUN., AUG., 17
The Band
Jeff Beck Group
Blood, Sweat and Tears
Joe Cocker
Crosby, Stills and Nash
Jimi Hendrix
Iron Butterfly
The Moody Blues
Johnny Winter
All programs subject to change without notice
Art Show—Paintings and sculptures on trees, on grass, surrounded by the Hudson valley, will be displayed. Accomplished artists, "Ghetto" artists, and would-be artists will be glad to discuss their work, or the unspoiled splendor of the surroundings, or anything else that might be on your mind. If you're an artist, and you want to display, write for information.
Crafts Bazaar—If you like creative knickknacks and old junk you'll love roaming around our bazaar. You'll see imaginative leather, ceramic, bead, and silver creations, as well as Zodiac Charts, camp clothes, and worn out shoes.
Work Shops—If you like playing with beads, or improvising on a guitar, or writing poetry, or molding clay, stop by one of our work shops and see what you can give and take.
Food—There will be cokes and hot-dogs and dozens of curious food and fruit combinations to experiment with.
Hundreds of Acres to Roam on—Walk around for three days without seeing a skyscraper or a traffic light. Fly a kite, sun yourself. Cook your own food and breathe unspoiled air.
Music starts at 4:00 P.M. on Friday, and at 1:00 P.M. on Saturday and Sunday—It'll run for 12 continuous hours, except for a few short breaks to allow the performers to catch their breath.
Please Print
Send me information on the WOODSTOCK MUSIC & ART FAIR
Send me ___ tickets for Fri., Aug. 15, at $7.00 each
Send me ___ tickets for Sat., Aug. 16, at $7.00 each
Send me ___ tickets for Sun., Aug. 17, at $7.00 each
Send me ___ 2 day tickets for Fri. & Sat., Aug. 15, 16, at $13.00 each
Send me ___ 2 day tickets for Sat. & Sun., Aug. 16, 17, at $13.00 each
Send me ___ Complete 3 day tickets for Fri., Sat., Sun., Aug. 15, 16, 17, at $18.00 each
Name
Address
City
State
Zip
Be sure to enclose a self-addressed, stamped envelope, with your check or money order (no cash please) payable to:
WOODSTOCK MUSIC, P.O. BOX 996
RADIO CITY STATION, NEW YORK 10020

14.6. Flyer for Woodstock Festival, 1967

manure smell of a real dairy operation. They imagined themselves entering a pastoral idyll not far from Dylan's sylvan retreat, of which they'd read in *Rolling Stone* and *Crawdaddy* and *Life, Time*, and *Newsweek*, a place renowned as an artists' colony, a place where celebrated musicians walked the streets in everyday attire, heading for breakfast or to buy a loaf of bread, a place where *they* could also be celebrities in everyday life.

Festival organizers played on this deception both indirectly and directly. There was never much interest in the actual Woodstock area. The planned site had been more than sixty miles from Woodstock in gritty Wallkill—scruffy acreage in transition from farmland to an industrial park, just off the rumble and congestion of Route 17, with a suburban shopping mall in view.

This did not prevent the organizers from continuing to promulgate the festival's locale as a space of rural beauty, relief from the urban landscape. "Hundreds of acres to roam on," promised their ad copy. "Walk around for three days without seeing a skyscraper or a traffic light. Fly a kite, sun yourself. Cook your own food and breathe unspoiled air. Camp out: water and restrooms will be supplied. Tents and camping equipment will be available at the Camp Store."[29]

In fact, the final site, at Max Yasgur's dairy farm, was far closer to that ideal than any of the organizers had imagined they might find, a canvas painted by man and nature for the pleasure of the traveler, made "to keep bringing new vistas into view . . . welcoming, warm, lush . . . fields and fields and fields," as one of the organizers described his first experience of the sight.[30]

Woodstock was, in other words, less a site than an amalgam of imaginative landscapes marked by that same duality of place and movement, of home and *hegira*. Woodstock signaled both a dreamscape and a destination, a pastorale through which pilgrims could wander and a village to which they could return. But that return could be, would be, transitory—a brief rejuvenation on an endless transient's quest.

The pilgrims and pleasure-seekers who made the trip brought with them a set of preconditions on which to base their experience of those three days: pictures in their heads, mental maps of the cultural terrain they, and the festival would come to occupy. But the clash of promotion, fantasy, and ambiguous reality left the experience unstable. It required something, or someone, to convert that confusion of signs, symbols and spaces into a coherent, overriding narrative.

It was Joni Mitchell, the most brilliant and evocative of singer-songwriters to come after Dylan, who found this synthesis and gave it voice. In her anthem to the festival, the narrator, herself a wanderer, "came upon a child of God," a fellow exile from the Garden of Eden, but one with a destination, a homely specific site—Yasgur's Farm—where, this pilgrim told her, he might *try and get my soul free*. His purposefulness seduced the narrator; she asked to join him. Two became a stream, a river, a vast ocean of pilgrims, "half a million strong," and the result was a collective, a community, all "stardust . . . golden," by their very coming-together transforming Yasgur's Farm into a Paradise reclaimed.

Everywhere there was song and celebration. The power of innocence in pilgrimage, multiplied into a vast community, did more than engender a festival in Mitchell's mythopoeic song. It transformed a nation, turning swords into plowshares or, in Mitchell's more appropriate acid-laced mutation, turning *bombers riding shotgun in the sky . . . into butterflies above our nation*. *Our* nation: Mitchell proposed that Woodstock could liberate America. It was a dream, and it carried the ambiguity of that word. As sung by Crosby, Stills, Nash & Young, Mitchell's song became an anthem of the counterculture, a declaration of the triumph of a spontaneous mass movement over the forces of repression and entrenched militarism. Wanderers who had been moving *away*, now found a destination and a purpose. It is easy to imagine, particularly listening to the version sung by "the boys" some eight months after the festival, and then watching the opening musical offering of the *Woodstock* film, released a few months later, that the counterculture had succeeded in coming together, in an Edenic American pastorale.

But Mitchell's song belongs in two very different places, sites not shown in the film and not consistent with the electric version driven by the push of multiple guitars and the high, angelic harmonies of the band. She wrote the song in a hotel room in New York City after having been left behind by "the boys"—Crosby, Stills, Nash, new member Neil Young, and producer-agent David Geffen—because (according to her) *they* (Geffen and CSNY manager Elliot Roberts) had decided it was too risky for her to try to get into the site, perform, and then return in time for a career-building appearance on *The Dick Cavett Show*.[31] For Mitchell, it was part of a more general patronizing pattern that goaded her: "I was the *girl* of the family and, with great disappointment, I was the one that had to stay behind."[32] So while Crosby, Stills, Nash and Young barreled in on a rented helicopter, gave their performance, and escaped, Mitchell herself spent the time in a Manhattan hotel, watching newscasts while waiting to go on TV to promote her most recent album, *Clouds*, released in May of that year. "The deprivation of not being able to go provided me with an intense angle on Woodstock," Mitchell told an interviewer:

> I was one of the fans. I was put in the position of being a kid who couldn't make it. So I was glued to the media. At the same time . . . I had been saying to myself, 'Where are the modern miracles? Woodstock, for some reason, impressed me as being a modern miracle, like a modern day fishes-and-loaves story. For a herd of people that large to cooperate so well, it was pretty remarkable, and there was tremendous optimism.[33]

And so, "glued to the media" in that hotel room, Mitchell wrote her song, with its Appalachian-modal melody line and its minor-key chords open to the space between voice and words, with the crackle and hiss of TV providing a counterpoint.

So many elements of the American moment collided there: the bland anonymity of a commercial hotel room; the mass-issue television set (by 1969 it was a color set but still a bit fuzzy, its colors off-kilter); the breathless news-story narratives of WCBS, WNBC, or WABC, with their helicopter views of the site and swooping shots of the long tentacles of abandoned cars along the roads leading to the festival; the male privilege and female subjugation that Mitchell experienced herself, dumped from the adventure; and behind all this, the veiled image of a woman unmoored for years from a place not unlike Bethel Woods, rootless, traveling, taking and losing, tired to exhaustion of the receding promises of that moment, and seeking to settle and make a new sort of home for herself, a process that she would memorialize in *Ladies of the Canyon*, the album that included her version of "Woodstock."

Studying the lyrics in the published anthology of Mitchell's songs and poems, pointedly devoid of punctuation and so flat of affect or voice, one senses the ambiguity of the song through the very struggle to put emphasis and pathos into the reading. The shifts from past tense to present to past and then, at the end, into the present imperative—*we've got to get ourselves back to the garden*—lean the song toward loss rather than celebration, and the final call seems all the more tinged by doubt.

Mitchell's performance of "Woodstock" at the Big Sur Folk Festival a few months later, on September 14, renders the song even more ambiguous for her own hesitations, particularly at the beginning. She is seated at an out-of-tune grand piano on an outdoor stage, and she strikes the first chords as if not sure of them, before her prologue: *Well everybody has heard about Woodstock and maybe a lot of you were there.* At this, she giggles, oddly, self-consciously, and then teaches her audience—some ten or fifteen thousand, tiny by comparison with the half-million at Bethel Woods a few months earlier—the chorus, implicitly inviting them to join her, breaking the performer-audience screen and turning the plangent elegy into a prayer.[34]

Her version at that moment still holds loss and possibility in balance. Her own hesitancy as she sings it, the audience's attempts to vocalize a really quite difficult chorus melody (with its surprising leaps of fifths and sixths and octaves), the badly miked, out-of-tune piano all contribute to its quality of childlike innocence and yearning. Sung as it was precisely *there*, at a scripted new-age event sponsored by the wealthy, elite Esalen Institute, the audience size and composition carefully controlled, the physical surroundings appropriately—and artificially—spectacular, "natural," the performance seems in retrospect precious.[35] It stands in mannered contradistinction to the site of its making—it seems to grope for an authenticity that might deny its origins in that hotel room. Instead, it seems part of a larger script, pushing political and social revolution aside, and replacing it with the sort of inner transformation—Eastern philosophy mashed in with transformative psychology—marketed by Esalen.

Between the Big Sur performance and the anthemic, hard-rock recording by Crosby, Stills, Nash & Young lies the shadow of that third festival, Altamont, held in December 1969 on a site not noted for picturesque beauty or transcendental associations. Originally planned by a consortium that included the Rolling Stones, Emmett Grogan and the Diggers, and the Grateful Dead, the Free Festival was intended as a "Woodstock West" and a reincarnation of the Human Be-In, sited in Golden Gate Park and featuring the Dead. There it would have fitted the Haight's tradition of concerts in the park, in which gently sloping meadows angled toward a stage, or the sloping amphitheater of Yasgur's Farm. But it too was relocated more than once, and unlike Woodstock, its changes of venue took it farther and farther from the pastorale.

The first shift—to the sterile, treeless, gritty Sears Point Raceway in Sonoma, California—was a wrenching one, erasing all associations with Haight-Ashbury and the Summer of Love. But even Sears was idyllic compared with the final site, rapidly chosen just two or three days before the festival date. Altamont Raceway was fully dedicated to the mechanical triumphalism so abhorred by the counterculture: it was an oval dirt racetrack,[36] even farther from San Francisco, in a landscape markedly more sterile and unpicturesque than Sears Point and at an even greater remove from the Haight. Moreover, its geography—a combination natural and man-made bowl, with a steep decline to what would become the stage—seemed at further odds with the bucolic sites of Golden Gate Park, Yasgur's Farm, and Big Sur's Esalen.

The violence and chaos of the Altamont Festival needed no rehearsing. The sheer naiveté of the Dead and the Stones in bringing in the Hell's Angels to police the stage only capped a long list of wild miscalculations surrounding the hasty and ill-considered choice of the raceway as a venue. An audience of three hundred thousand ranged down the hillsides, crammed so tightly at the front that they continually stumbled, fell, or were pushed onto the stage's low, unbarricaded edge. Bad acid and worse amphetamines passed through the crowd. Surrounded by an inhospitable landscape of dry hills, asphalt, and chain-link fencing, the festival started ugly and grew uglier as the day went on.

Crosby, Stills, Nash & Young played the festival. Indeed, they performed just before the Stones took the stage with their anthems to darkness and rage. Forced by the chaos to commandeer a pickup truck and drive themselves through the crowd to get to the stage, the band was too high to fully understand what surrounded them.[37] Guarded by drunken Angels who had commandeered the lip of the stage, Crosby, Stills, Nash & Young tried without success to reinvoke the pacifism of Bethel Woods with the plangent hopefulness of their signature songs. Shortly thereafter, they returned to the studio to finish recording *Déjà Vu*, complete with their rendering of "Woodstock."[38]

Though Joni Mitchell was still deeply involved with "the boys," she wasn't at Altamont; she was on the opposite side of the continent, performing that night in Syracuse, New York, on a college campus. But she heard about it from them. Just a week later, she appeared as the "surprise guest" at one of their concerts in Detroit. Late in December 1969, Mitchell went into the studio in Hollywood to record the tracks for *Ladies of the Canyon*, where she placed "Woodstock" at the end of the second side, just before her much-older and by then well-known "Circle Game."

Altamont permeates Mitchell's recorded version. Within it lies a painful contradiction between the innocent utopianism of the lyrics and the dark mood of the performance. It contains a reminder that Altamont, with its chaos, violence, bombast, and hubris, its tragic manifestation of the frailty of human innocence and human civility, took place just twelve miles from the other principal institution of Livermore, California: the Lawrence Livermore National Defense Laboratory, site of nuclear-weapons design and construction, and directed by nuclear warfare hardliner Edward Teller. Few people engaged with the West Coast antiwar and antinuclear movements were unfamiliar with Livermore's reputation as a nuclear warfare facility. By the time she recorded the song, Mitchell must have known how evocative of the long-shadowed tradition of Cold War atomic threats and atomic fear was her image of the "bombers riding shotgun in the sky." It was well within the range of her magical thinking for Mitchell to conceive that the environment, history and karma of Lawrence Livermore had infected Altamont, and through it, the counterculture, giving rise to the violence and cruelty of the day, and making all too clear the end of her fantasy that a music festival could in a moment liberate a soul, provide a home, and transform a nation.[39]

Taking the Hill: Kent State, 1970

Mitchell's version of "Woodstock" was released in April 1970. On the twenty-second of that month, the first American Earth Day celebration took place. A week later, the U.S. invasion of Cambodia brought antiwar protest to a fever pitch. The rhetoric of justification was tactical and military. On April 30, 1970, President Nixon went on national television to explain the invasion, pointing to a map of Vietnam and Cambodia, and speaking of "hit-and-run

14.7. Nixon explains the invasion of Cambodia, 1970. (Courtesy of the National Archives and Records Administration.)

attacks," "the enemy . . . concentrating his forces in . . . sanctuaries . . . encircling the capital . . ." and the American plan to "clean out these sanctuaries."

At the core of Nixon's speech was a deep anxiety about the end of America's place as a city upon a hill:

> *We will not be humiliated* . . . in an age of anarchy both abroad and at home . . . mindless attacks on all the great institutions which have been created by free civilizations in the last 500 years. Even here in the United States, great universities are being systematically destroyed. . . .
>
> If, when the chips are down, the world's most powerful nation—the United States of America—acts like a pitiful, helpless giant, the forces of totalitarianism and anarchy will threaten free nations and free institutions throughout the world.
>
> It is not our power, but our will and character that is being tested tonight.[40]

Nixon's rhetoric in that April 30 press conference reflected the confusion within American cultural and political institutions. Nixon's speech conjoined warfare on a vast scale at a great distance from the nation with the sporadic and largely ineffectual spasms of protest and low-level violence within the national boundaries. In both cases, the American reputation was threatened, America was "humiliated," its "will and character . . . tested." Only aggressive action could ensure that the small ragtag did not shame the righteous.

Less than a week later, on May 4, National Guard troops performed an advance-and-retreat dance with student protesters in the midst of the Kent State University campus until they finally turned and fired repeatedly and indiscriminately at protesters, onlookers, and students, killing four and wounding a number of others.

Nixon's conflation of domestic protest with the Vietnam conflict was only superficially absurd; at the level of myth and metaphor, it was deeply appropriate. For in both cases, the adversaries in the cultural dreamscape were shadowy, capable of injury at far greater effect than their numbers or their powers should have allowed. Nixon's hands, gesturing over the map of Southeast Asia, sought to counter the image of nearly invisible enemies emerging from holes in darkness, striking, then merging back into black night—the very image that the Yippie! planners at Chicago had sought to apply to their own strategies. In the bland, flat intensity of television studio lighting, Nixon presented a tactical argument, with a visual aid drawn from the newsreels and action movies of World War II (the C.O. standing at the map, his junior officers in a respectful semicircle, as he gestures the direct attack and the flanking move), even as his language, anxious of emasculation, called up that other picture, of loneliness and fear in a foreign landscape, powers diminished or lost, the security of American certainty stripped away.

Nixon's speech provided a template for Ohio's Republican governor, James Rhodes, to convey his desk-pounding, vitriolic response to anti-war protests at Kent State. Where Nixon had presented a benevolent if weak Cambodia overrun by North Vietnamese troops, Rhodes spoke of a campus beset by "outside agitators." Where Nixon presented the enemy as morally "intolerable," Rhodes spoke of protesters as "the worst sort of people we harbor in America." Where Nixon spoke of the necessity to "respond accordingly," Rhodes swore to use "every weapon possible to eradicate the problem."* Nixon's rhetoric had been inflammatory and the campaign one of escalation: Rhodes proposed the same.[41]

What he presented, however, was only one side in the conflict. On the other were the statements and gestures of protesters. The spate of rock-throwing and window-breaking in downtown Kent, Ohio, on Friday night, May 1, before the Monday massacre, may have been no worse than many student "riots" by fraternity brothers at homecomings in towns like Gainesville, Florida, or Columbus, Ohio, and there is significant evidence that much of the damage was the result of similarly drunken outbursts and cal-

---

* Rhodes made his statements at the press conference on Sunday, May 3, 1970, at which he announced the calling up of the National Guard.

low mobology: the first "rioters" emerged not from an opium den or a commune but from a frat bar, and the tricks of a local motorcycle club played into the early mix. But the outburst occurred in the midst of ongoing antiwar protests on campus, and within the context of the riots of the previous two years, with their emphases on race, antiwar and antigovernment grievances, the Kent events of that Friday and Saturday appeared to be local manifestations of an already tense cultural geography.[42]

For Kent State, and the town of Kent, were not elite enclaves. They were microcosms of the larger culture. Kent State was an increasingly suburban expansion campus, originally a land-grant teacher's college, and in 1970 still largely attended by first-generation college-goers whose families worked in the industrial jobs that undergirded the Ohio economy. Kent itself was an amalgam of college town and industrial suburb. It was twelve miles from Akron and thirty-eight miles from Cleveland. Neither fully dependent on the university for its economic life and cultural identity, nor large enough to absorb the campus (in 1970, the town's population was twenty-eight thousand, while Kent State's student body was close to twenty thousand), Kent was inherently unstable.

While there were mirror-image values reflected in the opposition groups staring each other down in Kent and on the campus, there was a fundamental distinction between them reflective of a far deeper and longer-standing tension in American political and cultural identity from the nation's very inception, and embodied in the Declaration of Independence. In Kent proper, and in the words of Governor Rhodes and President Nixon, was the original, English, Lockean declaration, expressed in the 1774 *Declaration and Resolves of the First Continental Congress*: "that they are entitled to life, liberty and property," reflecting the founders' embrace of John Locke, that "no one ought to harm another in his life, health, liberty, or possessions."[43] For those who sought to conserve "estates" or properties, the actions of wild college students with or without political motives breaking shop windows, throwing bottles and trashing stores, represented a fundamental violation of that American right to hold and preserve property and the covenant to respect the property of others.

Over the centuries, this conception of property rights had been more and more closely bound to the evolving notion of American democracy, as the ideals of upward economic and social mobility came increasingly to be attached to property, especially home ownership, which also was seen as a restraint on extremism. Remember Bill Levitt: "No one who owns his own house can be a Communist." Levittown's mortgage holders, and those in Kent, Ohio, believed that their real property could make possible their retirement and could free them to finance their children's higher education, hefting them up the ladder of opportunity.

In the town of Kent and in working- and middle-class communities throughout the nation, then, the campus protests seemed offensive and threatening, for they signaled not just a threat to hard-gained economic security for older and more conservative Americans, but also a schism in the social contract between generations. The disruptions threatened both American myths of upward mobility—individual and generational.

Moreover, those state college campuses where the protests were most noisy had been built with taxpayer money—they were the common property of the polity, and in particular of the generation that had worked to fund those buildings, greenswards, parking lots, and playing fields, especially at the young postwar state college campuses like U Cal Riverside, Cal State Fullerton, the University of Illinois at Chicago Circle, and Kent State.

Across the wall of grievance on the campus itself, where the protesters were amassed, a very different idea of *property* was emerging, in concert with the larger counterculture ideology. The protesters looked to Jefferson's transformation of Locke's language for the 1776 Declaration of Independence, in which "estates," "possessions," and "property" were banished and replaced with a broader and more communitarian conception of a common "pursuit of happiness." A devout Francophile, Jefferson had been steeped in the libertarian thinking of prerevolutionary French *philosophes*, who were variously associating that third universal right not as property, but as *Amitie, Fraternité, Union,* and *Charité*—a common desire for shared community. Jefferson had also looked to his Scottish-Presbyterian philosopher-mentor, Francis Hutcheson (as historian Garry Wills has pointed out), who also proposed the pursuit of happiness to be a communitarian venture, judged not by individual satisfaction but by a common "Public happiness," "the greatest happiness of the greatest number." The counterculturists were not simply rejecting property as a fundamental right: they were shifting away from individualism, especially economic individualism. Had Bill Levitt been asked (he wasn't), he'd have probably called them communists.

Jefferson was an appealing father figure for counterculture thinkers. He was university educated and a believer in higher education. He was a lover of nature and of the unspoiled landscape. He was a gentleman farmer, and—as the stories then had it—he abhorred slavery, gave his slaves rights not accorded blacks elsewhere in the continent, and freed them upon his death.*

---

* It would take a generation of post-utopian reform historians to complicate that picture of Jefferson.

And with his long hair cascading over his ears and over his collar, and his dandy's taste in costume, he looked as though he would have fit seamlessly into the street scene at the Haight or among the musicians backstage at Woodstock. The common knowledge the counterculture's utopians had imbibed from children's books, junior high school social studies texts, and high school history books, afforded them a founding father for their pursuit of a common good, a communal happiness.

At the same time, the protesters' call for the removal of National Guard troops from the campus reflected their understanding of the campus and its public space as a site for the invention of new forms of community. For them, *property* meant not goods and chattel—furniture, televisions, Thunderbirds, and picture windows—but rather a physical space on which to enact their community: a commons. They were claiming a place for their revolution, and that place was, if only for that moment, composed of a playing field, two hills, a parking lot, and a wooded area between classroom buildings.

Within these two Americas, then, Kent State's conflict was not simply a sideshow or a distraction, or even a symbolic culmination of tensions. It was a genuine insurrection and a genuine counterinsurgent response by the forces of American law and authority.

Yet close to the ground, it had also the quality of a drama, perhaps a passion play or a childhood reconstruction of some war movie seen at a Saturday matinee. For the protesters, and for the young guardsmen, Kent State's events seem to play out on a hazy geography, a landscape overlaid with resonant spaces of conflict. The students seek to "take the hill" and, taking it, jeer triumphantly at the Guardsmen. It is Ringolevio or War, all over again. The guardsmen march down to the open field, the field of skirmish and sporting battle—but only of practice, not actual event—and once there they turn to march back up to reclaim the high ground. They are failing at their manifest task—to dispel the protesters, to establish some semblance of order, to retake the common property of the state of Ohio back from those who have claimed it. None of their actions make sense in that regard. They are sufficient in number that any number of common stratagems should have worked—sealing perimeters, defining no-man's-lands, or even simply dispersing to avoid escalating tensions and hostilities. Instead, they play a slow-motion war movie—one of the many that demarcate the heroic Americans and their allies in the war of their elders, their supervisors, rhetoricians and commanding officers.

At the same time, they can feel that there is something wrong. They are pelted at times by stones; when they throw their grenades (tear gas this time, toy versions of the grenades tossed by the American soldiers in those movies they grew up watching on the screen or the TV), protesters retreat and return, or they grab the grenades and throw them back. When the cadre of G Troop makes its final march back up Blanket Hill, they are far from the protesters—far enough that the greatest immediate threat is a long-haired boy who has run forward into the open to give them the finger, perhaps fifty yards below them. The twenty-eight guardsmen turn, assume armed position, and shoot. Twenty shoot into the air. The gesture is ambiguous: are they recognizing, finally, that this is no game after all? Or are they reenacting the movie and television warning shot, over the heads of the Indians, the Confederates, the cattle rustlers?

Eight of the men shoot directly at the students. They too might make the defense that they'd forgotten this was real, that their guns were loaded. We can postulate two contradictory impulses that lead them to this deadly, criminal error. One is that articulated by Nixon: they have spent days *humiliated* by their opposition, harried by them, laughed at, jeered, stung, or even bruised by rocks thrown. They have been ill-led by their commanders and they have done nothing but march like caricatures of the Redcoats they read about in elementary school, whose lockstep marches reflected the impotence and failure of the English regime while harassed by the ill-clad and ill-armed yet perpetually victorious Americans, individuals who won the day by spontaneously forming a collective, then as spontaneously disappearing into the woods and fields. The guardsmen are also the domestic equivalent of the American soldiers Nixon refused to allow to be trapped by failure of nerve in Vietnam; their adversaries are the domestic equivalent of the VC and the NVA, appearing and disappearing, triumphant not by force of arms or display but by slipperiness, guile, violation of the rules.

All this may lead even the most disciplined soldier into irrational acts. But there is also that second impulse—the impulse to view this not as a *real* event but a *play*, a fictional enactment, a grown-up's version of War played in a new neighborhood. These guns—they aren't even BB guns. They are perhaps air rifles or plastic, wood and metal souvenirs of a trip to Disneyland and a happy moment in the souvenir shop. These boys are playing at soldiering,* and the losers who fall bloodily are far away, so far that it can seem as if they too are acting their roles.

---

* In the early twenty-first century, when so much of America's bloody work is done by national guardsmen, it's hard to remember that during the Vietnam Era, national guardsmen were known as "weekend warriors," and their most common work was mopping up after national disasters—floods, hurricanes, earthquakes. They trained rather casually, often with dummy weapons and often on college campuses, whose playing fields were readily available off-season.

Reading the reports from both sides, listening to the reminiscences, poring over the transcripts, one comes away with a general sense of the shock, even disbelief, felt on everyone's part. This wasn't supposed to actually happen. For both sides, Kent State became, if only for a few moments, not a real place at all, or rather, it became a real place so overlaid with myths, symbols, narratives and stories, with newsreels, movies, TV shows, amusement-park features, comic-book heroisms, textbook tales, that no one was walking on the real ground or shouting real threats or shooting real bullets. Until they were.

Ironically, the catastrophe put Kent State on the map. Today, the cultural landscape of the campus is awash in reminders: monuments official and unofficial, symposia and academic conferences, explanatory pamphlets and library exhibits, residues and rehearsals of the recurrent scarring battles over the meaning and the monumentality of the events there. In a parking lot, ill-designed low metal pillars with artificial flames—fluorescent lights, really—in their caps, mark the precise spots where the dead fell, and prevent the Toyotas and Hondas of teachers and students from marring the sites. Down the hill, a much-modified memorial, designed and redesigned by the architect Bruno Ast, offers a memory grove, benches, vistas marking the sight lines between combatants.

But the resonance is gone, the place is once again placeless. Its weight, its significance, emerged from a collision of meanings and urgencies on its topography—a shared declaration that this was land worth fighting for. That compact has since turned to dust and blown away, and what is left is a bland, utilitarian space—a grove of trees, a hillside, buildings, a practice field, a parking lot.

CHAPTER 15

Retreating to Utopia

A convenient if inaccurate narrative of the American counterculture would place the hippie back-to-the-land movement after those two violent *contretemps*, Altamont and Kent State. In this narrative, disillusioned youths turned from the possibility of changing the dominant culture and retreated to community-building on a smaller, more isolated scale. This is a gratifying narrative, not least because it tells the story the counterculture has told itself and the world about itself—or at least one of the stories. But a more nuanced account gives greater weight to the tension between individual hedonism and utopian community-building that I think lies at the heart of the counterculture's rise, its demise and its importance for understanding the imperial decades of American cultural history.

This is the story that repeats in the published reminiscences of the veterans of the rural communes in the oral histories preserved by the '60s Commune Project interviews, supervised by Timothy Miller and the Department of Religious Studies at the University of Kansas. It is also a theme that permeates the contemporaneous reports filling the bulk of the pages of *The Modern Utopian*, Dick Fairfield's periodical chronicling the movement in real time, beginning in 1966.[1]

The Modern Utopian was in some ways Dick Fairfield's autobiography-in-a-snapshot, its pages filled with reports of his excursions to one commune or another. Fairfield believed in the dream, but he had been in and out of communal experiences as far back as the mid-1960s, and his skepticism laced the reports.[2] By contrast, seeker Robert Houriet was more credulous. When communes failed to live up to their rhetoric or his hopes, one could feel his disappointment. Houriet toured a wide variety of communes in

1969 and 1970, publishing his report in 1971 as *Getting Back Together*. The communards, he concluded, shared a general sense of destiny:

> Somewhere in the line of history, civilization had made a wrong turn, a detour that had led into a cul-de-sac. The only way, they felt, was to drop out and go all the way back to the beginning, to the primal source of consciousness, the true basis of culture: the land. There they would again move forward, very slowly, careful not to take the wrong turn and keeping to ... the central spirit and consciousness that modern man had lost along the way. Reexamining, testing and adapting, they would evolve a micro culture.... Above all, they infused their rediscovered awareness of immanent divinity in to every action of daily life, seeking rituals and traditions with which to pass on to their children the timeless vision.[3]

Houriet points out an essential element of the movement: the draw of "the land." For the rural communes like Colorado's Drop City or New Mexico's New Buffalo and Libre or California's Morningstar or Vermont's Mullein Hill, this was a flagrant embrace of the old American promise proposed by Jefferson in his description of the perfect American republic as one consisting of "yeoman-farmers tilling the soil." And true to Jefferson's larger vision for America, the rural commune movement viewed itself as a clear and necessary antidote to the destructive corruption of American urban life.

But again, few of those who made or joined the counterculture communes drew their Jeffersonianism from his *Notes on the State of Virginia* or *Political Writings*. The generation of the counterculture imbibed the mythos of American privilege and virtue attached to free land from a cultural stew that did little to distinguish historical fact from necessary fiction, Harry Yount from Daniel Boone from Wild Bill Hickok, Lydia Child from Annie Oakley. Currier and Ives's *The American Farmer's Home* and *Westward the Course of Empire Makes Its Way* and other lithographs of the 1860s and '70s resurfaced as illustrations for elementary and middle school history textbooks, as did Edward Curtis's fictionalized images of American Indians as noble savages and proto-ecologists. Thanksgiving school plays had allowed the counterculture generation to act out the roles of America's first settlers, Myles Standish, Priscilla Mullins, and the Indian givers of turkeys and corn. Coming home from school they could turn on the TV to watch Owen Wister's foundational Western novel *The Virginian* (1902) in its 1946 Hollywood form, appearing on reruns next to the show of the same name, which ran from 1962 to 1971, sometimes as *The Men From Shiloh*. Every Sunday night,

15.1. Lisa Law, *Rainbow, New Buffalo Commune* (Photograph © Lisa Law.)

they could watch Disney's versions of the American settler, farmer, or rancher. On Wednesdays, they tuned in to *Wagon Train*.

These were the sources from which the vast majority of communards of the counterculture imagined their excurses—not the writings of Thomas Jefferson or Bronson Alcott or Ralph Borsodi.[4] And it is important to distinguish among very different types of communes, as Houriet and Fairfield both perspicuously did in their accounts: set in a wide continuum between highly focused (and often single-focused) communes—some committed to sexual liberation (Harrod East) some to spiritual or religious cultivation (the Christian communes, the Buddhist ashrams, and the like), some to economic or political goals (School of Living, Peace Action, Catholic Worker, New Left)—and the most inarticulate and temporary of assemblages. The majority of communes emerged more spontaneously than the focused "intentional communities." They embodied the multiple ideals and proposals of their members, and shifted direction as they lost some and gained others

and, as importantly, as local circumstances required that they abandon orthodoxy for pragmatism in order to survive.

Despite the heterogeneity of the movement—and commune historians
John Curl and Timothy Miller estimate that at its peak in 1970, there were
some 3,500 identifiable communes, housing as many as a million people,
double the transient population of Woodstock—there emerged out of the
'60s and early '70s a composite picture of the new communes, both within
the counterculture and in the broader culture: they were land-based, locating in rural settings or in Western landscapes with echoes of frontier heritage; they sought to find a simpler, more direct relationship to their environment in the food they ate, in their daily lives, and in the landscape; they
involved an economic collectivity, whether the Farm's requirement that all
property be shared or New Buffalo's more informal sharing of resources;
there was some ecstatic, universalist spiritual quest that motivated both individual and community.

Drop Out. This is often seen as the core impulse, linked to an apocalyptic
vision of impending social revolution. Drop City resident and commune-
movement historian John Curl describes the intertwining in this way:

> In its separatist aspect, 1960s communalism embraced the philosophy of
> "dropping out," having as little dependence as possible on the dominant
> system. In its social revolutionary aspect it saw large numbers abandoning
> the dying cities and moving out onto "liberated" land, interconnected com-
> munes around the country, where people could go who wanted to be out of
> the old culture and into something better.[5]

But from the first, the communes remained tightly dependent on the "old
culture," even when, in their more utopian moments, they sought self-
sufficiency. Their dependence began with the expectations they had and the
utopian dreams they held, which distilled mass-culture images of American agrarian settlement on one side, and American Indian primitivism and
tribalism on the other, into a contradictory romantic amalgam.[6]

This admixture of nostalgia, historical reenactment, and television
show revival played against the promise of wholesale social and cultural
reinvention that was the professed goal of the commune movement. A case
in point—and a significant one—is in the ways that men and women re-
entered highly structured roles. Fairfield, Houriet, and many others at the
time and afterward commented that women did the vast majority of the
cooking, cleaning, and child-rearing while often also taking on the responsibilities for gardening, and even water-gathering. Men left to do "men's

work" outside. Those women doing outside paid labor found themselves in the traditional woman's casual-labor pool—waitresses, housecleaners, baby-sitters. Sexual choices tended to remain tied to older roles: "the men stepped out with one of the single womyn, while their wives and partners took the kids home & waited for their return. . . . But when one of the family womyn took off for a tryst . . . there was hell to pay," as Black Bear communard Estrella Morning Star reported. In the cannibalization of Disney's Davey Crockett, the men were the hunters, the women stayed home in gingham, arm-deep in the washtub. In the back-to-the-Indians fantasy, the men were braves, free to roam the lands, the women squaws, tending the fires and the teepees or adobe pueblos. Little of the complex strangeness of *real* Native American lives came through—no born-for and born-to clans, no admixtures of patriarchal and matrilineal or matrilocal that were being lived out sometimes just a few miles from the communes of New Mexico, Colorado, and Arizona.[7]

This tension between a mass-culture-mediated romantic notion of life on the land (white settler or Indian noble savage) and the realities of food, shelter, clothing, and a semblance of law resulted in a near-endless string of disasters large and small, from sundered families and neglected children to tomato crops planted at the wrong time of year to failed negotiations with irrigation districts for necessary water, and, more tragically, to epidemics of fatal hepatitis and dysentery and the deaths of children and even infants from exposure, malnutrition, and fire. New Buffalo, located in New Mexico not far from both Pueblo and Navajo lands, attempted for its first years to emulate native foodways. "We had the Navahos' diet, but the Navahos were resigned to a forty per cent child mortality. . . . Our cultural conditioning puts more importance on the life of the individual than the tribe, and it's hard for us to accept the death of a child," reported New Buffalo resident "George" to Robert Houriet in 1969.[8]

The result of this tension between ideals and realities was often unresolvable. At the Farm, one of the central practices was natural childbirth, midwifery, and the acceptance of newborns into the group by any mother who gave birth there. One nursery went up in fire, killing two babies and grievously injuring others. Recounting the episode, resident Patricia Lapidus spoke briefly of "all the hardships and tragedy," then turned to the more upbeat "daily reminders of how great the whole experience of living in community was." On one side, one hears the almost relentless Farm insistence that all thoughts and expressions be positive and life-affirming. But there is also the sense that Lapidus had begun to shed that "cultural conditioning" New Buffalo George had pointed up.[9]

Communes that survived did so by parasitism—not just cultural, but political and economic as well. Foundational urban communal experiments like the Hog Farm and the Diggers had depended on the leavings of an excessive dominant consumer culture for their survival and their ethos. But for both, the process of scavenging, scouring restaurant garbage cans and grocery store dumpsters, and recycling reject clothing in giveaways was part of the political theater that formed their dominant rationales. Theirs was a spontaneous redistribution of wealth; their ability to make use of refuse was a pointed indictment of a culture of waste.

On the back-to-the-land communes, however, there was no particular way to enact that theatrical diatribe against consumer culture. Their existence was more-or-less predicated on a plan of eventual self-sufficiency, and so their dependency could only be seen as transitional, hypocritical, or a mark of failure. Some like New Buffalo intensely debated the question of dependency.[10] A few banned food stamps and other forms of cash dependence, but those tended to be trust-funder communes or vacation communes, hippie communal equivalents of weekender towns. Most of the working communes came to accept their parasitism uneasily as a temporary compromise on the way to their larger goals.

Contact beyond the borders of the commune was usually seen as part of a larger struggle to maintain forms of integrity and purity, set against the frank necessity for outside goods, outside help, outside cash. Interaction resulted in recontamination by the corrupt values and temptations of a bankrupt consumer capitalism. Small infractions took on looming significance, for purity is an absolute, not a relative, state. The consistent pilfering of common funds to buy the occasional candy bar or Coke produced a string of laments from the Farm to New Buffalo and Libre. Alcohol privately acquired and drunk outside of communal rituals was another symbol of the corrupting influence of the outside. Health codes and medical practices imposed on the communes were seen to threaten a lifestyle in which the body was held inviolate from technology and its artifices. Working at temporary jobs to bring in cash took workers from the labors needed to maintain the commune's independence (not least because seasonal labor tended to mirror the seasonal needs of the commune farms—planting, harvesting, and fuel gathering), and weakened the interdependent ties within the group.[11]

Even more damaging to the communes were the waves of countercultural tourism, most particularly between 1967 and 1974. Just as the Summer of Love overwhelmed the Haight-Ashbury experiments in community liberation, the arrival of thousands of transient visitors, peaking in summer and spiking during high school and college holiday periods, but threatening

15.2. Lisa Law, *Building the Communal House at New Buffalo, Arroyo Hondo, New Mexico,* August 1967. (Photograph © Lisa Law.)

even during the off-seasons, overwhelmed the fragile social, environmental, and economic ecosystems of the communes. Yet the communes also depended on the stream of outsiders to contribute ready cash, rides to and from town, news about the outer world, and converts to enliven the social, sexual, and community life.[12]

New Buffalo was in many ways typical. Communard Arthur Kopecky's journal entries describe the transition from a certain innocence to an increasingly divisive tension between members advocating "open" and "closed" communal life. Kopecky recounted a meeting early in the commune's history at which these issues were discussed: complete openness was philosophically ideal, but repeated encounters with opportunists, freeloaders, transient criminals and generally sick tickets already made this seem untenable. A closed-door policy allowed the community to develop organically from within and resolve tensions, yet enforcing such a policy involved forms of coercion and exclusion—fences, gates, warning signs, enforcers—that violated the basic tenets of New Buffalo. But to develop regulations allowing some but not others required all the trappings of a closed commune, plus a settled set of regulations that would have to be agreed to and then enforced. In the end, the meeting tailed off without consensus, and the commune continued to be buried in visitors.

Drop City had early embraced the open communal experience: "Drop City is not a fellowship of just our little group," founder "Curly" (Gene Bernofsky) said at one Droppers meeting. "Nobody's excluded from Drop City. We're just stand-ins for the whole humanship."[13] But theirs went beyond simply providing food, dope, and experience for visitors. Early Dropper "Rabbit" (Peter Rabbit) sought to make Drop City a byword and a destination. Under Rabbit's strength of conviction, Drop City published a newsletter, courted media attention and visits and, in 1966, held a three-plus-day Joy Festival, which simultaneously made the site a counterculture destination and overwhelmed many of the founders and early residents, who left to return to towns and cities or to establish or join other communes, notably, Libre. Within a few years, Drop City was dead.[14]

Drop City's Joy Festival was an early example of the destructive tensions between public celebration and private communitarianism. Rabbit's active courting of media attention, however, reflected a different sort of parasitism, that of audience and actor, or congregation and preacher. Communes that encouraged mass media attention, as had Drop City and others that appeared in *Time*, *Life*, and other mainstream media, did so at least in part to propagate their ideals and beliefs. But in the process, they—and the movement as a whole—began to develop a sense of themselves as celebrities, an awareness of their role as *representations*.

The San Francisco Mime Troupe and its offshoot the Diggers conceived of hippie confrontations as street theater, in keeping with their theatrical roots. Within the communes, however, any sense of playacting was exactly at odds with the professed goal of authenticity, directness, and actualization. They sought to make environments in which they were *not* oddities, rather than embracing the possibilities of their freakishness to shock and enliven the dominant culture.

And yet they could not, in the end, drop out. They were, finally, in a constant state of dialectical dependence on the dominant culture, on the outside world, not just for medicine, spare tractor parts, and cash, but for visitors to contribute to the till and acolytes to replace the disenchanted.

Some communes were absorbed by their surroundings. Some survived by becoming not hippie communes but farms and farm communities, adapting their practices to the realities of soil, climate, and market. And some reinvented themselves as tourist destinations, accepting the role and honing it so that rather than ending up spiritually, socially, and economically bankrupted by the washes of transients at their doors, they controlled the ebb and flow, directing it to the needs and goals of the commune. The communes around Taos gradually became a part of the picturesque tourist economy; visitors could see cowboys, Indians, and hippie communes all in one trip and could purchase memorabilia and souvenirs from all three, as well.

One of the most controversial of the proselytizing, self-dramatizing communes was the Farm, an evolving collective that began in San Francisco as a sort of seminar led by hippie-philosopher Stephen Gaskin. It eventually shifted to a traveling show preaching Gaskin's brand of spiritual communalism, and then settled on a large, stable tract of land in Tennessee, where, in much-modified form, it still remains.[15]

From the first, evangelizing was central to that commune's self-definition. The Farm's proselytizing was a complex mix of publicity and action. It is sometimes difficult to read Farm documents, as the stricture to remain always positive and uplifting lends a retrospective air of a public relations campaign to the material. But this is also an artifact of the ways that communards at the Farm, like those at Joy Festival-era Drop City and the core citizens of Esalen Institute in the years immediately after the 1969 post-Woodstock Big Sur Festival, embraced a notion of themselves as model citizens of the counterculture.

In this regard, the Farm shared much with Levittown, despite the many surface differences. Like Levittown, it was a community that found its communitarianism watched by the mass media and, through that lens, the nation and the world—and found itself perhaps a bit begrudgingly accepting its designation as a site of American reinvention. Like Levittown, it had its spokesman—huckster, salesman, visionary—to shape the image of the community and prescribe to residents their ideal behavior. Both communities embraced the notion of an evolving communitarianism that could operate in the face of the strain of American individualism, could make communitarianism seem like an evolution from individualism. And like Levittown, the Farm and many of the other public communes borrowed their self-image from the popular culture of American history, from the living dioramas of Colonial Williamsburg and the promise of continual American reinvention by heroic pioneers—Frederick Jackson Turner diluted by *Boys' Life* magazine and the juvenile histories on the shelves of the school library. Levittowners and Farmers alike embraced their designation as "pioneers."[16]

When the Farm finally failed as a self-sufficient enterprise, it lay moribund for a time and then reinvented itself as a counterculture tourist destination. In this regard, it was paralleling the Esalen Institute, which had with great success begun to market itself as a place for weekend spiritual, psychological, and social retreats for the weary mental worker of late-modern America. Once the locale for a fermenting mixture of psychological and spiritual practices, Esalen had evolved into a destination for wealthy seekers and would-be weekend hedonists who could receive a massage, take a Yoga workshop, experience an encounter session, and socialize in a hot tub for a hefty fee.

By the 1990s, the Farm was similarly proffering a wide range of retreats and workshops, from Mushroom People (organic mushroom farming) to Sustainable Life Retreats, and a wide array of products, including "Hippie Philosophy" wear (one shirt announces "The Hippies Were Right!") and Farm baseball caps and coffee mugs. The process of encouraging transients to embrace the communal philosophy and join the group, haphazard at other communes, has, in the twenty-first century, been institutionalized: twice a year, the Farm holds "Farm Experience Weekends" for prospective members.

The Farm's reincarnation refracts the prevailing tensions of the counterculture: between place and movement and between authenticity and ironic self-consciousness, shading at times to self-dramatization. These tensions played themselves out across a vast national stage, and in densely local places and moments: the Haight, Chicago '68, Woodstock, Altamont, Kent State, the rural communes. But while the counterculture may have presented itself as oppositional, an indictment of the dominant American culture of the postwar years, it carried most of the principal themes of that time within its own ideals and ideologies. And how could it not have done so? For its instigators and citizens were born, raised, and came into youthful maturity under the clouds of postwar America: the fear of nuclear annihilation, the sense of human destructibility on a global scale, the corresponding sense of the frailty of the individual, even as the mythos of the moment trumpeted American individualism as a vital and continuing force in the world.

And the citizens of the counterculture were children of the new mass media, with its pervasiveness, its ingratiating presence and its mastery of the art of manipulating common myths to affect new ends, political, social, economic, and cultural. Their parents had emerged from World War II as citizen-actors on a world stage, their everyday lives held up as models for the modern global future, even their kitchens celebrated by politicians as symbolic embodiments of an already achieved utopia. A bit dazzled, intimidated, and coerced by the attention, nevertheless they basked in it, as well. They came to believe in the significance of their roles—housewife, white-collar worker, PTA president, local politician, parent. And the children too grew up half-consciously aware of themselves as enacting their own lives on a stage. Coming of age, they set out to act a new play in the American drama and if, like their parents, their self-dramatizations, so often scripted by others than themselves, turned out to be less brilliant than they had hoped, they could still congratulate themselves in having been a part of a vast American reinvention.

*　*　*

The counterculture sought not just its own redemption but the redemption of the nation. To call that movement anti-American, a rejection of American values—indeed, to call it a "counter" culture at odds with the dominant American cultural ethos—is to miss the fundamental conservatism that lurked beneath its flamboyance and noise. The counterculture opposed not America but a particular brief era in American cultural transformation—the very period in which we have been immersed, from the atomic holocausts at Hiroshima and Nagasaki through the emergence of a new form of consumption economy with its promises of abundance and its undercurrent of fear, located in new spaces of plenty, both physical and imaginative: Levittown and *Lucy*, Macy's and *Life*, the Brill Building and "Up on the Roof."

In rejecting the dominant thrust of more than twenty years of American life, the counterculture's prime movers sought to redeem the nation and the culture by returning to its longest-held myths, narratives, and traditions: religious and spiritual, social, political, and cultural. Dressing often in the emblematic costumes of founding fathers as rendered in popular culture, public education, and the other forms of democratic cultural transmissions—from Benjamin Franklin's "granny glasses" to Daniel Boone's buckskins and Louisa May Alcott's gingham dresses—the counterculture's people evoked and reinterpreted the past in the present, cutting the cord of the present from the immediate past and reconnecting it to what they believed was a more continuous strand in which individuality and commonality found spontaneous convergence, in which radical democracy reinvented community mission, in which momentary life was bound to a higher purpose.

For critics of the movement, the counterculture's failing lay in its moral laxity, its flaccid embrace of pleasure over a sterner and more consistent dogma. But the hedonism of the counterculture was not, in its own eyes, a failure of will or of morality. It was instead an outgrowth of a telling admixture of religious ecstasy not seen since the tumultuous religious revivals of the "burned-over districts" of the nineteenth-century frontier, fermenting in contact with a form of nature-worship that had its roots in the transcendentalism of Thoreau and Emerson, catalyzed by an ebullient sensual celebration of self and identity that flowed from Walt Whitman.

This hedonism was also, more obliquely, the inheritance by one generation of the promises of the last. The generation born between the end of World War II and the Cuban missile crisis grew up surrounded by the promises of pleasure—everything from Lucky Strikes to Thunderbirds, Magnavox color televisions to Canadian Club whisky—blaring on the TV, filling the pages of magazines and newspapers, announced every few minutes on the radio. Those of that generation who founded or flirted with the counterculture rejected much of the surface material consumerism immersing them, substituting Acapulco Gold for Old Gold, New Buffalo for Levittown, but they embraced the pursuit of happiness as an inalienable American right. Like their parents, they swam in a warm sea of promises, but the deeper currents were cold: atomic annihilation, implacable enemies around the globe, flashpoints of chaos and violence around the corner, across the world, and on the living room televisions at 6 p.m. each weekday.

The counterculture Americans refused (for a time) the devil's bargain of prosperity purchased with fear. Their parents' generation, and their grandparents,' might rightfully accuse them of taking something for nothing. But this generation promised it would not devote itself to a mindless pursuit of pleasure. Its people chose a mindful pursuit of happiness, one that carried great costs: alienation from family, tradition and place; instability and insecurity in their most intimate relations; no clear sense of assurance that their next day would be anything like this one, or any one before it; the hard work, often marked by failure, of learning everything all over again, from scratch—how to till, plant, water, weed, and harvest a field, how to influence an election or a war, how to overhaul a carburetor or dig an outhouse, how to birth a baby and how best to raise that baby, how to talk down a psychotic roommate or find the money for the next day or the next meal.

More significant than the material pleasure promised by the commodity culture they grew up in was the search for spiritual and emotional emergence, and in this faith in transformation, the counterculture again laid claim to what it believed was a fundamental American trait. Its narrative was based on the contradictory myths of transcendence and authenticity that reached back to the earliest days of white settlement, and—in the communards' understanding, based in stereotype and mythos—of the Indians who had settled many centuries before the Pilgrims. For them, both these impulses were predicated on a return to the American land and its promise of rejuvenation and redemption.

The American story of personal and national salvation emerging from embrace of—and by—a benevolent Nature, is not simply the myth of the privileged, of Jefferson and Madison, of Frederick Edwin Church, John Gast, and Horace Greeley. Free land, freedom, and redemption interwove for slaves as well, emerging in the music of the spiritual but also in the post-emancipation calls for landed reparations. The lapsarian narratives of Native America, from Chief Joseph and Sitting Bull to the AIM manifestos of the 1960s laid claim, as well, to the myth of a redemptive American landscape. When the counterculture embraced these traditions, seeking (haphazardly, contradictorily) to draw them into one metanarrative, it was engaging in a long-standing stratagem of American rebels who presented themselves as revivalists of a creed in which America's particular blessing, and its particular mission, were to be found in its landscape.

The decade and a half that marked the ascendance, resonance, and decline of the counterculture in American cultural life also marked a dynamic reinvigoration of American myths and symbols, most notably those that revolved around the physical geography of the nation. For that, we have the counterculture to thank. The postwar promises of sociable suburban greenswards, automobile vacations to spectacular scenery, and nostalgic returns via television to older rural America had grown flat, tired, too often disappointing in their actuality. Indeed, it was the very lack of connection, tactility, authenticity, that had come to characterize an American landscape turned to fodder for propaganda, advertising and swindle. While on television *Green Acres* weekly declared the rural life a sham and a scam, counterculture communes were digging root cellars, swapping honey for ham, milking, weeding, harvesting.* While American vacationers were pulling off the road at photo opportunities marked by Kodak symbols on their road maps and confronting plaques showing them where to stand and what picture they'd get, counterculturists were waking to the sun, emerging from adobe structures they'd built themselves, and saying prayers of greeting to the vast sweeps ending in majestic ranges capped with snow. And when they left, they carried with them that awakened sense of having lived in the midst of sacrality. Long after the communes had been abandoned or turned to tourist traps, the reinvigoration of America's sense of miraculous occupation of a divinely granted place of beauty and promise remained.

The counterculture was awash in contradictions. Profoundly antiurban, it found its most potent and significant experiences played out in city spaces

* *Green Acres* ran almost precisely coterminous with the counterculture, debuting in 1965 and going off the air in 1971.

like San Francisco's Haight or New York's East Village, or in rural spaces rendered urban by the very influx of counterculture seekers—Woodstock, most famously, but also Altamont, and, paradoxically, many of the back-to-the-land rural communes that found themselves overwhelmed by visiting seekers. Trying to liberate themselves from the coercive powers of government and corporation alike, the counterculture's members found it necessary even in the most isolated and independent of communal environments to seek out and depend on the largesse of state and corporation: food stamps, surplus food, short-term employment (and the benefits of health care and unemployment insurance that came with it) and the beneficence of patrons. Fabled as a generation rejecting the materialism of its predecessor, the counterculture built many of its institutions on the generosity of parents' allowances and dynastic inheritances, or the institutional settings— universities most of all—paid for by parents and grandparents. Committed to a more fluid, generous, and inventive social and personal identity, it often mirrored the old tyrannies—especially when it came to the roles of women and men.

Yet what great American movement has made its mark without discovering its fabric to be woven of mutually exclusive strands, of hypocrisies and self-deceptions? Behind the surface contractions of talk and action lay a remarkably consistent foundation of myths and symbols that undergirded one of the most significant evangelical cultural revivals in American history. That this revival played out across a resonant cultural geography, that it sought, at its core, to reconnect American political, social, and cultural life to the great myths of the American land, suggests both how potent that tradition was, how influential even on those born and raised far from its locales, and how powerful a hold this mythos had on a nation long extricating itself from its older identity as open land and promised land.

The genius—or the luck—of the counterculture lay in part in locating its central identifying moments in sites that could be imaginatively transformed, with more or less effort, into modern instantiations of resonant historic spaces. The Summer of Love, and the spring that preceded it, took place at the juncture where an older, more gracious picturesque urbanism abutted a celebrated urban park that had been constructed to evoke the redemptive properties of American nature. When the battles of Chicago '68 were enacted the next summer, they too ranged across culturally laden artifices: from urban-industrial grid to manufactured picturesque and back again, evading and confronting forces of authority and alternately charming and repelling a wider audience watching on television or reading the daily newspaper dispatches. The countervalences of Woodstock and Altamont in

1969 both involved the "liberating" of unlikely sites. In both cases, though with opposite results, the desire to enact liberty—to free land; to offer the sustenance of food, shelter, clothing, and music for free; to behave with individual freedom without infringing on a common good—formed the core mission. A year later, the confusion of ownership that underlay the Kent State massacre of 1970 reflected much deeper deceptions on both sides as to the ease with which a site could be controlled and transformed.

After the violent dystopian outcomes at Altamont and Kent State, the promise of a universal transformation of the American experiment, a final chapter in "liberation" of the American landscape reemerged, in Vermont, California, Colorado, Massachusetts, Tennessee, Missouri, New Mexico, and, to a lesser extent, other states and regions of the country. The imperative: "drop out," which had for the most part been interpreted as a strategy of guerilla living *within* the dominant culture and its environments, came to have a more imperious cast, as a call to resuscitate an older tradition of Americans "lighting out for the territories" where, as Huck Finn imagined, the restrictions of a stultifying "civilization" lost their sway and the possibility of reinvention—personal, tribal, even national and transnational— seemed close at hand. What began as spontaneous experiments in anarcho- syndicalism, survived as examples of a long tradition of American utopias and intentional communities, from the Puritans through Brook Farm and into the communist experiments of the '30s. Wiping clear the slate of history, the communes failed; those that succeeded found themselves indebted to tradition and committed to continuation of history and not its rejection.

The landscapes of the counterculture were in many ways landscapes of reversal, denial and negation. Each of the sites I've named existed in more or less direct opposition to three powerfully evocative American spaces. One was the orderly grid of middle-class suburban life as it had been proffered and played out (more or less) after the end of the Second World War; this was the promised land into which most of the counterculture's population were born and raised, and to which they sought to escape.

Beneath and behind that land, lay the dystopic mental landscapes of atomic holocaust and global annihilation into which these children of the Cold War were inculcated, by mass media, by schooling, by government fiat and propaganda, by family. The signing of comprehensive test ban treaties and the ratcheting down of atomic fear in the '60s may have liberated the Cold War generation from their indenture to this geography of dread, but it did not disappear from their consciousness or their collective unconscious. Their mental maps of *away* still depended on that which they left. Traveling along the National Defense Superhighways westward toward the Haight, they crossed the western deserts where those atomic tests had taken place. On stage at Woodstock, after the Jefferson Airplane performed "Volunteers" (*one generation got old; one generation got soul; this generation got no destination to hold*), Crosby, Stills, Nash & Young recast the song they'd cowritten with Jefferson Airplane, "Wooden Ships," a parable about the possibility that the innocents of the counterculture might survive after global atomic warfare. A similar visionary utopianism marked their anthemic version of Joni Mitchell's "Woodstock."

For the Woodstock generation, the "bomber jet planes" in Mitchell's song weren't just the ones that carried nuclear weapons in airborne formation; they were also the massive bombers making their incursions into North Vietnam, Laos, and Cambodia, bombers that could at any time change their payloads from conventional to nuclear weapons. Like the other two spaces against which the counterculture defined its own mythic geography (test site and suburban cul-de-sac), Vietnam was a landscape both physical and imaginative, located at a great distance and also terrifyingly close at hand. For the young men born into the postwar era, Vietnam was a destination it was necessary to consider—a war zone voluntarily entered, passively encountered, resisted or denied, or, for the very lucky, a fate magically diverted, through deferment or the random chance of a high draft lottery number. For young women, Vietnam was a more indirect threat—to those they loved but also to their own agency and place within the dominant culture that regarded them, simultaneously, as special and as inferior.

Those abstractions gained concreteness through the medium of television, and most particularly through nightly news, which by the later '60s was running regular reports on the war, complete with images of dead and injured soldiers. This coverage grew more specific, less tied to the government messages of progress and impending victory after the Tet Offensive of 1968, when journalists stationed in Vietnam were finally successful in persuading network executives that the picture being presented on the screen did not correspond to conditions on the ground.

Within the suburban homes from which the counterculture's converts most often came, then, all three of these spaces intermingled in complex combinations of physical, imaginative, and symbolic form. A Levittown house had no basement fallout shelter as it had no basement; residents built theirs into the backyards or under additions that had dug-out basements, often for precisely this purpose. With their heritage of do-it-yourself creativity and their experience of common-value collectivity, Levittowners were excellent candidates for the many government publications and magazine articles detailing the relative ease and inexpensiveness of a home-built fallout shelter. Other postwar dwellings, those with concrete basement walls and floors, were demarcated as ideal sites for shelter kits and projects using the lumberyard lists found in published manuals. Children of the Cold War era grew up with that additional room in, or conspicuously *not in*, their homes. Either way, it was a repository of terror—dark, claustrophobic, a cinderblock coffin for themselves and their families.

With this countertext to the narratives of economic mobility and social stability, the generation that came of age between 1965 and 1973 had a powerful incentive to reverse the course promised to them. Between the atomic age and the Vietnam War there was an equivalently complex shading among fact, policy, belief, myth, and nightmare. The very public discussions concerning the use of atomic weapons in the Korean War remained firmly in the memories of older Americans. Throughout the mid-1960s, recurrent rumors that the Johnson and then the Nixon administrations were considering atomic escalation swept the country—and, as it turned out, with grounds.[17] But the landscape of Vietnam was more than a continuation of the Korean conflict, an exotic proxy war with Asian aliens, more than a potential site for the atomic trigger finger. It was in itself an exotic place of otherness, a locale for adventure, and the subject of stylized scripts of reassurance and triumphalism that played on television nightly news from the early '60s until the Tet Offensive. While common knowledge tends to attribute antiwar sentiment to television coverage, the coverage itself was for the most part anything but critical of the victory narratives coming out of the Pentagon and the Johnson and Nixon administrations. Blood, injuries, and bodies were rarely shown; most of the actual television footage—days old, as it was film-based and had to be processed in the States—focused on human-interest stories, while the networks continued to depend on material supplied them by government agencies for the larger reporting on progress of the war, battles, and tactics.[18]

That changed during and after the Tet Offensive, notably with graphic footage of a string of controversial moments, including the assassination of an alleged enemy informer by a South Vietnam Army officer and, in 1969, the public release of information about the brutal My Lai Massacre of civilians, mostly women, children, and old people, by U.S. forces.

The shift in focus of the television nightly scripts lagged behind a shift in sentiment that largely split along generational lines. While older Americans tended to accept at face value the reports of nightly news shows, the generation raised on television, the members of the so-called McLuhan Generation were already alert to the stylized and repetitive scripts of the war reports. They saw these, that is, *as scripts*, rather than as statements of truth or fact or even reasoned analysis. For that generation, military propaganda, government advocacy, and network television were elements of an integrated media-culture, and many of that generation were more than skeptical of the declarations that came from it.

Television was a form of artifice for these Americans, and it was not a form in which they could participate. They were too young, too far from the seats of power, too distant from the ideological convictions that afforded access to the systems of communication and the centralized locales where the dominant cultures truths were assembled and propounded.

America's television war, then, came to stand for the loss of democratic and personal agency in the new America; and for the inauthenticity of what was given in its stead. A generation whose smartest and most literate representatives had read George Orwell's 1984 in honors and college-prep high school English classes, understanding it not as a veiled allegory of anti-Communism but as a description of the artifice and duplicity of American culture, found themselves increasingly in search of that which they saw denied them in this artificial America. Believing themselves trapped in a prison of falsehoods (*Plastic America*, musician-visionary Frank Zappa called it), they embarked on a quest for truths.

As the most vocal and articulate spokespeople for the exodus described it, this was an eminently American emigration. Having been raised on the myths of American movement, of westering to freedom and cultural re-invention, from the Pilgrim narratives repeated each school year as Thanksgiving approached, to the tales of Daniel Boone and the warrior explorers of Manifest Destiny; having marched as Boy Scouts and Girl Scouts in Fourth of July parades in which the myth of Americans liberating a continent from the tyrannical hand of an effete, exhausted Europe played out in floats and marching songs and speeches; having listened to the stories of their parents and grandparents of a national and generational drama of rural life, hardship, bravery, and triumph closed to them; having grown up caught between the assurances of their privilege, even invincibility, and the experiences of global eradication and personal powerlessness, they sought to make a new narrative for themselves out of the same raw material and, in the process, to reinvent their nation and culture, returning it to its core myths and reinvigorating its fundamental symbols and narratives.

I have said that the counterculture came to define itself by negation, denial, and reversal, even as it sought, with often messianic, evangelical overtones to redeem the nation and the dominant culture. The counterculture sought to *negate* a corrupted America, choosing life over death, the communal and the tribal over alienated individualism or isolated huddling nuclear families, the spontaneous over the scripted.

The counterculture was a culture of *denial*, meant in two ways: as a culture based on refusal and rejection of dominant values, but also as a culture of denial in the psychoanalytic sense. For even as it sought to refuse the consumption materialism in which it had been immersed, it depended on that material wealth for its continued survival. More broadly, the counterculture (with a few notable exceptions, Dylan being one, Zappa another) sought to deny its deep dependence on the dominant culture as a source of its own ideals, and also as a term against which to define itself. Acid guru Timothy Leary's Trinitarian imperatives — "turn on, tune in, drop out" — proposed a sequence of personal and tribal liberation: to drop out required both forms of denial; absolute refusal of dominant values, but also a denial of the dialectical interdependence of the act of "countering" at the core of the counterculture.

This is the aspect of the counterculture that has lent itself to the easiest critiques, both during the era of its vibrancy and in the historical debates after the it mutated and disintegrated. But there remains a final and more benign, redemptive anticulture in the counterculture: *reversal*. The counterculture's utopian, evangelical goals were located in a desire to reverse what seemed the steep decline of American virtues, the loss of American innocence and American exceptionalism, and the squandering of a promise. Just as they had studied Orwell, analyzed Twain, and recited Walt Whitman, many of the counterculture's most articulate voices had read Winthrop's "Arbella Sermon," or at least the excerpts so often repeated by triumphalist politicians and the writers of their speeches. "We are as a city upon a hill," Winthrop had declared, and that was the line most commonly cribbed in the arguments for American blessing. But they had read further: "The eyes of all people are upon us. So that if we shall deal falsely with our God in this work we have undertaken . . . we shall be made a story and a by-word throughout the world . . . til we be consumed out of the good land whither we are a-going."[19] Born into the atomic age, with its terrors and its moral burdens, raised on the desolate plains and the walls and watchtowers that came with those burdens, they knew themselves to be the first American generation born "outside the Gates of Eden," as their poet laureate decried to them, and now they sought to redeem and, redeeming, return.

Imbedded in the counterculture's core was this redemptive evangelicalism. The often wrenching debates, the dramatic conflicts and differences within the counterculture, concerned the means by which this reversal was to be effectuated. And each of the positions in that debate had its precedents in American mythologies: symbols to be reapplied, narratives to be recast. For those who sought political change and embraced confrontation and revolution as the means, the long tradition of American rebellion provided a rich source of precedents, including the Boston Tea Party and the Whiskey Rebellion, and more recently the civil rights movement. For those who sought to transform through acts of irony and satire—Yippies and freaks, the Bread and Puppets Theater, the Diggers, the teach-ins and satiric ceremonies of the antiwar movement, for example—there was a long history of pamphleteering and ceremonial protest reaching back to Tom Paine (whom Dylan mentioned, obliquely, in "John Wesley Harding"). For those who sought to separate themselves entirely, forming alternative communities and utopian experiments, there was a similar history on which to draw.[20]

But the predominant population of the counterculture did not live in such sharply demarcated discourses of reversal. Theirs was a "soft" ideology of reversal, played out in lives as inconsistent, as personal, as hesitant and interrupted as the ones their parents had lived during the Cold War years. But the counterculturists also shared a core set of goals: to reverse the atomic age's manifest sense of normalcy overlaid on unconfronted terror, to reverse the ecological ravages of industrial-technological progress (they had read, or heard about, Rachel Carson's *Silent Spring*, if only echoed in Joni Mitchell's "Big Yellow Taxi"), to undo the dominate-and-destroy ethos of the American philosophy of nature, and to reverse the course of Vietnam and foreign policy and the expansionist ethos that underlay it.

But theirs was also a basic evangelicalism. In contrast to the lives of material prosperity and personal alienation that they believed were the inheritance of their parents' generation, they sought immersion, tactility, sensuality. In so doing, they sought to place their bodies and what their bodies demanded, in proximity to that which was not human—to "nature," but more pointedly, to the physical, the local. They sought to reclaim the American sense of place—of knowing, and being known by, *where they were*. If America had dissipated into a meta-place, they would reverse that course, as individuals, as spontaneous "tribes," and, eventually, as a culture.

In this quest, the counterculture was impeded by the very phenomenon it sought to reverse. For the members of this generation had little contact with the long tradition of American physicality. Their grandparents might have dug the mines or scrabbled in the drought-ridden earth of the Great Depression or escaped the ghettoes and *shtetls* of Europe, but that was a past negated by the transformative prosperity, growth, and geographical and economic reorganization of the postwar American into which they had been born. And so they would have to rediscover the most basic truths of a life lived in the midst of the land.

To say that they were doomed to fail without these lessons, this body of knowledge, is a cliché, a truism. I will propose something different: that their larger, more inarticulate goal was not doomed precisely because it was less determined, less absolute. To think of the counterculture as a revolutionary force in American cultural geography is not simply to locate their battles in symbolic sites—the Haight, Woodstock, Kent State, Drop City, New Buffalo, and the like. It is also to see this chapter in American history as a continuation of a narrative of reinvention that spanned the entire history of America.

The counterculture's confusing imperative was to continue that process while simultaneously testing its hypotheses in the grounded physical geographies of the nation. In abstract terms, the counterculture sought to reverse the gridding of America—not just the physical grids that had enabled its rapid development and its efficient exploitation of land and people, but the interior grids of bureaucratic rationality, corporate structure, economic and social discrimination—and in so doing, enable a culture of fluidity, dynamism, and adaptation.

What does failure mean in this context? For much of the counterculture, it meant *selling out*: the phrase is telling. When you sell, you lose one thing but gain some usable currency in return, currency that can be used in a wider arena. But to sell *out* carried the connotations of a greater loss—loss of community, loss of purpose, loss of ideals—and of removal: leaving the tribe. As the communes that survived suggested, selling out could mean selling oneself as a caricature, an entertainment, a commodity.

But in the larger sense, failure would, I think, mean not to have changed America and the world in that grandiose way that the counterculture sought to do so. But the counterculture *did* contribute to a transformation of America, even as it failed to convert all American souls to its gentle hedonism. We live today in a culture hypersensitized to global climate and ecological frailties; the air we breathe and the water we drink—if we are in the first world, the world the counterculture sought to redeem—is clean and safe. We debate the rights of the old and the infants and even the unborn, sensitized to issues of life, of humanity, of dignity and rights, with passion and sometimes with sophistication. These are not small inheritances, and they are the legacies of the counterculture.

Finally, though, the counterculture's goals of transcendence and authenticity, of sky and earth, of nomadicism and settlement did not take the form prophesized by their leaders, poets and mythmakers. Instead, a very different form of transcendence emerged: transcendence of place, of mate-riality, of narrative, but not on a spiritual plane or in a religious context. It was the very technological revolution the vast majority of the countercul-ture had rejected, that brought a further revolution in American cultural landscapes—neither physical nor spiritual, neither nomadic nor rooted, neither authentic nor imaginative, an alternative culture both seductively illusionistic and illusory, capable of manufacturing utopia and dystopia with equal conviction.

CHAPTER 16

Pong *versus* Computer Space, 1972

It was, first of all, a completely artificial object, as far from nature as one could imagine. Its face in prototype was a rather horrifying red that in production shifted to a bilious yellow with a hint of green. Body and sides: vinylized fake wood with a greasy sheen and feel to match. A TV set in a particle-board box, mounted at an angle to guarantee neck and back pain if you played it more than a few times, it was the first readily available computerized arcade video game: *Pong*.[1]

At idle, it was set to play itself—you could watch the dot languidly move from side to side, bouncing off the flat lines that were meant to be Ping-Pong paddles. And you could hear the odd electronic *doink* as the ball—if that's what you chose to call it—struck. There was only the one sound, set in three variations: dull, more dull, and punitive.

But it was seductive. Playing *Pong* was a novel experience. We should remember: it was almost entirely without precedent.* Its yellow console box mimicked the pinball games that surrounded it—games from Midway and Bally—games you played alone or alternated with others, games in which an actual ball moved and the sound of the flipper whacking that chrome

---

* As historians of the video game know all too well, *Pong* codeveloper Nolan Bushnell had actually seen a version of computerized tennis in a demo of Magnavox's Odyssey home-television game system, but the Odyssey was only released a month or so before *Pong* entered the bar scene, and its popularity was modest, to say the least. In addition, while the TV ads mentioned "tennis" as one of the simulated games, hockey was the featured sport, and Odyssey's tennis appeared only to offer a dull and repetitive straight-shot algorithm.

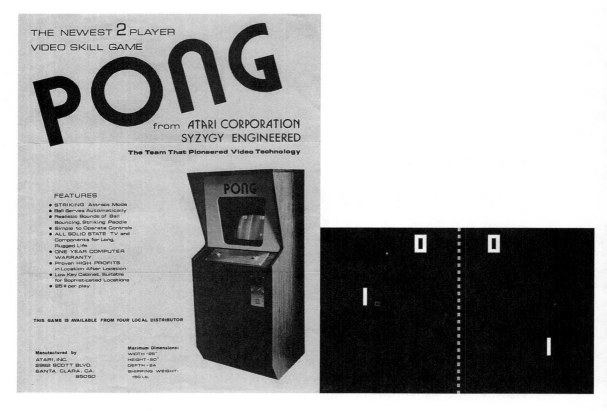

16.1. Original *Pong* arcade ad with a screenshot from a later iteration.

ball was reinforced by the ring of actual bells inside the machine. Putting muscle into those games had real effects—good players could persuade the ball to do feats of motion, but you risked the dreaded "tilt" that canceled you out if you went too far.

Pong was a Trojan horse among the pinball games. Its designers took the television screen and stripped it of its poverty-stricken attempts at illusion and verisimilitude. *Pong* used a black-and-white set. There was no depth to the scene you looked at. It wasn't even an approximation of an aerial view of a Ping-Pong table—it was flat and square, and the "net" was a faint strip of hyphens running bottom-to-top. Even the "ball" wasn't round—it was a fat pixel.

Yet *Pong*'s game play was deceptively deep. Al Alcorn, the principal developer under Bushnell, broke the flat lines of the "paddles" into eight hidden segments; each one returned the "ball" at a different angle. And he set the game so that, as long as no one missed, the speed of the ball's movement steadily increased.

The first *Pong* game appeared in Sunnyvale, California, in Andy Capp's Tavern, a bar frequented by a wide range of customers, from carpenters and truck drivers to defense engineers, computer people, and Stanford grad students. It was an instant hit.

Today, watching a video reproduction of seven and a half minutes of play is excruciating.[2] It is so slow, and the skill level required so rudimentary compared with what would come just three or four years later, that it seems unimaginable it would captivate millions and create an entire entertainment industry.

It had two imperatives silk-screened onto the metal play-face by the manufacturer: "Deposit Quarter" and "Avoid Missing Ball for High Score." The first instruction was clear enough. The second was oddly oblique, set in the cowardly negative. Your reward came not from hitting, but from avoiding the miss. To an America for which the word "avoid" had most commonly appended to "the draft," it might have seemed an odd choice of syntax.

Pong was a Vietnam-withdrawal diversion in other ways. Though the vast majority of its electronic components were descended from Cold War military weapons development, Space Race technologies, and Vietnam War machines, the game didn't reward killing or destroying anything. Its entire purpose was to skin you of your quarters. You could win, but only against your barroom buddy or your date. There wasn't any way to judge your abilities against the other millions playing it in bars across America. And it hid its difficulty beneath an inoffensive and reassuring slackness of rhythm. Until you put your quarter in, it was always a little behind the beat—it made you impatient. Even drunk, you were sure to find it too languid.

Here was a radically different form of play, based on a different conception of the relation of player to game. Whereas in the pinball game physical nuance and instinct made the master, in *Pong* the task was to reprogram mind and body to the mathematical algorithms that lay hidden beneath the dynamics of play. Great pinball players brought the console into their own physical space; *Pong* players sought to make themselves into robotic approximations of the algorithms of the game. *Here* the game seemed a better fit to the Cold War technoculture and its cousin, the corporate cubicle world.[3]

Yet there was also an odd physical sociability about *Pong* that wasn't shared by the pinball games nearby. Two people played *Pong* at once; to do this meant you stood shoulder to shoulder, and unless you were hyperconscious of your physical self, you were bound to rub, touch, bounce against your opponent. Indeed, to play well, you *had* to forget your physical self. The result was paradoxical; seeking prowess by dephysicalizing the bodily self, disembodying into algorithm, you were simultaneously made acutely physical, engaged in a contact sport that was closer to sex than to tag football. Yet to win meant to isolate yourself from the quotidian and the pleasurable.

So too with the other senses: the sound of *Pong*, its particular electronic *doink*, sped up in a virtuosic game to rapid-fire repetitions, had within it the underlying computer clock-tick that dictated the timing necessary to make the next shot and the next. In some ways, its sonic oddity and its visual screen called up the imagery of atomic apocalypse: radar screens, nuclear sub sonar pings, the hush of the nuclear war room. But *Pong* was played in a bar. There were so many other sounds impinging: the chink of glasses, the laughter of men and women, the blare of a TV, music from the jukebox or from the band in the room through the doorway behind you, even your own grunts and pants as you inhaled and exhaled around the implacable unheard tick of the computer clock that ruled all play. All those were distractions.

Pong proposed a new, ideal, posthuman identity, striving for a Zen-like absorption into a technology so rigid and determined that even the slightest form of human thought, feeling, or gesture marked failure. It was the direct opposite of both sides of the counterculture quest: it offered physicality purged of locality and spontaneity; it promised transcendence through denial of the authentic and embrace of the technocratic. There was nothing of the utopian about it. There was no promise of liberation; it allowed you to choose your prison.

Noland Bushnell and Al Alcorn chose Andy Capp's Tavern to try out their new game in part because it was on their pinball machine franchise route. It was easy to shoehorn it in, and the owner was an accommodating man. But there was another reason. Capp's Tavern was one of the few sites where one might find Bushnell's previous attempt at marrying barroom entertainment with computer logic: *Computer Space*.

Today, most critics consider *Computer Space* to be the very first commercial video game, and most would agree that it was a far better game than *Pong*—and whereas *Pong* was an evolutionary dead-end, *Computer Space* rapidly gave rise to the most popular form of arcade game play and spawned an increasingly complex and engaging string of space shoot-em-ups.

More than that, *Computer Space* emerged from the technocratic utopianism that had served as the counterfoil to the counterculture: men on the moon, space stations, space colonies, galactic imperialism. And it fed the paranoia of the time: even *out there* sinister civilizations sought to destroy us.

All that, and it was fun to play. *Computer Space* had the force of Nutting Associates behind it; as a consequence, it appeared in a beguiling guise: a

16.2. Industry trade ad for *Computer Space*. (Courtesy of The Strong, Rochester, New York.)

molded, streamlined case that was a cross between a custom Chevy and a stylized futuristic spaceship. Action was complex; one discovered the ways to thwart the flying saucers, to redirect the missiles, to hide behind the screen and emerge from above or below with a quick tap of the controller. There was nothing ponderous about it, no dictatorial regulation.

Of course beneath the game play *Computer Space* was algorithm-based, and the computer clock defined the best course of action for an aspiring player. But the game sought to hide that rigidity. It didn't take much—a few different courses taken by the flying saucers, set to randomized order, and most barroom aficionados had the feeling of anticipation and anxiety that came from expecting the unexpected.

On top of it, *Computer Space* used the rudiments of spatial illusion to break the tyranny of the flat TV screen on which play took place. The spaceship and the enemy saucers moved through the black depths of space punctuated by unwavering stars. Because your spaceship, the saucers, and the missiles all moved against this backdrop, they seemed to float in front of a gulf of infinite space—indeed, the stars seemed far, far away, even as the action took place in a determined distance—perhaps ten miles away, judging from the size of the ships and saucers.

The game had everything *Pong* did not: an evil enemy against whose forces you fought; a set of skills that drew from childhood games of cowboy and soldier; and longstanding literary, film, and television traditions of ambush and shoot-em-up. It was silly, but with a silliness that drew from the popular sci-fi literary and film forms—*Amazing Stories, Fantasy and Science Fiction* (known to all readers as *F+SF*), a host of bad space cowboy adventure movies, and some equally seductive TV shows, notably *Lost in Space* and *Star Trek*. It looked snazzy, too—it would have fit nicely on the flight deck of the Starship *Enterprise*.

But *Computer Space* was a flop. It just didn't draw the players away from the physicality of the pinball machine.

Bushnell and Alcorn didn't expect much better penetration with *Pong*. That's why they tried out their prototype in a familiar bar rather than seeking to sell it directly to Midway, Bally, or Nutting. When the news came back that people were waiting outside the bar in the morning for Capp to open up just so they could play the game, when the machine jammed after a week or less because it was overfull of quarters, Bushnell knew he had something transformational.

But he didn't know why—that is, why his more sophisticated, more stylish, more distinctive *Computer Space* had failed, and *Pong* had triumphed.

Bushnell's two games represent two faces of the virtual world that would turn out to dominate American entertainment and, in the process, train generations of players in the new regimes and protocols of the digital age.

One did so by stealth and illusion, imbedding itself in familiar traditions and genres. *Computer Space* was, after all, an adaptation of perhaps the oldest hacked game in the computer age's short history, emerging from the labs at MIT in the late '50s, migrating through each innovation and iteration of computer, moving from printed paper to screen, from toggle switches to joysticks. Its heritage lay in the technophilic world of the Cold War and the Space Age, from the sci-fi of Heinlein, Asimov, and Van Vogt. It was spatially illusionistic. It even had qualities of a Western taken out into space. You could dodge behind the screen; you could cut them off in a surprise run from the other side. It pitted Good against Evil—you against the invaders.

Put in your quarter, play against the computer; conquer its alienness with human wiles.

And then there was *Pong*. It demanded your obeisance, it trained you in the new posthuman condition, in which you learned to be meld yourself to the imperatives of the machine. And it did so flatly, without ingratiating itself to the familiar or flattering the player into thinking man was master.

And it won the contest. Oddly, it was *Pong* that defined computer space—stripped of illusion authentic to its algorithmic and computational condition—and *Computer Space* that posited its necessary dialectical opposition—a space of simulation, thriving on illusion. Together they would propose the virtual landscapes of the twenty-first century: Simerica.

CHAPTER 17

Simerica

In the second decade of the twenty-first century, we traverse an American landscape once again in transformation. We are on a frontier not spatial but temporal, or perhaps phenomenological. We engage its technologies, play with its toys, travel its spaces, work at its jobs, and embrace its sodalities with enthusiasm, even as we find ourselves surprised at odd turns, disoriented, sometimes lost. Even the generations born to Nintendo and Apple and the PC and the cell phone recognize they are inheritors and creators of a different world than existed even at their birth just two or three decades ago.[1]

We live in a cultural landscape of layers. We engage with the virtual world, but we occupy the physical, and in most cases, that physicality was made to be lived in differently than we do, now.

Ours is, then, a clumsy voyage along a once-again expanding frontier. We are impelled by continual promises (amplified by advertising) of a revolutionary utopia in which we are freed from the bounds of space and time, interconnected to the point where anomie and isolation will no longer define the human condition, and embodiment will be something we can enter and exit at will. So we stand on the platform, heads bent to the iPhones in our hands, watching the progress of the Ravenswood or the A Train or the next BART in from Fremont. We complain to all via Twitter that the Long Island Expressway is a parking lot, that the presenter at this meeting is using dual projectors to show identical PowerPoints even as he reads them off the iPad in front of him, that another jumper has gone off the High-5 interchange in Dallas and we are caught forever until the ambulances clear the sack of bloody clothes and flesh off the LBJ.

None of the sites we occupy in passing is amenable to our space-transcended selves. And so we travel between promise and condition, always awaiting the moment when our condition will accelerate to merge with the promise, while instead the promise accelerates at a pace just faster than any conceivable progress.

What distinguishes this epoch from its past is that promise of placelessness and dematerialization—freedom to move effortlessly in an ecstasy of perfect interconnection, all data available, the self a node in the infinitely expanding four-dimensional organism inanimate but so complex as to behave as if animate, organic yet still immortal, eternal, proffering eternality to the self connected into it. Yet the promise is that this digital realm is not simply neutral or benign but benevolent, even obeisant: a prosthesis, a servant, not a master or an addiction.

Consider for a moment two of the most important progenitors of this transformation: Will Wright and Jack Dorsey. Wright was a renegade city planner who started by trying to crunch urban infrastructure data to understand and remedy the crumbling cities of the '70s. By the turn of the millennium, his empire included not just virtual cities—*SimCity 2000*—but alternative suburban idylls entirely divorced from reality—*The Sims*. Jack Dorsey was a map-obsessed kid in St. Louis in the '80s when his family first got a PC Jr. and an Apple IIe. He began his life as a programmer by trying to figure out how to make maps of the physical within a crippled, barely legible graphical interface. Within a couple of years, he had developed programs that allowed taxi dispatchers to map the location of their cabs and match them to the locations of customers calling in for a ride. Ten years after that, he codeveloped Twitter. In both these cases, something flipped over, causing upheavals in the settled patterns of cultural behavior that have rippled out from one site into wider and wider reaches. Maps no longer approximate the physical; they replace it as sites for interaction, engagement, revolution, and sex.

And the promise expands. Soon we will become, fully, nodes between input and output. Wearing Google Glass eyewear, or what will no doubt replace it, we will simultaneously take in the digital world and transmit into it; we will order our prosthetic eye to record our experiences and then we will upload them into the cloud. (Even that word expresses the uneasy bifurcation between virtual and real, for the "cloud" is not insubstantial, illusory, transitory, but dense with data; still, we must express the sense that we are sending our self-constructed dramas into some magical ether.)

"Okay Glass: take a picture"; "okay Glass: record a video," our stand-ins order in the earliest advertising demo of the Google Glass.[2] Once again we are invited to declare ourselves the centers of dramas of invention—

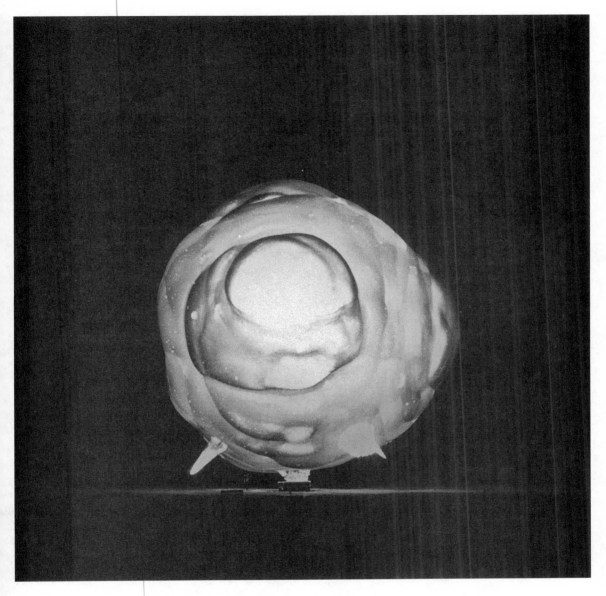

17.1. Harold Edgerton's photograph of a 1951 atomic test. (© MIT 2010. Courtesy of MIT Museum.)

self-invention, yes, but cultural invention, too. Just as the Levittown pioneers might today be called "first-adopters," today's first-adopters envision themselves as continuing the American pioneering spirit in the digital realm, traversing spaces or flying above them. In Google's first two-minute promotion for Glass, no fewer than thirteen separate forms of flight are pastiched, all of them recorded by Glass. Virtual *everywhere communities* of one, transcending the physical to take the role of some god (not flawed mortal, not Daedalus, not Icarus!) surveying the landscape with joyous detachment.

Perhaps we cannot even call this a landscape any more. The maps being made of the cyberworld reflect not a horizontal expanse—Frederick Jackson Turner's frontier "out there" ahead of a progressive movement of settlement, order, restriction—but an expanding bubble within which seethes a near-infinite collection of supercriticality. These are maps in name only; they are more like stop-motion representations, resembling nothing so much as Edgerton's pictures of the atom blasts over the suburban villas in the Nevada desert.

Figure 17.2 shows Microsoft data-mining engineer Matthew Hurst's

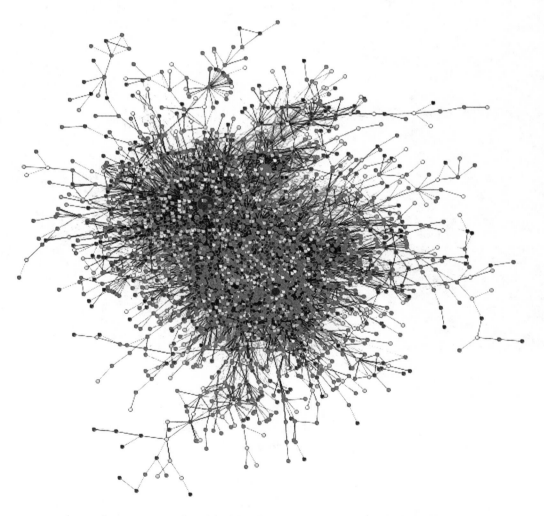

17.2. Matthew Hurst, visual model of the blogosphere, 2008. (Courtesy of Matthew Hurst.)

model of the blogosphere, ca. 2008. In its interactive version, each of the dots is "hot"—a hyperlink to a blog or a blog server (as of April 2010, some of the links were dead, but many were showing blog entries from that day).

In an online presentation, Hurst presented a number of other ways in which this blogosphere can be presented visually.[3] Here are two:

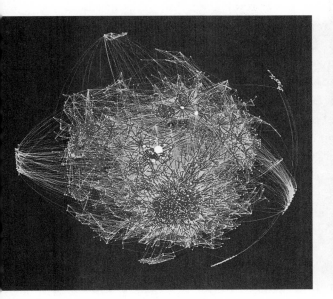 

17.3. and **17.4.** Matthew Hurst, visualization of the blogosphere, c. 2008. (Courtesy of Matthew Hurst.)

His imagery bears more than a simple visual relationship to Edgerton's pictures. For Hurst, the very "heat" of this exploding blogosphere comes from the ways each hot link releases energy, particulate ideas, that travel to arouse some stable identity into its own unstable criticality, where it too releases fragments: chain reactions not linear but spherical.

Hurst presents a visual poetics of the virtual. The lock-in of his images to algorithms in the virtual sphere makes what seems a scientifically accurate proposal for the existence of the virtual sphere not as metaphor but as condition.

This is the mythos of the new virtual culture, and Hurst's is one among an emerging body of iconographic visual formulations of that mythos. He was briefly the Giotto to this new culture, just as William Gibson was its Dante, and the elders like W. J. T. Mitchell and McKenzie Wark vie to be its St. Bonaventura or St. Augustine.

Between the disquisitions of the *philosophes* and the software patches of the engineers, between Hurst's expanding universe and his gnat's eyeball,

there is a level on which most of the occupants of the new culture operate on daily basis, a level approximating Photoshop's "flattened layers": of
promise, experience, local knowledge, received wisdom, mythology, and
pragmatics. It is this level where I find myself interrupted from writing by
a cell phone call from my daughter, just flown into BWI to compete in the
Cape May Marathon who tells me she is in a tow truck, the car she was riding in having been demolished by a driver texting on the freeway. She was
saved by the microprocessors that released airbags and the computers that
calculated the design of the safety cage of the Toyota Corolla in which she
sat with her friend Theresa, debating running nutrition.

As with space, so also with time. The rhythm of strums, the clatter of claw-
hammer banjo, the susurration of breath audible as the singer prepares for
the next phrase, the rattle and clap of the snare and the high hat, the shuffle
and rustle of the dancers: these are the sounds of music that builds upward
from the rhythms of human life, from heartbeat, from voices speaking back
and forth. Today musicians in the studio are bound to a computer's click
track; the drums are as likely to be samples or even full-on computerized
programs. The voice has been pitch-corrected by Auto-Tune. And not just
in the studio. The digital realm has advanced so far that even seemingly
spontaneous performed music in the pop world is running through processors, programs, and computers that reorganize the sound to conform to
the rigors of the bitmap, erasing the connection between the musical and
the organic. Plugged into the iPod Nano turned up high and hot, listening
alone, we train our hearts to beat in the absolute rhythms the digital realm
demands.

Here too hybrid forms are emerging, resistances and adaptations. My
son Taylor records his banjo transcription of the Bach cello suites into a
digital workstation while the instrument he plays has been made at a factory in China that tomorrow may be churning out a perfect replica of the
Martin D45 c. 1942 that I am playing, or a simulacrum of the stolid Midwestern chair that I'm sitting in as I write.

We who were born into the Cold War and its landscapes are uneasy with
this; we may tell ourselves we are ambivalent. Even those born into the digital age dance between accommodation and resistance. The recordings Taylor makes go onto cassette tapes, with all their wobble and hiss, because they
can fit in a pocket, because they are dispensable, because they remind every
listener that what is granted is not the illusion of utter connection but the
condition of distance from an authentic moment of listening, in a quiet
room, to a bearded young man holding a remnant of America's history of
slavery and the resistance to slavery in his big hands.

Not simply ambivalent: aware, at moments, usually unconscious, of the ways the quotidian and the taken-for-granted tie into a four-dimensional virtual sphere amenable to a map like Hurst's.

What remains, then, is a tentative history of the emergence of a new cultural landscape layered onto and transforming the older American cultural landscape of *places*, and of *things*.

Binaries

Perhaps it is a conceit, or perhaps a condition: the new American landscape seems composed of radiating binaries, the interstices of Hurst's supercritical expanding bubble. It is paradoxical. The very nature of the subatomic particle escaping the unstable home is the infinitude of vectors it may take. But the digital realm is, according to the common wisdom, a binary one, and so we follow its conceits. After all, the particle is both particle and wave; it is either entrapped or escaping; it either strikes or does not. So we can begin with binaries, though they will soon pile up with exceptions and interpenetrations until the conceit fails its duty to order new and unstable conditions.

The most basic binary lies between the physical and the virtual, and it divides into a further pair of pairings. One concerns the ways the digital realm required physical apparati, and those apparati required dedicated places located within physical spaces. The result was a transformation of the physical landscape to accommodate the virtual. The second concerns the way the digital sphere, brought into being to more fully and accurately map the physical realm, came to invent its own approximations of the physical, its own systems of representations and illusions, seeking to create an environment sufficiently convincing that it could vie with, even triumph over, the physical.

Manifest destiny. One might date the beginnings of the digital age by noting the point at which computers moved out of dedicated spaces and into the wider landscape, physical and cultural.

With their hot-running vacuum tubes, early Cold War computers required specialized environments for even the most rudimentary of work. Whirlwind, an MIT-developed machine operational by the early '50s, used twelve thousand vacuum tubes and required the development of a new system for archiving data, and a magnetic core memory, as the tubes were often unreliable. These computers were extraordinarily complex and expensive to develop, build and maintain. As a result, they were for the most part

17.5. Whirlwind/SAGE atomic shield antiballistic missile system, c. 1963. (Picture used with the permission of The Mitre Corporation. © The Mitre Corporation. All rights reserved.)

relegated to use in military operations. Whirlwind became the core of SAGE, the semi-automatic ground environment at the heart of the atomic-shield program in the United States.

By 1957, however, that had begun to change, when the Burroughs Corporation delivered the first all-transistor computer to Cape Canaveral, making possible an American intercontinental ballistic missile system capable of delivering atomic weapons globally.

This link between computers and atomic holocaust wasn't new.[4] One effect of this atomic-computer linkage, however, was to secrete the computers even further into interlocking mazes of physical space and social bureaucracy. Even as the development of integrated circuits and other forms of miniaturization made possible smaller and less expensive computer systems, the trend was in the other direction, toward conceiving ever more complex models of mutually assured destruction and more elaborately paranoid notions of enemy technologies and diabolical plans, requiring ever more complex and elaborate countermeasures, using greater and greater computer power.

The wartime and postwar atomic weapons initiative entrapped thousands of mathematically and scientifically brilliant young men (and a few young women) in these frustrating mazes, where they were often overlaid by layers of decreasingly competent and imaginative supervisors and censors. Many of these individuals had learned their crafts in the less-regulated environments of universities deeply indebted to the military contracting system and devoted to developing both the hardware and the human software for a next generation of defense contracting computation.

In the labs at these universities, notably at Stanford and MIT, a reaction began to take place. Rather than remain solitary or bureaucratically fixed, these men formed looser collaborative and collective groupings, social and intellectual at the same time, competitive but within a different realm than pure instrumentality, efficiency, or fear: they became hackers.[5]

Through them came ideas that struggled beyond the edge of the technology—playful experiments at redirecting the computer's power in ways not sanctioned or anticipated by the official triad who controlled the digital realm at that moment—corporate and military clients and owners, and the industry that developed the machines they required. In a complicated guerilla war fought in nanoseconds and on landscapes of computer code, these "developers" and "employees" snatched the machines away from their appointed tasks, and tested their possibilities and limitations.

At MIT, the Tech Model Railroad Club (generally nicknamed the TMRC) set up headquarters in the Kluge Room next to the room housing one of the earliest all-transistor computers, the TX-0; they had acquired one of the very first PDP-1 computers from the Digital Equipment Corporation in 1962. Smaller, running "tape" rather than computer program cards, and with a rudimentary video display, the PDP-1 became the platform for the very first game, the TMRC's 1962 *Spacewar*, a game without commercial outlet, played by hackers in the universities and tech corporations that had machines capable of running its then complex architecture, that was destined to become the basis for the first video games, notably *Computer Space*.

These early gamers found the process both exhilarating and frustrating: exhilarating because they knew, in ways the owners did not, the huge untapped possibilities of the digital realm, and frustrating because those possibilities lay on the far horizon, and only they were actively pushing the technology away from arithmetic and toward adventure, away from force and toward freedom.

It is worth pointing out that these technology collectives emerged at almost the same moment as the counterculture commune movement. It might seem that these were radical opposites—short-haired nerds working days at megacorporations like Bell/AT&T or major defense and atomic-weapons institutions, worshipping the absolute of the binary 01, while their long-haired, flamboyantly dressed, fluid counterparts were assembling in the pastoral landscape. But in fact the two had much in common. The hackers were, after all, committed to a radically democratic practice. They were contemptuous of the restraints of a corporate world. They believed in the free flow of information, including not just software code but hardware accessibility. They were as misogynistic as their brothers in the commune, though perhaps for different reasons. And they shared a fundamental utopianism and a sense of themselves as revolutionaries.

And the geeks were experimenters and subversives—though their focus was not on social possibility so much as informational liberation. Their experiments were first limited to those few places where the machines were big but the surveillance was lax, notably in the big universities where they were being trained to join the instrumentalist workforce. The arrival of "dumb terminals" and protocols of timesharing, however, began to disperse computer access, creating a new bifurcation, in which the actual computer, the mainframe, remained sequestered, but the user had access to its processes from a more remote spot. At MIT, this took place in 1964. Other universities and some corporations quickly adopted this architecture, and so did many military institutions. For the minions actually using the machine, this produced an odd disjunction. On the one hand, they had been exiled from the hushed, air-conditioned rooms where the actual machines were at work. Instead, they were in cubicles, with primitive keyboards and low-resolution screens that displayed rows and rows of code. Yet this exile also freed them. At a distance, invisible, they could commandeer the computer, compel it to do their bidding, with no one the wiser. A mere clerk, a *hack worker*, could hack into the system and wrest it away from its designated work and into other realms. Gaming hackers began toying with the computer's ability to make a huge number of calculations at the speed of light to see what other forms of play could be simulated on a computer.

Simulations at this early stage were not stunning successes. Either they devoted the computer's limited processing power to elaborate mathematical calculations (for example, how far a fly ball would travel if hit off a slider traveling at 84 miles per hour), or they produced an extremely primitive form of graphic on plotting paper or on the small, low-res TV screens into which operators peered. The simulations were slow, their illusionistic qualities close to nil. They were, as representations go, failures. The very idea of *immersion* was unthinkable.

The frustrations of visual simulation gave rise in 1975 to a sort of revanchism, in the form of the first fully successful text-based interactive game, Will Crowther's *Adventure*. Typically, Crowther had purloined workplace computers and computer time from the defense contractor BBN, where he was working at the time, and applied them to a personal quest—to produce a game that could entrance his young daughters.[6] *Adventure* involved imaginary travel through an underground cave-scape based on Crowther's spelunking activities in Kentucky's Mammoth Cave. Crowther took a Tolkienlike realm, adapted the wonk-addicts' *Dungeons & Dragons* game, and added wry sort of humor that masked the limitations of the computer's ability to recognize human language.

The game exploded across campus mainframes nationwide within the year, arrived at Stanford in 1977, was adapted and rendered more complex and dryly ironic by some of its players (notably Don Woods and Robert Pariseau), and in its transformed version attracted the attention of the Dynamic Modeling Group at MIT, four of whose members further complicated the gameplay and the underground landscape to produce *Zork!*, publically released in 1980, right in the midst of the first boom in personal computers— between the introduction of the Apple II in 1977 and the appearance of the IBM PC in 1981.

Zork! is critical because it helps to define that binary between *imaginative* landscapes, and *virtual* ones, and because it moved gaming from the workplace mainframe to the home-based minicomputer. Because it was entirely text-based, it required that the player engage in the sort of spatial landscape-creation that was found in literature and radio, rather than movies or television. Of course, both drama and television required leaps of faith, willing suspensions of disbelief, as the promise to substitute imagery for imagination could never reach some form of radical verisimilitude. Even a radio script encouraged the transliteration of words into images that characterized the landscapes of the radio *Gunsmoke* or of Bob Dylan's streets and landscapes.

Zork! was a strange sort of game, a combination of crippled limitation and radical innovation. Essentially, it presented you with a quest through a maze filled with puzzles to solve and no clear idea what your final objective was. There was no promise of a reward, just the pleasure of the process. Yet it was not like doing math or language puzzles; its scripts, brief as they were, could be spine-tinglingly foreboding, inducing increasingly frantic (and, as a result, inept) play, until you found yourself robbed by a trickster, eaten by a grue, or simply lost in a maze in the dark, with no idea where the exit was.

This quality of emotional engagement and imaginative fantasy put *Zork!* in the realm of radio plays and novels—and sly references throughout acknowledged its heritage. But it had the beginnings of what would become the grail of the virtual world—immersion in a seemingly infinite alternative realm from which you could not bear to escape. Reading a book, listening to a radio show, you knew that there lay beyond the mystery of the moment (*what will happen next?*) an awareness that the results were scripted, that you were carried along a predetermined path; you could even cheat, with a book, ruin everything by flipping to the end to see how it would turn out. You couldn't do that with *Zork!* To find out how it turned out, you had to stay with it to the end, and in so doing you found yourself in the midst of an increasingly engrossing world, exploring every nook and cranny, taking every path, until you ran out of real estate.

Zork! celebrated that combination of immersive and imaginative life. When the game's success prompted competitors to mine *Adventure* for their own versions, they sought to best the original by replacing the text-based play with some form of graphical experience. *Zork!*'s parent company, Infocom, responded by releasing a series of ads declaring the superiority of visual imagination to computerized animation. In one, the company accompanied its boasts with a color image that melded the human brain and the spectacular pictures of the mushroom cloud, and slyly appropriating the portentous language William L. Laurence had put in the mouth of Truman in August of 1945: "We have unleashed the power of the sun."[7]

At first, the imaginative won out over the virtual because it was better suited to the third revolution in hardware: the microcomputer, as it was called, or, the *home* or *personal* computer, as it rapidly came to be known. The Holy Trinity of 1977—the Apple II, the Tandy Radio Shack TRS-80, and the Commodore PET—all offered something close to a complete system at a price that, while high (above $600-$1,200 dollars, close to $3,000-$6,000 in 2014 dollars), was within reach of middle-class, suburban-dwelling American families, and thereby moved the digital realm out of the workplace and into the home.

At the workplace, the goals in the digital realm were instrumental: increased efficiency, fewer miscalculations by human workers, better surveillance of work, more rapid handling of larger and larger datasets. The impetus reinforced workplace compartmentalization, particularly around skill

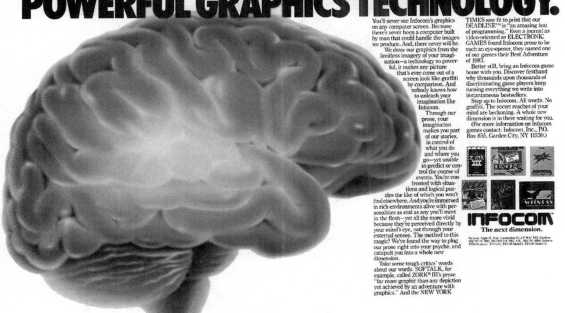

WE UNLEASH THE WORLD'S MOST POWERFUL GRAPHICS TECHNOLOGY.

You'll never see Infocom's graphics on any computer screen. Because there's never been a computer built by man that could handle the images we produce. And, there never will be.

We draw our graphics from the limitless imagery of your imagination—a technology so powerful, it makes any picture that's ever come out of a screen look like graffiti by comparison. And nobody knows how to unleash your imagination like Infocom.

Through our prose, your imagination makes you part of our stories, in control of what you do and where you go—yet unable to predict or control the course of events. You're confronted with situations and logical puzzles the like of which you won't find elsewhere. And you're immersed in rich environments alive with personalities as real as any you'll meet in the flesh—yet all the more vivid because they're perceived directly by your mind's eye, not through your external senses. The method to this magic? We've found the way to plug our prose right into your psyche, and catapult you into a whole new dimension.

Take some tough critics' words about our words. SOFTALK, for example, called ZORK® III's prose "far more graphic than any depiction yet achieved by an adventure with graphics." And the NEW YORK TIMES saw fit to print that our DEADLINE™ is "an amazing feat of programming." Even a journal as video-oriented as ELECTRONIC GAMES found Infocom prose to be such an eye-opener, they named one of our games their Best Adventure of 1983.

Better still, bring an Infocom game home with you. Discover firsthand why thousands upon thousands of discriminating game players keep turning everything we write into instantaneous bestsellers.

Step up to Infocom. All words. No graffiti. The secret reaches of your mind are beckoning. A whole new dimension is in there waiting for you. (For more information on Infocom games contact: Infocom, Inc., P.O. Box 855, Garden City, NY 11530.)

INFOCOM
The next dimension.

17.6. Ad for *Zork III!*, c. 1983.

sets, into which workers were trained, after which they were more-or-less locked into job categories.

By contrast with the workplace machine, the home computer promised itself as a liberating tool for the individual, a labor-saving machine that would generate increased leisure time and decreased stress. "The home computer that's ready to work, play and grow with you," read the banner headline for the ad trumpeting the Apple II inauguration. "Clear the kitchen table. Bring in the color T.V. Plug in your new Apple II®, and connect any standard cassette recorder/player. Now you're ready for an evening of discovery in the new world of personal computers. . . . You can learn to chart your biorhythms, balance your checking account, even control your home environment. Apple II will go as far as your imagination can take it."[8]

Like generations of household appliances, however, its promise of lessened labor translated into a more labor-intensive home environment. The

17.7. First ad for Apple II showing VisiCalc graphing of Dow Jones Industrials scenario, *Byte* Magazine, May, 1977. (Courtesy of Dan Bricklin.)

home computer was, in effect, a Trojan horse; what it secreted weren't physical invaders but mental and informational ones: habits of thought based in the bureaucratized workplace and digital briefcases brimming with tasks to be completed, skills to be mastered.

Two of the most vaunted early home computer programs brought new forms of white-collar menial work into the home, suggesting both a more efficient, workplace-like home, and a new site for office-work, which could be carried home on a floppy disk. VisiCalc, an "electronic spreadsheet" developed by Dan Bricklin and released for the Apple in June 1979, afforded the opportunity to "play" what-if scenarios with financials, keep bookkeeping within a computer, and bring accounting practices into the home amateur's domain.[9]

VisiCalc brought the efficiency of the workplace into the home, but it did so in a peculiar way—by affording the promise of work *as* play: not by coincidence did the software rapidly develop a slang language in which accounting scenarios were redefined as "playing with the numbers." Moreover, the promise of work entering the home was a utopian one—not the destruction of boundaries but the encouragement of leisure, by decreasing the amount of time the worker spent at the office or on the road, and by encouraging rapid shifts between work and play. Just as VisiCalc offered to break massively complex tasks into smaller, easier bits, so also the new homework computer would break home time down into smaller and more adaptable bites.

VisiCalc's counterpart was the word processing program, notably WordStar, which did for language-based work what VisiCalc did for the numerical

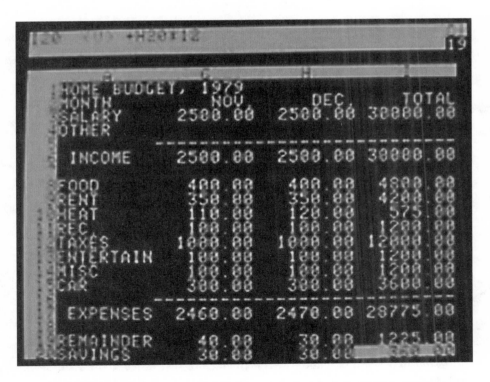

17.8. Detail of a screen shown in one of the first agency-based ads for VisiCalc. Screen shot shows "family budget" calculations.

Solve your personal energy crisis.
Let VisiCalc™ Power do the work.

With a calculator, pencil and paper you can spend hours planning, projecting, writing, estimating, calculating, revising, erasing and recalculating as you work toward a decision.

Or with VisiCalc and your Apple* II you can explore many more options with a fraction of the time and effort you've spent before.

VisiCalc is a new breed of problem-solving software. Unlike prepackaged software that forces you into a computerized straight jacket, VisiCalc adapts itself to any numerical problem you have. You enter numbers, alphabetic titles and formulas on your keyboard. VisiCalc organizes and displays this information on the screen. You don't have to spend your time programming.

Your energy is better spent using the results than getting them.

Say you're a business manager and want to project your annual sales. Using the calculator, pencil and paper method, you'd lay out 12 months across a sheet and fill in lines and columns of figures on products, outlets, salespeople, etc. You'd calculate by hand the subtotals and summary figures. Then you'd start revising, erasing and recalculating. With VisiCalc, you simply fill in the same figures on an electronic "sheet of paper" and let the computer do the work.

Once your first projection is complete, you're ready to use VisiCalc's unique, powerful recalculation feature. It lets you ask "What if?" examining new options and planning for contingencies. "What if" sales drop 20 percent in March? Just type in the sales figure. VisiCalc instantly updates all other figures affected by March sales.

Circle 301 on inquiry card

Or say you're an engineer working on a design problem and are wondering "What if that oscillation were damped by another 10 percent?" Or you're working on your family's expenses and wonder "What will happen to our entertainment budget if the heating bill goes up 15 percent this winter?" VisiCalc responds instantly to show you all the consequences of any change.

Once you see VisiCalc in action, you'll think of many more uses for its power. Ask your dealer for a demonstration and discover how VisiCalc can help you in your professional work and personal life.

You might find that VisiCalc alone is reason enough to own a personal computer.

VisiCalc is available now for Apple II computers with versions for other personal computers coming soon. The Apple II version costs just $99.50 and requires a 32k disk system.

For the name and address of your nearest VisiCalc dealer, call (408) 745-7841 or write to Personal Software, Inc. Dept. B, 592 Weddell Dr., Sunnyvale, CA 94086. If your favorite dealer doesn't already carry Personal Software products, ask him to give us a call.

PERSONAL SOFTWARE

VisiCalc was developed exclusively for Personal Software by Software Arts, Inc. Cambridge, Mass.

TM: VisiCalc is a trademark of Personal Software, Inc.

*Apple is a registered trademark of Apple Computer, Inc.

17.9. First agency-based ad campaign for VisiCalc. The screenshot in this ad shows business "sales flow" calculations. (Courtesy of Benji Edwards/Vintagecomputing.com.)

and arithmetic. WordStar had a horrific user interface, requiring vast amounts of memorization. It was slow, slower than most high-speed typists, and the words on the low-resolution, television-like CRTs of the Apple, TRS, PET and (after August 12, 1981) the IBM PC gave users headaches, eyestrain, and, for serious writers, sometimes permanent damage to their eyesight. But it had a tremendous advantage over every predecessor: it could back up and delete text. You could correct with it. You could cut and paste. The promise was similar to VisiCalc's: you could now truly "play" with words, phrases, sentences, paragraphs, ideas. Your failures could, and did, disappear by willful erasure.

VisiCalc made the Apple II a success; WordStar and its competition, WordPerfect, did the same for the IBM PC. By offering full-featured word processing, both WordStar and WordPerfect cemented the interpenetration of workplace and leisure space.

What may seem odd about this is the lack of resistance to the incursion. While most workplaces monitored computer use and punished hackers, in the home the computer rapidly and smoothly claimed its place. But that place itself is significant, both for where it was and for where it was not. PCs did not for the most part locate in living rooms or family rooms, in part because they would have competed with televisions that were used for shared viewing. Instead, they were relegated to the quasi-work, male-domain area of the study or the den. The very existence of such a separated space spoke volumes about the nature of these early consumers: upper-tier white collar workers who could afford suburban homes far larger than the Levittown houses of the past suburban revolution.

To some extent, this was a reflection of the male-centric workshop quality of early computers. Remember that the first-generation "home" computers were deeply uninviting. The earliest, like the Altair of 1975, operated with banks of switches rather than keyboards. Most were sold in the form of kits to be assembled and required mastery of soldering irons and electronics esoterica, from the different values of capacitors and resistors to the different pins of transistors. Even Apple's early versions were hardware tinkerers' dreams and everyone else's nightmares, sprouting cables and expansion cards outside their cases and projecting little more than strings of numbers and letters across their primitive screens. IBM's PC was uninviting at the software level—most programs required mastery of increasingly complex macro codes and the differences between a screen image and the printed product were extreme.

This changed when Apple's Macintosh model appeared in 1984, sporting a user-friendly "graphical user interface," or, GUI. But this was still relatively primitive: Apple effectively mimicked by symbolism the material parts of the computer, or their physical equivalents—files were signified by primitive "icons" representing manila file folders, and discarded files went into a mock trashcan. Atari's 1985 competitor, the GEM, went even further—disk drives were symbolized as file cabinets.

The Mac had another important feature: a mouse. Apple had tried pointing devices in its earlier Lisa but without much success. The Mac's mouse enabled a shift from text-based mnemonic keystrokes to the fabled "point-and-click" access. The result was a significantly more graphical and spatial *experience* of the graphical interface. At the same time, however, the addition of a mouse and mouse pad pushed the computer from a corner of the desk or table to grab a much larger portion of physical space.

The Mac was a success—and its novel approach pushed Microsoft, primary producer of software for IBM's PCs, to dramatically revise its own operating system. By the end of 1987, Microsoft was pushing Windows 2.0 along with companion programs, Word and Excel, that were conceptual clones of WordStar and VisiCalc.

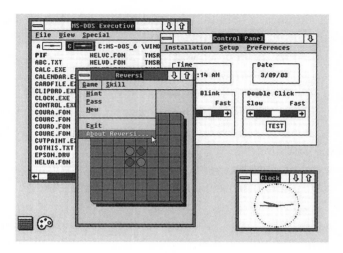

17.10. Windows 2.03, December 1987

Microsoft's GUI had a number of improvements. Windows could overlap each other, and could be moved with the aid of a mouse more easily than earlier GUIs. But Windows was, finally, little more than an inept replication of an unpleasant office cubicle, complete with its trash can; bland, pinup-free wall calendar; and modernist clock ticking the hours. Only its name betrayed Microsoft's attempt to ingratiate the computer into the home. And that was utter deception, for Microsoft's GUI didn't portray a window at all—just like Apple's GUI, and Amiga's, it was a desktop you looked disconsolately down on without even the distraction of lifting your head to look at the clock or calendar, counting down the hours till you could go home, the weeks and months till your vacation. You *were* home. This *was* vacation.[10]

Despite their lip service to home and family, PCs were, in design and purpose, workplace intruders. They weren't meant for noisy, distracting living rooms or high-traffic family rooms. They were difficult, frustrating tools. But they could be adapted, especially as the 1980s waned and the '90s loomed.

PCs went into dens and studies not just to avoid competing with television nor simply to reflect the hybrid nature of the machine, capable of switching binary paths between pleasant workplace and efficient home. They were also avoiding competition with a separate digital intruder: the game console. Nearly a decade before the PC, television and hi-fi manufacturer Magnavox had come out with a digital gaming system, 1972's Odyssey, that attached to the family television and allowed you to play a few primitive sports-simulation games: hockey, baseball, basketball, tennis, and, notably, table tennis. These were all quite similar (though some were made to seem different by overlaying templates on the television screen); they were essentially variants on what would become *Pong*, when Atari's Noland Bushnell purloined the idea after visiting an Odyssey demo. By the mid-1970s, upgrades of the Odyssey allowed two-player games and offered a greater range of game play. Then, in 1976, Fairchild Computers released a much more sophisticated gaming console system, followed shortly thereafter by the legendary Atari 2600. By 1980, when Mattel released its Intellivision system, and more potently by 1985, when Nintendo released its Nintendo Entertainment System in the United States, the digital realm had fully penetrated the middle-class American home in the name of sport, then recreation, then children's games, in family rooms, living rooms, and bedrooms.

Digital console home gaming systems weren't described in ways that betrayed their relationship to the PC in the den. Instead, they were rhetorically connected to the television system: they were *video game systems*. In this way they defined another social, cultural, and spatial binary: they were homely alternatives to the rough-and-tumble adolescent world of the video arcades and the arcade consoles that were to be found in pinball halls, amusement parks, penny arcades, and bars. *Pong* migrated early, in licensed versions for various home video game systems. So too with the evolutionary iterations of *Computer Space*, appearing as *Space Invaders* for the Atari, for example, in 1980. Nintendo's NES of 1985, in particular, clarified the promise of the home video game as a buttress to the house as haven—on the one side protecting the player from the workplace, on the other from the dangerous chaotic uncensored public life of streets and cities.

In part this migration from arcade to home computer took place because of the continued crippled nature of the virtual sphere in both. By now, there had developed a broad if largely unspoken consensus as to what the virtual digital domain should offer: the capability to produce some credible illusionism on graphic, sonic, visual, and spatial levels. Over time, this quality came to be called "immersion." Despite their dedicated nature—that is, their single-function role, unlike the multifunctionality promised by the PC—video game consoles and their games were surprisingly awful on a visual and illusionistic level. There were a number of reasons for this. Most important was price point. Video game systems sold well when they were reasonably priced—and somewhere around $300 (about $600 in 2013 dollars) in 1985 seemed about the spot. This limited the sophistication of the system itself, especially when it came to visuals and sound. On either side were further limits. Televisions were the display items of choice for these consoles, and TVs had limited graphic sophistication—refresh rates were slow, the pixels were quite large, and colors weren't easy to make accurate. Television's sound, moreover, was typically pumped through a three-inch speaker crammed under the screen. And with the addition of dedicated game cartridges, both price and limits on the hardware itself made for little in the way of sophisticated graphical "interfaces."

The obduracy of those limits suggested the great divide between the PC in the study and the console in the family room. For while video game systems made innovative leaps only rarely, personal computers were in a continuing, largely uninterrupted vector of innovation.

At first this widening gap appeared as a split between crippled virtuality and sophisticated imaginative play—between, say, *Donkey Kong* on Nintendo and *Zork!* on a PC. In the video game, flattened tawdry approximations of things—teeter-totter logs, an ape, barrels of burning oil. By contrast, the slow, often frustrating, fascinating process of trying to get out of imaginary cave-scapes like the Echo Room (room room room room . . .) or the Maze of Twisty Little Passages All Alike.

In *Zork!* there were moments of real, visceral panic, of surprise, hair-rising on your neck, jumping from the chair if a real person, casually wandering past the computer, touched you on the shoulder. In games like *Donkey Kong*, there was only the *Pong*-like frustration of a repeated task that sped

17.11. *Donkey Kong*, c. 1981

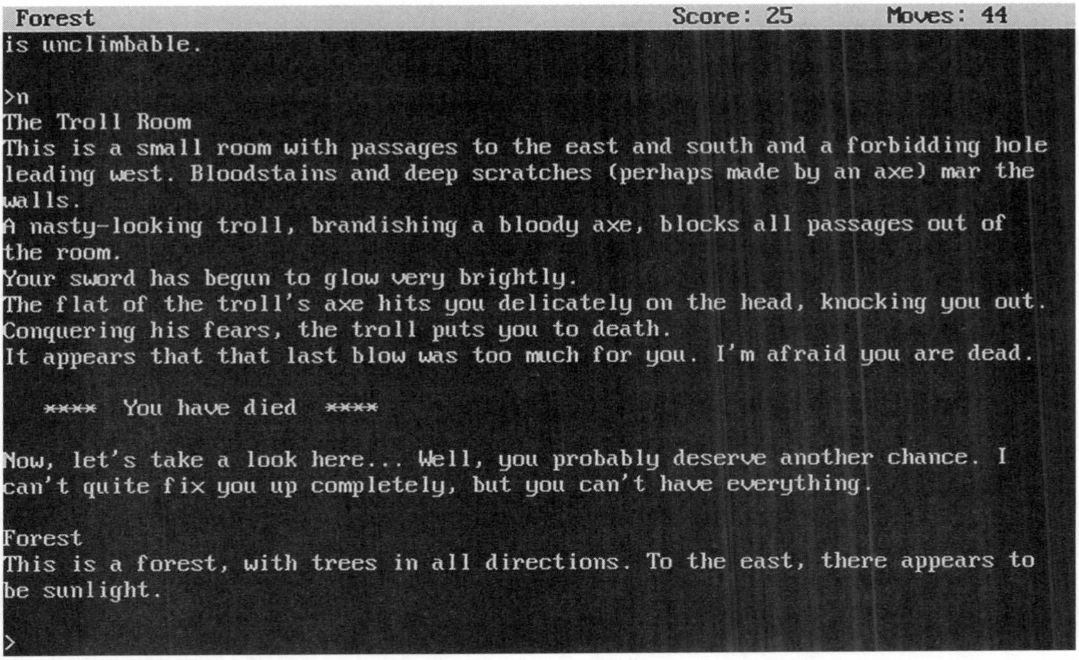

```
is unclimbable.

>n
The Troll Room
This is a small room with passages to the east and south and a forbidding hole
leading west. Bloodstains and deep scratches (perhaps made by an axe) mar the
walls.
A nasty-looking troll, brandishing a bloody axe, blocks all passages out of
the room.
Your sword has begun to glow very brightly.
The flat of the troll's axe hits you delicately on the head, knocking you out.
Conquering his fears, the troll puts you to death.
It appears that that last blow was too much for you. I'm afraid you are dead.

    ****  You have died  ****

Now, let's take a look here... Well, you probably deserve another chance. I
can't quite fix you up completely, but you can't have everything.

Forest
This is a forest, with trees in all directions. To the east, there appears to
be sunlight.
>
```

17.12. *Zork!*, c. 1981

up until it became too hard for you and you "died." When you died in *Zork!*, it was with a shiver; dying in *Donkey Kong* was simply a cap to frustration.

Most importantly, *Zork!* offered the illusion of genuine open-ended play, or at least of a world of many choices, each leading to many more choices, against which the console games could only look mechanical, even contemptuous. The "cheat-maps" to *Zork!*, to which most of us eventually resorted, once the frustration had overcome the wonder and we simply wanted to see what we might do, were remarkably big, elaborate.[11]

Imagination / Simulation

Zork! and its successors represented the most successful blending of the literary-imaginative and the computational. But it was the rapidly improving graphics capabilities of home computers that introduced the seductions of the virtual. Apple Computer's GUI was both the product and the engine. As importantly, Apple's desktop and Microsoft's Windows GUI for the IBM PC and its clones impelled innovations in the graphics hardware

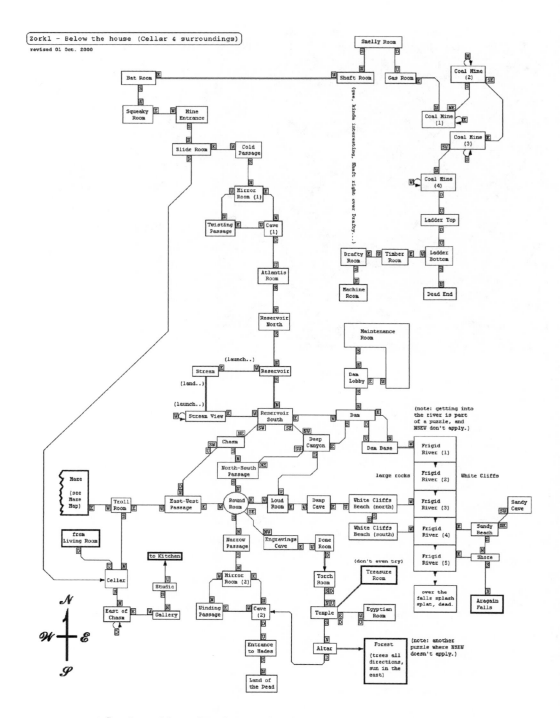

17.13. A flowchart of the *Zork!* underground world

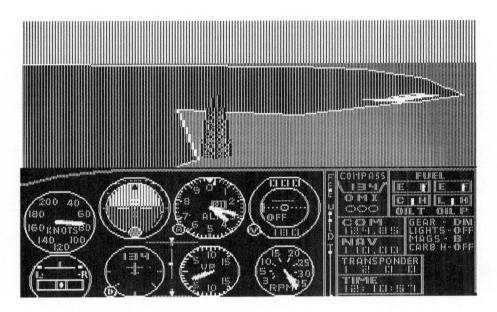

17.14. Microsoft *Flight Simulator*, cockpit view

sector. One result was the release by Microsoft of an oddly hybridic, visually based program somewhere between a pilot's training exercise and a Zen koan: *Flight Simulator*. Released for the Apple II in 1979 and then for the IBM PC in 1983, it used primitive graphics but introduced the idea of simulation at a visual rather than a purely computational level.

Within a year, Microsoft had responded to innovations in the PC and released version 2, which introduced color graphics, vastly improved simulation of speed, gravity effects, and the like, and a much larger array of aircraft and "scenarios" throughout the continental United States. With version 2, you could fly a Piper Cub from Nantucket to Neah Bay, Washington.

By the early '90s, software, hardware, corporate investment, audience size, and sophistication had placed digital gaming roughly where the novel was when Laurence Sterne published *Tristram Shandy* in 1759: as the central medium of a new social class in a new cultural era. Like the novel in Sterne's age, the digital game had multiple distribution channels—notably the video console and the computer, but also variants like the Game Boy. It had matured to the point of generating parodies and arousing widespread public concern over its morally degrading nature, as had the novel in Sterne's day. And it had a rapidly expanding range of genres: fantasy role-playing games, action games, adventures, strategy games like *Sid Meier's Civilization* (1991), and sports games, notably the hugely popular *John Madden Football*.

The games were played within the confines of the home. In some ways they represented the same structural relation of place to imaginative space as the television in the Levittown home offered—you were *here*, and through the technological object, you were transported *there*. In another way, though, these were games that accentuated your imprisonment in the home—like *Pong*, they insisted that you limit your physical and imaginative movement to conform to the requirements of the apparatus.

That changed dramatically in 1997, when *Ultima Online* went up for sale. It was the first sophisticated, commercially available game to appropriate already burgeoning online communities in which conversations and social interactions could occur in virtual "chat rooms" that could be conceived as contiguous rooms into which one could come and go (*PedalSteelPete has left the room*; *WiseWilly has entered the room*), either moving from one room to another or from the physical space of home to the virtual metahouse. Using modem technologies, and then, more efficiently, fiber optic and wired cable systems already piped into the home to improve the television experience, gaming franchises like *Ultima Online* joined the burgeoning virtual society within which the game served as simultaneously the virtual environment on which social systems could be built and housed, and the set of social and cultural laws and regulations that could structure "play" sufficiently to generate a form of civilization that existed outside of space and place. By the beginning of the twenty-first century, these MUD (multiple user domains)*, MMORPG (massively multiplayer online role-playing games) and MMRPG (massively multiplayer role-playing games) environs had begun to reach the limits of digitally transcendent self-creation, with the emergence of entrepreneurs selling digital tools and weapons, even virtual currency, for real dollars, and with the fabled appearance of "digital rape," with its foregrounding of philosophical questions about embodiment and exploitation.[12]

Such virtual environs, however, still left the physical participant locked in a physical environment, sitting on a chair, staring at a screen, tapping at a keyboard or pushing a mouse or groping with a handheld "controller." And while the digital counterculturists and utopians promised a grand new world freed of physical limitations, protean in its inventiveness, the reality of the virtual representation within which interaction occurred was disappointingly primitive and sketch-like. Even the most elaborate of these, *Second Life*, took years from its 2003 introduction to develop sophisticatedly immersive virtual environs.

* Often mistakenly, but accurately, called "multiple user dungeons."

The goal of immersion found its earliest and most consistent triumphs in the computer gaming sphere. The most revolutionary genres of game at the turn of centuries emerged with the rapid upswing in graphics technology and the promise of new experiences of immersion: simulations, or sims, and first-person-shooters, or FPSs. Both of these genres saw their first mature versions in 1993, with *SimCity 2000* from designer Will Wright, and *Doom*, from the collective id Software. Both afforded quantum leaps forward in the realms of illusionistic immersion. Both were intensely addictive. Both were the talk of the gaming world, spawning genetic lines that continue vigorously today, as the dominant modes of postmodern game play. And both contained within them forms of cultural atavism.

The End of History and the Return of the Repressed: Cold War Worlds in Virtual Space

It is common wisdom to set the digital age as successor to the atomic age. But the two interpenetrate. The digital age emerged from and served the atomic age, and the atomic age returns, with its ethical quandaries, its apocalyptic rhetoric, its deep individual and collective anxieties, and its dialectic of retreat and reform, even its spawn of countercultures utopian and dystopic in the virtual realm.

The interplay between Cold War weapons system development and the computer's hardware and software is common knowledge. Computers could assist in the immense task of arithmetical compilation and mathematical calculation necessary to weapons design. They could be used to calculate the thrust, vector, and arc of nuclear warhead-carrying intercontinental missiles. They could monitor the skies for incoming Soviet missiles. They could determine the timing, velocity and quantity of responses.

The hardware of atomic-age computing made possible more and more sophisticated doomsday scenarios and forms of brinksmanship diplomacy. These, in turn, drove the development of hardware and software to more efficiently manage the task of flirting with, and skirting, nuclear holocaust. While the hardware stayed within the physical confines of military bases and military contractor sites, the software rapidly emerged, in mutated form, from the secret spaces and regulated workplaces of national defense into the home-based leisure world of digital play.

By the middle 1980s, President Ronald Reagan's hard-line stance toward the Soviets—exemplified in his 1984 on-camera, pre-speech "humorous" microphone test: "We begin bombing in five minutes"—had brought a new wave of atomic anxiety after almost two decades of test bans had relaxed national concerns about atomic holocaust. In the midst of this reescalation of nuclear fear, game designer Chris Crawford shifted from video game designs directed at kids to produce a ponderous, and somber, nuclear strategy game, released in 1985: *Balance of Power.*

Crawford's intent was frankly polemical. His game would teach a generation of young computer gaming enthusiasts the basics of military and diplomatic history based on the premise that actual warfare in the nuclear age was folly, and that the appropriate way to win power and world standing was to forge alliances with other nations based on diplomacy and mutual national interests. *Balance of Power* was a strategy game. Its graphics were primitive and its mode of play referred back to board games, notably *Risk*, though with a nuclear warfare component. Players chose to lead either the United States or the Soviet Union, and had eight years to win imperial domination without escalating tensions to flashpoint, starting a nuclear war.

Particularly bizarre considering the previous history of video games and the subsequent trend of video and computer games, was Crawford's way of ending *Balance of Power* should the player trigger a nuclear holocaust. "You have ignited a nuclear war. And no, there is no animated display of a mushroom cloud with parts of bodies flying through the air. We do not reward failure."[13] The stern moralism of the narrative reflected a widening debate about the celebration of violence in video games, but Crawford was more concerned with what he saw as a trend toward marketing video games as places of godlike grandiosity, complete with the promise of infinite resurrection, while promoting them to a population of young, male players who in real life had little or no potency. Crawford's game, by contrast, was to educate and enlighten participants on complex matters of global diplomacy—a sort of atomic-themed edutainment that was surprisingly successful.[14]

Balance of Power was released into a wave of resurgent nuclear fear after two decades in which holocaust had receded. The Reagan era introduced a new generation of Americans to atomic anxiety and its associated feelings of powerlessness in a conflict supervised by unresponsive giants—governments, corporations, "interests" and "alliances."

Perhaps as importantly, the Reagan administration sought to reawaken America's sense of moral superiority, its long tradition of national exceptionalism. Not since John Kennedy had a major national political figure directly invoked Puritan John Winthrop's vision of an American "city upon a hill." Reagan made it a central theme of his national politics. The Reagan years brought a broader return to the Cold War vision of a world divided between good and evil, a world in which the phrase "with God on our side" could lose its ironic bite and serve instead as the basis of a call for national sacrifice and renewal.

By the later 1980s, the Soviet Union began a slow collapse, and by 1989, Reagan's "evil empire," the dialectical opposite that had helped define American identity and renew its central myths, had exploded into a welter of new nations, each far more concerned with its own stability and self-definition than with opposition to the United States. In Reagan's terms, the United States had "won," but in so doing had suddenly lost the anchor of a half-century of self-definition. At a moment of political triumph, there emerged a contrasting cultural moment, fraught with indecision and doubt.

The triumph of American ideals in a post–Cold War future was the topic of an influential essay by the political philosopher Francis Fukuyama. "The End of History?" appeared in the summer of 1989 in the neoconservative journal the *National Interest*. Fukuyama proposed that "what we may be witnessing is not just the end of the Cold War, or the passing of a particular period of postwar history, but the end of history as such: that is, the end point of mankind's ideological evolution and the universalization of Western liberal democracy as the final form of human government."

> But in the universal homogenous state, all prior contradictions are resolved and all human needs are satisfied. There is no struggle or conflict over "large" issues, and consequently no need for generals or statesmen; what remains is primarily economic activity.[15]

For Fukuyama, the end of this epochal struggle was not so much the emergence of a triumphant American utopia spreading to the globe, as a deeply disturbing cultural rupture marked by the sudden collapse of a decades-long paradigm of national purpose. "We might summarize the content of the universal homogenous state as liberal democracy in the political sphere combined with easy access to VCRs and stereos in the economic," wrote Fukuyama toward the end of the essay. What might VCRs and stereos offer as substitution for the heavy moral and ethical burdens—and, more importantly, the sense of portent, of common purpose—provided by the Cold War?

Here is Fukuyama's final paragraph, an explicit answer:

> The end of history will be a very sad time. The struggle for recognition, the willingness to risk one's life for a purely abstract goal, the worldwide ideological struggle that called forth daring, courage, imagination, and idealism, will be replaced by economic calculation, the endless solving of technical

problems, environmental concerns, and the satisfaction of sophisticated consumer demands. In the post-historical period there will be neither art nor philosophy, just the perpetual caretaking of the museum of human history. I can feel in myself, and see in others around me, a powerful nostalgia for the time when history existed. Such nostalgia, in fact, will continue to fuel competition and conflict even in the post-historical world for some time to come. Even though I recognize its inevitability, I have the most ambivalent feelings for the civilization that has been created in Europe since 1945, with its north Atlantic and Asian offshoots. Perhaps this very prospect of centuries of boredom at the end of history will serve to get history started once again.[16]

When Fukuyama wrote those words, it is doubtful that he had much experience in the digital world. Perhaps he did, however; he had children, born into the gaming age. Had he watched them as grade schoolers, flush-faced, white-knuckled, clenched-jawed in front of *The Legend of Zelda* or, perhaps later, argued over the appropriateness of the *Finish Him!* sequences in *Mortal Kombat!*, or purchased for them, in vain hopes of replacing violence with education and mental stimulation, *SimCity* or even *Balance of Power*, he might have seen what the triumph of consumer capitalism in the digital age might look like.

For Fukuyama had explicated the core of Cold War American culture: the way in which daily life, its times and spaces, its tasks and its pleasures, its images and myths, had been given form and significance by the underlying assumption of a great moral clash between two conceptions of civilization in which individual and collective action in the civilian world, in America's splendidly isolated continental landscape of wealth and potentiality, took on a soldierly cast.

The Levittowners came to understand themselves as embodying liberal democratic and consumer capitalist ideals and sought to live up to those ideals (sometimes admirably, sometimes ignobly). So also the avid moviegoers in the darkened theaters watching *Miracle on 34th Street* and the families devotedly setting aside their dinner hour each week to the antic struggles of Lucy and Ricky to make sense of their lives, the military publicists striving to construct a coherent national narrative out of the building and bombing of suburban houses in the desert, and the rock and rollers wresting outer space technology from warfare to universal communication and common pleasure: all believed their daily gestures were freighted with some small portion of moral significance, parts of a larger national responsibility to remake America as a city upon a hill once again. When the first generations of youth culture took over the radio, they used it to transmit their confusions as to how they could continue the mission of their parents, and indeed whether that mission had failed or had even been the right mission at all.

When the counterculture came to prominence, its influence far outran its numbers, for the critique of the Cold War generation at its heart struck at the very compact made between Cold War Americans and their time and culture.

The apostasy of the counterculture had lain not with its hedonistic behavior but with its underlying proposition that Cold War American's core beliefs, our behavior, our social systems, our houses and jobs and our very culture, were *not* freighted with moral import, were *not* the underlying themes, plots, and props of a gigantic global drama. Yet the counterculturists' claims—and their actions—betrayed the continued desire for a fundamental, exceptionalist, American purpose: to seek some individual happiness, some harmony with the land given us, some concord with our neighbors, some connection to the larger forces of God or gods.

Fukuyama's formulation was in its own way more dour: what if, having actually achieved our purpose, having won the war with the tools not just of atomic weapons and foreign aid but of Levittowns and *Lucy*'s, of Beach Boys and Brill Building promises transmitted to the world (*wouldn't it be nice to stay together?*), we now lost the underlying purpose to our actions, lost the script to the drama we had so earnestly acted out, nay, written and rewritten, rehearsed and revised, from sometime in the midst of World War II until the fall of our last implacable enemy?

Fukuyama's "end of history" was, more pointedly, an announcement of the end of American purpose as it had been defined for close to half a century. The collapse of the American narrative occurred at the moment when the technologies of the digital had reached a point of dramatic take-off: when improvements in that technology would far outstrip genuine needs for the new capacities, leaving them idle, available for play. Looking for solace, distraction, or a field for displacement, Americans—particularly the young male Americans whose place in America was perhaps most threatened—found their way to the virtual world, and they began to game.

Yet this gaming was not playful, or joyous, or redemptive. Perhaps the perfect case in point concerns a charming little nuclear war shareware game known as *Hovertank 3D*. Its premise, highly compressed, would seem to put it in the lineage of *Balance of Power* and *Trinity*: rescue innocent civilians from a city before the clock runs out and the Big One falls, nuking the city. But *Hovertank 3D* was closer to the opposite of those moralizing responses to nuclear fear. For one thing, it was one of the first true first-person shooters. Rather than presiding over negotiations to achieve world peace, or going back in time to engage in the moral debates over the development of atomic weaponry, you sat in a great big tank, loaded with firepower. For another, you weren't fighting the good fight out of some humanitarian gesture: you were a morally bankrupt mercenary hired by an organization whose goals weren't your concern, and you were paid by the rescue—but only the rescue of those whom your corporate bosses chose.

Hovertank 3D wasn't just a first-person shooter, it was among the first games to use a convincing illusion of movement in three dimensions. While the graphics at one level were primitive—walls were flat swaths of color, your refugees and enemies were pixilated cartoons—you moved within a convincingly-presented dynamic space. As you went forward, walls gave way, entrances and side corridors appeared, and as you turned into them, you left each area with a sense of space at your back—space that could harbor vicious enemies, atomic mutants out to get you, or perhaps one of your client's chosen refugees whom you'd not noticed as you went past them.

So there you were: ensconced in armor, your potency immensely amplified with weaponry, lumbering around a nuclear-mutant-infested pit hole of a future, picking up desperate powerless civilians for cash. Anyone vaguely versed in psychoanalytic ideas would suggest you were in the midst of a frenzy of compensatory acting-out, in which two powerful clusters of cultural repression were returning: the now-neutralized fear of a nuclear-holocaust future and the still-active condition of individual powerlessness and inconsequentiality.

Hovertank 3D was the product of a savvy collaboration of designers fully committed to the idea that the future of virtual gaming lay with escapist immersion, but immersion in a world that gained its energy and its addictive success from tapping the collective cultural unconscious—one bored, unhappy, purposeless American at a time. The design team was built around four brilliant apostates: John Romero, John Carmack, Tom Hall, and Adrian Carmack. Together, they developed a system for replicating dynamic movement in space in the virtual sphere and applying it to an increasingly sophisticated dystopian universe of post-atomic, post-historical violence, mutation, and moral anarchy. *Hovertank 3D* was their first salvo; their triumph, however, was *Doom*. And they named their company id Software.

Doom arrived on the digital scene in 1993. It far surpassed its predecessors in moral audacity, illusionistic immersion, and popularity. To build *Doom*, the designers ramped up their modeling program, rendering space, place, surface, and light with uncanny persuasiveness. They populated this

17.15. *Doom*, early gameplay scenario

world with a host of remorseless, conscienceless, murderous mutants.*
There were no allies, no friends, there was no one to protect or for whom to
sacrifice one's personal safety or moral integrity. There was just you against
them. With weapons ranging from the primitive (fists, knives) to the high-
tech-future (laser guns, the BFG4000), *Doom* offered every opportunity to
reenact (or, premonitorily, *enact*) every mass murder in human history and
imagination, from Jack the Ripper to *The Texas Chainsaw Massacre*.

On one level, *Doom* (and its successors in the super-immersive violent
first-person shooter genre) seemed to offer a displaced locale for the violence that could not be given sanction in warfare now that eternal peace
was soon to reign in the post-historical world. But if we return to Turner and
Fukuyama, we find in *Doom*, and in many of its dystopic offshoots, a further
dourness. Turner had proposed the movement of American purpose from

---

* "Monsters from the id" was the important quote that drove the choice of name. It referred
to the 1956 sci-fi cult movie *Forbidden Planet*, which had proposed the power of the id to create the very enemies around us.

the continent—the West—to the globe. Fukuyama may not have made the proposition, but as a neoconservative in the Reagan and first Bush eras, he was surrounded by people who saw the interstellar frontier as the proper next step, the necessary mission that would harness American energies and direct American purpose after winning the Cold War. In *Doom*, space became not a place of promise and vaulting ambition but one of genetic mutation and antihumanism where the only way for individual humans to survive was by regressing to primitive modes of self-preserving violence. In *Doom* and its successors, radical individualism, that base American value, mutated into sociopathic survivalism.

Mutation wasn't simply a metaphor in many of these games. The virtual world saw an explosion of games in which the player was immersed in the very landscape most feared during the Cold War—a post-nuclear wasteland populated by mutants or, in some cases, roving gangs of desperate survivors, retreated to tribalism and desperate conflict over the last pickings of the postapocalyptic age.[17]

Immersing oneself in a radiation-infused, mutant-spawning future was one form of the return of the Cold War's repressed scenarios. Strategy games, as well, quickly took the form of Cold War-turned-hot scenarios: *Balance of Power* without the antiwar sentiment. In other strategy/FPS/RPG hybrids, atomic weapons join the player's arsenal or are used by enemy forces— notably the *Strike* series, which began in 1992 with a war simulation scenario set in Desert Storm/Gulf War strategizing, evolved to *Soviet Strike* in 1996, with a post-Soviet demagogue assembling a nuclear strike force against the West, and then culminated in 1997's boldly titled *Nuclear Strike*.

The *Strike* franchise, one of a host of console-based games that emerged in the '90s, points up the power of the atomic-holocaust scenario to recur and then be overlaid on other forms of virtual immersion. *Strike* was actually an offshoot of a helicopter-simulation series that used an Apache assault copter in a highly sophisticated *Flight Simulator* descendent. So also with other genres of gaming. Even the seemingly benign *SimCity* series had, by 1994, developed a nuclear holocaust scenario: Barcelona, vaporized by nuclear terrorists, leaving the player of this "God game" simulation with the impossible task of decontaminating and rebuilding. As recently as 2008, some game franchises located firmly in morally safe historical settings had "ported" to the present, bringing atomic holocaust with them—games like *Call of Duty 4*.

Nuclear holocaust returned after the end of history, but without moral import. Instead, it became a part of the repertoire of the post-historical virtual world's promise of illusions of grandiosity, power, and agency to counteract the dissipation of an earlier era's mythos. You could inflict holocaust; you could witness it and then wade in to save the postapocalyptic world, or you could have it inflicted on you, and survive.

Or, by contrast, you could find yourself within the dystopia, a victim seeking to find some way out. This was the premise of the brilliant *Wasteland* (1988), in which a U.S.–USSR atomic war has rendered the world largely uninhabitable but for small sections, one of which, the American Southwest (including Las Vegas!), forms the setting for the game.[18]

Wasteland can be seen as a vestige of the Reagan-era resurgence of nuclear fear; its even more spectacular successor, the *Fallout* series, was firmly located in the post-historical moment of repetition and regression. *Fallout* was not authored by the same designers as *Wasteland*; instead it was a self-conscious attempt to extend and redirect the older game, undertaken by a team of designers headed by Tim Cain. After two highly successful forays, the team took the new graphics engines and the new multi-core processors and devised a game that married the "flat" endless game terrain made possible by the new technologies, with a sardonic take on post-nuclear apocalyptic life. With its much more sophisticated graphics and meticulous attention to detail, *Fallout 3* was a smashing success.

Cain was (and is) something of a model for the second generation of game designers. Cain came into the profession at a time when game design was a viable option for someone trained in computer science at a first-rate university. Cain was, in other words, exemplary of a generation of game

17.16. Washington DC in ruins: *Fallout 3*

designers who had been born with a Nintendo controller in their hands, who had taken apart the software code for their parents' programs, who had the mastery of gaming as a prerequisite for their vocation as designers, and who viewed computer games as a mass-culture art form arriving at a state of maturity and available for any number of tasks, from entertainment to consciousness raising.

Fallout designer Tim Cain was struggling to articulate a critique of the Cold War American premises of prosperity, progress, and moral exceptionalism; it was not until 2008's *Fallout 3*, that he and his team could fully explore the struggle to survive in a post-holocaust environment, and the questions about human conduct and dignity that arose.

By then, this set of issues had actually evolved into a game subgenre known as "survival-horror" in which impotence, not potency, became the character's defining trait, and the game's goal was not triumph but the canny and increasingly desperate hoarding of resources in order to survive against long odds. *Resident Evil* (1998) set the form; while it had no direct holocaust survival scenario, its setting was populated by genetic mutants, bred by the failure of modern scientists and bureaucrats to resist the call of *hubris*. As the genre evolved in the twenty-first century, it garnered games with paradoxically more specific atomic-holocaust scenarios. Most notable of these was 2007's *S.T.A.L.K.E.R.: Shadow of Chernobyl*, set within the "Zone of Alienation" surrounding the site of the Chernobyl nuclear disaster, not far from the city where the design team had its studio. A sequel focused squarely on the abandoned city of Pripyat at the center of the Chernobyl dead zone.

All these games conformed to the psychoanalyst's dream scenario: they offered escape from an unpleasantly impotent and meaningless daily life into a fantasy world that rapidly turned toward radical sociopathic grandiosity or toward nightmare desperation. But they took place in alternate universes to that of present-day America. In contrast there arose games with dystopic scenarios set in increasingly realistic simulacra of the contemporary world. Probably the most seductive and most controversial was the *Grand Theft Auto* series, first released in 1997 and reaching its acknowledged peak with *Grand Theft Auto IV* eleven years later.

Grand Theft Auto was the dystopian extrapolation of Fukuyama's post-historical world of purposeless consumption and boredom. In it, you countered boredom not by purchasing and consuming, but by stealing and consuming; not by escaping to fantasy but by descending into the turmoil of violence and radical individual selfishness of the most material sort. Theft led to sex, sex to murder, murder to prowess, prowess to more theft, theft to wealth, in a seemingly endless cycle.

GTA almost immediately garnered virulent protest, particularly from the neoconservative moral politicians of the later '90s and early '00s. On one hand, it rekindled arguments that the violence in video games would encourage violent action in the physical world. Much greater, however, was the revulsion at *GTA*'s studied absence of moral direction and encouragement of a worldview in which no larger purpose than immediate pleasure, excitement or revenge characterized the post-historical American condition.

The protests reflected a paradoxical interplay of fears: on one side, that the hyperagency of the game might awaken the player to his* powerlessness outside the virtual world, leading to a sort of revolutionary individualistic terrorism: becoming, in the language of that premonitory dystopian sci-fi writer John Brunner, a "mucker";[19] on the other that the fascinations of the game would so fully supplant the physical as to render it unimportant, leaving a wake of disobedient refuseniks holed up in their parents' basements when they should be out feeding the engines of late capitalism. Beyond this binary, however, was a third possibility: that the true danger of *Grand Theft Auto* lay in its mirroring of the new conditions of post-historical America.

Beyond Simulacra: Grand Theft Auto *and* The Sims

Grand Theft Auto reached its peak with its fourth version, released in 2008.[†] It was not simply that the franchise had exploited digital technology and game-design maturity to the fullest with each succeeding iteration. It was the way that this version embodied what had been implied by all preceding versions. It was, finally, radically *flat*, to borrow a phrase from game-design slang. For one thing, it was morally neutral. Unlike its predecessors in the franchise, the ease or difficulty of tasks no longer rewarded nuanced moral choices—on the contrary, the new improved software engine was utterly utilitarian, functionalist. It was radical free-market economics applied to the arena of human behavior.

---

* And here, until the arrival of Grrl gamers, almost all grandiose agency-granting immersive games were made by and for young men.

† *GTA V* is, to my mind, simply an extrapolation of *IV*, extending the flatness, improving the visuals, rendering the potential narrative lines more complex, without paradigm-shifting innovation. Rockstar's lengthy promotional video, released in 2012, makes their case, and mine: http://www.rockstargames.com/V/.

Version 4 was also flat in the virtual landscape—it was, finally, a game that was effectively without boundaries. If we hearken back to *Zork!* and its maps, we can see something of radicalism of this evolution. *Zork!*'s maps showed the trick; you thought you were wandering an infinite maze, but in fact it was quite limited, and those limitations were papered over with stratagems of language and of programming. With *GTA IV*, you would die in real time, in the physical world, before ever reaching the limits of the landscape and the options of the narrative.

In one of the most interesting texts on video game worlds, *Extra Lives* (2010), Tom Bissell describes in excruciating detail his descent into multiple addictions, first in Las Vegas, and then in Tallin, capital of the former Soviet republic of Estonia. Bissell's point is that of most literary recovery memoirs: video games, like cocaine, are addictive, destructively so. He is vague on the pleasures of the world to which he can now return, the world from which his addiction has allowed him to escape. From his book, we gather that he has worked at the edges of the knowledge economy—as a teacher of English in China, for example—that his bursts of writing production are not particularly satisfying, nor are their satisfactions to be trusted, and that his romantic and family life has not been marked by harmony, stability, or lasting comfort. His recovery from cocaine and gaming will, the recovery narrative form requires, lead him back to "normalcy": to the capacity for a middle-class family with children; to steady employment at work he does with increasing skill and efficiency; to a house he owns, and to a network of like-minded, sociable beings.

His is, in other words, a near-exact description of the future promised to the reunited family in *Miracle on 34th Street*, to the actors in the Levittown dream. It carries none of the rebelliousness or the rage of Dylan or the antic utopianism of the Diggers in the Haight or the earnest idealism of the communards of New Buffalo. Its arc is utterly clear: Bissell has learned his lesson. Cocaine and games may offer the initial rush of escape and excitement, the forbidden thrill of agency, of control over oneself and one's environment. But that is *maia*, illusion. Soon it will sour into a dystopian hell from which the only escape will be confession—*this* confession, the one you're reading now—followed by forgiveness, a chastened return to the fold.

Bissell cloaks *Extra Lives* in a peculiar jeremiad: he rails against the failure of games to satisfy the needs of the very form they occupy. They are, he tells us again and again, badly written. Their designers spend too much time on convincing rendering of hair, and too little on their promise of immersion in a believable virtual world, one that is convincingly built of the in-your-bones knowledge of the ways *this* world works, while taking that conviction into a place far distant. Yes, Bissell says, there are exceptions, and they are, to his taste, all hyperviolent, amoral FPSs or variants on that genre. If video gaming is a form of learning environment, Bissell implies, it's *watch out world*.

Bissell's final addiction was to *Grand Theft Auto IV*, perhaps the most triumphantly elaborate realization of the promise of free-will, open-landscape gaming. But *Grand Theft Auto IV* is also a game of immense moral peril, in which free-will play enables an utter amorality to dominate not just the world around you, but you, yourself. *Grand Theft Auto IV*, as Bissell describes it, is the ultimate video game. And yet it is the very addictive substance from which he must escape, begging forgiveness. Its very power over him reaffirms that it is he, and not the contemporary world, that is at fault.

Or almost. For despite Bissell's confessional tone, the real magnetic attraction in the picture he draws is to that virtual world, and his critique seems aimed not at the game itself but at the unhappy reality of physical boundedness, of mundane mortality. Never once does Bissell suggest that the real world, the post-historical America, is dull, stifling of creativity, without moral purpose, inhumane, disenfranchising, echoing with the portentous voices of propaganda and the seductive voices of advertising. Yet all his attention lies with his *other* world, with its free-will choices, its frontier violence and opportunism, its promises of wealth and pleasure and its threats of injury, punishment, and extinction. We know why he's chosen *GTA IV* over the real world, and no amount of redemption-narrative confessionalism can erase that awareness. After I read the book—more accurately, as I reached page 169—I went online to Steam* and bought the game.

Bissell's recovery confessional illuminates in stark relief some of the remaining complicated binaries that define the new virtual cultural landscape. One of these declares the Cold War era as a haven, a site for nostalgia, in contrast to the complex, uncertain era in which we live. These bursts of nostalgia present an America of the '50s and early '60s with a clear moral compass and a clean reputation, operating within an unambiguous sphere of right and wrong, of American and Soviet, capitalist and Communist. By contrast, the present is a time without moral clarity, in which too much choice, the *open world* of the video game, leaves us adrift.

Grand Theft Auto IV (and, even more extravagantly, 2013's *GTA V*, with its

---

* Those not initiated in twenty-first century gaming communities can go to Steampowered .com; there they'll find a huge array of downloadable games, access to multiplayer gaming domains, and the chance to create a gaming identity that can be accessed from any computer anywhere.

three points of view and fully open world, set in the insecure America of the Great Crash and its slow crawl of a play out) represented one example in a string of first-person, open-world shooters or mayhem games, in which the player inhabited a character of malleable moral character in an environment now so fully exploitative of the superior technologies of late-twentieth-century computers and consoles that game designers could create seamlessly convincing worlds of seemingly infinite choice through which that character could wander. These games find a common ancestry in the years immediately surrounding the collapse of the Soviet Union, and they form one side of a final binary with which we will end our travels, emerging, ourselves, into the confusing light of our own present moment, our America.

There is violence and power, and there is order and efficiency: *Doom* is countered by *SimCity 2000*, *Fallout 3* by *The Sims 3*. In the first, we roam a post-atomic dystopia; in the alternative, we return to the orderly city and then leave it for the comforts of a suburban home, a profession (practiced at some distance, off the stage of the game), to the making of a family and the founding of a dynasty.

If Bissell were to describe his post-recovery world, it would look something like *The Sims 3*, the most recent (as of 2013) of Will Wright's wildly successful real-world simulation games. Wright's simulation empire began in the late '70s with a little software machine designed to construct backgrounds for a game he was subcontracted to embellish—a game, tellingly, in which the Japanese had the chance to refight the Pacific Theater of World War II, island by island, and win—a game, needless to say, directed to a Japanese audience.[20] The result of that first experiment was released in more complex form and without the troubled underlying ideological baggage, as *Raid on Bungeling Bay* in 1984; the scenario-building software evolved into *SimCity*, released in 1989.

SimCity was a cute and deeply addictive little city-building simulation program: the player zoned areas commercial, residential or industrial, built roads and rail and mass transit, and watched over the city's expansion, modifying as circumstances changed and the city evolved. It was not a game you won or lost—you escaped into it, into its comforting orderliness and its promise that urban development, and by extension all of late-modern life, could be understood as a set of rational algorithms interacting with each other in predictable ways. There were, of course, certain ideological biases (Wright was living in Northern California; mass transit, not superhighways, was the way to go), but outside of those, even smart 7-year-olds could quickly immerse themselves in the game. It was, in fact, more like the purposeless play of childhood than the computer, console and arcade games of its era.

Through various iterations, though, Wright's simulations grew increasingly didactic—he would, perhaps, say, *educational*. The city simulations became more complex, requiring sewer systems, subways that could not necessarily be built wherever one wished to place them, cycles of decay in the built environment. And Wright's design team produced a stable of other games, from *Simfarm* and *Simant*, which taught the complexities of small economies and ecosystems, to the grandiose and less-successful *SimEarth*, which attempted to embody in software form the counterculture's cherished *gaia* concept—the belief that living things in right relation interacted to benefit the whole macroorganism of the planet.

Wright's software was deeply indebted to the counterculture, most directly to the gospel of ex-Digger and ex-Prankster Stewart Brand. Brand's *Whole Earth Catalog* had promoted a strange admixture of lifestyle austerity and simplification, and material consumption (it was loaded with products, though they were alternatives to the consumer products of their time—biodegradable soaps instead of Tide detergent; yurts rather than mobile homes). It emerged from, and was directed toward, the back-to-the-land communal wing of the American counterculture, but its power to mythologize that movement was far greater than its mere utility for the scattered counterculture communes of North America—it sold 1.5 million copies in 1972, suggesting the reach of that movement, at least as a construction of desire and curiosity if not direct action.[21]

Brand and Wright were part of a wave of utopian cyberfuturists; for them, the computer would liberate individual consciousness, enable new forms of communitarianism across physical spaces and national boundaries, and usher in a postmodern paradise of peace and love. Theirs too was a variant on Fukuyama's linking of liberal democracy with prosperity. They imagined that prosperity would emerge from a different economic model than free-market capitalism. In their utopia, dramatically increased efficiencies in production as a result of new technologies and the more appropriate use of what was already at hand (and the computer was an instrumental part of that revolution) would free up capital for rapidly improving global quality of life. Meanwhile, the opening of information frontiers would awaken new forms of global consciousness and widened vistas of human potential, supplanting greed and consumer desire (resulting in a new economy that eschewed frivolities for necessities). Sharing would replace owning, and spirituality and art would substitute for materialism and mass-entertainment.

For Wright, however, entertainment was still king, and he imagined that computer games could serve as Trojan horses, bringing new ways of thinking and imagining to households that might otherwise view the countercultural ideology with suspicion or contempt. His games were to be tools of empowerment rather than escapes from a world of disenfranchishment.

SimCity was the antidote to its contemporary, *Doom*. Its benign, *satori*-inducing Zen pacing and simplistic aphorisms bedded in binary code won it the gaming industry's highest awards. A slow seller at first, it became a hit, and as importantly, crossed computer gaming's gender barrier in ways that would revolutionize gaming. Previously, girls and women who played at all tended toward the fantasy-adventure games, with their puzzles and narrative lines, but even these required that female players take on male identities, not willingly but because there were no alternatives: the hero was the *hero*, never the *heroine*—even *The Legend of Zelda*'s protagonist wasn't Zelda, but Link, whose quest was to *rescue* Zelda, who was held captive, naturally, and in need of a good man. Not until 1996, with the emergence of *Tomb Raider*'s Lara Croft did the digital realm find a playable female protagonist—unless, that is, you want to count Ms. Pac-Man. *SimCity* didn't upend the gender imbalance; it rewrote the gaming rules to make a game that no longer privileged the masculine extremes of militarism, violence, greed, and competitiveness.

The full array of Wright rollouts, including games like *Spore* and *Sim-Earth*, weren't aimed *at* women, per se. They simply promoted a relatively testosterone-free worldview. Similarly, the franchise wasn't anticapitalist; after all, Wright didn't release his games as freeware or shareware, and they certainly weren't open-source coded. Wright and his acolytes and colleagues, including Stewart Brand, saw their mission as returning humankind to a sympathetically skeptical, curious, open-minded worldview. Wright's games would do so.

If one can imagine a gaming antidote to Fukuyama's boredom at the end of history, his vision of empty consumerism in increasingly stretched vacancies of "leisure" as work became less and less demanding on the individual with new technologies replacing inefficient human drudgery, Wright's empire of simulations would seem to fit the bill. But there was an inherent paradox to Wright's game design style: as each iteration, and each new and improved version of each iteration, emerged from the Maxis/Electronic Arts empire, the new became a more fascinating, seductive alternative to the real world. And the trend culminated in the first months of the new millennium, with the release, after a years-long frenzy of anticipation, of *The Sims*.

The Sims was nothing more and nothing less than a reconstruction of the Cold War's ideal huddling place—a suburban house on a quarter-acre lot on which you could build, socialize, romance, entertain, and be entertained, but which you could never leave.

Players of *The Sims 4* who did not start out on *The Sims*—that is, most players under the age of 20 and most over the age of 45—will miss the significance of this point. Recent versions and "expansion packs" of the game offer the opportunity to wander from lot to lot, to go for a jog from home to downtown gym to movie theater to restaurant, and then take a taxi home. In the original, however, Wright's team was faced with a notably less powerful stock of home computers on which their game could be played, and they decided to shrink the universe to a single home, and to make this little spot of heaven as deeply seductive, as fully satisfying, as possible.

The visual qualities shone, but that wasn't all. The visual quality of *The Sims* was a gentle satire, both on the soft-focus nostalgia for Levittown and its Cold War suburban counterparts and on the slick polyester surfaces that characterized most rendering in the digital domain. In that way, Wright and his people negated the critique of the visual sphere; it was almost cartoon-like, and its exaggerations and limits were to be forgiven.

Instead, they concentrated on what others had considered oddities: notably background noise and sonic nuance, and spoken language. Actually, these were inextricably linked parts of the game's appeal, for the designers had invented a gibberish, *Simlish*, that radically trumped previous attempts at convincing interaction between the player's projected character ("avatar," in game-speak) and the nondirected characters. What was so persuasive about the language was its sonic nuance—the ways consonants and vowels fit together, the ways questions, statements, conversations could be phrased with upthrusts and downdrafts to the flow. *The Sims*' designers even commissioned real alt-rock, pop, and Latino bands to reperform their music in Simlish, and the results were spot-on. Similarly with the sounds of appliances, of water flowing from faucets, of toilets flushing, and food processors whirring.

But all this took place within the limited sphere of one house. You could buy it, or you could build it, from a kit of parts. You were given a certain amount of money ("simoleons," they were called, one of many charmingly satiric puns and references in the game), and you chose where to spend it.

Rapidly you learned that there were laws of conduct, of cause and effect, in this little suburban world: you had better buy a bookshelf so you could read a cookbook and learn to cook or you'd starve, or light the house on fire. You'd better buy a chair and a bed to sleep in. You'd better check the newspaper for a job because you were already low on simoleons and your fridge was pretty empty, too.

There were two addictive components to *The Sims*. One was the verisimilitude—the slightly twisted, stylized replication that made you want to manipulate things to see what they sounded like, how they worked. The other was your obligation as a deity to make your sims happy and to learn the underlying laws of everyday life that made that possible. *The Sims* was, after all, a variant of the genre known as a god-game, a simulation in which you controlled the world or, in this case, a small distillate of it. *The Sims* taught you just how demanding, how interminable, and how exhausting, was the work of being a god.

First, there were the rules to learn. Use that toilet; flush it; clean it. Buy a smoke detector pretty soon, because even with cooking experience your sim was going to get ambitious, or distracted, while at the stove. Get a job. Find love. Get married. Sire children. Send them to school. Help them with their homework. Stay on time and make sure *they* stay on time, as well. Suck up to the headmaster of the private school so your kid got in, and did well. Earn more money; earn a promotion; learn what was necessary to get that promotion; follow the basic rules of the workplace. Shower before work. Dress well. And over the next iteration and the next, the geography your sims occupied expanded, and yours became more and more constrained. Make friends with coworkers, or at least pretend to do so. No, you didn't have to mow the lawn, but you did have to maintain your house and yard. Don't leave for long—there's work to be done, problems to be solved, crises to manage, happiness to replenish.

These were the rules of Cold War middle-class suburban life. Or, that is, they were the caricatures of those rules. It wasn't clear whether the designers were being gently satiric or whether Wright and Company were applying the didactics of *gaia* and the friendly nudging educational forms of the earlier sim games to the ideal life. If so, it was a radical retreat from the utopianism of *The Whole Earth Catalog*.

The Sims' game play was pretty much perpetual, but that didn't mean it wasn't goal-directed. You might win in any number of ways, according to the game itself, and these were in effect caricatures of the rigid and limiting definitions of success in the postwar middle-class American culture. There were new-age variants: you could marry same-sex partners or even engage in polyamorous relationships; you could adopt children as well as conceive them; you could live out your life in a Spartan, Thoreau-in-the-'burbs sort of way—but not in any really interesting way. After all, the point was to accumulate, and play with, *stuff*, with the archly caricatured versions of Best Buy and Home Depot and Crate & Barrel and (actually, by the third version of the game, in a triumph of product placement) Ikea.

And yet it mirrored in most respects the suburban life not as it was lived by the Levittowners or those in Skokie, Illinois, or (for the Beach Boys) Haw-

thorne, California, but as it was conceived in the placid and reassuring pan-
egyrics of the '50s suburban sitcoms, most notably *Father Knows Best* and,
even more directly, *Ozzie and Harriet*. There was just more opportunity for
more flamboyant achievement of the same materialist goals. In the end, you
triumphed by ascending the corporate ladder in some invisible workplace,
marrying up, maximizing your utilitarian knowledge, limiting your leisure
to what was necessary to reconstitute yourself so you'd be most cheerful and
efficient at work and buying the most stuff. *The Sims* was a virtual version of
the world that Fukuyama had so dreaded at the end of history.

The Sims was immensely popular. Within two years of its release, it was the
biggest selling game of all time, at 6.3 million copies. By 2005, as *The Sims 2*
began its own meteoric rise, there were 16 million copies of the first version
in circulation. As of early 2010, when the franchise entered its second decade, it had passed 125 million "units," and industry watchers expected it to
continue to ratchet up some 12 million units a year without flagging, for the
foreseeable future, and *The Sims 3* had ratcheted up no fewer than seventeen
expansion packs, ranging from celebrity tie-ins to *University Life*.[22] In 2014,
Maxis will leap into open-world gaming when it delivers *The Sims 4*.

Will Wright's design team didn't just devote itself to new versions of the
game; it also pushed out versions for nearly every possible type of graphics-
capable digital platform—not only computers and video consoles, but portable and hand-held players and, eventually, mobile phones, and musical
devices. By the end of the first decade of the twenty-first century, it was a
commonplace to see kids in the backs of minivans playing *The Sims* on the
pop-up screens of the seats in front of them; to see teenagers at concerts
playing *The Sims* on their Androids and iPhones; to see lawyers sitting in
the lobbies of government offices playing *The Sims* on their iPads. A digital
game borne into the American home, replicating the American home, now
carried that replica out into the physical world, overlaying the noise of subway trains or car horns with the reassuring sussurations of Simlish and the
comforts of a miniature world always on the verge of perfect orderliness
and comfort.

Something drove this popularity, something significant.

Repetition Compulsion: Playing The Sims

Bissell's confessional spoke little of the world to which he would reemerge
in recovery from his addiction to real cocaine and virtual nihilistic violence. So I will help him: he is going to *The Sims 4*.

I also will confess to an addiction: to the virtual world of *The Sims*. I have certainly played it as many hours as had Bissell his versions of *GTA*. But my experience is dramatically different than was his. He experienced *GTA* as a fantasy escape from the restrictions of middle-class life at the end of history. I was addicted to *The Sims* for its replication of that restricted world, and for the ways it stimulated and directed the same synapse connections as had my daily life when I lived in the suburbs. But just as my real life in that real world had been insistently and caustically commented on by my cultural historian's observing ego, so too the game play with which I reclaimed that experience was one marked by an almost schizoid self-observation.

In my case, daily play followed a certain rhythm. In the morning, I'd start the game with anticipation, pleasure, hope. I'd be delighted by the sounds (my daughter Molly and I used to speak Simlish to each other), by the things to manipulate; I'd look forward to earning a cache of simoleons to spend on something new. After a couple of hours, though, I'd get impatient, moving the game speed up to get to the next goal; fast-forwarding my sims' reading so they'd raise their cooking skill and learn a new recipe, or grunting with annoyance when a visitor came calling, interrupting the necessary task with another necessary task—sacrificing fun-building TV watching for friendship-building interactions with the neighbors at the door. After another hour or so, I'd be in a state of tense frustration, yearning to turn off the game, to escape its demands, but unable to leave things as they were. Then, finally, frustration would win out and I would exit. I'd look up from the computer screen at a sunstruck writing space cluttered with open books, legal pads, outlines pinned to the wall, guitars in the corner, cats on the rug, and it would all look a bit gray, washed out. I couldn't easily move from the game's colors, rhythms, and rules, to those outside of it, without feeling simultaneously like it was a diminishment of sorts, and a return to a messily unpredictable and complicated life, without clear goals. I yearned for the very thing I'd just left: a virtual world as orderly as a domestic sitcom from the '50s, in which, as here, all frustrations were small ones, unmarked by fear of global holocaust or individual injury, decline and death. My sims died; I didn't.

But to return was also untenable; that world, that simland, was too frustratingly limited. Its rules were too rigid, its demands on my autonomy too great. It was disturbingly like a critique of everyday American life, without the satisfactions of protest or the possibility of transformation. But wait. Even the drug of virtual agency quickly wore off. This was a god-game: I should have omnipotence, and omniscience, but I had neither. I could look down at the scenario, but from only a small number of camera angles. I

17.17. Dawn breaks over *The Sims 3*.

could observe action, but only within the narrow confines of this home, and this suburban lot. I couldn't go next door or see the workplace, or escape into a wider world. I was trapped.

The Sims was released on January 31, 2000, at the end of a short era of American peace and prosperity when it seemed the utopianism of the counterculture had found common cause with a technocracy liberated from militarism and now looking for new missions. But Americans do not abandon the old myths and symbols that easily. Where were the cowboys and wild ones, where was the frontier, where was the promise of personal mobility in this technocratically engineered program of steady, if slightly boring, material progress? Fukuyama said it well when he confessed to "a powerful nostalgia" for a more outsized drama, with Americans its most interesting heroes.

In the same month that George W. Bush took the Republican nomination for president (declaring, "In Midland, Texas, where I grew up, the town motto was, 'The sky's the limit,' and we believed it; there was a restless energy, a basic conviction that with hard work, anybody could succeed and everybody deserved a chance"), Wright's Maxis Software released *Livin' Large,* the first of a string of "expansion packs" that added more consumables and expanded the abilities of sims to act out in more extreme ways—notably, to remake themselves—sim-ing their simness. Its success might, in retrospect, be seen as a predictor of the way the election would go.

In January of 2001, George W. Bush gave his first inaugural address, articulating with eloquence the backward-looking, forward-driving America his campaign had come to exemplify:

> We have a place, all of us, in a long story—a story we continue, but whose end we will not see. It is the story of a new world that became a friend and liberator of the old, a story of a slave-holding society that became a servant of freedom, the story of a power that went into the world to protect but not possess, to defend but not to conquer. It is the American story—a story of flawed and fallible people, united across the generations by grand and enduring ideals. The grandest of these ideals is an unfolding American promise that everyone belongs, that everyone deserves a chance, that no insignificant person was ever born. Americans are called to enact this promise in our lives and in our laws. And though our nation has sometimes halted, and sometimes delayed, we must follow no other course. Through much of the last century, America's faith in freedom and democracy was a rock in a raging sea. Now it is a seed upon the wind, taking root in many nations. Our democratic faith is more than the creed of our country; it is the inborn hope of our humanity, an ideal we carry but do not own, a trust we bear and pass along.[23]

Two months after the inauguration, a second *Sims* expansion pack appeared—*House Party*, which combined two emerging trends in the new American economy: ever-more-conspicuous public consumption and display, and a Bush administration–fueled campaign to expand home ownership. As the ironic term "McMansion" was coined to describe outsize private homes with triple or quadruple stall garages and cavernous "family rooms," bought with easy credit and the promise of infinitely rising property values and stuffed with ever more-elaborate consumables, *The Sims: House Party* offered the opportunity to create outsize entertainment rooms with giant televisions and stereos, elaborate wet bars, swimming pools, and all the accoutrements simultaneously being built in the physical landscape of the American exurb.

Then the terrorist attacks of September 11, 2001, turned the Bush-era swagger and its Cold War–era rhetoric of American moral superiority and global mission in a darker and more paranoid direction. While the number of Americans killed, 2,819, was the largest military loss on American soil since the Civil War, it was a tiny fraction of the number of American soldiers killed in Vietnam. It was 1/16 the number of Vietnamese children estimated born deformed as a result of U.S. use of Agent Orange. Six years earlier, the Srebrenica massacres by Serbs of Bosnians had killed 8,000 civilians. Death statistics for 2001 in the United States: 42,000 highway deaths; 20,000 flu deaths; more than 15,000 murders. One violent coup in any other part of the globe, one natural disaster in an unprepared region reaped tenfold the number of innocents killed in 9/11.*

The intensity of national response to the terrorist bombings of the World Trade Center and the Pentagon in 2001 was far out of proportion, then, to the simple numbers. It is more easily understood as a complicated reaction to a larger sense of threat and injury that was triggered by the attacks, a sense of wounded virtue at the violation of the myth of national immunity. American exceptionalism—its moral gift and its geographical isolation— were to have protected America from attacks both military and ideological. We had fought, and won, the Cold War not just with military technology and investment, but with the moral superiority of our political, social and economic systems, and we believed that our national behavior in the drama on the world's stage had convinced the globe of our earnestness, our virtue, and our superiority as a cultural system and a historical entity. We were poised on the edge of a global revolution that would bring the combined powers of liberal democracy and free-market capitalism to every corner of the world. Our technologies had conquered the globe. Yet the fragility of our belief in ourselves and our mission manifested itself in the force and turbulence of our response to the terrorist attacks on that day. Over the following months and years, we would be drawn back to an older, more paranoid Americanism, and we would force the world to fit the mold of our older, more paranoid Manichaeism: for or against us, friend or foe, wounded but implacable force for good, or dark, demonic force for evil.

The frenzy of paranoid responses in the months after the attacks rekindled and replicated Cold War responses of decades before.[24] But there were differences. The Cold War's sense of siege had been based on a threat of genuine national and global immensity: atomic holocaust, whether willfully or accidentally ignited, that would eradicate the virtuous and the unvirtuous alike. After 9/11 no evidence surfaced of a similarly massive destructive force arrayed against us. The American rhetorical response to 2001's at-

* As of 2013, civilian deaths in Iraq after the American invasion were in a range between 113,876 and 124,696; see http://www.iraqbodycount.org/database/.

tacks bore little or no relation to the scale of the threat. Yes, there were tepid and sporadic discussions of the potential for nuclear terrorism and "dirty bombs" on American soil, but the vast preponderance of political speeches, journalistic essays, and common talk focused obsessively on further attacks on American symbols: hence the massive barriers around the White House and the Capitol, the surveillance at the Statue of Liberty and the Liberty Bell. Most broadly, it was the American sense of safe invulnerability that came under attack, and it was that feature of the attack that succeeded beyond the wildest expectations of the perpetrators of 9/11.

Within a year of the 9/11 attacks, *The Sims* had become the best-selling video game in history. This might seem unlikely, given the increasingly frustrating and limiting nature of the game play, as the novelty of its features wore off. Of course the cure for that was quintessentially consumerist— buy an expansion pack that allowed you more ways to shop, different raw materials with which to design and build your house, or even (in the case of *Apartment Life*) to live in something resembling an urban environment. What the expansion packs amplified was the capacity of the game to serve as a huddling-place, a retreat from a hostile world threatened by—already punctured by—unexpected, terrifying forces, largely invisible but utterly venomous. This was a picture of the world and America's place in it that was trumpeted by the voices of the Bush administration, particularly as the grotesque misstep of the Iraq invasion became clear. Even opponents of the Bush propaganda found themselves exhausted by the virulence of rhetoric and the shrill repetitive chant of the campaign.

Retreat to *The Sims* represented a significant trend in American cultural life. By 2008, the franchise had sold a hundred million copies, almost exactly the number of actual American households that year. At least once a day, we can estimate, some member of every computer- or video console-owning American household was returning to the quiet, restrictive, orderliness of a world modeled on the idealized postwar American utopia: the single-family home, presided over by adults who disappeared periodically into work-places invisible and inconsequential to the *real* life except for the wages their work brought—wages that enabled purchase of consumer goods, and thereby drove the stream of their continuous production.[25]

The Sims franchise replicated middle-class suburban life, with all its re-strictions and anxieties, its sense of eternal yearning, desire, and discontent. But it also eliminated from that sphere the full-on darkness that lay at the edges of the real American middle-class household, first in the Cold War, and then in the so-called War on Terror: the threat of undeserved, random injury or death, the eradication of the world, or at least of *your* world, which, in the solipsism of the post-9/11 American mind, *was* the end that mattered. In the confines of its bright, stylized, virtual landscape, we could reclaim, again and again, the promise of American progress, American prosperity, American exceptionalism.

Meditation: The Drama of Everyday Life

The post-9/11 world restarted history, though not to Francis Fukuyama's satisfaction. We are exhorted again to stand as a "city upon a hill," a model of Christian charity, and a demonstration of the perfect union of liberal democratic ideology and free-market capitalist economics. We are asked to consider our enemies savages, so opposed to the idea of humanism with its respect for a dignified human life that they are willing to sacrifice children or even themselves as, explosives strapped under their *hijabs*, they infiltrate the innocent, gently zealous missions of Americans abroad, Americans seeking only to improve the lot of those still far from the bright center. What are our shadowy enemies but regressive tribalists seeking to push the world back down the hill of civilization toward the brutal chaos of the primitive?

And yet, if we are so strong in virtue and they so weak, how can it be that we are so threatened, so beleaguered? How can they be winning against us? How can we have bankrupted ourselves in shadow wars with shadow enemies?

And what do we offer as our model? Is it, as Fukuyama said, nothing more than voting for televisual politicians, with archives of *American Idol* or *America's Most Wanted* awaiting us at home after our brief, pointless trip to the polls? With the mythic promises of upward mobility, property ownership, class fluidity, and individual and national reinvention shattered by the worst financial crash, and the most sustained economic bust, since the Great Depression, with wars on two fronts moving from debacle to debacle, we are hard-put to place ourselves as a shining example of hope to the world. We hold our breaths, waiting for the next sign that we have failed in our covenant.

This has become the new American fear, fear not of physical but of virtual annihilation, annihilation as a culture. Or, at least, diminishment and vulnerability which, to a national culture based on visible power and invulnerability, may be the same thing. America's symbols are under attack, America's myths, America's self-image.

It has been my proposal throughout this book that the defining quality of American cultural life between the end of World War II and the end of history was the belief that Americans were predestined to a dramatic vocation, to serve as actors on a stage of history. It is, and has been, a stage with sets we have had to build as we went along—suburban houses, television sets and the sets on which the TV sitcom is played, sets of songs played between commercials on the radio, sets of images played against each other, stages of new growth, far from the old centers, where new countercultures can emerge, rejuvenating the old ideals. We saw ourselves on stage acting out the drama of everyday life in pursuit of American happiness, acting *as if* material prosperity and a certain argumentative consensus could meld individual desire and community need into a harmonious chord.

Yet throughout this time, our dramas were always directed not to others, but to ourselves. We sought to imagine our America, to act it out, and then somehow to forget we were acting at all, forget our Levittowns and our atomic villages in Nevada were equally sets we had made on which to act our reinvention. The pop music of the first youth culture era reinvented our amateur drama: not in the Levittown home but out on the drag-racing streets or up on the urban roofs. When the counterculture's communalists made their entrance, they too set their lives as dramas—street performances by the San Francisco Mime Troupe became the street theater of the Diggers' Intersection Game; the communalists in New Mexico and Northern California, Tennessee and Oregon, played out their lives for the audiences of acolyte tourists on summer break or admiring, skeptical, or hostile witnesses from the dominant culture, out to get the pictures and the story for a Sunday feature or a weekly picture essay. Like their parents, they too believed that if they could act their roles successfully enough, convincingly enough, they could win the contest over America's direction, and they could at the same time convince themselves that the mundanities of brown rice, the indignities of pit toilets, and the tragedies of hepatitis and dysentery and infant mortality, were minor subtractions from a balance sheet in the reclamation of their beloved country.

And here we are, now, in the late stages of a return of the old, paranoid, America. Our dramas convince no one: not our opponents, not our friends, and—increasingly—not ourselves. We retreat to a simulacral world, where we enact caricatures of a past we no longer believe in. We are a culture beset by the very fears Puritan John Winthrop described as he ended the *Arbella* Sermon:

> If our hearts shall turn away, so that we will not obey, but shall be seduced, and worship other Gods, our pleasure and profits, and serve them; it is

propounded unto us this day, we shall surely perish out of the good land whither we pass over this vast sea to possess it.[26]

But these are dour thoughts for a sunny summer day. They are not portents or predictions; they are, instead, the premonitions that surround an anxious present. In this regard, this moment is not signally different than the moment that began our journey, the moment when Americans first confronted the power and peril of the atomic age. Just as then our triumph in a long-standing global battle has taken from us the easy comfort of an enemy to help us define, by negation, what we are not, and propose, by contrast, and out of necessity, what we are, and should, and will be. And so, set free of the comfort of an enemy of genuine consequence, we invent another, and another, seeking, always, only to invent and reinvent ourselves.

The present is not simple, and it is not simply binary: a redemptive past and a diminished future, a physical culture of powerlessness and propaganda from which we retreat to a virtual culture of grandiosity and false consciousness. *Second Life* may not be the utopian alternative to modern nationalism, capitalist greed, and social anomie it has been promised to be. *World of Warcraft* is more popular, and populous, than *Second Life*'s various desert islands and steampunk alt-cultures. We are shopping on our iPhones, not ending world hunger. But there *is* an iPhone app to end world hunger. We can learn the physics of atomic explosions on Wikipedia, and if we don't think the entry is clear enough, or accurate enough, we can sign on and edit it, joining a long string of contributors, giving up our personal contribution to a global knowledge commune.

The interpenetration of the virtual and the physical has had its utopian moments and, inevitably, its morose retractions. *Second Life*: who remembers when every corporation, every PBS show, was trumpeting its presence in that virtual world? Universities that thought they'd build their profitable online campuses there are retrenching, retreating or simply pretending they'd never made those fiscally foolish diversions of resources. Remember when Twitter and Facebook seemed to bring about a new spring of democratic uprising: in Egypt, now run (as of the moment I write this; by the time you read it, all will have changed) by a military that used to underwrite the previous hated regime, with women's rights perhaps even more at risk than before; in Syria, where brutal crackdowns, massacres, and scorched-earth retaliations have become the news you hear but turn from. With each of these uprisings, Americans left and right see the return of the American model, the city upon a hill, shining as a beacon for the globe to see. Technologies of communication born in the Cold War, evolved beyond recognition, provided the promise and the peril of another moment when America could imagine itself returning to its prominence as a moral model, its dramas the obsession of the world. And perhaps we are, but not in the simplistic way lauded by pundits and politicians. We are something more complicated, tenuous, and fragile.

We live, then, second lives, and third, and fourth—protean lives, threatened by the lingering traces of our mistakes, but also amenable to self-invention and renewal. Back in the earliest days of the virtual world, there were multiple user domains like The Well, where thousands struggled through glitches and freezes to imagine new forms of space-and-place-transcendent communities, communes of sorts, but without the hepatitis and the collapsing roof of the yurt or dome. These dreamers conceived of virtual places where they could be free of the bounds of their physical and their historical selves, embrace reinvention, form new communities of interest and engagement. Was this not what Turner described as the promise of the American frontier? Two decades later, MUDs and online communities were the ghettoes and subcultures of gamers and steam-punk enthusiasts. And then, across the gulf between one millennium and the next, between *then* and *now*, we have seen that promise renewed and globalized, on Facebook and Twitter, providing powerful tools for new communities, and perilous tools for stripping privacy and even personal safety.

Perhaps Fukuyama was wrong. Perhaps Turner will turn out to be right, and the new century will see the dissipation of the United States as a nation and the reinvigoration of *America* as a peril and a promise. America may lose its physical boundaries only to be transformed into layers of ideas, beliefs, images, myths; each of them resonant and seductive, yet each of them also open to reinterpretation, reinvention. That cultural landscape is hazy: it could be a desert or a garden, or something in between. It is and will be populated by Americans, or by those infected by the American imagination: a little cynical, skeptical, self-righteous, self-deprecating, impatient, but interested, engaged, argumentative, observant of the perilous beauty of a landscape we can never possess but yearn to be a part of, even as we are restive, impatient to go on. It's worth waiting around to see how it turns out.

Acknowledgments

I owe a great deal to many people and institutions, and I fear I will not honor all of them. I began this book more than twenty years ago; the central premise of the larger project appeared as a fragment of thought in an essay published in the journal *American Studies* in 1991, and the opening prologue spun off to become *Atomic Spaces: Living on the Manhattan Project*, published in 1997. Chapters on everything from the underground geography of Disney World to the manufactured topographies of Yellowstone and Jellystone passed through stages of research and field work, conception and draft, only to be jettisoned as the central themes became more distinct. During this long adventure I had the enthusiastic if sometimes puzzled support of the Art History Department and the College of Architecture and the Arts at the University of Illinois, Chicago. That faith in the project by my colleagues and friends made the piles of odd books and the sounds of video games and the portentous narrations of Cold War newsreels leaking from my office seem a natural part of the life of the scholar-teacher. David Sokol, Robert Munman, Virginia Miller, Hannah Higgins, Nina Dubin, Bebe Baird, and all the rest: thank you.

Others were more intimately involved with the forging of the argument and the gathering of material. Bob Bruegmann, my colleague, cowriter, and friend; Erika Doss, astute adjudicant and reader; Jeffrey Meikle, who read and read and read; Bradford Collins, always the ebullient enthusiast; my fellow humanists at UIC's Institute for the Humanities and the institute's always capable and supportive administrator, Linda Vavra; the purportedly anonymous evaluators of university fellowships and research grants: my deepest gratitude. The National Endowment for the Humanities funded the project not once but twice as it sprawled across disciplines and media. There are others and I apologize for not mentioning all of you. Certainly generations of students—undergrads and graduates both—listened, argued, suggested, and rekindled the project at critical moments.

The research institutions themselves deserve recognition: in times of darkening archives and closing doors, overworked staff always welcomed me at the Library of Congress, at the National Archives (especially the "new place," a shuttle bus away, where the raw newsreel footage emerged with its surprises), at the Chicago Historical Society (now the Chicago History Museum), at Department of Energy facilities in Oak Ridge and Hanford and Los Alamos, and at the remarkable National Archives Regional Depository in Eastpoint, Georgia, where Charlie Reeves took me around the vast Quonset hut on the front of a forklift and let me look at everything. The library staff at the University of Illinois, Chicago, took my requests with patience and enthusiasm.

The images in this book aren't just illustrations, as you know if you've made it this far: they are integral parts of the argument. If you look at the credit lines under the pictures, you will learn the names of a raft of wonderful people, all of whom helped me in various ways. The volunteers for the Levittown project, only a few of whom made it into the text, all deserve more credit than historians give when so-called democratic history is written. To all of them, but especially Charles Tekula, "Rusty" Arnesen, Sandy Adams, Frank Barning, and Brian McCabe, my humility and gratitude. The rights and reproduction people at the picture agencies and archives, so deeply feared by all of us, were unfailingly polite, cheerful, and often amenable to compromise when it came to rights pricing, making the book all the richer, visually and intellectually. The freelance photographers whose pictures showed us Hendrix—Gered Mankowitz and Bruce Fleming—and the unrivaled documentarian of the American counterculture, Lisa Law, were astonishingly generous. Their work deserves far wider celebrity than it has received, and I hope I can contribute to that expansion of repute.

When the world entered cyberspace, I was right there in hyperdrive, thanks in large part to my then five-year-old son, Taylor, who let me play his Nintendo and other video game machines in their various iterations for the next decade. Early on, I sent a note to a software developer for a small game company, and Will Wright's wife called me back to tell me I'd be hearing from him—around 2 a.m., when he got home. Will Wright did call me back, and for hours we talked about everything *SimCity*. By the time *The Sims* was out, he was far too celebrated a figure for me to dare impose on, but I garnered some of the courage necessary to venture as a cultural critic into the cyberworld from those conversations. The founding developers at id Software were equally generous. More recently, Dan Bricklin, the coinventor of VisiCalc and a towering feature in the Mt. Rushmore of software history, has set me straight and set me onto paths of tremendous interest. Not only those—so many developers, manual writers, programmers, designers, and production people have been willing to talk casually and directly about the worlds they inhabit and the worlds they have made. As the project came closer and closer to the present, I have to admit I leaned on my children, now grown, for more insights into the everyday life of the young and the cyberconnected. Molly Hales was my fellow explorer of version after version of *The Sims* and a stern taskmistress when it came to critiques of gender and culture in cyberspace and historical space. Taylor not only sent me regular updates on nuclear-themed and postapocalyptic gaming, he also gave me a subscription to *Steam*, without which I might have completed this book years earlier, but with far less nuance to that cyberchapter.

Early on—*very* early on—I met with an editor at the University of Chicago Press and pitched a book that seemed far from the collegiate gothic grandeur of that institution. Since that time, Susan Bielstein has risen far above mere editorship, yet she read every word numerous times, remonstrating, charming, wheedling, rewarding. As a result, this book is half as long as I wanted it to be, and far more than twice as good as I ever imagined. Late in the game she brought in a closer in the form of editor Anthony Burton, who was perhaps more forgiving than he should have been, but a great help nonetheless. Simultaneously deft and discreet, manuscript editor Mary Gehl put the final polish on the book you hold. My deep gratitude to the Press, but especially to Susan: I take pride in having done just about everything she told me to, but I take full responsibility for all the failings that no doubt remain in this labor of love.

As to love: my friend, my colleague, my wife, Maureen Pskowski, was more than a reader and critic, enthusiast and supporter. The marked-up printouts of chapter after chapter, a little the worse for wear during their trips by CTA and bus back and forth from the Art Institute, pushed me to revise and rethink. Her suggestions, often made in the form of offhand, even aphoristic turns of phrase, kept me up nights and dancing during the days. When there are points of real originality, the credit most likely goes to her.

Last, let me thank an entire generation: my parents'. All of us born into the postwar years know how foundational was the support and faith of that generation in the promise of ours. Veterans of Depression, deprivation, and war, of racial discrimination and threatening plutocracy, the best of that generation are often forgotten while the miserable few lay claim to their achievements. So to Ma and Pa, and to Catherine and Ed Pskowski, who treated all my adventures as worthy of their support, advice, and information, to the mothers and fathers of all my courageously contrarian, utopian friends, to the grandparents of my fervent, idealistic students: I raise my glass.

Notes

Chapter 1

1. Laurence's place in the context of the entire Manhattan Project is more extensively treated in my earlier book, *Atomic Spaces: Living on the Manhattan Project* (Urbana: University of Illinois Press, 1997).

2. The full text of the speech and accompanying press release are online at http://www.atomicarchive.com/Docs/Hiroshima/PRHiroshima.shtml.

3. William L. Laurence, "Nagasaki was the Climax of the New Mexico Test," *Life*, September 24, 1945, 30.

4. "What Ended the War," *Life*, September 17, 1945, 37.

5. Jonathan M. Weisgall, *Operation Crossroads: The Atomic Tests At Bikini Atoll* (Annapolis, MD: Naval Institute Press, 1994).

6. "What Ended the War," 37; Ernest K. Lindley, "Atomic Bomb, Greatest Show on Earth," *Newsweek*, February 4, 1946, 30.

7. James Michener, *Tales of the South Pacific* (New York: Fawcett Crest, 1974), 48.

8. The phrases appear in multiple magazine and newspaper articles, probably because they were lifted directly from military press releases and planted articles. The *New York Times* sometimes called Juda "king," and sometimes "chieftain," and even, once, "mayor." See "King Juda Might Be Puzzled," *New York Times*, March 3, 1946, 23. The final and most elaborate description is from "Atomic Age: The Goodness of Man," *Time*, April 1, 1946, 28, 100.

9. Military Cable, Wyatt to ComMarianas, February 18, 1946, *Manhattan Engineer District Records*, Box 28; National Archives Regional Depository, Eastpoint, Georgia, accessed August, 1990. The later report was part of the navy's official history of World War II, usually designated as Bureau of Ships, *An Administrative History of the Bureau of Ships During World War II*, 4 vols. (Washington DC: Department of Defense, 1952). Volume 4 concerns the postwar atomic tests at Bikini; the Wyatt reminiscence is found in volume 3, pp. 509-10. Weisgall includes a lengthy discussion concerning what exactly Wyatt might have said, and how the Bikinians understood his words, in *Operation Crossroads*, 104-15.

10. Lindley, "Atomic Bomb, Greatest Show on Earth, *Newsweek*, February 4, 1946, 28; Lt. (j.g.) E.J. Rooney, "The Strange People from Bikini; Primitive They Are, But . . . ,"*New York*

Times Magazine, March 31, 1946, 100; "Atom Bomb Island: Navy Moves Natives from Bikini, Target of Operation Crossroads," *Life*, March 25, 1946, 106.

11 "Atom Bomb Island . . . ," *Life*, March 25, 1946, 107; "Army and Navy—In A Blue Lagoon," *Time*, January 28, 1946, http://www.time.com/time/magazine/article /0,9171,855298,00.html; Carl Markwith, "Farewell to Bikini," *National Geographic*, July, 1946, 97-116.

12 "Atomic Age: The Goodness of Man, *Time*, April 1, 1946, 28.

13 The National Archives II in College Park, Maryland, has a complete collection of newsreels submitted for copyright purposes.

14 "Ready for Atom Tests at Bikini," *Universal Newsreel*, March 11, 1946, National Archives II, Motion Picture Section, Universal 19-484, College Park, Maryland. "First Pictures—Pacific Isle Waits Atom Bomb!," press release, March 11, 1946, National Archives II, Reference Section, College Park, Maryland.

15 "Ready for Atom Tests at Bikini," *Universal Newsreel*.

16 Ibid.

17 "Damage Foreshadows A-Bomb Tests," *Universal Newsreel*, June 6, 1946, National Archives II, Motion Picture Section, College Park, Maryland.

18 "First Pictures—Pacific Isle Waits Atom Bomb!" Press release for newsreel, "Ready for Atom Tests at Bikini," Reference Section, Motion Picture Section, National Archives II, College Park, Maryland.

19 Wyatt's report is quoted in Weisgall, *Operation Crossroads*, 107.

20 The Air Force films are located in the Motion Picture Section of the National Archives II, providing the opportunity to compare the raw footage with the finished newsreel. Some of the outtakes were reproduced in the mordantly ironic documentary *The Atomic Café* (1982), as the editors intercut the finished Paramount newsreel with the raw military footage from which it has been skillfully edited. A portion of the raw footage was also used in the still-arresting WGBH documentary *Radio Bikini* (directed by Robert Stone; 1988). The story itself, including the reminiscences of some of those who were there, is told in Jonathon Weisgall's *Operation Crossroads*, 106-13. Weisgall, an attorney, was the representative of the Bikinians in a series of lawsuits against the U.S. government in the '80s, and was listed as a coproducer of *Radio Bikini*.

21 These are William L. Laurence's words, first released in a military press release, "Atomic Bombing of Nagasaki Told By Flight Member," *Official War Department Release, Issue of September 9, 1945*, 4, repr. in William L. Laurence, *The Story of the Atomic Bomb* (Baltimore, MD: Wildside Press, 2009), 8, then published in various newspapers and magazines immediately after the Hiroshima and Nagasaki bombings. and reprinted in his book.

Chapter 2

1 "Atomic Age: Angel Food," *Time*, November 18, 1946, 31.

2 The naming of tests had its own tortuous history. Some tests operated under the aegis of the military, others the Los Alamos scientific teams, still others the Atomic Energy Commission. The scientists took pleasure inventing whimsical names; the military in imposing systems of code. But in every case, the necessity was to maintain a wall of secrecy around the purpose and nature of the test. Yet while the poetics of atomic tests may have originated in the desire to confuse, to disguise, the long list of titles conveyed reassurance as well: these unimaginably destructive, world-threatening weapons hid behind whimsical, humorous, sentimental, even mundane household vernacular forms. Who could fear "Teapot-Apple"? Or "Wigwam"?

There is no definitive discussion of the naming of tests. I have consulted a number of Department of Defense, U.S. Army, and AEC records to parse this enigma. An excellent general source for researchers in the atomic test era is U.S. Department of Energy, Nevada Operations Office, *United States Nuclear Tests: July 1945 through September 1992* (Oak Ridge, TN: U.S. Department of Energy Office of Scientific and Technical Information, 2000). Michon Mackedon's lacing, entertaining, mordant meditation on the tropes of the atomic era, aptly titled *Bombast: Spinning Atoms in the Desert* (Reno, NV: Black Rock Institute Press, 2010), has probably the best extended discussion of the ways the tests' names trivialized and normalized the enormity of the tests themselves; she is also acute on the ironies of names like "Starfish Prime," when starfish were among the first species genetically damaged by test radiation, or "Redwing-Navajo," when reservation Navajo were being paid two-thirds the wages of their white coworkers in the uranium extraction business that eventually rendered significant portions of the Navajo nation a radiation hazard wasteland from mine tailings and runoff contamination.

3 *Exercise Desert Rock*, U.S. Army Signal Corps, Staff Film Reports #177 of the Armed Forces (1951). The "Buster-Jangle" film's larger function—to reassure both soldiers and the wider American population that, in the narrator's final words, "it is possible to utilize an atomic weapon in close support of ground troops in those cases where the conditions surrounding its use are carefully considered and where participating troops are fully indoctrinated in the capabilities and effects of an atomic weapon"—was largely destroyed by its military bureaucratese and stiff filming. For this and other reasons, I am convinced it was a film directed not at civilian populations but toward appropriate military and political groups—the Senate Armed Services Committee, for example, and the Joint Chiefs of Staff.

4 This was the declaration of the official U.S. Geological Survey agronomist, Cyrus Thomas, writing in the *USGS Survey* of 1871. I have written more extensively about this cluster of myths and their effects in *William Henry Jackson and the Transformation of the American Landscape* (Philadelphia, PA: Temple University Press, 1988).

5 Charles Dana Wilber, *The Great Valleys and Prairies of Nebraska and the Northwest* (Omaha, NE: Republican Printing Company, 1881), 113.

6 These proposals were part of a fierce debate during the post–Civil War era of exploration, notably between two of America's greatest government surveyors, Ferdinand Vandeveer Hayden and John Wesley Powell. The best overall discussion of this clash of myths is found in William H. Goetzmann, *Exploration and Empire: The Explorer and the Scientist in the Winning of the American Wes.* (Denton, TX: Texas State Historical Society Reprint Press, 1997).

7 The newsreels produced by the U.S. Signal Corps are held at the Department of Defense Albuquerque office; many of them also are found, in whole or as edited portions of commercial newsreels, in the National Archives II in College Park, Maryland. A few have recently been uploaded to YouTube, though the sites appear and disappear with confusing rapidity. A full-length version, without copyright date, is titled *Department of Defense Presents: Military Participation On Buster-Jangle* (Hollywood: United States Air Force Lookout Mountain Laboratory, n.d.). The Troop Test Smoky reel was released with many others by the Department of Defense in the late '80s.

8 "Miss Atom Bomb," reproduced in the *Nevada Test Site History Newsletter*, December 2004, 1. The description of the picture-making process is found in Michael Childers, "Interview with Donald E. English, March 25, 2004," University of Nevada, Las Vegas, Oral History Project Archives.

9 Caption for Las Vegas News Bureau wire photo shot, dated May 8, 1952, of Candyce King, "Miss Atomic Blast" (private collection).

10 Richard L. Miller, *Under the Cloud: The Decades of Nuclear Testing* (New York: Free Press, 1986). The chapter on Plumbbob, pp. 251–293, is especially valuable.

11 This is a counternarrative of the American West best told by Richard White in his

important history, *It's Your Misfortune and None of My Own: A New History of the American West* (Norman, OK: University of Oklahoma Press, 1991).

12 Childers, "Interview with Donald E. English."

13 "Speaking of Pictures: Everywhere You Look, There's Danger in Las Vegas, *Life*, November 12, 1951, 37.

Chapter 3

1 *Miracle on 34th Street*, directed by George Seaton (1947; Los Angeles: 20th Century Fox, 1999), DVD.

2 "The Fortune Survey," *Fortune*, April 1946, 266–75.

3 Ibid.

4 "Dreams of 1946: Americans Yearn for Rosy Future of Rich Cars and Wondrous Homes," *Life*, November 25, 1946, 58.

5 Two standard works ably describe the wartime and immediate postwar role of women in the workplace and beyond: Susan M. Hartman, *The Home Front and Beyond: American Women in the 1940s* (New York: Macmillan, 1983), and, more recently, Doris Weatherford, *American Women and World War II* (Edison, NJ: Castle Books, 2008). On women in the demobilization economy, see especially Karen Anderson, *Wartime Women: Sex Roles, Family Relations, and the Status of Women during World War II* (Westport, CT: Greenwood Press, 1981), 154–75; and Weatherford, *American Woman and World War II*, 306–17. A marvelously polemical source is Julie A Matthaei, *An Economic History of Women in America: Women's Work, the Sexual Division of Labor, and the Development of Capitalism* (New York: Schocken Books, 1982). Matthaei argues that what she calls "the development of a system of commodity needs" began early in the twentieth century, with advertising serving "to convince home-makers that it was essential to acceptable family or home life" (235–36).

Once the war in Europe ended, large employers responded to the situation by firing their women workers, at roughly twice the rate they laid off their men. By the summer of 1945, it was a rout: in defense fields like shipbuilding and in the aircraft industries, the big contractors laid off three-quarters of their women workers in a matter of two or three months. The statistical information comes from Women's Bureau Bulletin 209, *Women Workers in Ten War Production Areas and Their Postwar Employment Plans* (Washington, DC: The Women's Bureau, 1946). See also Anderson, *Wartime Women*, 164.

6 "Amazons in the Arsenal," *Nation's Business*, July 1943, 65; "Aprons and Overalls in War," *Annals of the American Academy of Political and Social Science* 229 (Sept. 1943): 46–53; "Can the Girls Hold Their Jobs in Peacetime?" *Saturday Evening Post*, March 4, 1944, 28–29.

7 "American Women," *Life* January 29, 1945, 28–29; the responses were published in the February 19 issue on pp. 2–3. Margaret Mead, "What Women Want," *Fortune*, December 1946, 172–75.

8 "Women in America, Part 1," *Fortune*, August 1946, 5–6; "Women in America, Part 2," *Fortune*, September 1946, 5–6.

9 "Speaking of Pictures—Sentimental Advertisements Start a New Kind of Pinup Craze," *Life*, May 14, 1945; the ad is on the inside front cover, *Life*, May 7, 1945.

10 "Speaking of Pictures: Sentimental Advertisements Start a New Kind of Pin-Up Craze," *Life*, May 14, 1945, 12–13.

11 Back cover of *Life*, May 7, 1945.

12 The oddity of this has seemingly escaped most critics, yet the entire interior scene has the hallucinatory quality of a dream in which a small house unpacks into a huge one, in which impossible things happen. To make the light-struck interior sensible, the moviemakers had to add many more windows than any suburban house of 1946 could possibly have had; they even added an entire wall of windows to one side.

13 Shirley O'Hara, "Miracle in Herald Square," *New Republic*, June 2, 1947, 36.

14 John Mason Brown, "Wreathed Smiles," *Saturday Review of Literature*, July 12, 1947, 22–24.

Chapter 4

1 Editorial, *Newsday* (Long Island, NY), 1951, quoted in John Thomas Liell, "Levittown: A Study in Community Planning and Development" (PhD diss., Yale University, 1952), 272. Liell's research was drawn primarily from exhaustive questionnaires and interviews with residents; his assiduous research makes the dissertation still the best book on Levittown ever written, and it remains a pity that it has never been republished.

2 Pioneers recalled that the Levitt organization arranged for roving trucks that moved through the new neighborhoods selling the necessities—milk, bread, baby food, diapers, toilet paper—out of the back doors. By 1951, matters were better, but they weren't ideal. The Levitt organization had scaled back its grand plans for seven shopping centers, and what they built was markedly insufficient to the size of the community. Each of the centers housed five small shops and one larger one; the largest was about the size of a convenience store ("Community Facilities in Levittown," *American Builder*, November 1949, 82–85, 154).

3 Pictures of the Levitt portable stores can be found in the special collections of the Levittown Public Library; reminiscences about the first years, including descriptions of the travails of shopping, are recorded in the documentary *Building the American Dream*, directed by Stewart Bird (1994; Hempstead, NY: Hofstra University Television), DVD.

4 One pioneer remembered driving out on a weekend and seeing the model house; it was "floating in a sea of mud" and "it was adorable." Another recalled going for a drive with her husband and seeing with amazement "long lines of people just waiting to put down their down payment." Both stories are told in the Levittown documentary *Building the American Dream*; the reports of early residents are also drawn from e-mails sent to me via the Levittown webpage, available at http://www.uic.edu/~pbhales/Levittown. See also "Line Forms Early in Sale of Houses," *New York Times*, March 7, 1949.

5 Anyone wishing to read the full story of this phenomenon would probably best begin with Adam Rome, "Levitt's Progress: The Rise of the Suburban-Industrial Complex," chap. 1 in *The Bulldozer in the Countryside: Suburban Sprawl and the Rise of American Environmentalism* (New York: Cambridge University Press, 2001), which encapsulates both the historical and the historiographical precedents. Kenneth Jackson's *Crabgrass Frontiers: The Suburbanization of the United States* (New York: Oxford University Press, 1985) and Clifford Clark's *The American Family Home, 1800–1960* (Chapel Hill: University of North Carolina Press, 1986) are seminal generalist studies, while a more polemical but equally important text from the same era is Robert Fishman's *Bourgeois Utopias: The Rise and Fall of Suburbia* (New York: Basic Books, 1987). And there is, most recently, Dolores Hayden's mordant, often hilarious *A Field Guide To Sprawl* (New York: W. W. Norton & Company, 2004), and my colleague Robert Bruegmann's *Sprawl: A Compact History* (Chicago: University of Chicago Press, 2005), which places suburbanization and exurbanization within a bracingly wide context of time and globalized space. All of these point to the legal, economic, governmental, and historical precedents; Rome's book has an excellent up-to-date bibliography that includes both historical texts and contemporary secondary studies. On Levittown itself, we have still only two books, both with significant virtues and flaws. Barbara Kelly's *Expanding the American Dream: Building and Rebuilding Levittown* (Albany: State University of New York Press, 1993) focuses primarily on the processes of remodeling that characterized the life span of a Levittown house. Rosalyn Baxandall and Elizabeth Ewen's *Picture Windows: How the Suburbs Happened* (New York: Basic Books, 2000) takes Levittown as a type for the phenomenon

of suburbanization, with mixed results. More specific topics are addressed in books I've cited in later notes.

6 Caption to photograph accompanying "Up From the Potato Fields, *Time*, July 3, 1950, 67.

7 "Up From the Potato Fields," *Time*, July 3, 1950, 69.

8 This complaint is found in an undated, unsourced clipping in the special collection of the Levittown Public Library.

9 Christina Hodges and Christa Beranek, "Dwelling: Transforming Narratives at Historic House Museums," *International Journal of Heritage Studies* XVII, no. 2 (March 2011): 97–101; Diane Barthel, "Nostalgia for America's Village Past: Staged Symbolic Communities," *International Journal of Politics, Culture and Society* IV, no. 1 (Autumn 1990): 79–93; probably the most energetic critic-satirist of colonial Williamsburg was Ada Louise Huxtable, architecture critic for the *New York Times*; see "Dissent at Colonial Williamsburg: Errors of Restoration," *New York Times*, September 22, 1963.

10 Levittown received its due in a *Saturday Evening Post* pictorial feature long before it was even built, before the war ended, before VE-day, even: Boyden Sparkes, "They'll Build Neighborhoods, Not Houses," *Saturday Evening Post*, October 28, 1944, 11, 43, 44.

11 The original Levitt Cape Cods rented for just over $60 a month; it was not until the full implementation of FHA-VA loan programs that the Levitt establishment offered a purchase option; shopworn Cape Cods sold for $6,990; the 1947 ranch sold for $7,990.

12 Eric Larabee, "The Six Thousand Houses that Levitt Build," *Harper's*, September 1948, 84.

13 Writing in 1952, sociology graduate student John Thomas Liell reported that "Levittown's children have had a great effect on the development of the community. They are a source of contact, for with no fences they range freely from yard to yard. Through these contacts either friendships or antagonisms develop" (Liell, "Levittown," 221).

14 Letter to the editor, *Levittown Eagle*, June 21, 1951, quoted in Liell, "Levittown," 222.

15 *Levittown Tribune*, October 20, 1949, quoted in Liell, "Levittown," 223.

16 Many of these can be seen in photographs uploaded to Frank Barning, *Early Levittown NY and Beyond* (blog), http://theworldaccordingtofrankbarning.blogspot.com/.

17 Liell, "Levittown," 221.

18 Ibid.

19 Charlie Tekula provided my web project, *Levittown: Documents of an Ideal American Suburb* (http://www.uic.edu/~pbhales/Levittown), with a significant array of photographs, to which he appended extended commentaries; over a period of months, he also provided responses to specific questions concerning the pictures, but also more broadly concerning his family and his experiences in Levittown. My gratitude to him, and the others, many of whom preferred to remain anonymous, who responded to my calls for information and artifacts.

20 The discussion that follows concerning Rusty Arnesen's Levittown experiences come from written material he submitted with the photographs used on the *Looking at Levittown* web project, and follow-up e-mail interviews with the author.

21 Rusty Arnesen's contributions come from material he provided to the Levittown web project.

22 Harry Henderson, "Rugged American Collectivism: The Mass-Produced Suburbs, Part II," *Harper's Monthly*, December 1953, 80.

23 Cultural historian Peter Filene reports in an unpublished manuscript for a presentation that approximately sixty juvenile-delinquency "problem movies" were produced in the '50s ("Suburbia in the 1950s: Family Life in an Age of Anxiety," unpublished manuscript, MS Word, July 2011, http://www.dlt.ncssm.edu/lmtm/docs/suburbia/script .doc). A good policy study of the responses to the perceived fear is found in Jason Barnosky, "The Violent Years: Responses to Juvenile Crime in the 1950s," *Polity* 38, no. 3 (July 2006): 314–44.

24 The knifing was recalled by one of Frank Barning's informants.

25 Letter from Rusty Arnesen to the author, 1997.

26 This and a number of other pictures discussed in this chapter can be found at *Levittown: Documents of an Ideal American Suburb* (http://www.uic.edu/~pbhales/Levittown).

27 On the transformations of Levittown, the only fully satisfying book on the town is a rewarding source: Kelly, *Expanding the American Dream*.

28 "Model Home Completed in Manhasset," *New York Times*, March 3, 1935.

29 Letter from Brian McCabe to author, September 27, 2001. Accompanying materials used in the *Levittown* web project: http://tigger.uic.edu/~pbhales/Levittown/McCabe/.

30 "Same Rooms, Varied Decor," *Life*, January 14, 1952, 90–93.

31 The contest judges categorized all the contestants: 35 percent produced "modern" interiors, 20 percent "traditional," and—as *Life* paraphrased them—"45 percent were an eclectic mixture which in many cases turned out to be an unsuccessful hodgepodge."

32 "Levitt adds 1950 Model to His Line," *Life*, May 22, 1950, 141.

33 "Housewife's House: Designed by a Woman, It Puts Kitchen in the Center," *Life*, December 24, 1956, 134–35.

34 Levittown home advertisement, *New York Times*, September 25, 1949.

35 Sey Chassler, "A Town Takes Its Picture, *Collier's*, September 22, 1951, 34–35.

36 Ibid., 34.

37 The outfits are featured in a Civil Defense propaganda film, *Alert Today, Alive Tomorrow* (1956), filmed in what at first looks a good deal like a later, more remodeled Levittown, but is in fact Reading, Pennsylvania. It has resurfaced on YouTube (http://www.youtube.com/watch?v=c3ZnNsVyWMA). Guy Oakes discusses the newsreel-style film in the introduction to *The Imaginary War: Civil Defense and American Cold War Culture* (London: Oxford University Press, 1995), 4–6.

38 Ralph Martin, "How Individuality Got a Second Chance, *House Beautiful*, February, 1956, 96–98.

39 Harry Henderson, "Rugged American Collectivism," *Harper's Monthly*, December 1953, 80.

Chapter 5

1 A copy of the Levitt lease can be found in the Levittown Historical Society archives. It is reproduced in Lynne Mataresse, *The History of Levittown New York* (Levittown, NY: Levittown Historical Society, 1997), 37.

2 Two ads cut from newspaper real estate sections, handwritten "1950," no further information available. Private collection.

3 An interview with Ann Gilmore, who reports that she sought to rent in Levittown in 1948 and bought in Ronek Park in 1950, was originally published in 1997: Sidney Schaer, Ronek Park, "Equal Opportunity Suburb," *Newsday*, September 28, 1997, 19. Copies of the Ronek Park ads are shown in the documentary *Building the American Dream*, directed by Stewart Bird (1994; Hempstead, NY: Hofstra University Television), DVD.

4 Interview with Eugene Burnett in *Building the American Dream*.

5 Stewart Bird, interview with William Levitt, 1993, in Hofstra University Archives; excerpted at http://www.newsday.com/extras/lihistory/specsec/levint.htm (accessed August 2010). The site has since gone dark; portions of the interview are included in Bird's *Building the American Dream*.

6 The FHA's restrictions date back to the founding of the bureau in 1934. The full text of the instructions is widely published; a good overview can be found in Lawrence J. Vale, *From the Puritans to the Projects: Public Housing and Public Neighbors* (Cambridge, MA: Harvard University Press, 2000), 169–70.

7 Bernice Burnett is interviewed in *Building the American Dream*.

8 On the Levittown, Pennsylvania, racial conflicts, see David B. Bittan, "Ordeal in Levittown," *Look*, August 19, 1958, 84–86; Thomas J. Sugrue, "Jim Crow's Last Stand: The Struggle to Integrate Levittown," in *Second Suburb: Levittown, Pennsylvania*, ed. Dianne Harris, 175–99 (Pittsburgh, PA: University of Pittsburgh Press, 2010).

9 Burnett, interviewed in Bird, *Building the American Dream*.

Chapter 6

1 Cobbett S. Steinberg, *TV Facts* (New York: Facts on File, Inc., 1992), 141; Eric Barnouw, *The Golden Web: A History of Broadcasting in the United States 1933–1953* (New York: Oxford University Press, 1968), 284–297; Susan Kirsch Duncan, *Levittown: The Way We Were* (Huntington, NY: Maple Hill Press, 1999), 27.

2 Most of the general information and statistics on television use can be found in Erik Barnouw's encyclopedic three-volume history of American broadcasting: *A Tower in Babel: A History of Broadcasting in the United States To 1933* (New York: : Oxford University Press, 1966) covers radio broadcasting; *The Golden Web* traces the development of television in the context of radio's dominance; and *The Image Empire: A History of Broadcasting in the United States from 1953* (New York: Oxford University Press, 1970) focuses primarily on television. His single-volume history of television, *Tube of Plenty: The Evolution of American Television* (New York: Oxford University Press, 1976) is equally important, if less dense with detail. See esp. *The Golden Web*, 284–85.

3 An illustration in Lynn Spigel's *Welcome to the Dreamhouse* (Durham, NC: Duke University Press, 2001) confirms that even the copywriters and illustrators for the television set manufacturers saw the appropriate stance toward the television to be attentive, forward-leaning; see the reproduced ad, "Motorola TV Most Dependable," 46.

4 Harry Henderson, "The Mass-Produced Suburbs," *Harper's Magazine*, October 1953, 28.

5 Elizabeth Sweeney Herbert, "This Is How I Keep House in a Levittown Home," *McCall's*, April 1949, 41–44.

6 Ibid., 43.

7 William J. Baxter, "The Future of Television" (New York: Baxter International Economic Research Bureau, 1949). This was one of Baxter's periodic "bulletins," which ranged widely in topic and level of authoritativeness—a 1953 bulletin, titled "Today's Revolution in Weather," argued that a heat zone was moving northward in the United States and sought to extrapolate economic trends from this phenomenon. One of the most comprehensive surveys of the subject of America and television in the '50s was Leo Bogart, *The Age of Television: A Study of Viewing Habits and the Impact of Television on American Life*, 2nd ed. (New York: Frederick Ungar, 1958); see esp. "TV's Effects on Visiting and "Going Out" (101–6), "TV and Conversation" (106–7), and "TV and the Daily Routine" (107–8).

8 Henderson, "The Mass-Produced Suburbs," 29

9 Susan Kirsch Duncan, *Levittown: The Way We Were* (Huntington, NY: Maple Hill Press, 1999), 27.

10 Lynn Spigel, *Make Room For TV: Television and the Family Ideal in Postwar America* (Chicago: University of Chicago Press, 1992), 43.

11 Harry Hershfeld is quoted in Spigel, *Make Room For TV*, 117.

12 Henderson, "The Mass-Produced Suburbs," 28.

13 Tim Brooks and Earle Marsh, *The Complete Directory to Prime Time Network and Cable TV Shows* (New York: Ballantine Books, 1995), 820. See also Anna Everett's "Golden Age of Television," *Encyclopedia of Television* (Chicago: Museum of Broadcast Communications, 2009), 1000–4.

14 Ben Gross, quoted in Brooks and Marsh, *The Complete Directory to Prime Time Network and Cable TV Shows*, 60.

15 Brooks and Marsh, *The Complete Directory to Prime Time Network and Cable TV Shows*, 304; Alex McNeil, *Total Television: The Comprehensive Guide to Programming from 1948 to the Present* (New York: Penguin Books, 1996), 247. *Easy Aces* was perhaps the most bizarre of these scattershot experiments—it involved a married couple (the Aces) watching TV and commenting on it in real time. It was actually an adaptation to television of the Aces' popular radio show, with the addition of the television set as a source for ad-lib jokes; it died after one season.

16 Tewa was the name of a language-grouping of Puebloan peoples; they were among those pueblos that surrounded Los Alamos, often visited by Manhattan Project scientists and their wives. Tewa's test, while not televised live, was the subject of a portion of a high-production-standard, thirty-minute film produced by the Lone Mountain production team, of whom more discussion is found in later chapters. This included aerial photographs of the bombed remains of Bikini.

Chapter 7

1 Richard Miller, *Under the Cloud: The Decades of Nuclear Testing* (New York: Free Press, 1986), 159, reports that one light was left on. The rest of the material for this paragraph and the rest of the chapter comes from a wide variety of primary sources—newspaper articles, pieces, military propaganda, newsreel footage (located in the National Archives II, Video and Film Division). Strewn around the houses were a few standalone prototype bomb shelters and some fifty American cars, there to demonstrate that Detroit-made autos served as excellent A-bomb protection.

2 "Atomic Open House on Yucca Flat, *Life*, May 5, 1952, 36-39.

3 Michael Amrine, "Atomic Clouds Over America," *Science Digest*, June 1953, 23-30.

4 Leonard Slater, "Greasewood Fires and Man's Most Terrible Weapon," *Newsweek*, March 30, 1953, 31-31. From *Science Digest*: "Quite frankly, civil defense workers had told the press that it was also designed to dramatize the fact that dummies in the basement of House No. 2, the one which was a mile and a half from the explosion, would be able to survive this cosmic cataclysm, protected only by simple shelters costing less than $100. Reliable calculations forecast what actually happened: the basement shelters stood up" (Amrine, "Atomic Clouds Over America," 23).

5 Charles J. V. Murphy, "Outcasts of Yucca Flat," *Life*, March 30, 1953, 24. This is part of a larger spread, "A-Bomb vs. House," *Life*, March 30, 1953, 21-25.

6 "New Looks at the A-Bomb, *Life*, May 26, 1952, 49.

7 Caption released with publicity photograph, dated 5/1/1952. National Archives Record Group 127: Records of the U.S. Marine Corps, General Photograph File.

8 "When Atom Bomb Struck: Uncensored," *Life*, September 29, 1952, 19-25.

9 Ferenc Morton Szasz, "Atomic Comics: The Comic Book Industry Confronts the Nuclear Age," in *Atomic Culture: How We Learned to Stop Worrying and Love the Bomb*, ed. Scott C. Zeman and Michael A. Amundson, 11-31 (Boulder: University Press of Colorado, 2004); Szasz published a revised and expanded version in book form—*Atomic Comics: Cartoonists Confront the Nuclear World*. (Reno: University of Nevada Press, 2012), esp. 43-66.

10 "A-Bomb vs. House," 21, 24; Slater, "Greasewood Fires and Man's Most Terrible Weapon," 31. The history of televised broadcasting is a complex one. In February 1951, Los Angeles station KTLA secreted a camera crew atop a Las Vegas hotel, and in the early morning hours of February 1, 1951, relayed the first live telecast of an atomic explosion. As it was unauthorized, it caused a commotion. In 1952, KTLA was able to wangle official permission, and by some reports, the telecast went national, though *Life* and other magazines reporting the "Annie" shot of 1953 described it as the first nationally televised atomic tests.

11 "Eye Witness Account Given of Yucca-Flats 'Atomic Device' Explosion," *Iron County Record* LXIV, no. 15 (March 19, 1953): 1, 14. The account can be found online at http://udn.lib.utah.edu/cdm/compoundobject/collection/ironco3/id/102834/rec/12.

12 "A-Bomb vs. House," 21; Amrine, "Atomic Clouds Over America," *Science Digest*, June 1953, 23.

13 Amrine, "Atomic Clouds Over America," 24; Slater, "Greasewood Fires and Man's Most Terrible Weapon," 32.

14 Slater, "Greasewood Fires and Man's Most Terrible Weapon," 31.

15 Lynn Eden, *World on Fire: Organizations, Knowledge, and Nuclear Weapons Devastation* (Ithaca, NY: Cornell University Press, 2004), 166-68.

16 The best study of the fallout shelter movement is David Monteyne, *Fallout Shelter: Designing for Civil Defense in the Cold War* (Minneapolis: University of Minnesota Press, 2011); it is also the best analysis of the underlying campaign to link a hegemonic bureaucracy of the state to protection from unspoken terrors. Probably the best books on the general subject of atomic anxiety and American responses are Paul Boyer, *By the Bomb's Early Light: American Thought and Culture at the Dawn of the Atomic Age* (New York: Pantheon Press, 1985); and Spencer Weart, *Nuclear Fear: A History of Images* (Cambridge, MA: Harvard University Press, 1988). There is some discussion of the early years of atomic anxiety in Howard Ball, *Justice Downwind: America's Atomic Testing Program in the 1950s* (New York: Oxford University Press, 1986). Finally, Guy Oakes wrote tellingly of the concept of "emotion management" as a goal of civil defense campaigns in *The Imaginary War: Civil Defense and American Cold War Culture* (New York: Oxford University Press, 1994).

17 "When An Atomic Blast Hits Your Home or Auto," *U.S. News and World Report*, March 27, 1953, 38. The press releases can be found in the archives of the Los Alamos National Laboratory; other information on the Nevada test sites is found in the National Archives RG 326.4.4, currently held in the Riverside, California Regional Depository.

18 "When an Atomic Bomb Hits Your Home or Auto," 38-40.

19 *Life*, *Time*, *Newsweek*, *National Geographic*, and the rest all sampled the AEC pictures, and the results fulfilled the goal of that segment.

20 *Life*'s writer put it plainly. "If the aim was to awaken the nation to the importance of civil defense, it was less than an unqualified success. When the first nuclear device exploded at Alamogordo, observers had the sense of being close to the infinite. Now it is depressingly plain that the bloom is off infinity's rose. And this is a tragedy, when one considers the far more powerful weapons that are being built and the ignorance that envelops not only humanity in general but even the statesmen" (Murphy, "Outcasts of Yucca Flat," 24).

21 Amrine, "Atomic Clouds Over America," 23-30.

22 Ibid., 26 (original emphasis).

23 Ibid., 24, 25, 28, 29.

24 Samuel W. Matthews, "Nevada Learns to Live with the Atom," *National Geographic*, June 1953, 847, 849, 850.

25 Matthews, "Nevada Learns to Live with the Atom," 839-40.

26 Ibid., 843, 849.

27 Philip K. Fradkin, *Fallout: An American Nuclear Tragedy* (Tucson: University of Arizona Press, 1989), 5-6. The dosage and death estimates are taken from the National Cancer Institute/National Institutes of Health, *Estimated Exposures and Thyroid Doses Received by the American People From Iodine-131 in Fallout Following Nevada Atmospheric Bomb Tests* (Washington, DC: National Institutes of Health, 1997), http://www.cancer.gov/i131/fallout/contents.html.

28 Edgerton was working under contract for the Atomic Energy Commission, as part of a firm he had cofounded with a graduate student during the war. Edgerton, Germeshau-

sen, and Grier in this case used a film camera set to twenty-four frames per second, producing something over fifty separate images of the houses' demise.

29 Dwight D. Eisenhower, "Radio and Television Address to the American People on the State of the Nation," April 5, 1954. Online at *The American Presidency Project*, http://www .presidency.ucsb.edu/ws/?pid=10201.

Chapter 8

1 Betty Friedan's first salvo, the predecessor to *The Feminine Mystique* (New York: W.W. Norton, 1963), appeared as "Women Are *People*, Too!," *Good Housekeeping*, September 1960, 59-61, 161-62. The essential work on Friedan is Daniel Horowitz, *Betty Friedan and the Making of* The Feminine Mystique (Amherst: University of Massachusetts Press, 1998). Joanne Meyerowitz's essay, "Beyond the Feminine Mystique: A Reassessment of Postwar Mass Culture, 1946-1958," in *Not June Cleaver: Women and Gender in Postwar America, 1945-1960*, ed. Joanne Meyerowitz, 229-62 (Philadelphia, PA: Temple University Press, 1994), proposes a mass culture stream lauding women intellectuals, professionals and workers. Her argument, however, is to me insufficiently nuanced—it fails to contextualize those articles and "specials" *as* special, as tokens or contrasts set within a far wider context. Moreover, her argument removes these mass-market pieces from their material context—in the case of magazine articles, the effulgence of advertising copy and imagery that literally imprisoned the texts within a radically different, more conformist context.

2 Contextual information on television comes from the wide variety of television encyclopedias, fact books, and anthology appreciations that form standard fare for most TV critics' bookshelves. Three in particular deserve special mention for their factual accuracy, detail, and critical acumen. Tim Brooks and Earle Marsh have collaborated on *The Complete Directory to Prime Time Network and Cable TV Shows* (New York: Ballantine Books, 1995), which offers not only information on every television show, but such essentials as the prime-time schedule, the top rated programs of each season and of all television's history, and other more esoteric lists. Harry Castleman and Walter J. Podrazik's *Watching TV: Six Decades of American Television* (Syracuse, NY: Syracuse University Press, 2003) replicates some of this information, but valuably casts the history of TV as a narrative: each year's entry begins with a contextual essay, followed by a sometimes day-by-day rendering of the season, enabling one to get a sense of the call-and-response quality of popular culture at this moment in American history. Horace Newcomb is editor of the Museum of Broadcast Communications, *Encyclopedia of Television* (New York: Routledge, 2004) which, at 2,800 pages and 1,150 entries, is the most exhaustive, critically sophisticated, and indispensable of all television compilations.

3 *Hollywood Reporter* and *Variety* reviews are reproduced in Jess Oppenheimer, with Greg Oppenheimer, *Laughs, Luck . . . and Lucy: How I Came to Create the Most Popular Sitcom of All Time* (Syracuse, NY: Syracuse University Press, 1996), 161. "Sassafrassa, the Queen," *Time*, May 26, 1952, 62-64; "Beauty into Buffoon," *Life*, February 18, 1952, 93-94.

4 Oppenheimer, *Laughs, Luck . . . and Lucy*, 189.

5 Nielsen Ratings are reproduced in Brooks and Marsh, *The Complete Directory to Prime Time Network and Cable TV Shows*, 1258-60. The spread of television is outlined by the numbers in J. Fred MacDonald, *One Nation under Television: The Rise and Decline of Network TV* (New York: Wadsworth, 1993), http://jfredmacdonald.com/onutv.

6 Anyone looking for such a blueprint plan will turn to Mark Bennett's marvelous *TV Sets: Fantasy Blueprints of Classic TV Homes* (New York: TV Books/Penguin USA, 1996), 50.

7 Margaret Mead, "Male and Female," *Ladies Home Journal*, September 1949, 36-38.

8 Clifford B. Hicks, "If the A-Bombs Burst—Here Is What to Expect, What You Can Do

Today to Prepare Yourself, What You Can Do Then to Survive," *Popular Mechanics*, January 1951, 132–33.

9 Clifford B. Hicks, "If the A-Bombs Burst—Part II," *Popular Mechanics*, February 1951, 144–149, 246–49.

10 "Unaverage Situation, *Time*, February 18, 1952, 73.

11 "Sassafrassa, the Queen," 62–64.

12 On the fallout shelter as a cultural phenomenon, one article stands out: Sarah Lichtman, "Do-It-Yourself Security: Safety, Gender and the Home Fallout Shelter in Cold War America," *Journal of Design History* 19, no. 1 (2006): 39–55. Equally valuable is David Montayne, *Fallout Shelter: Designing for Civil Defense in the Cold War* (Minneapolis: University of Minnesota Press, 2011).

Chapter 9

1 "The Three Big *News* in Television!," full-page color ad for GE televisions, probably published in *Look* and *Life* (private collection).

2 This particular *House Beautiful* calendar was promoted by the Bank of Oshkosh, Wisconsin; identical versions were given out, with different bank imprints, throughout the U.S. (private collection).

3 This data is drawn from the *Statistical Abstracts for the United States*, (Washington, DC: Bureau of the Census) published at annual intervals; these numbers come from the 1960, 1963, and 1965 editions.

4 This was a trend that was visible as early as 1954, when a survey for the Advertising Research Foundation found 85 percent of televisions in the living room (another 12 percent were located in rooms like studies, dens, libraries and "rumpus rooms") while radios were dispersed fairly evenly throughout the house (Alfred Politz, *National Survey of Radio and Television Sets Associated with U.S. Households* [New York: Advertising Research Foundation, 1954], table 34).

5 William McPhee and Rolf Meyersohn did an extensive survey in 1955, *Futures for Radios* (New York: Columbia University Bureau of Applied Social Science Research, 1955), from which much of the information about radio in this chapter not drawn from the 1960 census and the *Statistical Abstracts* is derived.

6 This *Time* article is quoted in Michael Brian Schiffer's obsessive, opinionated, and thoroughly enlightening study of radio, *The Portable Radio in American Life* (Tucson: University of Arizona Press, 1991), 183.

7 This was the introductory price for the 1959 Philco "Slender Seventeen," advertised in *Look*, August 19, 1958, 2.

Chapter 10

1 The *Billboard* charts are found in individual issues of the magazine; the archive on which I drew is in the Music Collection of the McGill Library at Northwestern University, Chicago, Illinois. Joel Whitburn has reproduced the *Billboard* chart pages for a number of decades, as well, and the ability to page from week to week is invaluable. Joel Whitburn, *Joel Whitburn Presents the Billboard Hot 100 Charts: The Sixties* (Menonomee Falls, WI: Record Research, Inc., 1990).

2 John R. Pierce, "Telstar, A History," *SMEC Vintage Electrics*, 1990, republished online at http://www.smecc.org/john_pierce1.htm; James Early, "Telstar I: Dawn of a New Age," *SMEC Vintage Electrics*, 1990, http://www.smecc.org/james_early___telstar.htm; Eugene

O'Neill, "Commentary on the Telstar Project," July 13, 1991, http://www.smecc.org/eugene_o'niell_-_telstar.htm. "Space: Ailing TV Satellites 'Cured,'" *World News Digest*, January 23, 1963; "Telstar, Telstar Burning Bright, *Life*, August 3, 1962, 4; "Telstar is Silenced by Circuit Problem," *Aviation* Week, December 3, 1962, 31, 95; P. J. Klass, "Telstar Fault Located, Fixed from Earth," *Aviation Week* January 14, 1963, 32–33.

3 Daniel Boorstin, *The Image: A Guide to Pseudo-Events in America* (New York: Harper and Row, 1961); Eugene O'Neill, "Commentary on the Telstar Project," letter to the SMECC archive, http://www.smecc.org/eugene_o'niell_-_telstar.htm.

4 Daniel R. Glover, "NASA Experimental Communications Satellites, 1958–1995," chapter 6 in *Beyond the Ionosphere: The Development of Satellite Communications*, ed. Andrew J. Butrica (Washington, DC: The NASA History Series, NASA, 1997), 53. For Director Edward R. Murrow, USIA was not a propaganda agency but rather a provider of information in both directions—about the United States for the world, and about the world for the United States. Surveys like the USIA one that reported British citizens were more familiar with Telstar than Sputnik was in some ways typical of the complicated reality. The survey was a tendentious one, revelatory of the U.S. goal of outshining the USSR's achievements and then assuring a public forum for that triumph. But surveys like this one were also factors in government policy-making; President Kennedy, who had appointed Murrow, sought to emphasize "the American way of life" as an anti-Communist tool in the global Cold War. See Mark Haefele, "John F. Kennedy, USIA, and World Public Opinion," *Diplomatic History* 25, no. 1 (Winter 2001): 63–84.

5 "Casual," *New Yorker*, August 4, 1962, 23. The *New Yorker*'s reporter watched the dress rehearsal from the control rooms of the television network.

6 John Repsch, *The Legendary Joe Meek: The Telstar Man*. London: Cherry Red Books, 2001.

7 Ibid., 144–45.

8 Assorted Meek, Tornados and *Telstar* fan pages variously date the moment as July 10, July 11, or later.

9 Some information on Goddard and Meek is found in the obituary for Goddard in the *Guardian*, May 25, 2000, and in the obituary in the *London Times*, May 29, 2000; see also Repsch, *The Legendary Joe Meek*, 146–48.

10 Mike Berry (with The Outlaws), *Tribute to Buddy Holly* (His Master's Voice/The Gramophone Co., Ltd., London, 1961), a near-replica of Holly's own sound with a few grim lyrical twists, also has a livelier studio sound, though it's pretty clear it was recorded in the same studio as *Telstar*.

11 John F. Kennedy, News Conference 39, July 23, 1962, http://www.jfklibrary.org/Asset-Viewer/Archives/JFKWHA-114.aspx.

12 John F. Kennedy, "Address Accepting the Democratic Party Nomination for the Presidency of the United States," Los Angeles, July 15, 1960, http://www.presidency.ucsb.edu/ws/?pid=25966.

13 Kennedy's speech can be heard at http://er.jsc.nasa.gov/seh/ricetalk.htm; it is also archived in various audio formats by the National Archives at http://archive.org/details/jfks19620912 .

14 "Memorandum for Vice President [Lyndon Johnson, Chairman of the Space Council]," April 20, 1961, http://www.au.af.mil/au/awc/awcgate/key_docu.htm.

15 In addition to the standard literature on atomic testing cited in the first chapter, an invaluable source is found online: the Nuclear Weapon Archive, which offers detailed information and in many cases photographs of every American atomic test. The information for Starfish Prime is found at http://nuclearweaponarchive.org/Usa/Tests/Dominic.html.

16 Cecil R. Coale, "U.S. Atomic Veterans: Operation Dominic," *Atomic Veterans History Project*, originally online at http://www.aracnet.com/~pdxavets/cecil-co.htm (since

NOTES TO PAGES 207–212 445

removed). Discussion of Coale's findings and a fuller quotation from his report, drawn from the same source, is found in James Schmooch, *Global TV: New Media and the Cold War* (Urbana: University of Illinois Press, 2009), 132.

17 This estimate comes from Sakharov, the premiere Soviet atomic scientist: Andrei D. Sakharov, "Radioactive Carbon From Nuclear Explosions and Nonthreshold Biological Effects," *Science and Global Security* 01/1990: 175–86, originally published in Russian in the *Soviet Journal of Atomic Energy* 4, no. 6 (June 1958): 757–62; Sakharov had then used his extrapolations to argue to Krushchev against the exploding of this superweapon. See Gregory van der Vink, "The Road to a Comprehensive Test Ban Treaty" (working paper, Columbia International Affairs Online, January 1998), http://www.ciaonet.org /conf/nya02/nya02ah.html. Van der Vink reports that Sakharov had argued against the deployment even of the smaller 50–58-megaton bomb.

18 "Space Bomb in Color: Eerie Spectacle in Pacific Sky," *Life*, July 20, 1962, cover.

19 "As far away, the huge bomb exploded in space . . ." *Life*, July 20, 1962, 26–32; "Another wonder sears the sky," 33; "Man pursues his fiery destiny," 34.

20 Web researcher and publisher Cary Sublette's elaborate website, http://nuclearweapon archive.org contains data on virtually every test, not just by United States and Soviet authorities, but by every member of the atomic club. The documentary filmmaker Peter Kuran's series on atomic testing includes a volume devoted to the outer-space experiments: *Nukes in Space: The Rainbow Bombs* (Thousand Oaks, CA: Goldhill Home Media International, 2000).

21 In fact, the entire crisis was far more complex and, as Sheldon M. Stern has found in his close analysis of the secretly recorded "ExComm" meetings at which Kennedy discussed strategy with his experts, the U.S. bore a far greater brunt of responsibility, and the resolution was far less conclusive or triumphant (Sheldon M. Stern, *The Week The World Stood Still: Inside the Secret Cuban Missile Crisis* [Palo Alto, CA: Stanford University Press, 2005]).

22 This passage is cited in its entirety in John Szarkowski, *Winogrand: Figments from the Real World* (New York: Museum of Modern Art, 1988), 34. Winogrand showed me either the original or a copy in the mid-1970s while he was packing to leave Austin, Texas, for Los Angeles.

23 Ibid., 20. The story of the appliance store was one Winogrand told me in the mid-1970s.

24 Again, a conversation among Winogrand, Russell Lee, Lawrence Ivy, and myself, in the mid-1970s.

25 Joni Mitchell's version of "Woodstock" was released on her *Ladies of the Canyon* album; the quote from CSNY is excerpted from "Four Dead in Ohio," released as a single but banned from most AM radio; it helped to cement the bifurcation of youth culture between AM and FM people.

26 "Telstar Is Silenced by Circuit Problem," *Aviation Week*, December 3, 1962, 31, 95.

27 "Repair Job in Space: Telstar's Troubles," *Business Week*, January 12, 1963, 36.

28 Michael Brian Schiffer, *The Portable Radio in American Life* (Tucson: University of Arizona Press, 1991), 181.

Chapter 11

1 Bob Dylan, "Talkin' World War III Blues," *The Freewheelin' Bob Dylan* (1963). Special thanks to J. C. Bradford, pianist extraordinaire, for connecting this epigraph to the larger themes of the chapter.

2 Boorstin proposed that a feature of "modern" American culture was the development of what he termed "everywhere communities" based on patterns of consumption. His work, eloquently stated and fascinatingly illustrated, deserves far more credit than

it gets. Daniel Boorstin, *The Americans: The Democratic Experience* (New York: Vintage, 1974).

3 It was beaten out by Beach Boy pals Jan and Dean with "Surf City [USA!]," but it was really a victim of the band's own success—they'd broken the top 5 for a long run earlier in the summer, and "Surfin' USA" hadn't fallen out of the top 40 till mid-July, by which time the B-side was rising.

4 The listings are drawn from the *Billboard* "Hot 100," from the four weeks between September 7 and September 28, 1963. My thanks to the archivists at the music library at Northwestern University for having the foresight to keep these once-throwaway tabloids neatly bound, just across the stacks from Bach's *Well-Tempered Clavier* and the scores of Arnold Schoenberg's chamber pieces, providing me with something close to ecstatic dislocations of personal musical experience.

5 Ben Fong-Torres, *The Hits Just Keep On Coming* (San Francisco: Backbeat Books, 1997).

6 Ibid., 60–64. Information on the *Gavin Report* is also found in the seminal sociological study of the pop recording industry, R. Serge Denisoff, *Solid Gold: The Popular Record Industry* (New Brunswick, NJ: Transaction Books, 1975), 255–58.

7 As late as the early '70s, more than half of teenagers reported that their listening choices were dictated primarily by disc jockeys—R. Serge Denisoff quotes a study of Florida teenagers, 54 percent of whom declared the disc jockey their primary influence (Denisoff, *Solid Gold*, 253; Denisoff's lengthy discussion of the disc jockey's role in the industry is found on 219–50).

8 The 77-WABC station, and its principal New York rival 54-WMCA, both have extensive websites run by Allan Sniffen: http://www.musicradio77.com/index.html and http://http://www.musicradio77.com/wmca/home.shtml. These include sound files of "air checks" from October 1963, one for "Cousin Brucie" (Bruce Morrow, WABC), and one for B. Mitchel Reed (WMCA), which give a superb sense of the communities each deejay served. Cousin Brucie's antic persona is especially well represented, and the aircheck, which counts down the top 10 for that week, includes a number of references to specific high schools, including announcements, calendars, names of students and teachers, and the like. WINS, the third of these New York rival top-40 stations during the early and mid-1960s, does not as yet have its own site, but some airchecks are archived on the other two sites.

9 Weekly top 10 hits for the New York stations are found on their fan-maintained web pages, http://www.musicradio77.com and http://www.musicradio77.com/wmca/surveys.html.

10 The history of Aldon is recounted with verve by Ed Ward in his portion of Ed Ward, Geoffrey Stokes, and Ken Tucker, *Rock of Ages: The* Rolling Stone *History of Rock and Roll* (Englewood Cliffs, NJ: Rolling Stone Press/Prentice-Hall, Inc., 1986), 225–46. A surprisingly good chapter is found in David P. Szatmary's textbook survey, *Rockin' in Time: A Social History of Rock-and-Roll* (Upper Saddle River, NJ: Pearson/Prentice Hall, 2004), 63–69. Szatmary's bibliography is woefully inadequate, given how well salted with quotes his text is, and there are odd errors here and there. The standard work on the Brill Building is Ken Emerson, *Always Magic in the Air: The Bomp and Brilliance of the Brill Building Era* (New York: Viking Penguin, 2005). In addition, I've consulted a variety of industry web pages, including many of the "official" web pages of various artists, producers, and writers. But the themes of my discussion are entirely my own—Szatmary, for example, argues that the "girl-group" music was successful insofar as it proposed a fantasy of success and stardom to young female listeners, which might suggest an awareness of racial mutability rather than solidarity, and proposes that the lyrics themselves were fluff, citing Goffin's off-the-cuff (and off-the-wall) statement to *Time* in '63 that "lyrics will hurt a song if they're too adult, too artistic, too correct. You should shy away from anything too deep"(66). The original article, "Music: St. Joan of the Jukebox,"

appeared in the March 15, 1963, issue of *Time*, and is found online in the *Time* archive at http://www.time.com/time/subscriber/article/0,33009,870193,00.html.

11 Greg Shaw, "Brill Building Pop," in *The* Rolling Stone *Illustrated History of Rock & Roll*, ed. Anthony DeCurtis and James Henke, 143–52 (New York: Random House, 1992), 146.

12 Mann's second quote comes from Szatmary's *Rockin' in Time*, 66.

13 Timothy White, *The Nearest Faraway Place: Brian Wilson, the Beach Boys, and the Southern California Experience* (New York: Henry Holt, 1996), 230-38.

14 This is perhaps best chronicled in White, *The Nearest Faraway Place.*

15 Matthew Greenwald, "Brian Wilson's Legendary *Smile* Album—the History," *Analog Planet*, http://www.musicangle.com/feat.php?id=58.

16 This is detailed in a British ITV documentary for *The South Bank Show*, *The Making of Sgt. Pepper's Lonely Hearts Club Band* (1992), directed by Alan Benson.

Chapter 12

1 Most of the anecdotal and biographical information in this chapter is derived from Bob Dylan's authoritative biographies. Howard Sounes, *Down the Highway: The Life of Bob Dylan* (New York: Grove Press, 2001), is generally considered the most consistent. The more personal biography by Robert Shelton, *No Direction Home: The Life and Music of Bob Dylan* (New York: Da Capo Press, 2003), contains many anecdotal passages on these early years; whether they are to be trusted incontrovertibly is a matter for the reader's discretion. Clinton Heylin's *Bob Dylan: Behind the Shades Revisited* (New York: Harper Entertainment, 2003) is utterly fascinating and sprawling, combining fact, anecdote, interpretation, and quotation. Heylin's *Bob Dylan: The Recording Sessions 1960-1994* (New York: St. Martin's Press, 1995) is essential reading; Heylin's sleuthing puts him among the top ranks of detective-historians. More recently, he has expanded this work into two volumes, *Revolution in the Air: The Songs of Bob Dylan, 1957-1973* (Chicago: Chicago Review Press, 2009), and *Still On the Road: The Songs of Bob Dylan, 1974-2006* (Chicago: Chicago Review Press, 2010). Andy Gill's *Don't Think Twice, It's All Right: Bob Dylan, the Early Years* (New York: Thunder's Mouth Press, 1998) is an amalgam of biographical fact and song-by-song exegesis; the analysis of lyrics is sometimes thrillingly insightful, sometimes unconvincing, especially as Gill seeks intermittently to reduce the content of songs from universality to specificity. Much the same can be said of a more recent and more authoritative book, Sean Wilentz's *Bob Dylan in America* (New York: Doubleday, 2010); Wilentz moves between lengthy analyses of figures like Aaron Copeland and Jack Kerouac, and Heylin-like close reporting on studio sessions, with mixed success—though the work as a whole is indispensable and individual moments are epiphanies. His work, published well after this chapter was first written, is only marginally represented here. A vital resource for understanding just how fully Dylan steeped his work in multiple musical transitions, and how rapidly he made them his own is Todd Harvey's contribution for the American Folk Music and Musicians Series, *The Formative Dylan: Transmission and Stylistic Influences, 1961-1963* (London: Scarecrow Press, 2001). Admirable exegeses and analyses of Dylan's lyrics are provided by the three major sources: Mike Marqusee, *Wicked Messenger: Bob Dylan and the 1960s* (New York, Seven Stories Press, 2003), whose primary emphasis is on the political content and context for Dylan's work; Aiden Day, *Jokerman: Reading the Lyrics of Bob Dylan* (Oxford and New York: Basil Blackwell, 1988), which focuses on the way Dylan's lyrical output treats the modernist dilemma of identity, providing telling insights in the process; and Christopher Ricks, *Dylan's Visions of Sin* (New York: HarperCollins, 2003), a fascinating and often frustrating set of riffs on Dylan set in the context of the high literary tradition of which Ricks is a well-regarded scholar. Three anthologies of critical

writing and interviews provide a good background: Carl Benson, ed., *The Bob Dylan Companion: Four Decades of Commentary* (New York: Schirmer Books, 1998); Benjamin Hedin, *Studio A: The Bob Dylan Reader* (New York: W. W. Norton & Company, 2004); and Jim Ellison, *Younger Than That Now: The Collected Interviews With Bob Dylan* (New York: Thunder's Mouth Press, 2004), which is far from definitive (missing, for example, the crucial *Sing Out* interview of 1967, among others). For a largely comprehensive discography, one turns to Oliver Trager, *Keys to the Rain: The Definitive Bob Dylan Encyclopedia* (New York: Billboard Books, 2004), which, despite its title, does not include entries on Georgia Sam, Sarah Lownds, or Jesse Fuller; it is instead an alphabetically arranged series of sometimes pithy, sometimes extensive reports and critiques of every song in Dylan's repertoire.

For the "facts" and the ephemera, there are the fan sites, and they remind the visitor that the word was originally a contraction of "fanatic." Those I've depended on include *Expecting Rain* (http://expectingrain.com/), *Dylanbase* (http://www.dylanbase .com/), and the redoubtable journal *Isis*, which contains a wealth of interviews, reviews, critiques, essays, and the like, and maintains a robust website (http://www.bobdylanisis .com/). My spy in the fan world has been the assiduous and contentious Rick "Big Ricky" Greenwald, known by one and all within that shadowy cybercommunity of Dylanologists.

Finally, there tower two sources, impossible to emulate or to approach. Greil Marcus has written two wild, unimpeachable, personal, brilliant studies of Dylan: *Invisible Republic: Bob Dylan's Basement Tapes* (New York: Owl Publishing Group, 1998) and its reissued version, *The Old, Weird America: The World of Bob Dylan's Basement Tapes* (New York: Picador, 2001); and more recently, the sustained close-up, *Like A Rolling Stone: Bob Dylan at the Crossroads* (New York: Public Affairs, 2005). The other is Dylan himself, whose *Chronicles, Volume I* (New York: Simon and Schuster, 2004) is utterly remarkable.

For the lyrics and the music, I've depended on the records themselves, from which I have done careful transcriptions, rather than the standard authorized lyric sources, which reflect corrections, emendations, and errors galore and thus aren't accurate to the experience of the music in its historical context. Dylan's own official site, while valuable as a primary source, is not a useful or fully trustworthy resource for gaining historical accuracy—it is part of the much larger, lifelong project of self-construction that is central to Dylan's importance as a cultural figure.

2 In 1961, he told Izzy Young that he was combining "a lot of old jazz songs, sentimental cowboy songs, Top 40 hit parade stuff . . . old blues and Texas songs." (quoted in Heylin, *Bob Dylan: Beyond the Shades Revisited*, 71).

3 And it is safe to note that, extraordinary as was the version by Dave Van Ronk from which Dylan's was appropriated, the burly merchant mariner Van Ronk never proposed himself as that female narrator.

4 Calvin Trillin's description of the morning was written for the *New Yorker*'s "Talk of the Town" section and published in the September 7, 1963, issue. Dylan's performance receives no particular notice—it's Joan Baez's "wonderfully clear voice" that received his praise. The piece has been republished in Ann Charters, ed., *The Portable Sixties Reader* (New York: The Penguin Group, 2003), p. 61.

5 When Howard Sounes interviewed Wavy Gravy, he claimed to have been sitting next to Dylan as King spoke. But the claim is specious: he reported that he leaned over and told Dylan, "I hope he's over quick. Mahalia Jackson's on next," when in fact Jackson had already sung, followed by Rabbi Prinz of the American Jewish Congress, and then by A. Philip Randolph, who introduced King. See Sounes, *Down the Highway*, 140–41.

6 "TV: Coverage of March. Nielsen Reports 46% Higher Audience than in Normal Daytime Hours," *New York Times*, August 29, 1963. A good general study of the relationship between television and the civil rights movement, focused on the ways network TV

influenced the South, is William G. Thomas III, " Television News and the Civil Rights Struggle: The Views in Virginia and Mississippi," *Southern Spaces*, November 3, 2004, http://southernspaces.org/2004/television-news-and-civil-rights-struggle-views -virginia-and-mississippi#_edn47.

7 Probably the most complete analysis of the speech and its larger context of African American preaching is Elizabeth Vander Lei and Keith D. Miller's "Martin Luther King Jr.'s 'I Have a Dream' in Context: Ceremonial Protest and African American Jeremiad." *College English* 62, no. 1 (September 1999): 83-99. The reference to Carey is found on page 90, but the entire essay is an essential analysis of the speech and its place.

8 Ibid., 89-90.

9 A tradition used by others, including Ida B. Wells, as Vander Lei and Miller point out in "Martin Luther King Jr.'s 'I Have a Dream' in Context."

10 Cited in Marqusee, *Wicked Messenger*, 15.

11 King, quoted in Branch, *Parting the Waters*, 890-92.

12 David M. Lubin has brilliantly analyzed the cultural practices around Kennedy's assassination in *Shooting Kennedy: JFK and the Culture of Images* (Berkeley: University of California Press, 2003). Fashion historian Scott Jorgenson provides the information that Givenchy clothed all the Kennedy family with funerary garb.

13 Dylan, interviewed by Anthony Scaduto, quoted in Gill, *Don't Think Twice*, 43.

14 Quoted in Soames, *Behind the Shades Revisited*, 137.

15 This concert has been released nearly unedited as *The Bootleg Series, Vol. 6: Bob Dylan Live, 1964, Concert at Philharmonic Hall* (Columbia: 2004, CD), with a delightful appreciation by the historian Sean Wilentz who, at the age of 13, was in that audience. (A few weeks later, I, also 13, was in the audience at Woolsey Hall at Yale University in New Haven, for a reprise of that concert.)

16 Ginsberg speaking in D. A. Pennebaker's steely documentary tracking Dylan's 1965 English tour, *Don't Look Back* (1967).

17 I have excised for clarity's sake a complicating context—the reprising by Dylan of his mentor-hero Woody Guthrie's precedent song in which a narrator speaks to his mother: "Tom Joad." Guthrie's song is also very long, and it too reinterprets a previous epic—in Guthrie's case, John Steinbeck's *Grapes of Wrath*, which was also dependent on precedent, in the form of Dorothea Lange's photographs of migrant workers, made for the Farm Security Administration. Steinbeck and Guthrie celebrate their hero's activist declarations and his promise to be at the forefront of a revolution not of sensibility but of political action. This is exactly what Dylan's narrator rejects: *I got nothin', Ma, to live up to.*

18 All of the liner notes to Dylan's albums are published online at http://www.bobdylan .com/albums.

19 Nat Hentoff, "The Playboy Interview: Bob Dylan," *Playboy*, March 1966, 41-46 (quote, 46); this discussion ends what is one of the funniest and most biting of Dylan's performances.

20 Bobby Seale, *Seize the Time: The Story of the Black Panther Party and Huey P. Newton* (New York: Random House, 1968), 154, 181-87.

21 Ginsberg is quoted in Heylin, *Behind the Shades Revisited*, 287.

22 Dylan himself talked about this in an interview with musician and musicologist John Cohen shortly after the album was released:

> The scope opens up, just by a few little tricks . . . see on the album you have to think about it after you hear it . . . *All Along the Watchtower* opens up in . . . a stranger way, for here we have the cycle of events working in a rather reverse order.
>
> (JOHN COHEN AND HAPPY TRAUM, "Bob Dylan: The Sing Out Interview," *Sing Out*, October/November 1968, 13)

23 Ibid.

24 Deuteronomy 34:1-6.

Chapter 13

1 Robert Shelton, *No Direction Home* (New York: Da Capo Press, 1997), 59-60.

2 John McDermott, Billy Cox, and Eddie Kramer, *Jimi Hendrix Sessions: The Complete Studio Recording Sessions, 1963-1970* (Boston: Little Brown and Company, 1995), 49-50.

3 John McDermott with Edward E. Kramer, *Hendrix: Setting the Record Straight* (New York: Grand Central Publishing, 1992), 106-7, 136. This chapter is drawn from a wide range of works on Hendrix, including the definitive biographies: David Henderson, *Jimi Hendrix: Voodoo Child of the Aquarian Age* (Garden City, NY: Doubleday, 1978); McDermott and Kramer, *Hendrix*; Harry Shapiro and Caesar Glebbeek, *Jimi Hendrix Electric Gypsy* (New York: St. Martin's Press, 1991); and the most recent, Charles R. Cross, *Room Full of Mirrors: A Biography of Jimi Hendrix* (New York: Hyperion, 2005). The best interpretive study is Charles Shaar Murray, *Crosstown Traffic: Jimi Hendrix and the Post-War Rock 'N' Roll Revolution* (New York: St. Martin's Press, 1989). Important materials, both interpretive and biographical, are found in two rather lavish illustrated books: Keith Shadwick, *Jimi Hendrix Musician* (San Francisco: Backbeat Books, 2003), which delineates Hendrix's meteoric career on a month-by-month basis; and Adrian Boot and Chris Salewicz, *Jimi Hendrix: The Ultimate Experience* (New York: McMillan USA, 1995), which includes interesting memoirs and critical responses by a variety of cultural figures, along with a rich trove of photographs. Mitch Mitchell and John Platt, *The Hendrix Experience* (London: Hamlyn, 2000) provides extensive reminiscences by the Experience's drummer and Hendrix's longtime friend. Finally, John McDermott, Billie Cox, and Eddie Kramer have produced a valuable tracing of the recording process on a session-by-session basis in *Jimi Hendrix Sessions*. For the most part, I have skipped extensive footnoting of these sources in the following pages, because so much of the information is held in common by two or more of the works. The chapter also draws on my own experience as a Hendrix fan, involving numerous concerts with the Experience and its successor bands, including the Isle of Wight festival.

4 McDermott and Kramer, *Hendrix*, 163. McDermott and Kramer report that, in 1969, Hendrix confessed to a Frankfurt audience calling for the song: "Wait a minute: we recorded that a year ago and if you've heard it, we are very glad. But tonight, we're trying to do a musical thing, okay? That's a single, and we released it as a single, thank you very much for thinking about it but I forgot the words, that's what I am trying to say." There are other instances in which Hendrix chose to announce that he'd "forgotten" lyrics and so wouldn't sing, or wouldn't continue to sing, songs that bored or annoyed him—notably a session on the BBC's *Lulu Show*, where the hostess insisted that they perform "Hey, Joe," and Hendrix chose to forget the lyrics only after doing one of his finest feedback intros, after which the band performed Cream's "Sunshine of Your Love" stunningly, to the horror of the BBC producers (ibid., 159-60).

5 Kathy Etchingham with Andrew Crofts, *Through Gypsy Eyes—My Life, the Sixties, and Jimi Hendrix* (London: Gollancz Publishing, 1998), 110.

6 Johnny Winter's wild version of "Highway 61," with his signature hoarse, urgent "shout" voice and his virtuosic slide playing on his signature 1963 Gibson Firebird V, was released more than a year later, quite possibly inspired by the success of Hendrix's single.

7 A rare view of Hendrix in the back line behind Buddy and Stacey as they covered Booker T. and the MGs' hit "Shotgun" for the TV show *Night Train* in 1965 shows the guitarist in a heavily choreographed performance; it has surfaced on YouTube.

8 The 1970 census reported that Revere's population was 43,159, of which 38 were listed as "Negro," and all others as "White."

9 It's possible, in fact (and some of the biographies and musical histories of Hendrix and the group support the idea), that the decision to have Hendrix sing was insisted on by Chas Chandler and others who were collaborating with Hendrix in making the group's identity.

10 Karl Ferris's reminiscences concerning Hendrix and the album cover are found in numerous places on the web, notably, "Cover Story—Jimi Hendrix Experience's 'Are You Experienced?,' with photography by Karl Ferris," *RockpopGallery*, February 22, 2008, http://rockpopgallery.typepad.com/rockpop_gallery_news/2008/02/cover-story—j.html. Ferris himself self-produced a short video documentary, *The Karl Ferris Experience*, that can be found on YouTube at http://www.youtube.com/watch?v=Pp54sT9qGQk.

11 Kathy Etchingham with Andrew Crofts, *Through Gypsy Eyes—My Life, the Sixties, and Jimi Hendrix* (London: Gollancz Publishing, 1998), 110.

12 Shapiro and Glebbeek, *Jimi Hendrix Electric Gypsy*, 34–35.

13 The conflict is recounted in Henderson, *Jimi Hendrix: Voodoo Child of the Aquarian Age*, 123–29.

14 *Malcolm X., By Any Means Necessary: Speeches, Interviews, and a Letter by Malcolm X.*, ed. *George Breitman (New York: Pathfinder Press, 1989)*, 37 (original emphasis).

15 Christgau originally described Hendrix as "a psychedelic Uncle Tom," and it is that pejorative that persists in most writing, though the printed version in *Esquire* stands here. Christgau's lengthy essay in *Esquire*, written in July of 1967 but not published until the January 1968 issue, is reproduced in its entirety (though without illustrations or the inimitable *Esquire* design) on the web, http://www.robertchristgau.com/xg/music/monterey-69.php.

16 The original 1967 performance was recorded as soundtrack material for D. A. Pennebaker's documentary, *Monterey Pop* (released December 26, 1968) and currently available in DVD format as *Monterey Pop: The Criterion Collection* (June 13, 2006). The music was released in CD form as *Jimi Hendrix, At Monterey* (Geffen Records, 2007).

17 I first noticed this strange slip of the tongue not on the album, but at Hendrix's live performance at the Isle of Wight Festival in 1970. It was very cold that night, and Hendrix was rather frantically chewing gum while performing and I thought perhaps it was a speed-induced short circuit of the memory on his part. When I returned to the States and listened again to the album, I was struck that I had not noticed the misspeaking before. To those skeptics who find this analysis overreaching, I recommend that they see BBC video of the Isle of Wight performance uploaded recently to YouTube at http://www.youtube.com/watch?v=4wr8MmAT860 (Hendrix's performance begins at around 1 hour 11 minutes in). *All Along the Watchtower* has been edited out of the polished version, but a bootleg version is found at http://www.youtube.com/watch?v=04JR-kRD3k8; or the 1969 performance, barely comprehensible, from a concert in Munich, http://www.youtube.com/watch?v=V5GsX9uxhQo; despite the illegibility of the vocals, one can clearly hear Hendrix pause and then muff that phrase.

Chapter 14

1 The lines are from Dylan's "Subterranean Homesick Blues," released in 1965 as a single and appearing on the album *Bringing It All Back Home* (Columbia, 1965).

2 A string of books published in the '50s and early '60s had already begun to explore the American mythos of expansionism and Manifest Destiny, from Henry Nash Smith's *Virgin Land* (1950), Perry Miller's *Errand Into the Wilderness* (1956) and R. W. B. Lewis's *The American Adam* (1959), to a more strident and polemical second generation,

including works as seemingly disparate as Leo Marx's literary study, *The Machine in the Garden* (1967) and Roderick Nash's *Wilderness and the American Mind* (also 1967). These works began to be packaged together in courses and curricula in English and history departments and in the burgeoning field of American studies. In some cases, they were bundled with works more frankly nature-centric, from paperback "critical editions" of Thoreau's *Walden* and Emerson's *Nature* to Aldo Leopold's intimate *Sand County Almanac* (1949; paperback college edition 1968), and Rachel Carson's ringing polemic *Silent Spring* (1962; paperback college edition 1966), generally considered the single most important work in bringing the environmental movement into existence as a mass movement.

3   It is, however, striking to note that the Stewart Brand, founder of the *Whole Earth Catalog*, was a relatively long-standing citizen of the Haight, arriving around 1962 and remaining in that community through 1968, when his first catalog was issued.

4   Peter Coyote, *Sleeping Where I Fall: A Chronicle* (Berkeley, CA: Counterpoint, 1998), xii.

5   This segment is drawn from a variety of secondary and primary resources. Probably the best general study of the Haight during its heyday is Charles Perry, *The Haight-Ashbury* (1984; New York: Wenner Books, 2005). A valuable visual resource is Lisa Law, *Flashing on the Sixties* (San Francisco: Chronicle Books,. 1997) and the DVD version, *Flashing on the Sixties: A Tribal Document*, directed by Lisa Law (San Francisco: Flashback Productions, 1994). While Tom Wolfe's chronicle of the Merry Pranksters remains the best read of all the materials on the West Coast Counterculture, works that are more closely linked to the moment itself have appeared more recently. Notable is Paul Perry and Ken Babbs, *On the Bus: The Complete Guide to the Legendary Trip of Ken Kesey and the Merry Pranksters and the Birth of the* Counterculture (New York: Thunder's Mouth Press, 1990). Three volumes of excerpts from the voluminous footage taken by the Pranksters themselves have been released in DVD form: *Intrepid Traveler and his Merry Band of Pranksters Look for A Kool Place*, directed by Ken Kesey (Pleasant Hill, OR: Ken Kesey/key-z.com, 2 vols., 1999), and *The Acid Test* (Pleasant Hill, OR: Key-Z Productions, 1999). *The Oracle*, the seminal journalistic document of the Haight-Ashbury, has recently been reissued in its entirety on DVD as well: *The San Francisco Oracle*, facsimile ed. (New York: Regent Press, 2005). A wide variety of Digger materials has been uploaded to the Internet.

6   The trip was originally "planned" (an unlikely verb for such a group or process) to mark the publication of Kesey's monumental second novel, *Sometimes a Great Notion* (1964), a very different narrative of place and the loss of place, located in a very different mythic American landscape.

7   A significant part of Chicago's founding charter and its initial body of laws concerned what was allowed and what was forbidden on the streets, including children playing with hoops and commercial establishments setting signage or wares displays into the streets. Similar regulations accompanied most American city development, including that of San Francisco.

8   Golden Gate Park designer William Hammond Hall was a case in point of the paradoxical promises of American park design. He had trained in the military and had worked as a military and government topographer and surveyor, serving in the campaign to grid the nation's western lands and make them accessible to commercial, mining, agricultural, and ranching exploitation and settlement. Yet he was versed in the theories of the picturesque, which proposed a restorative mission to the landscape. With his partner, the horticulturist John McLaren, he developed a park that emphasized participation and engagement and not simply stunning visual effects—McLaren had declared that "his" park would have no "keep off the grass" signs.

9   This Digger broadside, "Where is PUBLIC," has been reproduced at the *Digger Archives*, http://www.diggers.org/bibscans/dp001_m8.jpg.

10   "Diggers' New Game: The Frame," *Berkeley Barb*, November 4, 1966, 1.

11 The sometimes evocative, sometimes obscurantist use of language, particularly the playing of nouns as verbs and verbs as nouns, and the interweaving of tyrannical past and present with liberated present and future, characteristic of Digger broadsides, represented an attempt to simultaneously render action in words, and prevent words from subverting or displacing actions; the Diggers considered their "actions" and those in which they participated, more important and more complete than the manifesto form found in the broadsides.

12 Quoted in Barney Hoskyns, *Beneath the Diamond Sky: Haight-Ashbury 1965–1971* (New York: Simon and Schuster Editions, 1997), 131.

13 See, for example, Herbert Gold, "Where the Action Is," *New York Times*, February 19, 1967.

14 Perry, *The Haight-Ashbury*, 116–24.

15 Hoskyns, *Beneath the Diamond Sky*, 155.

16 Coyote, *Sleeping Where I Fall*, 83.

17 Michael William Doyle, "Staging the Revolution: Guerrilla Theater as a Countercultural Practice, 1965–1968," in *Imagine Nation: The American Counterculture of the 1960s and '70s*, ed. Peter Braunstein and Michael William Doyle (New York: Routledge, 2002), 86–87.

18 General information on Chicago '68 comes from the following sources: Daniel Walker et. al., *Rights in Conflict: The Violent Confrontation of Demonstrators and Police in the Parks and Streets of Chicago During the Week of the Democratic National Convention of 1968* (New York: New American Library, 1968) (commonly called the *Walker Report* or the *Official Report*); David Farber, *Chicago '68* (Chicago: University of Chicago Press, 1988); Frank Kusch, *Battleground Chicago: The Police and the 1968 Democratic National Convention* (Westport, CT: Praeger, 2004); Larry Sloman, *Steal This Dream: Abbie Hoffman and the Countercultural Revolution in America* (New York: Dell, 1998); David Lewis Stein, *Living the Revolution: The Yippies in Chicago* (Indianapolis, IN: Bobbs-Merrill Company, 1969); and a number of web pages that have reproduced primary-source documents. I have also worked extensively with the collections in the archives of the Chicago History Museum, which includes, among many documents, a rich trove of photographs not yet fully catalogued or available online.

19 David Dellinger, quoted in Walker et al., *Rights in Conflict*, 10–11.

20 Cited in Farber, *Chicago '68*, 16–17.

21 Jerry Rubin to Allen Cohen, quoted in Doyle, "Staging the Revolution," 89–90.

22 Jerry Rubin, quoted in Farber, *Chicago '68*, 19–22 (emphasis added).

23 Quoted in Farber, *Chicago '68*, 22.

24 Davis's testimony is quoted in Walker et al., *Rights in Conflict*, 50.

25 The "Clearing of Clark Street" incident on Monday, August 26, when police and National Guard troops mounted a full-scale assault on protesters who had dispersed into Old Town, was the highlight. See Frank Kusch, *Battleground Chicago*, 78–83.

26 Walker et al., *Rights in Conflict*, 140–43, provides a description that has been corrected by study of photographs and documents. This revised version is well presented in Farber, *Chicago '68*, 184–85. I have also consulted the visual records in the Chicago History Museum archives to reassess the circumstances.

27 The most reputable source for unraveling the complex history of the Woodstock Music and Art Festival is Joel Makower, ed., *Woodstock: The Oral History, 40th Anniversary Edition* (Albany: State University of New York Press, 2009), which contains a stellar list of subjects interviewed and a healthily skeptical editing process by Makower; the interviews were done in 1989, at a moment when nostalgia and accurate recollection had begun to clash. Elliot Tiber's *Knock on Woodstock* (New York: Festival Books, 1994) is an amusing but unreliable memoir by a relatively peripheral if colorful figure; it was

the basis for the 2009 film, *Taking Woodstock*. Michael Land's *The Road To Woodstock: From the Man Behind the Legendary Festival* (New York: HarperCollins, 2009) is approximately as trustworthy as its subtitle implies, but is nevertheless full of information and interest. Mike Evans and Paul Kingsbury, *Woodstock: Three Days That Rocked the World* (New York: Sterling Publishing, 2009) is graphic, photographic, and reminiscent hagiography at its very best, as is Susan Reynolds, ed., *Woodstock Revisited: 50 Far Out, Groovy, Peace-Loving, Flashback-Inducing Stories from Those Who Were There* (Cincinnati, OH: Adams Media, 2009). One of the few valuable academic treatments of the subject is Andy Bennett, ed., *Remembering Woodstock* (Hampshire, UK: Ashgate Publishing, 1988), which contains scholarly essays of varying relevance and quality.

28   This may seem to romantics an exaggerated piling-up of small misfortunes in the face of some larger triumph. It was, however, the experience of my friends, colleagues and bandmates at the time. I was not there: I was doing double shifts at the Yale Experimental Animal Center cleaning cages and disposing of the dead, so that my friend and coworker John could go. I am for the most part quoting directly from his description of his weekend.

29   The circular is reproduced in Makower, *Woodstock*, 105.

30   "Yasgur says, 'You want'—I forget what he said—'you want something that has an angle?' . . . Now it's raining and we're going through and it's misty and we're on this back road. We drive onto the top of that hill, drive right onto the grass, get to the top and get out, look out. And all of a sudden the rain stops and the mist is, like, breaking up. And there it is. It's like a lake and a natural amphitheater and roads and woods . . . Whew. Michael and I looked at each other and said, 'This is it.' We were happy, we were smiling" (Makower, *Woodstock*, 115). Fellow associate Stanley Goldstein described the general area as one of the "few places in the world that are quite so lush and inviting, that there's contours sufficient to satisfy the eye and to keep bringing new vistas into view. But none of it is assaultive; none of it challenges you. It's very welcoming, warm, lush. . . . Max grew hay, the folks next door grew corn, and so far as the eye could see, there were fields and fields and fields . . . wherever you looked there was green and shade" (ibid., 115-16).

31   There is a great deal of confusion about the circumstances surrounding this event. Mitchell herself has recorded her sense of frustration and marginalization in later interviews, some of which are found on her official website, *jonimitchell.com*. She is also quoted by David Zimmer in *Crosby, Stills & Nash: The Authorized Biography* (New York: Da Capo Press, 1984), 99, 101-2. Valuable video footage, including her remembrance, but also—and more tellingly—containing most of the actual *Dick Cavett Show* footage, including the rather boorish crashing of the show by "the boys," can be seen on the DVD *Joni Mitchell, A Life Story: Woman of Heart and Mind*, directed by Susan Lacy (New York: Eagle Rock Entertainment, 2003). The most sympathetic and illuminating study of Mitchell, Sheila Weller's *Girls Like Us* (New York: Washington Square Press, 2008), reports that Mitchell had finished the song "by the time the boys got back" (291-92), though Crosby suggested that she wrote the song based on hearing "the boys" describe the event. I fall on the side of Weller (Zimmer, *Crosby, Stills & Nash*, 112).

32   Zimmer, *Crosby, Stills & Nash*, 109.

33   Ibid., 111.

34   The performance is found on a number of websites, including YouTube, at http://www .youtube.com/watch?v=IBqodL2OJ1A.

35   Jerry Hopkins, "Big Sur," *Rolling Stone*, October 18, 1969, 20-23.

36   This, according to Bill Owens, the photographer, who was working the festival.

37   "It was just fuckin' nuts . . . These gigs were all ridiculously unorganized . . . Crosby and Stills were standing on the front of the truck or on the running boards . . . just like,

y'know . . . parting the sea. I thought it was Fellini-esque" (Neil Young, interviewed in Jimmy McDonough, *Shakey: Neil Young's Biography* [New York: Random House, 2002], 318-20.

38 Zimmer, *Crosby, Stills & Nash*, 126-27.

39 A brief but excellent analysis of the song's musical and lyrical interactions is found in Lloyd Whitesell, *The Music of Joni Mitchell* (New York: Oxford University Press, 2008), 33-34: "Mitchell conceives the song as a lament for solo voice. . . . The long wordless vocal coda . . . gulps and throbs with loss."

40 Richard Nixon, "Cambodian Incursion Address,", transcript at *American Rhetoric*, http://www.americanrhetoric.com/speeches/richardnixoncambodia.html (emphasis added).

41 Governor Rhodes's remarks at the press conference are often cited. The transcript of the press conference is found in the Kent State University Archives, Box 63, folder M4C. Leigh Herington, who was a graduate of Kent State and at the time its assistant sports information director, most directly states what is considered common knowledge today. In an interview conducted on November 9, 1980, he declared that "when James Rhodes came to Kent on Sunday for the meeting at the fire station with local authorities—when the media showed up—he began to pound tables and put on an act. I have always felt he did that for the benefit of the Senate primary the following week" (Scott L. Bills, "Chain Reaction: 'A Series of Mistakes,' an interview with Leigh Herington," *Kent State/May 4: Echoes Through a Decade* [Kent, OH: Kent State University Press, 1982], 76-81).

42 This discussion of Kent State is based primarily on the official report, contained in the broader and more comprehensive *Report of the President's Commission on Campus Unrest* ("Scranton Commission"). (Washington, DC: US Government Printing Office, 1970); the section on Kent State is found at pp. 233-90. I have also used the standard books, though they are sometimes exaggerated or inaccurate, requiring sifting of one against the others and a close attention to the citations: William A. Gordon, *Four Dead in Ohio: Was There a Conspiracy At Kent State?* (Laguna Hills, CA: North Ridge Books, 1995); Philip Caputo, *13 Seconds: A Look Back at the Kent State Shootings* (New York: Chamberlain Brothers/Penguin Group, 2005); Scott L. Bills, ed., *Kent State/May 4: Echoes Through a Decade* (1982; Kent, Ohio: Kent State University Press, 1988); and Joseph Kelner and James Munves, *The Kent State Coverup* (New York: Harper & Row, 1980).

43 John Locke, *Two Treatises of Government* (1689); in one edition, Locke more precisely spoke of "lives, liberties and estates, which I call by the general name, property." Both Locke's treatises and the Declarations of the Continental Congress are easily found on the Internet, notably on *Project Gutenberg*.

Chapter 15

1 Stanley Krippner and Don Fersh, "Mystic Communes: The Mystical Experience and the Mystical Commune—18 Hip Religious Communes and the Beliefs of the People Who Inhabit Them," *Modern Utopian* 1.4, no. 2 (Spring 1970), unpaginated. A useful anthology from the journal, with some added and equally valuable items from the period and from recent scholars of the American commune, is Richard Fairfield, ed., *The Modern Utopian: Alternative Communities of the '60s and '70s* (Port Townsend, WA: Process Media, 2010).

2 Fairfield's "Special 3-in-1 Issue: Communes, U.S.A.," *Modern Utopian* 1.5, nos. 1-3 (1971), unpaginated, is perhaps the most encyclopedic of contemporaneous reports on communal life at that moment; Fairfield reported on forty-two currently active communes and included a critical history of the Oneida Community as well. The issue was later released as a book, *Communes, U.S.A.: A Personal Tour* (New York: Penguin, 1972).

3 Robert Houriet, *Getting Back Together* (New York: Coward, McCann and Geoghegan, 1971), xiii–xiv.

4 In this I am taking exception to Timothy Miller's account of "New Communards with Old Communal Ties," in *The 60s Communes: Hippies and Beyond* (Syracuse: Syracuse University Press, 1999), 8–13. The existence of a stray copy of Alcott in one commune's "library" does not constitute the sort of evidence needed to make such an argument, especially in the face of the far more powerful and universal mythos of American exceptionalism and utopianism that permeated American education and popular culture as the communards were growing up.

5 John Curl, *For All the People: Uncovering the Hidden History of Cooperation, Cooperative Movements, and Communalism in America* (Oakland, CA: PM Press, 2009), 324.

6 New Buffalo's experience with some tribal Indians was unusually benevolent; on the other hand, it was also often belied by other experiences, sometimes with drunken Indians who came through, often seeking the company of women, more alcohol, or money. John Curl's memoir, *Memories of Drop City* (New York: iUniverse, 2007) contains a harrowing description of Drop City drop-ins to a Ute Sundance, in which the tensions resulting from callow white hippies crashing Native American rituals over the preceding years (about 1965–1969) required delicate maneuvering. As illuminating are the encounters described by Arthur Kopecky in *New Buffalo: Journal from a Taos Commune* (Albuquerque: University of New Mexico Press, 2004), and the rather romanticized description of encounters with the Karoks by Black Bear Commune member Michael Tierra, in Don Monkerud et al., eds., *Free Land: Free Love: Tales of a Wilderness Commune* (Aptos, CA: Black Bear Mining and Publishing Company, 2000), 172–80, countered by the much darker descriptions of encounters contained in Robert Roskind's *Memoirs of an Ex-Hippie: Seven Years in the Counterculture* (Blowing Rock, NC: One Love Press, 2001).

7 Estrella Morning Star, "Free Luv & the Feminist Revolution: How the '60s became the '70s," in Monkerud et al., *Free Land: Free Love: Tales of a Wilderness Commune*, 151–55.

8 Quoted in Houriet, *Getting Back Together*, 170–71.

9 Patricia Lapidus, "The Letting Go and the Taking Hold," in *Voices from The Farm: Adventures in Community Living*, ed. Rupert Fike, 47–49 (Summertown, TN: Book Publishing Company, 1998), 49.

10 These recurrent debates are well-recorded in Kopecky's daily diaries, which form the bulk of his *New Buffalo*.

11 Outsiders mirrored the conflict. Health code violations on the communes were rightfully seen as threatening the welfare of the communities surrounding places like New Buffalo, Libre, and Drop City. Infectious agents in the water, unsanitary waste-water treatment, sickly commune children in the public school classrooms: all these contributed to an often vitriolic backlash. Young men and women willing to work at subsistence levels pushed down wage rates and competed with local workers. And crowds of visitors coming to gawk at or temporarily sample the hippie lifestyle overwhelmed local institutions and drove up prices. Food stamps were often the flash point, but the tension was far broader. The *Taos News* ran an article in February of 1970, "Do Hippies Love Us For Our Food Stamps?" to dispel some of the hostility by explaining that the program was federally funded, uniformly regulated from state to state, and could not be abrogated by local authorities. But the article veered toward the broader community fears—of contamination and invasion. One resident warned of "a greater influx of long hairs this summer . . . and there will be many who will come without any concept or regard of this community, with no notion of supporting himself, and will probably be a burden on all the cultures in the community, Indian, Spanish, Anglo and Hippie" (reproduced in Roberta Price, *Huerfano: A Memoir of Life in the Counterculture* [Amherst: University of Massachusetts Press, 2004], 72). Price also reproduced an article from

Fountain of Light, the Taos underground newspaper, detailing the food stamp process for communards, on the following page.

12   John Curl discusses the tension between "open" and "closed" communal structures in *For All the People*, 324-26.

13   Ibid., 58.

14   John Curl, *Memories of Drop City*, 108-9, 128-29, 148-49, 155-67. Fairfield, "Communes, U.S.A.," 93-99.

15   Richard Fairfield republished a lengthy ad taken by The Farm in a local Tennessee newspaper, in the *Modern Utopian*; it was reproduced in the anthology, Fairfield, *The Modern Utopian*, 43-46. Gaskin's own words were published as *The Monday Night Class* (Summertown, TN: Book Farm/Bookworks, 1970), and recently reissued with additional commentary; *The Monday Night Class* (Summertown, TN: Book Publishing, 2005). I also had access to a wide variety of materials disseminated by The Farm over its history.

16   Typical of that genre is the series published by Houghton Mifflin as "North Star Books," and including *Riders of the Pony Express* (1958), *Gold in California* (1958) and *Indian Wars and Warriors West* (1959).

17   Nina Tannenwald, "Nuclear Weapons and the Vietnam War, *Journal of Strategic Studies* 29, no. 4 (August 2006): 675-722. Probably the most important document was the recently declassified 1967 report, "Tactical Nuclear Weapons in Southeast Asia" (Washington, DC: Department of Defense, 1967), as well as a string of draft reports submitted to Secretary of Defense McNamara and/or submitted by him to President Johnson between 1965 and 1969.

18   The common wisdom in the military community is that the war in Vietnam was being won militarily and strategically, but was lost as a result of anti-war bias on the part of the television journalism community. This is most pointedly articulated in a 1984 report by the Command and Staff College of the Marine Corps: Major Cass D. Howell, *Television Coverage of the Vietnam War, and its Implications for Future Conflicts* (Washington, DC: Command and Staff College, 1984). A number of scholarly studies have conclusively rebutted this position, noting instead that, before the Tet Offensive of 1968, while television steadily increased its influence as a source of "trusted news," the reports on the Vietnam war were almost entirely positive, repeating without comment the press releases and daily briefing reports of the military and government representatives. See, for example, Clarence R. Wyatt, *Paper Soldiers: The American Press and the Vietnam War* (Chicago: University of Chicago Press, 1995), esp. 80-83; Daniel C. Hallin, *"The Uncensored War:" The Media and Vietnam* (New York: Oxford University Press, 1986), 13-156, esp. 109-111; and Peter C. Rollins, "The Vietnam War: Perceptions Through Literature, Film and Television," *American Quarterly* 36, no. 3 (1984): 419-32. One of the most controversial of writers on U.S. proxy wars, Bruce Cumings, also reports that the television coverage was predominantly prowar: see Bruce Cumings, *War and Television* (New York: Verso Books, 1994), 83-84.

19   John Winthrop, "A Modell of Christian Charity [the 'Arbella Sermon']," 1630, full text online at http://religiousfreedom.lib.virginia.edu/sacred/charity.html .

20   The most comprehensive anthology of American communalism is Donald E. Pitzer, *America's Communal Utopias* (Chapel Hill: University of North Carolina Press, 1997).

Chapter 16

1   The best general study of *Pong* is found in Steven L. Kent's *The Ultimate History of Video Games* (Roseville, CA: Prima Publishing, 2001), 37-48. *Pong* gets a typically incisive treatment in J. C. Herz, *Joystick Nation: How Videogames Ate Our Quarters, Won Our Hearts, and Rewired Our Minds* (Boston: Little, Brown and Company, 1997), notably in

her second chapter, "A Natural History of Video Games," 14. There is a marvelously breathless G4tv.com bio of Noland Bushnell on YouTube at http://www.youtube.com /watch?v=fd2DcV8akBQ, and a mesmerizing "demo" of the original arcade *Pong* also available at http://www.youtube.com/watch?v=pDrRnJOCKZc. Other tribute web pages and segments from books, notably John Sellers, *Arcade Fever: The Fan's Guide to the Golden Age of Video Games* (Philadelphia, PA: Running Press, 2001); and Bill Kurtz, *The Encyclopedia of Arcade Video Games* (Atglen, PA: Schiffer Publishers, 2003), provided context.

2 http://www.youtube.com/watch?v=pDrRnJOCKZc

3 The most thoughtful and dense philosophical discussion of the digital game system and its implications is McKenzie Wark, *Gamer Theory* (Cambridge, MA: Harvard University Press, 2007); on the algorithmic, see the second chapter, "Allegory: On *The Sims*."

Chapter 17

1 There is a burgeoning—and as rapidly obsolescing—literature on cyberspace and the digital domain; a short list would take up pages. Sherrie Terkle's trilogy of books reaches back to the very first theorizing about the computer as a cultural tool: *The Second Self: Computers and the Human Spirit* (New York: Simon and Schuster, 1984) was followed by the central text, *Life on the Screen: Identity in the Age of the Internet* (New York: Simon and Schuster, 1995); most recently she published *Alone Together: Why We Expect More From Technology and Less From Each Other* (New York: Basic Books, 2011). Janet Murray's *Hamlet on the Holodeck: The Future of Narrative in Cyberspace* (Cambridge, MA: MIT Press, 1998) is a relatively early exploration of the changing shape of imaginative production under the onslaught of the virtual. Allucquere Rosanne Stone's major work appeared at about this same moment—*The War of Desire and Technology at the Close of the Mechanical Age* (Cambridge, MA: MIT Press, 1996)—as did N. Katherine Hayles's *How We Became Posthuman: Virtual Bodies in Cybernetics, Literature, and Informatics* (Chicago: University of Chicago Press, 1999) and Julian Dibbell's *My Tiny Life: Crime and Passion in a Virtual World* (New York: Holt Paperbacks, 1999). A few works have sought to include the spatial in the analysis of cyberspace. Martin Dodge and Rob Kitchin released two similar works in 2001: *Mapping Cyberspace* (London and New York: Routledge, 2001) and *Atlas of Cyberspace* (New York: Addison-Wesley, 2001). Vincent Mosco's provocative—but to my purposes, unsatisfying—work was published in 2004 as *The Digital Sublime: Myth, Power and Cyberspace* (Cambridge, MA: MIT Press, 2004). That same year saw the release of William J. Mitchell's *Me++: The Cyborged Self and the Networked City* (Cambridge, MA: MIT Press, 2004); this work updated and expanded his influential earlier work, notably *City of Bits: Space, Place and the Infobahn* (Cambridge, MA: MIT Press, 1996). The trend in overlaying the virtual on the physical, known generally as "augmented reality," and exemplified by Google Glass, is investigated in the upcoming book by Dieter Schmalstieg and Tobias Hollerer, *Augmented Reality* (Indianapolis, IN: Addison-Wesley Professional, forthcoming). Any further list would be an exercise in near-immediate irrelevance.

2 Available at http://www.google.com/glass/start/how-it-feels/.

3 Hurst's work is found online at http://datamining.typepad.com/gallery/blog-map -gallery.html; it was discussed in a May 2007 issue of *Discover* magazine (Stephen Ornes, "Welcome to the Blogosphere," http://discovermagazine.com/2007/may /map-welcome-to-the-blogosphere), and Jeffrey R. Young, "Human Trails in Cyberspace," *Chronicle of Higher Education* 52, no. 43 (2006): A18.

4 The very earliest work on the Manhattan Project had also required banks of "computers," as the military called them: young women, recruited from secretarial pools and

other sites of menial white-collar office labor on the grounds that they were efficient and uncurious, then located at rows of desks, to do the often-tedious arithmetic work, usually with mechanical adding machines, necessary to convert theory into practice. Peter Bacon Hales, *Atomic Spaces: Living on the Manhattan Project* (Urbana: University of Illinois Press, 1997), 214–19, esp. 215–16; Richard Feynman, *Surely You're Joking, Mr. Feynman* (New York: W. W. Norton, 1985), 125–26.

5 The best and most comprehensive book on the subject of hackers and their history is Steven Levy, *Hackers* (Sebastopol, CA: O'Reilly Media, 2010), esp. 3–60.

6 Aside from *Wikipedia*, which is highly reliable when it comes to arcana of computers and gaming (for obvious reasons), the best description of Crowther's development of the game is found in Tristan Donovan, *Replay: The History of Video Games* (East Sussex, UK: Yellow Ant, 2010), 50–52. Oddly, Steven L. Kent's oral-history-based *The Ultimate History of Video Games* (Roseville, CA: Prima Publishing, 2001) gives little interest to Crowther or *Adventure*; even more bizarre is J. C. Herz's confused and inaccurate description of the game as a collective effort c. 1967 (J. C. Herz, *Joystick Nation* (New York: Little, Brown, 1997), 10–11).

7 William L. Laurence/Harry S. Truman, "Statement by the President of the United States [announcing the atomic bombing of Hiroshima]," August 6, 1945, online at http://www.pbs.org/wgbh/americanexperience/features/primary-resources/truman-hiroshima/.

8 Apple computer ad in *Byte*, December 1977, 16.

9 Dan Bricklin comments: "We were aiming at both personal and business use and had photos showing each. We all knew that an Apple II needed a 'checkbook program' and that was one use shown. (Quicken ended up taking the crown there and has been very successful.) We also knew very well how helpful VisiCalc would be for business (many of the principals involved in making and marketing it were MBAs)" (communication with author, March 13, 2013).

10 Though this early Microsoft GUI did include a graphically crippled version of *Reversi*, the campaign to include small game applets, notably virtual solitaire and an addictive little time-waster called *Minesweeper* did not take off until 1990.

11 These maps are found at http://www.lafn.org/webconnect/mentor/zork/zorkText.htm.

12 Probably the most famous early account of the clash between the real and the virtual in these MUDs is Julian Dibbell's "A Rape in Cyberspace," *Village Voice*, December 21, 1993, republished in Dibbell's *My Tiny Life: Crime and Passion in a Virtual World* (New York: Holt Paperbacks, 1999), 11–32.

13 Quoted in Donovan, *Replay*, 144.

14 *Balance of Power* sold very well in a time of gaming market collapse (250,000 games sold) despite its admonitory tone suggested that the game had hit on something. And Crawford's game wasn't alone. That same year, *Zork!*'s creative team released its last text-based game, the highly regarded *Trinity*. Like *Balance of Power*, though in markedly different fashion, *Trinity* pushed the dangers of atomic warfare to the forefront of the gaming world; it began in a London park just moments before an atomic attack and left it to the player to move through the space-time continuum in order to avert global holocaust. Donovan also reports this brief antinuclear gaming didactic: Donovan, *Replay*, 142–46.

15 Frances Fukuyama, "The End of History?," *National Interest*, Summer 1989, 2–5. Vincent Mosco discusses Fukuyama quite differently in *The Digital Sublime*, 56–62.

16 Fukuyama, "The End of History?," 3.

17 This theme was earliest embodied not in the gaming world but in that vestigial medium, the movies, in the form of the *Mad Max* series. The first, released in 1979 as a low-budget Australian action film, had no real backstory; it was not until the second, released as *The Road Warrior* in 1981, that the nuclear postapocalyptic theme took shape, though still imprecisely. *Mad Max: Beyond Thunderdome*, released in 1985, brought the

backstory front and center by describing a full narrative of atomic holocaust and dystopian chaos, pockmarked here and there with the hesitant attempts to rebuild some civilization on the ruins.

18 "More real than your worst nightmare . . . neon lights never made Las Vegas glow like this . . ." read the package description.

19 John Brunner, *Stand on Zanzibar*, (Garden City, NY: Doubleday, 1968).

20 My history of Wright's empire is informed by a series of interviews I did with him over a decade ago; these informed two earlier analyses of *SimCity* and *The Sims*; one appeared as part of an essay written to introduce Bob Thall's *The Perfect City*; the other was presented at the College Art Association national convention in 2001 and published in expanded form in the Spring/Summer 2001 issue of *The Bulletin of the Allen Art Museum*.

21 Andrew G. Kirk, *Counterculture Green: The* Whole Earth Catalog *and American Environmentalism* (Lawrence: University Press of Kansas, 2007) tells the story in exhaustive detail.

22 Brendan Sinclair, "*The Sims* Turns 10, Tops 125 Million Units," February 4, 2010, *Gamespot*, http://www.gamespot.com/news/6249485.html.

23 The full text of the speech can be found online at John T. Woolley and Gerhard Peters, *The American Presidency Project* originating from the University of California at Santa Barbara, http://www.presidency.ucsb.edu/ws/?pid=25853.

24 Richard Hofstadter, "The Paranoid Style in American Politics," *Harper's*, November 1964, 77–86.

25 I'm over *The Sims*. The many add-on packs, from *Pets* to *World Adventures*, have sought to inveigle me, and those like me, who have played so passionately, seem obvious, cheap, diminished. Instead, I have moved to *Fallout 3* and its quasi-successor, *Fallout: New Vegas*. Here the radical flatness and infinite or near-infinite geography of the gameplay mirror *GTA IV*, with a mordant satiric edge. There's a certain satisfaction in seeing Washington, DC in ruins; even more satisfying is to hear the unctuous patriotism of the nation's self-declared "president" on the virtual radio. The game is rife with postapocalyptic jokes, references, and scenes. On every front, technology has failed—bioterrorism and genetic engineering, "survivability" initiatives, robotic nuclear-cleanup machines: all have turned out to render more harmful the already-toxic wasteland that is the consequence of technological utopianism combined with political grandiosity.

   Fallout 3 takes on the caricatures of American political mission; *New Vegas* does the same for laissez-faire capitalism, which has set up shop in the ruins of Nevada's gambling cities. In both cases, the pleasure lies in a strange slippage between the horrors that surround you as you play, and the sardonic intelligence that lies behind and weaves through the game itself. Bracing satires on the grandiosities of the era of American superiority, these games render politics in the real world all the more surreal, and they make it bearable, for a couple of hours, a long, intense weekend, till even this begins to seem snide, and you click the quit key without saving, exhausted with moral exhaustion turned to play. I am waiting for *Fallout 4*.

26 Online at http://religiousfreedom.lib.virginia.edu/sacred/charity.html.

Index

manhood, in America, 168-71, 180, 191

Manifest Destiny, 10, 36-37 261; in pop culture, 312-14; invoked by Kennedy to call for American conquest of outer space, 210

Mankowitz, Gered, photographs The Jimi Hendrix Experience, 297-98

Mann, Barry, 238, 241, 243

March, "Little" Peggy, 225, 242-43

March on Washington for Jobs and Freedom, 261, 262-69; media treatment, 264;

Martha & the Vandellas, 245, 299

Masakela, Hugh, plays Monterey Pop Festival, 309

Mason, Dave, 290

Maxis Software, 416

McCabe, Brian, 95, 101-2, 102

McCartney, Paul, 291-92

McHarg, Ian, 314

McKenzie, Scott, 282, 322

McLuhan, Marshall, 286

Mead, Margaret, 54, 176

Meek, Joe, 207-8, 222-23

Merry Pranksters, 316-18

Mertz, Ethel, 166, 184

Mertz, Fred, 166, 184

Michener, James, 19-20

Microsoft. See Excel; Flight Simulator; Windows; Word

Miller, Timothy, 350

Miracle on 34th Street (movie), 7, 10, 43-71, 83, 93-94, 165, 171-72, 220, 229, 404, 412; Alfred, 59-60; Doris Walker, 43-44, 50-51, 55-58, 62, 66-62, 66, 67; Fred Gailey, 46, 50, 58, 62, 66-67, 66, 67; Kris Kringle, 43-44, 45, 46-48, 47, 60-61, 62-63, 64, 66, 68-70; and credit economy, 68-69; as Christmas allegory, 68-69; as commentary on postwar economy, 45, 61, 68-71; city in, 63-64; Macy's Thanksgiving Day Parade, 43; Macy's as setting and character, 58-64, 68; Mr. Sawyer, 61; Mr. Shellhammer, 44, 56, 58; suburban ideal represented, 45-49, 62-63, 64-67 Susie Walker, 46-50, 47, 62, 65-67, 66, 67;

Miss Atomic Bomb contest, 38-39

"Miss-Cue," 38, 38

MIT: and Cold War research, 383-84; hacker movement, 385-87. See also Tech Model Railroad Club

Mitch Ryder and the Detroit Wheels, 299

Mitchell, Joni, 222, 311; 332, 334-36; appears on Dick Cavett Show, 335; performs at Big Sur Folk Festival, 336; writes "Woodstock," 334-336

Mitchell, Mitch, 296-300. See also Jimi Hendrix Experience

MMORPG (massively multiplayer online role-playing game), 400

MMRPG (massively multiplayer role-playing game), 400

Moab, Plain of, 288

mobe. See mobilization

mobilization: and Chicago '68 protests, 324-28; Pentagon protest of 1967, 324

Moby Dick, as source for "Bob Dylan's 115th Dream," 272

Modern Utopian (Fairfield, Dick), 347

"Monster Mash, The" (Pickett, Bobby [Borris]), 204

Monterey Pop Festival, 282, 307; antithesis of Gathering of the Tribes/Human Be-In, 321-22

Moondog. See Freed, Alan

Morning Star, Estrella, 351

Morningstar commune, 348

Moses, Robert, 316

Motown, 245, 299

mouse, computer, 393

"Mr. Tambourine Man" (Dylan, Bob), 272-73

MUD, 400

Mullein Hill commune, 348

Mumford, Lewis, 93

mushroom cloud, 11, 14, 16, 29, 32, 40, 145-146, 152, 154, 156, 161, 237, 278, 388; cake, 31-32; hat, 32, 38; in Laurence's first "official" report, 16; in virtual world, 402

"My Boyfriend's Back" (The Angels), 231

Mydans, Carl: photographs Starfish Prime test, 213

Nagasaki, atomic bombing of, 15, 25-26, 146, 148

NASA, 204, 206

"Nashville Skyline," 257

National Guard, 269; role at Kent State disturbances, 340-41, 343-45

National Interstate and Defense Highways Act, 185, 361-62

National Geographic: covers Operation Crossroads Bikini atoll test, 22; covers Nevada tests, 34, 40; reports on Upshot-Knothole-Annie atomic test, 155-61

National Mobilization to End the War in Vietnam. See mobilization

Native American culture. See American Indians

Neihardt, Paul, 313-14

Nelson, Rick, 174-75, 257

NES. See Nintendo

Nevada testing grounds, 17, 34-42; decision to develop, 34-35

Nevins, Al, 238. See also Aldon Music

New Buffalo commune, 348, 349, 350, 351, 352, 353, 353

Newark riots, 282

Newport Folk Festival: 1963, 262; 1965, 275